ALL THINGS TO ALL CULTURES

All Things to All Cultures

Paul among Jews, Greeks, and Romans

Edited by

Mark Harding and Alanna Nobbs

WILLIAM B. EERDMANS PUBLISHING COMPANY
GRAND RAPIDS, MICHIGAN / CAMBRIDGE, U.K.

© 2013 Mark Harding and Alanna Nobbs
All rights reserved

Published 2013 by
Wm. B. Eerdmans Publishing Co.
2140 Oak Industrial Drive N.E., Grand Rapids, Michigan 49505 /
P.O. Box 163, Cambridge CB3 9PU U.K.

Library of Congress Cataloging-in-Publication Data

All things to all cultures : Paul among Jews, Greeks, and Romans /
edited by Mark Harding and Alanna Nobbs.
pages   cm
Includes bibliographical references and index.
ISBN 978-0-8028-6643-1 (pbk. : alk. paper)
1. Bible. Epistles of Paul — Criticism, interpretation, etc. 2. Paul, the Apostle, Saint.
I. Harding, Mark.   II. Nobbs, Alanna, 1944–
BS2650.52.A45   2013
225.9′2 — dc23
2013031431

www.eerdmans.com

To our colleagues near and far

"For now we see in a mirror, dimly, but then we will see face to face"

1 Corinthians 13:12

Contents

Foreword   ix
Alanna Nobbs

Contributors   xi

Abbreviations   xv

1. Paul in the Twenty-First Century   1
   Murray J. Smith

2. Paul: An Outline of His Life   34
   David L. Eastman

3. The Archaeology of the Pauline Mission   57
   Cavan W. Concannon

4. Pauline Letter Manuscripts   84
   Brent Nongbri

5. Paul among the Jews   103
   Paul McKechnie

6. Paul among the Greeks   124
   Christopher Forbes

7. Paul among the Romans   143
   James R. Harrison

8. The Letter to the Romans   177
   Michael F. Bird

9. The Corinthian Correspondence   205
   L. L. Welborn

10. The Letter to the Galatians   243
    Greg W. Forbes

11. The Thessalonian Correspondence   269
    Murray J. Smith

12. The Later Pauline Letters: Ephesians, Philippians, Colossians, and Philemon *Ian K. Smith*	302
13. The Pastoral Epistles *Mark Harding*	328
14. Pauline Theology *Timothy J. Harris*	353
Appendix 1: Paul in the Book of Acts *Paul W. Barnett*	392
Appendix 2: A Tabular Analysis of Paul's Asian Epistles *Paul W. Barnett*	396
Index of Ancient People	399
Index of Places	401
Index of Scholars	402

Foreword

The Apostle Paul generated controversy during his lifetime and in the early centuries of the spread of Christianity. His writings and legacy have been revered, maligned, set aside, re-interpreted, not to mention scrutinized for authenticity, and never more than since the late nineteenth century in New Testament research.

This collection is not meant to be comprehensive in any way, but it does represent a range of scholarly reflections on several facets of St Paul's life, ministry and influence. All contributors have links in varying degrees with the Australian College of Theology and/or the Department of Ancient History at Macquarie University (often with both institutions). The research collaboration of these two institutions has been fruitful and is ongoing. It extends well beyond the authors whose chapters are published here and in the preceding work with the same editors as this volume, *The Content and Setting of the Gospel Tradition* (Eerdmans, 2010). We hope to bridge some of the gap which can occur between Classical/Ancient History studies and those of the New Testament.

The Ancient History Department at Macquarie has long had a focus on the Greco-Roman setting of the New Testament. Its Ancient Cultures Research Centre series, *New Documents Illustrating Early Christianity* (ten volumes to date), now published by Eerdmans, discusses evidence for the background of the New Testament in published inscriptions and papyri. The Society for the Study of Early Christianity, also based in the Research Centre, funds annual conferences, seminar series and an international Visiting Scholar in the field. The Centre has had a long-term interest too in the papyri from Egypt which bear on the history of Christianity. Many of the essays included in this volume illustrate the fruits of the historical enquiry fostered there.

The ACT has been a major provider of theological education since its establishment by the General Synod of the Anglican Church of Australia in 1891. The ACT operates nationally as a network of affiliated colleges. Each college has its own well-qualified academic staff teaching a range of disciplines, including the New Testament and its Greco-Roman and Jewish setting. Five of the fourteen contributors to this volume are full-time ACT academic staff members. Several others enjoy honorary associate status at ACT colleges.

The provenance of several of the contributors demonstrates also the strong links which have been forged in the past decade with North American Biblical scholars, via the annual North American and the International Society of Biblical Literature Meetings.

The varied views expressed in the individual chapters are the work of their authors. All the chapters were independently and anonymously peer reviewed and revised in the light of comments received. The views expressed are those of the authors of the individual contributions. This means that the positions taken in the individual chapters are not necessarily in agreement with one another, Pauline chronology being a good example. Readers are given the relevant arguments and a range of up to date modern references, in order to be able to pursue for themselves the many facets of our understanding of the life and mission of St Paul.

Thanks are due to the Board of Directors of the Australian College of Theology for a subvention towards formatting and indexing, and to Philip Walker-Harding for his meticulous attention to this aspect of the publication. The resources of the Ancient Cultures Research Centre at Macquarie University were also used in the preparation of the volume. As always the representatives of our publisher William B. Eerdmans have been understanding and helpful.

Our thanks are due to the contributors and to all colleagues, friends, and family who have assisted both them and the editors. It is fitting that Mark Harding's name be listed first, not merely for alphabetical reasons but for the major effort he contributed during the editorial process.

Alanna Nobbs
Professor of Ancient History
Macquarie University
20 May 2013

CONTRIBUTORS

Mark Harding

Mark Harding is an Honorary Associate of Macquarie University. Since 1996 he has been the Dean of the Australian College of Theology. He has postgraduate degrees from London University, Macquarie University, and Princeton Theological Seminary where he completed a Ph.D. in New Testament in 1993. He is the author of *Tradition and Rhetoric in the Pastoral Epistles* (Peter Lang, 1998) and *Early Christian Life and Thought in Social Context* (T. & T. Clark, 2003).

Alanna Nobbs

Alanna Nobbs is Professor of Ancient History and deputy Director of the Ancient Cultures Research Centre at Macquarie University. Her teaching, research interests and publications are in Greek and Roman historiography (including New Testament background), and in the history of Christianity especially as seen through the papyri.

Paul W. Barnett

Paul Barnett is an ancient historian and a prominent writer on the rise of Christianity and the historical Jesus. He is the author of a large number of monographs on the New Testament, including the commentary on 2 Corinthians in the New International Commentary on the New Testament series (Eerdmans, 1997), *Jesus and the Rise of Christianity* (IVP Academic, 1999), *The Birth of Christianity* (Eerdmans 2005), and *Paul: Missionary of Jesus* (Eerdmans, 2008). He is an Honorary Associate in Ancient History at Macquarie University, Lecturer Emeritus at Moore College, Sydney, Teaching Fellow at Regent College, Vancouver, and a visiting scholar at several colleges affiliated with the Australian College of Theology.

Michael F. Bird

Michael F. Bird is Lecturer in Theology at Ridley Melbourne College of Mission and Ministry in Victoria, Australia. He is a graduate of Malyon College and the University of Queensland. His previous publications include *Jesus and the Origins of the Gentile Mission* (T. & T. Clark, 2007), *The Saving Righteousness of God* (Paternoster, 2007), *A Bird's-Eye View of Paul* (IVP, 2008), and *Jesus is the Christ* (IVP, 2013). He also serves as co-editor for the *Journal for the Study of Paul and His Letters*, *The Story of God Bible Commentary*, and the *New Covenant Commentary Series*.

Cavan W. Concannon

Cavan Concannon is Visiting Assistant Professor and American Council of Learned Societies New Faculty Fellow in the Departments of Religion and

Classical Studies at Duke University. He was formerly Post Doctoral Fellow in Early Christianity in the Department of Ancient History at Macquarie University. His forthcoming book *"When You Were Gentiles: Specters of Ethnicity in Roman Corinth and Paul's Corinthian Correspondence* will be published by Yale University Press in 2014.

David L. Eastman

David L. Eastman is an Assistant Professor of Religion at Ohio Wesleyan University. He has postgraduate degrees from the University of St Andrews, the Université de Poitiers, Gordon-Conwell Theological Seminary, and Yale University, where he completed a Ph.D. in Ancient Christianity in 2009. He is the author of *Paul the Martyr: The Cult of the Apostle in the Latin West* (SBL/Brill, 2011) and is the Book Review Editor for the *Journal of Early Christian Studies*.

Christopher Forbes

Christopher Forbes is a Senior Lecturer in Ancient History at Macquarie University, where he teaches New Testament history, Hellenistic history and Greco-Roman history of ideas. He completed his Ph.D. in Ancient History at Macquarie University under the supervision of Professor E. A. Judge in 1987. His thesis was published by Mohr Siebeck in 1995 as *Prophecy and Inspired Speech in Early Christianity and its Hellenistic Environment*. He has published various articles on the intellectual and cultural context of the early Christians and is a regular contributor to the conferences of the Society for the Study of Early Christianity held annually at Macquarie University.

Greg W. Forbes

Greg Forbes is the head of the Department of Biblical Studies at the Melbourne School of Theology, an affiliated college of the Australian College of Theology, where he has taught for 20 years. He currently lectures in Greek, New Testament, and Hermeneutics. After completing an undergraduate degree and a Research Masters degree in Theology with the Australian College of Theology, he was awarded a Ph.D. from Deakin University for a thesis on the parables in Luke's Gospel. Greg's published works include *The God of Old: The Role of the Lukan Parables in the Purpose of Luke's Gospel* (Sheffield Academic, 2000), a commentary on 1 Peter in the Asia Bible Commentary Series (Asia Theological Association, 2006), and a commentary forthcoming in the Exegetical Guide to the Greek New Testament series (Broadman and Holman) on 1 Peter.

Timothy J. Harris

Tim Harris is an Adjunct Lecturer in New Testament at Charles Sturt University, and Assistant Bishop in the Anglican Diocese of Adelaide. He was previously Dean of Bishopdale Theological College in Nelson, New Zealand, and New Testament Moderator for the Australian College of Theology from 2004 until

2012. His Flinders University Ph.D. thesis reflects his ongoing interests and research in Pauline theology, with the title "The Subversion of Status: A Pauline Theology of Humility and Deference in Graeco-Roman Perspective, with Special Reference to Stoicism and Epictetus".

James R. Harrison

James Harrison, Director of Research (Sydney College of Divinity), completed his Ph.D. in Ancient History at Macquarie University under the supervision of Professor E. A. Judge and Dr Chris Forbes in 1997. His book *Paul's Language of Grace in Its Graeco-Roman Context*, published by Mohr Siebeck, was the 2005 Winner of the Biblical Archaeology Society Publication Award for the Best Book Relating to the New Testament published in 2003 and 2004. His latest monograph, published by Mohr Siebeck in 2011, is *Paul and the Imperial Authorities at Thessalonica and Rome: A Study in the Conflict of Ideology*. He is also the co-editor, with Dr Stephen Llewelyn, of *New Documents Illustrating Early Christianity Volume 10* (Eerdmans 2012). James is an Honorary Associate at Macquarie University and a regular contributor to the conferences of the Society for the Study of Early Christianity held annually at Macquarie University.

Paul McKechnie

Paul McKechnie is an Associate Professor (CoRE) in Ancient Cultures at Macquarie University. He teaches Greek and Roman history, and early Christianity, and has research interests in Ptolemaic Egypt and the early Christian churches. His published works include *The First Christian Centuries* (Leicester, 2001).

Brent Nongbri

Brent Nongbri is a Research Fellow in the Department of Ancient History at Macquarie University. He is the author of *Before Religion: A History of a Modern Concept* (Yale University Press, 2013) and has published several articles on early Christian manuscripts in *Harvard Theological Review*, *Novum Testamentum*, the *Journal of Biblical Literature*, and the *Bulletin of the American Society of Papyrologists*.

Ian K. Smith

Ian Smith was appointed Principal of the Presbyterian Theological Centre (Sydney), an affiliated college of the Australian College of Theology, in 2010. He has been a lecturer in New Testament at the Centre since 1995. He has served as the Head of the Department of Bible and Languages of the Australian College of Theology from 2006 until 2010. He holds postgraduate degrees from the University of New England, the Australian College of Theology, and the University of Sydney where he completed a Ph.D. in New Testament in 2002. He is the author of *Heavenly Perspective: A Study of the Apostle Paul's Response to a Jewish Mystical Movement at Colossae* (T. & T. Clark, 2006).

Murray J. Smith

Murray Smith lectures in Biblical Studies (Greek and New Testament) at the Presbyterian Theological Centre (Sydney). He holds Masters degrees from the University of Sydney (Reformation History) and Macquarie University (Early Christian and Jewish Studies). His Macquarie University Ph.D. concerns "Jesus and the Logic of his Coming in Earliest Christianity."

L. L. Welborn

Larry L. Welborn is Professor of New Testament and Early Christianity at Fordham University and Honorary Professor of Ancient History at Macquarie University. He is the author of several books, including *Politics and Rhetoric in the Corinthian Epistles* (Mercer, 1997), *Paul, the Fool of Christ: A Study of 1 Corinthians 1–4 in the Comic-Philosophic Tradition* (T. & T. Clark, 2005) and *An End to Enmity: Paul and the "Wrongdoer of Second Corinthians* (de Gruyter, 2011). He is currently preparing the *Hermeneia* commentary on *First Clement*. With Dale B. Martin, he serves as book series editor of *Synkrisis: Comparative Approaches to Early Christianity in Greco-Roman Culture*, published by Yale University Press.

ABBREVIATIONS

Details of all papyri referred to in this volume (especially chapter 4) can be accessed in: John F. Oates et al, *Checklist of Editions of Greek, Latin, Demotic and Coptic Papyri, Ostraca and Tablets* (5th ed., BASPSup 9; Oakville: American Society of Papyrologists, 2001).

Note also the regularly updated on-line resource of: John F. Oates, Roger S. Bagnall, Sarah J. Clackson, Alexandra A. O'Brien, Joshua D. Sosin, Terry G. Wilfong, and Klaas A. Worp, *Checklist of Greek, Latin, Demotic and Coptic Papyri, Ostraca and Tablets*: http://library.duke.edu/rubenstein/scriptorium/papyrus/texts/clist.html (May, 2013).

Details of inscriptions referred to in this volume (especially chapters 7 and 11) can be accessed at the on-line resource sponsored by the American Society of Greek and Latin Epigraphy: http://www.bbaw.de/forschung/ig/ectypa/1syllabus.html (May, 2013).

For abbreviations of works not listed below, see: Siegfried M. Schwertner, *Internationales Abkürzungsverzeichnis für Theologie und Grenzgebiete* (2nd ed.; Berlin: de Gruyter, 1992).

1 Apol.	Justin, *First Apology*
1 Clem.	*1 Clement*
1 En.	*1 Enoch*
1QS	*Rule of the Community*, from Qumran cave 1
2 Bar.	*2 Baruch*
2 En.	*2 Enoch*
A.J.	Josephus, *Antiquitates Judaicae*
AAR	American Academy of Religion
AB	Anchor Bible
ABD	David Noel Freedman, ed. *The Anchor Bible Dictionary*. 6 vols. New York: Doubleday, 1992
ABR	*Australian Biblical Review*
Adv. indoct.	Lucian, *Adversus indoctum*
AE	*Année épigraphique*. Paris: Presses universitaires de France, 1888–
Aen.	Virgil, *Aeneid*
AJA	*American Journal of Archaeology*
AJP	*American Journal of Philology*
AnBib	Analecta biblica
Ann.	Tacitus, *Annals*
ANRW	H. Temporini and W. Haase, eds. *Aufstieg und Niedergang der römischen Welt: Geschichte und Kultur Roms im Spiegel der neueren Forschung*. Berlin: de Gruyter, 1972–
Ant. rom.	Dionysius of Halicarnassus, *Antiquitates romanae*
Ant.	Plutarch, *Antonius*

Apg	Apostelgeschichte
Apol.	Seneca, *Apolocyntosis*
Astron.	Manilius, *Astronomica*
ATR	*Anglican Theological Review*
Att.	Cicero, *Epistulae ad Atticum*
Aug.	Suetonius, *Divus Augustus*
b. Erubin	Babylonian Talmud, *Eruvin*
b. Shabbat	Babylonian Talmud, *Sabbat*
B.J.	Josephus, *Bellum judaicum*
BA	*Biblical Archaeologist*
BBR	*Bulletin for Biblical Research*
BDAG	Frederick W. Danker, ed. *A Greek-English Lexicon of the New Testament and Other Early Christian Literature*. 3rd edn. Chicago: University of Chicago Press, 2000
BeO	*Bibbia e oriente*
BGU	*Aegyptische Urkunden aus den Königlichen Staatlichen Museen zu Berlin, Griechische Urkunden*. 15 vols. Berlin, 1895–1983
Bib	*Biblica*
BIFCS	The Book of Acts in Its First Century Setting
BJRL	*Bulletin of the John Rylands University Library of Manchester*
BR	*Biblical Research*
BSA	*Annual of the British School at Athens*
BSac	*Bibliotheca sacra*
BTB	*Biblical Theology Bulletin*
BZ	*Biblische Zeitschrift*
C. Ap.	Josephus, *Contra Apionem*
Caes.	Aurelius Victor, *De Caesaribus*
Carm. saec.	Horace, *Carmen saeculare*
CBQ	*Catholic Biblical Quarterly*
CBQMS	Catholic Biblical Quarterly Monograph Series
CBR	*Currents in Biblical Research*
CEV	Contemporary English Version
CIL	*Corpus inscriptionum latinarum*
CITM	Christianity in the Making
Claud.	Suetonius, *Divus Claudius*
Clem.	Seneca, *De clementia*
CNT	Commentaire du Nouveau Testament
ConBNT	Coniectanea neotestamentica
CP	*Classical Philology*
CR:BR	Currents in Research: Biblical Studies
CTR	*Criswell Theological Review*
De arch.	Vitruvius, *De architectura*
De comp. med. sec. loc.	Galen, *De compositione medicamentorum secundum locus*
De spect.	Martial, *De spectaculis*
Dial.	Justin, *Dialogue with Trypho*
Diogn.	*Diognetus*

DocsAug	V. Ehrenberg and A. H. M. Jones. *Documents Illustrating the Reigns of Augustus and Tiberius*. 2nd Edition. Oxford: Clarendon Press, 1955
DPL	G. F. Hawthorne and R. P. Martin, eds. *Dictionary of Paul and His Letters*. Downers Grove: Intervarsity Press, 1993
Eng.	English
Ep.	Pliny the Younger, *Epistles*
Ep. Tars.	Ps. Ignatius, *Epistle to the Tarsians*
Ep.	Seneca, *Epistulae morales*
Eph.	Ignatius, *To the Ephesians*
Epict. diss	Arrian, *Epicteti dissertationes*
Esd	Esdras
ESV	English Standard version
ET	English translation
Eth. eud.	Aristotle, *Ethica eudemia*
Eth. nic.	Aristotle, *Ethica nichomachea*
EvQ	*Evangelical Quarterly*
ExpT	*Expository Times*
fl.	flourished
Flacc.	Philo, *In Flaccum*
frg(s).	fragment(s)
Geogr.	Strabo, *Geographica*
Ger.	German
Gk.	Greek
Haer.	Irenaeus, *Adversus haereses*
Heb.	Hebrew
Herm. Vis.	Shepherd of Hermas, *Vision*
Hist. c. pag.	Orosius, *Histories against the Pagans*
Hist. eccl.	Eusebius, *Historia ecclesiastica*
Hist.	Tacitus, *Historiae*
HSCP	Harvard Studies in Classical Philology
HTR	*Harvard Theological Review*
HTS	Harvard Theological Studies
HUT	Hermeneutische Untersuchungen zur Theologie
I.Eph.	H. Engelmann, H. Wankel, and R. Merkelbach. *Die Inschriften von Ephesos*. Bonn: Rudolf Habelt, 1979–1984
IBR	Institute for Biblical Research
IG	*Inscriptiones graecae*. Editio minor. Berlin. 1924–
Ign. *Eph.*	Ignatius, *To the Ephesians*
ILS	*Inscriptiones latinae selectae*
Inst.	Quintillian, *Institutio oratorica*
Int	*Interpretation*
IT	Charles Edson, ed. *Inscriptiones graecae Epiri, Macedoniae, Thraciae, Scythiae, Pars II Inscriptiones Macedoniae, Fasciculus I Inscripitones Thessalonicae et viciniae*. Berlin: de Gruyter, 1972
JAAR	*Journal of the American Academy of Religion*
JAARSup	*Journal of the American Academy of Religion Supplements*

JBL	*Journal of Biblical Literature*
JECS	*Journal of Early Christian Studies*
JETS	*Journal of the Evangelical Theological Society*
JGRChJ	*Journal of Greco-Roman Christianity and Judaism*
JHS	*Journal of Hellenic Studies*
JJS	*Journal of Jewish Studies*
JPTSup	Journal of Pentecostal Theology Supplement Series
JQR	*Jewish Quaterly Review*
JR	*Journal of Religion*
JRelS	*Journal of Religious Studies*
JRS	*Journal of Roman Studies*
JSJ	*Journal for the Study of Judaism in the Persian, Hellenistic, and Roman Periods*
JSNT	*Journal for the Study of the New Testament*
JSNTSup	Journal for the Study of the New Testament: Supplement Series
JSP	*Journal for the Study of the Pseudepigrapha*
JTS	*Journal of Theological Studies*
Jub.	*Jubilees*
Jul.	Suetonius, *Divus Julius*
KJV	King James version
L.A.B.	*Liber antiquitatum biblicarum (Pseudo-Philo)*
Lat.	Latin
Legat.	Philo, *On the Embassy to Gaius*
Liv. Pro.	*Lives of the Prophets*
LNTS	Library of New Testament Studies
LXX	Septuagint
m.	*Mishnah*
Marc.	Tertullian, *Adversus Marcionem*
Mart. Ign.	*Martyrdom of Ignatius*
Met.	Ovid, *Metamorphoses*
MM	James H. Moulton and George Milligan. *The Vocabulary of the Greek Testament Illustrated from the Papyri and Other Non-Literary Sources*. London: Hodder & Stoughton, 1930
Mor.	Plutarch, *Moralia*
Most.	Plautus, *Mostellaria*
Nat.	Pliny the Elder, *Natural History*
NIB	*New Interpreter's Bible*
NIBC	New International Bible Commentary
NIDNTT	Colin Brown, ed. *New International Dictionary of New Testament Theology*. 3 vols. Grand Rapids: Eerdmans, 1975–1978
NIV	New International Version
NovT	*Novum Testamentum*
NovTSup	Novum Testamentum Supplements
NPNF	*Nicene and Post-Nicene Fathers*
NRSV	New Revised Standard Version
NT	New Testament
NTS	*New Testament Studies*

NTTSD	New Testament Tools, Studies and Documents
OCD	S. Hornblower and A. Spawforth, eds. *Oxford Classical Dictionary*. 3rd edition. Oxford: Oxford University Press, 1996
Oct.	ps.-Seneca, *Octavia*
OGIS	W. Dittenberger, ed. *Orientis graeci inscriptiones selectae*. 2 vols. Leipzig: S. Hirzel, 1903–1905
Or.	Dio Chrysostom, *Orationes*
OT	Old Testament
P.Oslo	Oslo Papyri
P.Oxy.	Oxyrhynchus Papyri
P.Ryl.	Rylands Papyri
P.Tebt.	Tebtunis Papyri
P.Lond.	London Papyri
PE	Pastoral Epistles
Phil.	Polycarp, *To the Philippians*
Polyb.	Polybius
PSB	*Princeton Seminary Bulletin*
PSI	*Papiri Greci e Latini, Pubblicazioni della Societa italiana*
Pss. Sol.	Psalms of Solomon
Rab. Post.	Cicero, *Pro Rabirio Postumo*
RB	*Revue biblique*
ResQ	*Restoration Quarterly*
RevExp	*Review and Expositor*
Rhet.	Aristotle, *Rhetorica*
Rhet. ad Her.	*Rhetorica ad Herennium*
RHPR	*Revue d'histoire et de philosophie religieuses*
RIC	C. H. V. Sutherland and R. A. G. Carson. *The Roman Imperial Coinage*. Revised ed. London: Spinks & Son, 1984
RTR	*Reformed Theological Review*
Sat.	Horace, *Satirae*
SB	*Sammelbuch griechischen Urkunden aus Ägypten*
SB	F. Preisigke, et al eds., *Sammelbuch griechischer Urkunden aus Aegypten*. 1915–
SBL	Society of Biblical Literature
SBLDS	Society of Biblical Literature Dissertation Series
SEG	*Supplementum epigraphicum graecum*
SFSHJ	South Florida Studies in the History of Judaism
sg.	singular
SIG	W. Dittenberger, ed., *Sylloge inscriptionum graecarum*. 4 vols. 3rd ed. Leipzig: S. Hirzel, 1915–1924
Sir	Sirach
SJT	*Scottish Journal of Theology*
SNTSMS	Society for New Testament Studies Monograph Series
Socratic Ep.	Socratic Epistles
SPAW	Sitzungsberichte der preussischen Akademie der Wissenschaften
Strom.	Clement of Alexandria, *Stromata*
StudBL	Studies in Biblical Literature
T. Abr.	Testament of Abraham

T. Dan	*Testament of Dan*
T. Jud.	*Testament of Judah*
T. Levi	*Testament of Levi*
T. Mos.	*Testament of Moses*
TAM	Ernst Kalinka, et al, eds. *Tituli Asiae Minoris*. Vienna: Hoelder, Pichler, Tempsky, 1901–
TAPA	*Transactions of the American Philological Association*
TDNT	Kittel Gerhard, and Gerhard Friedrich, eds. *Theological Dictionary of the New Testament*. 10 vols. Translated by Geoffrey W. Bromiley. Grand Rapids: Eerdmans, 1964–1976
ThStKr	*Theologische Studien und Kritiken*
Tib.	Suetonius, *Tiberius*
TNIV	Today's New International Version
TynB	*Tyndale Bulletin*
TZT	*Tübinger Zeitschrift für Theologie*
v(v).	verse(s)
Vir. ill.	Jerome, *De viris illustribus*
Vit. Apoll.	Philostratus, *Vita Apollonii*
Vit. soph.	Philostratus, *Vitae sophistarum*
WBC	Word Biblical Commentary
WGRWSup	Writings from the Greco-Roman World Supplements
Wis	Wisdom of Solomon
WTJ	*Westminster Theological Journal*
WUNT	Wissenschaftliche Untersuchungen zum Neuen Testament
ZNW	*Zeitschrift für die neutestamentliche Wissenschaft*
ZST	*Zeitschrift für systematische Theologie*
ZTK	*Zeitschrift für Theologie und Kirche*

1. Paul in the Twenty-First Century

Murray J. Smith

The apostle Paul was a controversial figure from the start. His letters provide ample evidence of the debate that almost universally followed his proclamation of the gospel, and the earliest sources indicate that his letters themselves generated further discussion (2 Pet 3:16). This lively conversation did not die with the apostle. It has been going on now for almost two thousand years. The result is that our current readings of Paul are shaped, more than we often realize, by those of Augustine, Luther, Calvin, Wesley, and a host of others down through the centuries. Indeed, the discussion of Paul and his letters shows no signs of abeyance. In recent years, the literature on Paul at both scholarly and popular levels has grown exponentially. This chapter attempts, then, what has been called—by one who knows well—an "impossible task."[1] It traces the major contours of Pauline scholarship over the last century and a half, with an emphasis on the present state of Pauline research. It is hoped that this sketch may lead to greater understanding of the apostle himself, and of the letters through which we principally know him.[2]

To provide a kind of outline for this sketch, we take as a starting point the review of the literature on Paul offered almost exactly one hundred years ago by Albert Schweitzer.[3] In characteristic fashion, Schweitzer summed up and dismissed the vast bulk of scholarship on Paul to 1911 and set the trajectory for what was eventually to become the majority consensus of the twentieth century. As Schweitzer saw things, the great question for interpreters of Paul is how to make sense of Paul's place between the Jewish proclamation of Jesus, and the significantly Hellenized Christian orthodoxy that developed in the second century.[4] As Schweitzer recognized, this "great and still undischarged task"

---

[1] D. E. Aune, "Recent Readings of Paul Relating to Justification by Faith," in D. E. Aune, ed., *Rereading Paul Together: Protestant and Catholic Perspectives on Justification* (Grand Rapids: Baker, 2006), 188.
[2] For alternative recent reviews, see: M. Zetterholm, *Approaches to Paul: A Student's Guide to Recent Scholarship* (Minneapolis: Fortress, 2009); N. T. Wright, "Paul in Current Anglophone Scholarship," *ExpT* 123 (2012): 367-81. For an interesting discussion between some major recent interpreters of Paul, see M. F. Bird, *Four Views on the Apostle Paul* (Grand Rapids: Zondervan, 2012).
[3] A. Schweitzer, *Geschichte der Paulinischen Forschung: von der Reformation bis auf die Gegenwart* (Tübingen: Mohr [Siebeck], 1911).
[4] A. Schweitzer, *Paul and his Interpreters: A Critical History* (trans. W. Montgomery; London: A. & C. Black, 1912), v.

involves seeking answers to two central and related questions which have dominated Pauline scholarship in the modern era. The first question is whether Paul's thought is more Jewish or more Greek; whether the gospel he proclaimed is shaped more by the Jewish proclamation of Jesus, and Paul's own Pharisaic background, or by the worldview of his primary audience as apostle to the Gentiles. The touchstone issues within this debate have been the extent to which Paul develops (or even replaces) the original proclamation of Jesus, and the nature of Paul's understanding of the Jewish law. Whatever the precise focus, a great deal of discussion has crystallized around this question of the continuity and discontinuity between Paul and first-century Judaism. The second question Schweitzer identified is related to the first, and concerns the center of Paul's theology: to what extent is it possible to identify a generative principle at the heart of Paul's thought, by which the remainder of his writing might be understood and explained? Schweitzer considered only two major candidates for such a center—justification by faith and participation in Christ. It is a credit to Schweitzer's insight that these have remained the two major options in a great deal of subsequent scholarship, even if in the days since Schweitzer a host of other possibilities have also been suggested.

These two fundamental questions are interrelated, and the following discussion highlights the connections between them. Part 1 focuses on that stream in scholarship which has seen Paul primarily in terms of his *break with* Judaism, and which has tended to posit justification by faith as the heart of his thought. Part 2 examines the parallel stream in scholarship which has seen Paul primarily in terms of his *continuity with* Judaism, and which has tended to identify participation in Christ as central to Paul's theological vision. Since, however, the full picture is not so simple, Part 3 examines recent developments in Pauline scholarship, outlining the great diversity of approaches now in play, and the range of readings of Paul and his letters that have emerged. The conclusion offers a summary of the current state of play in Pauline scholarship, and some suggestions for the way ahead.

1. Paul, the Apostle to the Gentiles and Justification by Faith

1.1. Paul against the Judaizers: F. C. Baur and the Tübingen School

The course for much modern study of Paul was set by F. C. Baur, Professor of New Testament at Tübingen (1826–1860).[5] In answer to the question of whether Paul's thought is more Jewish or more Greek, Baur unequivocally argued that Paul's gospel took its lead from Hellenistic thought. On the basis of 1 Cor 1:11-

---

[5] See esp. F. C. Baur, "Die Christuspartei in der korinthischen Gemeinde, der Gegensatz des petrinischen und paulinischen Christenthums in der ältesten Kirche, der Apostel Petrus in Rom," *TZT* issue 4 (1831): 61-206; F. C. Baur, *Paulus, der Apostel Jesu Christi: Sein Leben und Wirken, seine Briefe und seine Lehre* (Stuttgart: Becher & Müller, 1845). The second edition (1866) of this work was translated as *Paul the Apostle of Jesus Christ: His Life and Works, His Epistles and Teachings: A Contribution to a Critical History of Primitive Christianity* (2nd ed.; London: Williams & Northgate, 1873).

12, Baur posited a sharp division between Jewish Christianity (Cephas and the "Christ party") and Gentile Christianity (Paul and Apollos). Deploying the categories of Hegelian philosophy, Baur argued that Paul set his universal, law-free gospel for the Gentiles (the antithesis) against ethnocentric, law-laden, Jewish Christianity (the thesis), and that this opposition became the defining feature of the early Christian movement until the tension was eventually resolved at the end of the second century in the emergence of the orthodox, hierarchical Church (the synthesis).

In this context, it is no surprise that in answer to the second question Baur, in keeping with his Lutheran heritage, identified justification by faith as the center of Paul's thought. According to Baur, "the essential principle of Christianity first attained a decided place in its struggle against Judaism."[6] In opposition to the merit-based works righteousness of his Jewish-Christian opponents (led by James, Peter, and the rest of the Jerusalem apostles), Paul proclaimed the gospel of God's free grace. Baur argued further that Paul's authentic teaching is only to be found where a sharp conflict between Jewish and Gentile Christianity is in evidence, and where Paul responds by laying out his characteristic doctrine of justification by faith. This assumption led Baur to recognize only Galatians, Romans, and the Corinthian letters as authentic, and to reject the authenticity of the others letters attributed to Paul, on the grounds that they make little of justification by faith (e.g. 1–2 Thessalonians), or are directed against second-century Gnostic opponents (the prison letters, the pastoral letters).[7]

The view that Paul sharply opposes law and Gospel, Judaism and Christianity, was not new with Baur, but had deep roots in earlier Christian readings of the NT, not least in the Lutheran tradition. Indeed, Baur's implicitly negative evaluation of first-century Judaism as a legalistic religion opposed to the gospel of grace pervaded a great deal of both Catholic and Protestant biblical scholarship.[8] Baur's thesis, however, especially as it was later elaborated by his followers in the Tübingen school, made the opposition between law/Judaism and Gospel/Christianity the primary explanation for the history of early Christianity down to the end of the second century.

1.2. Paul among the Greeks: The History of Religions School

The dominance of Baur's thesis in German scholarship eventually gave way to the influence of the *Religionsgeschichtliche Schule* (history of religions school). This new approach argued that Paul, and early Christianity with him, is best understood in the context of the evolving religions of the Roman Empire.

In answer to the first question regarding whether Paul's thought is more Jewish or Greek, the scholars of the history of religions school agreed with Baur and the Tübingen school, but went much further. They assumed the prevailing

---

[6] Baur, *Paul the Apostle*, 1.267.
[7] See esp. F. C. Baur, *Die sogenannten Pastoralbriefe des Apostels Paulus aufs neue kritisch untersucht* (Stuttgart and Tübingen: J. G. Cotta'schen Verlagshandlung, 1835).
[8] See esp. F. W. Weber, *Jüdische Theologie auf Grund des Talmud und verwandter Schriften, gemeinfasslich dargestellt* (Leipzig: Dürffling & Franke, 1897).

negative evaluation of first-century Judaism, and argued not only that Paul's gospel was opposed to Jewish Christianity, but that its inner dynamic was actually derived from the worldview of the Greeks. The first to argue this case was O. Pfleiderer, who suggested that "Paul's theology would not have been what it is, if he had not drawn deeply on Greek wisdom as this was made available to him through the Hellenized Judaism of Alexandria."[9] Pfleiderer thus gave birth to a view that has long persisted in Pauline scholarship, namely, that (1) Paul was the first to introduce foreign Hellenistic ideas into the Christian gospel; (2) this led to an irreconcilable contradiction within Paul's own thought; and (3) Paul's gospel was a radical departure from the teaching of Jesus.[10]

Pfleiderer's arguments were adopted and developed by a whole generation of German scholars. A. Eichhorn and W. Hietmüller, for example, argued that Paul's view of the sacraments derived from neither Jewish practice nor the preaching of Jesus, but from Hellenistic religion.[11] R. Reitzenstein, similarly, maintained that Paul's view of Jesus as the divine-human redeemer grew out of the Hellenistic mystery religions and a supposed Gnostic myth of redemption.[12] And in the same way W. Bousset, in his influential *Kyrios Christos*,[13] insisted that Paul cut the Christian faith off from its roots in Jewish apocalyptic eschatology and, turning to the Hellenistic mystery religions, ensured that "the center of gravity of the faith began to shift from the future into the present."[14] In particular, Bousset suggested that Paul's great innovation was to replace the mystery cult's veneration of the "Lords" Sarapis, Osiris, and Mithras, with the worship of a new "Lord," Jesus of Nazareth. Like others in the history of religions school, Bousset insisted that Paul radically hellenized Jesus' original proclamation of the kingdom of God. In all of this, the history of religions school developed and extended a central tenet of Baur's thesis, namely, the formative influence of Greek thought on Paul's gospel.

In relation to the second major question regarding Paul's theology, however, the history of religions school departed from Baur's emphasis on justification by faith. While the prominence of this theme in at least some of the Pauline letters could not be denied, proponents of the history of religions school argued that

---

[9] O. Pfleiderer, *Das Urchristentum* (Berlin: G. Reimer, 1887), 170.
[10] Cf. S. Neill and N. T. Wright, *The Interpretation of the New Testament 1861–1986* (2nd ed.; Oxford: Oxford University Press, 1988), 171-72. For a recent presentation of this view, see A. N. Wilson, *Paul: The Mind of the Apostle* (New York: Norton, 1997).
[11] A. Eichhorn, *The Lord's Supper in the New Testament* (trans. Jeffrey F. Cayzer; Atlanta: Society of Biblical Literature, 2007); trans. of A. Eichhorn, *Das Abendmahl im Neuen Testament* (Leipzig: Mohr [Siebeck], 1898); W. Heitmüller, *Taufe und Abendmahl bei Paulus* (Göttingen: Vandenhoeck & Ruprecht, 1903). Cf. Pfleiderer, *Das Urchristentum*, 303-6.
[12] R. Reitzenstein, *Die hellenistischen Mysterienreligionen: ihre Grundgedanken und Wirkungen* (Leipzig, Berlin: Teubner, 1910), 55-56. In a later work Reitzenstein pushed the origins of Paul's gospel further east to Iranian Zoroastrianism, and a supposed "Iranian myth of redemption." See R. Reitzenstein, *Das iranische Erlösungsmysterium: religionsgeschichtliche Untersuchungen* (Bonn: Marcus & Weber, 1921). Though now widely discredited, this whole approach continues to find occasional support in the popular literature (e.g. T. Freke and P. Gandy, *The Jesus Mysteries: Was the "Original Jesus" a Pagan God?* [New York: Harmony, 2000]).
[13] W. Bousset, *Kyrios Christos: Geschichte des Christusglaubens von den Anfängen des Christentums bis Irenaeus* (Göttingen: Vandenhoeck & Ruprecht, 1913).
[14] Cited in Neill and Wright, *Interpretation*, 177.

Paul's teaching on justification by faith stood side by side with an equally significant emphasis on the mysterious presence of Christ in the church through the sacrament. Bousset, for example, explained Paul's apparent lack of interest in the historic events of the life of the earthly Jesus as a result of his preoccupation with the Lord's presence among his people, especially in the worship of the gathered community. The inevitable result was that Paul's teaching on justification was relegated to the periphery of his thought.

1.3. Paul, the Apostle of Personal Decision: Rudolf Bultmann

These currents in German scholarship converged in the work of a remarkable NT scholar, Rudolf Bultmann, Professor of New Testament at Marburg University (1921–1951), perhaps the most influential interpreter of Paul in the twentieth century.

In relation to the first question, regarding whether Paul is best understood in the categories of Jewish or Greek thought, Bultmann maintained in his influential *New Testament Theology* that Paul's theology belongs firmly in its Hellenistic context.[15] He assumed, like many before him, that first-century Judaism was a religion of legalistic works-righteousness,[16] and argued, like proponents of the history of religions school, that at his conversion the apostle to the Gentiles abandoned the categories of his Jewish worldview and embraced a gospel expressed in the language and categories of the Greek world. Paul's gospel was therefore fundamentally different from the kingdom of God proclaimed by Jesus.[17] In particular, Bultmann argued, Paul came to understand the cross of Christ as "God's judgment upon his self-understanding" prior to his conversion, indeed, nothing less than "God's condemnation of his Jewish striving after righteousness by fulfilling the works of the law."[18] In the light of the cross of Christ, Paul rejected his previous Jewish worldview, including Jewish apocalyptic eschatology, with its historical and communal hope for the restoration of Israel in the land under the leadership of the Messiah, and opted instead for the Greek categories of a timeless, individual, and spiritual salvation.

In relation to the second question, however, Bultmann—like Baur before him—saw Paul's teaching about justification by faith as central to his message. Bultmann's reading of Paul here relied on a unique blend of Lutheran theology and German existential philosophy. On the one hand, as the son of a Lutheran pastor, it is perhaps not surprising that Bultmann attributed to Paul a radical distinction between the law of Moses, which exposes sinners to God's judgment, and the gospel of Christ, which brings salvation. Moreover, in his reading of Rom 3:21-26 and a host of other key passages, Bultmann showed his debt to the Lutheran understanding of justification in forensic terms, according to which

---

[15] R. Bultmann, *Theology of the New Testament* (trans. K. Grobel, 2 vols.; New York: Scribner, 1951, 1955), 1:187. ET from the German original: R. Bultmann, *Theologie des Neuen Testaments* (2 vols.; Tübingen: Mohr [Siebeck], 1948–1953).
[16] Bultmann, *TNT* 1:262-64.
[17] Bultmann, *TNT* 1:189.
[18] Bultmann, *TNT* 1:187.

God's eschatological judgment in favor of believing sinners is declared in the present.[19] The only hope for sinners, he wrote, is to receive the righteousness that is "bestowed upon the faith which appropriates the grace of God and not upon the works of the law."[20] On the other hand, Bultmann developed this Lutheran reading of Paul in conversation with the existential philosophy of his friend and colleague at Marburg (1922–1928), Martin Heidegger. Deploying Heidegger's categories, Bultmann organized Paul's thought under two headings: "existence prior to the revelation of faith" (Paul's justification by works) and "existence under faith" (Paul's justification by faith).[21] These two modes of existence, Bultmann insisted, are utterly opposed to each other. In Heidegger's terms, the first mode of existence is "inauthentic" (*uneigentlich*) because it fails to respond to the Word of God by the decision of faith. Such inauthentic existence describes human life prior to the revelation of faith, whether in its Gentile form of total disregard for God, or in its Jewish form of works-righteousness.[22] In contrast, the second mode of existence is "authentic" (*eigentlich*) because, through the decision of faith, it submits to God's judgment in the cross.

All of this formed a part of Bultmann's broader program of "demythologization," according to which he attempted to strip the NT gospel of its ancient mythical "husk" and to present its simple "kernel" in terms more readily understandable in the modern world. Bultmann identified the ancient mythic husk of Paul's doctrine of justification in terms of its associations with the Jewish cult and the Gnostic redeemer myth. He therefore rejected as "pagan" the notion of Christ's death as a propitiatory sacrifice, and argued that the real kernel of Paul's teaching is to be found in the individual's decision of faith.[23] Given this hermeneutic, it is no surprise that Bultmann moved away from the traditional emphasis on God's work in Christ as the objective ground of justification, and emphasized the believer's subjective appropriation of justification through the decision of faith.[24] Indeed, Bultmann's remarkable synthesis of Lutheran tradition and modern existentialist philosophy enabled him to present Paul's theology in profoundly anthropocentric terms.[25] While this approach exerted an enormous influence for a time, it was ultimately unable to account for the radically Christocentric nature of Paul's theological vision. With the benefit of hindsight, it is clear that Bultmann's analysis represents the zenith of the whole stream of scholarship in which Paul was understood primarily in terms of his opposition to Judaism and his debt to Hellenism. A fundamentally different approach to Paul, however, came to dominate the scholarship of the post-war period.

---

[19] Bultmann, *TNT* 1:272-79.
[20] Bultmann, *TNT* 1:264.
[21] Bultmann, *TNT* 1: chs. 4–5.
[22] Bultmann, *TNT* 1:239.
[23] Bultmann, *TNT* 1:287, 296.
[24] Bultmann, *TNT* 1:302.
[25] Bultmann, *TNT* 1:190-91.

2. Paul, the Hebrew of Hebrews: Participation in Christ

This fundamentally different interpretation of Paul placed the apostle firmly in his Jewish context. Although it was advanced by only a small minority of scholars throughout the nineteenth and early twentieth centuries, after the World War II the Jewishness of Paul, and the fundamental continuity of his gospel with the religion of Judaism and the teaching of Jesus, began to emerge as an increasingly strong consensus. This interpretation, in turn, has engendered significant new debates of its own.

2.1. Paul, Jewish Prophet of Being-in-Christ: Albert Schweitzer

Albert Schweitzer (1875–1965) was one of the first scholars in our period to argue that Paul's announcement of the gospel, like Jesus' earlier proclamation of the kingdom, was thoroughly Jewish. Schweitzer's first work, titled *Geschichte der Paulinischen Forschung* (1911), offered—like his earlier *Geschichte der Leben-Jesu-Forschung*—an iconoclastic summary and critique of nineteenth-century German scholarship on the apostle.[26] Schweitzer's own substantive treatment of Paul had to wait almost twenty years, until the publication of *Die Mystik des Apostels Paulus* in 1930.[27]

In relation to the first question, Schweitzer argued that Paul's gospel was in "complete agreement" with the very Jewish proclamation of Jesus: it was rooted in Jewish apocalyptic, and dominated by the eschatological expectation of the coming Messiah.[28] Schweitzer was for this reason scathing of the approach adopted in the history of religions school:

> those who labor to explain [Paul] on the basis of Hellenism, are like a man who should bring water from a long distance in leaky watering cans in order to water a garden lying beside a stream.[29]

To Schweitzer's mind, the quest to understand Paul by comparing him with the Hellenistic mystery religions was misguided, especially since a complete explanation for his thought was ready to hand in Jewish apocalyptic eschatology and the proclamation of Jesus.[30] Nevertheless, Schweitzer readily acknowledged that although "Paul was not the Hellenizer of Christianity . . . his eschatological mysticism of the Being-in-Christ . . . gave it a form in which it could be Hellenized."[31] Significant here was Schweitzer's insistence that Paul saw Christ as "the end of the law" (Rom 10:4): although the Jewish law continues to bind those outside of Christ, "the law ceases where the Messianic Kingdom begins"

---

[26] Schweitzer, *Paulinischen Forschung*.
[27] Schweitzer, *Die Mystik des Apostels Paulus* (Tübingen: Mohr [Siebeck], 1930).
[28] Schweitzer, *Mysticism*, xxiv.
[29] Schweitzer, *Mysticism*, 140. Cf. Schweitzer, *Mysticism*, 27 offers the following criticism of Reitzenstein: "before the poor apostle can get a word in, he has overwhelmed him with a shower of parallel passages from the Hellenistic literature."
[30] Schweitzer, *Mysticism*, 113.
[31] Schweitzer, *Mysticism*, ix.

and therefore "the law is no longer valid for those who are in Christ Jesus."[32] Thus, though Paul's proclamation was thoroughly Jewish, his law-free gospel paved the way for the later de-Judaizing of the Christian message.

This "eschatological mysticism of the Being-in-Christ" was Schweitzer's answer to the second question, that of the center of Paul's thought. According to Schweitzer:

> The fundamental thought of Pauline mysticism runs thus: I am in Christ; in Him I know myself as a being who is raised above this sensuous, sinful, and transient world and already belongs to the transcendent; in Him I am assured of resurrection; in Him I am a Child of God . . . Being-in-Christ is conceived as a having died and risen with Him, in consequence of which the participant has been freed from sin and from the law, possesses the Spirit of Christ, and is assured of resurrection . . . this "being-in-Christ" is the prime enigma of the Pauline teaching: once grasped it gives the clue to the whole.[33]

For Schweitzer, the mystical doctrine of dying and rising again with Christ lies at the heart of Paul's thought. The centrality of this "being-in-Christ" logically follows from Paul's "idea of predestination to the Messianic kingdom."[34] Though apprehended by faith, entered into through baptism, and celebrated in the Lord's Supper, the participation of the elect in Christ is foreordained and thus ultimately independent of human apprehension. According to Schweitzer, Paul's great "achievement was to grasp, as the thing essential to being a Christian, the experience of union with Christ."[35] The necessary corollary of this emphasis on the centrality of "being-in-Christ," however, was the relegation of Paul's teaching about justification by faith to the periphery. Like William Wrede before him,[36] Schweitzer argued that:

> the doctrine of righteousness by faith is . . . a subsidiary crater, which has formed within the rim of the main crater—the mystical doctrine of redemption through the being-in-Christ.[37]

That is to say, according to Schweitzer, Paul's doctrine of justification by faith was a "battle doctrine" drawn from him by the opposition of Jewish agitators, rather than a central element of his thought.[38]

Schweitzer's case endeared him to neither the academy nor the church. Writing as he did at the time when the history of religions school exercised great influence, his case for a Jewish Paul largely fell on deaf ears. His emphasis on union with Christ as the center of Paul's theology, while in many ways similar to the emphasis of Reformed theology from Calvin onwards, faced a cold reception

---

[32] Schweitzer, *Mysticism*, 188-89.
[33] Schweitzer, *Mysticism*, 1, 3.
[34] Schweitzer, *Mysticism*, 101.
[35] Schweitzer, *Mysticism*, 377.
[36] W. Wrede, *Paulus* (Halle: Gebauer-Schwetschke, 1904).
[37] Schweitzer, *Mysticism*, 225.
[38] Schweitzer, *Mysticism*, 205-26.

in Lutheran Germany, especially since Schweitzer's construction (unlike that of Reformed theology), involved the relegation of justification by faith to the periphery. In a later time, under different conditions, Schweitzer's insights came to be appreciated. But prior to World War II, the vast majority of Christian scholarship on Paul, both Catholic and Protestant, continued to posit a sharp break between Paul and his Jewish forbears.

2.2. *The Jewish Paul: the Post-war Paradigm Shift*

a) Early Voices

Schweitzer was, to be sure, not a lone voice in early twentieth-century scholarship. The Reformed branch of Protestant theology had, following Calvin, long emphasized the deep continuity between the way of salvation presented in the Old Testament (OT), and that offered in Christ in the New. More specifically, there were significant protests against the caricature of Judaism in Christian theology and scholarship before World War II, most significantly from C. G. Montefiore[39] and G. F. Moore,[40] who argued that first-century Judaism was not a religion of legalistic works-righteousness, but one of grace. Nevertheless, such protests, like that of Schweitzer, were largely ignored.

The situation was different, however, after World War II. The horrors of the holocaust sensitized the academy and the church to Christian mistreatment of Jews. The result was a new openness to the case for the Jewishness of Paul's gospel made earlier by Schweitzer, Montefiore, and Moore, and a long overdue re-evaluation of first-century Judaism in Christian scholarship. At the same time, the beginnings of the post-modern rediscovery of narrative and to community opened the way for new readings of Paul which were more sensitive to the "story of Israel" and "church as community" emphases in his letters.

b) Paul the Jewish Rabbi: W. D. Davies

The first to pursue these lines of argument after the War was the Welsh-born, Cambridge-trained scholar W. D. Davies, who spent the majority of his academic career in the United States (Duke University 1950–1955; 1966–1981; Princeton University 1955–1959; Union Theological Seminary, New York 1959–1966). Davies' major work *Paul and Rabbinic Judaism*[41] has been said to mark "a

---

[39] C. G. Montefiore, "Rabbinic Judaism and the Epistles of St Paul," *JQR* 13 (1900–1901), 161-217; C. G. Montefiore, *Judaism and St. Paul: Two Essays* (London: Max Goschen, 1914).
[40] G. F. Moore, *History of Religions: Judaism* (International Theological Library 2; Edinburgh: T. & T. Clark, 1914); cf. G. F. Moore, "Christian Writers on Judaism," *HTR* 14 (1921): 197-254; G. F. Moore, *Judaism in the First Centuries of the Christian Era: The Age of the Tannaim* (3 vols.; Cambridge, Mass.: Harvard University Press, 1927–1930).
[41] W. D. Davies, *Paul and Rabbinic Judaism: Some Rabbinic Elements in Pauline Theology* (London: SPCK, 1948). The work is now in its 4th edition: W. D. Davies, *Paul and Rabbinic Judaism: Some Rabbinic Elements in Pauline Theology* (4th ed.; Philadelphia: Fortress, 1980).

watershed in the history of scholarship on Paul and Judaism,"[42] and to be "one of the few epoch-making books in modern Pauline studies."[43] Davies' major achievement was to demonstrate, via analysis of the Jewish sources, that Schweitzer's instinct was correct: Paul is best understood in his first-century Jewish context.

In relation to first-century Judaism, Davies maintained that the traditional Protestant (Lutheran) reading of Paul as the arch-critic of Judaism produces an inaccurate caricature of Judaism as a lifeless religion of legalistic works-righteousness. In relation to Paul's own thought, Davies argued, in contrast to Schweitzer, that Paul is best located not within the matrix of apocalyptic Judaism, but within the Rabbinic Judaism that emerged from the Pharisaism of Paul's own day. On this basis, Davies insisted that Paul saw the Christian faith not as the "antithesis of Judaism but its fulfillment."[44] Indeed, Davies saw deep continuity between the biblical narrative and Paul's gospel: Paul interpreted the problem of the human condition in relation to the fall of Adam and Jewish ideas about the "evil impulse";[45] Paul's language about dying and rising with Christ reflects not Hellenistic mystery religions, but Jewish ideas about Israel's solidarity with the Messiah;[46] Paul's teaching about the Christian life presents it as a recapitulation of the story of Israel.[47] In all of this, Paul's originality lay not in a radical departure from Judaism, but in his declaration that the "age to come," long expected in Judaism, had now arrived in Jesus, the Jewish Messiah. This involved for Paul a renewal of the people of God, by the gift of the Spirit, to include Gentiles, and a renewal of the Jewish law in the "law of the Messiah" (Gal 6:2). In answer to the first question, then, Davies wrested Paul from those who had placed him amongst the Greeks, and planted him "firmly back into the soil of his native Judaism."[48]

In this context, it should be no surprise that Davies answered the second question by identifying the union of believers with Christ, the second Adam, as the center of Paul's thought. Indeed, Davies agreed with Schweitzer that justification by faith, while not unimportant, is a subsidiary element in the apostle's thought, and one which was only drawn from him in the polemical context of his argument with Judaizers.[49] It is at this point, however, that Davies has been rightly criticized. For while it is now hard to argue with his case for Paul's Jewishness, Davies' failure to account for Paul's radical—at times vehement—critique of Judaism, is a major oversight. Significant discussion of Paul's critique of Judaism is conspicuous by its absence in Davies' work. He

---

[42] E. P. Sanders, *Paul and Palestinian Judaism: A Comparison of Patterns of Religion* (Phildelphia: Fortress, 1977), 7.
[43] Neill and Wright, *Interpretation*, 412.
[44] D. R. A. Hare, "W. D. Davies," in Donald K. McKim, ed., *The Dictionary of Major Biblical Interpreters* (Downers Grove: IVP, 2007), 352.
[45] Davies, *Rabbinic Judaism*, 17-35.
[46] Davies, *Rabbinic Judaism*, 36-57.
[47] Davies, *Rabbinic Judaism*, 146.
[48] So N. T. Wright, *What Saint Paul Really Said: Was Paul of Tarsus the Real Founder of Christianity?* (Oxford: Lion, 1997), 16.
[49] Davies, *Rabbinic Judaism*, 221.

provides only a very limited treatment of those passages in which Paul declares that a person is "justified by faith apart from works of the law" (Rom 3:28), or critiques the "works of the law" or Israel "according to the flesh." It would appear, then, not that Davies' swung the pendulum back too far in the direction of Paul's Jewishness, but that in rightly emphasizing Paul's Jewishness, he failed to adequately account for what is distinctly Christian about the apostle to the Gentiles.

c) Paul and the Robust Conscience: Krister Stendahl

The next significant contribution to this emerging "new perspective on Paul" came from Krister Stendahl, a Swedish Lutheran scholar based at Harvard University. In a provocative essay of 1963 titled *The Apostle Paul and the Introspective Conscience of the West*, Stendahl, like Moore, argued that the Protestant categorization of Judaism as a religion of works-righteousness is unfounded, and owed more to Luther's critique of sixteenth-century Catholicism than to Paul's critique of first-century Judaism:

> For the Jew, the law did not require a static or pedantic perfectionism but supposed a covenant relationship in which there was room for forgiveness and repentance and where God applied the measure of grace.[50]

This reappraisal of first-century Judaism required a corresponding reappraisal of Paul's theology. Stendahl argued that the emphasis on the doctrine of justification in the Western Christian tradition from Augustine to Luther and beyond was an outworking of the "introspective conscience of the West," and foreign to Paul. From a survey of Pauline texts, Stendahl argued that Paul, in fact, had a "robust conscience."[51] Put briefly, Paul did not struggle with Augustine's or Luther's guilt problem. Thus, while Luther was interested in individual salvation, and asked the question how he could find a gracious God, Paul was more interested in salvation history, and asked the question of how Gentiles can find a place in God's covenant community. Thus, according to Stendahl, justification by faith is not the heart of Paul's teaching, intended as the salve to the guilty conscience of individual sinners, but a polemical and pastoral doctrine designed to defend the rights of Gentile believers as full members of the people of God, and heirs of God's promises to Abraham.[52]

d) Paul, Apostle of God's Victory in Christ: Ernst Käsemann

These developing trends in Pauline scholarship found a new and creative synthesis in the writings of Ernst Käsemann, Professor of New Testament at

---

[50] K. Stendahl, "The Apostle Paul and the Introspective Conscience of the West," *HTR* 56 (1963): 201.
[51] K. Stendahl, "Introspective Conscience," 200.
[52] Cf. K. Stendahl, *Paul Among Jews and Gentiles* (London: SCM Press, 1976), 2.

Mainz (1946–1951), Göttingen (1951–1959), and Tübingen (1959–1971), a member of the German Confessing Church under the Nazis, a life-long advocate of socio-political action in the name of Christ, and also a student of Bultmann. Käsemann's interpretation of Paul is a brilliant but ultimately unstable synthesis. In it, he weaves together emphases inherited from the Lutheran tradition interpreted through Bultmann, with emphases taken from the protest associated with Schweitzer.

On the one hand, in answer to the first question, Käsemann insisted with Schweitzer, that Paul must be understood in the framework of Jewish apocalyptic, which he famously suggested was "the mother of all Christian theology."[53] In a series of publications climaxing in his influential 1973 commentary *An die Römer*,[54] Käsemann argued that Paul's gospel proclaimed the Lordship of God in the Messiah, and so stood in deep continuity with the prophets of Israel, and with the kingdom proclamation of Jesus himself.[55] On the other hand, Käsemann insisted with the Lutheran tradition, and with Bultmann, that Paul's doctrine of justification remains central to his thought, standing over against all human pride and self-justification, including Jewish boasting in the law.[56] For Käsemann, then, Paul's gospel was rooted in Jewish apocalyptic, and announced to the entire world that the sovereign Lord would judge not only the Gentiles, but also even his own covenant people. The cross of the Messiah pronounced God's judgment on all human pride, including Jewish pride, and it was only in submitting to that judgment, through faith in Christ, that all people, Gentile and Jew alike, might be justified before God. Thus like Baur, the history of religions school, Bultmann, and others in that stream of scholarship, Käsemann gave due weight to Paul's significant critique of Judaism. Unlike that school, however, Käsemann saw that Paul, like the prophets before him, opposed Judaism *from within*.[57]

This novel reconstruction grew out of Käsemann's conviction that Paul's righteousness language must be set a larger canvas than was otherwise recognized. Paul's gospel, according to Käsemann, announced God's victory, in Christ, over all the powers of evil on a cosmic scale. This victory over the powers of evil includes victory not only over sin and death, but also over the law, by which human beings attempt to establish their own righteousness before God, and

---

[53] E. Käsemann, "The Beginnings of Christian Theology," in *New Testament Questions of Today* (London: SCM Press, 1969), 102.

[54] See esp. E. Käsemann, "The Righteousness of God in Paul," in *New Testament Questions of Today* [London: SCM, 1969], 168-82; trans. of "Gottesgerechtigkeit bei Paulus," *ZTK* 58 (1961): 367-78; E. Käsemann, "Justification and Salvation History in the Epistle to the Romans," in *Perspectives on Paul* (London: SCM, 1971), 60-78; trans. of E. Käsemann, "Rechtfertigung und Heilsgeschichte im Römerbrief," in *Paulinische Perspektiven* (Tübingen: Mohr [Siebeck], 1969), 108-39; E. Käsemann, *Commentary on Romans* [trans. Geoffrey William Bromiley; 4th ed.; Grand Rapids: Eerdmans, 1980]); trans. of E. Käsemann, *An die Römer*, Handbuch zum Neuen Testament (Tübingen: Mohr [Siebeck], 1973).

[55] Käsemann, "Justification," 74-75.

[56] Käsemann, "Justification," 76 argues, against Stendahl, that "Salvation history must not take precedence over justification. It is its sphere. But justification remains the center, the beginning, and end of salvation history."

[57] Cf. Neill and Wright, *Interpretation*, 419: "Paul opposed *from within* a Jewish framework *rethought* in the light of the cross."

so by their "pious claims and works . . . attempt to bring God into dependence on us."[58] Thus when Paul declares at Rom 1:16-17 that the gospel reveals the "righteousness of God" (δικαιοσύνη θεοῦ), he speaks not merely of God's gift to those in Christ, thus shattering all proud religious pretensions, but more importantly of God's power to transform their lives and, ultimately, to set things right in his world.[59] Put another way, Käsemann insisted, against Bultmann, that the "gift" of righteousness cannot be separated from the giver.

The result of all this was that, in relation to Paul's teaching on justification, Käsemann stood, self-consciously, "between two fronts."[60] On the one hand, though he is clearly indebted to the Lutheran tradition, including not least his own teacher Bultmann, he pushed beyond the boundaries of a forensic and individualist understanding of justification to stress what he saw as its transformative, corporate, and cosmic dimensions.[61] On the other hand, while he affirmed with Stendahl and others that Paul's doctrine of justification was highly polemical in character,[62] he was not content to limit its significance to the margins of theology as a curiosity of first-century Jew-Gentile polemics, insisting instead on its timeless character as "the center, the beginning, and end of salvation history."[63] In Käsemann's influential writings, then, the stage was set for the rise of the new perspective on Paul, and also for its eclipse in a range of post-new perspective interpretations of the apostle to the Gentiles.

2.3. The New Perspective on Paul

The origins of the new perspective on Paul are usually traced to the publication of E. P. Sanders' book titled *Paul and Palestinian Judaism* (1977). This perspective takes as its starting point the conviction of Schweitzer, Davies, Stendahl, and Käsemann that Paul is best understood within his Jewish context. But in reality this involves two new perspectives: a re-evaluation of the nature of first-century Judaism as a religion of grace rather than of legalistic work's righteousness; and a corresponding reinterpretation of Paul. In relation to the first of these new perspectives (on Judaism), there is basic agreement that the old (Lutheran) perspective, according to which Paul opposed the grace of the gospel to the law of Moses, and the faith of the Christian to the works of the Jew, cannot do justice to the evidence. In this respect, it is possible to understand the new perspective, at least in part, as a "Reformed protest (Judaism and the law as positive and God-

---

[58] Käsemann, "Justification," 72.
[59] Käsemann, "Righteousness of God," 180: the "righteousness of God" is "God's sovereignty over the world revealing itself eschatologically in Jesus"; Käsemann, "Justification," 74-75.
[60] Käsemann, "Justification," 76, n. 27.
[61] Käsemann, "Justification," 74 critiques the "individualist curtailment of the Christian message"; Käsemann, "Righteousness of God," 176 confesses that, unlike Bultmann, he finds himself "totally unable to assent to the view that Paul's theology and his philosophy of history are oriented towards the individual."
[62] Käsemann, "Justification," 71: it is "impossible to overstress the polemical character of Paul's doctrine of justification"; Käsemann, "Justification," 74: "Stendahl and his friends are right in protesting against the individualist curtailment of the Christian message."
[63] Käsemann, "Justification," 76.

given) against a Lutheran theology (Judaism as the wrong sort of religion, the law as negative)."[64] In relation to the second new perspective (on Paul), however, the debate is more complex, such that the "new perspective on Paul" is, at best, an umbrella term.[65] In terms of exegesis, the flashpoints have been the meaning of key Pauline words and phrases, especially "righteousness of God," "justification," "works of the law," "faith," and "faith of Christ." In terms of biblical theology, the key issues have been the nature of righteousness language in the Christian canon, the relationship between the law and the gospel in Paul's thought, the extent to which Paul anticipates the Reformation doctrine of the imputation of Christ's righteousness, and the role of Christian obedience in the final justification of believers. For the sake of brevity, the following survey briefly outlines the (at points very different) interpretations of Sanders, J. D. G. Dunn, and N. T. Wright, who are commonly acknowledged as the three leading voices within the new perspective on Paul, before surveying the range of the responses to this new wave in Pauline scholarship.[66]

a) E. P. Sanders

E. P. Sanders completed his Th.D. at Union Theological Seminary, New York (1966) and held teaching posts at McMaster University (1966–1984), the University of Oxford (Dean Ireland's Professor of the Exegesis of Holy Scripture: 1984–1989), and Duke University (Arts and Sciences Professor of Religion: 1990–2005). In a series of publications from 1973 onwards, climaxing in two major works titled *Paul and Palestinian Judaism* (1977) and *Paul, the Law, and the Jewish People* (1983),[67] Sanders sought to unseat the then dominant Protestant understanding of first-century Judaism, exemplified in the work of Bultmann, and

---

[64] Wright, "Current Anglophone Scholarship," 369; cf. N. T. Wright, *Justification: God's Plan and Paul's Vision* (London: SPCK, 2009), 53.
[65] Reviews of the debate, from varying perspectives, are offered by M. B. Thompson, *The New Perspective on Paul* (Cambridge: Grove Books, 2002); G. P. Waters, *Justification and the New Perspective on Paul: A Review and Response* (Phillipsburg: Prebyterian & Reformed, 2004); S. Westerholm, *Perspectives Old and New on Paul: The "Lutheran" Paul and his Critics* (Grand Rapids: Eerdmans, 2004); Aune, "Recent Readings," 188-245; J. K. Beilby, P. R. Eddy, and S. E. Enderlein, "Justification in contemporary debate," in James K. Beilby and Paul R. Eddy, eds., *Justification: Five Views* (Downers Grove: IVP, 2011), 53-82; K. L. Yinger, *The New Perspective on Paul: An Introduction* (Eugene: Wipf & Stock, 2011). For a brief review of reactions and discussion at a popular/church level, see P. R. Eddy, J. K. Beilby, and S. E. Enderlein, "Justification in Historical Perspective," in Eddy and Beilby, *Justification*, 13-15.
[66] E.g. Aune, "Recent Readings," 205; J. Piper, *The Future of Justification: A Response to N. T. Wright* (Wheaton: Crossway, 2007), 27. Note, however, Wright, *Justification*, 12, who emphasizes that a larger number of scholars have contributed to the development of the "new perspective."
[67] E. P. Sanders, "Patterns of Religion in Paul and Rabbinic Judaism: A Holistic Method of Comparison," *HTR* 66 (1973): 455-78; E. P. Sanders, "The Covenant as a Soteriological Category and the Nature of Salvation in Palestinian and Hellenistic Judaism," in R. Hamerton-Kelly and R. Scroggs, eds., *Jews, Greeks, and Christians* (Leiden: Brill, 1976), 11-44; Sanders, *Paul and Palestinian Judaism*; E. P. Sanders, "On the Question of Fulfilling the Law in Paul and Rabbinic Judaism," in E. Bammel, ed., *Donum Gentilicum* (Oxford: Oxford University Press, 1978), 103-26; E. P. Sanders, *Paul, the Law, and the Jewish People* (Philadelphia: Fortress, 1983).

to offer a corresponding re-reading of Paul.[68]

To begin with, Sanders argued that first-century Judaism was not a legalistic religion of merit-based works-righteousness. On the contrary, he insisted, the rabbinic sources reveal a religious system which he described as "covenantal nomism." In Sanders' words:

> Covenantal nomism is the view that one's place in God's plan is established on the basis of the covenant and that the covenant requires, as the proper response of man, his obedience to its commandments, while providing means of atonement for transgression.[69]

According to Sanders, the variegated Judaisms of the first century shared a fundamental understanding of the covenant as the key soteriological category.[70] In this context, he insisted that first-century Jews understood that God had elected Israel purely by grace. First-century Jews did not understand themselves as miserable sinners in need of salvation, but as God's chosen people. They did not obey the law in order to earn God's favor, but as an expression of their covenant with him, and as a means of maintaining their place among the chosen people. They believed that "salvation comes by *membership* in the covenant, while obedience to the commandments *preserves* one's place in the covenant."[71] Like Paul, therefore, first-century Jews understood that salvation is by grace; it is not earned by meritorious obedience.[72] Putting all of this together, Sanders made a crucial distinction between "getting in" and "staying in."[73] In first-century Judaism, he argued, obedience to the law was never a means of getting in to favor with God; it was, however, the necessary requirement of staying in the covenant: "keeping the law is always the *condition* for remaining in the covenant, never the means of earning God's grace."[74]

Sanders asserted that his re-reading of first-century Judaism required a significant re-reading of Paul. The crucial question raised by his analysis, for Pauline studies, was why, if Judaism taught salvation by grace, did Paul ultimately reject it? Put another way, if Paul's Jewish contemporaries were not trying to earn their salvation by obedience to the law (the common Protestant view), then who, or what, was Paul opposing when he declared that justification is "by faith apart from works of the law" (Rom 3:28)? Sanders own answer to this question was straightforward, but has ultimately proved unsatisfying. He suggested, with Stendahl, that Paul's primary critique of Judaism was a salvation-historical one.[75] Paul's "real attack on Judaism," Sanders suggested, was focused on the "the idea of the covenant" which restricted salvation to the Jews.[76] Put

---

[68] Sanders, "Patterns of Religion," 455 n. 1.
[69] Sanders, *Paul and Palestinian Judaism*, 75.
[70] Sanders, "Covenant," 39.
[71] Sanders, "Covenant," 41.
[72] Sanders, *Paul and Palestinian Judaism*, 543.
[73] Sanders, *Paul an the Jewish People*, 6.
[74] Sanders, "Covenant," 40; cf. Sanders, *Paul and Palestinian Judaism*, 420.
[75] Sanders, *Paul an the Jewish People*, 140.
[76] Sanders, *Paul an the Jewish People*, 55.

simply, Judaism had failed because it had failed to recognize that in Messiah Jesus God offers salvation for all, Jew and Gentile alike. Or, in Sanders' memorable words: "this is what Paul finds wrong in Judaism: it is not Christianity."[77]

For this reason, despite Paul's agreement with Judaism on the question of grace and works, Sanders argued that "Paul presents *an essentially different type of religiousness from any found in Palestinian Jewish literature.*"[78] Paul's "pattern of religion" does not fit the covenantal nomism, which Sanders found in Palestinian Judaism;[79] it is a "change of entire systems."[80] In particular, Sanders argued that Paul's christocentric theology differed from Judaism in three important respects. First, while the covenant was the key soteriological category in Judaism,[81] it played only a minor role in Paul's thought,[82] being replaced by Paul's "participationist eschatology" according to which participation in Christ by faith is the key soteriological category.[83] Second, in terms of the human predicament, while Judaism began with the presumption of God's favor under the covenant, and understood sin as transgression, which can be rectified by atonement and renewed obedience,[84] Paul began with the paradox of a crucified Messiah (the solution), and surmised from this the plight of humanity in bondage to sin.[85] Third, while Judaism employed righteousness language to speak of the maintenance of right relationships within the covenant,[86] for Paul righteousness or justification was "a *transfer term*," referring to the transfer of believers from the power of sin to the kingdom of God through their participation in Christ.[87] The result of all of this, of course, was that Sanders, like Schweitzer before him, rejected the Protestant (Lutheran) emphasis on justification by faith as the center of Paul's thought, and gave that place instead to Paul's teaching about participation in Christ.[88] In the final analysis, Sanders argued that the difference between Judaism and Paul was primarily a question of salvation history: "what is wrong with the law, and thus with Judaism, is that it does not provide for God's ultimate purpose, that of saving the entire world through faith in Christ."[89]

---

[77] Sanders, *Paul and Palestinian Judaism*, 552; Sanders, *Paul and the Jewish People*, 47.
[78] Sanders, *Paul and Palestinian Judaism*, 543 (italics original).
[79] Sanders, *Paul and Palestinian Judaism*, 513-14, 543.
[80] Sanders, *Paul and Palestinian Judaism*, 550.
[81] Sanders, "Covenant," 39.
[82] Sanders, "Patterns of Religion," 476.
[83] Sanders, *Paul and Palestinian Judaism*, 552.
[84] Sanders, *Paul and Palestinian Judaism*, 547.
[85] Sanders, *Paul and Palestinian Judaism*, 482, 484; cf. 547: Paul's characteristic understanding of sin is not as transgression of the covenant but as "a power from which one must be freed in order to be saved."
[86] Sanders, *Paul and Palestinian Judaism*, 544.
[87] Sanders, *Paul and Palestinian Judaism*, 544.
[88] Sanders, *Paul and Palestinian Judaism*, 434-42, 502-8.
[89] Sanders, *Paul an the Jewish People*, 47.

b) J. D. G. Dunn

Despite Sanders' enormous influence, it was J. D. G. Dunn, Lightfoot Professor of Divinity at the University of Durham (1982–2003), who first popularized the phrase "new perspective on Paul" with the title of his 1982 Manson Memorial Lecture.[90] Since then, Dunn has argued his case in an impressive series of publications on Paul and his letters in the context of early Christianity, including a large commentary on *Romans* (1988) and a major study of the *Theology of the Apostle Paul* (1998).[91] In essence, Dunn has taken Sanders' interpretation of first-century Judaism as his starting point, pushed this reading further, and then offered a different, and ultimately more influential, re-reading of Paul.

In relation to first-century Judaism, Dunn's initial new perspective essay supported Sanders' work in undermining "one hundred years of falsely placing Paul and Judaism in fundamental antithesis."[92] In the same essay, Dunn clearly agreed with Sanders in rejecting the Lutheran hermeneutic which had dominated Pauline scholarship,[93] and adopted Sanders' categories of getting in and staying in as a description of covenantal nomism in first-century Judaism.[94] On the other hand, Dunn suggested that Sanders "failed to take the opportunity his own mold-breaking work offered," namely, "to explore how far Paul's theology could be explicated in relation to Judaism's covenantal nomism."[95] Dunn thus criticized Sanders for replacing the "Lutheran Paul" with an "idiosyncratic Paul who in arbitrary and irrational manner turns his face against the glory and greatness of Judaism's covenant theology and abandons Judaism simply because it is not Christianity."[96]

In terms of Paul's own theology, Dunn sees a much greater degree of continuity with Judaism than Sanders ever envisaged. In particular, Dunn argues that Paul was not against the idea of covenant, or against the law, but against a

---

[90] Published as: J. D. G. Dunn, "The New Perspective on Paul," *BJRL* 65 (1983): 95-122. Note, however J. D. G. Dunn, "The New Perspective: Whence, What, Whither?," in J. D. G. Dunn, ed., *The New Perspective on Paul* (Grand Rapids: Eerdmans, 2008), 7 n. 24 where Dunn himself points out that the phrase was actually coined several years earlier by N. T. Wright in his 1978 Tyndale New Testament Lecture, delivered at Tyndale House, Cambridge on 4 July 1978 and later published as N. T. Wright, "The Paul of History and the Apostle of Faith," *TynB* 29 (1978): 61-88.

[91] Key works include: J. D. G. Dunn, "The Incident at Antioch (Galatians 2:11-18)," *JSNT* 18 (1983): 3-57; J. D. G. Dunn, "Works of the Law and the Curse of the Law (Galatians 3:10-14)," *NTS* 31.4 (1985): 523-42; J. D. G. Dunn, *Romans 1–8* (Dallas: Word, 1988); Dunn, *Romans 9–16*; J. D. G. Dunn, *Jesus, Paul, and the Law: studies in Mark and Galatians* (London: SPCK, 1990); J. D. G. Dunn, *The Partings of the Ways: Between Christianity and Judaism and their Significance for the Character of Christianity* (London: SCM Press, 1991); J. D. G. Dunn, "How New was Paul's Gospel? The Problem of Continuity and Discontinuity," in L. Ann Jervis and Peter Richardson, eds., *Gospel in Paul: Studies on Corinthians, Galatians, and Romans for Richard N. Longenecker* (Sheffield: Sheffield Academic Press, 1994); J. D. G. Dunn and A. M. Suggate, *The Justice of God: A Fresh Look at the Old Doctrine of Justification by Faith* (Grand Rapids: Eerdmans, 1994); J. D. G. Dunn, *The Theology of Paul the Apostle* (Grand Rapids: Eerdmans, 1998); J. D. G. Dunn, *The New Perspective on Paul* (rev. ed.; Grand Rapids: Eerdmans, 2008).

[92] Dunn, "New Perspective," 98.
[93] Dunn, "New Perspective," 95-96.
[94] Dunn, "New Perspective," 99.
[95] Dunn, "New Perspective," 100.
[96] Dunn, "New Perspective," 101.

particular Jewish *attitude* to the law. What Paul rejected was Jewish *nationalistic exclusivism*, which boasted in its exclusive membership of the covenant over against other nations, and which distorted the law into a means of excluding Gentiles.[97] In particular, Paul's polemic against the works of the law (e.g. Gal 2:16; 3:2, 5, 10; Rom 3:27; 4:2; 9:32; 11:6) was directed not at the law itself, but at the Jewish use of certain elements of the law (especially circumcision, food laws, and Sabbath) as badges of covenant membership or boundary markers designed to exclude Gentiles.[98] Paul's problem with these works was that, when allowed to retain significance in the church, they disastrously divided the single body of Christ.

The results of this reconstruction for Paul's teaching on justification by faith are significant. Dunn stresses that Paul's teaching about justification must be understood in the context of his mission to the Gentiles. As a polemic against Jewish nationalistic exclusivism, it expresses "Paul's fundamental objection to the idea that God has limited his saving goodness to a particular people."[99] In Dunn's words:

> [J]ustification by faith is the banner raised by Paul against any and all such presumption of privileged status before God by virtue of race, culture or nationality, against any and all attempts to preserve such spurious distinctions by practices that exclude and divide.[100]

That is, according to Dunn, justification by faith includes an important ecclesiological or sociological dimension: faith in Christ rather than works of law is the badge of membership in the new covenant people of God.[101] Nevertheless, Dunn has more recently affirmed that justification by faith is not merely an ecclesiological or sociological principle, but also involves the "vertical" dimension of a sinner's standing before God.[102] Even at this point, however, Dunn believes a significant modification to the traditional Protestant understanding is necessary. In particular, he sees in Paul an emphasis on future justification on the basis of Spirit-enabled Christian obedience that is lacking in traditional Protestant formulations. As Dunn puts it:

> Paul's theology of justification by faith alone has to be qualified as final justification by faith *and* works accomplished by the believer in the power of the Spirit.[103]

Although this is a significant departure from Reformation teaching, Dunn has most recently insisted that the new perspective, at least his version of it, was never designed to undermine the traditional Reformation understanding of

---

[97] Dunn, *The Partings of the Ways*, 137-38.
[98] Dunn, "New Perspective," 114, 117, 120; Dunn, "Works of the Law," 528.
[99] Dunn and Suggate, *The Justice of God*, 28.
[100] Dunn, *New Perspective*, 205.
[101] Dunn, "New Perspective," 194-98.
[102] Dunn, "Whence, What, Whither?" 85.
[103] Dunn, "Whence, What, Whither?" 85.

justification by faith as God's declaration that those in Christ are right with himself. It was, rather "primarily an attempt to highlight a missing dimension of Paul's doctrine of justification."[104]

c) N. T. Wright

N. T. Wright is currently Research Professor of New Testament and Early Christianity at St Mary's College, University of St Andrews, Scotland, having held a number of university teaching posts (McGill 1981–1986; Oxford 1986–1993) and offices in the Church of England (Dean of Lichfield 1994–1999; Canon Theologian Westminster Abbey 2000–2002; Bishop of Durham 2003–2010) following the completion of his Oxford University doctoral thesis on Paul's Letter to the Romans (1981).[105] Wright's contribution to the new perspective on Paul began with his 1978 Tyndale New Testament Lecture titled *The Paul of History and the Apostle of Faith*.[106] Through a long line of publications, both scholarly and popular,[107] he has a made a significant impact on Pauline studies already,[108] even if his major work is yet to come.[109] Although advocating a "new view" of the apostle Paul, Wright has also been at pains to emphasize, especially in more recent publications, that he considers himself to stand in the Reformed Protestant tradition, and to be offering a corrective to certain emphases in that tradition

---

[104] J. D. G. Dunn, "New Perspective Response," in Beilby and Eddy, *Justification*, 119-20; cf. Dunn, "Whence, What, Whither?," 96.

[105] N. T. Wright, "The Messiah and the People of God: A Study in Pauline Theology with Particular Reference to the Argument of the Epistle to the Romans" (Oxford University, 1981).

[106] Wright, "Paul of History," 61-88.

[107] N. T. Wright, "Justification: The Biblical Basis and its Relevance for Contemporary Evangelicalism," in Gavin Reid, ed., *The Great Acquittal: Justification by Faith and Current Christian Thought* (London: Collins, 1980), 13-119; N. T. Wright, *The Epistles of Paul to the Colossians and to Philemon: An Introduction and Commentary* (Leicester: IVP, 1986); N. T. Wright, *The Climax of the Covenant: Christ and the Law in Pauline Theology* (Edinburgh: T. & T. Clark, 1991); N. T. Wright, "Romans and the Theology of Paul," in David M. Hay and E. Elizabeth Johnson, eds., *Pauline Theology, Volume III* (Minneapolis: Fortress, 1995), 30-67; Wright, *Saint Paul*; N. T. Wright, "Paul's Gospel and Caesar's Empire," in Richard A. Horsley, ed., *Paul and Politics: Ekklesia, Israel, Imperium, Interpretation: Essays in Honor of Krister Stendahl* (Harrisburg: Trinity Press International, 2000), 160-83; N. T. Wright, "Romans," in Leander Keck, ed., *New Interpreter's Bible* (Nashville: Abingdon, 2002); N. T. Wright, *Paul: In Fresh Perspective* (Minneapolis: Fortress, 2005); N. T. Wright, "New Perspectives on Paul," in Bruce L. McCormack, ed., *Justification in Perspective: Historical Developments and Contemporary Challenges* (Grand Rapids: Baker, 2006); Wright, *Justification*; N. T. Wright, "Justification: Yesterday, Today, and Forever," *JETS* 54.1 (2011): 49-64; N. T. Wright, "Israel's Scriptures in Paul's Narrative Theology," *Theology* 115.5 (2012): 323-29; N. T. Wright, "Paul and the Patriarch: The Role of Abraham in Romans 4," *JSNT* 35 (2013): 207-41. Wright's popular level *For Everyone* commentary series on the New Testament is also now complete.

[108] The significance of Wright's contribution may be judged by the fact that the 2010 Wheaton Theology Conference was dedicated to a consideration of his work, the proceedings of which are now published as N. Perrin and R. B. Hays, *Jesus, Paul, and the People of God: A Theological Dialogue with N. T. Wright* (London: SPCK, 2011).

[109] The next promised volume in Wright's comprehensive *Christian Origins and the Question of God* series is to deal with Paul and his theology.

rather than a wholesale rejection of it.[110]

On the question of first-century Judaism and Paul's critique of it, Wright is in basic agreement with Sanders and Dunn. As early as 1978 he affirmed, with Sanders, that traditional Pauline scholarship "has manufactured a false Paul by manufacturing a false Judaism for him to oppose."[111] According to Wright, first-century Jews were not seeking to earn their salvation by meritorious works, but were confident to the point of presumption in their status as God's elect;[112] Israel's "meta-sin" was not her attempt to earn favor with God by obedience, but her attempt to "confine grace to one race" by turning the symbols of her covenant with God (Sabbath, dietary laws, circumcision) into "badges of superiority," and so effectively excluding Gentiles from any share in the blessing promised to Abraham.[113] In partial agreement with Dunn, Wright argues that by the phrase works of the law Paul intends the law "seen as that which defines Israel over against other nations."[114] His polemic against works of the law is, then, not directed against the law itself, nor against a Jewish attempt to earn salvation by keeping the law, but against a kind of Jewish presumption which saw salvation as the inalienable right of the Jews and the Jews alone. Similarly, Paul's contrast between faith and works was not a contrast between believing and doing in the traditional Lutheran sense, but between relying on Jesus and relying on the law. The problem with Judaism, as Paul saw it, was not works-righteousness in the sense of the attempt to earn salvation by moral effort, but works-righteousness in the sense of Jewish national exclusivism.[115]

It is in his reading of Paul's positive teaching, however, that Wright has made his major contribution. The main distinctive of Wright's approach is his insistence that Paul's letters must be read in the context of the covenant, which he explicates in biblical theological terms as "God's single plan through Israel for the world."[116] For this reason Wright is critical of the way in which later theology has screened out the "Jewish, Messianic, covenantal, Abrahamic, history of Israel overtones" of Paul's theology.[117] In this context, it is no surprise that Wright argues that God's righteousness, both in the Old Testament and in Paul, refers to "God's own faithfulness to his promises, to the covenant."[118] Paul's break with Judaism, he says, did not come in the shape of his theology, but in its content.[119] Like Judaism, Paul's theology was grounded in God's gracious covenant, envisaged covenant members living in response to God's grace, and looked

---

[110] E.g. Wright, "New Perspectives," 247-48, 262; Wright, *Justification*, 72-73, 252.
[111] Wright, "Paul of History," 78.
[112] Wright, "New Perspectives," 263.
[113] Wright, *Climax of the Covenant*, 240, 243.
[114] Wright, "Romans," 480-81: "works of law" is "Torah seen as that which defines Israel over against other nations witnessed by the performance of the works that Torah prescribes—not only Sabbath, food laws, and circumcision, though these are obvious things that, sociologically speaking, give substance to the theologically based separation."
[115] E.g. Wright, *Justification*, 53-58.
[116] Wright, *Justification*, 18.
[117] Wright, *Justification*, 62.
[118] Wright, *Saint Paul*, 96; cf. Wright, *Justification*, 52.
[119] Wright, *Saint Paul*, 132.

forward to a final judgment according to works.[120] Unlike Judaism, however, Paul declared that in Jesus the long-awaited Jewish Messiah had come, and that therefore the great final age, in which God's promise of blessing would go out to all nations, had now arrived. For this reason, the badge of membership in the true people of God was no longer the Jewish works of the law but faith in the Messiah.[121] Paul's burden was to affirm that salvation is by "grace not race."[122]

On this basis, Wright advances a fourfold understanding of justification in Paul. He argues, firstly, that the Greek δικ- root has its origins in Hebrew law court imagery and that righteousness or justification in this law court setting "*does not denote an action which transforms someone* so much as *a declaration which grants them a status*"; it is "the status that someone has when the court has found in their favor."[123] At this point, Wright clearly affirms the Reformation understanding of justification as a forensic declaration, over against the Augustinian/Roman Catholic view of justification as moral transformation. Secondly, Wright argues that this law court language can only be understood within the broader framework of God's covenant with Israel, his "single plan through Israel for the world."[124] In this context, justification refers to God's final vindication of his true people in fulfillment of his covenant promise, demonstrating that those who trust in Jesus the Messiah are, in fact, the true descendants of Abraham. Related to this, thirdly, Wright insists that Paul's teaching about justification must be set within his eschatology: justification is, above all, the verdict God will pass over his covenant people, those who trust in Jesus, *on the final day*.[125] Finally, as already indicated in the second and third points, Wright argues that Paul's teaching about justification is intimately related to his Christology. Jesus is the long awaited Jewish Messiah, who did what Israel was always meant to do, who offered God the obedience he required, and whose death and resurrection, as Israel's representative and substitute, enabled God's "single plan through Israel for the world" to proceed.[126] Jesus' resurrection was, therefore, his own vindication or justification, encompassing within it the justification of all those who belong to him.[127] In this sense, although justification properly refers to the verdict of the final day, in Christ "the verdict of the final day (is) brought forward into the present on the basis of the Messiah brought forward into the present, and the resurrection brought forward into the present."[128]

None of this seems particularly controversial, until one realizes that it leads Wright to three positions that have attracted significant criticism. He argues, first, that "justification," for Paul, does not primarily refer to a person's salvation, narrowly understood, but to God's declaration that those in Christ are members of

---

[120] Wright, *Saint Paul*, 19; Wright, "New Perspectives," 253.
[121] Wright, *Saint Paul*, 132.
[122] Wright, *Climax of the Covenant*, 168, 194, 238.
[123] Wright, *Justification*, 70, 69.
[124] Wright, *Justification*, 74.
[125] Wright, *Justification*, 79.
[126] Wright, *Justification*, 83.
[127] Wright, *Justification*, 80.
[128] Wright, *Justification*, 189; cf. 223.

his family, included in the covenant, having been forgiven their sins.[129] Wright argues, second, that "justification," for Paul, does not include the idea of the "imputed righteousness of Christ."[130] And he argues, third, that final justification is in some sense based on the believer's Spirit-inspired obedience.[131] In these three controversial conclusions, however, Wright is not alone. His views are therefore best discussed in the context the ongoing debates regarding the "new perspective." It is to those debates that we must now turn.

2.4. Responses to the New Perspective on Paul: Issues of Ongoing Debate

Responses to the new perspective on Paul have varied widely. At one end of the spectrum, a number of scholars, such as M. Thompson, D. Garlington, and K. Yinger wholeheartedly embrace both the new perspective label and the re-reading of Judaism and Paul that it implies.[132] At the other end of the spectrum, a number of other scholars, such as T. R. Schreiner, M. A. Seifrid, C. P. Venema, J. Piper, D. Moo, and M. Horton, while allowing for various nuances, continue to argue that the Protestant Reformers understood Paul better than the advocates of the newer view.[133] In the middle, other scholars, such as M. Bird, have sought to find a kind of "*via media* between reformed and revisionist readings of Paul."[134] At the same time, it is increasingly recognized that the debate has shifted significantly beyond the initial battle lines drawn up between the old and new perspectives so that, at least since 2001, writers such as B. Byrne and M. Bird have begun to speak of a "Post-New Perspective Perspective,"[135] and others, such as F. Watson and D. Campbell, have offered positions that they consider go "beyond the new

---

[129] Wright, *Saint Paul*, 119, 121-122, 125; cf. Wright, "New Perspectives," 260; Wright, "Romans," 481.

[130] Wright, *Saint Paul*, 98; Wright, *Justification*, 64, 82, 180-81, 186-87.

[131] Wright, *Saint Paul*, 129; Wright, *Paul: In Fresh Perspective*, 121, 148; Wright, "New Perspectives," 260.

[132] Thompson, *New Perspective*; D. Garlington, *In Defense of the New Perspective on Paul: Essays and Reviews* (Eugene: Wipf & Stock, 2005); B. Colijn, "Justification by Faith(fulness)," in *Images of Salvation in the New Testament* (Downers Grove: IVP, 2010); Yinger, *New Perspective*.

[133] T. R. Schreiner, *The Law and its Fulfillment: A Pauline Theology of Law* (Grand Rapids: Baker, 1993), 11; M. A. Seifrid, "Blind Alleys in the Controversy over the Paul of History," *TynB* 45 (1994): 74; C. P. Venema, *The Gospel of Free Acceptance in Christ: An Assessment of the Reformation and "New Perspectives" on Paul* (Edinburgh: Banner of Truth Trust, 2006); D. J. Moo, "Justification in Galatians," in Andreas J. Köstenberger and Robert W. Yarbrough, eds., *Understanding the Times: New Testament Studies in the 21st Century, Essays in Honor of D. A. Carson on the Occasion of His 65th Birthday* (Wheaton: Crossway, 2011), 192; M. Horton, "Traditional Reformed View," in Beilby and Eddy, *Justification*, 83-111. For a survey of such views to 2004 see Westerholm, *Perspectives*, 201-25.

[134] M. F. Bird, "Justification as Forensic Declaration and Covenant Membership: A Via Media Between Reformed and Revisionist Readings of Paul," *TynB* 57.1 (2006): 109-30; cf. M. F. Bird, "What Is There between Minneapolis and St Andrews? A Third Way in the Piper-Wright Debate," *JETS* 54.2 (2011): 299-310; M. F. Bird, "Progressive Reformed View," in Beilby and Eddy, *Justification*, 131-57.

[135] B. Byrne, "Interpreting Romans Theologically in a Post-'New Perspective' Perspective," *HTR* 94 (2001): 227-41; M. F. Bird, "When the Dust Finally Settles: Reaching a Post-New Perspective Perspective," *CTR* 2 (2005): 57-69.

perspective."[136] The result of all of this is that a number of distinct but related issues remain the subject of significant debate. In what follows we briefly outline the state of play on six key questions.

First, the nature of both first-century Judaism, and Paul's critique of it, remains in dispute. On the one hand, Sanders' arguments against the old perspective on Judaism as a religion of works-righteousness have won widespread acceptance. Where Sanders' reconstruction is basically accepted, the tendency is to see Paul's polemic against the works of the law as primarily directed at Jewish presumption and ethnocentrism.[137] On the other hand, a large number of scholars, with S. Gathercole, acknowledge that Sanders has rightly drawn attention to the significance of grace and the covenant in first-century Judaism, but continue to argue that "alongside the emphasis on God's gracious election . . . there is nevertheless a firm belief in final vindication on the basis of works."[138] Indeed, D. A. Carson, in his summative conclusion to the most sustained and comprehensive critique of the new perspective on Judaism to date, judges "not that Sanders is wrong everywhere, but that he is wrong when he tries to establish that his category is right everywhere."[139] Carson finds that first-century Judaism was characterized by a "variegated nomism," and argues that Sanders' broad category of "covenantal nomism" papers over "huge tracts of works-righteousness or merit theology."[140] And many scholars, likewise, continue to understand the target of Paul's polemic to at least include Jewish legalism and merit-righteousness, even if a simultaneous attack on Jewish ethnocentrism cannot be ruled out.[141]

---

[136] F. Watson, *Paul, Judaism, and the Gentiles: Beyond the New Perspective* (Grand Rapids: Eerdmans, 2007), 12-26; D.A. Campbell, *The Deliverance of God: An Apocalyptic Rereading of Justification in Paul* (Grand Rapids: Eerdmans, 2009), 202-3.

[137] Cf. D. A. Carson, "Summaries and Conclusions," in D. A. Carson, Peter T. O'Brien, and Mark A. Seifrid, eds., *Justification and Variegated Nomism: Vol. 1, The Complexities of Second Temple Judaism* (Grand Rapids: Baker, 2001), 505: "at least in the Anglo-Saxon world, it is not going beyond the evidence to say that the new perspective is the reigning paradigm."

[138] S. J. Gathercole, "After the New Perspective: Works, Justification, and Boasting in Early Judaism and Romans 1–5," *TynB* 52 (2001): 304; cf. S. J. Gathercole, *Where is Boasting? Early Jewish Soteriology and Paul's Response in Romans 1–5* (Grand Rapids: Eerdmans, 2002); D. J. Moo, "'Law,' 'Works of the Law,' and Legalism in Paul," *WTJ* 45 (1983): 73-100; D. J. Moo, *The Epistle to the Romans*, (Grand Rapids: Eerdmans, 1996), 211-17; R. H. Gundry, "Grace, Works, and Staying Saved in Paul: A Response to E. P. Sanders' Thoughts on Getting in and Staying in According to Palestinian Judaism and Paul," *Biblica* 66 (1985): 1-38; T. R. Schreiner, "'Works of the Law' in Paul," *NovT* 33.3 (1991): 217-44; F. Avemarie, *Tora und Leben: Untersuchungen zur Heilsbedeutung der Tora in der frühen rabbinischen Literatur*, Texte und Studien zum antiken Judentum (Tübingen: Mohr [Siebeck], 1996); F. Avemarie, "Bund als Gabe und Recht," in *Bund und Tora: zur theologischen Begriffsgeschichte in alttestamentlicher, frühjüdischer und urchristlicher Tradition*, Friedrich Avemarie and Hermann Lichtenberger, eds., (Tübingen: Mohr [Siebeck], 1996), 163-216; F. Avemarie, "Erwählung und Vergeltung: Zur optionalen Struktur rabbinischer Soteriologie," *NTS* 45 (1999): 108-26; M. A. Seifrid, *Christ, Our Righteousness: Paul's Theology of Justification* (Downers Grove: IVP, 2000), 16; Venema, *The Gospel of Free Acceptance in Christ*, 299-301; Piper, *Future of Justification*, 145-61.

[139] Carson, "Summaries and Conclusions," 543.

[140] Carson, "Summaries and Conclusions," 545.

[141] Cf. Bird, "Via Media," 109 who argues that Paul is simultaneously concerned to combat both Jewish ethnocentrism and merit-righteousness.

Second, there is significant debate regarding the meaning and significance of righteousness language in Paul, especially in relation to Paul's declaration of the "righteousness of God" (δικαιοσύνη θεοῦ: Rom 1:17; 3:5, 21-22; 10:3; 2 Cor 5:21; Phil 3:9). These debates predate the rise of the new perspective and its critics, but have received fresh impetus from the recent discussions. On the one hand, a number of scholars continue to defend the traditional Reformation reading, which interprets "righteousness of God" (δικαιοσύνη θεοῦ) as God's gift of righteousness to those who trust in Christ.[142] This reading goes back at least to Augustine,[143] received a major impetus from Luther and Calvin,[144] and has been advocated by scholars from a range of confessional positions ever since.[145] An alternative reading, however, according to which the "righteousness of God" (δικαιοσύνη θεοῦ) refers to God's own righteous character or actions has recently gained increasing support.[146] This reading also claims ancient precedent in the writings of Ambrosiaster,[147] and was championed by a number of prominent scholars prior to the rise of the new perspective.[148] Wright's reading of the "righteousness of God" as God's "covenant faithfulness" is one example of this view, but it should be noted that this reading is not unique to Wright, nor to the new perspective.[149] Finally, attempting to mediate this debate, some scholars, including Dunn, have followed Käsemann in understanding δικαιοσύνη θεοῦ to denote both God's saving power, and the gift of righteousness created by that power.[150]

---

[142] E.g. D. A. Carson, "Atonement in Romans 3:21-26," in Charles E. Hill and Frank A. James, eds., *The Glory of the Atonement: Biblical, Historical and Practical Perspectives: Essays in Honor of Roger Nicole* (Downers Grove: IVP, 2004), 124-25. Grammatically speaking, this reading relies on reading θεοῦ as either: (1) a genitive of source (origin), giving the meaning "a righteousness that comes from God (as a gift)"; or (2) an objective genitive with the sense of righteousness that "counts" before God.

[143] Augustine, *The Spirit and the Letter*, 15.9, cited in G. L. Bray, ed., *Romans* (Downers Grove: IVP, 1998), 99.

[144] M. Luther, "Preface to the Complete Edition of Luther's Latin Writings," in *Luther's Works, Volume 34* (St Louis: Concordia, 1960), 336-37; J. Calvin, *The Epistles of Paul the Apostle to the Romans and the Thessalonians* (Edinburgh: St. Andrews Press, 1961) on Rom 3:21.

[145] E.g. Bultmann, *TNT* 1:285; G. Bornkamm, *Paul* (trans. D. M. G. Stalker; London: Hodder & Stoughton, 1971), 138; H. Conzelmann, *An Outline of the Theology of the New Testament* (London: SCM, 1969), 218-20; C. E. B. Cranfield, *A Critical and Exegetical Commentary on the Epistle to the Romans* (6th ed.; 2 vols.; Edinburgh: T. & T. Clark, 1975–1979) 1:96-99.

[146] This reading relies on reading the genitive θεοῦ as either: (1) an adjectival, possessive genitive, referring to an aspect of God's own character; or (2) a verbal, subjective genitive, referring to God's righteous acts.

[147] Ambrosiaster, *Commentary on Paul's Epistles*, cited in Bray, *Romans*, 99.

[148] C. K. Barrett, *A Commentary on the Epistle to the Romans* (London: A. & C. Black, 1957), 29; W. G. Kümmel, *The Theology of the New Testament According to its Major Witnesses, Jesus-Paul-John* (Nashville: Abingdon, 1973), 198.

[149] Wright, "Romans," 398. Cf. S. K. Williams, "The 'Righteousness of God' in Romans," *JBL* 99.2 (1980): 285; R. B. Hays, "Justification," *ABD* 3:1129; M. F. Bird, *The Saving Righteousness of God: Studies on Paul, Justification, and the New Perspective* (Milton Keynes: Paternoster, 2006), 15-16.

[150] Käsemann, "Righteousness of God," 167-93; cf. J. C. Beker, *Paul the Apostle: The Triumph of God in Life and Thought* (Philadelphia: Fortress, 1980), 262-64; Dunn, *Romans 1–8*, 41-42; Moo, *The Epistle to the Romans*, 74; T. R. Schreiner, *Romans* (Grand Rapids: Baker, 1998), 63-71.

Third, the meaning and significance of Paul's teaching about justification is hotly contested. To begin with, there is no consensus on how the concept should be defined: should justification be understood broadly, to include the whole Christian doctrine of salvation, or narrowly, to encompass only the teaching of those Pauline passages where the δικ- root appears?[151] In terms of the substantial issue, the old Reformation debate continues: should Paul's justification language be understood, with Augustine and the Roman Catholic tradition, to mean both "declare righteous" and "make righteous" or, with the Protestant Reformers, in exclusively forensic terms, to mean "reckon as righteous"? There is now a relatively widespread consensus, across confessional lines, that the verb δικαιόω, like its Hebrew antecedent (צדק), is a forensic and declarative term, drawn from the law court setting, and carrying the sense "declare righteous" or "vindicate."[152] A significant minority of Pauline scholars, however, spurred on by Käsemann, argue that Paul's justification language includes reference to moral transformation.[153] In response, a number of Reformed scholars argue, following Calvin, that while moral transformation is indeed important for Paul, the apostle's teaching is best understood if we consider justification and moral transformation ("sanctification") as inseparable but distinguishable benefits of union with Christ.[154] Yet further, there is also significant debate about whether justification in Paul is best understood as a future verdict anticipated in the present in Christ (so Wright),[155] a present verdict to be confirmed in the future (so Piper),[156] or a process which spans the whole period between a believer's initiation into Christ and the consummation (so P. Stuhlmacher).[157] Finally, there is not yet agreement on the question of whether Paul's justification language is primarily language about the sinner's standing before God, as traditional readings would insist, or

---

[151] Cf. Moo, "Justification in Galatians," 161.

[152] For a concise summary of the evidence, see Bird, *Saving Righteousness*, 17-18. The forensic understanding is supported, for example, by: (1) "Traditional Protestant" scholars: Moo, *The Epistle to the Romans*, 227-28; Horton, "Traditional Reformed View," 91-92; (2) "New Perspective" scholar: Wright, *Justification*, 69-71; (3) J. A. Fitzmyer, "The Letter to the Romans," in R. E. Brown, Joseph A. Fitzmyer, and Roland E. Murphy, eds., *The New Jerome Biblical Commentary* (London: Geoffrey Chapman, 1995), 241-44. Sanders, *Paul and Palestinian Judaism*, 198-99 demonstrates the forensic meaning in the Jewish literature, but argues that Paul uses the language differently as a "transfer term" (544).

[153] Käsemann, "Righteousness of God,", 168-82; D. B. Garlington, *Faith, Obedience, and Perseverance: Aspects of Paul's Letter to the Romans* (Tübingen: Mohr [Siebeck], 1994), 155-61; Dunn, *The Theology of Paul the Apostle*, 344; P. Stuhlmacher, *Revisiting Paul's Doctrine of Justification: A Challenge to the New Perspective* (Downers Grove: IVP, 2001), 62-67; M. J. Gorman, *Inhabiting the Cruciform God: Kenosis, Justification, and Theosis in Paul's Narrative Soteriology* (Grand Rapids: Eerdmans, 2009); V.-M. Kärkkäinen, "Deification View," in Beilby and Eddy, *Justification*, 229-32.

[154] Calvin, *Institutes* 3.16.1. Cf. R. B. Gaffin, "Union with Christ: Some Biblical and Theolgocal Reflections," in A. T. B. McGowan, ed., *Always Reforming: Explorations in Systematic Theology* (Downers Grove: IVP Academic, 2006), 271-88; M. S. Horton, *The Christian faith: A Systematic Theology for Pilgrims on the Way* (Grand Rapids: Zondervan, 2011), 587-687; Moo, "Justification in Galatians," 176-77.

[155] Wright, *Justification*, 79, 189; cf. 223.

[156] Piper, *Future of Justification*, 101-16.

[157] Stuhlmacher, *Revisiting Paul's Doctrine of Justification: A Challenge to the New Perspective*, 62-63; cf. Dunn, *The Theology of Paul the Apostle*, 386.

primarily language about the inclusion of Gentiles among the covenant people, as argued by advocates of the new perspective.[158] While there is recognition on both sides that both vertical and horizontal dimensions are significant, the question of emphasis remains.[159]

Fourth, and closely related to these discussions, a significant debate surrounds the question of whether Paul's teaching about justification can support the traditional Protestant affirmation that God imputes the righteousness of Christ to sinners who believe. Wright resolutely rejects the notion that Christ's moral obedience is imputed to sinners. The main problem Wright sees with the language is that it relies on medieval conceptions of grace and righteousness,[160] and implies that righteousness is some kind of substance or commodity that can be shared between parties, rather than a status conferred by the declaration of a judge.[161] In place of this construction, Wright prefers to speak of justification as God's declaration that those who are in Christ by faith are right with him, and members of his covenant family, because of their participation in Christ, their representative head.[162] God is able to justify sinners in Christ because—as their representative—what is "true for him is true for them":[163] in Christ's death their sin is condemned; in Christ's resurrection they are vindicated.[164] It is, therefore, Christ's death and resurrection alone which are reckoned to the one who believes.[165] Here Wright's thought is close to the traditional Reformed emphasis on justification as a forensic aspect of the believer's union with Christ, even if he rejects the idea that Jesus' "active obedience" counts for others, and demurs from the term "imputation." Indeed, R. H. Gundry and Seifrid, who have otherwise been critical of the new perspective, concur with Wright at this point.[166] And more recently, Bird has proposed the category of "incorporated righteousness" to emphasize the believer's union with Christ as the ground of their righteousness.[167]

---

[158] E.g. Wright, *Saint Paul*, 119; cf. 121-22, 125; cf. Wright, "New Perspectives," 260; Wright, "Romans," 481.

[159] Compare the essays of M. Horton and J. D. G. Dunn in Beilby and Eddy, *Justification*, 83-111 and 176-201, respectively. Cf. also the definition of Bird, "Progressive Reformed View," 132, which seeks to integrate the two emphases: "justification is the act whereby God creates a new people, with a new status, in a new covenant, as part of the first instalment of the new age."

[160] Wright, *Justification*, 187.

[161] Wright, *Saint Paul*, 98; Wright, *Justification*, 186-87.

[162] Wright, *Justification*, 64 emphasizes the correspondence between his own reading at this point, and that of the Reformers, not least Calvin, who understood justification as one of the benefits of being "in Christ" (e.g. Calvin, *Institutes* 3.16.1).

[163] Wright, *Justification*, 82.

[164] Wright, *Justification*, 180-81.

[165] Wright, *Justification*, 205-6.

[166] Seifrid, *Christ, Our Righteousness*, 173-75; R. H. Gundry, "The Nonimputation of Christ's Righteousness," in Mark Husbands and Daniel J. Treier, eds., *Justification: What's at Stake in the Current Debates?* (Downers Grove: IVP, 2004), 17-45; cf. also D. Garlington, *Studies in the New Perspective on Paul: Essays and Reviews* (Eugene: Wipf & Stock, 2008), 172-233; see also A. E. McGrath, *Iustitia Dei: A History of the Christian Doctrine of Justification* (2nd ed.; Cambridge: Cambridge University Press, 1998), 207-13 who traces the formulation to Melanchthon.

[167] M. F. Bird, "Incorporated Righteousness: A Response to Recent Evangelical Discussion Concerning the Imputation of Christ's Righteousness in Justification," *JETS* 47.2 (2004): 253-75; cf. Bird, *Saving Righteousness*, 60-87.

At the same time, the doctrine of the imputation of Christ's righteousness has been defended by Piper, Carson, and Horton, among others.[168] While these scholars acknowledge that the doctrine of the imputation of Christ's righteousness cannot be established in a straightforward manner from the text of Paul's letters, they nevertheless argue that when Paul speaks of justification he intends not only the remission of sins, but also the imputation of Christ's active obedience to sinners who trust in him.

Fifth, and related to the discussion regarding justification and imputation, the place of the believer's obedience in his or her final justification before God remains in dispute. Dunn and Wright have both emphasized, in different ways, the significance of the believer's Spirit-enabled works in relation to their final justification before God. Indeed, until quite recently, Wright has regularly spoken of justification as God's verdict on the final day, passed "on the basis of the entire life."[169] By this language, Wright insists that he intends nothing other than the Spirit-enabled Christian obedience which accompanies true faith, demonstrates a person's membership in the covenant, and in no way merits salvation.[170] Nevertheless, in his more recent writings, Wright has been more careful to present Christ alone as the basis of the believer's justification, and to adopt the Pauline language of judgment "in accordance" with works.[171] At the same time, a number of other scholars, including Yinger, Seifrid, Gathercole, and Kirk, assign an instrumental role of some kind to works in final justification, even as they emphasize that these works are only enabled by the Holy Spirit.[172] This view has, however, drawn sharp criticism from a number of scholars, not least among them Piper, whose book-length critique of Wright emphasizes that while the believer's obedience is the necessary fruit and evidence of their union with Christ, it may in no way assigned an instrumental role as any basis of final justification.[173]

Sixth, a related but distinct debate surrounds the crucial Pauline phrase "faith of Christ" (πίστεως Ἰησοῦ Χριστοῦ), which occurs seven times in Paul's letters (Rom 3:22, 26; Gal 2:16 x2; 3:22; Eph 3:12; Phil 3:9).[174] The phrase has

---

[168] J. Piper, *Counted Righteous in Christ: Should We Abandon the Imputation of Christ's Righteousness?* (Wheaton: Crossway, 2002); Piper, *Future of Justification*, 75; D. A. Carson, "The Vindication of Imputation: On Fields of Discourse and Semantic Fields," in Mark Husbands and Daniel J. Treier, eds., *Justification: What's at Stake in the Current Debates* (Downers Grove: IVP, 2004): 77-78; Horton, "Traditional Reformed View," 98-105.

[169] Wright, *Saint Paul*, 129; cf. Wright, *Paul: In Fresh Perspective*, 111-13, 121, 148; Wright, "New Perspectives," 260.

[170] Wright, *Justification*, 124, 223.

[171] Wright, *Justification*, 223, 251; cf. Wright, "Yesterday, Today, and Forever," 61.

[172] K.L. Yinger, *Paul, Judaism, and Judgment According to Deeds* (Cambridge: Cambridge University Press, 1999), 288; Seifrid, *Christ, Our Righteousness*, 148, 180, 182; S. Gathercole, "A Law unto Themselves: The Gentiles in Rom 2:14-15 Revisited," *JSNT* 85 (2002): 27-49; Gathercole, *Where is Boasting?*, 134; J. R. D. Kirk, *Unlocking Romans: Resurrection and the Justification of God* (Grand Rapids: Eerdmans, 2008), 223-27.

[173] Piper, *Future of Justification*, 110, 117-32; cf. Bird, *Saving Righteousness*, 174.

[174] For recent reviews of the debate, see: D. Hunn, "Debating the Faithfulness of Jesus Christ in Twentieth-Century Scholarship," in M. F. Bird and P. M. Sprinkle, eds., *The Faith of Jesus Christ: Exegetical, Biblical, and Theological Studies* (Milton Keynes: Paternoster, 2009), 15-32; M. C. Easter, "The Pistis Christou Debate: Main Arguments and Responses in Summary," *CBR* 9.1 (2010): 33-47.

traditionally been interpreted anthropocentrically as an objective genitive, with reference to the believer's faith: "faith in Jesus Christ."[175] In recent years, however, an alternative interpretation has gained increasing acceptance. This reading interprets the phrase Christocentrically, as a subjective genitive, referring to the "faith of Jesus Christ" in the sense of the "faith(fullness) *exercised by* Jesus Christ." Although advocates of this reading can be found earlier,[176] a major impetus was provided in 1983 by the publication of R. B. Hays' major study *The Faith of Jesus Christ*.[177] Good arguments have been made on both sides, and recognizing this, some scholars, such as M. Hooker, have suggested that Paul's understanding of "faith of Christ" is "a concentric expression, which begins, always, from the faith of Christ himself, but which includes, necessarily, the answering faith of believers, who claim that faith as their own."[178] Here again, it should be noted that although the question is related to those surrounding the new perspective on Paul, the debate is not as simple as new perspective verses old; significantly, Dunn and Wright have argued different sides on the issue.[179]

3. Paul among Jews, Greeks, and Romans: Alongside and Beyond the Perspectives Old and New

Alongside and beyond the debates regarding the new perspective on Paul, a great deal of Pauline scholarship since World War II can be seen as the result of the attempt to understand Paul first and foremost as a Pharisaic Jew, convinced of the Messianic identity of Jesus, and proclaiming the gospel of the Messiah's death and resurrection in the Greco-Roman world. In this final section, we survey scholarly contributions to the understanding of Paul as he lived and worked among Jews, Greeks, and Romans.

3.1. Paul and Judaism

The post-war consensus that Paul's gospel is rooted in the soil of Judaism produced a great deal of reflection upon the nature of Paul's relationship to

---

[175] For a history of translations of the phrase, see G. E. Howard, "Notes and Observations on the 'Faith of Christ'," *HTR* 60 (1967): 461. Amongst recent commentators who prefer the objective genitive reading, see e.g. J. Murray, *The Epistle to the Romans: The English Text with Introduction, Exposition, and Notes* (London: Marshall, Morgan & Scott, 1974), 370-71; Moo, *The Epistle to the Romans*, 224-25; Schreiner, *Romans*, 184-86.
[176] Howard, "Faith of Christ," 459-65; M. Barth, "The Faith of the Messiah," *Heythrop Journal* 10 (1969): 363-70.
[177] R. B. Hays, *The Faith of Jesus Christ: An Investigation of the Narrative Substructure of Galatians 3:1–4:11* (Chico: Scholars Press, 1983); now republished as: R. B. Hays, *The Faith of Jesus Christ: The Narrative Substructure of Galatians 3:1–4:11* (2nd ed.; Grand Rapids: Eerdmans, 2002).
[178] M. D. Hooker, "Pistis Christou," *NTS* 35 (1989): 341.
[179] Compare, in relation to Rom 3:22, Dunn, *Romans 1–8*, 166-67 arguing for "faith in Jesus Christ" and Wright, "Romans," 470 arguing for "the faithfulness of Jesus the Messiah." Cf. more recently J. D. G. Dunn, "ΕΚ ΠΙΣΤΕΩΣ: A Key to the Meaning of ΠΙΣΤΙΣ ΧΡΙΣΤΟΥ," in J. Ross Wagner, C. K. Rowe, and A. Katherine Grieb, eds., *The Word Leaps the Gap: Essays on Scripture and Theology in Honor of Richard B. Hays* (Grand Rapids: Eerdmans, 2008), 364 and Wright, *Justification*, 178.

Paul in the Twenty-First Century

Judaism in general, and to the Scriptures of Israel in particular.

In the context of the post-modern rediscovery of narrative, and the rise of literary criticism of the biblical texts, Hays seminal study of 1983 developed the earlier insight of C. H. Dodd, and argued that Paul's theology exhibits a narrative substructure shaped by the story of Israel, and reaching its climax in the life, death, and resurrection of Messiah Jesus.[180] Hays' approach finds a parallel in the work of an increasing number of scholars, including especially B. Witherington,[181] K. Grieb,[182] and Wright,[183] all of whom emphasize, in various ways, the way in which Paul presents God's action in Messiah Jesus, and by the Spirit, as the climax of the story of Israel found in her Scriptures. Related to this, a great deal of work has concentrated on Paul's use of the Scriptures of Israel. Significant studies from (again) Hays[184] and C. D. Stanley[185] have ignited a lively debate surrounding the question of the sense in which Paul might be considered faithful to the original intention of the Scriptures he cites, and the extent to which he intends to evoke the context of his Scriptural citations.[186]

Further, attention to the way in which Paul's narrative theology is shaped by the Scriptures of Israel is related to a second major focus of scholarly attention, namely, the relationship between Jewish monotheism and Paul's high Christology. Groundbreaking studies here are R. Bauckham's *God Crucified* (1998)[187] and L. Hurtado's *Lord Jesus Christ* (2003)[188] which argue in different ways that Paul's "christological monotheism" can be understood as a natural, albeit remarkable, outgrowth of Second Temple Jewish theology which, even prior to the rise of Christianity, exhibited a range of tendencies that enabled Paul and the other early Christians to include Jesus "within the identity of the one true God."

Related to these developments, but essentially independent of them, a significant third stream of scholarship has sought to read Paul's theology in the

---

[180] C. H. Dodd, *According to the Scriptures: The Sub-structure of New Testament Theology* (London: Nisbet, 1952); Hays, *Faith of Jesus Christ*.

[181] B. Witherington III, *Paul's Narrative Thought World: The Tapestry of Tragedy and Triumph* (Louisville: Westminster, 1994).

[182] A. K. Grieb, *The Story of Romans: A Narrative Defense of God's Righteousness* (Louisville: Westminster John Knox, 2002).

[183] Most recently: Wright, "Paul's Narrative Theology," 323-29.

[184] R. B. Hays, *Echoes of Scripture in the Letters of Paul* (New Haven: Yale University Press, 1993).

[185] C. D. Stanley, *Paul and the Language of Scripture: Citation Technique in the Pauline Epistles and Contemporary Literature* (Cambridge: Cambridge University Press, 1992).

[186] See especially R. B. Hays, *The Conversion of the Imagination: Paul as Interpreter of Israel's Scripture* (Grand Rapids: Eerdmans, 2005); S.E. Porter and C.D. Stanley, eds., *As it Is Written: Studying Paul's Use of Scripture*, Symposium (Atlanta: Society of Biblical Literature, 2008); S. Moyise, *Paul and Scripture: Studying the New Testament Use of the Old Testament* (Grand Rapids: Baker Academic, 2010); C. D. Stanley, ed., *Paul and Scripture: Extending the Conversation* (Atlanta: Society of Biblical Literature, 2012).

[187] R. J. Bauckham, *God Crucified: Monotheism and Christology in the New Testament* (Carlisle: Paternoster, 1998); cf. R. Bauckham, "Paul's Christology of Divine Identity," in R. Bauckham, ed., *Jesus and the God of Israel: God Crucified and Other Studies on the New Testament's Christology of Divine Identity* (Grand Rapids: Eerdmans, 2008), 182-232.

[188] L. Hurtado, *Lord Jesus Christ: Devotion to Jesus in Earliest Christianity* (Grand Rapids: Eerdmans, 2003).

context of Jewish apocalyptic. The most significant study here was J. C. Beker's *Paul the Apostle: the Triumph of God in Life and Thought* (1980).[189] Beker argued that Paul used the "symbolic" terms of apocalyptic to apply his conviction about the cosmic triumph of God in Christ to particular contingencies in the situation of his readers. This suggestion, that Paul's theological hermeneutic is best understood in terms of the interface between "coherent center" and "contingent interpretation," has proved quite influential. Since Beker, the conviction that Paul is best understood in the context of Jewish apocalyptic has received further eloquent and extended defense from J. Louis Martyn and, most recently, D. Campbell, among others.[190]

Finally, discussion of Paul's relation to Judaism inevitably also involves discussion of the old question of the relation between Paul and Jesus. On the specific question of how much Paul is indebted to traditions about the historical Jesus, a number of scholars have argued that Paul knew relatively little of Jesus' teaching, even as others, such as D. Wenham and S. Kim have sought to demonstrate, in response, that Paul knew well the historical proclamation of Jesus.[191] On the broader question of the congruence between Jesus' proclamation of the kingdom, and Paul's proclamation of Jesus, the older view, exemplified by history of religions school, that Paul's teaching was essentially different from that of Jesus, has now given way to a widespread consensus, influenced especially by J. Jeremias and W. G. Kümmel, which recognizes that despite significant developments "Paul did develop the central insights of the teaching of Jesus and the central meaning of his life and death in a way that truly represented their dynamic and their fullest significance."[192]

3.2. Paul and Greco-Roman Society and Empire

In the light of the significant post-war consensus that Paul's theology must be understood in the context of Judaism and its Scriptures, the older attempt of the history of religions school to derive Paul's thought from the Greco-Roman mystery religions has given way to new explorations of the ways in which Paul engages polemically with the Greco-Roman world, even as he lived and worked within the confines of its socio-political realities.

---

[189] Beker, *Paul the Apostle*; cf. also J. C. Beker, *The Triumph of God: The Essence of Paul's Thought* (trans. L. Stuckenbruck; Minneapolis: Fortress, 1990).

[190] See, esp. J. L. Martyn, *Galatians: A New Translation with Introduction and Commentary* (New York: Doubleday, 1997); J. L. Martyn, *Theological Issues in the Letters of Paul* (London: Continuum, 2005); Campbell, *Deliverance of God*; cf. D. A. Campbell, "An Apocalyptic Rereading of 'Justification' in Paul: Or, An Overview of the Argument of Douglas Campbell's 'The Deliverance of God' by Douglas Campbell," *ExpT* 123 (2012): 382-93.

[191] D. Wenham, "Paul's Use of the Jesus Tradition: Three Samples," in D. Wenham, ed., *The Jesus Tradition Outside the Gospels Gospel Perspectives* (Sheffield: JSOT, 1984), 7-38; D. Wenham, *Paul: Follower of Jesus or Founder of Christianity?* (Grand Rapids: Eerdmans, 1995); S. Kim, "Sayings of Jesus," in G. F. Hawthorne and R. P. Martin, eds., *DPL* (Downers Grove: IVP, 1993), 474-92; S. Kim, "The Jesus Tradition in 1 Thess 4:13–5:11," *NTS* 48.2 (2002): 225-42.

[192] J. G. Barclay, "Jesus and Paul," in *DPL*, 492-503.

In this regard, the pioneering work of A. Deissmann and E. A. Judge set the trajectory for a range of approaches to Paul and his letters that have come to be known as the social-scientific study of the apostle to the Gentiles.[193] Seminal studies in this area were those of B. L. Malina,[194] G. Theissen,[195] and W. A. Meeks,[196] each of which attempts to situate Paul within his social and cultural milieu, and to show how Paul's theology was hammered out and applied within the realities of the Greco-Roman world of the first century. More recent studies have explored, for example, the material realities under which Paul's church planting took shape,[197] the contours of Paul's mission in the Greco-Roman world,[198] and the economic goals and realities entailed in his collection for the saints of Jerusalem.[199]

A further development of this approach has been a renewed interest in the extent to which Paul's letters might be shaped by the conventions of Greco-Roman epistolary and rhetorical techniques. Following the early work of Deissmann, who explored the significance of the documentary papyri for the understanding of the New Testament,[200] J. White,[201] and D. Aune,[202] among others, began to explore the implications of this for the interpretation of Paul's letters. A significant and ongoing debate exists, however, between those, such as S. Porter, who see Paul's letters as primarily epistolary in character,[203] those like G. A. Kennedy and Witherington, who understand them as rhetorical pieces in written form,[204] and those such as R. F. Collins, who offer a mediating position.[205]

---

[193] A. Deissmann, *Light from the Ancient East* (trans. L. R. M. Strachan; 1927; repr., Grand Rapids: Baker, 1978); A. Deissmann, *Paul: A Study in Social and Religious History* (trans. W.E. Wilson; London: Hodder & Stoughton, 1926); E. A. Judge, *The Social Pattern of Christian Groups in the First Century* (London: Tyndale Press, 1960); now reprinted in D. M. Scholer, ed., *Social Distinctives of the Christians in the First Century: Pivotal Essays by E. A. Judge* (Peabody: Hendrickson, 2008), 1-56. Cf. also E. A. Judge and J. R. Harrison, *The First Christians in the Roman World: Augustan and New Testament Essays* (Tübingen: Mohr [Siebeck], 2008).

[194] B. L. Malina, *The New Testament World* (Atlanta: John Knox, 1981).

[195] G. Theissen, *The Social Setting of Pauline Christianity* (Philadelphia: Fortress, 1982).

[196] W. A. Meeks, *The First Urban Christians: The Social World of the Apostle Paul* (New Haven: Yale University Press, 1983).

[197] R. F. Hock, *The Social Context of Paul's Ministry: Tentmaking and Apostleship* (Philadelphia: Fortress, 1980); J. Murphy-O'Connor, *St. Paul's Corinth: Texts and Archaeology* (rev. and enl. ed.; Collegeville: Liturgical Press, 2002); J. Murphy-O'Connor, *St. Paul's Ephesus: Texts and Archaeology* (Collegeville: Liturgical Press, 2008).

[198] E. J. Schnabel, *Paul the Missionary: Realities, Strategies, and Methods* (Downers Grove: IVP, 2008).

[199] E.g. most recently: J. M. Ogereau, "The Jerusalem Collection as Κοινωνία: Paul's Global Politics of Socio-Economic Equality and Solidarity," *NTS* 58.3 (2012): 360-78.

[200] Deissmann, *Light*.

[201] J. L. White, *Light from Ancient Letters: Foundations and Facets* (Philadelphia: Fortress, 1986).

[202] D. E. Aune, *The New Testament in Its Literary Environment* (Philadelphia: Westminster, 1987).

[203] S. E. Porter and S.A. Adams, eds., *Paul and the Ancient Letter Form* (Leiden: Brill, 2010).

[204] G. A. Kennedy, *New Testament Interpretation through Rhetorical Criticism* (Chapel Hill: University of North Carolina Press, 1984); B. Witherington III, *New Testament Rhetoric: An Introductory Guide to the Art of Persuasion in and of the New Testament* (Eugene: Cascade, 2009). See also the pioneering work in this area of H. D. Betz, *Galatians: A Commentary on Paul's Letter to the Churches in Galatia* (Philadelphia: Fortress, 1979).

In addition to emphasizing the social location of Paul's mission and message, social-scientific approaches have explored how "Paul's engagement with the society of his day often took the form of a provocative reinterpretation of his society's dominant cultural symbols."[206] This has, in turn, produced a range of studies of the way in which Paul engaged polemically with the Greco-Roman world in general, and with the imperial propaganda of the Roman empire in particular.[207] Particularly fruitful studies in this area have explored, for example, the way Paul engaged with the popular philosophies of his day,[208] challenged the Greco-Roman ethical norms of the city of Corinth,[209] subverted Roman ideas of imperial benefaction by his language of grace,[210] challenged imperial claims to final authority by his announcement of the *parousia* of Christ,[211] and offered an alternative social vision for the city of Rome.[212]

4. Conclusion

For all the complexity of these debates, which can at times be quite bewildering, the early twenty first century is an exciting time to be engaged in the study of Paul and his letters. The lively discussions of the last decades have loosened the stranglehold of traditional interpretations of all varieties, and breathed new life into the study of this most controversial Apostle. If the result is that we return to the letters of Paul with fresh eyes, ready to learn again from the man from Tarsus, that can only bode well for the future of both the academy and the church. The way forward must surely be to go back, time and again, to Paul's own letters, to pay close attention to his use of language in its first-century context, to read each section as part of the narrative whole, and to listen to this very Jewish apostle to the Gentiles proclaiming God's victory in Christ, with ears attuned to hear the echoes of the Scriptures of Israel, and eyes open to see his polemical engagement with the Greco-Roman world.

---

[205] E.g. R. F. Collins, "'I Command That This Letter Be Read': Writing as a Manner of Speaking," in Karl P. Donfried and Johannes Beutler, eds., *The Thessalonians Debate: Methodological Discord or Methodological Synthesis?* (Grand Rapids: Eerdmans, 2000), 319.

[206] S. C. Barton, "Social-Scientific Approaches to Paul," in *DPL* 892-900.

[207] E.g. R. A. Horsley, ed., *Paul and Empire: Religion and Power in Roman Imperial Society* (Harrisburg: Trinity Press International, 1997); Wright, "Gospel and Empire," 160-83; W. Carter, *The Roman Empire and the New Testament: An Essential Guide* (Nashville: Abingdon Press, 2006). Note also, however, the criticisms of this approach by S. Kim, *Christ and Caesar: The Gospel and the Roman Empire in the Writings of Paul and Luke* (Grand Rapids: Eerdmans, 2008).

[208] A. J. Malherbe, *Paul and the popular philosophers* (Minneapolis: Fortress, 1989).

[209] B. W. Winter, *After Paul Left Corinth: The Influence of Secular Ethics and Social Change* (Grand Rapids: Eerdmans, 2001).

[210] J. R. Harrison, *Paul's Language of Grace in its Graeco-Roman Context* (Tübingen: Mohr [Siebeck], 2003); cf. J. R. Harrison, "Paul, Eschatology and the Augustan Age of Grace," *TynB* 50.1 (1999): 79-91.

[211] J. R. Harrison, *Paul and the Imperial Authorities at Thessalonica and Rome: A Study in the Conflict of Ideology* (Tübingen: Mohr [Siebeck], 2011).

[212] J. R. Harrison, "Augustan Rome and the Body of Christ: A Comparison of the Social Vision of the *Res Gestae* and Paul's Letter to the Romans," *HTR* 106.1 (2013): 1-36.

Recommended Reading

Aune, D. E. "Recent Readings of Paul Relating to Justification by Faith." Pages 188-245 in *Rereading Paul Together: Protestant and Catholic Perspectives on Justification.* Edited by D. E. Aune. Grand Rapids: Baker, 2006. Pages 188-245.

Beilby, J. K., and P. R. Eddy, eds., *Justification: Five Views.* Downers Grove: IVP, 2011.

Bird, M. F. *Four Views on the Apostle Paul.* Grand Rapids: Zondervan, 2012.

Dunn, J. D. G. *The Theology of Paul the Apostle.* Grand Rapids: Eerdmans, 1998.

Hafemann, S. J. "Paul and His Interpreters." Pages 666-79 in *Dictionary of Paul and His Letters.* Edited by Gerald F. Hawthorne and Ralph P. Martin. Downers Grove: IVP, 1993.

Ridderbos, H. N. *Paul: An Outline of His Theology.* Grand Rapids: Eerdmans, 1975.

Sanders, E. P. *Paul and Palestinian Judaism: A Comparison of Patterns of Religion.* Philadelphia: Fortress, 1977.

Schnelle, U. *Apostle Paul: His Life and Theology.* Grand Rapids: Baker, 2005.

Schreiner, T. R. *Paul, Apostle of God's Glory in Christ: A Pauline Theology.* Downers Grove: IVP, 2001.

Witherington, B., III. *Paul's Narrative Thought World: The Tapestry of Tragedy and Triumph.* Louisville: Westminster, 1994.

Wright, N. T. *Paul: In Fresh Perspective.* Minneapolis: Fortress, 2005.

Wright, N. T. "Paul in Current Anglophone Scholarship." *Expository Times* 123 (2012): 367-81.

Yinger, K. L. *The New Perspective on Paul: An Introduction.* Eugene: Wipf & Stock, 2011.

Zetterholm, M. *Approaches to Paul: A Student's Guide to Recent Scholarship.* Minneapolis: Fortress, 2009.

2. Paul: An Outline of His Life

David L. Eastman

Mapping out the chronology of the life of the apostle Paul remains one of the enduring puzzles in New Testament studies. The number of proposed chronologies, even over just the past half-century, is impressive.[1] This is well-tilled ground, yet it is ground that continues to demand the attention of Pauline scholars. What is at stake is not just the chronology *per se*, but also related issues such as the date and place of composition of the epistles, the attempt to establish the development of Pauline thought over time, the usefulness (or lack thereof) of the material in Acts, and the authenticity (or lack thereof) of material in the disputed letters, such as the facts concerning the end of Paul's life.[2] As we will see, however, a definitive Pauline chronology is impeded by challenges at every turn, particularly the problem of establishing the sources and the relative dearth of fixed data points. I will address each of these challenges at length before turning to the construction of my own proposed chronology.

1. Sources

Before we can begin constructing a chronology, we must establish which sources will and will not be used. Both canonical and extra-canonical sources claim to recount details of Paul's life, and scholars have agreed that the evidence within the New Testament must be given priority over demonstrably later church traditions. This agreement gives preference to the corpus of thirteen letters traditionally ascribed to Paul and the biographical information contained in the Acts of the Apostles, but how do these relate to each other? Three basic models have been employed:

1. Acts as the basis of the chronology, with details from the epistles fit into that structure.

---

[1] In addition to the works cited in the footnotes and bibliography here, see also the summaries of previous scholarship in Rainer Riesner, *Paul's Early Period: Chronology, Mission Strategy, Theology* (trans. Doug Stott; Grand Rapids: Eerdmans, 1997), 3-28; Mark A. Seifrid and Randall K. J. Tan, *The Pauline Writings: An Annotated Bibliography* (IBR Bibliographies 9; Grand Rapids: Baker, 2002), 31-37.

[2] Many of these issues will be explored here in varying degrees of detail, and the footnotes will direct interested readers to additional bibliography.

2. The undisputed Pauline epistles as the sole basis of the chronology, with the disputed letters and Acts being completely (or at least largely) disregarded.
3. The undisputed Pauline epistles provide the primary framework for a chronology, and details from the disputed letters and Acts are used only when they are judged to be reliable and consistent with what is otherwise known.

The first model was the approach of most scholars prior to the nineteenth century. Because Acts gives an extensive account of Paul's career and was seen as historically reliable, it was logical to start with that chronology and then fill in the gaps from the letters. Beginning in the nineteenth century, however, scholars began to question the authorship of some letters in the Pauline corpus and the reliability of the narrative in Acts. Critical presuppositions and perceived discrepancies with details from undisputed Pauline letters (more on this below) caused many to conclude that the authors of the pseudonymous epistles and Acts had no connection with the historical Paul.[3] Therefore, the second model emerged.[4] Proponents of this model have argued that the disputed epistles and Acts should not be used in constructing a Pauline chronology, for they reflect nothing more than later traditions driven by theological interests. The third model presents something of a middle way. Critical assessments of the disputed letters and Acts still leave the undisputed epistles in a privileged position, but this is not to say that the other sources can have no value, particularly when they agree with, or seem to fill in a connection left missing by, the undisputed letters. For all these approaches, extra-canonical evidence is brought in only in a subsequent phase.

The first approach is still in use today primarily in conservative confessional contexts, where readers approach issues of historicity and authorship through traditional models. If Acts is read as the product of a real-life companion of Paul, then it must be treated on equal authority with the letters. Critical scholars generally take the second or third approach. Some choose the second method in order to establish a clear line of demarcation between historical and unhistorical sources. This perspective represents a vigorous application of the historical-critical method, yet even these scholars often end up at least considering possible contributions from the other canonical materials. They find it difficult to complete a Pauline chronology without at least some reference to Acts in particular. Most critical scholars today employ the third approach or some variation thereof. [5] They share

---

[3] Not all scholars have abandoned this first approach. See e.g. Riesner, *Paul's Early Period*, who describes the chronological framework in Acts as "strikingly reliable," particularly in the "we" sections, while the data from the Pauline epistles are "unable to provide even a marginally secure date for the apostle's life" (quotations on p. 412).

[4] The pioneering study from this perspective was John Knox, *Chapters in a Life of Paul* (rev. ed.; Macon: Mercer University Press, 1987).

[5] See e.g. Walter F. Taylor Jr., *Paul, Apostle to the Nations: An Introduction* (Minneapolis: Fortress, forthcoming), 21-40.

doubts about the authorship of some of the epistles but recognize that the pseudepigraphical letters and Acts may contain some authentic Pauline traditions.[6] This study will take a version of the third approach.

2. The Pauline Epistles

The traditional Pauline corpus contains thirteen letters, yet modern critical scholarship divides these into two broad categories: undisputed (or "pillar") epistles and disputed (or pseudonymous) epistles. The undisputed corpus consists of seven letters (in canonical order): Romans, 1 and 2 Corinthians, Galatians, Philippians, 1 Thessalonians, and Philemon. The other six letters are disputed: Ephesians, Colossians, 2 Thessalonians, 1 and 2 Timothy, and Titus.[7] Scholars have made this division based on studies of vocabulary, writing style, and perceived theological emphases or differences.[8] Even if one takes the corpus of seven undisputed epistles as reliable, there are still complexities. We know, for example, that 1 Corinthians is not Paul's first letter to the Corinthians (1 Cor 5:9). And 2 Corinthians, although considered authentic, is seen by many as a patchwork of two letters (chapters 1–9 and 10–13), which may actually be preserved in reverse order. In this reading chapters 1–9 may be a response to the Corinthians' reaction to a "tearful letter" from Paul that is preserved, at least in part, in chapters 10–13. Other, even more intricate models for 2 Corinthians exist, all of which would have an impact on a chronological reconstruction of Paul's life and ministry. Beyond these considerations, the undisputed corpus poses other challenges. The letters provide incomplete biographical information and very few (if any) clear chronological indicators. Even the location of writing is not always clear. And from a methodological perspective, there is a problem in assuming that autobiographical information should be used as if it were objective and

---

[6] In regard to Historical Jesus studies, Dale Allison Jr. has recently argued that authentic memories of Jesus can be found in "sentences that he did not utter and stories that never took place. If we really want to recover and reconstruct Jesus, then, we will cast our nets far wider than the [traditional, historical-critical] criteria can ever reach" ("It Don't Come Easy: A History of Disillusionment," in Chris Keith and Anthony Le Donne, eds., *Jesus, Criteria, and the Demise of Authenticity* [London: T. & T. Clark, 2012], 199). Allison thus speculates that the authentic Jesus can be present even in disputed sayings and stories. Scholars who use the third method would likewise argue that authentic Pauline traditions might be found in letters he did not personally write and in stories related by the author of Acts, even if that person did not know Paul personally.

[7] Some scholars divide the letters into three categories: undisputed, disputed, and spurious. There is, therefore, a range of certainty on various letters. Colossians and 2 Thessalonians are considered by some the most likely of the disputed letters to be authentic. The Pastoral Epistles (1 and 2 Timothy, Titus) are generally considered the least likely, although some have argued that each epistle should be considered individually, not as part of a group, and that elements of authentic Pauline material may be contained within them. See e.g. Jerome Murphy-O'Connor, *Paul: A Critical Life* (Oxford: Clarendon, 1996), 356-59, where he argues that 2 Timothy is close in language and perspective to the undisputed Pauline epistles and is the only authentic of the three Pastorals.

[8] This is not the place to explore the complexities of this approach, yet it should be noted that not all scholars agree on this methodology or its outcomes.

Paul: An Outline of His Life

unfiltered. Paul is highly rhetorical in his writings, so we must recognize that this rhetorical stance could extend to biographical details in his letters.

What do we do, then, with the disputed letters? The undisputed Paulines may well merit the pride of place, but if, for example, disciples of Paul lie behind the authorship of the disputed epistles or at least the traditions contained within them, then these may well tell us additional details that the apostle himself did not record. The complexities of the Pauline corpus itself, therefore, can be dizzying, but our problem of sources is only amplified when we consider the evidence from Acts.

3. The Acts of the Apostles

The author of Acts (traditionally identified as Luke) dedicates over half his work to the career of Paul, from his early days as a persecutor of the followers of Jesus, to his missionary journeys and eventual arrest and transport to Rome. The Lukan narrative provides itineraries, spans of time, a few possible date ranges, and even claims to eyewitness testimony, yet many critical scholars doubt its overall usefulness. This skepticism results from comparative readings of Acts versus the undisputed Pauline epistles on issues such as Paul's theology, the presentation of his apostleship (or relative lack thereof in Acts), the different emphases on his ability to perform miracles as proof of his apostleship, and his ability or inability as a public speaker. Too much can be made of some of these categories, yet there remains one undisputable fact that is of primary interest for our study here: There is disagreement between Acts and the epistles on several biographical and chronological details. The most evident of these disagreements concerns Paul's visits to Jerusalem.

According to the undisputed epistles, Paul made two trips to Jerusalem and was planning a third, while there are five Jerusalem visits in Acts. Not only does the number of visits vary, but there are also other important differences concerning the circumstances of these visits.

PAULINE VISITS TO JERUSALEM IN THE UNDISPUTED EPISTLES AND ACTS	
In the undisputed epistles	**In Acts**
After his Damascus road experience, Paul went to Arabia (Nabatea) and then returned to Damascus. Three years later he made his first trip to Jerusalem. **Visit 1** (Gal 1:18-20): Paul visits Jerusalem for 15 days and meets with Cephas (Peter) and James, but none of the other apostles. After a journey through Syria and Cilicia, 14 years later, Paul went to Jerusalem with	After his Damascus road experience, Paul stays in Damascus and successfully argues with other Jews about the messiahship of Jesus. After an undetermined amount of time (literally, "After many days had passed"), he escapes an assassination plot in Damascus and goes to Jerusalem. **Visit 1** (9:26-29): Paul comes to Jerusalem, but the disciples all avoid him out of fear. Finally Barnabas takes him to

37

Barnabas and Titus "in response to a revelation."	the apostles and vouches for his change of life. They accept him, and he preaches openly among them. He eventually must also leave Jerusalem out of fear for his life.
Visit 2 (Gal 2:1-10): Paul presents the gospel that he had been preaching to the Gentiles in a private meeting with the Jerusalem leaders. Titus is accepted without being circumcised, and Paul overcomes a disturbance caused by "false believers" who were attempting to undermine "the freedom we have in Christ Jesus" (a likely reference to legal observance). He learns nothing new about the gospel from the Jerusalem leaders. James, Cephas, and John recognize his ministry to the uncircumcised and offer the right hand of fellowship to Barnabas and him. They ask only that Paul and Barnabas remember the poor.	Paul goes to Tarsus and stays there until Barnabas comes to take him to Antioch. Here the believers were first called "Christians."
	Visit 2 (11:27-30; 12:25; 24:7): Paul and Barnabas go to Jerusalem to deliver a collection for the believers there who were suffering from famine. They deliver it to the elders and then return to Antioch.
	Paul and Barnabas embark on the first missionary journey to Cyprus and southern Asia Minor, then return to Antioch for a lengthy stay. When some Judeans come to Antioch and insist that circumcision is required for salvation, Paul and Barnabas debate with them and finally decide to take the matter to the leaders in Jerusalem.
On subsequent journeys, Paul collects money from Gentile churches to support the believers in Jerusalem impacted by a famine. This is intended to be a means of building unity between Jewish and Gentile believers.	
Visit 3 (Rom 15:25-29): Paul plans a visit to deliver the collection for the Jerusalem community before leaving for Rome and then Spain. However, he never confirms this visit in his letters.	**Visit 3** (15:1-29): Paul and Barnabas report to the apostles and elders what God had done in converting the Gentiles. After some debate, Peter and James declare that the Gentile mission is the fulfillment of Scripture. The apostles and elders in Jerusalem send a letter back with Paul and Barnabas stating that the only requirements for Gentile converts are abstinence from food sacrificed to idols, from blood, from strangled animals, and from fornication. Paul and Barnabas take this as a victory for their mission and return to Antioch.
	Paul and Silas (Silvanus) leave for the second missionary journey to Cilicia, Asia Minor, Macedonia, Greece (Achaia), and back to Asia Minor. They eventually return to Caesarea Maritima.
	Visit 4 (18:22): Acts says only that Paul "went up" from Caesarea and greeted the church before he "went down" to Antioch. The author does not mention Jerusalem by name, but most scholars agree that a

	Jerusalem visit is implied here. It was standard usage in that time to speak of "going up" to Jerusalem,[9] and no Christian community is known in Caesarea or its environs. Thus, the author of Acts seems to imply that Paul went out of his way to greet the Jerusalem church, perhaps to report on his second journey.
	After spending some time in Antioch, Paul sets out for the third missionary journey to western Asia Minor, Macedonia, Greece (Achaia), and back to Asia Minor (where he is joined by a group that included Timothy). The group then sails to Tyre before making additional stops at Ptolemais and Caesarea Maritima.
	Visit 5 (21:15–23:30): Paul and others go to Jerusalem to report to James and the elders the further success of the mission, during which many Gentiles and Jews had come to believe. Paul must answer the charge that he is encouraging Jewish believers to ignore the Mosaic law and circumcision, so he performs a vow in the temple as a show of good faith. Soon after some Jews from Asia Minor stir up trouble for Paul, and he is arrested and put on trial before finally being sent to Caesarea Maritima to appear before the Roman governor Felix.

Both sources agree that Paul's first visit to Jerusalem occurred after his Damascus road experience, but the timing and circumstances are otherwise different. Acts has Paul going to Jerusalem "after many days," while Paul claims the interval was three years. One may postulate that Luke simply does not know the exact length of time and therefore leaves it somewhat vague, but the differences do not end there. According to Paul, his first visit is very limited in scope. He meets with only two of the Jerusalem leaders, while in Acts Paul is openly received by all the apostles after some initial hesitation. The default is to favor Paul's own words, but some caution is in order. In Galatians Paul is arguing for his apostolic authority as one who received his gospel "not from man . . . but through a revelation of Jesus Christ" (1:11-12). Therefore, it is rhetorically significant that his apostleship is independent of the Jerusalem church. He does not need the approval of the apostles, as he is at pains to show. This may be accurate, but we must consider that Paul has

---

[9] E.g. Mark 10:32 and parallels; John 2:13; 5:1.

perhaps understated his interactions in Jerusalem as part of his self-defense.[10] Thus, we are reminded of the importance of reading even first-person accounts with great care.

Paul's second visit in Acts does not appear as such in Paul's writings, although it is possible that this difference reflects the particularities of Lukan chronology. We know from Paul's writings that he was involved in gathering a collection for famine sufferers in Judea (see visit 3 in the Pauline column and 1 Cor 16:1-4; 2 Corinthians 8–9). For him, this was an important project for improving relations between Jewish and Gentile converts. We also know that Luke is not always bound by chronological order.[11] Thus, it is possible that Paul's visit 2 in Acts should be connected to the anticipated visit 3 in Paul's own writings, which was meant to include the delivery of the collection from the Gentile churches for the believers in Judea.[12] These brief references in Acts 11, 12, and 24 may be the only vestiges in the Lukan account of one of Paul's major personal projects. Yet whether or not one accepts this connection as viable, it must be said that the second visit in Acts is not specifically corroborated by Paul's letters.

Scholars generally agree, however, that Paul's visit 2 and Luke's visit 3 refer to the same event, the so-called Apostolic Council to determine the restrictions and requirements for Gentile converts. Paul's account in Galatians is less specific on the details and makes no mention of a letter from the Jerusalem leaders. But here again, Paul is careful to emphasize his independence from Jerusalem's authority. The leaders there add nothing to his gospel, and he learns nothing from them. They simply grant their blessing to what Paul and Barnabas had already been doing and teaching. The Acts account suggests a more interactive exchange, in which Paul, Barnabas, and the Jerusalem leaders all agree on the value of the Gentile mission. The outcome is a letter with the authority of Jerusalem behind it. Paul's victory here is the confirmation not of his total independence from—but rather his successful collaboration with—the Jerusalem leaders.

Paul's epistles offer no parallel to visit 4 in Acts, and visit 5 can be connected to the letters only indirectly. It is possible that Luke is attempting to fill in the story of Paul's intended visit to Jerusalem and Rome (Rom 15:22-29), yet the circumstances in Acts are quite different from what Paul

---

[10] Cf. Acts, where Luke is trying to show Paul's continuity with the Jerusalem community and emphasizes the public nature of this visit.

[11] In his Gospel, for example, Luke re-orders Jesus's visits to Capernaum and Nazareth. In Mark and Matthew, Jesus visits Capernaum and heals Peter's mother-in-law (Mark 1:29-31; Matt 8:14-15), and then later returns to Nazareth and teaches in the synagogue (Mark 6:1-6; Matt 13:54-58). In Luke the order is reversed, with Jesus reading in the synagogue at Nazareth before he even gets to Capernaum. This detail might escape notice, except that in Luke's account Jesus expects the crowd to demand, "Do here in your home town what we heard you did in Capernaum" (4:23). Luke is the only author to include this reference to the healing at Capernaum, yet in his chronology Jesus does not even come to Capernaum until 4:31. Thus, the Lukan Jesus anticipates from the crowd a request to repeat a miracle that he has not even performed yet in Luke's narrative.

[12] Richard I. Pervo, *Acts: A Commentary* (Minneapolis: Fortress, 2009), 297-98.

anticipates. In Romans Paul indicates that he will deliver the collection to Jerusalem and then stop in Rome to gather supplies and help for his mission to Spain. In Acts, however, there is no mention of the collection, and Paul goes to Rome only because he is transferred there as part of his legal appeal—the latter being a situation he could not have foreseen.

By now the point should be clear enough. The question of Paul's journeys to Jerusalem, and indeed the nature of his relationship with the Jerusalem leaders as a whole, reveals some significant differences between the data in Paul's letters and the narrative in Acts. We may rightly give preference to the undisputed epistles, which still must be read carefully and critically. However, we cannot completely disregard Acts if we want to build a Pauline chronology, for while the undisputed letters give autobiographical details, they do not provide a single specific date that can be used as an anchor for this chronology. As Karl Donfried has stated, "Inevitably, if one is to establish a possible chronology of this period, there will have to be some dependence on Acts," for Luke does provide some possible dates.[13] We will explore these dates later in this chapter.

4. Extra-canonical Sources

Other texts also claim to provide details about Paul's life and activities. The earliest of these is a letter traditionally known as *1 Clement*, which dates from the end of the first century or the very beginning of the second century A.D..[14] Because many critical scholars also date Acts and some of the disputed Pauline epistles to this general time period, *1 Clement* could be roughly contemporaneous with some of these canonical texts. It deserves serious consideration, therefore, yet the information it provides is highly disputed.

1 Clement is a letter from the church in Rome to the church in Corinth, written in response to reports that factionalism among the leadership had led to deep schism in the Corinthian community. No specific author is identified by name, but tradition ascribes this letter to a certain Clement.[15] We know that the group of presbyters in Rome at one point had a secretary named Clement,[16] so perhaps this figure is in mind. The most relevant section of the letter for our purposes appears in a lengthy list of biblical examples of jealousy and strife:

> On account of jealousy and envy the greatest and most righteous pillars were persecuted and fought to the death. Let us place before our eyes the noble apostles. . . . On account of jealousy and conflict Paul pointed the way to the

---

[13] Karl Paul Donfried, "Chronology: The Apostolic and Pauline Period," in Karl Paul Donfried, *Paul, Thessalonica, and Early Christianity* (Grand Rapids: Eerdmans, 2002), 101.
[14] The traditional date is A.D. 95–96, although L. L. Welborn suggests a broader range of A.D. 80–140 ("Clement, First Epistle of," *ABD* 1:1060).
[15] Eusebius, *Hist. eccl.* 3.15-16; 4.23.11, citing Dionysius of Corinth; Irenaeus, *Haer.* 3.3.3.
[16] Herm. *Vis.* 2.4.3. Cf. the above references in Eusebius, who identifies him as Rome's third bishop, and Irenaeus, who lists him as the fourth bishop.

prize for perseverance. After he had been bound in chains seven times, driven into exile, stoned, and had preached in both the East and in the West, he received the noble glory for his faith, having taught righteousness to the whole world and having gone even to the limit of the West. When he had borne witness (μαρτυρήσας)[17] before the rulers, he was thus set free from the world and was taken up to the holy place, having become the greatest example of perseverance.[18]

The author provides few specific details about Paul's death, but the comments that he had reached "the limit of the West" (τὸ τέρμα τῆς δύσεως) and then stood "before the rulers" (ἐπὶ τῶν ἡγουμένων) prior to his death have prompted significant scholarly debates. These debates focus on whether or not *1 Clement* should be read as indicating that Paul succeeded in his desired trip to Spain (Rom 15:24-28) and then died in Rome. I have argued elsewhere in favor of reading this passage as evidence of a Roman tradition that Paul went to Spain.[19] The "limit" or "end" of the West is clearly Spain in a number of sources from the first century B.C. through the second century A.D., so I conclude that the authors of *1 Clement* are using it in the same way. No Roman author would have used "the limit of the West" to refer to Rome, which was at the center of the world, not its periphery. Of course, *1 Clement* cannot be used to *prove* that Paul went to Spain, merely that this tradition existed.[20] The idea that Paul went "before the rulers" (ἐπὶ τῶν ἡγουμένων) likewise cannot be taken as evidence that Paul died in Rome. This is the traditional reading, but the phrase could also be an allusion to Acts 9:15, where the Lord describes Paul as "my chosen instrument for carrying my name before the Gentiles [or nations] and kings and the sons of Israel." There is no specific link to Rome as the site of Paul's death in *1 Clement* or indeed in any other source prior to the *Acts of Paul* (A.D. 180–190).[21] *1 Clement*, therefore, may well inform us about some early Roman traditions, but there

---

[17] By the end of the first century A.D., there is no evidence that the verb μαρτυρέω had taken on the technical meaning of "dying as a martyr." See Boudewijn Dehandschutter, "Some Notes on *1 Clement* 5,4-7," in A. A. R. Bastiaensen, A. Hilhorst, and C. H. Kneepkens, eds., *Fructus Centesimus: Mélanges offerts à Gerard J. M. Bartelink à l'occasion de son soixante-cinquième anniversaire* (Instrumenta Patristica 19; Dordrecht: Kluwer, 1989), 83-89.
[18] *1 Clement* 5.2-7.
[19] David L. Eastman, *Paul the Martyr: The Cult of the Apostle in the Latin West* (WGRWSup 4; Atlanta: Society of Biblical Literature, 2011), 18-19, 144-46.
[20] The first explicit reference to a Pauline visit to Spain is in the *Acts of Peter* (ca. A.D. 180). See Eastman, *Paul the Martyr*, 146.
[21] Glenn E. Snyder ("Remembering the *Acts of Paul*" [Ph.D. diss., Harvard University, 2010], 60-64) argues that the martyrdom account may have been composed as early as the reign of Trajan, but this would still likely post-date *1 Clement*. Notable also here is the presence of a potential rival tradition to the claims of Rome as Paul's martyrdom site. See Helmut Koester, "Paul and Philippi: The Archaeological Evidence," in Charalambos Bakirtzis and Helmut Koester, eds., *Philippi at the Time of Paul and after His Death* (Harrisburg: Trinity Press International, 1998), 65; Allen D. Callahan, "Dead Paul: The Apostle as Martyr in Philippi," in Bakirtzis and Koester, *Philippi*, 77-80. Callahan specifically highlights the omission of a reference to Paul's death in Rome in *1 Clement* as "a curious silence on the part of a Roman Christian writing no more than a generation after the apostle's death" (citation at p. 77).

are not sufficient grounds for definitively including these in a Pauline chronology.[22]

In late antiquity Christians produced numerous texts that purportedly gave details of Paul's background, life, travels, and eventual death. From the second through the sixth century, for example, there are no fewer than nine texts that give accounts of Paul's death. We may add to that number stories about other parts of Paul's life, as well as references in texts that are not primarily about Paul but still include supposed biographical information. These texts give us no basis for treating them as historically reliable, even if other later authors and commentators depend on them. References to Paul in patristic authors such as Irenaeus, Tertullian, Eusebius of Caesarea, John Chrysostom, Augustine, and others are often so deeply indebted to the later sources that their works are of no value in reconstructing Paul's life.

5. Fixed Dates?

An important step toward building our chronology is exploring references to events that may establish a specific date or at least a limited range of dates. In Paul's letters, as mentioned earlier, there are no specific dates, but a detail in 2 Corinthians might provide a range of dates for the time in Damascus following his call/conversion experience.[23] In 2 Corinthians 11 Paul defends the authority of his apostleship by recounting the many hardships he has endured for the gospel. He then states, "In Damascus the ethnarch of Aretas the king was guarding the city of Damascus in order to arrest me, but I was lowered down in a basket through a window in the wall and escaped his hands" (2 Cor 11:32-33). Here an autobiographical detail from Paul can be cross-referenced to an historical figure known from other sources, namely Aretas the king.

Scholars agree that the king mentioned here must be the Nabatean king Aretas IV. The Jewish historian Josephus records that he ruled from 9 B.C. to A.D. 40. Nabatea is a region southeast of the Dead Sea, and this is probably the region Paul has in mind when he refers to his three years in Arabia (Gal 1:17). The reference to an ethnarch means that Aretas IV controlled Damascus and had installed a sort of governor to oversee local affairs, because

---

[22] Ignatius of Antioch, *Rom.* 4.3 and Irenaeus, *Haer.* 3.3.2-3 are other second-century sources that connect Paul with Rome but do not mention his martyrdom there. Ignatius, for example, contrasts himself as "a condemned man" with Paul who was "free." Because Ignatius was going to Rome to be martyred, we might expect him to compare himself with Paul, not draw a contrast, if he was to be killed in the same city. In the pseudepigraphical *Epistle to the Tarsians*, "Ignatius" reflects an awareness of the tradition of Paul's death in Rome (*Ep. Tars.* 3.3). The likewise spurious *Martyrdom of Ignatius* states that the bishop rejoices when he lands at Puteoli on his way to Rome, because he desires to follow in the footsteps of Paul (*Mart. Ign.* 5.3). None of these, however, demonstrates anything other than later traditions.

[23] Scholars debate whether Paul's experience on the road to Damascus should more properly be described as his "call" (in the pattern of prophets of the Hebrew Bible) or his "conversion." The event seems to have elements of both, so I will employ the compound term throughout this chapter.

Damascus was an important economic center but was rather far from the Nabatean capital. If Aretas died in A.D. 40, then his death would provide a definite *terminus ad quem* (latest possible date) for Paul's escape. It is possible to limit the range of dates even further, because Nabatea did not control Damascus for Aretas' entire reign. The standard scholarly view has been that the Roman emperor Caligula (A.D. 37–41) gave Damascus to Aretas to take care of as a client king of Rome. The Romans used such client kings on the eastern frontier as a way of creating a buffer with their Parthian enemies. From this perspective, A.D. 37 would be the *terminus a quo* (earliest possible date), because this is when Caligula came to power, so Paul's escape from Damascus would have occurred between A.D. 37 and 40.

Another theory, however, suggests that Aretas actually gained control of Damascus for a short time in A.D. 36–37. Proponents of this approach argue that there is no evidence that Caligula ever gave Damascus to Aretas, while it can be shown that Aretas launched a successful military campaign against Herod Antipas in 36 and held the city for less than a year.[24] If Paul is describing events that occurred during Aretas' brief but independent control of Damascus (which would have allowed the king to install an ethnarch), then he must have escaped Damascus in late A.D. 36 or early A.D. 37. This would give us a solid date for constructing the larger chronology. For example, Paul tells us that there was a three-year gap between his call/conversion on the road to Damascus and his return to and eventual escape from Damascus, so we can conclude that the initial call/conversion happened in A.D. 33/34.[25] This theory might also explain *why* the ethnarch was trying to arrest Paul. If the apostle had already spent three years in Nabatean territory preaching his message about Jesus as the Jewish Messiah, then he had probably caused as much commotion there as he did in other cities. Perhaps he had to flee Nabatea and return to Damascus as a safe zone, but when Aretas gained control of the city, the king was once again able to pursue Paul as a troublemaker.[26] This would explain why Paul then goes directly to Jerusalem, a city outside Aretas's reach. The available evidence cannot prove the details of this reconstruction, yet this approach has much in its favor and will be adopted as an anchor point for our chronology.

The other possible datable events in Paul's biography all come from the Acts of the Apostles, so they must be used with caution but cannot be completely ignored. In Acts 11, a prophet named Agabus predicts a severe famine, which in the Lukan narrative prompts Paul's second visit to Jerusalem along with Barnabas to bring aid to the Jerusalem community. Luke states that

---

[24] Glen W. Bowersock, *Roman Arabia* (Cambridge, Mass.: Harvard University Press, 1983), 65-69; Douglas A. Campbell, "An Anchor for Pauline Chronology: Paul's Flight from the 'Ethnarch of King Aretas' (2 Corinthians 11:32-33)," *JBL* 121.2 (2002): 279-302. Campbell notes that, regrettably, the classicist Bowersock "has received little attention from Pauline scholars" (p. 281 n. 7). This may indeed be yet another case in which the artificial division of academic disciplines has created an unfortunate gap in the scholarly discourse.

[25] Campbell, "Anchor," 300-1.

[26] Campbell, "Anchor," 299-300.

this famine "took place during the reign of Claudius" (11:28). Numerous famines are recorded in the eastern Mediterranean during the reign of the emperor Claudius (A.D. 41–54).[27] The most damaging of these famines occurred in the mid 40s A.D.. It hit Egypt first, and it was only a matter of time before Judea felt the impact of the food shortage. The Roman historians Suetonius and Pliny, as well as the Jewish historian Josephus, make reference to such a famine, as do some papyri from Egypt.[28] In Judea this famine is dated to A.D. 46–48.[29] At first glance, it may appear that Luke provides a clear date for the alleged (in his chronology) second visit of Paul to Jerusalem, but the situation is not as simple as that. If we read Acts 11:27-30 carefully, we discover that the language is obscure on the precise timing of the various elements of the story. The events as Luke tells them are as follows: (1) Agabus' prophecy; (2) The famine occurs; (3) The disciples decide to send aid to Judea; and (4) Paul (here Saul) and Barnabas deliver the aid. Luke does not specify how much time passes between each of these events. Clearly Luke suggests a gap between the prophecy and the famine, but how long a gap? Once the famine begins in 46 or 47, how long does it take the other believers to realize that this is the predicted famine? And then how long does it take them to get organized to make the collection and organize the delivery to Judea? All these elements of the story would take time. Thus, even if we accept that Luke is referring to the famine of 46 or 47, we need not—in fact perhaps should not—assume that the visit of Paul and Barnabas to Jerusalem would have taken place in that same year.[30] Luke's narrative here, therefore, is ultimately unable to provide us with a fixed point, even if we take the story at face value. And as I have indicated above, it is probable that Luke has moved the collection for Jerusalem to this earlier point in Paul's life, so the account in Acts cannot provide a fixed date for building a chronology.

Another case is Acts 13, where Luke states that Paul and Barnabas encountered a magician on the island of Cyprus who "was with the proconsul, Sergius Paulus, a discerning man" (13:7). The proconsul summons them to hear what they have to say and "believed, because he was amazed at their

---

[27] See e.g. Bruce Winter, "Acts and Food Shortages," in David W. J. Gill and Conrad Gempf, eds., *The Book of Acts in Its Graeco-Roman Setting* (BIFCS 2; Grand Rapids: Eerdmans, 1994), 59-78; Pervo, *Acts*, 296-97 and bibliography. None of these was "worldwide," as Acts describes it, yet we should not let a Lukan exaggeration cause us to miss the possible connection to other sources.

[28] Suetonius, *Claud.* 18; Pliny the Elder, *Nat.* 5.58; Josephus, *A.J.* 3.320-21; 20.51-53; 101. According to Josephus, queen Helena of Adiabene (not to be confused with the mother of Constantine) saw the suffering of the people in Jerusalem and purchased dried figs and wheat at her own expense and had them sent to the city. Eusebius (*Hist. eccl.* 2.12) claims that she was honored with monuments in Jerusalem as a result of her generosity. On the Egyptian and Judean evidence see Kenneth S. Gapp, "The Universal Famine under Claudius," *HTR* 28.4 (1935): 258-65; Winter, "Acts and Food Shortages," 62-71.

[29] Theodor Zahn, *Introduction to the New Testament* (Edinburgh: T. & T. Clark, 1909), 3:459-63.

[30] As Zahn (*Introduction*, 459) notes, "The language in 11:29 and the analogy of other collections (1 Cor 16:2; 2 Cor 8:10, 9:2) justify us in supposing that a year or more elapsed before the collection was completed, and that it was not sent until much later."

teaching about the Lord" (13:12). Given that proconsuls usually served terms of one year (and never more than two years), information about the career of this proconsul could provide a specific date for this encounter at the beginning of Paul's first missionary journey. Two inscriptions from Cyprus have been identified as possible links to this figure. Both have complicated histories of scholarship that we need not rehearse in detail here.[31] The result of this scholarly debate is that neither can be definitively linked to Sergius Paulus or definitively eliminated from possibly referring to this proconsul.[32] For all the work that has been invested in this epigraphical evidence, the results remain inconclusive. A third inscription that has sparked much consideration was preserved on a boundary stone found in Rome. It was put in place to delimit the bank of the Tiber during the reign of Claudius.[33] The name Sergius Paulus appears among the list of those charged with placing these stones. Could this inscription refer to the figure from Acts at an earlier stage in his political career? For over a century scholars have debated the point. Alanna Nobbs has argued that this Sergius Paulus is "quite feasibly . . . identifiable with the proconsul of Acts," for the date of the inscription is appropriate (she accepts the date A.D. 41–47), and there is evidence that at least one other member of the boundary stones committee went on to hold the position of proconsul in Asia.[34] Scholars have lined up on both sides of this question,[35] yet even if the Tiber inscription is accepted as referring to the eventual proconsul of Cyprus, it does not help us assign a specific date to the events of Acts 13. Acts is the only outside literary source that refers to Sergius Paulus, but there is unfortunately no way to determine the year in which he would have served as proconsul. Here again, therefore, a potentially datable detail in Acts ultimately proves unhelpful.

A more promising case of dating a government official comes from Acts 18:12-17. Paul is in Corinth and is brought by a group of Jews before the proconsul, Gallio, because he was causing a disturbance by teaching against the Jewish law. Gallio refuses to become involved in "questions about words and names and your own law" and tells them to attend to it themselves. He sends them all away, and Paul goes free. Is it possible to date precisely the year of Gallio's proconsulship? In this case, the answer is affirmative. An

---

[31] From Soli: *IGR* 3, 353 no. 930. From Chytri/Kythri: *SEG* 30 (1980): 1605. The most important secondary literature on the dating of these inscriptions is Terence Mitford, "Some Published Inscriptions from Roman Cyprus," *BSA* 42 (1947): 201-30; "Roman Cyprus," *ANRW* 2.7.2: 1285-1384; Justin Taylor, "St Paul and the Roman Empire: Acts of the Apostles 13-14," *ANRW* 2.26.2: esp. 1194; Douglas A. Campbell, "Possible Inscriptional Attestations to Sergius Paul[l]us (Acts 13:6-12), and the Implications for Pauline Chronology," *JTS* 56.1 (2005): 1-29.

[32] Many scholars had eliminated the Soli inscription from consideration after the publication of Mitford's "Roman Cyprus," but Campbell ("Possible Inscriptional Attestations," 2 n. 3) has argued that this dismissal was done on grounds that are "clearly rather weak."

[33] *CIL* 6.31543; republished in Arthur E. Gordon and Joyce S. Gordon, *Album of Dated Latin Inscriptions* (Berkeley: University of California Press, 1958), 1:98.

[34] Alanna Nobbs, "Cyprus in the Book of Acts," in David W. J. Gill and Conrad Gempf, eds., *The Book of Acts in its Graeco-Roman Setting* (Grand Rapids: Eerdmans, 1994), 284-89 (quotation on 289).

[35] See the bibliography in Nobbs, "Cyprus," 285 nn. 21-23.

inscription found in the Greek city of Delphi, an important center for the cult of Apollo, mentions a proconsul named Gallio and can be reliably dated:

> Tiberius [Claudius] Caesar Augustus Germanicus, [Pontifex maximus in his tribunician] power [year 12, acclaimed emperor for] the 26th time, the father of the country, [consul for the 5th time, censor, sends greetings to the city of Delphi.] I have for long been zealous for the city of Delphi [and favorable to it from the] beginning, and I have always observed the cult of the [Pythian] Apollo. [But with regard to] the present stories, and those quarrels of the citizens of which [a report has been made by Lucius], Junius Gallio my friend, the [pro]consul [of Achaia] . . .[36]

The text has been partially reconstructed (elements in square brackets are reconstructions), but the critical data for Pauline chronology are secure: the name of Gallio and the fact that Claudius was proclaimed proconsul for the 26th time. Such proclamations could occur multiple times in the same year, and evidence from other inscriptions allows us to date the 26th proclamation, and therefore this inscription, to the period between January 25 and August 1 of A.D. 52.[37] This means that Gallio was proconsul during this same period. We also know that proconsuls served one or (in rare cases) two-year terms that began in the summer, around July 1. It is very unlikely that Gallio could have begun his proconsular year and been mentioned in an inscription by Claudius within the same month (i.e. between July 1 and August 1, A.D. 52), so scholars conclude that Gallio must have served from around July 1 of A.D. 51 to July 1 of 52.[38] Therefore, if Luke is accurate when he says that Paul appeared before Gallio, then this would have occurred some time within that twelve month period. We cannot be any more specific than that,[39] but even this level of precision is significant, for it would place Paul in Corinth at a particular date that may then be used to situate other events relative to it. As I have stated above (and as scholars have reiterated), we must use this potential date with some caution, because Luke is demonstrably less concerned with chronology than we as historians might want him to be.[40]

---

[36] W. Dittenberger, *SIG*, 801 D. This English translation is taken from C. K. Barrett, ed., *The New Testament Background* (rev. ed.; San Francisco: Harper & Row, 1989), 51. See also Jerome Murphy-O'Connor, *St. Paul's Corinth: Texts and Archaeology* (Collegeville: Liturgical Press, 1983), 149-60.
[37] Robert Jewett, *A Chronology of Paul's Life* (Philadelphia: Fortress, 1979), 39.
[38] If he served for two years, which we have no way of verifying, then the date range could be July of A.D. 50 to July of A.D. 52, but a two-year term is unlikely. See e.g. Taylor, *Paul*, 36-37.
[39] Cf. for example the reconstructions by George Ogg, *The Chronology of the Life of Paul* (London: Epworth, 1968), 104-11; and Joseph A. Fitzmyer, *The Acts of the Apostles* (AB 31; New York: Doubleday, 1998), 622-23. Both attempt to limit this event to a narrow range of several months, but their arguments necessarily remain speculative.
[40] See e.g. Gerd Lüdemann, *Paul, Apostle to the Gentiles: Studies in Chronology* (Philadelphia: Fortress, 1984), 160. Lüdemann does grant that the "denial of the historicity of a trial before Gallio does not automatically mean denial of every sort of relationship between the apostle to the Gentiles and the proconsul." Dixon Slingerland ("Acts 18:1-18, the Gallio Inscription, and Absolute Pauline Chronology," *JBL* 110.3 [1991]: 439-49) dismisses the event as unhistorical. He then proceeds to argue that even if the Pauline trial were granted, the possible range of dates

Luke's account of Paul's time in Corinth also includes a reference to an expulsion of the Jews from Rome by the emperor Claudius. Luke tells us that this explains the presence in Corinth of Aquila and Priscilla, who had been forced to leave the capital (Acts 18:1-2). Most historians agree that Suetonius refers to this or a similar edict: "He expelled the Jews from Rome, because they were constantly making disturbances at the instigation of Chrestus."[41] Suetonius does not date this edict, however, so we must look elsewhere for further evidence. The Roman historian Cassius Dio, writing at the beginning of the third century, corroborates Claudius' troubles with some Jews in the city, yet he claims that the emperor could not remove all of them because of their sheer numbers. Thus, he merely forbade them from holding meetings.[42] Cassius Dio dates this prohibition to A.D. 41, which has led some scholars to connect this date to the Suetonius account and Acts 18.[43] There is a problem, however, in that Suetonius describes an expulsion, and Cassius Dio specifically says that this was not possible (at least not in 41). Some scholars have attempted to harmonize these references by arguing that Suetonius technically says the emperor expelled only those Jews directly involved in the disturbances (against Luke's claim that "all" the Jews were impacted), and Cassius Dio confirms that a general expulsion would have been impossible.[44] Thus, if one disregards Luke's "all," then Suetonius and Cassius Dio can be rectified.

Not all are content with this harmonization, so they rely on the work of the fifth-century Christian historian Orosius, who says the Jews were expelled from Rome in the ninth year of Claudius' reign, A.D. 49.[45] Those who appeal to Orosius contend that Suetonius and Cassius Dio are talking about different events, with the former referring to a later expulsion. Indeed, the majority of scholars has adopted 49 as the reference date for Acts 18:1-2.[46] Here again

---

would extend to A.D. 49–54, well beyond the consensus of 50/51–52. His arguments for expanding the range are themselves highly speculative and unpersuasive, in particular due to his imprecise handling of the Delphi inscription. For a critical response to Slingerland, see Jerome Murphy-O'Connor, "Paul and Gallio," *JBL* 112 (1993): 315-17. On the negative presentation of the Jews in this passage, see Slingerland, "'The Jews' in the Pauline Portion of Acts," *JAAR* 54 (1986): 305-21.

[41] Suetonius, *Claud.* 25. This reference to Chrestus as a possible variant on Christus (Christ) has led many scholars to suggest that the "disturbances" in question surrounded missionary activities in the synagogues of Rome. For a critique of this reading of Suetonius, see H. Dixon Slingerland, *Claudian Policymaking and the Early Imperial Repression of Judaism at Rome* (SFSHJ 160; Atlanta: Scholars Press, 1997), 151-217.

[42] Cassius Dio, *Hist.* 60.6.6.

[43] E.g. Lüdemann, *Paul,* 164-73; Irina Levinskaya, *The Book of Acts in Its Diaspora Setting* (BIFCS 5; Grand Rapids: Eerdmans, 1996), 171-82; Pervo, *Acts,* 446 who considers this date "more probable." This date would also link the Roman situation with a controversy in Alexandria, where Claudius did threaten the Jews in that same year.

[44] E.g. Gerd Lüdemann, *The Acts of the Apostles* (Amherst: Prometheus, 2005), 236.

[45] Orosius, *Hist. c. pag.* 7.6.15.

[46] E.g. Peter Lampe, *From Paul to Valentinus: Christians at Rome in the First Two Centuries* (trans. Michael Steinhauser; Minneapolis: Fortress, 2003), 11-16; Hans-Jürgen Wolter, *Die Zeit des Apostel Paulus: Eine paulinische und frühchristliche Chronologie* (Regensburg: Roderer, 1996), 7, 48-50; Calvin J. Roetzel, *Paul: The Man and the Myth* (Columbia: University of South

there are problems, however, for Orosius claims that his source for the date is Josephus. Josephus, however, does not mention this expulsion under Claudius, which prompts some scholars to dismiss the Orosius passage entirely from consideration.[47] Furthermore, the historian Tacitus does not mention this expulsion in his recitation of the events of 49, while he does refer to a similar event in A.D. 19 under Tiberius.[48] Why would he recount such an event in 19 yet omit it in 49, if it in fact occurred? Proponents of the A.D. 49 theory recognize these potential objections but hold that, on balance, their view is more likely to be correct. The A.D. 49 theory also has the added benefit of lining up with the dates of Gallio. If Aquila and Priscilla were forced out of Rome in 49, then Paul would likely have met them in Corinth in 49/50. Acts tells us that he stayed in Corinth for at least 18 months, and this timeline would still have Paul in the city at the time of Gallio's proconsular year(s) of 50/51–52. In the absence of further evidence, the issue cannot be definitively resolved as to whether Acts 18 refers to 41 or 49 (or some other date entirely). We are left making an educated guess, in spite of what had held promise as a possible fixed point of chronology.[49]

A final passage to which some point concerns Porcius Festus' date of arrival as procurator in Jerusalem. According to Acts 24:47, Festus succeeded Felix, who had ruled for two years. If the date could be established, then we may have some information on the precise date of Paul's arrest and trial in Jerusalem. Both Tacitus and Josephus confirm that Felix was procurator for two years,[50] as Luke states, but beyond that they offer no help. A reference in Josephus might favor a date of 59 or later,[51] but the details of his account are not entirely clear on this point. Using the limited data available, scholars generally arrive at a date between A.D. 55 and 61.[52] Arguments for greater precision have been made,[53] but these inevitably rely on speculation and/or

---

Carolina Press, 1998), 178-83; Riesner, *Paul's Early Period*, 412; Murphy-O'Connor, *Paul*, 9-10; Aldo Moda, "Paolo prigioniero e martire: per una cronologia degli ultimi anni," *BeO* 31.2 (1989): 63-66; Jewett, *Chronology*, 37-38.

[47] Gerd Lüdemann, "Das Judenedikt des Claudius (Apg 18,2)," in Claus Bussmann and Walter Radl, eds., *Der Treue Gottes trauen. Beiträge zum Werk des Lukas* (Freiburg: Herder, 1991), 289-98; Dixon Slingerland, "Suetonius Claudius 25.4, Acts 18, and Paulus Orosius' 'Historiarum Adversum Paganos Libri VII': Dating the Claudian Expulsion(s) of Roman Jews," *JQR* 83.1/2 (1992): 127-44. Both are highly dependent on Adolf von Harnack, "Chronologische Berechnung des Tages von Damaskus," *SPAW* 37 (1912): 675-76.

[48] Tacitus, *Ann.* 2.85. Unfortunately, the section of his work on A.D. 41 has not survived.

[49] For a summary of the issues and arguments related to dating this expulsion, see John M. G. Barclay, *Jews in the Mediterranean Diaspora from Alexander to Trajan (323 BCE–117 CE)* (Berkeley: University of California Press, 1996), 303-6; Donfried, "Chronology: The Apostolic and Pauline Period," 111-12.

[50] Tacitus, *A.J.* 13.14; Josephus, *A.J.* 20.182.

[51] Josephus, *A.J.* 20.179, 182.

[52] Pervo, *Acts*, 608.

[53] Those who prefer a date between 55 and 57 include Lüdemann, *Acts*, 219; Ernst Haenchen, *The Acts of the Apostles: A Commentary* (Philadelphia: Westminster, 1971), 70-71; and Hans Conzelmann, *Acts of the Apostles* (Philadelphia: Fortress, 1987), 195. Dates from 58 to 60 have been argued by Joel Green, "Festus, Porcius," *ABD* 2:794-95; D. B. Saddington, "Roman

other indications in Acts (thus creating the problematic situation of assigning a precise date to an event based on other imprecise dates). As with most of the examples above, we are again left without a precise date.

In approaching the construction of a chronology, then, Paul's own words in 2 Cor 11:32-33 seem to provide one reference point. Of the possible anchor points in Acts, however, only the trial before Gallio can be dated with much precision. As discussed above, some historians attempt to use no material from Acts, but the dearth of evidence compels us to use this material, even if cautiously, if we want to construct a chronology that is anything beyond a few scarce points on a timeline.

6. A Chronology of Paul's Life

Despite all the caveats and challenges noted above, the construction of a chronology of Paul's life remains an important pursuit toward understanding both the apostle and the development of early Christianity more broadly. Indeed, if we change our focus from historical anchor points to points of potential overlap and convergence between the undisputed epistles and Acts, then a more viable picture begins to emerge.

OVERLAP BETWEEN PAUL'S UNDISPUTED LETTERS AND ACTS[54]		
Pauline reference	**Event**	**Acts reference**
Gal 1:11-17; 1 Cor 9:1; 15:8[55]	Vision of the risen Christ on the road to Damascus and call/conversion	9:1-22; 22:6-11; 26:9-23
2 Cor 11:32-33	Escape from Damascus	9:23-25
Gal 1:18-20	Journey to Jerusalem	9:26-29
Gal 1:21-22	Journey to Syria and Cilicia	9:30 (Caesarea and Tarsus)
Gal 2:1-10	Journey to Jerusalem after 14 years; Apostolic Council	15:1-30[56]
Gal 2:11-14 (including the conflict with Peter)	Paul returns to Antioch	15:30-35 (but no conflict with Peter mentioned)
Gal esp. 4:13; 1 Cor 16:1	Journey through Galatia	16:6
Phil; 1 Thess 2:2; 2 Cor 11:9	Preaching in Philippi	16:11-40
1 Thess esp. 2:2; Phil 4:15-16	Preaching in Thessaloniki	17:1-9
1 Thess 3:1	Journey to Athens	17:15-34

Military and Administrative Personnel in the New Testament," *ANRW* 2.26.3: 2428-29; Murphy-O'Connor, *Paul*, 22-23; Jewett, *Chronology*, 41-44.

[54] This chart is informed by similar summaries in Taylor, *Paul*, 33, and Raymond E. Brown, *An Introduction to the New Testament* (New York: Doubleday, 1997), 424.

[55] Paul gives no full description of the experience to match Acts, but in Galatians he makes reference to his revelation and later return to Damascus, while in 1 Corinthians he mentions the vision of Christ twice.

[56] Acts does not mention the lapse of fourteen years.

1 Cor esp. 1:26-28; 2:1-5	Preaching in Corinth	18:1-18
1 Thess 1:1; 3:6	Timothy and Silas/Silvanus come to Corinth	18:5
Gal 4:13	Journey through Galatia	18:23
1 Cor 16:12 (by Paul)	Apollos sent to Corinth	18:27 (by Priscilla and Aquila)
1 Cor 16:1-9	Preaching in Ephesus	19:1–20:1; 20:31
1 Cor 16:3-8; 2 Cor 1:15-16	Planned visits to Macedonia, Corinth, Jerusalem	19:21 (with Rome added)
2 Cor 2:13; 7:5; 9:2-4	Preaching in Macedonia	20:1-2
Rom 15:26; 16:1; 2 Cor 13:1	Preaching in Greece (Achaia)	20:2-3
Rom 15:25-28 (planned only)	Journey to Jerusalem	21:15–23:30
Rom 15:22-24, 28-29 (planned only)	Journey to Rome	27:1–28:31

Agreement between these sources is not unassailable proof of historicity, but multiple attestation has been a staple of critical biblical scholarship for over a century. When applied here, it gives us reasonable grounds for beginning to put meat on the bones, so to speak, of our chronology.

We know nothing of the chronology of Paul's life prior to the Damascus Road experience. Scholars estimate that Paul (then Saul) was born in the first few years of the Common Era, making him roughly a contemporary of Jesus. Paul never identifies Tarsus as his hometown in his letters, but there is no reason to doubt Luke's claim about this in Acts. Most scholars estimate that Jesus may have died in A.D. 30,[57] so all of Paul's activities persecuting the followers of Jesus would have to post-date that event.

Below is a chart representing five of the numerous chronologies proposed by scholars,[58] along with my own proposed chronology. Riesner and Witherington represent more traditional chronologies based on Acts, with the other three proposing revisions of various sorts. As the chart reflects, there is clustering around certain events early in Paul's life, such as the date of his call/conversion and the first trip to Jerusalem. In addition, there is some concern for having Paul in Corinth in the years 51/52, in order to match the Gallio reference discussed above, yet there is not total agreement on which journey of Paul to Corinth is in play here. When it comes to dating Paul's travels, there is considerable variety. Some combine or split the traditional three journeys and the additional travels into different configurations, and

---

[57] Karl Paul Donfried, "Chronology of the Life of Jesus," *ABD* 1:1015-16. For examples of other possible dates see e.g. Brown, *Introduction*, 429.

[58] See the insert at back of Jewett, *Chronology*. Lüdemann, *Paul*, 262-63 provides two separate sets of dates, depending on whether one dates the crucifixion to A.D. 27 or 30. The dates based on A.D. 30 are indicated in parentheses. He also divides Paul's journeys differently, making it difficult to reflect the details precisely in this chart. Murphy-O'Connor, *Paul*, 1-31. Riesner, *Paul's Early Period*, 322. Ben Witherington III, *The Acts of the Apostles: A Socio-Rhetorical Commentary* (Grand Rapids: Eerdmans, 1998), 81-86. Witherington represents a traditional chronology that places considerable weight on the chronology of Acts.

Lüdemann fails to include any of the Roman material, for it is not reflected in the undisputed Pauline corpus. What follows the chart are explanations of how I have arrived at some of the key (particularly disputed) dates.

	Jewett	Lüdemann	Murphy-O'Connor	Riesner	Witherington	Eastman
Call/conversion	34	30 (33)	33	31/32	33/34	33/34
First visit to Jerusalem	37	33 (36)	37	33/34	37	36/37
Syria and Cilicia	37–46	34 (37)	37–?	34–42	37–46	37–?
First Missionary Journey	(included in above)			45–47	48	?
Second visit to Jerusalem after 14 years (Council)	51	47 (50)	51	48	49	50/51
Second Missionary Journey	46–51	36– (39–) (Corinth in A.D. 41[59])	46–51	49–51/52	50–52	50/51–53
Third Missionary Journey	52–55	48–50 (51–53)	52–54	52–55	53–57	53–55
Through Macedonia to Corinth	56–57	50–52 (53–55)	54–56	55–57	(included in above)	56–57
Third visit to Jerusalem; arrest and 2-year imprisonment	57–59	52 (55)	57?–61?	57–59	57–59	57–59
Voyage to Rome	59–60		61–62	59	59–60	59–60
Imprisonment in Rome	60–62		62–64	60–62	60–62	60–62
Spain			64			62–63[60]
Return trip to the East			64–66?		62–64	63–64[60]
Death	62		67		65–68	62–68[60]

7. Call/conversion and First Jerusalem Visit

Earlier in this chapter I argued for dating Paul's escape from Damascus to the end of 36 or the early months of A.D. 37 based on the Aretas reference. This starting point gives us two dates. First, we know that Paul's escape and subsequent trip to Jerusalem happened three years after his call/conversion (Gal 1:17-18), so we can count backwards to calculate the date of this event to 33/34. We can also date his first trip to Jerusalem to 36/37, for this seems to have followed his Damascus escape directly.

8. First Missionary Journey

We have no chronological indications for what is traditionally known as the first missionary journey, so it is impossible to settle on concrete dates. Paul and Acts agree that Paul's first missionary travels were in Syria and Cilicia (Gal 1:21-22; Acts 9:30), but Luke then claims that after a year in Antioch (Acts 11:26), Paul went forth with Barnabas on the first journey through Cyprus into Galatia (13:1-14:28). Paul never mentions an additional journey,

---

[59] The A.D. 41 date corresponds to the Edict of Claudius and the expulsion of the Jews from Rome.
[60] These are hypothetical dates, as explained in the discussion that follows.

so some disregard Acts. However, arguments from silence are always problematic, and Paul's silence is not necessarily grounds to dismiss out of hand the additional material in Acts.[61] In the absence of specific chronological evidence, I follow Jewett, Lüdemann, and Murphy-O'Connor in leaving the dates for the first journey open to further debate and inquiry.[62]

9. Second Jerusalem Visit (Jerusalem Council)

Counting Paul's fourteen-year absence from his first trip to Jerusalem (Gal 2:1) yields a date of 50/51.[63] I am among the many scholars who connect the Jerusalem visit of Gal 2:1-10 with the account in Acts 15:1-30, even if not all the details agree between the two renderings of the events.

10. Second Missionary Journey

In Acts Luke tells us that Paul's initial visits to Macedonia and Achaia (the second journey) take place after the Jerusalem Council (as reflected in Witherington), yet Jewett, Lüdemann, and Murphy-O'Connor depart from Acts in placing these travels prior to the Council. This difference is informed by their perspectives on an unresolved debate within Pauline scholarship, namely whether Galatians was written to those in North Galatia or South Galatia. The arguments are complex,[64] but the main points for our purposes are the following: In Galatians Paul states that he had already visited them (4:13) and that—at the Jerusalem Council—he had defended the gospel that he had preached to them (2:5). Thus, Paul must have visited the recipients of Galatians prior to the Jerusalem Council. This point is important because in Luke's chronology, Paul does not evangelize North Galatia (on the second journey) until after the Jerusalem Council. This leaves two possibilities: (1) Galatians is written to South Galatia. In that case there is no conflict with Acts, for South Galatia is the very region visited by Paul on his first journey. The gospel that he defended in Jerusalem is the one he preached in South Galatia prior to the Council on the first journey; (2) Galatians is written to North Galatia, and therefore Luke must have altered the chronology of the

---

[61] As Donfried has noted, Acts may be used carefully "when it does not contradict assertions made by the apostle" ("Chronology: The Apostolic and Pauline Period," *ABD* 1:1017). In this case there is no direct contradiction.

[62] Witherington arrives at A.D. 48 by the following calculation: The Jerusalem Council happened in 49 (by his reckoning) in response to what Paul and Barnabas were preaching on the first journey. There must be a year between the Syria-Cilicia journey and the first journey (the year in Antioch), so the Syria-Cilicia journey must have ended in 46, followed by a year in Antioch (A.D. 47) and then the first journey in 48.

[63] Cf. Lüdemann's minority position that the fourteen-year period should begin at the time of Paul's call/conversion.

[64] Recent summaries of the arguments on both sides can be found in Martinus de Boer, *Galatians* (Philadelphia: Westminster John Knox, 2011), 4-11 (favors the North Galatia hypothesis); Thomas R. Schreiner and Clinton E. Arnold, *Galatians* (Grand Rapids: Zondervan, 2010), 22-29 (favor the South Galatia hypothesis).

second journey. Paul's second journey must have taken place before the Council, thus allowing Paul to teach the gospel that he then had to defend in Jerusalem. Advocates of both positions admit that the evidence is inconclusive on the audience of Galatians, so it would be methodologically problematic to appeal to this as the basis of a major chronological adjustment. Therefore, I have placed the second missionary journey shortly after the Jerusalem Council (following Acts), which also places Paul in Corinth at the appropriate time for the trial before Gallio in A.D. 51/52.[65]

11. Later Journeys and Imprisonments

From the placement of the second journey flows the placement of the third journey, the subsequent trip through Macedonia to Corinth (which Witherington attaches to the third journey), and Paul's arrest and travel to Rome. Here again, despite the concerns about Acts, scholars employ the data from Luke's narrative on the length of Paul's stay in Ephesus (Acts 19:8-10; 20:31), his imprisonment following arrest in Jerusalem (Acts 24:27), and the length of his imprisonment in Rome (Acts 28:30). For these latter years of Paul's life, my reconstruction closely aligns with those of Jewett and Witherington.

12. After Rome?

Neither the undisputed Pauline epistles nor Acts contain any information concerning what happens to Paul after his arrival in Rome. Many (e.g. Jewett) assume that Paul is killed after the two-year imprisonment there, but there is no evidence to support this assumption. Others (e.g. Murphy-O'Connor) believe that Paul was released and fulfilled his desire to go to Spain (Rom 15:22-24, 28-29).[66] Some patristic authors believed this, as well, and this alleged Pauline visit was the basis for the apocryphal *Life and Conduct of the Holy Women Xanthippe, Polyxena, and Rebecca*.[67] To this point we have not engaged the disputed Pauline letters, but here they may come into play. The Pastoral Epistles (1 and 2 Timothy, Titus) contain references to Pauline travels that do not fit within the frameworks of the undisputed letters or Acts. Some simply dismiss these as spurious (e.g. Lüdemann), while Murphy-

---

[65] Advocates of moving the second journey before the Jerusalem Council (and the North Galatia hypothesis) point out that a post-Council second journey makes the chronology very crowded in the A.D. 50s. This observation is correct, but the fact that we may perceive his travels as crowded is not in and of itself sufficient grounds for moving this journey in the chronology.

[66] Murphy-O'Connor, *Paul*, 359-63.

[67] Eastman, *Paul the Martyr*, 144-48. See my forthcoming new translation with commentary of these *Acts* for the forthcoming collection *More Christian Apocrypha: A New Anthology of Untranslated Christian Apocryphal Texts*, ed. Tony Burke and Brent E. Landau (Eerdmans, forthcoming). An important article (also forthcoming) is Richard I. Pervo, "Dare and Back: The Stories of Xanthippe & Polyxena," in Ilaria Ramelli and Judith Perkins, eds., *Early Christian and Jewish Narrative: The Role of Religion in Shaping Narrative Forms* (Tübingen: Mohr [Siebeck], fothcoming). Dr. Pervo was kind enough to show me an advanced copy of this article.

O'Connor and Witherington are willing to entertain the possibility that these letters might contain some authentic traditions.[68] I agree with Murphy-O'Connor and Witherington that we cannot simply dismiss the possibility that there are authentic chronological details within the Pastoral Epistles, even if the authorship is disputed by the majority of critical scholars. Indeed, we know that we do not have all of Paul's epistles,[69] so it is possible that the Pastorals could preserve some biographical details that would have otherwise been lost to us. On the other hand, given the doubts about authorship, it is prudent to proceed only with great caution regarding the implications for Pauline chronology. At the end of the day, neither the evidence for the trip to Spain nor the information from the Pastorals is secure enough to warrant historical confidence. Therefore, these journeys and their dates must remain hypothetical and are indicated as such in the chart.

13. Death

Only later traditions identify Rome as Paul's place of execution and Nero as the primary agent in his death. If these traditions are to be believed, then the death of Nero himself (June 6, A.D. 68) would provide the *terminus ante quem* for Paul's martyrdom. Roman historians record that Nero executed numerous Christians as part of his cover-up of the fire of A.D. 64,[70] yet this kind of indiscriminate persecution does not fit with the later accounts of Paul's death, in which the emperor specifically targets the apostle (sometimes alongside Peter) for a direct offense against Nero's authority (and with no mention of the fire). There is certainly no specific evidence against the idea that Paul died in Rome under Nero,[71] yet the fact that a tradition is repeated numerous times does not make it historically reliable. Thus, I have again given only a hypothetical range of dates.[72]

14. Conclusion

Establishing a reliable Pauline chronology remains an elusive task for New Testament scholars. The combination of incomplete chronological data on the

---

[68] Murphy-O'Connor, *Paul*, 363-66; Witherington, *Acts*, 85-86. See also Lindsey P. Pherigo, "Paul's Life after the Close of Acts," *JBL* 70 (1951): 277-84.

[69] The most famous example is the fact that what we call 1 Corinthians is actually Paul's (at least) second letter to the Christians there (1 Cor 5:9).

[70] Tacitus, *Ann.* 15.44; Suetonius, *Nero* 16.2.

[71] Cf. the suggestion of a Philippian martyrdom, as indicated above in n. 19.

[72] I am currently working on an article exploring the dates given for Paul's death in the various apocryphal acts and passion accounts. The dates range from A.D. 57 to 69, and this variety reinforces my conviction about the need to proceed with caution on offering a date. Modern reconstructions propose a variety of dates, as well. Several are reflected in the chart above and are roughly consonant with one another, but others are quite divergent. Bartosz Adamczewski (*Heirs of the Reunited Church* [Frankfurt: Peter Lang, 2010], 81-82), for example, has proposed a martyrdom date of A.D. 49, a view that faces significant chronological challenges. It is beyond the scope of this chapter to explore all these scholarly debates here.

one hand, and conflicting chronological data on the other, presents formidable challenges. We rightly give preference to—but cannot rely solely upon—the undisputed Pauline epistles, and the use of Acts and the disputed epistles requires caution. Donfried has concluded that "there can be no absolutely definite chronology of this period,"[73] and others have taken this to its logical conclusion by jettisoning altogether the notion of a fixed chronology.[74] What I have presented here is an approximation of Paul's chronology based on the evidence, yet there is always hope that new discoveries will lead to new insights. Until more evidence comes to light, however, we are not able to push the question forward to a viable and satisfactory solution.

Recommended Reading

Donfried, Karl Paul. "Chronology: The Apostolic and Pauline Period." Pages 99-117 in *Paul, Thessalonica, and Early Christianity*. Grand Rapids: Eerdmans, 2002.
Jewett, Robert. *A Chronology of Paul's Life*. Philadelphia: Fortress, 1979.
Knox, John. *Chapters in a Life of Paul*. Rev. ed. Macon: Mercer University Press, 1987.
Lüdemann, Gerd. *Paul, Apostle to the Gentiles: Studies in Chronology*. Philadelphia: Fortress, 1984.
Murphy-O'Connor, Jerome. *Paul: A Critical Life*. Oxford: Clarendon, 1996.
Ogg, George. *The Chronology of the Life of Paul*. London: Epworth, 1968.
Riesner, Rainer. *Paul's Early Period: Chronology, Mission Strategy, Theology*. Grand Rapids: Eerdmans, 1997.
Tatum, Gregory. *New Chapters in the Life of Paul: The Relative Chronology of his Career*. Catholic Biblical Quarterly Monograph Series 41. Washington: Catholic Biblical Association, 2006.
Wolter, Hans-Jürgen, *Die Zeit des Apostel Paulus: Eine paulinische und frühchristliche Chronologie*. Regensburg: Roderer, 1996.

---

[73] Donfried, "Chronology," *ABD* 1:1017.
[74] E.g. Gregory Tatum, *New Chapters in the Life of Paul: The Relative Chronology of his Career* (CBQMS 41; Washington: Catholic Biblical Association, 2006).

3. The Archaeology of the Pauline Mission

Cavan W. Concannon

The interconnectedness of biblical interpretation, archaeological materials, and the interests of contemporary readers of the bible requires that biblical scholars think critically about the role that each should play in the study of Paul. This chapter examines the archaeology of the Pauline mission, but does so from a different perspective than what might typically fall under this heading, asking about how and why we look at archaeological materials to interpret Paul and his letters.

I begin by briefly considering the history of the use of archaeology in the study of the Christian Scriptures and Paul's mission. I examine the development of classical archaeology as a discipline alongside and in conversation with biblical studies. In particular, I look at how both disciplines inherited problematic ideologies of pilgrimage and elite tourism. By understanding these intertwined histories and their ideologies, we might hope to find new avenues with which to pursue a richer conversation between New Testament scholars and classical archaeologists. I then lay out how we might, following feminist biblical interpreters, gaze differently on archaeology and how such a gaze can change the study of early Christianity. The way forward for those who want to take the importance of archaeological work seriously is to use archaeology to place early Christians within the dynamic and diverse landscapes of the Roman Empire, as participants in, and not distinct from, the production and transformation of Roman provincial culture. To see how we might envision the use of archaeology otherwise, I then move on to short studies of four "Pauline" cities (Thessaloniki, Philippi, Ephesos, and Corinth), where I highlight scholarship that is producing new insights and frameworks for the study of early Christianity.[1]

---

[1] The approach that I take here is rooted in my own work with feminist biblical and archaeological studies. See, for example, my *"When You Were Gentiles": Ethnicity in Roman Corinth and Paul's Corinthian Correspondence* (New Haven: Yale University Press, forthcoming). In particular, I am interested in how an interdisciplinary approach to the study of the Pauline materials can offer us ways of "gazing upon the invisible," those people, practices, and spaces that have been obscured from view by the kyriarchal and colonialist histories and interests of both biblical studies and archaeology.

1. Archaeology, Pilgrimage, and the Study of the New Testament

Both the academic study of early Christianity and the practice of Mediterranean archaeology are modern intellectual products, coming of age in post-Enlightenment Europe and alongside the rise of European colonialism.[2] Though excavations of classical sites occurred during the Italian Renaissance, archaeology as it is practiced today began to flourish in the late nineteenth century.[3] Prior to that time connections were made between the European elite and the classical lands of Italy and Greece through cultured "tourism." During the Renaissance, the Grand Tour inspired European intellectuals with the grandeur of ancient Rome.[4] Travel to the region often was done in a romantic spirit, with a major influence on travelers' perceptions being the fictional *Voyage of Anacharsis the Younger in Greece*, published in 1788 by the abbé Jean-Jacques Barthélemy.[5] By the nineteenth century, increasing access to rail and steam-powered travel in the Mediterranean lead to a renewed appreciation of Greek history and a desire to experience the sites of classical Greece and imperial Rome or the sacred topography of the Holy Land.[6] These changes in transportation allowed for a certain amount of democratization in travel to the Mediterranean and the Holy Land. Travel to classical lands was part of the

---

[2] On the origins of the study of religion, see Tomoko Masuzawa, *The Invention of World Religions: Or How European Universalism Was Preserved in the Language of Pluralism* (Chicago: University of Chicago Press, 2005).

[3] Some of the earliest excavations were driven not by the search for knowledge of the ancient world, but for antiquities and art that could be displayed in the homes of the European elite. See, for example, the relationship between collecting and the Grand Tour in James Buzard, "The Grand Tour and After (1660–1840)" in Peter Hulme and Tim Youngs, eds., *The Cambridge Companion to Travel Writing* (Cambridge: Cambridge University Press, 2002), 40-41.

[4] The Tour moved from England, through France via Paris to Geneva to the ancient cities of Italy and then back via Austria, Germany and the Low Countries (Buzard, "The Grand Tour," 38-39). Glen W. Bowersock, *From Gibbon to Auden: Essays in the Classical Tradition* (Oxford: Oxford University Press, 2009), 16, notes, for example that Gibbon went on the Grand Tour in 1764 and credited this tour with the inspiration behind his *Decline and Fall of the Roman Empire*.

[5] Stephen L. Dyson, *In Pursuit of Ancien Pasts: A History of Classical Archaeology in the Nineteenth and Twentieth Centuries* (New Haven: Yale University Press, 2006), 66-67. Other popular "guides" to the romantic travel experience were produced around this time, including Marie-Gabriel Florent August's *Voyage pittoresque de la Grèce*. Dyson describes Florent August's romantic view of Greece as "impressionistic" and "fuzzy." Margarita Díaz-Andreu, *A World History of Nineteenth-Century Archaeology: Nationalism, Colonialism, and the Past* (Oxford: Oxford University Press, 2007), 82, suggests that "the enlightened elites [of Europe] imagined Greece as the land of nature, genius, and freedom as opposed to their own experience of living in an artificial, overspecialized, and authoritarian world."

[6] Bowersock, *From Gibbon to Auden*, 126; Buzard, "The Grand Tour," 47-48. Mark Humphries, *Early Christianity* (New York: Routledge, 2006), 58, notes that cordial relations between Europe and the Ottoman Empire also opened up the eastern Mediterranean to travel in this period. By the last third of the eighteenth century, the earlier "Grand Tour" had begun to shift from the domain of aspiring male aristocrats to include women and children (Buzard, "The Grand Tour," 42). The Tour's itinerary focused on Rome and not Greece. As Buzard, "The Grand Tour," 39-40, notes, this was due to British pretensions to "Roman" power: "As their overseas empire expanded, well-off Britons drew parallels between their nation's current position and that of the ancient Roman Empire. They styled their age an 'Augustan' one and expected men of taste to admire and imitate Roman models."

production of elite identity in northern Europe and spurred interest in the acquisition and collection of ancient artifacts. The acquisition of ancient artifacts was also part of the creation of national identity. In early nineteenth-century France, the acquisition of ancient artifacts by the state was viewed as emblematic of progress and the development of an imperial national identity.[7]

At the same time that archaeology was emerging as a new academic field and archaeologists were unearthing vast quantities of new artifacts, the study of early Christianity was emerging as a field of study distinct from theology in the burgeoning departments of religious studies in European and American universities. While biblical scholars debated the value and the use of parallels in the study of the New Testament they began to use archaeological evidence as another kind of "literary" parallel, as in the work of Adolf Deissmann. In the latter case, scholars saw archaeological excavations as a window onto the world of the bible, an opportunity to "walk in the footsteps of Paul" similar to the tourists who followed the path of the Grand Tour. Deissmann famously highlighted what he saw as the benefits of such a scholarly pilgrimage: "Even to-day the traveler who follows the footsteps of the apostle Paul from Corinth past the ruins of Ephesus to Antioch and Jerusalem, finds much revealed to him in the sunshine of the Levant which he would not necessarily have seen at Heidelberg or Cambridge."[8] A few examples taken from Corinth illustrate some of the ways in which this romantic spirit animated both biblical scholars and the archaeologists who looked to Christian scholars, lay readers, and tourist/pilgrims as audiences for their discoveries.

In the third volume of his history of early Christianity, Ernest Renan describes his visit to Corinth as part of a larger itinerary that took him to a number of sites associated with early Christianity.[9] Unlike other famous archaeological sites, Corinth's remains lay mostly under several meters of sedimentary deposit, aside from a few freestanding columns from the Temple of Apollo, until excavations began in 1896. Because he toured the Corinthia before the excavations began, Renan's description of Corinth knows nothing of the topography of Corinth as we know it today and relies instead on a romanticized literary reconstruction of the city.

Renan's account of Corinth focuses on the mobility of the city due to trade and its mixing of races, social classes, and moralities. The population, he

---

[7] "Antiquities of the Great Civilizations had been judged as symbols of progress, emblems of the first steps on a long historical route which led to civilization and the French nation and, therefore, to freedom" (Díaz-Andreu, *Nineteenth-Century Archaeology*, 80).

[8] Gustav Adolf Deissmann, *Light From the Ancient East: The New Testament Illustrated by Recently Discovered Texts of the Graeco-Roman World* (New York: Hodder and Stoughton, 1910), 1-2. The German edition was first published in 1908, with the English translation following in 1910. Deissmann's earlier work had involved two volumes of *Bibelstudien* (1895 and 1897) that involved studies of inscriptions and papyri. On Deissmann's use of "light" in his work, see Ward Blanton, *Displacing Christian Origins: Philosophy, Secularity, and the New Testament* (Chicago: University of Chicago Press, 2007), 107-12. For Blanton, Deissmann "employs the image of an unmodern light from the East in order to critique modern academic productions as a form of alienated—and alienating—labor" (108).

[9] Ernest Renan, *Saint Paul* (trans. Ingersoll Lockwood; History of the Origins of Christianity 3; New York: G. W. Carleton, 1875), 145-52.

writes, was "very mixed. It was composed of a collection of those people, of all sorts and origins, who liked Caesar . . . in a word, one of those mixed cities which were no longer native lands."[10] Kenchreai, Corinth's southern port, is defined by its orientation to the East (it was "inhabited principally by orientals") and it is because of this geographical orientation that Renan locates the Jewish population there (including Prisca and Aquila, though they would have come to Lechaion from Rome).[11] Since there was little else in the landscape to give him a sense of the city and its built environment, Renan seizes on features of the landscape to romanticize the spot: "The beautiful rock of Acro-Corinth, the white summits of Helicon and Parnassus, refreshed [Paul's] gaze for a long while."[12] We might characterize Renan's description of Acro-Corinth as fitting within the emerging travel-writing style of the "picturesque," combining an aestheticized travel narrative with a description of the picturesque beauty of the landscape.[13] Renan's description of the Corinthian landscape and its people is shaped by the romantic outlook of a scholar walking in the footsteps of Paul. At the same time, Renan searches the geographic landscape, since he lacked any evidence for the city's built environment, for features that might be put to historical use, such as the orientation of Kenchreai as a magnet for Jewish immigrants.[14]

When we come to the early period of Corinth's excavations, we see a similar recourse to a romanticized biblical past, though at this point this past is conjured by both biblical scholars and the Corinthian archaeologists for Christian audiences in the United States. When the excavations at Corinth by the American School of Classical Studies began in 1896 there was little at the site that could be used to orient the archaeologists to the city center or to Pausanias' description of the city in his *Periegesis*.[15] This made the first excavation season difficult, turning up only a few finds in comparison with other excavations underway at Olympia or Athens.[16]

---

[10] Renan, *Saint Paul*, 145.
[11] Renan, *Saint Paul*, 146. On the troubling anti-Semitism of Renan's work, see Shawn Kelley, *Racializing Jesus: Race, Ideology, and the Formation of Modern Biblical Scholarship* (New York: Routledge, 2002), 83-87.
[12] Renan, *Saint Paul*, 148.
[13] On the "picturesque," see Buzard, "The Grand Tour," 42-47.
[14] Similar to Renan's romantic evocation of landscape is that of Deissmann, *Light From the Ancient East*, 286, who writes of Corinth, as one among many impressive religious sites in the ancient world: "There Corinth lies, above the gleaming beauty of her rock-crowned gulf, not unlike Eleusis, only vaster, severer, more masculine, possessing the oldest temple on Greek soil, and overhung by the defiant mass of the Acrocorinthus."
[15] In his description of the site at the beginning of the excavations, Edward Capps, "The Recent Excavations at Corinth," *The Biblical World* 8.3 (1896): 233, says, "Today a little handful of wretched hovels occupies the site, and only the seven columns of the old temple and the potsherds which every footstep turns up in the loose soil reveal the fact of its ancient habitation."
[16] Though the Corinthian theater was discovered in the first excavation season (trench XVIII), the excavators did not uncover an abundance of monuments or materials (Rufus Richardson, "The Excavations at Corinth in 1896," *AJA* 1.6 [1897]: 455-80). Some terracotta figurines and small statuary were found near the theater, as well as some Latin inscriptions. But compared to other excavations of the time, it would take several more seasons before the site would begin producing greater returns.

Of the reports that came out of this first season, it is interesting to note how the findings of the archaeologists were presented to different audiences. Writing in the journal *The Biblical World*, which regularly published reports from the excavations at ancient Corinth from the very first season, Edward Capps, who eventually became professor of Greek at Princeton (1907) and director of the American School (1918–1939) speaks directly to the journal's Christian audience:[17]

> Possibly one of the houses [uncovered in the first season] which the future visitor to the uncovered city will see was the house of Chloe, messenger from which told Paul of the dissensions which prompted the first letter to the Corinthians, while another may be the home of Stephanas, the first-fruits of Achaea. The excavators have already dubbed one of the houses found "the house of Sosthenes the brother," though, to tell the truth, it does not appear that Sosthenes was a resident of Corinth.[18]

The discovery of these houses was cast by the excavators in biblical terms for an audience interested in recovering connections to a biblical world, even to the point of misreading the text of 1 Corinthians itself and assuming that Sosthenes was a resident of Corinth.[19]

The question of audience becomes more pronounced when we look at how the head of the excavations for 1896, Rufus Richardson, is quoted in reference to these same houses for the not specifically Christian audience of *The American Journal of Archaeology and of the History of the Fine Arts* in the same year (1896): "We have uncovered several houses. In one of these was a fine floor and walls of good stucco. We put the house down as belonging to the Corinth of the time of Paul."[20] Though Paul remains the temporal marker for these houses, the description does not engage in flights of biblical fancy, nor is there mention of nicknaming one of the houses after Sosthenes. At other times, mention of Paul, Sosthenes, and the first-century houses disappears altogether, as in Richardson's official report of the 1896 excavations in the *American Journal of Archaeology*.[21]

---

[17] Capps was the director of the American School from 1918–1939. He graduated from Yale in 1891 and taught at Yale, Harvard, Johns Hopkins, and the University of Chicago before taking up a professorship at Princeton in 1907. He was the founding editor of Classical Philology while at Chicago. For a summary of Capps' tenure as the chair of the American School, see Louis E. Lord, *A History of the American School of Classical Studies at Athens, 1882–1942* (Cambridge, Mass.: Harvard University Press, 1947), 130-270.

[18] Capps, "Recent Excavations at Corinth," 237.

[19] There are two Sosthenes mentioned in connection with Paul. The first is found alongside Paul in the greetings of 1 Cor 1:1, where he is called a "sibling" (ἀδελφός). The second is named in Acts 18:17 as a head of the Corinthian synagogue (ἀρχισυνάγωγος). Whether the latter ever existed, it is difficult to imagine that the Sosthenes of Acts 18:17 was the same person as the Sosthenes in 1 Cor 1:1, since the former is beaten by the crowd for his opposition to Paul and Luke knows of no story about his eventual conversion to Paul's camp.

[20] Rufus Richardson, "Notes from Corinth," *The American Journal of Archaeology and of the History of the Fine Arts* 11.3 (1896): 372.

[21] Richardson, "The Excavations at Corinth in 1896," 455-80. In his next report from 1898, no mention is made of Paul, Sosthenes, or the houses (Rufus Richardson, "The Excavations at

The temptation to read the life of Paul into the archaeological materials coming from the Corinthian excavations did not come solely from the archaeologists. In the excavations of 1898 the excavators found a marble slab on the Lechaion road, the inscription of which can be reconstructed as [ΣΥΝΑ]ΓΩΓΗ ΕΒΡ[ΑΙΩΝ] ("Synagogue of the Hebrews").[22] The inscription itself, which now hangs in the courtyard of the Corinth museum, could not be connected with any specific building and its lettering was deemed to be from a period well after the time of Paul. Nevertheless, the possibility of drawing a connection between the inscription and the synagogue in which Paul preached (Acts 18:4-7), proved too great for a number of scholars of early Christianity. For example, writing in 1939, well after the official publication and dating of the inscription,[23] Harold Willoughby evokes the romanticism of one walking in Paul's footsteps: "[At Corinth] we can actually stand on the Bema of Gallio, inspect the market where consecrated meat was offered for sale, walk the pavement laid by Erastus the Aedile, and read the inscription over the entrance to the Jewish synagogue."[24] The temptation to link Acts 18 to a physical object is part of the legacy of Christian pilgrimage and elite European tourism that continues to affect the use of archaeological materials in historical reconstructions. The connection has found its way into a number of commentaries on 1 Corinthians and continues to be recited by tour guides leading groups of Christian audiences through the Corinth museum.[25]

Corinth in 1898: Preliminary Report," *AJA* 2.3/4 [1898]: 233-36). The 1897 season lasted only a week before shutting down with the outbreak of war between Greece and Turkey over Crete (Thomas Day Seymour, et al., "Sixteenth Annual Report of the Managing Committee of the American School of Classical Studies at Athens," *American Journal of Archaeology* 1.2 (1897): 91-92).

[22] Benjamin Dean Merritt, *Corinth VIII.3: Greek Inscriptions, 1896–1927* (Cambridge, Mass.: Harvard University Press, 1931), no. 111; Richard E. Oster, "Use, Misuse, and Neglect of Archaeological Evidence in Some Modern Works on 1 Corinthians (1 Cor 7:1-5; 8:10; 11:2-16; 12:14-26)," *ZNW* 83 (1992): 55-58; Helmut Koester, "Corinth," in Helmut Koester, ed., *Cities of Paul: Images and Interpretations from the Harvard New Testament Archaeology Project [CD-ROM]* (Minneapolis: Fortress, 2005).

[23] The original publication of the inscription in 1903 dated the inscription to the first century and made the connection with the synagogue of Acts 18 (Benjamin Powell, "Greek Inscriptions from Corinth," *AJA* 7.1 [1903]: 60-61, no. 40). It is this dating, later corrected by Merritt in the official publication that seems to have influenced the reconstructions of biblical scholars. See, for example, Deissmann, *Light From the Ancient East*, 13-14, n. 7).

[24] Harold R. Willoughby, "Archaeology and Christian Beginnings," *BA* 2.3 (1939): 33-34. The structure identified as the Bema was once the city's rostrum, not the "seat" of Gallio (Acts 18:12). See Erich Dinkler, "Das Bema zu Korinth: Archäologische, Lexikographische, Rechtsgeschichtliche und Ikonographische Bemerkungen zu Apostelgeschichte 18, 12-17," *Marburger Jahrbuch für Kunstwissenschaft* 13 (1944): 12-22. For a balanced examination of the Corinthian meat market (*macellum*) referred to by Willoughby, see Henry J. Cadbury, "The Macellum of Corinth," *JBL* 53.2 (1934): 134-41. On the question of Erastus the *aedile*, see below.

[25] Even so shrewd an interpreter as Conzelmann was taken in by the synagogue inscription. See Hans Conzelmann, *1 Corinthians: A Commentary on the First Epistle to the Corinthians* (Philadelphia: Fortress, 1975), 12. See also Oster, "Use, Misuse, and Neglect," 55-58, for more examples. A less bold, but no less problematic, interpretation of the synagogue inscription suggests that, though the inscription is from a later synagogue, the synagogue of Paul's day was probably in the general vicinity. See, for example, Meritt, *Corinth VIII.3: Greek inscriptions,*

These examples from Corinth help us to see the complicated and problematic relationship that exists between biblical scholars and archaeological research. Because many biblical scholars look to archaeology as a means of proving details from the bible, archaeological materials are often consumed in biblical studies without due consideration or critical reflection. In some cases this is even encouraged by archaeologists themselves, who may see benefits from such publicity and have little invested in the theological debates around the Bible and its interpretation. Biblical scholars, such as Henry Cadbury and Erich Dinkler, occasionally pushed back against archaeological interpretations.[26] But the dangers, rooted in the ideological and disciplinary histories of both biblical studies and archaeology, still remain, particularly for those who approach material evidence from the ancient world with the sole purpose of constructing a background or interpretation of Paul and his letters.

2. Where Do We Direct Our Gaze?

When Deissmann set to making the non-literary remains of the ancient world (his "Light from the Ancient East") shine on the out-of-touch scholarship of Heidelberg or Cambridge,[27] he sought to change what his fellow biblical scholars looked for and saw in the texts of the New Testament. Having dwelt at length upon problems that have come from using archaeological materials to interpret the New Testament, I turn now to focus upon the possibilities that might come from an interdisciplinary approach that looks otherwise at what archaeology and early Christian studies can see together. Rather than use Deissmann's image of the light that shines a path through the darkness, I suggest instead, following Melanie Johnson-DeBaufre, that we think in terms of "gazing upon the invisible."[28]

1896–1927, no. 111 and William A. McDonald, "Archaeology and St. Paul's Journeys in Greek Lands: Corinth, " *The Biblical Archaeologist* 5.3 (1942): 41. Since we can connect the inscription to no surviving building and since the inscription is of such poor quality that it is not likely to have been part of a building set up so close to the center of town, we should be cautious in assuming a connection between the find spot and its original location.

[26] Henry J. Cadbury, "Erastus of Corinth," *JBL* 50.2 (1931): 42-58, offered a rare, early resistance to the identification of the Erastus who laid a pavement near the Theater in return for his election as *aedile* with the Erastus mentioned by Paul in Rom 16:23. Dinkler, "Das Bema zu Korinth," 12-22, offered a compelling critique of Oscar Broneer's claim that the Rostrum in the Forum would have been the site for Paul's trial before the Bema in Acts 18.

[27] Deissmann, *Light From the Ancient East*, 1-2.

[28] Johnson-DeBaufre, "'Gazing Upon the Invisible': Archaeology, Historiography, and the Elusive Women of 1 Thessalonians," in Laura Nasrallah, Charalambos Bakirtzis, and Steven J. Friesen, eds., *From Roman to Early Christian Thessalonikē: Studies in Religion and Archaeology* (Cambridge, Mass.: Harvard Theological Studies, 2010), 73-108. Johnson-DeBaufre takes this phrase from Connie H. Nobles, "Gazing upon the Invisible: Women and Children at the Old Baton Rouge Penitentiary," *American Antiquity* 65 (2000): 5-14. She is also indebted to the work of Elizabeth A. Castelli and Hal Taussig, "Drawing Large and Startling Figures: Reimagining Christian Origins by Painting like Picasso," in Elizabeth A. Castelli and Hall Taussig, eds., *Reimagining Christian Origins: A Colloquium Honoring Burton L. Mack* (Valley Forge: Trinity Press International, 1996), 3-20.

To parse this somewhat paradoxical phrase, I suggest three ways that it can help us to orient our thinking about the relations between archaeology and early Christian studies. First, to gaze upon the invisible requires attention to how we gaze, how we observe, look, see, collect, analyze, and present the materials that we collect and study.[29] Johnson-DeBaufre uses the metaphor of the camera lens to describe the varying ways in which we might attend to our gaze: "Depending on how we move our lens, objects slide back and forth toward the edges or the center or even out of the frame altogether."[30] In other words, how we look determines what we see and thus requires that we pay attention to how we direct our historical gaze and what our gaze leaves out.[31]

Second, we might direct our gaze, following Johnson-DeBaufre's lead, to making the invisible visible. Deissmann's eastern light shone on the dark scholarship of continental Europe so as to make the poorer classes out of which Christianity arose visible. Obscured by the dogmatism of elite scholars, whose vision was directed solely toward elite, literary texts, Deissmann opined, to mix our metaphors, that "The lower class is seldom allowed to speak."[32] To go beyond Deissmann's focus on economic class, Johnson-DeBaufre reminds us that attention to archaeological remains can also make visible those who have been obscured by a focus on the elite: women, slaves, the poor, immigrants, and all those who stood outside the small circle of elite males who produced the writings that have survived from antiquity.[33] That such people "were there" should no longer need to be argued; rather, "[i]t should be a critical presupposition for interpretation."[34]

Finally, though archaeology can show us that wo/men were present in the daily life of ancient cities and rural landscapes, we must also direct our gaze to the invisible as invisible. This means recognizing that some historical occlusions are not able to be overcome and so require us to come at old questions with new frameworks and imagine new possibilities for writing history.[35] Though women, slaves, and children can be "visible" in the

---

[29] Johnson-DeBaufre, "Gazing Upon the Invisible," 74: "Observing . . . tensions between material visibility and discursive invisibility opens a valuable space for examining the relationship between archaeological research and early Christian historiography."

[30] Johnson-DeBaufre, "Gazing Upon the Invisible," 77.

[31] This assumes, following Castelli and Taussig, "Drawing Large and Startling Figures," 14, "that objectivity in the study of Christian origins is impossible."

[32] Deissmann, *Light From the Ancient East*, 6.

[33] Johnson-DeBaufre, "Gazing Upon the Invisible," 73. On the term wo/men, which Johnson-DeBaufre uses to describe those who have been occluded by patriarchal ancient texts and modern scholarship, see Elisabeth Schüssler Fiorenza, *Rhetoric and Ethic: The Politics of Biblical Studies* (Minneapolis: Fortress, 1999). In their review of feminist archaeology in the 1990s Margaret W. Conkey and Joan M. Gero, "Programme to Practice: Gender and Feminism in Archaeology," *Annual Review of Anthropology* 26 (1997): 414-16, call this the "locate-the-women" approach.

[34] Johnson-DeBaufre, "Gazing Upon the Invisible," 92.

[35] Those whose voices have been left out of the mainstream historical record cannot be simply revived by a positivistic historical process and put on display; rather, writing a history of the forgotten and invisible requires an approach that takes into account Giorgio Agamben's observations about the unforgettable:

archaeological record, their representations and their voices are constrained by the perspectives of the elite males who dominated ancient society and modern scholarship. As such, one way of gazing at the invisible might involve "analyzing the dialectic between human life as socially constructed and the very materiality of human life."[36] Another avenue might follow the lead of feminist biblical critics, who have sought to shift the focus of interpretation away from the intention of authors like Paul and toward the possibilities for those who heard Paul and reacted to his letters.[37] Such an approach might meld archaeological and literary analysis to construct audiences negotiating the multiple spaces of ancient civic and rural landscapes in ways that differed significantly from the elite males whose perspectives historical writing has long privileged.[38]

3. What Do We See When We Look?

Having thought about how we might look otherwise at the possibilities for studying early Christianity, I turn now to discuss the work of a few scholars of early Christianity, aggregated around particular "Pauline" cities (Thessaloniki, Philippi, Ephesos, and Corinth), who make use of archaeological materials in ways that might help us to gaze otherwise on Paul's letters and their reception. This is not meant to be an exhaustive list by any means, as there is a great deal of good work being done across the landscape of early Christian studies beyond even the study of Paul;[39] however, I do intend that the work discussed below might serve as examples for future study.

[O]ne should remember that the tradition of the unforgettable is not exactly a tradition.... The alternatives at this juncture are therefore not to forget or remember, to be unaware or become conscious, but rather, the determining factor is the capacity to remain faithful to that which having perpetually been forgotten, must remain unforgettable. It demands [*esige*] to remain with us and be possible for us in some manner.

See Giorgio Agamben, *The Time That Remains: A Commentary on the Letter to the Romans* (Stanford: Stanford University Press, 2005), 40.

[36] Conkey and Gero, "Programme to Practice," 418.

[37] "I recommend taking difference among Paul's audience seriously and considering the multiple ways that such a teaching could be heard, regardless of precisely what Paul meant" (Johnson-DeBaufre, "Gazing Upon the Invisible," 95). Such an approach is suggested by the work of Schüssler Fiorenza, *Rhetoric and Ethic* and Antoinette Clark Wire, *The Corinthian Women Prophets: A Reconstruction Through Paul's Rhetoric* (Minneapolis: Fortress, 1990).

[38] "It should be a critical presupposition that they found ways to survive and—in their own ways, not always highly visible or imaginable to us—to create spaces in which to act.... I suggest placing certain aspects of the letter alongside an understanding of mobile and diverse community members who were not consigned to one space and did not carry a singular identity, but rather moved through the spaces of the ancient city and regularly negotiated multiple identities such as status, wealth, gender, and tribe" (Johnson-DeBaufre, "Gazing Upon the Invisible," 98-99).

[39] To name just a few, see L. Michael White, *The Social Origins of Christian Architecture* (2 vols.; Harvard Theological Studies 42; Valley Forge: Trinity Press International, 1996); Mark Humphries, "Trading Gods in Northern Italy," in Helen Parkins and Christopher Smith, eds., *Trade, Traders, and the Ancient City* (New York: Routledge, 1998); Steven J. Friesen, *Imperial Cults and the Apocalypse of John: Reading Revelation in the Ruins* (Oxford: Oxford University Press, 2001); Laura S. Nasrallah, *Christian Responses to Roman Art and Architecture: The*

The studies that I have highlighted tend to cluster around four methodological foci that I think it useful to name from the start. First, these studies are conspicuously interdisciplinary in their approaches to studying Paul's writings. These interdisciplinary approaches do not limit themselves to archaeology, but are in dialogue with sociology, anthropology, critical geography, and feminist and post-colonial theory.[40] Second, the scholarship that I have highlighted often takes a local focus to the interpretation of Paul's letters. Rather than drawing haphazardly on archaeological materials from around the wider Greco-Roman world to elucidate particular Pauline passages, the scholarship highlighted here places Paul's letters within a local, civic context as part of the interpretive process.[41]

Third, a local approach must aim toward imagining early Christian communities as participants in a dynamic and changing context, rather than constructing a static background against which to read Pauline texts.[42] Early Christians were one among many groups who navigated and negotiated the civic landscape of ancient cities. To assume that early Christianity emerged *sui generis* in direct confrontation with Judaism or "paganism" is to reinscribe a longer history of Protestant theology as historical analysis.[43] One of the

---

Second-Century Church Amid the Spaces of Empire (New York: Cambridge University Press, 2010); Cavan W. Concannon, "Ethnicity, Economics, Diplomacy in Dionysios of Corinth," *HTR* (April 2013). For lack of space, I will also not be able to give attention to the excellent work on Paul that falls outside of the cities I have selected. See, for example, Peter Oakes, *Reading Romans in Pompeii: Paul's Letter at Ground Level* (Minneapolis: Fortress, 2009); Brigitte Kahl, *Galatians Re-Imagined: Reading with the Eyes of the Vanquished*, (Paul in Critical Contexts; Minneapolis: Fortress, 2010); Davina C. Lopez, *The Apostle to the Conquered: Reimagining Paul's Mission* (Paul in Critical Contexts; Minneapolis: Fortress, 2010).

[40] Many of the scholars, though not all, have been influenced by Helmut Koester, a student of Bultmann, who has been a driving force for training early Christianity students in an interdisciplinary approach in the tradition of the "History of Religions" School.

[41] Though this approach has a longer history, Koester has played an integral part in developing this type of scholarship. See his, *Paul and His World: Interpreting the New Testament in its Context* (Minneapolis: Fortress, 2007), 55; Steven J. Friesen, *Twice Neokoros: Ephesus, Asia, and the Cult of the Flavian Imperial Family* (Religions in the Graeco-Roman World 116; New York: Brill, 1993), 5-6), particularly through organizing and publishing proceedings from interdisciplinary conferences focusing on particular Greek cities (Charalambos Bakirtzis and Helmut Koester, eds., *Philippi at the Time of Paul and After His Death* (Harrisburg: Trinity Press International, 1998); Helmut Koester, *Pergamon: Citadel of the Gods: Archaeological Record, Literary Description, and Religious Development* (Harvard Theological Studies 46; Harrisburg: Trinity Press International, 1998); Helmut Koester, ed., *Ephesos, Metropolis of Asia: An Interdisciplinary Approach to its Archaeology, Religion, and Culture* (Harvard Theological Studies 41; Cambridge, Mass.: Distributed by Harvard University Press for Harvard Theological Studies/Harvard Divinity School, 1995); Koester., *Cities of Paul*. Peter Pilhofer, *Die frühen Christen und ihre Welt* (WUNT 145; Tübingen: Mohr [Siebeck], 2002), 9, has called this a *lokalgeschichtliche Methode* (a "local history method").

[42] L. Michael White and John T. Fitzgerald, "Quod est comparandum: The Problem of Parallels," in John T. Fitzgerald, T. H. Olbricht, and L. Michael White, eds., *Early Christianity and Classical Culture: Comparative Studies in Honor of Abraham J. Malherbe* (Leiden: Brill, 2003), 37-39.

[43] Jonathan Z. Smith, *Drudgery Divine: On the Comparison of Early Christianities and the Religions of Late Antiquity* (Jordan Lectures in Comparative Religion 14; Chicago: University of Chicago Press, 1990), 1-35. As Koester, *Paul and His World*, 41, has noted, most New Testament scholars have sought to "use archaeological data in order to anchor texts from the

important legacies of the "History of Religions" School is the observation that Christianity was, from its very inception, a diverse and loosely connected set of communities that participated in the language, culture, morality, and cultic practices of the Roman world.[44] Rather than using archaeology to construct a "pagan" environment that Paul attacked, a more fruitful approach assumes that Paul and his audiences participated in the dynamic context of civic life and attempts to understand that landscape in all of its complexity.[45]

Finally, by placing early Christian communities within their civic landscapes, the work that I highlight below offers us the opportunity to write history that does not place Paul at the center of analysis. An approach that focuses on the dynamic context of which early Christian communities were a part allows us to use archaeological evidence to imagine what was available for early Christian audiences to think with when they heard and interpreted Paul's letters, reimagining early Christian communities as diverse and dynamic sites for discourse and debate.[46]

New Testament in a particular historical situation and in a specific location; thus they are nothing but a continuation of 'biblical archaeology.'" Using archaeology as a means of prooftexting the biblical text fails to recognize the difficulties of taking the fragmentary and haphazard evidence derived from excavations and assuming that one has a clear and complete picture of the ancient world and its impact on the production of Paul's letters: "But to move from geographically restricted archaeological information to the interpretation of a New Testament writing is a complex and difficult, perhaps even impossible, venture" (Koester, *Paul and His World*, 55).

[44] "In that New Testament scholarship for many decades had been preoccupied with the theology of the New Testament, insights into non-Christian religions of that period were often used as a negative foil for the elaboration of the superiority of early Christian theological insights. . . . A history-of-religions approach will be unwilling to accept a fundamental distinction among Christian theology, Judaism, and pagan cults. . . . Individual forms of organization, of religious rituals, and of literary and architectural expressions may differ in many instances. But it still remains one and the same Greco-Roman world and one and the same development of the history of religions and culture, to which all these religions belong." (Koester, *Paul and His World*, 42).

[45] Castelli and Taussig, "Drawing Large and Startling Figures," 12, offer a proposal to counter this tendency: "that reimagining Christian origins must involve a refusal to marginalize the social, religious, and cultural context of early Christianity into a flattened category of 'backgrounds.' Instead, the cubist portrait of Christian origins will include rich, interdisciplinary attention to the complex material and ideological frameworks in which Christianity first emerged."

[46] A focus on the reception rather than the intent of Paul's letters has been advocated by feminist biblical scholars for a number of years. Wire, *Corinthian Women Prophets*, offers an early example of a literary approach to reconstructing a particular audience for 1 Corinthians. Not all studies of potential audiences for Paul's letters are specifically feminist in orientation. Oakes, *Reading Romans in Pompeii*, uses studies of domestic space in Pompeii to reconstruct several different hearers of Paul's Letter to the Romans. He offers a similar reconstruction of readers in Philippi. See Peter Oakes, "Jason and Penelope Hear Philippians 1:1-11," in Christopher Rowland and Crispin H. T. Fletcher-Louis, eds., *Understanding, Studying, and Reading: New Testament Essays in Honour of John Ashton* (Sheffield: Sheffield Academic Press, 1998), 199-212. We also might use archaeological material to think beyond Paul by examining how later Christians heard, interpreted, and remembered Paul's writings. Such an approach coheres with the call by Castelli and Taussig, "Drawing Large and Startling Figures," 9, that "the romanticizing privilege afforded the 'New Testament era' of the first century must be supplanted by a broader focus on the first few centuries of Christian activity and thought." Laura Nasrallah's work on the interpretation of 1 Thessalonians in the Late Antique architecture and

4. Associations and Sacred Laws in Thessaloniki

Founded by Cassander in 316/5 B.C., Thessaloniki was one of the major cities of Macedonia in the Roman period.[47] The city sat at a major node of ancient trade and travel, at the point where the Via Egnatia met the Thermaic Gulf.[48] After the Romans took control of Macedonia, Thessaloniki became the capital of the province. It was initially an important military center, later developing into a hub for trade and communication.[49] It became important again when Galerius made it his regional capital, evidenced by the monumental architecture that is still extant. The city was laid out in a generally Hippodamian fashion, with streets moving east/west and north/south and moving up along the slope of the terrain as it rises up from the Thermaic Gulf.[50] The city's second-century Forum has been excavated, as well as large structures built during the reign of Galerius, along with a number of smaller (and quicker) rescue excavations. The most famous of these brought to light the city's Sarapeion.[51] The city's Forum was built in the second century on two levels along the side of the hill, involving the use of terracing that created a long cryptoporticus under the south side of the upper level that was used for storage.[52]

One of the challenges of studying early Christianity in Thessaloniki is the paucity of archaeological information available from the first century.[53] This

---

art of Thessaloniki offers an example of how archaeology and New Testament studies can enrich how we write the broader histories of early Christianity. See Laura S. Nasrallah, "Empire and Apocalypse in Thessaloniki: Interpreting the Early Christian Rotunda," *JECS* 13.4 (2005): 465-508; Laura Nasrallah, "Early Christian Interpretation in Image and Word: Canon, Sacred Text, and the Mosaic of Moni Latomou," in Nasrallah, Bakirtzis, and Friesen, *From Roman to Early Christian Thessalonikē*, 361-96.

[47] Before its refoundation under Cassander, the city was likely known as Therme.

[48] Built in the 130s B.C., the Via Egnatia was originally intended as a military road, allowing the Romans to deploy troops more quickly across great distances. See John Vanderspoel, "Provincia Macedonia," in Joseph Roisman and Ian Worthington, eds., *A Companion to Ancient Macedonia* (Oxford: Blackwell, 2010), 264-67. Over time, the road also allowed for enhanced trade and mobility for non-military personnel. On the conditions of travel on the Via Egnatia, see Aelius Aristides, *Sacred Tales*, 2.60-61.

[49] The city and the province of Macedonia played a crucial part in the Civil Wars of the Late Republic, first as a base for Pompey to regroup after Caesar's crossing of the Rubicon and later when it was controlled by Brutus, who took control of the province after Caesar's death. After the defeat of Antony at Actium, the province was given over to Crassus. The province's military importance waned through the early years of the principate as the Romans expanded their control of the territory up to the Danube. This created a buffer zone between Macedonia and the frontier and so the province no longer needed to be actively garrisoned.

[50] Michael Vickers, "Hellenistic Thessaloniki," *JHS* 92 (1972): 156-70; Helmut Koester, "Thessalonike," in Koester, *Cities of Paul*.

[51] Helmut Koester, "Egyptian Religion in Thessalonikē: Regulation for the Cult," in Nasrallah, Bakirtzis, and Friesen, *From Roman to Early Christian Thessalonikē*, 133-50.

[52] Though the second-century Forum is an engineering achievement, it is not itself a uniquely Thessalonikan phenomenon; "[r]ather, it mirrors the widespread tendency of the Roman imperial period to transform the older open agora of the Greek city into the shape of an enclosed forum" (Koester, *Paul and His World*, 46).

[53] Koester, *Paul and His World*, 56; Christine M. Thomas, "Locating Purity: Temples, Sexual Prohibitions, and 'Making a Difference' in Thessalonikē," in Nasrallah, Bakirtzis, and Friesen,

paucity of data is the result of the continuous habitation of the city from antiquity to the present, meaning that the excavations in the city have been haphazard and sporadic. The spotty archaeological evidence, combined with a lack of texts written to or about the city and its inhabitants, means that we have very little information about the cultic life of Thessaloniki. For example, there is no archaeological evidence for Jews in the city outside of a fifth-century Samaritan inscription and the account of Acts 17:5-9.[54]

Because of the lack of a robust picture of the city's layout, those who seek to make use of archeological materials in their study of early Christianity at Thessaloniki have often stretched the available evidence.[55] For example, Karl Donfried has argued that several Thessalonikan inscriptions referencing the worship of Dionysos and a herm with an insertion hole for a phallus suggest that Dionysiac orgies were sufficiently central to Thessalonikan cultic life that they explain Paul's concern in 1 Thess 4:4 with men controlling their own vessel (τὸ ἑαυτοῦ σκεῦος) and his warning against drunkenness in 5:7.[56] Such uses of archaeological materials to elucidate 1 Thessalonians neglect to account for the absence of a complete picture of cultic life in Thessaloniki that is available in the archaeological and textual record.[57] Because we do not have enough information, we cannot offer a clear picture of Dionysiac cultic activity in Thessaloniki, its place among other cults of the city, or the extent to which the cult was practiced in ways unique to the city itself.[58] As a result, the

---

From Roman to Early Christian Thessalonikē, 110-13; Johnson-DeBaufre, "Gazing Upon the Invisible," 74-75.

[54] Koester, *Paul and His World*, 56-57. Luke is not completely ignorant of some aspects of civic life in Thessaloniki, however; he correctly names the local officials known as politarchs (Acts 17:6).

[55] Thomas, "Locating Purity," 110, notes in reference to previous studies, "New Testament scholars have tended to overestimate the representative value of the evidence. . . . [T]he extant artifacts cannot provide a clear picture of the major features of religious life in Thessalonikē."

[56] For the inscriptions honoring Dionysos, see Charles Edson, ed., *Inscriptiones Thessalonicae et viciniae (= IG X/2.1)* (Berlin: de Gruyter, 1972), nos. 28, 59, 259, 503, 06. For discussion of the herm and criticism of Donfried, see Koester, *Paul and His World*, 39-40. See also the critical appraisal of Thomas, "Locating Purity," 110-12, particularly n. 8.

[57] Further, as Johnson-DeBaufre, "Gazing Upon the Invisible," 83-84, has noted, what archaeological evidence is marshaled in Donfried's reconstruction ignores epigraphic evidence of women's cultic participation and leadership collected in Charles Edson's earlier work. As Johnson-DeBaufre points out, prominent women figure prominently in Charles Edson, "Cults of Thessalonica (Macedonia III)," *HTR* 41.3 (1948): 153-204. She argues that Donfried's "narrative interweaving of archaeology, literary texts, and scholarship invites a series of erotic/exotic wo/men to saunter into the reader's historical imagination." In contrast to their role in the cults that Edson chronicles, the Thessalonikan women in Donfried's reconstruction are found in "references to 'nocturnal initiations' of Isis, priestesses who honor the fertile phallus, 'divine women' who nurse Dionysos, Bacchic frenzies with dancing maidens, and the hieros gamos ('sacred marriage')" (84).

[58] Robert Jewett, *The Thessalonian Correspondence: Pauline Rhetoric and Millenarian Piety* (Philadelphia: Fortress, 1986), 161-78, engages in a similarly loose use of archaeological materials in claiming that local elite appropriation of the cult of Kabiros created a millenarian response from the common citizenry of Thessaloniki. For a critical response to Jewett, see Koester, *Paul and His World*, 40-41, 57-58. Johnson-DeBaufre, "Gazing Upon the Invisible," 85-86, is similarly critical of Jewett, though she suggests a possible usefulness of his millenarian framework.

evidence fails to offer us enough material "to distinguish between characteristics of religious life that are peculiar to Thessaloniki and those that are merely instances of more broadly distributed features of religious life in the Roman Empire."[59]

Though there is not a great deal of physical evidence for cultic practice in Thessaloniki, several scholars of early Christianity have found creative ways to reimagine the cultic context of the city. In what follows I highlight two recent contributions drawn from the edited volume *From Roman to Early Christian Thessalonikē*,[60] which is itself a model for interdisciplinary study of archaeology, religion, society, and politics in ancient cities. In her contribution to the volume, Christine Thomas has offered an approach that deals specifically with the paucity of evidence from the city.[61] Approaching early Christianity in Thessaloniki as one of many other cultic groups concerned with issues of purity, Thomas deploys the work of critical geographer Henri Lefebvre, who argues that geography is both spatial and discursive.[62] Drawing on inscriptional evidence of "sacred laws," which she considers widespread and systematic enough to be consistent in the practice of traditional Greek religion across regions, Thomas compares the ways in which the laws mark the physical boundaries between sacred and profane, pure and impure, moral and immoral, with the language of purity and sanctification that peppers Paul's first Letter to the Thessalonians. Thomas thus shows how Paul's rhetoric of purity was part of broader contestations over the topography of the sacred that would have been part of cultic practice in Thessaloniki and beyond.[63]

Another avenue for research into early Christianity in Thessaloniki might come via the epigraphic record of the city. The epigraphic record boasts forty-four inscriptions of the imperial period that mention thirty-nine different voluntary associations, all of which have been recently edited and published

---

[59] Thomas, "Locating Purity," 111.
[60] Nasrallah, Bakirtzis, and Friesen, *From Roman to Early Christian Thessalonikē*.
[61] Thomas, "Locating Purity," 109-32.
[62] "[T]he social construction of space includes both spatial practices and spatial discourses. The first, spatial practice, includes production and reproduction of items in physical space and the ways that people live and move in space. The second, spatial discourse, is all the things that people say, think, and imagine about space. The two are involved in a reciprocal and dynamic relationship, in which practice and discourse influence and change one another" (Thomas, "Locating Purity," 113). Thomas draws on Henri Lefebvre, *The Production of Space* (Cambridge: Blackwell, 1991), 1-67.
[63] Thomas' approach offers the further benefit of treating Paul's Thessalonikan audience as moral and cultic agents in their own right. In line with feminist critiques highlighted above, Thomas is critical of interpreters who focus solely on Paul, which results in analyses that place undue weight on Jewish purity laws as the background against which to read Paul's rhetoric. By contrast, Thomas argues, "A tacit assumption seems to reign with New Testament scholarship that Gentiles possessed no independent system of moral values. . . . The standard anti-Gentile tropes employed by Paul are consequently taken at face value as a description of actual Gentile behavior" (Thomas, "Locating Purity," 118-19). By focusing on Greek sacred laws, Thomas is able to show that Paul's Gentile audience in Thessaloniki was not a "tabula rasa" but would have perceived their participation in the cult of Christ through their own previous experiences of morality, ethics, and proper cultic practice.

by Pantelis Nigdelis.[64] Ascough has used this material to elucidate issues that arose within the Thessalonian correspondence, suggesting that the community dealt with similar issues that frequently arose in ancient voluntary associations.[65] Ascough focuses on how Paul's rhetoric seems to presuppose common concerns about order, food, membership, and death. Future work on voluntary associations in Thessaloniki might begin to think about the expectations and experiences of association life that Paul's audience in Thessaloniki brought with them. Such an approach, which takes seriously Ascough's argument that Paul may have converted a local trade association to a "cultic" association in honor of Jesus, would look to how the Thessalonians themselves may have constructed their own identities and practices in relation to their experience of the new "cult" of Jesus and their communal experiences as a voluntary association.

5. Figuring Romans in Philippi

Bearing the name of the Macedonian king Philip II, who took control of the city from the Thasians in 356 B.C., Philippi was a Roman colony in Macedonia, situated along the Via Egnatia near a fertile agricultural region and the metal mines of Mt. Pangaion.[66] The town was the site of the Battle of Philippi in 42 B.C., which saw the defeat of Cassius and Brutus, and was soon converted into a colony by Antony, who settled some veterans in the new colony. After Antony's defeat at Actium, Augustus renamed the colony Colonia Augusta Iulia Philippensis and settled another batch of Antony's veterans.[67] The Via Egnatia, which is still visible at the site next to the modern road, connected Philippi to the military supply routes moving toward the frontiers and to the coastal port of Neapolis on the Aegean coast.[68]

---

[64] Pantelis M. Nigdelis, "Voluntary Associations in Roman Thessalonikē: In Search of Identity and Support in a Cosmopolitan Society," in Nasrallah, Bakirtzis, and Friesen, *From Roman to Early Christian Thessalonikē*, 13-48.

[65] I deal here specifically with Richard S. Ascough, "Of Memories and Meals: Greco-Roman Associations and the Early Jesus-Group at Thessalonikē," in Nasrallah, Bakirtzis, and Friesen, *From Roman to Early Christian Thessalonikē*, 49-72. This represents a summary and updating of Ascough's earlier studies that build upon his Ph.D. dissertation: Richard S. Ascough, "The Thessalonian Christian Community as a Professional Voluntary Association," *JBL* 119 (2000): 311-28; Richard S. Ascough, *Paul's Macedonian Associations: The Social Context of 1 Thessalonians and Philippians* (WUNT 2.161; Tübingen: Mohr [Siebeck], 2003).

[66] My description of Philippi relies on Helmut Koester, "Philippi," in Koester, *Cities of Paul*; Chaido Koukouli-Chrysantaki, "Colonia Iulia Augusta Philippensis," in Bakirtzis and Koester, *Philippi at the Time of Paul and After His Death*, 4-36, and Peter Oakes, *Philippians: From People to Letter* (SNTSMS 110; Cambridge: Cambridge University Press, 2001), 1-50. Among the most important sources for these reconstructions are Paul Collart, *Philippes, Ville de Macédoine: depuis ses origines jusqu'à la fin de l'époque romaine* (Travaux et Mémoires 5; Paris: École Française d'Athènes, 1937), and Paul Lemerle, *Philippes et la Macédoine Orientale à l'époque chrétienne et byzantine: Recherches d'histoire et d'archéologie* (Bibliothèque des Écoles Françaises d'Athènes et de Rome 158; Paris: Bocard, 1945).

[67] Koukouli-Chrysantaki, "Colonia Iulia Augusta Philippensis," 8-9.

[68] Luke has Paul arriving at Philippi via Neapolis, where he arrived by boat from Alexandria Troas (Acts 16:11).

Our knowledge of the city from the first century is surprisingly limited. The city likely developed along the lines laid out by the earlier Macedonian plan.[69] The Forum that is visible in the current excavations dates to the time of Marcus Aurelius and overlays what would have been a similar Forum of the first century.[70] The Forum's north side sits alongside the Via Egnatia, showing the close connection between the road and the city's economic life. Outside of the city center, the layout of the first-century city is confused by later building phases, which include several large, early Christian basilica complexes. To the north of the Forum was the city's theater, which was built in the fourth century B.C. and renovated in the second century A.D.[71] The acropolis of Philippi offers evidence for a number of cults important to the city, including evidence for women's participation in the city's cultic life. Evidence for cults of Diana, Isis, and Silvanus are found, along with a great number of rock reliefs, clustered at various points and carved into the face of the acropolis.[72]

Scholars of early Christianity have produced a number of excellent studies of Philippi and its early Christian community.[73] De Vos and Oakes have produced interesting studies of the history, demographics, and politics of Philippi.[74] Oakes in particular has called attention to the Roman imperial context of the production and reception of Paul's letter, a theme that we will return to below. Notable as well is the work of Pilhofer, whose two volume work on Philippi includes a volume dedicated to cataloguing all the extant inscriptions from the city, making it an invaluable resource for scholars.[75]

Alongside this body of work are two monographs by Joseph Marchal that explore Philippi and its Christian community from a feminist, postcolonial

---

[69] Koukouli-Chrysantaki, "Colonia Iulia Augusta Philippensis," 14. Oakes, *Philippians*, 14-50, offers a model for the development of Philippian demographics, which he then uses to reconstruct the likely composition of the Pauline community.

[70] The Forum measures roughly 100 x 50 meters and is surrounded by shops, a curia, several temples, and a library (Koester, "Philippi"). There are indications that the first-century Forum had a slightly larger central area (Koukouli-Chrysantaki, "Colonia Iulia Augusta Philippensis," 15-16).

[71] Koukouli-Chrysantaki, "Colonia Iulia Augusta Philippensis," 18.

[72] On the these cults and their importance for women's participation in the cults of Philippi, see Valerie A. Abrahamsen, "Women at Philippi: The Pagan and Christian Evidence," *Journal of Feminist Studies in Religion* 3.2 (1987): 17-30; Valerie A. Abrahamsen, "Christianity and the Rock Reliefs at Philippi," *BA* 51.1 (1988): 46-56; and Joseph A. Marchal, *Hierarchy, Unity, and Imitation: A Feminist Rhetorical Analysis of Power Dynamics in Paul's Letter to the Philippians* (Lieden: Brill, 2006), 73-82.

[73] In his study of the province of Macedonia, Vanderspoel, "Provincia Macedonia," 271 n. 55, writes that, beyond guidebooks available at museum bookshops, "books about Philippi tend to focus on early Christianity and the visit of the apostle Paul."

[74] Craig Steven De Vos, *Church and Community Conflicts: The Relationships of the Thessalonian, Corinthian, and Philippian Churches With Their Wider Civic Communities* (SBLDS 168; Atlanta: Scholars Press, 1999), 233-50, 75-87; Oakes, *Philippians*, 1-76. See also Lukas Bormann, *Philippi: Stadt und Christengemeinde zur Zeit des Paulus* (NovTSup 78; New York: Brill, 1995), and the collected volume Bakirtzis and Koester, *Philippi at the Time of Paul and After His Death*.

[75] Peter Pilhofer, *Philippi I: Die erste christliche Gemeinde Europas* (WUNT 87; Tübingen: Mohr [Siebeck], 1995), and Peter Pilhofer, *Philippi II: Katalog der Inschriften von Philippi* (WUNT 119; Tübingen: Mohr [Siebeck], 2000).

The Archaeology of the Pauline Mission

perspective, particularly examining the intersections of empire, ethnicity, and gender.[76] Marchal's work takes seriously the Roman imperial context to which Paul's Letter to the Philippians was directed and within which it was heard, constructing a complex picture of Philippian politics through examination of unity rhetoric, military imagery, and the city's colonial history.[77] In the revised version of his dissertation, Marchal reconstructs the cultic life of Philippi, focusing particularly on evidence for women's leadership in the city's cults.[78] He shows how women held leadership positions in many Philippian cults, suggesting that "any other movement introduced to Philippi would have to contend with *expectations* about women's roles," which should lead us to expect women's leadership in the community to which Paul writes.[79]

In his later book, Marchal builds upon his earlier reconstruction of Philippi and women's cultic participation to offer a feminist, postcolonial interpretation of Philippians. He redescribes Philippi through the framework of "contact zones," by which he means "social spaces where disparate cultures meet, clash, and grapple with each other, often in highly asymmetrical relations of domination and subordination."[80] Marchal uses Philippi as a contact zone to examine dynamics of travel, imitation, mimicry, and citizenship that occur in Philippians. In addition he attends to how we might reconstruct women's leadership in the Philippian community, focusing particularly on the figures of Euodia and Syntyche (Phil 4:2-3). Because of his attention to the intersections of gender and empire, Marchal offers two cautionary observations that must guide such reconstructions of voices other than Paul's.[81] First, Marchal argues, citing Gyatri Spivak, that we must be

---

[76] Marchal, *Hierarchy, Unity, and Imitation*; Joseph A. Marchal, *The Politics of Heaven: Women, Gender, and Empire in the Study of Paul* (Minneapolis: Fortress, 2008). See also Joseph A. Marchal, "Mimicry and Colonial Differences: Gender, Ethnicity, and Empire in the Interpretation of Pauline Imitation," in Laura Nasrallah and Elisabeth Schüssler Fiorenza, eds., *Prejudice and Christian Beginnings: Investigating Race, Gender and Ethnicity in Early Christian Studies* (Minneapolis: Fortress, 2009), 101-27.

[77] Paul and the Roman Empire has been a persistent topic of conversation among scholars for several years, building particularly on a series of collected papers from the Paul and Politics Section of the Society for Biblical Literature. See Richard Horsley, ed., *Paul and Empire: Religion and Power in Roman Imperial Society* (Harrisburg: Trinity Press International,1997); Krister Stendahl, et al., *Paul and Politics: Ekklesia, Israel, Imperium, Interpretation: Essays in Honor of Krister Stendahl* (Harrisburg: Trinity Press International, 2000); Richard A. Horsley, ed., *Paul and the Roman Imperial Order* (Harrisburg: Trinity Press International, 2004).

[78] Marchal, *Hierarchy, Unity, and Imitation*, 73-112. Marchal builds on earlier work by Lilian Portefaix, *Sisters Rejoice: Paul's Letter to the Philippians and Luke-Acts as Received by First-Century Philippian Women*, (ConBNT 20; Stockholm: Almqvist & Wiksell, 1988), Valerie A. Abrahamsen, *Women and Worship at Philippi: Diana/Artemis and Other Cults in the Early Christian Era* (Portland: Astarte Shell Press, 1995).

[79] Marchal, *Hierarchy, Unity, and Imitation*, 81.

[80] Marchal, *The Politics of Heaven*, 92.

[81] "[B]ecause there are few resources besides Paul's letters to develop concepts of these first-century communities in various imperial cities, most mainstream Pauline scholars have rhetorically acquiesced and operated as if there were no community outside of what Paul describes. When and if other participants are considered, they are treated as 'bit players' to our main character, the missionary adventure hero Paul" (Marchal, *The Politics of Heaven*, 106).

careful not to be "the first-world intellectual masquerading as the absent nonrepresenter who lets the oppressed speak for themselves."[82] Marchal also cautions that we must also avoid reconstructions that valorize the voices of those other than Paul. Speaking of his own reconstructions of Euodia and Syntyche within the Philippian community, Marchal notes, "Recognizing Euodia's and Syntyche's potential position(s) in the intersecting kyriarchal orders of first-century Philippi, though, should not simply lead to an unqualified valorization of them as decolonizing feminist subjects," since women have themselves been a part of colonizing missions in modern empires.[83] Because empires often involve the appropriation of agency of their subjects in the recreation of imperial power relations, one has to imagine those that we reconstruct as "both resistant and complicit, both colonized and colonizing."[84] Marchal's work brings to the forefront the ways in which empire, gender, and ethnicity are intertwined in the contact zone of Philippi and shows how taking these entanglements seriously impact how we go about reconstructing both Paul's rhetoric and the communities to which he wrote.

6. Slaves and Cultic Practice in Ephesos

The city of Ephesos was one of the largest cities in the ancient world, situated along the coast of Asia Minor where the Kaÿstros River met the sea.[85] Under Augustus the city was made the capital of the province (29 B.C.) and saw its population and size grow due to its importance as a trading center.[86] Its location gave the city access to overland trade routes to Sardis and up the Kaÿstros and Meander Valleys (after the silting up of Miletos' harbor), as well

---

[82] Marchal, *The Politics of Heaven*, 94. Marchal cites from Gayatri Spivak, "Can the Subaltern Speak?" in P. Williams and L. Chrisman, eds., *Colonial Discourse and Postcolonial Theory* (New York: Harvester Wheatsheaf, 1993).
[83] Marchal, *The Politics of Heaven*, 107.
[84] Marchal, *The Politics of Heaven*, 108. In her reconstruction of the Corinthian positions on power and knowledge, Elizabeth A. Castelli, "Interpretations of Power in 1 Corinthians," *Semeia* 54 (2006): 209, offers a similar caveat: "I do not understand the opposing views of power here to be egalitarian/utopian vs. hierarchical, but rather as different conceptual models."
[85] The city was said to have been founded in 1100 B.C. by migrating Ionians who settled on the slopes of Mount Pion alongside Karian and Lydians who clustered around the area that would become the Artemision (Koester, "Philippi"). Paul Trebilco, *The Early Christians in Ephesus from Paul to Ignatius* (Grand Rapids: Eerdmans, 2007), 17, estimates that the city was home to between 200,000 and 250,000 people in the Roman period, making it the third largest city after Rome and Alexandria.
[86] Strabo, *Geogr.* 14.1.24. On the government and history of the city in the Roman period, see Sviatoslav Dmitriev, *City Government in Hellenistic and Roman Asia Minor* (Oxford: Oxford University Press, 2005), 265-86. Trebilco, *Early Christians in Ephesus*, 15, notes the growth in building during the first two centuries of the Empire. The city had, like many other Greek cities, experienced the turbulence of the Civil War years. See Peter Scherrer, ed., *Ephesus: The New Guide* (Istanbul: Ege Yayinian, 2000), 21-22). The importance of the city to the Romans is seen in the city's receipt of the first cult of Roma and Divus Iulius in the province (Dmitriev, *City Government*, 265).

as to seaborne trade.[87]

Unlike Thessaloniki, where continual inhabitation of the site has made excavation difficult, Ephesos has been well excavated and our knowledge of the city's history is extensive. The first excavations at Ephesos began in 1863 under John Turtle Wood, uncovering the theater, the processional way, and the Temple of Artemis.[88] The Austrian Archaeological Institute took over the excavations in 1895 and continues to manage the ongoing excavations.[89] A visitor to the city by sea in the early empire would have seen an impressive harbor complex, with shops, a gymnasium, and an Olympieion, backed by a view of the massive theater, which was cut into the slopes of Mt. Pion.[90] Adjacent to the theater was the Tetragonos Agora, around which was the library of Celsus and the city's Sarapeion. Moving up Kouretes Street from the Celsus Library, one would pass the Terrace Houses on the right and the Varus Baths on the left before coming upon the State Agora, built in the small valley between Mt. Pion and Mt. Koressos. The State Agora boasted a small Odeion, a large, terraced Sebasteion, and a bath complex.[91] The Artemision, which was an important part of the city's cultic and festive life, sat to the northeast of the city, on the other side of Mt. Pion and below the ruins of the Basilica of St. John.[92]

The cultic life of Ephesos was diverse, with temples and inscriptions honoring a number of deities.[93] The most important to the life of the city was the cult of Artemis, located at the Artemision.[94] Another frequently discussed feature of cultic life in Ephesos has been the imperial cult, which is

---

[87] Koester, "Philippi." Trebilco, *Early Christians in Ephesus*, 17-18, discusses Ephesian trade and its use as a center for official communication in the Roman Empire.

[88] Koester, "Philippi." After World War II, D. G. Hogarth excavated further at the Artemis Temple.

[89] Albrecht Gerber, *Deissmann the Philologist* (BZNW 171; Berlin: de Gruyter, 2010), 155-206, shows the role that Adolf Deissmann played in helping to maintain the excavations at Ephesos.

[90] For this tour through the city, I am indebted to the excellent guide to the excavations of Scherrer, *The New Guide*, and to Koester, "Philippi."

[91] The State Agora came into use during the reign of Augustus and measured 160 x 58 meters. See Scherrer, *The New Guide*, 74-87. On the north it was lined by the Basilica Stoa and its western end was dominated by the Sebasteion.

[92] On the Artemision, see Scherrer, *The New Guide*, 44-57. The major procession of the Artemis cult entered the city at the Magnesian gate near the State Agora and wound its way through the city around the base of Mt. Pion before returning to the Artemision (Koester, "Philippi.")

[93] Dieter Knibbe, "Ephesos: nicht nur die Stadt der Artemis. Die 'anderen' ephesischen Götter," in S. Sahin, E. Schwertheim and J. Wagner, eds., *Studien zur Religion und Kultur Kleinasiens: Festschrift für Friedrich Karl Dörner* (Leiden: Brill, 1978), 2.489-503; Richard E. Oster, "Ephesus as a Religious Center under the Principate, I. Paganism before Constantine," *ANRW* II 18.3: 1661-728; Christine M. Thomas, "At Home in the City of Artemis: Religion in Ephesos in the Literary Imagination of the Roman Period," in Koester, *Ephesos, Metropolis of Asia*, 81-117; Dmitriev, *City Government*, 265-86.

[94] Dieter Knibbe, "Via Sacra Ephesiaca: New Aspects of the Cult of Artemis Ephesia," in Koester, *Ephesos, Metropolis of Asia*, 141-55; Guy McLean Rogers, "The Mysteries of Artemis at Ephesos," in Barbara Brandt and Karl Krierer, eds., *100 Jahre Österreichische Forschungen in Ephesos* (Österreichische Akademie der Wissenschaften Philosophisch-Historische Klasse Denkschriften 260; Wien: Österreichische Akademie der Wissenschaften, 1999), 241-50; Trebilco, *Early Christians in Ephesus*, 19-30.

monumentally represented by the large Sebasteion on the western end of the State Agora.[95] The Egyptian cults were also prominent in the cultic life of the city, as seen by the Sarapeion to the west of the Tetragonos Agora.[96] Our evidence for a Jewish population comes from several passages in Josephus and Philo and inscriptions dating at the earliest to the late second century.[97] Josephus claims there was a Jewish community in Ephesos in the third century B.C. (*C. Ap.* 2.39; *A.J.* 12.119) and includes several discussions of decrees issued by various Roman officials that relate to Jewish conflicts over rights in Ephesos (*A.J.* 14.185-267; 16.160-78). Regardless of what we can know from the literary and archaeological evidence, it makes sense to assume that there was a sizable Jewish population in Ephesos in the first century.[98]

The paradox of studying early Christianity in Ephesos is that, though we suspect that a large portion of the New Testament and a sizable number of early Christian texts were written to, about, or in Ephesos, it is very difficult to find agreement on exactly what should comprise the list of texts that can be used in reconstructing the Christian communities there.[99] For example, reconstructions of early Christianity in Ephesos vary dramatically depending on whether one thinks that Ephesians was written by Paul and/or to Ephesos or whether it was written later and directed toward another city.[100] Similarly, accounts of early Christianity in Ephesos differ greatly depending on how much historical reliability one accords to Luke's account of Paul in Ephesos in Acts 18:18-21; 19:1-40.[101] Because of the complexity involved in weighing

---

[95] On the history of the imperial cult in Ephesos, see Friesen, *Twice Neokoros*. In a development of this important study, Friesen has drawn on evidence for the imperial cult from the province as a whole in his study of Revelation (Friesen, *Imperial Cults*, 23-132).

[96] Scherrer, *The New Guide*, 149-50. The association of the site with Sarapis was made by Keil in 1926 and remains likely, though unconfirmed. On the Egyptian gods in Ephesos, see Oster, "Ephesus as a Religious Center," 1677-81; James Walters, "Egyptian Religions in Ephesos," in Koester, *Ephesos, Metropolis of Asia*, 281-310; Sarola A. Takács, "Isis and Serapis in Ephesos," in Brandt and Krierer, *100 Jahre Österreichische Forschungen in Ephesos*, 269-74; James Walters, "The Coincidence of the Expansion of Christianity and the Egyptian Cults in Imperial Ephesos," in Brandt and Krierer, *100 Jahre Österreichische Forschungen in Ephesos*, 315-24.

[97] On the evidence from Philo and Josephus, see Trebilco, *Early Christians in Ephesus*, 37-44; Mikael Tellbe, *Christ-Believers in Ephesus: A Textual Analysis of Early Christian Identity Formation in a Local Perspective* (WUNT 242; Tübingen: Mohr [Siebeck], 2009), 65-72. On the inscriptional evidence, see Tellbe, *Christ-Believers in Ephesus*, 73-75.

[98] Tellbe, *Christ-Believers in Ephesus*, 75, offers an estimate from 10,000 to 25,000 for the Jewish population in Ephesos. Trebilco, *Early Christians in Ephesus*, 50-51, is more cautious, noting that our ability to measure population size is severely limited by the nature of our sources and evidence.

[99] See, for example, the summary of recent scholarship in Tellbe, *Christ-Believers in Ephesus*, 3-52.

[100] In this case, we might compare the accounts of Rainer Schwindt, *Das Weltbild das Epheserbriefes: Eine religionsgeschichtlich-exegetische Studie* (WUNT 148; Tübingen: Mohr [Siebeck], 2002), who favors an Ephesian address for Ephesians, and Koester, *Paul and His World*, 254, who follows the lack of reference to Ephesos in the earliest manuscripts of Eph 1:1. Trebilco, *Early Christians in Ephesus*, 89-94, rejects the idea that Ephesians was addressed to Ephesos, but adds the interesting theory that it was written in Ephesos as part of a Pauline letter collection in the city.

[101] Trebilco, *Early Christians in Ephesus*, 104-7, thinks that the Acts account is largely reliable. Tellbe, *Christ-Believers in Ephesus*, 27-30, similarly is open to the historicity of the Acts

the evidence, it is difficult to determine what might be mobilized to reconstruct the history of early Christianity at Ephesos.

Though there are difficulties in writing a traditional history of early Christianity in Ephesos, the forthcoming dissertation of Katherine Shaner from Harvard University offers a promising way forward.[102] Shaner's work focuses on slaves and their participation in (and leadership of) cultic practices and communities in Ephesos. Through the use of archaeological, epigraphic, and literary sources, Shaner treats the Christian communities in Ephesos as one among many groups in which slaves negotiated their status and participated in or even lead cultic practices. For example, Shaner shows how the rhetoric of 1 Timothy, generally regarded as written in or to Ephesos at the beginning of the second century A.D., attempts to constrain the role of slaves in the community in ways analogous to the contemporary regulation of public slaves' participation in the local cult of Artemis.[103] Such attempts to constrain the roles of slaves in cultic practices and associations stand alongside evidence from Delos and Pliny's famous letter to Trajan in regard to female, slave *ministrae* of the Christians in Bithynia (*Ep.* 10.46). These sources envision a cultic landscape in which slaves could serve as leaders in cultic practices and associations. What makes Shaner's work useful for future studies of early Christianity in Ephesos is the way in which she brings together textual and archaeological materials to offer something like a "thick description" of slavery and its relation to cultic practice in Ephesos that sees Christian texts like 1 Timothy as one among many working to constrain or enable, describe or occlude, slaves and their roles in communal institutions and associations. Future work might be broadened to other aspects of how early Christians and their texts participated in the daily life of Ephesos.

7. Women and the Poor in their Place in Corinth

Destroyed by the Romans in 146 B.C. and rebuilt as a colony in 44 B.C., Corinth was a crucial node in the movement of goods, people, and ideas in the eastern Mediterranean. Because of its unique location along the narrow Isthmus connecting mainland Greece to the Peloponnesos, Corinth acted as a bridge to ease the movement of Italian commodities to the East and vice versa, while also creating a more efficient means of administrative and

---

account, largely relying on the evidence of Luke's attention to the *Lokalkolorit* ("local color") of Ephesos. Tellbe approvingly cites the work of Peter Lampe, "Acta 19 im Spiegel der ephesischen Inschriften," *BZ* 36 (1992): 59-76, in this regard. Koester, *Paul and His World*, 255-59, by contrast, argues that Acts offers little reliable information about Paul's stay in Ephesos, but that Luke's sources do tell us something about the history of early Christianity in the city.

[102] I want to thank the author for sending me early drafts of her work.

[103] In particular, Shaner focuses on an inscription by the Roman proconsul Paullus Fabius Persicus that was put up in several places in the city (including the theater and the commercial agora) in the late first century A.D. For the text of the inscription, Shaner follows Friedrich Karl Dörner, *Der Erlaß des Statthalters von Asia Paullus Fabius Persicus* (Greifswald: Hans Adler, 1935), 37-40.

military communication.[104] Via its two ports, Kenchreai and Lechaion, Corinth controlled maritime trade routes that avoided treacherous sailing routes around the southern tip of the Peloponnesos.[105]

The city's demographic makeup is connected to its role in facilitating trade between Italy and the Greek East. In the archaeological record from Corinth, there is strong evidence for bilingualism within the city, with Greek as the language of the street and Latin as the language of monumentality, set out for public display on prominent buildings and inscriptions.[106] Greek was the common tongue of most inhabitants; Latin was generally the language

---

[104] For a discussion of Corinth as a "bridgehead," see Susan E. Alcock, *Graecia Capta: The Landscapes of Roman Greece* (New York: Cambridge University Press, 1993), 169. On the specific trade routes that moved through Corinth, see (Kathleen Warner Slane, "East-West Trade in Fine Wares and Commodities: The View From Corinth," *Rei Cretariae Romanae Fautorum acta* 36 (2000): 306 and Kathleen Warner Slane, "Corinthian Ceramic Imports: The Changing Patter of Provincial Trade in the First and Second Centuries A.D.," in Susan Walker and Averil Cameron, eds., *The Greek Renaissance in the Roman Empire: Papers from the Tenth British Museum Classical Colloquium* (London: University of London Institute of Classical Studies, 1989), 224. Corinth's position on the Isthmus also allowed it to control the movement of overland trade between Greece and the cities of the central Peloponnesos.

[105] Of Lechaion, Pausanias says that it had a sanctuary and a bronze image of Poseidon (II.3). According to Charles K. Williams II, "Roman Corinth as a Commercial Center," in Timothy E. Gregory, ed., *The Corinthia in the Roman Period: including the papers given at a Symposium held at The Ohio State University on 7–9 March, 1991* (Journal of Roman Archaeology Supplementary Series 8; Ann Arbor: Journal of Roman Archaeology, 1994), 46, the harbor at Lechaion was remodeled under Claudius: "The interior harbor and the creation of the two huge sand hills by the harbor were . . . also part of the design of Claudius' engineers." Of Kenchreai, Pausanias notes a temple and stone statue of Aphrodite, a bronze image of Poseidon on the harbor's mole, harborside temples of Asclepius and Isis, and a stream called Helen's Bath (II.3). Apuleius says that Kenchreai had a safe harbor and was crowded with a great population (*magno frequentatur populo*) in the second century (*Metamorphoses* X.35). For recent archaeological research on Kenchreai, see Joseph L. Rife, et al., "Life and Death at a Port in Roman Greece: The Kenchreai Cemetery Project 2002–2006," *Hesperia* 76 (2007): 143-81 and Joseph L. Rife, "Religion and Society at Roman Kenchreai," in Steven Friesen, Daniel N. Schowalter, and James Walters, eds., *Corinth in Context: Comparative Studies on Religion and Society* (Leiden: Brill, 2010), 391-432.

[106] See the important study of Benjamin Millis, "The Social and Ethnic Origins of the Colonists in Early Roman Corinth," in Friesen, Schowalter, and Walters, *Corinth in Context*, 13-36. It has long been noted that the bulk of the inscriptions from Corinth in the first two centuries after its colonization are in Latin. See John H. Kent, *Corinth VIII:3: The Inscriptions, 1926–1950* (Princeton: American School of Classical Studies at Athens, 1966), 18-19. This has been used to suggest that Corinth was a "Roman" city that only later was diluted by the arrival of Greek immigrants and by the Philhellenism of Hadrian's reign. Millis examined evidence from graffiti, *dipinti*, curse tablets, mason's marks, and funerary inscriptions that suggested Greek was the language of daily use in Corinth. Based on Millis' work, we can then see the prominence of Latin on Corinth's monumental architecture as part of the elite's attempt to display a connection to Roman culture and power. As Greg Woolf, "Monumental Writing and the Expansion of Roman Society in the Early Empire," *JRS* 86 (1996): 32 has argued, epigraphy is often used to address anxieties around identity, an anxiety that was no doubt felt by a colonial elite made up of mainly Greek freedmen and Italian traders. Monumental writing in Latin in the city center was a strategic mode for the city and its elite to present themselves as bearing a unified, Roman identity, despite the realities on the ground.

used to mark elites and local benefactors as Roman.[107] The demographics of the city's elite strengthen this observation about the bilingualism of the city. Antony Spawforth's work on the demographics of the early elite suggests that the bulk of the colony's elite came from two groups that would be best able to manage commerce between Greece and Rome: Greek freedmen from prominent Roman families and *negotiatores*, Italian trading families that had been operating in the Greek East for several centuries.[108] These two groups were well positioned to capitalize on the opportunities presented by Corinth's position, which would require an ability to navigate ethnic, cultural, and social interactions between Greeks, Romans, and Italians.[109]

The excavations at Corinth have been directed by the American School of Classical Studies at Athens since 1896. The excavations have focused on the public spaces in the city center, unearthing the city's Forum, a number of prominent temples, an odeion, a theater, a gymnasium complex, and a large sanctuary of Demeter and Kore. Though the excavations have focused on the public spaces of the city, the excavators have examined several villas, basilicas, graveyards, and pottery evidence that give indications of life in Roman Corinth outside of the city's monumental center.[110] In addition to the regular publications of the American School and the scholars associated with it, several recent publications by scholars of the New Testament and early Christianity have helped to push the boundaries of how to craft an interdisciplinary dialogue between archaeologists, classicists, and early Christian studies. I will discuss several of these contributions below, but it is worth noting the two volumes of conference proceedings, edited by Steven Friesen, Daniel Schowalter, and James Walters (2005 and 2010).[111] Both collections bring together interdisciplinary contributions to the study of Corinth from classical to Byzantine times using a variety of textual and archaeological evidence and methods. Rather than starting with the goal of interpreting Paul's letters to the Corinthians, these collections focus on examining the local history of Corinth, making the Christian community there part of and not distinct from the life of the city.[112] Turning to some of the

---

[107] As Richard Hingley, *Globalizing Roman Culture: Unity, Diversity, and Empire* (New York: Routledge, 2005) 47, notes, such acts of euergetism allowed local elites to "negotiate their own power simultaneously in local and in imperial contexts."

[108] Antony Spawforth, "Roman Corinth: The Formation of a Colonial Elite," in A. D. Rizakes, ed., *Roman Onomastics in the Greek East: Social and Political Aspects: Proceedings of the International Colloquium Organized by the Finnish Institute and the Centre for Greek and Roman Antiquity, Athens, 7–9 September 1993* (Meletemata 21; Athens: Kentron Hellenikes kai Romaikes Archaiotetos Ethnikon Hidryma Ereunon, 1996).

[109] For a more detailed discussion of trade, bilingualism, and the demographics of Corinth, see my *"When You Were Gentiles."*

[110] The results of the American School's excavations are regularly published in official volumes and in the school's journal *Hesperia*.

[111] Daniel N. Schowalter and Steven J. Friesen, *Urban Religion in Roman Corinth: Interdisciplinary Approaches* (Harvard Theological Studies 53; Cambridge, Mass.: Harvard Theological Studies; Distributed by Harvard University Press, 2005) and Friesen, Schowalter, and Walters, *Corinth in Context*.

[112] Such a project, which builds on the shoulders of earlier collections edited by Helmut Koester, namely: Koester, *Ephesos*; Koester, *Pergamon*; Bakirtzis and Koester, *Philippi at the Time of*

recent contributions to the study of early Christianity in Corinth, I want to highlight two scholars whose work touches on questions of economics, space, and gender.[113]

The economic makeup of the communities to whom Paul wrote has long been a point of contention among scholars of early Christianity. Earlier generations of scholars assumed that Christianity was, from its start, a proletarian movement made up mostly of those at the bottom of the economic ladder.[114] The work of Edwin Judge, Gerd Theissen, and Wayne Meeks created what has been called the New Consensus in Pauline studies, arguing that early Christian groups were peopled by individuals from multiple social and economic levels.[115] In a recent series of articles Steven Friesen has challenged the New Consensus and argued that the communities to whom Paul wrote were made primarily of people at or near subsistence level.[116] A crucial piece of Friesen's argument revolves around the person of Erastus the οἰκονόμος τῆς πόλεως, from whom Paul sends greetings while staying in Corinth in Rom 16:23.[117] Erastus' identity shows the dangers of an approach that uncritically deploys archaeological evidence to link up with the text of the New Testament.

In April of 1929 the excavators at Corinth discovered an inscription near the theater that mentioned an Erastus who was a Corinthian *aedile,* one of the

---

Paul and After His Death. A parallel collection building off of Koester's leadership in this realm is the previously mentioned Nasrallah, Bakirtzis, and Friesen, *From Roman to Early Christian Thessalonikē.*

[113] Though I will not discuss it, mention must also be made of the work of Richard DeMaris. In two parallel articles, DeMaris has made a compelling case for thinking about the role of mystery cults in the landscape of Corinthian religion. See Richard E. DeMaris, "Demeter in Roman Corinth: Local Development in a Mediterranean Religion," *Numen* 42.2 (1995): 105-17 and Richard E. DeMaris, "Corinthian Religion and Baptism for the Dead (1 Corinthians 15:29): Insights from Archaeology and Anthropology," *JBL* 114.4 (1995): 661-82. In a more recent monograph, DeMaris has taken a more interdisciplinary approach by looking at ritual in Corinth, focusing on water and its relation to ritual practice in Corinth, the Corinthian *ekklēsia,* and the broader Roman world. See Richard E. DeMaris, *The New Testament in its Ritual World* (New York: Routledge, 2008).

[114] See, for example, the discussion of Deissmann's work above.

[115] Edwin A. Judge, *The Social Patterns of Christian Groups in the First Century* (London: Tyndale, 1960); Gerd Theissen, *The Social Setting of Pauline Christianity: Essays on Corinth* (Philadelphia: Fortress, 1982); Wayne Meeks, *The First Urban Christians: The Social World of the Apostle Paul* (New Haven: Yale University Press, 1983).

[116] Steven J. Friesen, "Poverty in Pauline Studies: Beyond the So-called New Consensus," *JSNT* 26.3 (2004): 323-61; Steven J. Friesen, "Prospects for a Demography of the Pauline Mission: Corinth among the Churches," in Daniel N. Schowalter and Steven J. Friesen, eds., *Urban Religion in Roman Corinth: Interdisciplinary Approaches* (Cambridge, Mass.: Harvard Theological Studies, Distributed by Harvard University Press, 2005), 351-70; Walter Scheidel and Steven J. Friesen, "The Size of the Economy and the Distribution of Income in the Roman Empire," *JRS* 99 (2009): 61-91. Friesen's work is in dialogue with Justin J. Meggitt, *Paul, Poverty, and Survival* (Edinburgh: T. & T. Clark, 1998). For a response to Meggitt's work, see Gerd Theissen, "Social Conflicts in the Corinthian Community: Further Remarks on J. J. Meggitt, *Paul, Poverty, and Survival,*" *JSNT* 25.3 (2003): 371-91.

[117] Steven J. Friesen, "The Wrong Erastus: Ideology, Archaeology, and Exegesis," in Friesen, Schowalter, and Walters, *Corinth in Context,* 231-56.

elected magistracies in a Roman colony.[118] Shortly after its discovery and publication, many New Testament scholars began to herald the discovery as evidence for the existence of a wealthy Corinthian official in the Corinthian community.[119] In particular, Gerd Theissen's reconstruction of Erastus' life and psychology has been the most influential.[120]

In contrast to those who see a direct connection between the two Erasti, Friesen has offered a powerful counter-argument through a nuanced study of both archaeological and philological materials. Friesen reexamined the evidence for dating the Erastus inscription to the first century, finding that it is more likely to have come from the middle of the second century.[121] This makes it too late to be associated with the Erastus of Rom 16:23. Having shown that Erastus the *aedile* cannot be associated with Paul's Erastus, Friesen examines the description of Erastus in Rom 16:23 as an οἰκονόμος τῆς πόλεως.[122] He shows that the offices of *aedile* and *oikonomos* cannot be equated, the latter being an office often filled by public slaves. Whether we assent to Friesen's characterization of early Christian communities made up of those at or near subsistence level, it is no longer possible to assume that the Erastus that Paul mentions is evidence for a Corinthian follower of Jesus from the ranks of the local elite.[123] Friesen's contribution, however, goes beyond this exegetical point, offering a model of how an early Christian scholar can draw on archaeological materials only after a long process of studious analysis and careful interpretation. Further, he challenges scholars to account for the

---

[118] Kent, *Corinth VIII.3: The Inscriptions, 1926–1950*, no. 232.

[119] We saw above the romantic aura with which Willoughby, "Archaeology and Christian Beginnings," 33-34, described the pavement of Erastus. Cadbury, "Erastus of Corinth," 42-58, was one of the few who challenged the identification of the Erastus of the inscription with that of Rom 16:23.

[120] Theissen, *The Social Setting of Pauline Christianity*. For a summary of Erastus' characterization in New Testament studies of Corinth, see Friesen, "The Wrong Erastus," 232-35.

[121] Friesen, "The Wrong Erastus," 236-45. Friesen shows that there is no evidence for a first century dating apart from the connection with Paul's Erastus. The earliest publications by the archaeologists assumed a connection and reasoned for a first century dating from there. In addition, there is no evidence for a connection between the blocks on which the inscription is carved and the plaza to which it is connected. The pavement of the plaza (just to the east of the theater) has a different alignment to the blocks of the inscription, suggesting that the largest block (A) was moved to the courtyard sometime after the pavement was laid and used for a different purpose (239). It was Oscar Broneer who discovered Block A in the courtyard in 1929 and it was also Broneer who brought the other blocks (B and C) to the courtyard and aligned them with Block A to join the inscription together (236). Though they were not originally used in the present orientation with the plaza, the blocks did come from the same stone as the pavement, so they were probably in a different location. But the pavement itself overlays a latrine of Hadrianic date, which means that the pavement for the plaza could not have been laid before the mid-second century (242). Friesen further considers the medium of Latin pavement inscriptions, compiling a list of all known examples in the empire. Though most of these examples (nineteen in all) come from the time of Augustus, there are examples of inscriptions from later periods.

[122] Friesen, "The Wrong Erastus," 245-49.

[123] On recent attempts to build on Friesen's work, adding different metrics for measuring poverty and inequality, see Oakes, *Reading Romans in Pompeii*, and Bruce Longenecker, *Remember the Poor: Paul, Poverty, and the Greco-Roman World* (Grand Rapids: Eerdmans, 2010).

ideological positions that shape how they reconstruct early Christian communities. Rather than presuming an "ideology of upward mobility," we ought to presume an "ideology of inequality" to account for the socio-economic status of those drawn to early Christianity.[124]

A second example of interesting work to come out of early Christian studies in Corinth is Jorunn Økland's *Women in their Place*.[125] Økland examines evidence for women's cultic practice in Corinth, including the orientation of temple and ritual space, and places this alongside the broader discourse of gender in the Roman world. This approach takes account both of the local context of Corinth and the larger discursive constructs through which social and cultic space was perceived, structured, and experienced. Økland then turns to Paul's rhetoric in 1 Corinthians 11–14, particularly paying attention to the way in which he seeks to shape the ritual practice of the community, effectively transforming a household gathering into a ritualized sanctuary space. Paul's ritualizing rhetoric in 1 Corinthians 11–14 also works to limit the leadership roles of women in the community, constrain their behavior, and prescribe their attire. Økland's study offers an important example of how to study an early Christian community by taking account the ways in which gender and space shape the rhetoric and practice of community life (and vice versa). A further step forward could build upon Økland's framework to reimagine not just Paul's rhetorical goals but also those of the Corinthians who heard, reacted to, and resisted Paul's own rhetoric.[126]

8. Reading Paul Otherwise

In this chapter I have argued that an archaeology of the Pauline mission has to be more than a scholarly tour in the footsteps of Paul. Many scholars of early Christianity and classical archaeologists alike have participated in a larger history of pilgrimage and tourism in search of Paul. The scholars that I have highlighted above demonstrate how we might gaze otherwise on Paul, the communities to which he wrote, and the broader history of early Christianity in conversation with scholars in other disciplines. To do so is to allow us to see early Christian communities as part of, and not distinct from, the dynamic and diverse landscapes of civic life in the early Roman Empire.

Recommended Reading

Alcock, Susan E. *Graecia Capta: The Landscapes of Roman Greece*. New York: Cambridge University Press, 1993.

---

[124] Friesen, "The Wrong Erastus," 256.
[125] Jorunn Økland, *Women in Their Place: Paul and the Corinthian Discourse of Gender and Sanctuary Space*, (JSNTSup 269; New York: T. & T. Clark, 2004).
[126] On the possibilities for reconstructing a Corinthian response to Paul, see Wire, *Corinthian Women Prophets* and Schüssler Fiorenza, *Rhetoric and Ethic* (105-28).

Ascough, Richard S. *Paul's Macedonian Associations: The Social Context of 1 Thessalonians and Philippians*. Wissenschaftliche Untersuchungen zum Neuen Testament 2.161. Tübingen: Mohr (Siebeck), 2003.

Concannon, Cavan W. *"When You Were Gentiles": Specters of Ethnicity in Roman Corinth and Paul's Corinthian Correspondence*. New Haven: Yale University Press, forthcoming.

Deissmann, Gustav Adolf. *Light From the Ancient East: The New Testament Illustrated by Recently Discovered Texts of the Graeco-Roman World*. New York: Hodder and Stoughton, 1910.

DeMaris, Richard E. *The New Testament in its Ritual World*. New York: Routledge, 2008.

Friesen, Steven J., Daniel N. Schowalter, and James Walters, eds. *Corinth in Context: Comparative Studies on Religion and Society*. Novum Testamentum Supplements 134. Leiden: Brill, 2010.

Koester, Helmut, ed. *Ephesos, Metropolis of Asia: An Interdisciplinary Approach to its Archaeology, Religion, and Culture*. Harvard Theological Studies 41. Cambridge, Mass.: Distributed by Harvard University Press for Harvard Theological Studies/Harvard Divinity School, 1995.

Koester, Helmut. *Pergamon: Citadel of the Gods: Archaeological Record, Literary Description, and Religious Development*. Harvard Theological Studies 46. Harrisburg: Trinity Press International, 1998.

Nasrallah, Laura S., Charalambos Bakirtzis, and Steven J. Friesen, eds. *From Roman to Early Christian Thessalonikē: Studies in Religion and Archaeology*. Cambridge, Mass.: Harvard Theological Studies, 2010.

Nasrallah, Laura S. *Christian Responses to Roman Art and Architecture: The Second-Century Church Amid the Spaces of Empire*. New York: Cambridge University Press, 2010.

Oakes, Peter. *Reading Romans in Pompeii: Paul's Letter at Ground Level*. Minneapolis: Fortress, 2009.

Økland, Jorunn. *Women in Their Place: Paul and the Corinthian Discourse of Gender and Sanctuary Space*. Journal for the Study of the New Testament Supplement Series 269. New York: T. & T. Clark, 2004.

Schowalter, Daniel N., and Steven J. Friesen, *Urban Religion in Roman Corinth: Interdisciplinary Approaches*. Harvard Theological Studies 53. Cambridge, Mass.: Distributed by Harvard University Press for Harvard Theological Studies/Harvard Divinity School, 2005.

Spawforth, Antony. "Roman Corinth: The Formation of a Colonial Elite." Pages 167-82 in *Roman Onomastics in the Greek East: Social and Political Aspects: Proceedings of the International Colloquium Organized by the Finnish Institute and the Centre for Greek and Roman Antiquity, Athens, 7–9 September 1993*. Edited by A. D, Rizakes. Athens: Kentron Hellenikes kai Romaikes Archaiotetos Ethnikon Hidryma Ereunon, 1996.

White, L. Michael. *The Social Origins of Christian Architecture*. 2 vols. Harvard Theological Studies 42. Valley Forge: Trinity Press International, 1996.

4. Pauline Letter Manuscripts

Brent Nongbri

Like all the documents that make up the New Testament, the letters attributed to the apostle Paul have reached us by way of transmission through a number of ancient manuscripts (when I say "manuscripts" here, I refer to handwritten copies of texts made before the introduction and spread of the printing press in Europe in the mid-fifteenth century). None of these manuscripts are exactly identical to one another, and no single one of them is the "original" copy of the letters.[1] What we read in most modern English editions of the Bible (the NRSV, the NIV, etc.) are translations of what scholars call an "eclectic" Greek text, a text made up of bits and pieces of lots of manuscripts, although it reproduces no actual, single manuscript from the ancient world.[2] In fact, most editions of ancient texts work this way when multiple copies of the ancient manuscripts survive. What makes Paul's letters, and indeed all the documents that make up the New Testament, different from other ancient literature is that we have many, many more manuscript copies of them than we have for most other ancient texts.

The letters attributed to Paul are preserved in ancient manuscripts of several different languages—Greek, Latin, Coptic, Syriac, and others. This chapter will focus on the manuscripts of Paul's letters written in Greek, the language in which the letters were composed.[3] In what follows, I will discuss

---

[1] The idea of a single "original" version of any of Paul's letters is problematic for a number of complicated reasons. For a discussion of some of these difficulties, see E. J. Epp, "The Multivalence of the Term 'Original Text' in New Testament Textual Criticism," *HTR* 92 (1999): 245-81; repr. in E. J. Epp, *Perspectives on New Testament Textual Criticism: Collected Essays, 1962–2004* (Leiden: Brill, 2005), 551-93. I discuss this point in more detail later in the chapter.

[2] The eclectic text most commonly used by scholars of the New Testament is the twenty-eighth edition of *Novum Testamentum Graece* (Stuttgart: Deutsche Bibelgesellschaft, 2012), originally edited by Eberhard Nestle and more recently produced by the Institute for New Testament Textual Research in Münster. Scholars generally refer to it by the shorthand designation "Nestle-Aland," and it is often abbreviated as "NA28." Other important older eclectic texts include those of B. F. Westcott and F. J. A. Hort, *The New Testament in the Original Greek* (New York: Harper & Brothers, 1881) and Constantin von Tischendorf, *Novum Testamentum Graece* (Leipzig: Giesecke & Devrient, 1869–1894).

[3] For information on the various ancient translations of Paul's letters, see D. C. Parker, *An Introduction to the New Testament Manuscripts and their Texts* (Cambridge: Cambridge University Press, 2008), 264-67, and B. M. Metzger, *The Early Versions of the New Testament: Their Origin, Transmission, and Limitations* (Oxford: Clarendon, 1977).

the different ways that scholars classify these manuscripts and describe some features of a few especially important manuscripts of Paul's letters. I will also briefly outline how scholars go about determining the oldest recoverable text of Paul's letters and survey some textual problems raised by the differences in the various manuscripts. I will conclude by giving an overview of different theories about how and when copies of Paul's letters began to be gathered into the kinds of collections that constitute the vast majority of our surviving manuscripts. Throughout, I will try to illustrate the complex relationship that exists between the modern translations most people read today and the ancient manuscripts.

Modern Bibles contain thirteen documents explicitly attributed to Paul (or to Paul and co-authors): Romans, 1 Corinthians, 2 Corinthians, Galatians, Ephesians, Philippians, Colossians, 1 Thessalonians, 2 Thessalonians, 1 Timothy, 2 Timothy, Titus, and Philemon. The letter "To the Hebrews" does not explicitly name an author, and early Christians were divided about whether or not Paul wrote it. Nevertheless, Hebrews is present as a part of most ancient Greek manuscript collections of Paul's letters. We also possess ancient copies of other letters attributed to Paul, including an epistle to the Laodiceans, an additional letter to the Corinthians (often called 3 Corinthians), as well as a set of letters between Paul and the Roman philosopher Seneca.[4] Some of these letters are included in ancient Latin and Syriac collections of Paul's letters, but they are not regularly present in the Greek manuscripts; so for the most part, they will be left out of the following discussion.[5]

1. Classifications of Manuscripts

There are about eight hundred Greek manuscripts (or fragments of manuscripts) of Paul's letters known today.[6] These range in size from complete or nearly complete copies of collections of Paul's letters to tiny scraps of a single letter.[7] Almost all of these manuscripts are (or were at one

---

[4] For further information on these texts, see the relevant pages in J. Fitzgerald and W. A. Meeks, eds., *The Writings of St. Paul* (2nd ed.; New York: Norton, 2007).

[5] Modern scholars debate whether or not Paul actually wrote some of these letters. There is general agreement that Paul wrote Romans, 1 and 2 Corinthians, Galatians, Philippians, 1 Thessalonians, and Philemon. Most scholars regard Laodiceans, 3 Corinthians, the correspondence of Paul and Seneca, 1 and 2 Timothy, and Titus as forgeries written in Paul's name by later authors. There is no consensus on whether or not Paul wrote Colossians and Ephesians. The Letter to the Hebrews, as I mentioned, does not claim to be by Paul, and few modern scholars would claim Pauline authorship for this letter. On the practice of forgery in the Christian tradition, see Bart Ehrman, *Forgery and Counterforgery: The Use of Literary Deceit in Early Christian Polemics* (Oxford: Oxford University Press, 2012).

[6] This number is constantly growing as manuscripts are identified. For up to date statistics, readers should consult the list of manuscripts (Handschriftenliste) at the website of the Münster Institute for New Testament Textual Research at http://intf.uni-muenster.de/vmr/NTVMR/ListeHandschriften.php.

[7] About fifty Greek manuscripts (mostly dating from the eleventh century to the fifteenth century) contain the whole New Testament. For a list and discussion, see D. D. Schmidt, "The

time part of) codices, that is, books. While most ancient letters were written on unbound sheets of papyrus, early Greek literary works were actually written on papyrus rolls (scrolls). The use of the codex for the production of literary texts was just getting underway in the late first century when Paul's letters were beginning to be copied and circulated, but by the time of our earliest surviving manuscripts of Paul's letters (probably the third century), the codex appears to have been the most common means of transmitting Christian texts.[8]

These manuscripts can look quite different from the type of printed pages to which most modern readers are accustomed. The system of division into numbered verses so common in modern Bibles, for example, was not a feature of ancient manuscripts (the division of the text into numbered verses first occurred in a 1551 printed edition of the Greek New Testament).[9] Many manuscripts of Paul's letters are written in what is called *scriptio continua*, that is, there are no spaces between words or punctuation marks, just strings of letters. It takes practice to gain facility with this kind of writing, and some combinations of letters can be open to multiple interpretations. Consider the following: GODISNOWHERE. The letters could be construed as "God is now here" or as "God is nowhere." Many manuscripts of the New Testament also employ contractions for certain words now generally called *nomina sacra*.[10] Many manuscripts, however, (especially later manuscripts) contain various reading aids such as word divisions, punctuation marks, chapter divisions, and even introductions to the individual letters.[11]

Scholars classify these manuscript copies of Paul's letters in different ways. One chief division of these manuscripts places them in four groups: minuscules, majuscules, papyri, and lectionaries. The vast majority of our

---

Greek New Testament as a Codex," in L. M. McDonald and J. A. Sanders, eds., *The Canon Debate* (Peabody: Hendrickson, 2002), 469-84. A small group of what are called majuscule manuscripts (to be discussed below) of the fourth and fifth centuries also contain Paul's letters as part of a larger "New Testament" collection.

[8] For a recent sensible discussion of the development and spread of the codex in the Roman world, see R. Bagnall, *Early Christian Books in Egypt* (Princeton: Princeton University Press, 2009). One scholar has even suggested that the production of a collection of Paul's letters was an impetus for the increased popularity and spread of the codex format among Christians. For that argument, see H. Gamble, "The Pauline Corpus and the Early Christian Book," in W. S. Babcock, ed., *Paul and the Legacies of Paul* (Dallas: Southern Methodist University Press, 1990), 265-80.

[9] See B. M. Metzger and B. D. Ehrman, *The Text of the New Testament: Its Transmission, Corruption, and Restoration* (4th ed.; New York: Oxford University Press, 2005), 149-50.

[10] For a good discussion of this phenomenon, see K. Haines-Eitzen, *Guardians of Letters: Literacy, Power, and the Transmitters of Early Christian Literature* (New York: Oxford University Press, 2000), 91-94.

[11] For Paul's letters, the chief reading aids found in the manuscripts themselves are the so-called "Marcionite Prologues" to the letters and the "Euthalian Apparatus." On these two features of the manuscripts, see N. A. Dahl, "The Origin of the Earliest Prologues of the Pauline Letters," *Semeia* 12 (1978): 233-77; repr. in Nils A. Dahl, *Studies in Ephesians: Introductory Questions, Text- and Edition-Critical Issues, Interpretation of Texts* and Themes (eds. D. Hellholm, V. Blomkvist, and T. Fornberg; Tübingen: Mohr [Siebeck], 2000), 179-209; and Nils A. Dahl, "The 'Euthalian Apparatus' and the Affiliated 'Argumenta,'" in Dahl, *Studies in Ephesians*, 231-75.

ancient copies of Paul's letters are from codices that scholars describe as "minuscules," a type of manuscript characterized by a neat, cursive form of Greek handwriting. These manuscripts were produced beginning around the ninth century and continued to be produced up to and beyond the invention of the printing press. Scholars identify these manuscripts by numerical designations (thus, 312 refers to a minuscule manuscript of Paul's letters copied in the eleventh or twelfth century and now in the British Library).[12] The second major category in this system of classification is the group of manuscripts known as "majuscules" or "uncials." These manuscripts are characterized by clear, regular, capital lettering and are usually assigned dates from roughly the fourth century through the ninth century. To distinguish between the minuscules and the majuscules, scholars identify the majuscules by means of a numeral prefaced by a zero, although some of these pieces are better known by a particular name or by a letter associated with an older classification system (for example, the Bible generally known as "Vaticanus," to be discussed in more detail below, is abbreviated both as 03 and with the letter "B").[13] The third grouping in this method of classification is designated not by style of handwriting but rather by the type of material on which the manuscript was copied. These are the papyri, named for the reed-like papyrus plant from which they are made (minuscules and majuscules were generally written on parchment, that is, treated animal skins). This distinction can cause some confusion, since many of the papyri are in fact written in fine majuscule characters. To date, over 30 different Greek papyrus fragments of Paul's letters have been published. They range in date from perhaps as early as the third century to the seventh or eighth century and are identified in this volume and more generally by a number preceded by the capital letter P. The manuscript designated P^{49}, for example, is a single fragmentary leaf of a copy of Ephesians usually assigned to a date in the third century and now kept at Yale University's Beinecke Library.[14] The final grouping of manuscripts in this classification system consists of the lectionaries. These manuscripts do not contain a continuous text of the documents of the New Testament but rather select verses for liturgical use (thus instead of handwriting or type of writing material, it is rather *function* that is the defining feature of the lectionaries, which, again, can invite some confusion since the lectionaries are written in minuscule hands). They are abbreviated by a script letter "L" (*l* or ℓ) followed by a number. The majority of lectionary manuscripts contain passages from the gospels, but there are a number, such as the twelfth-century

---

[12] The codex also contains a variety of medical recipes after the Letter to the Hebrews. Digital images of 312 may be viewed online at http://www.bl.uk/manuscripts/FullDisplay.aspx?index=1&ref=Add_MS_5116.

[13] A fuller designation of the codex is Bibliothecae Apostolicae Vaticanae codex Vaticanus Graecus 1209. The Vatican produced a photographic facsimile of the codex in 1999. See *Bibliorum sacrorum Graecorum codex Vaticanus B* (Rome: Istituto poligrafico e Zecca dello Stato, 1999).

[14] For digital images of P^{49}, see http://beinecke.library.yale.edu/papyrus/oneSET.asp?pid=415.

lectionary designated *l* 809, that contain selections from Paul's letters.[15] I shall say more about individual examples of each of these types of manuscripts momentarily, but first I want to introduce a second way that scholars classify these manuscripts.

As I already mentioned, no two manuscripts contain exactly identical texts, but the manuscripts do show different degrees of similarity and difference with one another, with the result that scholars divide them into "families" or "types" or "clusters." Strictly speaking, it is not the manuscripts themselves that are classified in this way but rather the text that a manuscript contains. The exact characteristics of these textual clusters are debated by specialists, but the system outlined below is in wide use among scholars who study the documents that make up the New Testament.[16] The majority of Greek manuscripts of Paul's letters contain what is called the "Byzantine Text" (also sometimes called the Koine Text or the Syrian Text). It is generally slightly longer and more polished than other textual clusters. Readings characteristic of the Byzantine Text are absent in the writings of Christian authors who wrote before the middle of the third century, but they are overwhelmingly popular in Christian writers in the east after the early fifth century, which suggests that this version of the text arose between the late third century and the early fifth century.[17] Most, but not all, of the minuscule manuscripts preserve texts of the Byzantine cluster. Several majuscule manuscripts of Paul's letters contain what scholars have come to call the "Western Text." This text more closely resembles the early Latin translations of the New Testament (the so-called "Old Latin" version, which is to be distinguished from the more familiar "Vulgate" Latin translation associated with the work of the Christian scholar Jerome in the early fifth century). As we shall see below, some of these manuscripts are actually bilingual, containing both Greek and Latin texts. The "Western" text seems to have taken shape before the middle of the second century, as it is found in the writings of such figures as Marcion and Justin Martyr, two Christian authors active in Rome in the middle of the second century. Scholars designate some manuscripts as representing a third textual type, the "Alexandrian" type. This text had arisen by the end of the second century. It is found in the writings of Clement, who wrote in Alexandria in the late second century, and Origen, a

---

[15] For an image and discussion of *l* 809, see B. M. Metzger, *Manuscripts of the Greek Bible: An Introduction to Palaeography* (New York: Oxford University Press, 1981), 126-27. For further discussion of Pauline lectionaries, see Parker, *An Introduction to the New Testament Manuscripts and their Texts*, 263-64.

[16] Scholars working at the Institute for New Testament Textual Research now use a rather different vocabulary for speaking about textual transmission and variation, the "Coherence-Based Genealogical Method." For an introduction to this method, see http://www.uni-muenster.de/INTF/Genealogical_method.html. For another method of recovering the early text of Paul's letters and mapping the history of the textual transmission, see S. C. Carlson, "The Text of Galatians and its History" (Ph.D. diss., Duke University, 2012). Carlson's summary of the Coherence-Based Genealogical Method on pp. 53-58 is also admirably clear and concise.

[17] The clearest discussion of these issues remains B. F. Westcott and F. J. A. Hort, *The New Testament in the Original Greek, Introduction, and Appendix* (New York: Harper & Brothers, 1882), 90-115.

Pauline Letter Manuscripts

Christian scholar who was active in the first half of the third century, first in Alexandria in Egypt and then later in Caesarea Maritima in Palestine.[18]

The vast majority of scholars regard the Byzantine textual type as a later derivative from the Western and Alexandrian types. This relationship is most easily illustrated by what scholars call Byzantine "conflation" readings. For example, in Rom 6:12, manuscripts of the Western cluster read, "Therefore, do not let sin reign in your mortal bodies so that you should obey *it*." Manuscripts of the Alexandrian cluster read, "Therefore, do not let sin reign in your mortal bodies so that you should obey *its passions*." Manuscripts of the Byzantine cluster read, "Therefore, do not let sin reign in your mortal bodies so that you should obey *it in its passions*." The Byzantine version appears to combine the readings of the Western and Alexandrian types and thus appears to be derivative from these types. Determining the precise relationship between the Western textual type and the Alexandrian textual type is a challenge that still puzzles professional textual critics today.[19] I should close this discussion of classification by again emphasizing that various aspects of these schemes of categorization are contested by different specialists, but they are still regularly used by most critical scholars of the New Testament. A discussion of individual manuscripts will illustrate some of the difficulties and ambiguities.

2. Individual Manuscripts

As I mentioned earlier, most minuscules have a version of the "Byzantine" type of text, and thus most textual critics regard this group of texts as the least helpful in determining early forms of the Pauline letters. There are, however, some exceptions. Among the minuscule manuscripts of Paul's letters, the one designated by the number 1739 is especially important. In its present state, 1739 contains Acts, the "Catholic" epistles, and Paul's letters. A typical feature of these minuscule manuscripts is the presence of colophons, notes to the reader from the scribe who copied the text. Just before the Letter to the Romans in 1739, the scribe wrote a note (or copied a note) that tells the reader that the fourteen letters of Paul were "copied from a most ancient exemplar," and that in fact much of the text of Romans was derived from the excerpts and homilies of Origen available to the scribe.[20] If 1739 represents a text of Paul's

---

[18] For the text of the four gospels, especially the text of the Gospel of Mark, some scholars recognize a fourth textual type, the "Caesarean" text, supposedly the text known to Origen when he was in Palestine. This textual type does not exist for the Pauline letters, and many, perhaps most, textual critics now find it doubtful that this text is identifiable in any manuscripts of the gospels either.

[19] See E. J. Epp, "Issues in New Testament Textual Criticism: Moving from the Nineteenth Century to the Twenty-first Century," in D. A. Black, ed., *Rethinking New Testament Textual Criticism* (Grand Rapids: Baker Academic, 2002) 17-76; repr. in Epp, *Perspectives on New Testament Textual Criticism*, 641-97.

[20] For a collation of 1739 (that is, a collection of its variant readings) as well as the Greek text of this scribal note, see K. Lake and S. New, *Six Collations of New Testament Manuscripts* (Cambridge, Mass.: Harvard University Press, 1932), 199-219.

letters known to Origen, then even though 1739 was itself copied in the tenth century, the text it preserves would be much, much older than that preserved in most other tenth-century manuscripts. Thus, it is important to note that the age of a manuscript itself is not the only factor that determines its usefulness for reconstructing the earliest recoverable text of Paul's letters.

There are several important majuscule manuscripts that contain Paul's letters. I will describe just a few of them below. I have already mentioned Codex Vaticanus (abbreviated as B or 03), which has been kept at the Vatican since at least the late fifteenth century. Its history before that point is unknown, but it was probably copied in Egypt or Caesarea at some point in the fourth century. It contains both the Old and New Testaments, and almost certainly originally contained all of the standard canonical Pauline letters, although it is now defective, missing the latter portion of Hebrews, as well as 1 and 2 Timothy, Titus, and Philemon. In the opinion of the textual critic Bruce Metzger, the text of Paul's letters in Vaticanus displays "a distinctly Western element."[21] In Codex Vaticanus, Paul's letters are divided into numbered chapters that continue sequentially through the set of letters. Yet, in Vaticanus itself, Hebrews comes after 2 Thessalonians, but the chapter numbers of Hebrews are out of sequence and clearly indicate that in the manuscript from which Vaticanus was copied (or in an ancestor of that manuscript), Hebrews was placed between Galatians and Ephesians.[22] Like nearly all ancient manuscripts of the New Testament, Vaticanus displays a number of alterations by later users of the manuscript. One example of this phenomenon in Vaticanus is especially noteworthy. At Heb 1:3, the scribe who first copied this portion of the codex wrote that Jesus "reveals all things" (Greek: *phanerōn te ta panta*). A later user of the manuscript changed it to the more common reading: Jesus "bears all things" (Greek: *pherōn te ta panta*). A still later user of the manuscript restored the earlier reading and wrote a note in the margin: "Ignorant and wicked man! Leave the old reading alone and don't change it!"[23]

Another codex likely copied in the fourth century that provides an important copy of Paul's letters is Codex Sinaiticus (abbreviated by the Hebrew letter *aleph*, א, or by the number 01). Like Codex Vaticanus, it is a complete Bible. It was preserved at St. Catherine's monastery in Egypt, and was discovered there by the famous textual critic Constantine von Tischendorf in the nineteenth century. The bulk of the manuscript is now kept at the British Library in London.[24] Sinaiticus is the oldest surviving manuscript that preserves a complete text of the thirteen letters attributed to Paul as well as the Letter to the Hebrews (which comes after 2 Thessalonians and before 1 Timothy in this manuscript). The text of the Pauline letters in Sinaiticus is

---

[21] Metzger, *Manuscripts of the Greek Bible*, 74.
[22] See the discussion in Metzger and Ehrman, *The Text of the New Testament: Its Transmission, Corruption, and Restoration*, 69.
[23] For a digital image of this note, see http://www-user.uni-bremen.de/~wie/Vaticanus/note1512.html.
[24] Digital images of Codex Sinaiticus can be viewed online at http://codexsinaiticus.org/en/.

basically of the Alexandrian type. Yet another important representative of the Alexandria textual cluster for Paul's letters is the fifth-century majuscule manuscript (again of the whole Bible) called Codex Alexandrinus (A or 02), which is also now housed at the British Library.[25]

Codex Ephraemi Syri Rescriptus (abbreviated C or 04) is now held in Paris. It is called *rescriptus* ("rewritten") because it is what scholars refer to as a palimpsest. The writings of Ephraem the Syrian were copied into the manuscript in the twelfth century, but they were not copied on to fresh pages. Instead, they were copied on to pages of a fifth or sixth-century Greek majuscule manuscript of the Bible that had been partially erased. Fortunately, under the newer writing, much of the older writing is still visible, including Paul's letters. This manuscript is especially interesting in regard to the Letter to the Romans. The copyist, who regularly set the beginnings of sense units into the left margin, included a high concentration of these breaks and indentations in the verses we now call Rom 3:27–4:2.[26] The effect is something like presenting lines in a play, with individual characters' parts marked off by the indentations.[27] These sorts of physical features of manuscripts can provide clues to how ancient readers understood Paul's writings. I should also point out that it is equally interesting to notice the things *not* marked off by indentation in the ancient manuscripts. For example, many modern translations of the New Testament set off Phil 2:6-11 with special indentation to suggest that it is somehow different from the surrounding text (scholars generally refer to these verses as a "hymn"). Yet, to my knowledge, no ancient manuscript indents or otherwise marks this passage in a way that would indicate it is somehow different from the material surrounding it.[28]

As I mentioned earlier, some majuscule codices of Paul's letters are examples of diglots, that is, manuscripts written in two languages. Three especially important diglot manuscripts consisting chiefly of Paul's letters are Codex Claromontanus (abbreviated as D^{Paul} or 06), Codex Augiensis (F^{Paul} or 010), and Codex Boernerianus (G^{Paul} or 012).[29] Codex Claromontanus, which was probably copied in the fifth century, presents the Greek and Latin texts on facing pages. Codex Boernerianus, which was copied in the ninth century, is an interlinear text, in which the Latin translation is written above each line of

---

[25] Digital images of Codex Alexandrinus can be viewed online at http://www.bl.uk/manuscripts/Viewer.aspx?ref=royal_ms_1_d_viii_fs001r.
[26] Digital images of Codex Ephraemi Syri Rescriptus can be viewed online at http://gallica.bnf.fr/ark:/12148/btv1b8470433r.
[27] On this point, see S. K. Stowers, *A Rereading of Romans: Justice, Jews, and Gentiles* (New Haven: Yale University Press, 1997), 231-34.
[28] For a discussion of these issues, see the fascinating article by M. Peppard, "'Poetry,' 'Hymns,' and 'Traditional Material' in New Testament Epistles, or How to Do Things with Indentations," *JSNT* 30 (2008): 319-42.
[29] The superscript "Paul" (or occasionally just "P") distinguishes these codices from Codex Bezae, Codex Boreelianus, and Codex Harleianus, codices of the gospels which are also abbreviated as D, F, and G, respectively.

Greek.[30] The pages of Codex Augiensis, also copied in the ninth century, contain double columns of Greek and Latin. These codices are the main representatives among the Greek manuscripts for the Western Text of Paul's letters. They seem to be closely related to one another. A strong case has been made that Augiensis and Boernerianus are derived from a common ancestor.[31] That ancestor manuscript and Claromontanus also seem to derive from a still earlier (fourth century?) manuscript.[32] Thus, in spite of the relatively late date of Augiensis and Boernerianus, these manuscripts are of considerable importance when discussing the earliest recoverable text of Paul's letters.

In the late nineteenth and early twentieth century, archaeological excavations in the dry sands of Egypt began to yield a massive amount of writing preserved on papyrus. These finds included everything from classic literature to documents of everyday life—letters, receipts, magical spells, certificates of marriage and divorce, and a whole host of other kinds of writing. Also discovered were many fragments of early Christian literature, both documents of the New Testament and non-canonical Christian literature. To date there are 35 published papyrus fragments of Paul's letters, but some of these were likely parts of the same codices, such as P^{15} and P^{16}, fragments of 1 Corinthians and Philippians, respectively, which share similar handwriting and textual affinities and were found together at Oxyrhynchus in Egypt.[33] Thus, we have papyrus fragments representing roughly 30 different manuscripts of the epistles of Paul.

Of the surviving papyrus fragments of manuscripts of Paul's letters, by far the most important is P^{46}, a well preserved codex containing substantial portions of nine of the letters attributed to Paul. Prior to its publication, P^{46} was divided on the antiquities market and sold to different buyers. At present, some leaves of the codex are kept at the University of Michigan Library, and some are kept at the Chester Beatty Library in Dublin.[34] It appears to have

---

[30] Digital images of Codex Claromontanus can be viewed online at http://gallica.bnf.fr/ark:/12148/btv1b84683111. Digital images of Codex Boernerianus can be viewed online at http://www.slub-dresden.de/index.php?id=5363&tx_dlf[id]=2966.

[31] See W. H. P. Hatch, "On the Relationship of Codex Augiensis and Codex Boernerianus of the Pauline Epistles," *HSCP* 60 (1951): 187-99.

[32] See N. A. Dahl, "0230 (= PSI 1306) and the Fourth-century Greek-Latin Edition of the Letters of Paul," in E. Best and R. McL. Wilson, eds., *Text and Interpretation: Studies in the New Testament Presented to Matthew Black* (Cambridge: Cambridge University Press, 1979), 79-98; repr. In Dahl, *Studies in Ephesians*, 211-30.

[33] For a list of papyrus fragments of Paul's letters, see Parker, *An Introduction to the New Testament Manuscripts and their Texts*, 258, table 8.1. To his list should be added three recently published pieces: P^{123} (containing 1 Cor 14:31-34 and 15:3-6, assigned to the fourth century), P^{124} (containing 2 Cor 11:1-4, 6-9, assigned to the sixth century), and P^{126} (containing Heb 13:12-13, 19-20, assigned to the fourth century). Also, Parker's entry for P^{118} lists a date of "X?" This seems to be an error. Different scholars have assigned P^{118} to dates ranging from the second century to the fifth or sixth century. Again, the most up to date listing is to be found in the online Handschriftenliste at http://intf.uni-muenster.de/vmr/NTVMR/ListeHandschriften.php.

[34] Digital images of the pages of P^{46} kept at the University of Michigan can be viewed online at http://quod.lib.umich.edu/cgi/i/image/image-idx?type=bbaglist;view=bbthumbnail;bbdbid=1942765957.

been copied some time in the third or early fourth century.[35] P^{46} seems to have been what is called a single-quire codex. That is, it consisted of a single stack of papyrus sheets folded over once and stitched along the fold. In its current state, P^{46} is missing pages at its beginning and end, but since its pages are numbered and it was most likely a single quire, the original size of the quire can be calculated (it would have had 104 leaves, which would be 208 pages). P^{46} contains (in this order):

Pages 1-41:	Romans (the first 14 pages are missing)
Pages 41-64:	Hebrews
Pages 64-117:	1 Corinthians
Pages 118-45:	2 Corinthians
Pages 146-58:	Ephesians
Pages 158-68:	Galatians
Pages 168-76:	Philippians
Pages 176-84:	Colossians
Pages 184-94:	1 Thessalonians (the text is incomplete, and we can assume 14 pages are missing at the end).

The content of the missing pages at the end of P^{46} is a puzzle. There is no conceivable way the remainder of the quire could have space for the other letters commonly contained in Greek manuscripts of letters attributed to Paul (2 Thessalonians, 1 Timothy, 2 Timothy, Titus, and Philemon). The missing pages could likely only fit 2 Thessalonians and perhaps Philemon. It is thus highly probable that the single quire of P^{46} did not contain the so-called Pastoral Epistles (1 Timothy, 2 Timothy, and Titus).[36] The text of P^{46} does not fall very neatly into any of the textual clusters described above, but it does seem to side more frequently with manuscripts of the Alexandrian cluster against those of the Western cluster.

The excellent state of preservation of P^{46} is something of an oddity among the papyrus manuscripts of Paul's letters. At the other end of the spectrum are pieces like P^{87} and P^{32}, which are assigned to the same general date range as P^{46}. These pieces, however, are nowhere near as well preserved as P^{46}. P^{87} is a tiny scrap (roughly 4 x 5 cm) of Paul's Letter to Philemon. [37] This small fragment is all we have of a codex that (presumably) contained an entire collection of Paul's letters. P^{32} is a small corner (about 11 x 5 cm) of a page

---

[35] On the date of P^{46}, see S. R. Pickering, "The Dating of the Chester Beatty-Michigan Codex of the Pauline Epistles (P^{46})," in T. W. Hillard et al., eds., *Ancient History in a Modern University, Volume 2: Early Christianity, Late Antiquity, and Beyond* (Grand Rapids: Eerdmans, 1998), 216-27. Pickering offers a good discussion of the many difficulties involved in trying to assign dates to manuscripts on the basis of handwriting.

[36] For an in depth discussion of this issue, see E. J. Epp, "Issues in the Interrelation of New Testament Textual Criticism and Canon" in McDonald and Sanders, *The Canon Debate*, 485-515; reprinted in Epp, *Perspectives on New Testament Textual Criticism*, 595-639.

[37] For a digital image of P^{87}, see http://www.uni-koeln.de/phil-fak/ifa/NRWakademie/papyrologie/PKoeln/PK12r.jpg.

containing bits of the first and second chapters of Titus.[38] These pieces are more representative of the state of preservation of the papyrus copies of Paul's letters.

It is also important to recognize that some papyrus fragments of Paul's letters were not actually part of a continuous text of Paul's letters. For example, P^{10}, a sheet of papyrus excavated in the Egyptian town of Oxyrhynchus, contains the first seven verses of Paul's Letter to the Romans copied out in crudely shaped letters on the top third of the sheet. The remainder of the sheet is blank save for a short note in different handwriting below the verses from Romans. It appears to be an exercise copied out by a school child.[39] Another papyrus, P^{99}, is part of a codex containing Greek grammatical lessons. The section of this codex that we call "P^{99}" is a bilingual dictionary with words and phrases from some of Paul's letters translated from the Greek into Latin. It seems to be a kind of educational handbook.[40]

3. Textual Problems in the Pauline Letters and Determining the Earliest Recoverable Text

What we read in most English versions of Paul's letters is a translation of what many scholars believe is the earliest recoverable text of the letters. As I said at the outset, astute textual critics have acknowledged that the idea of an "original text" of any of the documents of the New Testament is highly problematic. They prefer to speak of the earliest recoverable text or the initial text. The difference is more important than it might seem. Since our earliest manuscripts of Paul's letters probably come from the third century, the best that textual critics can do is to try to discern what the text looked like at that point in time. Quotations of Paul's letters by Christian authors of the second century may make it possible to ascertain what the text of some passages in the letters looked like in the middle to late second century, but that is as early as the evidence goes.[41] Given that this is the case, to speak of recovering the "original text" of any of Paul's letters would presume that the texts of Paul's letters circulating in the late second century were identical to those written by

---

[38] For a digital image of P^{32}, see the website of the John Rylands University Library at http://enriqueta.man.ac.uk:8180/luna/servlet and search for "Titus."

[39] An image of this papyrus is available online at http://pds.lib.harvard.edu/pds/view/7456384. For further information about this piece, see A. Luijendijk, "A New Testament Papyrus and Its Documentary Context: An Early Christian Writing Exercise from the Archive of Leonides (P.Oxy. II 209/ P^{10})," *JBL* 129 (2010): 575-96.

[40] For an edition of the text with facsimile images, see Alfons Wouters, *The Chester Beatty Codex AC 1499: A Graeco-Latin Lexicon on the Pauline Epistles and a Greek Grammar* (Leuven: Peeters, 1988).

[41] The use of quotations of Paul's letters in the writings of Christian authors of the second century is somewhat problematic, since our texts of those authors are just as unstable as our texts of Paul's letters. For a discussion of the difficulties of this evidence, see G. D. Fee, "The Use of the Greek Fathers for New Testament Textual Criticism" in B. D. Ehrman and M. W. Holmes, eds., *The Text of the New Testament in Contemporary Research: Essays on the status quaestionis* (Grand Rapids: Eerdmans, 1995), 191-207.

Paul, or by Paul and his associates (see, for example, 1 Cor 1:1 and 2 Cor 1:1) or by one of Paul's secretaries (see Rom 16:22), in the middle decades of the first century. Such an assumption would seem quite problematic, judging by the amount of variation preserved in the later manuscripts that we do possess and the comments of Origen concerning the state of the manuscripts known to him at the end of the second century. In regard to the gospels, Origen wrote, "The differences among the manuscripts have become great, either through the negligence of some copyist or through the perverse audacity of others; they either neglect to check over what they have transcribed, or, in the process of checking, they make additions or deletions as they please."[42]

There are a number of substantial differences among the texts preserved in the Greek manuscripts of Paul's letters. When textual critics attempt to establish the earliest recoverable text of a given passage, they use both "external" and "internal" criteria. The internal criteria deal with issues like the immediate context of the passage and the author's writing style; the external criteria concern the manuscripts. Scholars "weigh" the manuscript evidence; that is, they do not simply count up the manuscripts supporting one reading versus the manuscripts containing another reading and select the winner (doing so would almost always result in selecting the reading of the Byzantine Text). Rather, they consider factors like the antiquity of the manuscript evidence for a given reading and the breadth of support for a given reading. In many cases conclusions based on these internal and external criteria conflict, and scholars who want to make decisions about the earliest recoverable text must dismiss some of the evidence. To take just one example, in most of the earliest manuscripts containing 1 Thess 2:7, the verse reads as follows: "We were infants among you, like a nurse caring for her children." The manuscript evidence, or external support, for this reading is overwhelmingly strong: P^{65}, Sinaiticus, Vaticanus, Syri Rescriptus, Claromontanus, Boernerianus, Augiensis, and others have this reading. Yet other manuscripts, like 1739, have "gentle" (Greek: *ēpioi*) instead of "infants" (Greek: *nēpioi*). The situation is complicated by the fact that the preceding word ("we were," Greek: *egenēthēmen*) ends with a *nu* ("n"), the one letter that differentiates between the terms *ēpioi* and *nēpioi*. Nevertheless, given that the idea of being "gentle as a nurse" was a common theme in the writings of ancient philosophical teachers, it is not surprising that the majority of English translations give preference here to the internal criteria (context and sense of the passage) and translate the verse as follows: "We were gentle among you,

---

[42] The quotation is found in Origen's *Commentary on Matthew*, book 15, chapter 14. The translation is that of B. M. Metzger in "Explicit References in the Works of Origen to Variant Readings in New Testament Manuscripts," in J. N. Birdsall and R. W. Thomson, eds., *Biblical and Patristic Studies in Memory of Robert Pierce Casey* (Freiburg: Herder, 1963), 78-95; repr. in B. M. Metzger, *Historical and Literary Studies: Pagan, Jewish, and Christian* (Leiden: Brill, 1968), 88-103. As Metzger discusses (*Historical and Literary Studies*, 88 n. 2), even this passage of Origen itself contains textual discrepancies among the Greek and Latin manuscripts in which it is preserved!

like a nurse taking care of her children" (RSV).[43] These are the sorts of judgment calls that scholars regularly make in trying to establish the earliest recoverable text of Paul's letters.

The preceding example may seem trivial, but there are several more substantial textual variations in Paul's letters. I will mention just a few here. The most prominent textual variant in the Pauline letters concerns the ending of the Letter to the Romans, which takes a number of different forms. The verses that appear in modern translations as Rom 16:25-7 are found in many manuscripts at the conclusion of chapter 14 (that is, after Rom 14:23). In P^{46}, these verses appear at the end of Romans 15. Some manuscripts include the verses twice; others lack them entirely. This state of affairs has led some scholars to speculate that shorter versions of Romans (lacking chapter 15 or chapter 16 or even both of those chapters) may well have circulated in antiquity and in fact may be older than the longer more familiar form of the letter.[44] Other scholars have suggested that the longer version of Romans is older and was later shortened by the removal of chapter 16, with its long list of personal greetings in order to make the letter appear to be directed to more than just the assemblies of Rome. Such a notion finds support from other textual variations in Romans. Some manuscripts of Romans (including Boernerianus and manuscripts known to Origen) lack the phrases "in Rome" at 1:7 and "who are in Rome" in 1:15. This phenomenon is taken by some as evidence that Romans was altered to make it less like a letter to one particular historically situated group and more like a universally applicable theological essay.[45]

Other more minor variations are also noteworthy. For example, verses 34 and 35 in chapter 14 of 1 Corinthians ("Women should be silent in the churches . . . If there is anything they desire to know, let them ask their husbands at home. For it is shameful for a woman to speak in church.") appear in different places in different manuscripts. Some manuscripts, including Claromontanus, Boernerianus, and Augiensis, place these verses after 1 Cor 15:40. While, to my knowledge, no manuscript of 1 Corinthians lacks these verses, the fact that they appear in different in different locations in different manuscripts has suggested to some scholars that they might be later insertions and not part of earlier copies of Paul's letters.

As I mentioned, when scholars try to ascertain what the earliest recoverable text might be, the ages of the manuscripts are taken into

---

[43] See Metzger and Ehrman, *The Text of the New Testament*, 328-30; and A. J. Malherbe, "'Gentle as a Nurse': The Cynic Background to 1 Thess 2," *NovT* 12 (1970): 203-17. It is interesting to note that the most recent edition of Nestle-Aland (unlike the 26th edition) opts for the reading "infants" (*nēpioi*).

[44] For a thorough treatment of the problem, see H. Y. Gamble, *The Textual History of the Letter to the Romans: A Study in Textual and Literary Criticism* (Grand Rapids: Eerdmans, 1977).

[45] N. A. Dahl, "The Particularity of the Pauline Epistles as a Problem in the Ancient Church," in *Neotestamntica et Patristica. Eine Freundesgabe. Herrn Oscar Cullmann zu seinem 60 Geburtstag überreicht* (Leiden: Brill, 1962), 261-71; repr. in N. A. Dahl, *Studies in Ephesians (Introductory Questions, Text and Edition-Critical Issues, Interpretation of Texts and Themes* (David Hellholm et al., eds.; Tübingen: Mohr [Siebeck], 2000), 165-78).

consideration. But as we already saw (in the case of 1739), the age of a manuscript does not always equate to the age of the text copied on it. P^{46} offers another opportunity to illustrate the complexity of the problem. Most modern translations of Phil 1:9-11 read something like this: "And this is my prayer, that your love may overflow more and more with knowledge and full insight to help you to determine what is best, so that in the Day of Christ you may be pure and blameless, having produced the harvest of righteousness that comes through Christ Jesus for the glory and praise of God" (NRSV). This translation is in agreement with Codex Vaticanus, Sinaiticus, and a number of other manuscripts. The diglot manuscripts Boernerianus and Augiensis, however, have a different reading at the end of the verse: "for glory and praise *for me.*" At that point in the text, P^{46} reads, "to the glory of God and praise for me." This group of words in P^{46} is thus a conflation, since it seems to have been produced by combining the reading of the Alexandrian cluster and the Western cluster, which suggests that the reading found in Boernerianus and Augiensis must be older than that found in P^{46} (this hypothesis is strengthened by the fact that the fourth-century Latin author known as Ambrosiaster also had the reading of "glory and praise for me" (*gloriam et laudem mihi*). The lesson, again, is that the oldest manuscript does not necessarily preserve the oldest text.[46] These are just a few examples of the many variations in our manuscripts of Paul's letters and the ways that scholars approach them.

4. Theories about the Collection of Paul's Letters

A final issue requires some consideration. We have evidence for collections of Paul's letters with varying sets of letters or a different ordering of the letters. Compare, for example, the contents and ordering of the following manuscript copies:

P^{46}	Sinaiticus	Claromontanus	Boernerianus
Romans	Romans	Romans	Romans
Hebrews	1 Corinthians	1 Corinthians	1 Corinthians
1 Corinthians	2 Corinthians	2 Corinthians	2 Corinthians
2 Corinthians	Galatians	Galatians	Galatians
Ephesians	Ephesians	Ephesians	Ephesians
Galatians	Philippians	Colossians	Philippians
Philippians	Colossians	Philippians	Colossians
Colossians	1 Thessalonians	1 Thessalonians	1 Thessalonians
1 Thessalonians	2 Thessalonians	2 Thessalonians	2 Thessalonians

---

[46] For more detailed discussion of these verses, see B. Nongbri, "Two Neglected Textual Variants in Philippians 1," *JBL* 128 (2009): 803-8.

[2 Thessalonians]⁴⁷	Hebrews	1 Timothy	1 Timothy
[Philemon]	1 Timothy	2 Timothy	2 Timothy
	2 Timothy	Titus	Titus
	Titus	Philemon	Philemon
	Philemon	Hebrews	[Laodiceans]⁴⁸

We have already seen that there is evidence for additional collections with still more varied contents and orders (such as the indications that in an ancestor of Codex Vaticanus Hebrews was found between Galatians and Ephesians). Why do the manuscripts have these peculiar shapes? It is important to remember first of all that we do not possess copies of all the letters that Paul wrote. Some have not survived. In 1 Cor 5:9, Paul mentions that he had written a letter to Corinth *before* 1 Corinthians was written. This earlier letter is lost to us. Furthermore, some of the letters we do possess seem to be composed of fragments of different letters. The prime example of this phenomenon is the text we now call 2 Corinthians. Many scholars believe 2 Corinthians actually contains fragments of six or more separate letters.[49] This situation raises several questions related to the surviving manuscripts of Paul's letters: Who would have edited Paul's letters in this way? When and why would they have done so? Is such editing somehow related to the collecting of the other letters? It also highlights an issue I mentioned briefly at the outset, the problem of the "original text." If 2 Corinthians actually contains parts of several different letters, what does it mean to speak of the "original" text of 2 Corinthians? Does that mean the earliest version of the composite letter? Or the earliest version of one or more of the letters that make it up? These are difficult questions with which even experienced scholars struggle to come to terms.

There are a number of different theories of how the letters of Paul came to be collected and copied into the type of continuous manuscripts that have survived antiquity. Some scholars suggest that Paul made an initial collection of some of his own letters and edited them himself.[50] We know of other ancient collections of letters that were initiated by the authors themselves. Perhaps the most famous example is the collection of Cicero. If Paul collected and edited his own letters for a broader audience, he would fit the pattern of

---

[47] As I noted earlier, P⁴⁶ breaks off toward the end of 1 Thessalonians. It appears that there only would have been space in the single quire of P⁴⁶ for 2 Thessalonians and Philemon, but this assessment is necessarily speculative.

[48] On page 100 of this codex, the ending of the Letter to Philemon is followed by the title "The Letter to the Laodiceans begins . . ." but the Greek then breaks off and another treatise fills the next several pages.

[49] For a more detailed treatment of these issues, see the contribution on 2 Corinthians by Laurence Welborn in this volume. Some scholars have argued that the versions of Philippians and Romans preserved in the manuscripts are also composite letters assembled from portions of other letters.

[50] This theory has most recently been argued by David Trobisch, *Paul's Letter Collection: Tracing the Origins* (Minneapolis: Fortress, 1994).

highly educated elite men of the Roman age who brought together their letters with the goal of publishing them for a wider audience. Yet, there is no direct evidence that such a process took place in Paul's case. That is to say, there is no statement in Paul's writings comparable to Cicero's comment to his friend Atticus: "There is no collection of my letters, but Tiro [Cicero's slave] has about seventy, and some can be got from you. Those I ought to see and correct, and then they may be published."[51] Other scholars have argued that Paul's letters were collected immediately after his death by an admirer. Another popular proposal is that there were multiple different local collections of Paul's letters in different cities that only later found their way into the more comprehensive collections familiar to us.[52] Given the limited evidence that we possess (recall that our earliest surviving manuscripts of Paul's letters are likely no earlier than the third century), it is not possible to rule out any of these suggestions. Nevertheless, it is still worthwhile to survey the data we do possess.

One point seems reasonably clear: The letters attributed to Paul, although they were addressed to individual churches or multiple churches in a given civic area, circulated among multiple groups. This much is indicated by the instructions in Col 4:16: "When this letter has been read among you all, see to it that it is read among the Laodiceans and that you all also read the letter from the Laodiceans," presumably referring to a letter written in Paul's name in the possession of the Laodiceans. At some point in the late first or early second century, it seems that individuals or groups began making collections of these letters. For instance, some time in the first half of the second century, Polycarp, the leader of a Christian community in Smyrna (a city in Asia Minor), wrote a letter to Christians in Philippi, in which he mentions "the letters" (plural) that the Philippians received from Paul.[53] This statement

---

[51] *Letters to Atticus* 16.5. The text and translation are from the Loeb edition of E. O. Winstedt, *Cicero: Letters to Atticus* (London: William Heinemann, 1961 [orig. 1918]). Even Cicero's statement here is not secure evidence that Cicero himself ever did *actually* carry out the collection and publication of his letters. See the discussion in M. Beard, "Ciceronian Correspondences: Making a Book Out of Letters," in T. P. Wiseman, ed., *Classics in Progress: Essays on Ancient Greece and Rome* (Oxford: Oxford University Press, 2002), 103-44. A more certain example would be the letters of Pliny the Younger, a Roman aristocrat active in the late first and early second century. The first book of his collected letters begins with a cover letter stating the origin of the collection: "You have often urged me to collect and publish any letters of mine which were composed with some care. I have now made a collection . . ." For a Latin text and translation, see the Loeb edition of B. Radice, *Pliny: Letters, Volume 1: Books 1–7* (Cambridge, Mass.: Harvard University Press, 1969).
[52] For further details of these theories, see E. H. Lovering, Jr., "The Collection, Redaction, and Early Circulation of the *Corpus Paulinum*" (Ph.D. diss., Southern Methodist University, 1988).
[53] See Polycarp's *Letter to the Philippians* 3.2. For a Greek text and English translation, see the edition of B. D. Ehrman in the Loeb Classical Library, *The Apostolic Fathers* (Cambridge, Mass.: Harvard University Press, 2003). Chapter 47 of *1 Clement*, a letter written from followers of Jesus at Rome to the Corinthian congregation(s) at perhaps the end of the first century, mentions a letter from Paul to the Corinthians (which overlaps at least partly with 1 Corinthians), indicating that at least some of Paul's Corinthian correspondence was known at Rome (for text and translation, see Ehrman, *The Apostolic Fathers*). 2 Pet 3:15-16 also refers to "letters" of Paul that are "difficult to interpret," which would seem to indicate knowledge of a collection of Paul's

suggests the existence in the early second century of a collection of Paul's letters in Smyrna, though one that differed from the collections now known to us, which contain only a single letter from Paul to the Philippians. We do not have any direct evidence for the process by which Paul's letters were collected at this early stage, but we do have some evidence for the manner in which another collection of letters was produced by a network of early Christian communities. Ignatius was a Christian from Antioch who, like Paul, wrote a series of letters to assemblies in Asia Minor and Rome. Ignatius was likely active in the first quarter of the second century. After Ignatius had died, Polycarp, in his own letter to the Philippians that I have already mentioned, wrote the following: "Just as you requested, we are sending you the letters of Ignatius, which were sent to us by him, as well as other letters of his that we possess. These are attached to this letter."[54] Thus, at the instigation of someone in Philippi, Polycarp produced a collection of Ignatius' letters (although it seems that a smaller collection had already been gathered in Polycarp's home city, Smyrna). It is easy to imagine a similar kind of process taking place to bring about a collection (or multiple different local collections) of Paul's letters. What seems most likely to me is the theory of a gradual accumulation of different collections. Copies of one or more of these local collections of letters may then have eventually found their way to a scholarly center like Alexandria where higher quality, more comprehensive copies were produced.[55] I want to emphasize, however, that this scenario is highly speculative.

We are on somewhat firmer ground when it comes to the evidence from the middle of the second century. We have a reasonably good idea of the contents of at least one collection of Paul's letters known in the city of Rome at that time. Around the year 140, a Christian called Marcion of Sinope (Sinope is an area in what is now northern Turkey) came to Rome and promoted what has been called the first Christian canon, a closed group of texts that apparently consisted of a short version of Luke's Gospel, a composition by Marcion himself called "The Antitheses," and a collection of Paul's letters that appears to have included (apparently in this order) only Galatians, 1 and 2 Corinthians, Romans, 1 and 2 Thessalonians, Laodiceans (generally thought to be the letter usually called Ephesians), Colossians and

---

epistles. This piece of evidence is, however, not very useful because the date of 2 Peter is notoriously hard to establish. The first explicit evidence for its existence is not until Origen (late second or early third century), who seems to have regarded 2 Peter as a forgery. See Eusebius, *Hist. eccl.* 6.25.8 (a text and translation of the passage is available in the Loeb Classical Library edition, *Eusebius: The Ecclesiastical History* [London: Heinemann, 1932]).

[54] See Polycarp's *Letter to the Philippians* 13.2.

[55] The thesis that Paul's letters were edited at Alexandria is most closely associated with G. Zuntz, *The Text of the Epistles: A Disquisition upon the Corpus Paulinum* (London: Oxford University Press, 1953). Zuntz assumed that there was a Christian scriptorium in Alexandria by the end of the second century, but this thesis has been strongly challenged by Haines-Eitzen, *Guardians of Letters*, 77-104.

Philemon, and Philippians.⁵⁶ Some scholars believe that Marcion made this collection himself, since the placement of Galatians at the head of the collection seems to fit well with one of Marcion's main concerns, an attack on what he regarded as the "old" law. Others, however, have argued that Marcion did not create this particular collection of Paul's letters but claim instead that such a collection of Paul's letters was already in existence, and it just happened to suit Marcion's needs.⁵⁷ Whatever the case may be, the order of Marcion's collection of Paul's letters helps to relativize the more common order and raises the question of how the placement of Romans at the beginning of the collection of Paul's letters in modern translations tends to affect our overall reading of Paul's letters. Marcion's collection of Paul's letters seems to have stimulated the production of other more inclusive collections of Paul's letters. The writings of Irenaeus, the bishop of Lyon in the latter part of the second century, contain citations from thirteen of the fourteen letters generally attributed to Paul in the Greek manuscripts (only reference to Philemon is missing), suggesting that he probably had access to a collection of fourteen letters.⁵⁸

5. Conclusion

The manuscripts of Paul's letters, like the manuscripts of other parts of the New Testament, are crucial pieces of evidence not only for the study of the earliest followers of Jesus but also for the study of late antique and medieval Christianity. The manuscripts are both the means by which scholars try to establish an early text of Paul letters and fascinating artifacts in and of themselves. The many variations in the manuscripts attest to a complex history of transmission. The letters of Paul as we encounter them in modern Bibles are thus not really the starting point for interpretation. Rather, they are already the *result* of centuries of interpretations by the numerous modern translators of the Greek texts, the many modern editors of the ancient manuscripts, and the countless ancient scribes who copied the manuscripts. Becoming familiar with the manuscripts leads to a much richer understanding

---

⁵⁶ For information about Marcion, we must rely on the writings of other later Christians who were quite hostile to him and his followers. For details about Marcion's collection of Paul's letters, we rely primarily upon works written against Marcion by Tertullian, a Christian who wrote in north Africa in the late second and early third centuries, and Epiphanius, a Christian leader in Cyprus in the fourth century. For a Latin text and English translation of Tertullian's treatise *Against Marcion*, see Ernest Evans, *Tertullian: Adversus Marcionem* (2 vols.; Oxford: Clarendon, 1927). For Epiphanius, see the Greek text of Karl Holl, revised by Jürgen Dummer, *Epiphanius II: Panarion (haereses 34-46)* (2nd ed.; Berlin: Akademie-Verlag, 1980) and the English translation by Frank Williams, *The* Panarion *of Epiphanius of Salamis: Book I (Sects 1-46)* (2nd rev. ed.; Leiden: Brill, 2009).
⁵⁷ See John J. Clabeaux, *A Lost Edition of the Letters of Paul: A Reassessment of the Text of the Pauline Corpus Attested by Marcion* (Washington: Catholic Biblical Association, 1989).
⁵⁸ See Bruce M. Metzger, *The Canon of the New Testament: Its Origin, Development, and Significance* (Oxford: Clarendon, 1987), 154.

of the letters attributed to the apostle Paul and their legacy among early Christian readers.

Recommended Reading

Bagnall, Roger S. *Early Christian Books in Egypt.* Princeton: Princeton University Press, 2009.
Carlson, Stephen C. "The Text of Galatians and its History." Ph.D. diss., Duke University, 2012. Online: http://dukespace.lib.duke.edu/dspace/handle/10161/5597.
Gamble, Harry Y. *Books and Readers in the Early Church: A History of Early Christian Texts.* New Haven: Yale University Press, 1995.
Jongkind, Dirk. "The Text of the Pauline Corpus." Pages 216-31 in *The Blackwell Companion to Paul.* Edited by Stephen Westerholm. Malden: Wiley-Blackwell, 2011.
Parker, D. C. *An Introduction to the New Testament Manuscripts and their Texts.* Cambridge: Cambridge University Press, 2008. Pages 246-82.
Pickering, S. R. "The Dating of the Chester Beatty-Michigan Codex of the Pauline Epistles (P^{46})." in *Ancient History in a Modern University, Volume 2: Early Christianity, Late Antiquity, and Beyond.* Edited by T. W. Hillard et al. Grand Rapids: Eerdmans, 1998.
Royse, James R. "The Early Text of Paul (and Hebrews)." Pages 175-203 in *The Early Text of the New Testament.* Edited by Charles E. Hill and Michael J. Kruger. Oxford: Oxford University Press, 2012.
Royse, James R. *Scribal Habits in Early Greek New Testament Papyri.* New Testament Tools, Studies, and Documents 36. Leiden: Brill, 2008. Pages 199-358.
Zuntz, Günther. *The Text of the Epistles: A Disquisition upon the Corpus Paulinum.* London: Oxford University Press, 1953.

5. Paul among the Jews[*]

Paul McKechnie

This chapter addresses a topic which has been of enhanced scholarly interest since Krister Stendahl's *Paul among Jews and Gentiles* (1976) and E. P. Sanders' *Paul and Palestinian Judaism* (1977).[1] Interest is not diminishing. Just the reverse: 2009 saw the publication of Pamela Eisenbaum's *Paul was not a Christian* and Magnus Zetterholm's *Approaches to Paul*,[2] along with Richard I. Pervo's *Acts: a Commentary*,[3] while 2010 brought Mark D. Given's *Paul Unbound* and David J. Rudolph's article on Paul's "rule in all the churches."[4] In 2011, John M. G. Barclay's *Pauline Churches and Diaspora Jews*, a collection of Barclay's papers, continued the task of putting "Pauline believers and Diaspora Jews/Judaeans into a comparative framework."[5]

Faced with such an *embarras de richesses*, this chapter will follow a narrow path, seeking not to cover subject matter belonging to other chapters in this book—particularly not those on Paul's life, Paul's theology, or the Letter to the Romans. Two areas of concern will be dealt with: first, the road to Damascus: where Paul came from, and where he went after the incident that happened on it; and second, how Paul interacted with Jews, from when Barnabas brought him to Antioch, until the time when he was in Rome awaiting trial before Caesar. The chapter as a whole is not a theological discussion, which is to say that it is not about Paul and *Judaism*, but an exploration based (for the most part) on biblical *narrative*: "Paul among the Jews," therefore, in the sense of what Paul did, and what happened to him—with some reference to why.

---

[*] I wish to thank my colleagues Drs. Cavan Concannon, Bernard Doherty, and Chris Forbes, and an anonymous referee, for valuable help with this chapter. They should not be assumed to agree with anything said here.
[1] K. Stendahl, *Paul among Jews and Gentiles* (Philadelphia: Fortress, 1976); E. P. Sanders, *Paul and Palestinian Judaism: A Comparison of Patterns of Religion* (London: SCM, 1977).
[2] P. Eisenbaum, *Paul Was Not a Christian: The Original Message of a Misunderstood Apostle* (New York: HarperOne, 2009); M. Zetterholm, *Approaches to Paul: A Student's Guide to Recent Scholarship* (Minneapolis: Fortress, 2009).
[3] R. I. Pervo, *Acts: A Commentary* (Minneapolis: Fortress, 2009).
[4] M. D. Given, ed., *Paul Unbound: Other Perspectives on the Apostle* (Peabody: Hendrickson, 2010); D. J. Rudolph, "Paul's 'Rule in All the Churches' (1 Cor 7:17-24) and Torah-Defined Ecclesiological Variegation," *Studies in Christian-Jewish Relations* 5 (2010): 1-23.
[5] J. M. G. Barclay, *Pauline Churches and Diaspora Jews* (Tübingen: Mohr [Siebeck], 2011), 9.

1. Is Saul Also Among the Prophets?[6]

Saul of Tarsus, in or about A.D. 34, was advancing beyond his contemporaries in Judaism.[7] Paul was in Jerusalem, in his twenties, at the time when Stephen the deacon was killed by stoning after his hearing in the Sanhedrin,[8] because his (Paul's) studies under Rabbi Gamaliel I[9] were still ongoing.[10] Paul's account in Galatians of his "previous way of life in Judaism," which involved his persecuting the Church of God and trying to destroy it, treats his advance in Judaism seamlessly with his zeal for the traditions of his ancestors: a zeal shown, in the learned circles Paul was part of, through studying the Bible.

Gamaliel, Saul's teacher, was at the heart of the world of Jewish learning, even though only small traces of his ideas are echoed in the Mishnah;[11] it says in *Pirke Avot* that Johanan ben Zakkai "received the Torah from Hillel and from Shammai"[12]—a schematic pronouncement, which appears to disregard a generation or so, since Hillel died about A.D. 10, whereas Johanan was young enough in 70, when Jerusalem fell, to move to Jamnia, set up the school known as "The Vineyard," and lay down precedents which shaped the practice of the Jewish religion in the absence of the Jerusalem temple.[13]

Paul's association with Gamaliel has sometimes been presented in effect as an absurdity—for example by Helmut Koester, who, in the course of expounding his view that "the Book of Acts contributes very little to our knowledge of Paul's origin and education," says that Acts 22:3 "indicates that Paul grew up in Jerusalem and studied there with the famous rabbi Gamaliel I. Since the first part of this information is not trustworthy, the second is pure invention."[14]

Koester's view is that Luke, author of Luke and Acts, belonged to the third generation of Christianity, and composed Acts using written sources (he was "certainly not a travel companion and fellow-worker of the apostle

---

[6] 1 Sam 10:9-12; cf. 19:24.
[7] Gal 1:14.
[8] Acts 7:56-60.
[9] Acts 22:3.
[10] Note also that Paul's sister's son was in Jerusalem in 58 to warn him of a plot against his life (Acts 23:16-22): Paul's family, based in Tarsus when he was born, may have relocated to Jerusalem, where Paul said (Acts 22:3) he was brought up.
[11] *m. Pirke Avot* 1.16: "Rabban Gamaliel said: 'Provide yourself with a teacher and remove yourself from doubt, and do not accustom yourself to give tithes by estimation'"; at *m. Yebamoth* 16.7 it is recorded that Nehemiah of Beth-delee told Rabbi Akiva: "I have it in tradition from the elder Rabbon Gamaliel, that a woman may re-marry on the evidence of a single witness, or of that of a woman or slave." Gamaliel's son Simeon said, "Studying Torah is not the most important thing, rather fulfilling it" (*m. Pirke Avot* 1.17): if he learnt this from his father, it might account for his father's being little quoted.
[12] *m. Pirke Avot* 2.9.
[13] For instance in relation to where it was proper to sound the ram's horn (*shofar*) when New Year's Day (*Rosh Hashanah*) fell on the Sabbath (previously, only in Jerusalem; after the destruction of the temple anywhere where there was a court [*beth din*]): *m. Rosh Hashanah* 4.1-3.
[14] Helmut Koester, *Introduction to the New Testament: History and Literature of Early Christianity, Volume 2* (Berlin: de Gruyter, 1982 [repr. 2000]), 107.

Paul"). [15] But the hypothesis that Luke wrote Acts in ca. 62 [16] accounts for the fact, otherwise hard to explain, that Acts does not complete the story of Paul's appeal to Caesar: the assumption about Acts here will be that Harnack was right, as to date, and that Acts is a document of the (first or) second, not the third, Christian generation. [17]

I will not restate Harnack's argument at length, because where dating Acts is concerned, "of making many books there is no end." [18] In brief, however, he observes that Acts ends in 62, when Paul has spent two years living at Rome, [19] and that the ending may frustrate readers who wish they could read about what happened when Paul's case came up before the emperor. Harnack accounts for the unexpected non-conclusion of Acts by arguing that the book was composed and circulated while Paul was still awaiting his hearing, and that the aim of circulating it at that time was to build awareness of Paul in the churches, and gather support for him, in advance of his case being resolved. This argument I find compelling.

2. The Big Change in Paul's Life

After the occasion when he looked after the coats of the witnesses who testified against Stephen, [20] Saul "began to destroy the Church" at Jerusalem, dragging men and women off to prison. [21] Planning to do something similar to followers of the Way in Damascus, Saul obtained letters from the high priest to the Damascus synagogues, and set off to travel there. [22] On the road, he underwent the experience which changed the direction of his life. The debate over whether this experience ought to be called a "conversion" or a "call," as Krister Stendahl argued, [23] remains unresolved. [24] Stendahl's point is that Paul

---

[15] Koester, *Introduction to the New Testament, Volume 2*, 49-50.
[16] Argued for by Adolf Harnack (*Neue Untersuchungen zur Apostelgeschichte und zur Abfassungszeit der synoptischen Evangelien* [Leipzig: Hinrich, 1911], 64-65), after Harnack changed his mind about a date in the 70s.
[17] The fullest recent discussion of the question of date is perhaps Richard I. Pervo, *Dating Acts: Between the Evangelists and the Apologists* (Santa Rosa: Polebridge, 2006), which places Acts ca. 115 (343-46); an appendix (359-63) summarizes which modern scholars have dated Acts when, from Friedrich Blass (56 or 60), to John Townsend (ca. 140 or later).
[18] Eccl 12:12.
[19] Acts 28:30.
[20] Acts 7:58.
[21] Acts 8:3.
[22] Acts 9:1-2.
[23] Stendahl, *Paul among Jews and Gentiles*, 7-23.
[24] John M. G. Barclay ("Paul Among Diaspora Jews: Anomaly or Apostate?" *JSNT* 60 (1996): 89-119, at 110), avoids engaging in the debate by using the term "transformation." N. T. Wright in a conference paper argues that "Krister Stendahl's suggestion that we should think of Paul's 'call' as opposed to his 'conversion' misses the point. For Paul, the word 'call' denoted not merely a vocation to a particular task but also, more fundamentally, the effective call of the gospel, applied by the Spirit to the individual heart and life and resulting in a turning away from idolatry and sin and a lifelong turning to God in Christ in believing allegiance" (N. T. Wright, "New Perspectives on Paul" (paper presented at the tenth Edinburgh Dogmatics Conference, Edinburgh 25–28 August 2003), n.p. [cited 27 June 2011].

"received a new and special calling in God's service" on the road to Damascus,[25] but that the event, which in the biblical text plays out in a way similar to the prophetic calls of Isaiah, Jeremiah, and Ezekiel, was not a "conversion from one 'religion' to another."[26]

Acts, notoriously, gives three accounts of Saul's experience on the road to Damascus, at 9:1-19; 22:4-16; and 26:9-19: accounts which are difficult to harmonize in detail, since (for example) it appears at Acts 9:7 that Saul's travelling companions "heard the voice but saw no one," whereas at Acts 22:9 those who were with him "saw the light but did not hear the voice of the one who was speaking."[27] Stendahl, perhaps correctly, takes the view that "what a man reveals about himself is on the whole more accurate than what is recounted by others,"[28] and therefore gives priority in his discussion to Galatians 1 where Paul says at verse 16 that through this experience God revealed his son to him "so that [he] might proclaim him among the Gentiles."

Stendahl's argument for "call, not conversion" set the cat among the academic pigeons. Alan F. Segal, in *Paul the Convert*, views Paul as a convert in the terms argued for by A. D. Nock in *Conversion*.[29] Conversion, Segal observes, need not mean moving from one religion to another: to become an Essene, he argues, Josephus would have had to become a convert, because "Essene membership came only by conversion."[30] More recently, Pamela Eisenbaum is sympathetic to rejecting the idea of Paul being converted, and cites Stendahl in the first footnote of her book.[31] She infers that "Paul was not a *Christian*—a word that was in any case completely unknown to him because it had not yet been invented."[32] At this point she seems to have recourse to a merely semantic distinction: the word was invented only a little later, at Antioch, where Barnabas and Saul had been teaching[33]—so that Paul was in on the ground floor,[34] as far as the word "Christian" was concerned.

Online: http://www.ntwrightpage.com/Wright_New_Perspectives.pdf.

[25] Stendahl, *Paul among Jews and Gentiles*, 7.

[26] Stendahl, *Paul among Jews and Gentiles*, 8-9.

[27] Charles W. Hedrick ("Paul's Conversion/Call: A Comparative Analysis of the Three Reports in Acts," *JBL* 100 [1981]: 415-32) attributes the differences to "Lucan corrections and improvements" (432).

[28] Stendahl, *Paul among Jews and Gentiles*, 7-8.

[29] Alan F. Segal, *Paul the Convert: the Apostolate and Apostasy of Saul the Pharisee* (New Haven: Yale University Press, 1990), 72-75; cf. A. D. Nock, *Conversion: The Old and the New in Religion from Alexander the Great to Augustine of Hippo* (Oxford: Clarendon, 1933).

[30] Josephus *Vita* 9-12 (= 32-67), and Segal, *Paul the Convert*, 83. Segal also argues (82) that Josephus' commitment from his nineteenth year to being a Pharisee does not count as a conversion.

[31] Eisenbaum, *Paul was not a Christian*, 3 n. 1.

[32] Eisenbaum, *Paul was not a Christian*, 4.

[33] Acts 11:25-26.

[34] Barclay (*Pauline Churches and Diaspora Jews*, 3 n. 1) writes that "the adjective 'Christian' is a convenient, and sometimes unavoidable, anachronism when speaking of the first generations of 'believers'"—which draws a fine line. Really it is barely even an anachronism.

3. Shammai, Hillel, or the Fourth Philosophy?

Paul told Agrippa II at Caesarea that he had "belonged to the strictest sect of our religion and lived as a Pharisee."[35] In the gospels, the Pharisees are more prominent than the Sadducees, and the only story centring on Jesus' interaction with Sadducees is the one about the question over the woman and the seven brothers, each of whom died and left the next one to take the widow in levirate marriage. Whose wife would she be, in the resurrection? A question arising from an erroneous assumption, Jesus suggested.[36] "Sadducees and Pharisees" can appear together in Jesus' pronouncements,[37] but there are more stories of Jesus in conflict with (only) the Pharisees.

Josephus, who describes the four "philosophies" which Jews followed in his lifetime,[38] shows the Pharisees ahead on points from the Sadducees, the Essenes, and the followers of the "fourth philosophy," which Judas the Galilean started. Judas' followers agreed with the Pharisees on most things, except that they refused to acknowledge any earthly ruler other than God.[39] As for the Pharisees, Josephus says:

> ... they are able greatly to influence the masses of the people. Whatever the people do about divine worship, prayers, and sacrifices, they perform according to their direction. The cities give great praise to them on account of their virtuous conduct, both in the actions of their lives and their teachings also.[40]

The Sadducees, who disagreed with the Pharisees on important matters (life after death; the role of tradition/commentary on Scripture), had to appear to be in agreement with the Pharisees' ideas, Josephus says, when they took public office, in order to be acceptable to the people.[41] The Essenes were a small enough minority for it to be possible for Josephus to count them—or at least, to count those who led a celibate life (Josephus is apparently referring to Qumran), of whom there were four thousand.[42]

Jacob Neusner observes that the Sadducees, Pharisees, and Essenes, as "class and sectarian divisions," had an inner life which "would have astonished the Roman administration,"[43] an administration formed from a ruling class which (until after the Jewish War) lacked a Josephus to explain to it the vitality of Israel. In the case of the Pharisees, the *Havurah*

---

[35] Acts 26:5.
[36] Matt 22:23-32; Mark 12:18-27; Luke 20:27-39.
[37] "Watch out, and beware of the yeast of the Pharisees and Sadducees" (Matt 16:6 [cf. Mark 8:15; Luke 12:1]).
[38] Josephus *A.J.* 18.11-25.
[39] Josephus *A.J.* 18.23-25.
[40] Josephus *A.J.* 18.15.
[41] Josephus *A.J.* 18.16-17.
[42] Josephus *A.J.* 18.18-22.
[43] Jacob Neusner, *A Life of Yohanan ben Zakkai, ca. 1–80 CE* (2nd ed.; Leiden: Brill, 1970), 24.

("fellowship") existed to maintain their distinctiveness and a superior level of observance of the law. As Neusner summarizes it:

> The basis of this society was meticulous observance of the laws of tithing and other priestly offerings as well as the rules of ritual purity even outside the temple where they were mandatory. The members undertook to eat even profane foods (not sacred tithes or other offerings) in a state of rigorous levitical cleanness. At table, they compared themselves to temple priests at the altar. These rules tended to segregate the members of the fellowship, for they ate only with those who kept the law as they thought proper. The fellows thus mediated between the obligation to remain within the common society and equally important precepts on religious observance. By keeping the rules of purity the fellow separated from the common man.[44]

Dating from the second century B.C. or earlier,[45] the party of the Pharisees in the days of Jesus and Paul had within it a degree of diversity in terms of how the Bible was read and the law of Moses interpreted.[46] The House of Shammai and the House of Hillel were the most important schools of thought. As the Mishnah says in *Pirke Avot*, "Hillel and Shammai received the Torah from [Shemayah and Avtalion]."[47] Shammai took over as president of the Sanhedrin after Hillel died, about A.D. 10. Shammai and his followers were the leading interpreters of the law from then until the time of the destruction of the temple in 70. Mishnah *Shabbat* records an occasion when Shammai's followers had better numbers at a meeting, and were able to use them to establish some principles:

> The following are among the decisions enacted in the Upper Hall of Hananiah, the son of Hezekiah, the son of Giorion, when they [the sages] went thither, and went up to visit him. On that occasion the sages present were counted, and [the sages of] the school of Shammai were found to be more numerous than [those of] the school of Hillel. On that day eighteen enactments were decreed.[48]

But majority voting was not the usual method of deciding on what the Bible meant, and in the long run the principles of the House of Hillel gained general acceptance, as the Talmud says:

---

[44] Neusner, *Life of Yohanan ben Zakkai*, 23.
[45] Neusner, *Life of Yohanan ben Zakkai*, 25.
[46] For present purposes there will be no attempt to draw the fine line between Pharisees and *hakhamim* whose existence Martin Goodman infers ("Josephus and Variety in First-Century Judaism," in *Judaism in the Roman World: Collected Essays* [Leiden: Brill, 2007], 33-46; first published in *Proceedings of the Israel Academy of Sciences and Humanities* 7.6 [2000]: 201-13). There, he observes (39) that "there is . . . no explicit evidence that Hillel or Shammai considered themselves to be Pharisees" and argues for a distinction between the Pharisees and those identified in Tannaitic texts as *hakhamim*, even while the kinds of Judaism which Pharisees and *hakhamim* respectively followed "must have been very similar" (44).
[47] *m. Pirke Avot* 12.
[48] *m. Shabbat* 1.4.

May, then, the rigorous ordinances of two Tanaim be applied to one case? Have we not learned in a Boraitha, that at all times the Halakha prevails according to the school of Hillel, but he who wishes to act in accordance with the school of Shamai, may follow that school exclusively both in the lenient and the rigorous ordinances, and he who wishes to act in accordance with the school of Hillel may follow that school exclusively in both lenient and rigorous ordinances. He who only follows the more lenient ordinances of both schools is a sinner, and he who follows only the more rigorous ordinances of both schools is referred to by the passage (Ecclesiastes 2:14) as "the fool walketh in darkness."[49]

This passage shows that each House gave a spectrum of rulings, some rigorous, some lenient. In retrospect, rabbinic teachers saw the disagreements between Hillel and Shammai as embodying a creative tension: "Which controversy was an example of being waged in the service of God? Such was the controversy of Hillel and Shammai."[50]

N. T. Wright argues that Paul's zeal places him as a student who leaned towards the House of Shammai rather than the House of Hillel.[51] A difficulty with this view is that his teacher Gamaliel I was the grandson or son of Hillel, and Wright's view is that "after his conversion, [Paul] changed in several notable respects, becoming in some ways apparently closer to Hillel."[52] The great care over tithing, and over ritual purity of food and garments, which was enacted through the *Havurah*, was shared by both Houses, although they differed on how long an individual had to stay in the novitiate stage of membership[53]—so that it is clear that the distance between the Houses was relatively small, and perhaps a situation in which a pupil of Hillel's grandson Gamaliel had a preference for Shammai's method of interpreting biblical law could be contemplated without much difficulty.

Shammai's second maxim, after "Make your study of Torah a fixed habit," was "Say little and do much."[54] Application of that principle might have been seen as consistent with what Paul did when he hauled sinners off to be imprisoned; in New Testament retrospect, however, Paul appeared as "a blasphemer, a persecutor, and a man of violence."[55] But in 1999, Mark R.

---

[49] *b. Erubin* 1.

[50] *m. Pirke Avot* 5.20.

[51] N. T. Wright, "Paul, Arabia, and Elijah (Galatians 1:17)," *JBL* 115 (1996): 683-92 at 685-86.

[52] N. T. Wright, *The New Testament and the People of God* (Minneapolis: Fortress, 1992), 202; Wright refers to earlier discussion arguing for Paul as a follower of either House, in Joachim Jeremias, "Paulus als Hillelit" in E. E. Ellis and M. Wilcox, eds., *Neotestamentica et Semitica: Studies in Honour of M. Black* (Edinburgh: T. & T. Clark, 1969), and in F. F. Bruce, *Paul: Apostle of the Heart Set Free* (Grand Rapids: Eerdmans, 1977), respectively.

[53] *Tosefta Demai* 2.12: "Until when is a man accepted? The House of Shammai say, For liquids, thirty days; for clothing, twelve months. The House of Hillel say, For either, thirty days." Cf. Jacob Neusner, *Fellowship in Judaism: The First Century and Today* (London: Valentine, Mitchell, 1963), 25-28.

[54] *m. Pirke Avot* 1.15.

[55] 1 Tim 1:13.

Fairchild proposed a more radical view of Paul's place in the spectrum of Jewish factions, arguing that he was a Zealot. The word (ζηλωτής) is used in connection with Paul at Gal 1:14 and Acts 22:3, where English translations tend to avoid the technical term;[56] but rendering the word as "zealous" rather than "Zealot" is defensible in both those places, and its use to describe Paul is not enough by itself to prove that he was associated with Judas the Galilean's party.

In Josephus' description of the "fourth philosophy," as he calls Judas the Galilean's party (to distinguish it from Essenism, Sadducaism, and Pharisaism), he says: "This school agrees in all other things with the Pharisaic notions, except that they have an unconquerable passion for liberty, and say that God is to be their only Ruler and Lord."[57] The "fourth philosophy" has usually been identified as being the same thing as the party of the Zealots. Richard A. Horsley and John S. Hanson, however, argue that the two phenomena are not the same: they argue that the Zealots "originated as a coalition of brigand groups entering Jerusalem from the countryside in late 67,"[58] after the beginning of the first Jewish War.

Horsley and Hanson place the "fourth philosophy" as an intellectual movement, "composed of, or at least led by, Pharisaic and other teachers,"[59] and they distinguish it sharply from the "bands of brigands"[60] who jelled into the force which took control of Jerusalem between 67 and 69.[61] But Fairchild's objection that the "fourth philosophy," the bandits, the Sicarii, and the Zealots were probably not as unconnected as Horsley and Hanson say they were has considerable force,[62] so that it seems best not to follow Horsley and Hanson, except by agreeing that the word "Zealot" must have gained a new and more precise meaning after 67.

Being a Zealot, assuming that Josephus is right, would not have involved Paul subscribing to different religious theories than a Pharisee. Fairchild's argument for placing him as a Zealot rests on other grounds:[63] he notes the two places where Jerome says that Paul's parents' home town was Gischala,[64] the last city captured in Galilee by Titus at the end of the first Jewish War;[65] and he argues that when Paul's parents were moved from there to Tarsus (as Jerome says they were), they had been sold as slaves, in the course of the

---

[56] In the NRSV, for example: ". . . *zealous* for the traditions of my ancestors" (Gal 1:14); ". . . *zealous* for God" (Acts 22:3).
[57] Josephus *A.J.* 18.23-25.
[58] Richard A. Horsley and John S. Hanson, *Bandits, Prophets, and Messiahs: Popular Movements at the Time of Jesus* (San Francisco: Harper & Row, 1985), 220.
[59] Horsley and Hanson, *Bandits, Prophets, and Messiahs*, 198.
[60] Horsley and Hanson, *Bandits, Prophets, and Messiahs*, 217.
[61] Horsley and Hanson, *Bandits, Prophets, and Messiahs*, 218-19.
[62] Mark R. Fairchild, "Paul's Pre-Christian Zealot Associations: A Re-examination of Gal 1:14 and Acts 22.3," *NTS* 45 (1999): 514-32, at 518 n. 22.
[63] Fairchild, "Paul's Zealot Associations," 515-17.
[64] Jerome, *Comm. Philm.* 5.23 and *Vir. ill.* 5.
[65] Josephus *B.J.* 4.84.

Romans' establishment of control of Galilee.[66] When Fairchild speculates that Paul "was born a citizen"[67] at Tarsus because he was born after his parents had been manumitted, he seems not to have registered that Jerome wrote of Paul being deported from Gischala with his parents. Martin Hengel, however, deals with the point, citing Photius' explanation that Paul was conceived at Gischala but born in Tarsus.[68] Like Fairchild, Hengel does not argue against Paul's connection with the town of Gischala.

Galilee in general, and Gischala in particular, may constitute a relatively strong point in favor of Paul as a Zealot. John of Gischala was a "very cunning and knavish person"[69] of whom Josephus disapproved; but John hardly measured up to Josephus' picture of the followers of the "fourth philosophy" as agreeing with the Pharisees:

> . . . the food was unlawful that was set upon his table, and he rejected those purifications that the law of his country had ordained; so that it was no longer a wonder if he, who was so mad in his impiety towards God, did not observe any rules of gentleness and common affection towards men.[70]

So, although Fairchild's observation that Paul tended in his letters to keep his association with Tarsus in the background (it being mentioned only in Acts[71]) is well made[72] and his explanation of why the term "Zealot" is not used, perhaps avoided, at Phil 3:5-6 is persuasive[73] his case for Paul as a Zealot remains inconclusive. Wright draws attention to the way "the words 'zeal' and 'zealous' were . . . used in connection with all sorts of Jews who were zealous for God and the Torah, and some of whom carried their 'zeal' to the lengths of violence"[74]—but cautions that not all were connected with "the Zealots."

4. The Road from Mount Sinai

After his call, and "several days" in Damascus,[75] Paul (as he says himself) "went away at once into Arabia, and afterwards . . . returned to Damascus."[76] Not until A.D. 106 was there a Roman province of Arabia, but the geographical term was well understood, and referred to the area to the south

---

[66] Fairchild, "Paul's Zealot Associations," 519.
[67] Acts 22:28.
[68] Martin Hengel, *The Pre-Christian Paul* (Philadelphia: SCM, 1991), 14, citing Photius at n. 106 (cf. Photius *Epistles* 246, lines 1-10).
[69] Josephus *B.J.* 2.585.
[70] Josephus *B.J.* 7.264.
[71] Acts 9:11, 30; 11:25; 21:39; 22:3.
[72] Fairchild, "Paul's Zealot Associations," 516: ". . . one may detect Paul's embarrassment that his days in Tarsus could be seen as a detriment to his exemplary Jewish credentials."
[73] Fairchild, "Paul's Zealot Associations," 528.
[74] Wright, *New Testament and the People of God*, 180.
[75] Acts 9:19.
[76] Gal 1:17.

of the provinces of Judaea and Syria, whose principal city was Petra, and which extends down into the Sinai Peninsula. Paul, when he discusses the allegorical meaning of the two mothers of Abraham's children, Hagar and Sarah, explains that Hagar is "from Mount Sinai, bearing children for slavery. Now Hagar is Mount Sinai in Arabia," he adds, "and corresponds to the present Jerusalem."[77]

In his discussion of Paul's sojourn in Arabia, Wright draws attention to correspondences between Paul's retreat into Arabia and what Elijah did after killing the prophets of Baal:[78] travelling for forty days and forty nights to the mountain of God.[79] Paul returned to Damascus after his time in Arabia,[80] and, as Wright notes,[81] Elijah, too, was sent from Mount Horeb (= Sinai) to "the wilderness of Damascus."[82] Wright's argument is that Paul did not travel to Arabia to commence his mission to the Gentiles,[83] but, in effect, to contemplate the limitations of zealous and violent action and to seek a way of reordering his own life.

Magnus Zetterholm perhaps goes too far in doubting whether Paul during his "several days" in Damascus began at once to "proclaim Jesus in the synagogues, saying 'He is the Son of God.'"[84] Zetterholm characterizes this as "working as a missionary,"[85] and hesitates to take it at face value because of the "rather long process of resocializing, including the social as well as the cognitive aspects" which he argues that Paul must have undergone. Paul, however, had been struck blind, not dumb. While Zetterholm's argument about Paul's "process of resocializing" is persuasive, it need not imply that Paul experienced inability to speak on the subject which mattered to him. The longer process of resocializing, however, was incomplete, from the viewpoint of some of his contemporaries, in about 37, three years after Paul's call, when, having been let down in a basket to get out of Damascus and away from King Aretas' attempt to have him arrested,[86] he arrived in Jerusalem and stayed with Cephas (Peter) fifteen days. In Galatians, Paul makes the point that the only apostles he saw on that visit were Peter, and James the Lord's brother[87]—but Acts puts a different gloss on the visit, saying that the disciples were all afraid of him, and he had to be introduced to the apostles by

---

[77] Gal 4:24-25.
[78] 1 Kgs 18:20-40.
[79] 1 Kgs 19:8.
[80] Gal 1:17.
[81] Wright, "Paul, Arabia, and Elijah," 686-87.
[82] 1 Kgs 19:15.
[83] Wright, "Paul, Arabia, and Elijah," 687.
[84] Acts 9:20.
[85] Zetterholm, *Approaches to Paul*, 20.
[86] 2 Cor 11:32; cf. Acts 9:23-25. On this incident see L. L. Welborn, "The Runaway Paul," *HTR* 92 (1999): 115-63, observing (116) that "the promise of the passage for historical knowledge has hitherto failed to fulfil the historian's hope," and presenting a detailed argument (120-161) to the effect that narrating this incident was an important move in relation to Paul's strategy of presenting himself as "a fool" in 2 Corinthians.
[87] Gal 1:19.

Barnabas,[88] who informed them that he had been speaking in the name of Jesus in Damascus.

Where Paul in Galatians says that he "went into the regions of Syria and Cilicia,"[89] Acts writes of him being sent off to Tarsus.[90] He was there a dozen years or more. Going to Tarsus after his fifteen-day visit to Jerusalem, even if Paul would have been reluctant to call it "going home," was consistent with his sense of being called to "proclaim [Jesus] among the Gentiles."[91] Damascus, which Paul had left, was in the province of Syria; but his mention in Galatians of going into Syria surely refers to his move, after he had been in Cilicia a good many years, to Antioch, when Barnabas brought him there,[92] after early preaching in Antioch had resulted in "a great number [becoming] believers and [turning] to the Lord."[93]

5. The Road from Antioch

At Antioch, Paul spent a year meeting with the church and teaching a great many people, after Barnabas had brought him there.[94] This was the service (διακονία) after completing which the two of them returned to Jerusalem.[95] This was fourteen years on from Paul's call—if this journey to Jerusalem with Barnabas is the one referred to in Galatians, where Paul writes that he went in response to a revelation, and explained to "those who seemed [to be leaders]" (τοῖς δοκοῦσιν) the gospel he was preaching to the Gentiles.[96]

Acts narrates what followed: chapters 13–20 deal with Paul's travels from when the church at Antioch commissioned them ("Set apart for me Barnabas and Saul for the work to which I have called them")[97] until the time when Paul left Asia,[98] heading for Jerusalem, and the sequence of events which would bring him to Rome. These eight chapters provide the substance of what is

---

[88] Acts 9:26-27.
[89] Gal 1:21.
[90] Acts 9:30.
[91] Gal 1:16.
[92] Acts 11:25.
[93] Acts 11:21.
[94] Acts 11:26.
[95] Acts 12:25.
[96] Gal 2:1-2. The majority view would be that this passage refers to the council at Jerusalem described in Acts 15 (e.g. John Knox, "'Fourteen Years Later': A Note on the Pauline Chronology," *JR* 16 [1936]: 341-49 at 341); the difficulties with that view are, first, that the visit described in Galatians is a private meeting (Gal 2:2), while the council in Acts involves "the whole assembly" (15:12), and second, that the idea of Paul consulting the acknowledged leaders about the gospel he preached to the Gentiles only *after* his journey into Pisidia appears less logical than the idea that he would consult before he and Barnabas set sail from Antioch. Accordingly it is assumed here that "Gal 2:1-2 = Acts 12:25." Pervo at *Acts: A Commentary*, 317 n. 7 views Acts as "quite possibly dependent on Galatians here." The difference in listings of personnel (Paul, Barnabas, Titus vs. Paul, Barnabas, John Mark) does not seem to be much of a difficulty.
[97] Acts 13:1-3.
[98] Acts 20:38.

known about how Paul related to Jews in the Diaspora, and to Gentiles in their world. Paul visits eight named synagogues (at Salamis,[99] Antioch of Pisidia,[100] Iconium,[101] Thessalonica,[102] Beroea,[103] Athens,[104] Corinth,[105] and Ephesus[106]), receiving varying responses.

Acts 13–20 has been constructed with care as a showcase for Paul's activity in defining and spreading the gospel.[107] It begins with a miracle (the blinding of Bar-Jesus/Elymas at Paphos[108]) and a sermon (given by Paul in the synagogue at Antioch of Pisidia[109]), and ends, similarly, with a miracle and a sermon: the raising of Eutychus at Troas,[110] followed by Paul's address, given at Miletus, to church elders from Ephesus.[111] There is, then, a marked element of patterning in how the story is told. This feature functions to draw attention to Paul's sermon at Antioch of Pisidia: included as a programmatic statement introducing the theme which is developed through the travel narrative as a whole, it represents the content of the "gospel for the Gentiles" which Paul had run past the Jerusalem brethren before setting out.

Now is the time to add that the views of those who have argued that Paul cannot have preached in synagogues[112] are treated as implausible in this chapter: the majority view,[113] which accepts the historicity of Paul's preaching in synagogues, is followed. Recently, however, a second and arguably complementary idea has been put forward by Douglas A. Campbell, who argues that Gal 5:11 (". . . why am I still being persecuted if I am still preaching circumcision?") implies that Paul used to preach circumcision. Campbell's view is that at a date prior to the writing of Galatians, Paul

---

[99] Acts 13:5: "When they arrived at Salamis, they proclaimed the word of God in the synagogues of the Jews"—implying more than one synagogue at Salamis, or at least in Cyprus.
[100] Acts 13:14.
[101] Acts 14:1.
[102] Acts 17:1.
[103] Acts 17:10.
[104] Acts 17:17.
[105] Acts 18:4.
[106] Acts 18:19; 19:8.
[107] Zetterholm perhaps goes too far in presuming that Paul and John (Mark) "acted as assistants to Barnabas on the mission journey," and adding, "It was not yet a question of independent missionary work for Paul" (*Approaches to Paul*, 22): by the time they sail from Paphos at Acts 13:13, the party is "Paul and his companions"—although this comes after Paul has called blindness down on Elymas, a mighty act which perhaps made it clearer than it had been hitherto who was to take the lead.
[108] Acts 13:6-11.
[109] Acts 13:16-47.
[110] Acts 20:7-12.
[111] Acts 20:17-35.
[112] For example Walter Schmithals in *Paul and James* (trans. D. M. Barton; Naperville: Alec R. Allenson Inc., 1965), who writes at 59-60: "In spite of Acts, Paul did not engage in a mission to the Jews . . ."
[113] As taken for instance by Zetterholm at *Approaches to* Paul, 22, and by Segal at *Paul the Convert*, 222. Wayne A. Meeks, *The First Urban Christians: the Social World of the Apostle Paul* (New Haven: Yale University Press, 1983), 168, seems to adopt an agnostic position, writing of "the author of Acts . . . imagining Paul trying in every place first to win the Jewish community whole," then adding, "Perhaps that happened, but Paul says nothing of it."

expected non-Jewish male converts to adopt full Jewish law-observance.[114] His argument in favor of this view is that those who have ruled it out, have done so in reliance on "the Lutheran reading" (Krister Stendahl's phrase) of Paul, whereby the apostle *could not* have changed his mind on this important point.[115] Campbell's discussion, however, establishes only a necessary, but not a sufficient, condition towards demonstrating his case (if it is *not impossible* that Paul changed his mind, it is not thereby proven that he *did*). A further weakness is that Campbell does not take the step of attempting to integrate the phase in Paul's preaching whose existence he posits into an updated narrative of Paul's life. In summary, Campbell's idea that Paul at some (early) point advocated circumcision for Gentile men who turned to Christ cannot be dismissed out of hand, but has perhaps not yet been shown to be more likely than the alternative.

The Antioch of Pisidia sermon starts with a haggadic narrative commencing from the election of Israel and the sojourn in Egypt, but moving forward via Saul son of Kish and David son of Jesse, to Jesus, endorsed by John but put to death and buried. Paul speaks of God raising Jesus from the dead, and proceeds to his conclusion:

> Let it be known to you therefore, my brothers, that through this man forgiveness of sins is proclaimed to you; by this Jesus everyone who believes is set free from all those sins from which you could not be freed by the law of Moses.[116]

Then a coda to the sermon warns against unbelief, Paul quoting Habakkuk: ". . . in your days I am doing a work, a work that you will never believe, even if someone tells you."[117]

This sermon is directed at a mixed audience in a Jewish context, Paul starting to speak by saying: "You Israelites, and others who fear God . . ." A. T. Kraabel in 1982 argued that synagogues in Asia Minor were likely to be more like the Sardis synagogue community than the Roman Jewish community, which was mostly of servile origin. At Sardis, where a synagogue of late Roman date was excavated, the Jewish community was "prosperous" and "an influential group within the city."[118] Antioch of Pisidia was a smaller

---

[114] Douglas A. Campbell, "Galatians 5:11: Evidence of an Early Law-Observant Mission by Paul?" *NTS* 57 (2011): 325-47 at 340.

[115] Campbell, "Galatians 5:11," 342-44.

[116] Acts 13:38-39.

[117] Acts 13:41, cf. Hab 1:5.

[118] A. T. Kraabel, "The Roman Diaspora: Six Questionable Assumptions," *JJS* 33 (1982): 445-64 at 457. Andrew R. Seager writes of the synagogue at Sardis "in its initial form" being completed about the second half of the second century A.D. ("The Building History of the Sardis Synagogue," *American Journal of Archaeology* 76 [1972]: 425-35 at 432); more recently, Jodi Magness has argued for the main hall and forecourt of the (excavated) synagogue being constructed in the sixth century, not the fourth ("The Date of the Sardis Synagogue in Light of the Numismatic Evidence,"*American Journal of Archaeology* 109 [2005]: 443-47 at 443), but she notes (447 n. 12) a coin of Marcus Aurelius (A.D. 161–180) or Commodus (A.D. 180–192) found in the bedding of the floor of stage 2 of the building. Though not completed in its

and less rich city than Sardis, but the synagogue congregation included "many Jews and devout converts to Judaism" who followed Paul and Barnabas after the meeting at which Paul laid out his program:[119] and then, the next week, "almost the whole city gathered to hear the word of the Lord" and "the Jews ... were filled with jealousy."[120]

Mark D. Nanos, analysing Paul's own writing about the Jews, comments that:

> Paul's rhetoric, addressed to non-Jews, is often developed in conflict with rival Jewish groups and their interpretations of how to live Jewishly, which emerge because of his Jewish coalition's claims that non-Jews, by way of their response to the gospel of Christ, have become included in Jewish communities, in Judaism, as equal members, apart from them becoming Jews, that is, without undertaking proselyte conversion.[121]

This argument points in the direction of Nanos' finding (same page) that "Paul's criticism was not of Judaism." The case is persuasively made; but Nanos, using in his chapter the Pauline text with relatively little reference to Acts, perhaps makes too little of the dialectic implicit in the Antioch of Pisidia incident. The Jews drove Paul out of the region, though not until "as many [Gentiles] as had been destined for eternal life became believers,"[122] and then the same thing happened at Iconium, where "a great number of both Jews and Greeks became believers," but some of the people of the city sided with the unbelieving Jews, and an attempt to "mistreat . . . and stone" them was forestalled for a while by Paul and his companions fleeing again.[123]

However sophisticated an attempt at synthesis Paul was to reach in his writings of the fifties, the antithesis generated by Paul's opponents in Antioch of Pisidia and Iconium had a powerful impact. The stoning which Paul in 2 Corinthians lists among the troubles he has undergone as a minister of Christ came from them, when they caught up with him in Lystra.[124] This observation does not, however, locate Paul as a victim. To achieve his strategic aim, "he was willing to precipitate local breaches with the synagogues," as E. A. Judge says,[125] even at the cost of Jewish members of the churches Paul established being excluded from the synagogue. Acts is explicit about unbelief being part

---

originally projected form, then, the synagogue was undergoing redevelopment on a new plan between 161 and (probably) the end of the second century.

[119] Acts 13:43.
[120] Acts 13:44-5.
[121] Mark D. Nanos, "Paul and Judaism: Why not Paul's Judaism?" in Mark D. Given, ed., *Paul Unbound: Other Perspectives on the Apostle* (Peabody: Hendrickson, 2010), 117-60, at 157.
[122] Acts 13:48-50.
[123] Acts 14:1-5.
[124] Acts 14:19-20; cf. 2 Cor 11:25.
[125] E. A. Judge, "Judaism and the Rise of Christianity: A Roman Perspective," *TynB* 45.2 (1994): 355-68 at 366: the strategic aim being (in Judge's words) "the 'grafting in' of new branches to Israel's olive tree, and the restoration of the old ones (Rom 11:17-24)."

of the motivation of the Jews from Antioch and Iconium, although jealousy is also mentioned.

And yet Paul's dangers and punishments almost certainly did not all result from reactions to his preaching. Stanley Kent Stowers writes that the punishment of thirty-nine lashes which Paul underwent five times[126] ". . . could only have been caused by Paul's attempts to win Jews to belief in the crucified messiah."[127] But his view seems to be mistaken: the Mishnah, in the place where it defines how and when the punishment of flogging[128] is to be imposed, lists a number of offences to which the sentence is appropriate—but preaching divergent ideas in the synagogue is not among them.[129] Among the offences for which one could be flogged (which included sex with the wrong person, eating temple offerings while unclean, cutting one's hair for the dead, and being tattooed), the most clearly applicable in Paul's case is the offence of eating untithed produce[130]—since he in effect says that he did it, or rather, he says that he "opposed [Cephas] to his face" at Antioch because Cephas *ceased* eating with Gentiles,[131] which meant eating untithed produce. After a visit to Derbe, Paul and Barnabas revisited the disciples in Lystra, Iconium, and Antioch before travelling back towards the coast and preaching in Perga; next, they sailed from Attalia to Syrian Antioch.[132]

The council at Jerusalem, which came in 49 or 50, "some time" after their return to Antioch,[133] was a pivotal moment. It was not precipitated directly by the interactions Paul had had with synagogues in Antioch of Pisidia, and Iconium; but the discussions arose from the agenda Paul had on his journey to Pisidia—because Paul's assertion in Pisidian Antioch that "everyone who believes is set free from all those sins from which you could not be freed by the law of Moses"[134] ran counter to what unnamed "individuals . . . from Judea" came and taught at Syrian Antioch.[135] The issue of overarching principle was already settled, according to Acts, in that Peter had already explained to the circumcised believers his vision at Joppa, as the reason why he had eaten with Gentiles at Cornelius' house in Caesarea.[136] The conclusion

---

[126] 2 Cor 11:24.
[127] Stanley Kent Stowers, "Social Status, Public Speaking, and Private Teaching: The Circumstances of Paul's Preaching Activity," *NovT* 26 (1984): 59-82 at 64. Stowers is right, however, to add (same page) that "[T]his text also shows that Paul continued to present himself as a Jew and submit to the authority of the synagogue."
[128] Deut 25:1-3.
[129] Even the matter of what would have counted as divergent was contestable: as Jacob Neusner notes (*Life of Johanan ben Zakkai*, 25-26): "no such thing as 'normative Judaism' existed, from which one or another 'heretical' group might diverge . . . In the end two groups emerged, the Christians and the rabbis, heirs of the Pharisaic sages. Each offered an all-encompassing interpretation of Scripture, explaining what it did and did not mean."
[130] *m. Makkoth* 3.1-6; eating untithed produce listed at 3.2.
[131] Gal 2:11-12.
[132] Acts 14:20-26.
[133] Acts 14:28.
[134] Acts 13:39.
[135] Acts 15:1.
[136] Acts 11:2-17.

drawn was that "God has given even to the Gentiles the repentance that leads to life."[137] But it could still be argued that food and circumcision were separable issues. James' decision was largely in Paul's favour. Judge refers to it as "conditional endorsement" of the move to include Gentiles without requiring circumcision. He sees bans of Christians from synagogues as a consequence of this decision, and adds, as the next stage in the broad sequence of events, that "The Jewish authorities (where possible) use their civil standing to dissociate themselves from the churches, which go underground, and can thus be discovered by the Romans as a threat."[138]

Equally striking in the context of the Acts narrative is that as soon as James' "conditional endorsement" has been given, Paul (back in Lystra, where he had survived the attempt to stone him, and visiting for the third time) circumcises Timothy.[139] This happened, it may be surmised, before Paul formulated his "rule in all the churches" (against, *inter alia*, seeking to be circumcised if one was uncircumcised when called),[140] and the reason given is "because of the Jews who were in those places, for they knew that his father was a Greek."[141] Richard I. Pervo notes in relation to James' "conditional endorsement" that an "unstated subsidiary point is that all the obligations of Torah remain in effect for Jews," and adds that "Acts 16:1-3 will bear this out."[142] Paul did have to think about not being stoned again;[143] and the incident fits in with the tendency Laurence M. Wills observes for the Jews in Acts to be pictured as the agents of *stasis* and disorder,[144] while Romans in general appear as reasonable figures.[145]

Travelling to Macedonia made a new start possible. At Philippi Paul and his companions apparently found no synagogue to attend on the Sabbath. Pervo raises the possibility that the word προσευχή (place of prayer: which they had expected to find by the river) may mean nothing different from

---

[137] Acts 11:18.
[138] Judge, "Judaism and the Rise of Christianity," 364.
[139] Acts 16:1-3.
[140] 1 Cor 7:17-20.
[141] Acts 16.3.
[142] Pervo, *Acts: A Commentary*, 379. It may be thought that the lucidity of this argument is undermined when Pervo adds (388), "From Acts one would infer that Timothy was considered a Gentile by local Jews, who knew that his father was such." On page 388 n. 22 Pervo summarizes positions taken on whether Jewish descent was treated as being matrilineal at the relevant date: Shaye J. D. Cohen concluding that Timothy was not Jewish, and Irina Levinskaya arguing that on balance the matrilineal principle should be accepted as having been in force. A sword which might cut this Gordian knot would be the inference that Paul himself (*au fait* with the teaching of the best contemporary interpreters of the Law of Moses) took the view that Timothy was Jewish and ought to be circumcised.
[143] Pervo, looking at this another way, says, "One must ask what Paul could possibly do to provoke further injury to his reputation among the local Jews, who were last seen hurling stones at him. Circumcision would provide no more protection for Timothy than it had for Paul" (*Acts: A Commentary*, 388).
[144] Note also Pervo (*Acts: A Commentary*, 371) on Acts 15:1: "Luke . . . characterizes them as dangerous outside agitators."
[145] Lawrence M. Wills, "The Depiction of the Jews in Acts," *JBL* 110 (1991): 631-54, at 636-38 and passim.

συναγωγή (synagogue), and "Luke has simply varied his terminology,"[146] but this is improbable, particularly because the experience Paul and the others have at Philippi is a distinctive one in comparison with what happened at the eight named synagogues in Acts 13–20. For one thing, they meet some women, but men are unmentioned;[147] and for another, the person who invites them to stay at her home is a "worshipper of God," that is, a Gentile. Indeed, Paul and Silas are the only Jews referred to at Philippi: the owners of the slave-girl whose spirit of divination Paul casts out tell the magistrates that "These men are disturbing our city: they are Jews and are advocating customs that are not lawful for us as Romans to adopt or observe."[148]

At Thessalonica, in contrast to everywhere else Paul had so far visited in Europe (Philippi, Amphipolis, Apollonia), there was a synagogue. The story there echoes the story of Paul at Antioch of Pisidia. Because of the success of Paul's preaching, "the Jews became jealous,"[149] provoked a riot, and (failing to find Paul and Silas) brought Jason, at whose house they were staying, in front of the city authorities.[150] Beroea is a coda to Thessalonica, as Iconium was to Antioch of Pisidia. Jewish antagonists follow Paul and Silas there "to stir up and incite the crowds"—that is, local people in general, not the synagogue congregation, since Paul's message had been welcomed eagerly by the Jews at Beroea. The chief target was Paul, so that it was possible for Silas and Timothy to stay behind when Paul went on to Athens.[151]

At Athens the synagogue scarcely plays a role in the drama: Paul did "[argue] in the synagogue with the Jews and the devout persons,"[152] but it was his discussions in the marketplace which led to his well-known address to the Areopagus—a Gentile and philosophical occasion.[153] After Athens, Acts bespeaks a shift in sentiment, and violence against Paul and his companions seems to cease to be effective. At Corinth, unprecedentedly, Paul spends a year and a half teaching the word of God;[154] and although Paul shakes the dust from his clothes in protest against opponents in the synagogue, they do not prevent him from moving into Titius Justus' house, next door.[155] Even bringing Paul up before the proconsul of Achaea fails to deliver the desired results for his opponents:[156] "Gallio paid no attention to any of these things" (Acts 18:17)—not even to violence against Sosthenes, the official of the synagogue (ἀρχισυνάγωγος), who presumably was responsible for bringing the case, and who apparently had no more than equivocal support from his

---

[146] Pervo, *Acts, A Commentary*, 402 n. 19.
[147] Acts 16:13-15.
[148] Acts 16:16-21.
[149] Acts 17:5, cf. 13:45.
[150] Acts 17:6-9.
[151] Acts 17:10-14.
[152] Acts 17:17.
[153] Acts 17:17-34.
[154] Acts 18:11.
[155] Acts 18:1-7.
[156] Acts 18:12-17.

constituency.[157]

Paul stayed at Corinth for "a considerable time" before leaving for Syria.[158] On the way, at Ephesus for the first time, Paul's discussion with the Jews at the synagogue was productive enough for them to ask him to stay longer;[159] but he, after visiting Jerusalem and Antioch, went to Galatia and Phrygia for the fourth time, "strengthening all the disciples."[160] Wills argues that, in the second half of Acts, "[a]n important organizing principle—perhaps the most important organizing principle of the narrative—is a repeating cycle of three dramatic moments: positive missionary activity, opposition and constriction, and release and expansion."[161] On this scheme, the Ephesus narrative in chapters 19–20 would count as a sustained phase of expansion. Paul spoke in the synagogue for three months before the controversy he caused led to his moving to the lecture hall of Tyrannus for two years, so that "all the residents of Asia, both Jews and Greeks, heard the word of the Lord."[162] As Pervo notes, Paul at Ephesus "does not announce a turn to the Gentiles."[163] The riot, when it follows,[164] is caused by Gentiles, not Jews.

The journey through Greece at the beginning of Acts 20,[165] briefly dealt with like the long fourth visit to Galatia and Phrygia, is a reminder (if reminder were needed) that Acts is a structured narrative, drawing out a sequence of significant events which the author intends to foreground. Paul's list of his own troubles in 2 Corinthians hints that events which Acts omits brought untold dramas.[166] But within the pattern created by the text of Acts, things have moved forward by the time of Paul's journey back to Jerusalem. In chapter 13, he travelled to a backwater (Antioch of Pisidia) and laid out his gospel to Jews and Gentiles in the synagogue, but in chapter 20 he can call church elders to him[167] from one of the great cities of the eastern Mediterranean. He has built a church in Asia, by "[testifying] to both Jews

---

[157] Wills comments, "This Sosthenes is not likely a convert to Christianity and is also not likely the same as the Sosthenes in 1 Cor 1:1. The beating he receives at the hands of the citizenry is seen by Luke as the just punishment for bringing false charges" ("Depiction of the Jews in Acts," 637). Pervo (although discussing the possibility that Gentiles were involved) adopts the view that those who beat Sosthenes were Jews (*Acts: A Commentary*, 454 and n. 93), and preaches a little sermon: "For Christian readers of today, this episode should bring discomfort . . . Christians should repudiate the sentiment herein expressed . . . Apology, rather than apologetics, is in order" (455).
[158] Acts 18:18.
[159] Acts 18:19-20.
[160] Acts 18:22-23.
[161] Wills, "Depiction of the Jews in Acts," 639, with table 1 at 640-42.
[162] Acts 19:8-10.
[163] Pervo, *Acts: A Commentary*, 470. At *Dating Acts* 104-5, with table 4.24, Pervo summarizes the places where Acts speaks of going to the Jews first and turning to the Gentiles "only in the face of rejection."
[164] Acts 19:21-41.
[165] Acts 20:1-4.
[166] 2 Cor 11:23-27.
[167] Acts 20:17.

and Greeks about repentance toward God and faith towards our Lord Jesus."[168]

6. The Road to Rome

Back in Jerusalem, Paul was in another world—a world (on the positive side) with "thousands of believers . . . among the Jews, all zealous for the law."[169] Not that Jerusalem was less dangerous than the Diaspora environment, and in the medium term Jesus' brother James, who in Acts 15 had conditionally endorsed the move to include Gentiles in the Christian community without circumcision, was to be killed (in 62, five years or so after Paul's return to Jerusalem), on the authority of the High Priest Ananus son of Ananus, when Festus, the Roman procurator, had died in office.[170] James' first move, when he met Paul, was to advise him to join with four men of James' community in discharging their (Nazirite) vow—as a demonstration that he (Paul) "observe[d] and guard[ed] the law."[171]

Even if James' sense of what would avoid damage to community relations in Jerusalem was in principle correct, Paul's past caught up with him. Jews from Asia claimed that he had brought Greeks into the temple, and incited a riot in which Paul was seized, dragged out of the temple, and beaten.[172] His arrest, which saved him from being killed then and there,[173] began the sequence of interactions with the Roman authorities and the Jerusalem temple authorities which ended with Paul being taken to Rome to appear before the emperor.

In the cities of the Greek-speaking Diaspora, Jewish communities had relatively little influence. A low point is reached in the narrative of Acts at Corinth, where Gallio refuses to listen to the Jews' case, and even pays no attention when Sosthenes is beaten in front of him. But matters were different at Jerusalem. As I have observed elsewhere, Josephus describes six cases (some of them diplomatic matters, others legal cases) from Judaea dealt with before emperors at Rome after the death of Herod Agrippa I (A.D. 44) and before the cessation of sacrifices on behalf of the emperor at the temple (66).[174] It is worth noting that the Jewish side won or obtained a favorable diplomatic resolution of five of the six cases, the exception being "Jews of Caesarea Maritima vs. Antonius Felix."[175] This dispute was ended, probably in 61, by Nero issuing a rescript which annulled the equal civil rights (to those of Syrians/Greeks) which Jews at Caesarea, the capital of the province of

---

[168] Acts 20:21.
[169] Acts 21:20.
[170] Josephus *A.J.* 20.199-203; cf. Eusebius *Hist. eccl.* 2.23.1-19.
[171] Acts 21:22-24.
[172] Acts 21:27-32.
[173] Acts 21:31-35.
[174] Paul McKechnie, "Judaean Embassies and Cases before Roman Emperors, A.D. 44–66," *JTS* 56 (2005): 339-61 at 339-58.
[175] McKechnie, "Judaean Embassies and Cases," 353-56.

Judaea, previously had. (This outcome, Josephus called "the cause of the troubles which afterwards came upon our nation."[176]) But the Caesarea case was the only one of the six to which the Jerusalem priesthood was not a party.

In brief, the Jerusalem priesthood was influential at Rome. To recall the summary given in my earlier article:

> In order to rule in favor of the Jerusalem priests in the middle decades of the first century, the emperors ruled against three procurators of Judaea, a legate of Syria, and Claudius' personal friend Agrippa II. Over about two decades the political priority which was accorded to giving judgments favorable to the Jerusalem priests appears to have been consistently high.[177]

Tension in Judaea was high, and in the event war was not avoided. But while it was still possible to keep a lid on the situation, Claudius, and then Nero, tried to do so. This is the background to the narrative of Acts 23–26: the appearance before the Sanhedrin, the plot to kill Paul, the move to Caesarea, Paul's appearances before Felix then (two years later) Festus, the appeal to Caesar, and the hearing before Agrippa II. Tertullus, appearing before Felix on behalf of the Jerusalem priests, did his best to broaden the case against Paul: "We have . . . found this man a pestilent fellow, an agitator among all the Jews throughout the world, and a ringleader of the sect of the Nazarenes. He even tried to profane the temple, and so we seized him."[178]

Tertullus' move to make the matter political, calling Paul "an agitator among all the Jews throughout the world," was vital. It made the case sound like something an emperor might be interested in, and so circumvented the danger that Felix would brush it off as of no importance to a Roman judge. As to legal technicalities, Justin J. Meggitt even argues that "it is problematic whether [Paul] was being accused of any crime under Roman law at all."[179] Later, indeed, when Paul became Festus' responsibility, he and Agrippa were concerned, before sending Paul to Rome, to state the charges.[180] It was a delicate matter, and Festus had to avoid seeming careless or irresponsible—so that the question of what crime might be involved was less important than an evaluation of political risk.

And so Paul was sent, under guard, to Rome. There he was welcomed by believers before he even reached the city;[181] but three days after arriving, he called together the local leaders of the Jews (τοὺς ὄντας τῶν Ἰουδαίων πρώτους) to see him,[182] and explained that his present confinement (and his forthcoming hearing) were "for the sake of the hope of Israel."[183] Not having

---

[176] Josephus *A.J.* 20.184.
[177] McKechnie, "Judaean Embassies and Cases," 361.
[178] Acts 24:5-6.
[179] Justin J. Meggitt, *Paul, Poverty, and Survival* (Edinburgh: T. & T. Clark, 1998), 94.
[180] Acts 25:10-27.
[181] Acts 28:14-15.
[182] Acts 28:17.
[183] Acts 28:20.

received letters from Judaea about Paul, the leaders were prepared to hear him speak further about his (Nazarene/Christian) sect, and came "in great numbers" on the appointed day. "From morning until evening he explained the matter to them," Acts says.[184] And at Rome, as elsewhere, "Some were convinced by what he had said, while others refused to believe."[185] By now there is long precedent for Paul's answer; indeed, it has come to summarize "Paul among the Jews": "this salvation of God has been sent to the Gentiles: they will listen."[186]

Recommended Reading

Barclay, John M. G. *Pauline Churches and Diaspora Jews*. Tübingen: Mohr (Siebeck), 2011.

Campbell, Douglas A. "Galatians 5:11: Evidence of an Early Law-Observant Mission by Paul?" *New Testament Studies* 57 (2011): 325-47.

Fairchild, Mark R. "Paul's Pre-Christian Zealot Associations: a Re-Examination of Gal 1:14 and Acts 22:3." *New Testament Studies* 45 (1999): 514-32.

Hengel, Martin. *The Pre-Christian Paul*. Philadelphia: SCM, 1991.

Horsley, Richard A., and John S. Hanson, *Bandits, Prophets, and Messiahs: Popular Movements at the Time of Jesus*. San Francisco: Harper & Row, 1985.

Judge, E. A. "Judaism and the Rise of Christianity: A Roman Perspective." *Tyndale Bulletin* 45.2 (1994): 355-68.

McKechnie, Paul. "Judaean Embassies and Cases before Roman Emperors, A.D. 44–66." *Journal of Theological Studies* 56 (2005): 339-61.

Meeks, Wayne A. *The First Urban Christians: the Social World of the Apostle Paul*. New Haven: Yale University Press, 1983.

Nanos, Mark D. "Paul and Judaism: Why not Paul's Judaism?" Pages 117-60 in *Paul Unbound: Other Perspectives on the Apostle*. Edited by Mark D. Given. Peabody: Hendrickson, 2010.

Neusner, Jacob. *Fellowship in Judaism: The First Century and Today*. London: Valentine, Mitchell, 1963.

Pervo, Richard I. *Acts: A Commentary*. Minneapolis: Fortress 2009.

Stendahl, Krister. *Paul among Jews and Gentiles*. Philadelphia: Fortress, 1976.

Wright, N. T. "Paul, Arabia, and Elijah (Galatians 1:17)." *Journal of Biblical Literature* 115 (1996): 683-92.

---

[184] Acts 28:21-23.
[185] Acts 28:24.
[186] Acts 28:28.

6. Paul among the Greeks

Christopher Forbes

When Saul of Tarsus looked at the world around him, he saw two basic categories of people: Jews and Greeks. He used a variety of essentially synonymous terms to describe these two classes: *Iudaios* and *Hellen*, *Iudaioi* and *Ethne*, and the metaphors *he peritome* and *he akrobustia*. Occasionally he used other terms: *barbaros* (Rom 1:14, Col 3:11), *Galatai* (Gal 3:1), *Makedones* (2 Cor 9:4), and *Skythes* (Col 3:11). Several of these terms are unclear or puzzling to us. Does *Iudaios* indicate what we would call ethnicity, being "a Jew," or has it more to do with geographical origins, being "a Judean"?[1] The plural *Ethne* is often translated in modern Bibles as "the Gentiles,"[2] but means more literally "the (other) nations." There are Jews, and there are the Nations, foreigners.

Once only, in Rom 1:14, does Paul describe himself as owing a metaphorical debt to both "Greeks and Barbarians." That is a distinction which would have been more natural to a Greek than to a Jew. There were Greeks, and there were *non*-Greeks, the *barbaroi*, the people who do not speak Greek but make "bar-bar-bar" noises.[3] Once he adds the term *Skythes*, "Scythian," a term Greeks used for non-Greek peoples on the north-eastern borders of their mental map of the world. For Paul, the distinction between Greeks, barbarians, and even the most remote barbarians, the Scythians, had been radically relativized in Christ.[4] Much more commonly however, his worldview uses characteristically Jewish categories. "Jews" and

---

[1] On this topic see, among others, Steve Mason, "Jews, Judaeans, Judaizing, Judaism: Problems of Categorization in Ancient History," *JSJ* 38 (2007): 457-512.

[2] "Gentiles" simply transliterates the Latin *gentiles*, which is a perfectly good translation of the Greek *ethne*.

[3] The same two-way distinction is made by Philo of Alexandria, an approximate contemporary of Paul, and a Greek-educated Jew. Philo (e.g. *Life of Moses* 2.25-27) describes his own Jewish people as "barbarians" with no apparent self-consciousness. By Philo's time, it would seem, the term had lost its pejorative flavor. It had once meant what we mean by it, "savage," uncivilized person, but by Philo's time it could indicate simply a person whose primary language was not Greek.

[4] Col 3:9-11: "you have stripped off the old self with its practices and have clothed yourselves with the new self, which is being renewed in knowledge according to the image of its creator. In that renewal there is no longer Greek and Jew, circumcised and uncircumcised, barbarian, Scythian, slave and free; but Christ is all and in all!" (NRSV) I make no judgment about the authorship of Colossians. If it is not Pauline, this passage is an entirely reasonable extension of Paul's thought.

"Greeks/Gentiles" can also be described as "the circumcision" (ἡ περιτομή) and "the uncircumcision" (ἡ ἀκροβυστία). More literally, the terms used are "the circumcised" and "the foreskinned."[5] Paul finds these categories entirely natural despite the facts that (1) neither category applied to the approximately fifty percent of the population who were women; and (2) a number of non-Jewish national or ethnic groups also circumcised their men.[6] These details are irrelevant to Paul: for him "the circumcised" are Jews, and everybody else is "foreskinned."

Most striking, however, is his simple antithesis between "Jews" and "Greeks." Paul usually writes as if Jews and Greeks between them comprise the totality of humanity. In 1 Cor 1:22-24 he first contrasts Jews and Greeks (Jews demand signs and Greeks desire wisdom), then Jews and "the nations" (a stumbling block to Jews and foolishness to the nations), and then Jews and Greeks again (those who are called, both Jews and Greeks), all in the one sentence. "The nations" are identified simply as "Greeks." Baffling though it is, Paul never once mentions "Romans" as a category—not even when writing to the Christians in Rome! Are we to presume that Paul thinks Romans are just one of many kinds of "barbarians," as might be suggested by Rom 1:13-15? Or are they a variety of Greeks?[7] Why do the Romans, the current masters

---

[5] See, for example, Gal 2:6-9: when the Jerusalem leaders saw that Paul "had been entrusted with the gospel for *the uncircumcised*, just as Peter had been entrusted with the gospel for *the circumcised* (for he who worked through Peter making him an apostle to *the circumcised* also worked through me in sending me to *the nations*)," they agreed "that we should go to *the nations* and they to *the circumcised*." Acts 10:28 adds one more term to this mix. Peter is described as contrasting Jewish men (ἀνδρὶ Ἰουδαίῳ) with "other tribes/peoples" (ἀλλοφύλῳ). Once again, there is the one universalizing term for everyone who is not Jewish.

[6] Herodotus, writing for a Greek audience in the fifth century B.C., noted that "The Egyptians and those who have learned it from them are the only people who practice circumcision" (Herodotus 2.36.3). In other passages he specifies that the Egyptians "practice circumcision for cleanliness' sake; for they would rather be clean than more becoming" (2:37:2) and that "the Colchians and Egyptians and Ethiopians are the only nations that have from the first practiced circumcision. The Phoenicians and the Syrians of Palestine acknowledge that they learned the custom from the Egyptians, and the Syrians of the valleys of the Thermodon and the Parthenius, as well as their neighbors the Macrones, say that they learned it lately from the Colchians. These are the only nations that circumcise, and it is seen that they do just as the Egyptians. But as to the Egyptians and Ethiopians themselves, I cannot say which nation learned it from the other. . ." (2.104.2-4). In the first century B.C. Diodorus Siculus paraphrases Herodotus' material (Diodorus Siculus 1.8.2-3, 1.55.5; cf. 3.32), and early in the first century A.D. Strabo claims that Egyptians and Jews (who he believes have Egyptian origins) both circumcise (περιτέμνειν) male children and "excise" (ἐκτέμνειν) female children. Philo of Alexandria was aware of the "circumcision" of women in Egypt in his time (*Questions and Answers in Genesis* 3.47); cf. Josephus, *C. Ap.* 1.169; 2.142, who is aware of the evidence of Herodotus.

[7] Intriguingly, at least one Greek intellectual in the century before Paul thought precisely this. Writing in the late first century B.C. in Rome (but for a Greek audience), Dionysius of Halicarnassus, literary critic and historian, wrote his *Roman Antiquities* with the explicit aim of demonstrating to his fellow-Greeks that "to this day almost all the Greeks are ignorant of the early history of Rome and the great majority of them have been imposed upon by sundry false opinions grounded upon stories which chance has brought to their ears and led to believe that, having come upon various vagabonds without house or home and barbarians, and even those not free men, as her founders, she in the course of time arrived at world domination . . . I shall in this Book show who the founders of the city were, at what periods the various groups came together

of the Mediterranean world, not merit a category of their own?[8] This is especially puzzling given that (1) the Acts of the Apostles reports that Paul was himself a Roman citizen; and (2) his letters to the Romans, Corinthians, and Philippians are written to cities which were Roman colonies, and Roman as much as or more than they were Greek.

To understand this peculiar conceptual framework, we need to examine it both from a cosmopolitan Greco-Roman perspective and from a more specifically Jewish perspective. What defined someone as a "Greek"?

1. "Greeks" in the Hellenistic and Roman Period

In the fifth and fourth centuries B.C. the answer to the question was reasonably simple. A Greek was someone native to the Greek homelands of (modern) Greece, the Greek Islands, and the Mediterranean coast of modern Turkey (or from the regions colonized by such people from Sicily and southern Italy to Crete, the Bosphorus, and the south-western coast of the Black Sea). Such people shared a common language, though in differing dialects, and a cultural heritage of poetry and myth. They had no political unity. Greeks lived in more than a thousand independent "city-states," but they shared a language and a culture. On the margins of the Greek world were various peoples who the Greek mainstream might have considered more or less Greek, in much the same way that Londoners might have doubts about Highland Scots being "British" (and, of course, vice versa!). One of those marginal peoples, however, the Macedonians, were about to transform the very idea of "Greekness."

Starting in 358 B.C., King Philip of Macedon organized a professional standing army[9] and began to extend Macedon's power into the mainstream of the Greek world. In a generation he had come to dominate the whole region, and was preparing for a confrontation with the huge Persian Empire, which for two centuries had ruled the region from modern Pakistan to Turkey from its heartland in Iran. When Philip was assassinated in 336 B.C., most Greeks expected his achievements to evaporate, but his twenty year old son Alexander rapidly re-asserted Macedon's position of dominance in the Greek world. He then announced a pan-Hellenic war of revenge on the Persians for their invasions of Greece, a century and a half previously. It made fine propaganda, but probably not even Alexander himself could have predicted the overwhelming military success which followed. Between 334 and 322

---

and through what turns of fortune they left their native countries. By this means I engage to prove *that they were Greeks and came together from nations not the smallest nor least considerable*." See Dionysius of Halicarnassus, *Ant. rom.* 1.4.2-5.2 (trans. E. Cary; Cambridge, Mass.: Harvard University Press, 1937), 1:15-17, emphasis mine.

[8] The question is raised provocatively by J. Barclay, in "Why the Roman Empire was Insignificant to Paul," in his *Pauline Churches and Diaspora Jews* (Tübingen, Mohr [Siebeck], 2011), 363-87.

[9] In this period Greek armies (with the exception of that of Sparta) were citizen militias, the equivalent of the National Guard or the Army Reserve. They were brave and reasonably well-trained, but they were not the equals of full-time professional troops.

B.C., Alexander led his father's veteran Macedonian troops on an unparalleled march of conquest, which placed Macedonians and their Greek allies firmly in control of an empire which reached from Macedon in the north of Greece, through Turkey, Syria, Lebanon, Israel, Egypt, Jordan, Iraq, Iran, Afghanistan, Pakistan, and to the boundaries of modern India. Over the generations which followed, Greek language and culture became dominant across this entire region. The distinction between Macedonians and other Greeks soon ceased to have any significance. And though the Kings who followed Alexander made little or no effort to spread Greek culture to the native peoples, those peoples (at least at the elite level) soon began to take on elements of Greek culture for themselves. Thus began the long-term trend known as "Hellenization": the diffusion of Greek language (*"koine"* or "common" Greek), education, art, architecture, lifestyle, and ideals. It started with the urban elites of the local peoples, and eventually penetrated down, in many places, even to the village level. The long-term result of this broad trend by Paul's time was that a Greek:

> came to mean someone who spoke flawless Greek and embraced Greek culture and institutions, regardless of national origin. . . . After two or three generations, the Greek-educated descendants of . . . former 'barbarians' might gain acceptance as 'Hellenes,' including grants of citizenship.[10]

We know, for example, that at least some Jews resident in Alexandria had achieved citizen status, with all its privileges, and many more coveted this prize.[11]

From the point of view of the wider world, then, the definition of "Greek" had broadened considerably by the first century A.D. From a Jewish point of view, the picture was different. From earliest times Jews had believed themselves chosen by God from among the nations, a people "set apart." Many aspects of their ancestral law (e.g. food taboos, rules against intermarriage) had acted to reinforce this sense of separation. After the conquests of Alexander, however, the Jewish people found themselves facing, not a variety of neighbouring nations and cultures, but one sophisticated, highly successful dominant culture. They were surrounded by the new cosmopolitan Greek culture in its local manifestations, which between 322 and 198 B.C. meant the Ptolemaic empire, based in Alexandria in Egypt. From 198 B.C. on it meant the Seleucid empire, based in Antioch in north Syria. Whether the

---

[10] C. D. Stanley, "Neither Jew nor Greek: Ethnic Conflict in Graeco-Roman Society," *JSNT* 64 (1996): 113-14.

[11] This group included several members of the family of Philo of Alexandria, a near-contemporary of Paul, and (most probably) Paul's friend and colleague Apollos, described in Acts as "a native of Alexandria . . . a learned man" (Ἀλεξανδρεὺς τῷ γένει, ἀνὴρ λόγιος, literally "an Alexandrian and a man of words." We would say, "a man of letters"). On Apollos' status see B. W. Winter, *Philo and Paul among the Sophists* (2nd ed.; Grand Rapids: Eerdmans, 2002), 175-76. For the attempts of other Alexandrian Jews to gain citizenship, see (among others) A. Kasher, *The Jews in Hellenistic and Roman Egypt: The Struggle for Equal Rights*, (Tübingen: Mohr [Siebeck], 1985).

Jewish people found this Hellenistic Greek culture attractive, threatening, or a combination of the two, they could not help being influenced by it. This applied both to the scattered communities of Jews living in various Hellenistic cities,[12] the "Diaspora," and to Jews still living in their ancestral homeland.

The interactions between Jewish and Hellenistic culture were complex, but for a variety of reasons, the mid-second century B.C. saw a major crisis develop. A campaign to encourage the urban elite of the Jewish nation to conform to cosmopolitan Hellenistic norms was initiated by a group within the Jewish elite themselves. It was eventually extended and enforced nationwide by the Seleucid overlord, Antiochus IV Epiphanes. His "persecution" of more traditional Jews led to a successful nationalist Jewish revolt against the Seleucids.[13] This revolt led to the establishment of an independent Jewish monarchy (the "Hasmonean state"), which for a time became a successful middle-ranking power in the region.

The success of the Hasmoneans and their championing of various Jewish communities outside their own borders were two factors which led to increasing tensions between Diaspora Jewish communities and their (predominantly Greek) neighbours. Wider factors seem to be involved as well. Many Jewish communities had acquired the patronage of the Romans, who were steadily encroaching on both the Hellenistic monarchies and Greek civic independence in this period. Such patronage can only have exacerbated tensions between Greek citizen-bodies, Greek civic authorities, and their Jewish minorities. Christopher Stanley documents approximately fifteen known cases of such civil disturbances in the first century B.C., and another six in the first century A.D. before the outbreak of the Jewish Revolt in 66 A.D.[14] Such struggles with their Greek neighbours strongly reinforced the Jewish view that the world which mattered to them was made up of two significant groups, themselves as Jews, and "the Greeks." Nobody else really mattered. It did not particularly concern Jews in Paul's day whether the "Greeks" with whom they had to deal were ethnically Greek in any technical sense: they spoke Greek, championed Greek culture, and were the citizens and officials of Greek cities. If it walks like a duck and quacks like a duck, it's a duck—or in this case, a Greek.

We have seen, in outline, the factors from the Hellenistic Greek side, and from the Jewish side, which shaped Paul's bi-polar ethnic world view. Next we need to examine Paul's own engagement with Greek culture. After this we

---

[12] We know of substantial Jewish communities living in Greek cities all across the Hellenistic world, with varying degrees of cultural integration with their neighbors. The largest and best known community was that in Alexandria in Egypt, where by the first century A.D. Jews may have made up between 20 and 25 percent of the population.

[13] The story is told, in some detail but from rather different points of view, in the books known as 1 and 2 Maccabees, which may be found in the Greek appendix to the Hebrew Bible (now known as the "Apocrypha"). For the complex and controversial question of this, the "Maccabean revolt," see the commentaries on 1 and 2 Maccabees, and D. J. Harrington, *The Maccabean Revolt: Anatomy of a Biblical Revolution* (Wilmington: Michael Glazier, 1988).

[14] See the evidence cited by C. D. Stanley, "'Neither Jew nor Greek': Ethnic Conflict in Graeco-Roman Society," *JSNT* 64 (1996): 101-24, esp. 102-3 and 121-22.

will consider the ways in which that worldview continued to shape his approach, even as he formed his mixed Jewish and "Greek" communities, the "assemblies of the nations" (Rom 16:3), in which he believed the distinction between Jew and Greek was to be relativized and replaced by a new unity "in Christ." Finally we will discuss the striking ways in which Paul's "conceptual map" underpins his sense of his own role in the purposes of his God.

2. Paul's Level of Engagement with Greek Culture

The question of Paul's level of Greco-Roman education has been controversial since antiquity. The second, third, and fourth-century church fathers, themselves members of a highly literate elite, are often defensive about the ways New Testament writers such as Paul did not seem to measure up to the standards of the high literary culture of their day.[15] More recently, modern scholars have debated the extent of Paul's engagement with the elite level of culture known to us from Greco-Roman literature. Adolf Deissmann (writing from the 1890s and into the 1930s) instead located Paul and his converts within the context of the papyri discovered in Egypt in the late nineteenth and early twentieth century. The New Testament writers were understood as being literate, but not literary.

Since Deissmann wrote, his basic insights have been refined considerably, and our understanding of the processes of Greek education in the Hellenistic and Roman period has also improved. Scholarship now often proceeds by describing the literary techniques taught at the various stages of the Greek curriculum, and asking which of these can be identified in Paul's own writings. Does Paul make use of maxims,[16] anecdotes,[17] and the techniques of characterization[18] and comparison?[19] If so, he had probably completed at least

---

[15] See, for example, John Chrysostom, *On the Priesthood* 4.6-7.

[16] On Paul's use of Greco-Roman maxims, see R. A. Ramsaran, "Paul and Maxims," in J. P. Sampley, ed., *Paul and the Greco-Roman World: A Handbook* (Harrisburg: Trinity Press International, 2003), 429-56.

[17] For Paul's use of *chreiae*, "anecdotes," see B. Mack, *Anecdotes and Arguments: The Chreia in Antiquity and Early Christianity* (Claremont: Institute for Antiquity and Christianity, 1987), R. F. Hock and E. N. O'Neil, eds., *The Chreia in Ancient Rhetoric* (2 vols.; Atlanta: Society of Biblical Literature, 1986–2002), V. K. Robbins, "The Chreia," in D. E. Aune, ed., *Graeco-Roman Literature and the New Testament: Selected Forms and Genres* (Atlanta: Scholars Press, 1988), 1-23. See also D. F. Watson, "Rhetorical Criticism," in D. E. Aune, ed., *The Blackwell Companion to the New Testament* (Malden: Wiley-Blackwell, 2010), 171-72, though he is mainly concerned with the *chreiae* of the gospels.

[18] On Paul's use of rhetorical characterization, see S. K. Stowers, "Romans 7:7-25 as a Speech-in-Character (προσωποποιία)," in T. Engberg-Pedersen, ed., *Paul in His Hellenistic Context* (Minneapolis: Fortress, 1995), 180-202, and "Apostrophe, Προσωποποιία, and Paul's Rhetorical Education," in J. T. Fitzgerald et al., eds., *Early Christianity and Classical Culture: Comparative Studies in Honor of Abraham J. Malherbe* (Leiden: Brill, 2003), 351-69, and R. F. Hock, "Paul and Greco-Roman Education," in Sampley, *Paul in the Greco-Roman World*, 198-227, esp. 210-11.

[19] On Paul's use of rhetorical comparison, see my "Comparison, Self-Praise, and Irony: Paul's Boasting and the Conventions of Hellenistic Rhetoric," *NTS* 32 (1986): 1-30, and "Paul and Rhetorical Comparison," in Sampley, *Paul and the Greco-Roman World*, 134-71.

the "secondary" level of Greek education, where such skills were taught by a graded series of exercises known as the *Progymnasmata*.[20] Such an argument is imperfect, of course. A literate person such as Paul may have made use of conventional literary forms and techniques he picked up informally, as well as those in which he had been formally trained. Presumably he would use them more flexibly and comfortably the better his formal training, but this would depend on his own innate skills and degree of practical experience as well.

Further, the argument may also be inconclusive because Paul may have known much that he did not use. In Corinth, at least, we know he made an in-principle decision *not* to make use of rhetorical techniques or other learning which he felt would obscure the heart of his message (1 Cor 2:1-5). This strongly implies that he felt he had access to such rhetorical techniques. He *could* have made use of them, but deliberately decided not to do so. This point has often been obscured by an overly-literal reading of 2 Cor 10:10 and particularly 11:6, "I may be untrained in speech, but I am not in knowledge (ἰδιώτης τῷ λόγῳ, ἀλλ' οὐ τῇ γνώσει)." A surprising number of scholars still seem to take what Paul says here seriously, despite the fact that (1) the comment comes in the middle of one of the most obviously rhetorical sections in all his letters; and (2) virtually identical comments are made by orators such as Dio Chrysostom, whose rhetorical competence is not in doubt.[21] Ancient literary critics distinguished as many as eleven different grades of irony,[22] and Paul is here engaged in a highly sophisticated ironic parody of the claims of his opponents. The rhetorical skill he displays in this passage strongly suggests at least some degree of formal rhetorical training, not to mention considerable natural aptitude!

How aware does Paul appear to be of the kinds of Greek literature used in various stages of Greek education? Does he quote from, or allude to the standard authors known to all school children?[23] If he does, he has either

---

[20] On these works, several of which have survived down to our time, see G. A. Kennedy, *Progymnasmata: Greek Textbook of Prose Composition and Rhetoric* (Leiden: Brill, 2003). Most scholars see Greek and Roman education as being divided into three successive phases, roughly equivalent to our idea of primary, secondary, and tertiary education. "Primary" education, usually undertaken in the home, taught elementary literacy and numeracy. "Secondary" education was taught by a *grammaticus*, and included advanced reading and writing, as well as a range of other subjects. "Tertiary" education, only available to the elite, focused on rhetoric and philosophy. On all this see R. F. Hock, "Paul and Greco-Roman Education" and R. A. Kaster, "Notes on 'Primary' and 'Secondary' Schools in Late Antiquity," *TAPA* 113 (1983): 323-46.

[21] See, for example, Dio Chrysostom, *Discourse* 32.39. A. B. du Toit is quite correct to comment that "Paul's remark in 2 Cor 11:6 about his being "untrained" (ἰδιώτης) should not be taken at face value. It was his tongue-in-cheek reference to a derisive remark of his opponents," See "A Tale of Two Cities: 'Tarsus or Jerusalem' Revisited," *NTS* 46 (2000): 397.

[22] See the references in my "Comparison, Self-Praise, and Irony," 11-12.

[23] U. Schnelle claims (*Apostle Paul: His Life and Theology* [Grand Rapids: Baker Academic, 2005], 75) that "Only once (1 Cor 15:33) does he specifically cite Greek literature, when he refers to a popular proverb of Euripides, found in Menander's comedy Thais: 'Bad company ruins good morals.'" S. E. Porter and A. W. Pitts, by contrast, suggest a list of eight quotations, though their list includes two examples in letters not generally thought to be Pauline, and three in speeches attributed to Paul in Acts. See their "Paul's Bible, his Education, and his Access to

learned them in formal schooling or picked them up in conversation, or from collections of "quotable quotes" (anthologies or compilations).[24] If he does not, or only does so rarely, he may know them but not wish to use them,[25] or he may not know much about them at all.[26] The question is not easy to resolve. Certainly Paul rarely quotes from the standard Greek authors. He quotes from or alludes to the traditions of the words of Jesus more often,[27] and from the Septuagint, the Greek translation of the Hebrew Bible,[28] *far* more often.

The question of Paul's level of formal Greek education is also related to the issue of the geographical location of his formative years. According to Acts (9:10, 30; 11:25; 21:39; 22:3), Paul was born in Tarsus in Cilicia, but was "brought up" (ἀνατεθραμμένος, Acts 22:3) in Jerusalem. What (if any) level of education had Paul completed in Tarsus?[29] The question matters because, if he left Tarsus as a young child and spent his formative years in Jerusalem, Aramaic would be his primary language, and the Hebrew Bible would in all likelihood be the basis of his education. If on the other hand his formative years were spent in Tarsus, his mother tongue would almost certainly be Greek. His understanding of the Bible would most likely be based on the Greek Bible, the Septuagint (see n. 27, above), and the level of Greek

---

the Scriptures of Israel," *JGRChJ* 5 (2008): 19.

[24] See the brief discussion of anthologies in Greco-Roman and Jewish education in Porter and Pitts, "Paul's Bible," 27-31.

[25] Thus Porter and Pitts, "Paul's Bible," 19-20. Porter and Pitts suggest two arguments to support their case that Paul's failure to quote more Greek literature is not decisive: (1) the likelihood that an author will quote or allude to literature he knows is genre-dependent, and in at least *some* other cases (Plato and Epicurus) letters seem not to be the place for quotations; and (2) "Pagan literature held little authority in the eyes of the apostle and his congregations." Neither argument is fully persuasive. In response to (1), Paul *does* quote, but what he quotes is the Greek Bible. In regard to (2), even if pagan literature was not held to be authoritative, a neatly turned quotation or allusion could still be useful, as the few probable examples show. This question seems to me to need more careful examination.

[26] Thus E. P. Sanders, "Paul Between Judaism and Hellenism," in J. D. Caputo and L. M. Alcoff, eds., *St. Paul among the Philosophers* (Bloomington: University of Indiana Press, 2009), 74-90 esp. 80.

[27] The question of how often Paul quotes the words of Jesus is a controversial one. However, the great majority of scholars would be happy to accept that Paul at least alluded to the sayings of Jesus a dozen to twenty times, and some would claim far more. See, for example, J. D. G. Dunn, "Jesus Tradition in Paul," in B. Chilton and C. A. Evans, eds., *Studying the Historical Jesus* (Leiden: Brill, 1994), 155-78, D. Wenham, "The Story of Jesus Known to Paul," in J. B. Green & M. Turner, eds., *Jesus of Nazareth, Lord and Christ* (Grand Rapids: Eerdmans, 1994), 297-311, or S. Kim, *Paul and the New Perspective: Second Thoughts on the Origin of Paul's Gospel* (Grand Rapids: Eerdmans, 2001), ch. 8.

[28] The Septuagint is so called because of the legend that it was the work of seventy translators, whose work took seventy days. In fact it was most probably translated by a number of different groups, working in Alexandria over more than a generation, somewhere in the period 280–240 B.C. It is usually referred to with the abbreviation "the LXX," the Roman numerals for seventy.

[29] The question was formulated in the influential work of W. C. van Unnik, *Tarsus or Jerusalem. The City of Paul's Youth* (trans. G. Ogg; London: Epworth Press, 1962), though see now A. B. du Toit, "A Tale of Two Cities;" A.W. Pitts, "Hellenistic Schools in Jerusalem and Paul's Rhetorical Education," in S. E. Porter, ed., *Paul's World* (Leiden: Brill, 2008), 19-50; and Porter and Pitts, "Paul's Bible," 9-40.

education and culture to which he had immediate access would be considerably greater. A Greek education was available (to those of sufficient means) in Jerusalem,[30] but Tarsus was a "university town" which, according to the first-century geographer Strabo, could rival even Athens and Alexandria.[31]

The question cannot be resolved, however, simply on the basis of the brief reference in Acts 22:3. We have been trying to find some way to test the level of Paul's engagement with Greek education with a degree of objectivity. His use of particular rhetorical techniques in his letters is one such method. His quotations of, or allusions to, standard Greek literature are another indicator. The way he uses his most common source of quotations and allusions, the Septuagint, is a third, but that is an issue too complex to be dealt with effectively here.[32]

A fourth indicator of Paul's educational level may be found in his creative use of the terminology and concepts of the popular philosophy of his day. Considerable work in this area has been done by A. J. Malherbe,[33] as well as by a number of his students (e.g. J. T. Fitzgerald, C. E. Glad),[34] and others.[35] Recently, however, two new approaches have developed. Troels Engberg-Pedersen has revitalized the study of parallels between Paul's worldview and Stoicism, the dominant philosophical tradition of his time.[36] Most recently, a

---

[30] See the references in M. Hengel, *The Pre-Christian Paul* (Philadelphia: Trinity Press International, 1991), 57-62.

[31] Strabo, *Geography* 14.5.13. He specifically mentions schools of both philosophy and rhetoric.

[32] The literature on Paul's use of the Old Testament is immense. See, for example, M. D. Hooker, "Beyond the Things that are Written? St Paul's Use of Scripture," *NTS* 27.3 (1981): 295-309; R. B. Hays, *Echoes of Scripture in the Letters of Paul* (New Haven: Yale University Press, 1993); S. E. Porter and C. D. Stanley, eds., *As it is Written: Studying Paul's Use of Scripture* (Atlanta: Society of Biblical Literature, 2008). More recently scholarship has focused on either Paul's use of the Old Testament in particular letters or shorter passages in his letters, or on his use of particular Old Testament books or passages.

[33] Malherbe's work is extensive. For representative examples see his *Social Aspects of Early Christianity* (2nd enl. ed.; Philadelphia: Fortress, 1983); *Paul and the Popular Philosophers*, (Philadelphia: Fortress, 1988); and *Paul and the Thessalonians: The Philosophic Tradition of Pastoral Care* (Philadelphia: Fortress, 1987). A full list may be found in J. T. Fitzgerald et al., eds., *Early Christianity and Classical Culture: Comparative Studies in Honour of Abraham J. Malherbe* (Leiden: Brill, 2003), 41-46.

[34] Along with work such as "Paul, the Ancient Epistolary Theorists, and 2 Corinthians 10–13: The Purpose and Literary Genre of a Pauline Letter," in D. L. Balch et al., eds., *Greeks, Romans, and Christians: Essays in Honor of Abraham J. Malherbe* (Minneapolis: Fortress, 1990), 190-200, and "The Catalogue in Ancient Greek Literature" in S. E. Porter and T. H. Olbricht, eds., *The Rhetorical Analysis of Scripture: Essays from the 1995 London Conference*, (Sheffield: Sheffield Academic Press, 1997) 275-93. Fitzgerald has edited several extremely useful collections of essays. See, for example, J. T. Fitzgerald, ed., *Greco-Roman Perspectives on Friendship*, (Atlanta: Scholars Press, 1997), and *Passions and Moral Progress in Greco-Roman Thought* (New York: Routledge, 2008). C. E. Glad's *Paul and Philodemus: Adaptability in Epicurean and Early Christian Psychagogy* (Leiden: Brill, 1995) strikingly illustrates the unexpected directions study of the intellectual context of Paul's ideas can take.

[35] For a useful survey, see G. E. Sterling, "Hellenistic Philosophy and the New Testament," in S. E. Porter, ed., *Handbook to Exegesis of the New Testament* (Leiden: Brill, 1997), 313-58.

[36] See T. Engberg-Pedersen, *Paul and the Stoics*, (Louisville: Westminster John Knox, 2000) and *Cosmology and Self in the Apostle Paul: The Material Spirit* (Oxford: Oxford University Press,

number of studies have examined the cases where Paul's vocabulary and ideas seem to be related more to Platonic philosophy than to Stoicism.[37] We know that in Paul's day Platonism was entering a period of revival,[38] so it is not *a priori* implausible that he might have had either direct or indirect contact with Platonic terminology and ideas.

In my view, however, the study of Paul's intellectual context can be taken even further. I have argued that it is possible to detect Middle-Platonic cosmological concepts similar to those expressed by (among others) Philo and Plutarch in Paul's understanding of the "principalities and powers" (Rom 8:38-39; 1 Cor 15:24-28, 54-57; Gal 3:23–4:11; Eph 1:21; 3:10; 6:10-18; Col 1:16-18; 2:8-23) which dominate the world of those who do not belong to Christ.[39] If this case is accepted, then there is evidence of influence from popular philosophical ideas from a wide range of traditions in Paul's letters. Some of these are ethical concepts, some anthropological, others cosmological. Does this mean we need to argue that Paul had received a broad philosophical, as well as a rhetorical education? I do not think so. Rather, we need to think of Paul as being aware of the kinds of terminology and ideas which concerned popular philosophy in his time.[40] We do not know enough

---

2010) as well as numerous articles. See also R. M. Thorsteinsson, "Paul and Roman Stoicism: Romans 12 and Contemporary Stoic Ethics," *JSNT* 29 (2006): 139-61, and S. K. Stowers, "Matter and Spirit, or, What is Pauline Participation in Christ?" in Eugene F. Rogers, ed., *The Holy Spirit: Classic and Contemporary Readings* (Malden: Wiley-Blackwell, 2009), 91-105, and T. Rasimus et al., eds., *Stoicism in Early Christianity* (Grand Rapids: Eerdmans, 2010). Engberg-Pedersen's work has opened a new chapter in the discussion. For older scholarship in this area, see M. Colish, "Stoicism and the New Testament: an Essay in Historiography," *ANRW* II 26.1: 335-79.

[37] See, for example, H. D. Betz, "The Concept of the 'Inner Human Being' (ὁ ἔσω ἄνθρωπος) in the Anthropology of Paul," *NTS* 46 (2000): 315-41: "Whether Paul was aware of the origin of the concept in Plato and how he first learned about it, cannot be determined ... While retaining the terms of ἔσω and ἔξω ἄνθρωπος, he reconfigured them conceptually, in order to preclude a split in the person between an immortal soul and a material body," (340); Emma Wasserman, "The Death of the Soul in Romans 7: Revisiting Paul's Anthropology in Light of Hellenistic Moral Psychology," *JBL* 126.4 (2007): 798-816; and briefly S. K. Stowers, in "The Concept of 'Community' and the History of Early Christianity," in *Method and Theory in the Study of Religion* 23 (2011): 238-56, esp. n. 7, 243: "Paul's basic idea here is assimilation to Christ, a concept that he almost certainly borrowed from Platonism as did Philo (e.g., 2 Cor 3:18; Rom 8:29)."

[38] On the nature of this transformation, see T. Engberg-Pedersen, "Setting the Scene: Stoicism and Platonism in the Transitional Period in Ancient Philosophy," in Rasimus et al., *Stoicism in Early Christianity*, 1-14. For other isolated but intriguing evidence of a Platonic "revival" in this period, see G. H. R. Horsley, ed., *New Documents Illustrating Early Christianity* (vol. 4; Macquarie University: Ancient History Documentary Research Centre, 1987), 70-71.

[39] See C. Forbes, "Pauline Demonology and/or Cosmology? Principalities, Powers, and the Elements of the World in their Hellenistic Context," *JSNT* 85 (2002): 51-73. "Middle Platonism" is a term which refers to a diverse group of Platonic philosophers who, starting in the mid-first century B.C., moved away from the skeptical tradition of the previous two centuries of Platonic thinking. They focused instead on the explanation and development of ideas from Plato's works. Philo of Alexandria and Plutarch, mentioned in the text, are two of the better known Middle Platonists.

[40] "I do not wish to suggest that Paul has formally studied philosophy or is *au fait* with the technicalities of Middle Platonic cosmological thinking. I would argue, rather, that he is working

about the ways in which such ideas and terminology circulated outside the realm of higher education to come to strong conclusions about how Paul came into contact with them. In our own day one does not need to have formally studied Jean-Paul Sartre to use the term "existential," or Michel Foucault to use the term "deconstruction." We must likewise presume that in Paul's day some understanding of philosophical terms and concepts trickled down into the conversation of the intelligent layman. This is clearly an area which deserves further study.

In recent years a number of scholars have suggested that Paul is to be understood as a "Diaspora Pharisee," someone whose family maintained a strong Jewish identity in Tarsus, and who was sent (or taken) to Jerusalem by his parents for the best Pharisaic education available. Were they already Pharisees, and was Paul already a Pharisee before he went to Jerusalem? Though scholars may not all mean quite the same thing by the phrase "Diaspora Pharisee,"[41] they all intend to emphasize at least that Paul's early Jewish education was more focused on the Greek Bible than the Hebrew Bible. This is entirely reasonable. However, I have serious reservations about the portrayal of Paul as a "Diaspora Pharisee" if this means locating any real Pharisaic education in the Diaspora. We have no other evidence to suggest that Pharisaic communities or schools were to be found in the Jewish Diaspora, and even given the limits of our knowledge of first-century Pharisaism, it is hard to see how a strong Pharisaic regime could be maintained in a Diaspora community.[42] The purity regulations would be

---

creatively between the angelology and demonology of his Jewish heritage, and the worldview of the thoughtful Greco-Roman philosophical amateur . . . I would suggest that Paul, himself in part a product of decades of intelligent engagement with Hellenistic Judaism and Greco-Roman culture, is here working towards his own synthesis" (Forbes, "Pauline Demonology and/or Cosmology?" 73).

[41] This approach should probably be traced to the portrayals of Paul by H. J. Schoeps and S. Sandmel, though they do not use the term. J. Becker, *Paul: Apostle to the Gentiles* (Louisville: Westminster John Knox, 1993), 40-51, argues that as a Diaspora Pharisee, Paul draws heavily on mainstream Pharisaic teaching, but in all likelihood both learned and formulated these ideas in Greek. Paradoxically, he also argues that Paul was probably taught Aramaic in his Tarsian education (52). E. P. Sanders seems to use the phrase primarily in relation to his claim that Paul is unaware of the text of the Hebrew Bible where it differs from the Greek translation. C. J. Roetzel ("Oikoumene and the Limits of Pluralism in Alexandrian Judaism and Paul," in J. A. Overman and J. S. MacLennan, eds., *Diaspora Jews and Judaism* [Atlanta: Scholars Press, 1992], 163-82 and esp. 165 n. 10) argues more simply that Paul is a "Septuagint Jew." But whatever Paul's knowledge of the Hebrew Bible, clearly Paul's *congregations*, if biblically literate at all, would be far more familiar with the Septuagint. Schnelle, *Apostle Paul*, 64, describes Paul as a "Pharisee in the Diaspora" but does not make it clear whether he thinks Paul *became* a Pharisee in the Diaspora.

[42] G. Stemberger argues that "We have no other evidence for Pharisees in the Diaspora, but we cannot draw any conclusion from this accidental silence of the sources, even though the observance of various religious laws, above all in the realm of purity, would have been very difficult in the Diaspora" (*Jewish Contemporaries of Jesus: Pharisees, Sadducees, Essenes* [trans. A. W. Mahnke; Minneapolis: Fortress, 1995], 112). In this context, what do we make of Jesus' comment in Matt 23:15 about Pharisees crossing land and sea to make converts? Cf. Becker, *Paul, Apostle to the Gentiles*, 39, who though he does not exclude the possibility of a Jerusalem education for Paul, still comments that "Paul could also have easily received an

extremely onerous in a Diaspora setting. As Martin Goodman points out, we know of only two Pharisees even living in the diaspora: Paul himself, and Josephus,[43] and Paul was hardly strictly observant!

In summary, there is considerable evidence to suggest that Paul had a good broad Greek education up to at least the "secondary" level, and at least some real exposure to the rhetorical curriculum. Further, he had at least an intelligent layman's interest in and some knowledge of the terminology and concepts of several "schools" of philosophy. It is therefore most reasonable to argue that Paul could have had quite a degree of both Greek and Jewish education before coming to Jerusalem, both most probably conducted in Greek. His Greek education *could* have been extended in Jerusalem, though no concrete evidence proves that it was. All the evidence we do have suggests that Paul's education in Jerusalem focused heavily on the law of Moses and Pharisaic interpretations of it.

Paul's broad engagement with the Greek culture of his audience is obvious in his letters. His metaphors of the Christian life as athletics (e.g. 1 Cor 9:24), his military metaphors (e.g. 1 Cor 9:7; Phil 2:25; Eph 6:11-17), his metaphor of citizenship (e.g. Phil 3:20; Eph 2:12), his use of the range of metaphors common in popular philosophy discussed above, and a range of other features of his letters illustrate the degree to which a characteristically Greek view of the world came naturally to Paul. Yet in a number of striking ways, the deeply Jewish presuppositions of Paul's worldview also remain visible. We are often tempted to see these two aspects of Paul's cultural heritage, the Greek and the Jewish, as existing in tension. For Paul, however, they form an integrated backdrop for his thinking.[44] What is remarkable is the degree to which he expects his (cosmopolitan Greek or Greco-Roman) audience to share his particular "ethnic prejudices." To this question we now turn.

3. The Continuing Influence of Jewish Ethnic Presuppositions in Paul's Worldview

For Paul, Jews are defined by their shared history and culture/religion, while "the (other) nations"/Greeks/the uncircumcised are defined by their lack of these privileges. "The nations" are the ones who, having rejected the

---

education in the Pharisaic sense at any large diaspora synagogue, even in Tarsus." I do not know of any evidence which supports this claim.

[43] M. Goodman, "Diaspora Reactions to the Destruction of the Temple," in J. D. G. Dunn, ed., *Jews and Christians: The Parting of the Ways, A.D. 70–135* (Grand Rapids: Eerdmans, 1999), 29. B. Chilton and J. Neusner concur: "the evidence for Pharisees in the Diaspora is scarce at best" ("Paul and Gamaliel," *BBR* 14.1 [2004]: 1-43 esp. 34), and A. Edrei and D. Mendels give an even stronger formulation: "there is certainly no evidence that the sects existed in the diaspora" ("A Split Jewish Diaspora: Its Dramatic Consequences II," *JSP* 17 [2008]: 181).

[44] On this issue see the useful comments of S. E. Porter in section 2 of "Exegesis of the Pauline Letters, including the Deutero-Pauline Letters," in Porter, *Handbook to Exegesis of the New Testament*, 505-12, and the broader discussion in the various essays in T. Engberg-Pedersen, ed., *Paul Beyond the Judaism/Hellenism Divide*, (Louisville: Westminster John Knox, 2001).

knowledge of God, are prey to idolatry and its moral and social consequences (Romans 1–2).[45] That "the nations (ἔθνη), *who did not strive for righteousness, have attained it* . . ." (Rom 9:30) could well have sounded highly patronising to a thoughtful Greco-Roman audience. Was "righteousness" not one of the four "cardinal virtues" of the Greek tradition? In 1 Cor 5:1 Paul comments that "It is actually reported that there is sexual immorality among you, and of a kind that is not found even among the nations (οὐδὲ ἐν τοῖς ἔθνεσιν)." The presumption that "the nations" might (in other ways) have been sexually immoral, as a generalisation, could well have been quite offensive. Certainly Paul would have been willing to admit that Jews had characteristic failings as well (Rom 2:17-24), but this may not have appeased a hostile Greek audience! When Paul reminds the Corinthians that "wrongdoers will not inherit the kingdom of God," naming fornicators, idolaters, adulterers, male prostitutes, sodomites, thieves, the greedy, drunkards, revilers, robbers, and that "none of these will inherit the kingdom of God, and this is what some of you used to be" (1 Cor 6:9-11a), he is listing what many Jewish moralists considered the characteristic failings of "the nations" as a whole.[46]

First and foremost, normally, came idolatry. As Paul puts it in 1 Cor 12:2: "You know that when you were (!) the nations (ἔθνη), you were enticed and led astray to idols that could not speak." In Galatians 2:15 he comments to a predominantly Gentile audience that "We ourselves are Jews by birth and not Gentile sinners" (φύσει Ἰουδαῖοι καὶ οὐκ ἐξ ἐθνῶν ἁμαρτωλοί). The phrase, literally "not from among the sinful nations," could hardly have sounded "politically correct"! In Eph 4:17 when Paul advises his audience that "you must no longer live as the nations live (μηκέτι ὑμᾶς περιπατεῖν καθὼς καὶ τὰ ἔθνη περιπατεῖ), in the futility of their minds," he takes it for granted that his audience will accept that the description is a fair one. The one concession Paul appears willing to make is that "When Gentiles (ἔθνη), who do not possess the law, do instinctively what the law requires, these, though not having the law, are a law to themselves" (Rom 2:14). Such people's consciences might well "accuse or perhaps excuse them on the day when, according to my gospel, God, through Jesus Christ, will judge the secret thoughts of all" (Rom 2:15-16).

What is intriguing here is Paul's assumption that his audience, the congregations of his converts, predominantly made up of "the nations," will accept that his characterisation of them as idolatrous and sinful used to be the truth. Paul assumes that, in the light of their new identity "in Christ," all that has changed. They had "turned to God from idols, to serve a living and true God, and to wait for his Son from heaven, whom he raised from the dead—Jesus, who rescues us from the wrath that is coming" (1 Thess 1:9-10). But that leads us to the question of Paul's understanding of his own role as "an

---

[45] For a case that Paul is thinking more of Genesis 18 and the sins of Sodom than of Genesis 1–3 and "the Fall" more generally, see P. F. Esler, "The Sodom Tradition in Romans 1:18-32," *BTB* 34 (2004): 2-16.

[46] See, for example, Wisdom 12–14, or Philo, *de Abrahamo* 134-35, though Philo traces what he sees as "characteristic gentile vices" back to luxury rather than idolatry.

apostle to the nations." How did a Jewish Christian such as Paul understand the purposes of the Jewish God for "the nations," and his own role in those purposes?

4. Paul as "An Apostle to the Nations" and His Understanding of his Role in the Purposes of Israel's God

In different ways in his own letters and in the Acts of the Apostles, Paul describes himself, or is described, as a preacher to "the nations," who nonetheless gives priority to the Jews. Three times in his letter to the churches in Rome Paul affirms that God's message and its consequences, and Paul's preaching of them, is "to the Jew first and also to the Greek" (Ἰουδαίῳ τε πρῶτον καὶ Ἕλληνι; Rom 1:16, cf. Rom 2:9-11).[47] Paradoxically, in the next sentence he continues, "God shows no partiality." God is not partial, but it seems He does have priorities! Of the twenty-two times Paul uses the terms "Jew/s" and "Greek/s"[48] in close conjunction, in only four cases does he put the term "Greek" (or its equivalent) first.[49] Not unnaturally, Paul the Jew normally thinks of the Jews first.

In Acts, Luke regularly represents Paul as beginning his missionary preaching in synagogues, among Jews (and Gentile sympathizers), and only stepping outside this predominantly Jewish context when forced to do so by opposition.[50] The author of Acts puts into Paul's and Barnabas' mouths the comment (13:46) that "It was necessary that the word of God should be spoken first to you (Jews). Since you reject it and judge yourselves to be unworthy of eternal life, we are now turning to the Gentiles. For so the Lord has commanded us, saying, 'I have set you to be a light for the Gentiles, so that you may bring salvation to the ends of the earth'."[51]

To supplement these two pictures of Paul, we need to note that he clearly thinks that his preaching to *Gentiles* has a place in God's plans for the *Jews*.

A common understanding of Paul argues that his gospel of grace and salvation "without the law" liberated Christianity from the ethnic exclusivism

---

[47] It is important to remember, as L. E. Keck points out, that "both passages (i.e. 1 Cor 9:19-23 and 2 Cor 11:24) show that Paul did not construe his apostleship to Gentiles to entail ignoring fellow Jews" ("The Jewish Paul among the Gentiles: Two Portrayals," in Fitzgerald et al., *Early Christianity and Classical Culture*, 461-82, esp. 473).

[48] Or their functional equivalents "Jews" and "nations," or "circumcised" and "uncircumcised." The references are as follows: Rom 1:16; 2:9, 10; 3:9, 29; 4:9; 9:23; 10:12; 11:11(?), 25; 15:8-12, 25; 1 Cor 1:22-24 (x3); 7:18-19 (x2); 10:32 (N.B. with a new third category: Jews, Greeks, and the "Assembly of God," which is in some sense neither!); 12:13; Gal 2:15; 3:28; 1 Thess 2:15.

[49] The four cases are Rom 9:30; Gal 2:6; Eph 2:11-12; and Col 3:11. Two factors may well modify the force of this comparison of references: (1) contextual features of Paul's argument (e.g. emphasis) may determine the order in which the terms are used; and (2) the question of the authenticity of particular letters may alter the balance a little. The general picture, however, remains clear.

[50] See Acts 13:5 (a partial exception: Barnabas and Saul are summoned by the Proconsul); 13:14-48, 14:1-5, 19; 16:13-15; 17:1-8, 10-14; 18:1-6.

[51] Cf. Acts 18:6; 19:8-10; 28:23-31.

of Judaism. According to this view, Judaism was essentially ethnocentric. Gentiles could only be "saved" by converting to Judaism, which involved breaking all ties with their previous religion/cultural heritage so as to "become Jews." For men, the crucial steps were proselyte baptism and circumcision. For women, proselyte baptism was the only ceremonial requirement. For both men and women, this "conversion" involved a commitment to keep the law of Moses. Pauline Christianity, however, did away with the "particularism" of Judaism, opening the way for it to become a universal religion.

The problem with this view, attractive though it may be to modern Gentile Christians,[52] is that it reverses the vector of Paul's argument. Paul certainly does talk about the breaking down of the barriers between Jews and Greeks/the nations, but not by "universalizing" the message. Membership of the true people of God is offered to non-Jews in terms of adoption into the family of God and via inheritance metaphors,[53] membership of the people of Israel or the offspring of Abraham[54] and grafting into the cultivated olive tree.[55] Paul can even speak of his Gentile audience having ceased to be Gentiles (*without* undergoing circumcision). Thus he says to the Corinthians (1 Cor 12:2): "You know that when you *were* pagans (ἔθνη ἦτε),[56] you were enticed and led astray to idols that could not speak."[57] More commonly, however, he thinks of them as still being members of "the nations," but as

---

[52] This view has also proven popular to a number of modern intellectuals from outside traditional Christian circles. See now the discussion in Caputo and Alcoff, *St. Paul among the Philosophers*, but for an early criticism see N. A. Dahl, "The One God of Jews and Gentiles (Romans 3:29-30)", in his *Studies in Paul: Theology for the Early Christian Mission* (Minneapolis: Augsburg Fortress, 1977), 178-91.

[53] Adoption references: Rom 8:15; 8:29; 9:4; Gal 4:5; Eph 1:5. Inheritance references: Rom 4:13-14; 8:17; 1 Cor 6:9-10; 15:50; Gal 3:18, 29; 4:1, 7, 30; 5:21; Eph 1:11, 14, 18; 5:5; Col 1:12; 3:24; Tit 3:6-7. For recent discussion see J. C. Walters, "Paul, Adoption, and Inheritance," in Sampley, *Paul in the Greco-Roman World*, 42-76; T. J. Burke, *Adopted into God's Family: Exploring a Pauline Metaphor* (Downers Grove: IVP, 2006); and C. Johnson-Hodge, *If Sons then Heirs: A Study of Kinship and Ethnicity in the Letters of Paul* (New York: Oxford University Press, 2007).

[54] Membership of the people of Israel: Rom 9:24-26; offspring of Abraham: Gal 3:29; "God's own people": Eph 1:14.

[55] Grafting references: Rom 11:17-24. It is worth remembering, as T. L. Donaldson points out, that the NRSV translation of 11:17, "some of the branches were broken off, and you, a wild olive shoot, were grafted *in their place* to share the rich root of the olive tree" should instead be translated "among them." Gentiles do not displace or replace Jews. They *join* believing Israel. Thus, correctly, the NIV ("some of the branches have been broken off, and you, though a wild olive shoot, have been grafted in *among the others*"), and the ESV ("some of the branches were broken off, and you, although a wild olive shoot, were grafted in *among the others*") (emphasis mine). See T. L. Donaldson, "'Riches for the Gentiles' (Rom 11:12): Israel's Rejection and Paul's Gentile Mission," *JBL* 112.1 (1993): 81-98, esp. 84.

[56] "Pagans" (NIV, NRSV) is a poor translation. The Latin *paganus* only comes to have its modern meaning in the fourth century A.D., and the term's use here obscures Paul's characteristic language. His audience was "(from among) the nations."

[57] Similarly in Eph 4:17 (if it is Pauline) the author says: "Now this I affirm and insist on in the Lord: you must no longer live as the Gentiles live (μηκέτι ὑμᾶς περιπατεῖν καθὼς καὶ τὰ ἔθνη περιπατεῖ), in the futility of their minds." The implication is that his audience is no longer to consider themselves as τὰ ἔθνη. They are now "in the Lord," which involves a completely new identity.

having that identity subsumed into their new identity "in Christ." The vector of Paul's argument is not from the people of Israel (particular) out to the wider world of the nations (universal), but from outsider status (the nations) to insider status (descendants of Abraham, Rom 4:9-12, 16-17; Gal 3:7, because they are now in Christ 3:15-18, 29; 4:31).[58] "Israel" as a category is not done away with in favour of a new, universal category. Rather the nations are given entry into the privileges of the people of Israel, properly understood.[59] As Gal 3:13-14 and 26-29 formulate the issue:

> 13 Christ redeemed us from the curse of the law by becoming a curse for us . . . 14 in order that in Christ Jesus *the blessing of Abraham might come to the Gentiles* . . . 26 in Christ Jesus you are all children of God through faith. 27 As many of you as were baptized into Christ have clothed yourselves with Christ. 28 There is no longer Jew or Greek, there is no longer slave or free, there is no longer male and female; for all of you are one in Christ Jesus. 29 And if you belong to Christ, *then you are Abraham's offspring* (literally "seed"), heirs according to the promise (NRSV, emphasis mine).[60]

Only rarely does Paul talk about the new, trans-national people of God in contrast to the old ethnic categories.[61]

The nations, then, are being brought within the circle of "the people of God," even while "national Israel" has to a large extent rejected the message of their Messiah. But for Paul this historical irony is only temporary. The time will come when God will prove himself faithful to his ancient promises to Israel. "All Israel" will be saved.[62] And Paul hopes, by his preaching to "the nations," to be part of the process by which this will occur. This becomes clear in two ways: (1) in the motif of "jealousy" in Rom 10:19; 11:11, 14;[63]

---

[58] Thus D. B. Martin: "As remarkable as it is, given the past two thousand years of European and world history, Paul promises the adoption of the gentiles into Israel, not the rejection of Israel in favor of a new people, nor even the creation of a new, nonethnic universal people" ("The Promise of Teleology, the Constraints of Epistemology, and Universal Vision in Paul," in Caputo and Alcoff, *St. Paul Among the Philosophers*, 101). But adoption may not be "into Israel," but into the wider "family of God." This family Paul describes as the "seed of Abraham" (Rom 4:13-18), who was the "father of many nations" (v. 18), not just one.

[59] On the complexities of Paul's argument here, see D. K. Buell and C. J. Hodge, "The Politics of Interpretation: The Rhetoric of Race and Ethnicity in Paul," *JBL* 123.2 (2004): 235-51. Note that it is *not* the case that "foreigners must be included among Israel" (D. B. Martin, "The Promise of Teleology, the Constraints of Epistemology, and Universal Vision in Paul," 100). As noted above, they are included among the "seed of Abraham," who was "the father of many nations," *not* only of Israel. Rom 11:17-23, the "grafting in of the wild olive branches," seems to me to be too general a metaphor to support Martin's formulation, and the one use of the term "Israel" in the passage (v. 23) speaks against it. For Paul "Israel" remains an ethnic descriptor.

[60] On this passage see W. S. Campbell, *Paul and the Creation of Christian Identity* (New York: T. & T. Clark, 2008), 61, with whose interpretation I am in broad agreement.

[61] See, for example, 1 Cor 10:32: "Give no offence to Jews or to Greeks or to the church of God" (καὶ Ἰουδαίοις . . . καὶ Ἕλλησιν καὶ τῇ ἐκκλησίᾳ τοῦ θεοῦ).

[62] Precisely what Paul means by "all Israel" here is unclear. All Israel at the time God acts? All faithful Israelites from across history? Or even more than this? Paul does not say enough for us to be certain.

[63] On this motif see R. H. Bell, *Provoked to Jealousy: The Origin and Purpose of the Jealousy*

and (2) in Paul's actual practice in bringing representative converts "from among the nations," and offerings of money from the "assemblies of the nations" to Jerusalem.

In Romans 10 and 11 Paul introduces the idea that the conversion of "the nations" will lead to national Israel being "provoked to jealousy," and hence to their conversion. He raises the theme of jealousy in a quotation from Deut 32:21, suggesting that God will act in judgement on (but with an eye to the restoration of) his rebellious people by making them envy unnamed foreigners. He supplements this with a citation of Is 65:1-2 to connect the "jealousy" theme with God's unexpected grace to covenant outsiders. But the core of his argument comes in Rom 11:11, where he reverses a number of common Jewish expectations to do with the order of events in God's ultimate restoration of his people.

Most Second Temple Jewish expectation, drawing on passages from the prophets such as Isaiah 2; 56:6-8; 60, Jeremiah 31, and Mic 4:2-7, had God's redemption and vindication of Israel lead to either the return of the tribes in exile and/or the pilgrimage of the (repentant) nations to Jerusalem to acknowledge the God of Israel.[64] Instead of this, Paul argues that the coming of the nations to Jerusalem, brought about by God's unexpected grace to them, is what will provoke rebellious Israel to jealousy, and thus lead to their final redemption. Most importantly, he seems to believe that his own bringing of "the offering of the nations" (Romans 15:16), his collection for "the poor among the saints," and his bringing to Jerusalem of members of the "assemblies of the nations" (such as Sopater, Aristarchus, Secundus, Gaius, Timothy, Tychicus and Trophimus, Acts 20:4, cf. Acts 21:29, and Titus, Gal 2:1-3) were in some sense signs that this process was under way.[65] The conversion of Gentiles and their bringing of their "tribute" to Jerusalem, were for Paul a fulfilment of prophecy, and a clear sign that God was bringing his purposes (which must surely include all Israel) to their completion.

Thus, for Paul, the fundamental binary distinction between Jews and "the nations" (characterized as "Greeks") was in the process of being dissolved. Paul's own profound engagement with both Jewish and Hellenistic Greek culture had prepared him for the role of an "apostle to the nations." This was a role he came to see as central to God's plans "for the Jew first, but also for the

---

Motif in Romans 9–11 (Tübingen: Mohr [Siebeck], 1994.
[64] For discussions of this widespread view, see for example R. D. Aus, "Paul's Travel Plans to Spain and the 'Full Number of the Gentiles' of Rom 11:25," *NovT* 21.3 (1979): 232-62.
[65] I do not think that Paul believed that this fulfillment of prophecy was something exclusive to him. He worked, after all, as part of a large co-operative exercise in the "Gentile mission." Nor do I believe that he thought his own relatively small-scale actions would bring on the eschatological repentance of Israel. Rather, I suggest, he saw his actions as part of a wider work of God which would climax in that eschatological repentance. The suggestion has recently been made that Paul believed that his Gentile converts were, in some sense, representative of the lost Northern tribes of Israel, scattered among the nations. See J. A. Staples, "What do the Gentiles have to do with 'All Israel'? A Fresh Look at Romans 11:25-27," *JBL* 130.2 (2011): 371-90. For a similar view see D. I. Starling, *Not My People: Gentiles as Exiles in Pauline Hermeneutics* (Berlin: de Gruyter, 2011). If such a view is accepted, it would tie together the two themes of the expectation of Gentile pilgrimage to Mount Zion and of the restoration of "all Israel."

Greek." That order had been temporarily reversed, so that for now, despite Paul's ongoing efforts among his own people, he saw his task as focussing on "the uncircumcised." Nonetheless he never stopped believing in the faithfulness of the God of Abraham to the promise that through Abraham all the peoples of the world would be blessed. For Paul this could only mean that those peoples would be included within the family of Abraham, on the same basis as Abraham himself: the faithfulness of God and their own responsive faith in God's Christ. God was the God of the nations, for there was only one God (Rom 3:29-30). Abraham was the father of many nations, "of all of us" (Romans 4:16-18),[66] both circumcised and uncircumcised (Rom 4:11-12). Eph 2:12-15 develops what Rom 10:12, 1 Cor 12:12-13, and Gal 3:28-29 formulate in condensed form. God is in the process of—no, has done away with—the importance of the distinction between Jew and Gentile, creating one new humanity with full access to God. Those who had no part in the community of Israel (πολιτεία, Eph 2:12) are now fellow citizens (συμπολῖται, 2:19), co-heirs, sharers in the one body and in the promise (συγκληρονόμα καὶ σύσσωμα καὶ συμμέτοχα τῆς ἐπαγγελίας, 3:6: note the four συν- compounds). When the full number of the nations has come in (Rom 11:25—and the process is already underway!) then the principle enunciated in Gal 3:28 will reach its fulfilment. There is neither Jew nor Greek, for they are all one in Christ Jesus.

Recommended Reading

Barclay, J. "Why the Roman Empire was Insignificant to Paul," in his *Pauline Churches and Diaspora Jews* (Tübingen, Mohr [Siebeck], 2011), 363-87.
Buell, D. K., and C. J. Hodge. "The Politics of Interpretation: The Rhetoric of Race and Ethnicity in Paul." *Journal of Biblical Literature* 123.2 (2004): 235-51.
Burke, T. J. *Adopted into God's Family: Exploring a Pauline Metaphor*. Downers Grove: IVP, 2006.
Campbell, W. S. *Paul and the Creation of Christian Identity*. New York: T. & T. Clark, 2008.
Du Toit, A. B. "A Tale of Two Cities: 'Tarsus or Jerusalem' Revisited." *New Testament Studies* 46 (2000): 375-402.
Engberg-Pedersen, T., ed. *Paul Beyond the Judaism/Hellenism Divide*. Louisville: Westminster John Knox, 2001.
Engberg-Pedersen, T. "Setting the Scene: Stoicism and Platonism in the Transitional Period in Ancient Philosophy." Pages 1-14 in *Stoicism in Early Christianity*. Edited by T. Rasimus et al., eds. Grand Rapids: Eerdmans, 2010.
Johnson-Hodge, C. *If Sons then Heirs: A Study of Kinship and Ethnicity in the Letters of Paul*. New York: Oxford University Press, 2007.
Mason, Steve. "Jews, Judaeans, Judaizing, Judaism: Problems of Categorization in Ancient History." *Journal for the Study of Judaism* 38 (2007): 457-512.
Pitts, A.W. "Hellenistic Schools in Jerusalem and Paul's Rhetorical Education." Pages 19-50 in *Paul's World*. Edited by S. E. Porter. Leiden: Brill, 2008.
Porter, S. E., and A. W. Pitts. "Paul's Bible, his Education and his Access to the Scriptures of Israel," *Journal of Greco-Roman Christianity and Judaism* 5 (2008): 9-40.

---

[66] On this passage see Campbell, *Paul and the Creation of Christian Identity*, 63.

Porter, S. E., and C. D. Stanley, eds. *As it is Written: Studying Paul's Use of Scripture.* Atlanta: Society of Biblical Literature, 2008.

Sampley, J. P., ed. *Paul and the Greco-Roman World: a Handbook.* Harrisburg: Trinity Press International, 2003.

Stanley, C. D. "Neither Jew nor Greek: Ethnic Conflict in Graeco-Roman Society." *Journal for the Study of the New Testament* 64 (1996): 101-24.

Stanley, C. D. "The Ethnic Context of Paul's Letters." Pages 177-201 in *Christian Origins and Hellenistic Judaism.* Edited by S. E. Porter and A. W. Pitts. Leiden: Brill, 2012.

Starling, D. I. *Not My People: Gentiles as Exiles in Pauline Hermeneutics.* Berlin, de Gruyter, 2011.

7. Paul among the Romans

James R. Harrison

1. The Triumph of Augustus and the Emergence of the Julio-Claudian Conception of Rule

With the triumph of Octavian over Antony and Cleopatra at the battle of Actium (31 B.C.), a century of bloody civil war and social chaos came to an end. The grateful Roman public and Senate pressed unprecedented honors and powers upon the undisputed victor and heir of the Julian house, the newly named Augustus (27 B.C.).[1] Undoubtedly, the expectation was that no military rival, present or future, would be able or willing to challenge Augustus for the leadership of Rome and that the peace, so decisively established by the victor, would remain a permanent feature of his rule. An unparalleled "age of grace" ensued with the advent of Augustus as the ruler of Rome and her empire. The extravagant favor of Augustus to his clients in the capital and overseas not only outstripped all previous Roman benefactors but also became the paradigm for all beneficence in the future.[2]

Consequently, the Julian house was depicted in providential, prophetic, teleological, and cosmological terms. At first blush, some of these motifs may have sounded vaguely familiar to contemporary auditors conversant with Jewish and early Christian eschatology.[3] The cyclical "Golden Age" had dawned in the principate of Augustus and, by the time of Paul's writing of Romans (ca. A.D. 55–57), it had returned in its fullness with the accession of the young Nero to power in A.D. 54.[4] This was reinforced ideologically by the application of the language of election, newness, and eternity to the dynasty of the Julio-Claudian rulers.[5] A series of providentially defining events in their

---

[1] On Augustus as *triumphator* (conqueror, vanquisher), see J. R. Harrison, *Paul and the Imperial Authorities at Thessalonica and Rome: A Study in the Conflict of Ideology* (Tübingen: Mohr [Siebeck], 2011), 133-38.
[2] See J. R. Harrison, "Paul, Eschatology, and the Augustan Age of Grace," *TynB* 50.1 (1999): 79-91.
[3] See Harrison, *Paul and the Imperial Authorities.*
[4] On the *saeculum* and the "Golden Age," see Harrison, *Paul and the Imperial Authorities*, 97-104.
[5] Harrison, *Paul and the Imperial Authorities*, 118-21, 142-44, 317-19; J. R. Harrison, "Paul, Theologian of Electing Grace," in S. E. Porter, ed., *Paul the Theologian* (Pauline Studies 3; Leiden: Brill, 2006), 77-108.

reigns also underscored their divine legitimation.[6]

Subtle differences in honorific rituals marked the approach of clients to the ruler in the Greek East and in the Latin West. In the East, grateful clients redeployed and expanded the accolades of the Hellenistic ruler cult in order to honor the Roman rulers: specifically, "son of god," "lord," "savior," "benefactor," "epiphany," "salvation," "hope," "joy," "peace," "grace," and "good news," among others.[7] In the capital, however, the republican quest for "glory" on the part of the Roman nobles was depicted as having found its culmination in the vastly superior glory of the princeps and his family.[8] Further, the statue program of the *forum Augustum* depicted Augustus as the *Pater Patriae* (Father of the Country) who had surpassed all the achievements of the great men of Roman history, Julian and republican.[9]

This propaganda was reinforced in the architecture and iconography of the capital and the provinces. The carved reliefs of defeated barbarians on the Augustan triumphal arches in the Greek East and in the Latin West highlighted the victory of the princeps and the Julian house over his enemies.[10] The erection of Augustus' self-eulogy, the *Res Gestae*, at his mausoleum at Rome and at three sites in provincial Galatia ensured that the princeps had articulated his understanding of his achievements for posterity well in advance of his later detractors.

The interrelation of sacred space in Rome also conveyed symbolic messages about the ruler. Three examples will suffice. First, a few hundred meters away from the site of the *Res Gestae*, which highlighted Augustus' domination of the nations (3.1-2; 4.3; 13; 25-33), was Agrippa's monumental map displaying the extent of the Roman empire and its peoples.[11] The motif of the conquest of the nations was also employed in the iconography of the Temple of Apollo Sosianus situated on the Palatine. Two northern barbarian captives, possibly Illyrians and part of Augustus' 29 B.C. triple triumph (*Res Gestae* 4.1; 30.1), are shown on a frieze block sitting on a parade float, hands bound behind their backs, ready to be hoisted mid-air for exhibition in Augustus' triumphal procession.[12]

---

[6] Harrison, *Paul and the Imperial Authorities*, 128-33.
[7] Harrison, *Paul and the Imperial Authorities*, 47-69; J. R. Harrison, "Paul and the Imperial Gospel at Thessaloniki," *JSNT* 25.1 (2002): 71-96.
[8] Harrison, *Paul and the Imperial Authorities*, 201-69; J. R. Harrison, "Paul and the Roman Ideal of Glory in the Epistle to the Romans," in U. Schnelle, ed., *The Letter to the Romans* (Leuven: Leuven University Press/Uitgenerij Peeters, 2009), 329-69.
[9] P. Zanker, *The Power of Images in the Age of Augustus* (Ann Arbor: University of Michigan Press, 1999), 210-15; E. A. Judge, "The Eulogistic Inscriptions of the Augustan Forum: Augustus on Roman History," in E. A. Judge, *The First Christians in the Roman World: Augustan and New Testament Studies* (ed. J. R. Harrison; Tübingen: Mohr [Siebeck], 2008), 165-81; Harrison, *Paul and the Imperial Authorities*, 170-77.
[10] For discussion, see J. R. Harrison, "'More Than Conquerors' (Rom 8:37): Paul's Gospel and the Augustan Triumphal Arches of the Greek East and Latin West," *Buried History* 47 (2011): 3-21.
[11] R. Hingley, *Globalising Roman Culture: Unity, Diversity and Empire* (New York: Routledge, 2005), 79.
[12] See K. Bradley, "On Captives Under the Principate," *Phoenix* 58.3-4 (2004): plate 1; Zanker, *The Power of Images*, 70, fig. 55.

Second, there was symbolic connection between the two circular buildings in the Campus Martius: Augustus' mausoleum and the Agrippan Pantheon. The latter building was dedicated to all the gods and included, among other cult statues to the deities (Mars, Venus, and the gods), a statue to the recently divinized Julius Caesar (Cassius Dio 53.27.2-4). Visitors to the Pantheon would have had direct sightline from the door of the temple to the mausoleum. P. E. J. Davies sums up the significance of the spatial relations thus: "The axial connection between his mausoleum and the Pantheon, two circular buildings, expressed the progression from mortal to immortal status: Augustus, like Julius Caesar, and like Romulus on the very Marsh of Capra, would not die but achieve apotheosis."[13]

Also in the Campus Martius was set the *horologium Augusti*, the giant sundial designed by the astrologer Facundus Navius.[14] This monument, dedicated to the Sun (*CIL* VI. 709), was placed between the *ara Pacis Augustae* and the (later) *columna Antonini Pii*. The symbolic importance of the monument is seen the inscription accompanying the sundial: *Aegypto in potestatem populi Romani redacta Soli donum dedit* (*CIL* VI 702: "On the occasion of Egypt's submission to the power of the Roman people he gave a gift to the Sun").[15] The sundial celebrates Augustus' victory at Actium (31 B.C.) that secured peace in the Greek East, whereas the *ara Pacis Augustae*, strategically placed nearby, eulogizes Augustus' establishment of peace in the Latin West.[16] Thus, as C. E. Newlands observes, "control over time was closely linked with military control" throughout the empire.[17] It is hard not to draw the inference from the imperial propaganda that Augustus had become the "Lord of time" by being the "Lord of the battlefield."

Third, the modest house of Augustus on the Palatine was located nearby a model of Romulus' hut,[18] thereby underscoring Augustus' status as the "new Romulus," the traditional founder of Rome, along with Aeneas.[19] Both founding figures, Aeneas and Romulus, were also featured in the statue program of the *forum Augustum* and in the iconography of the *ara Pacis Augustae*. In sum, the ideology of Julio-Claudian rule would have had

---

[13] P. E. J. Davis, *Death and the Emperor: Roman Imperial Funerary Monuments from Augustus to Marcus Aurelius* (Austin: University of Texas Press, 2004), 140, 142.

[14] Additionally, see Ammianus Marcellinus 17.4.12; Strabo 17.805; Pliny the Elder, *Nat.* 30.6.71.

[15] Cited, in abbreviated form here, in C. E. Newlands, *Playing with Time: Ovid and the Fasti* (Ithaca: Cornell University Press, 1995), 24.

[16] On the *ara Pacis Augustae*, see Zanker, *The Power of Images*, 172-83; C. Gates, *Ancient Cities: The Archaeology of Urban Life in the Ancient Near East and Egypt, Greece and Rome* (New York: Routledge, 2003), 339-42.

[17] Note the further observation of Newlands (*Playing with Time*, 24): "The names of the winds and zodiacal signs on the pavement around the obelisk are in Greek, a sign of Hellenistic learning. The obelisk thus specifically commemorated Augustus' military and cultural control over the Graeco-Roman world."

[18] Gates, *Ancient Cities*, 337; M. Beard et al., eds., *Religions of Rome, Volume 1: A History* (Cambridge: Cambridge University Press, 1998), 189-92; S. Walker, "The Moral Museum: Augustus and the City of Rome," in J. Coulston et al., eds., *Ancient Rome: The Archaeology of the Eternal City* (Oxford: Oxford University School of Archaeology, 2000), 61-75, esp. 62-64.

[19] Horace, *Carm. saec.* 41-60; Suetonius, *Aug.* 7.2.

interesting intersections with Paul's eschatological gospel of the crucified, risen, ascended, and returning Lord of all. A strong sense of prophetic fulfillment animated the Roman and early Christian meta-narrative of history and their respective culminations in Augustus and Christ, notwithstanding the fact that Roman worldview was cyclical and the Jewish-Christian view was, by contrast, linear.[20]

Paul's narrative theology, with its Jewish eschatological and apocalyptic roots, reveals the panorama of the ideological conflict. The ruler's election by the Roman gods and his providential appointment to rule was challenged by Paul's meta-narrative about God's electing grace being extended through Israel to the nations. God's justification of Abraham, the father of the nations, led to the eschatological gathering of a counter-imperial family of nations ruled over by the messianic Root of Jesse. In a paradoxical upending of the imperial reciprocity system, Christ the dishonored benefactor had defeated the ruling powers of sin and death, with the result that his death on behalf of his ungrateful dependents transferred to them the glory and righteousness that had become the preserve of the Julio-Claudian house. Indeed, the Roman ruler was held hostage to the Adamic reign of sin and death and would face divine judgment along with the rest of humanity. Thus the Senate's decision to apotheosize some of the Julio-Claudian rulers and their family members upon their death was a meaningless honorific accolade without any substance.

Moreover, the reign of Christ's grace and the newness of his Spirit filling the church represented an overflow of beneficence in the present age that not only outstripped the iconic Augustan age of grace but also rendered obsolete its much fêted revival under Nero. While the Roman ruler was to be obeyed and honored by believers, Paul, in line with the Jewish Scriptures, demoted the ruler to servant status. Concomitantly, Paul elevated the body of Christ in importance over Nero's "body of state," transferring to the risen and ascended Jesus many of the ruler's titles and to the body of Christ many of the ruler's functions.

It is therefore likely that an ideological conflict existed between Paul's gospel and the Julio-Claudian conception of history. Presumably Paul would have been aware of this collision in having to handle the pastoral issues generated by the impact of the imperial cult upon believers, including those who were part of the *familia Caesaris* (family of Caesar), in the house churches of the Greek East and Latin West.[21] However, several important questions have to be addressed at the outset (sections 2-3 below) before we describe the theological and social consequences of this ideological conflict in the epistle to the Romans as a case study (section 4). First, what have New Testament scholars said about Paul's critique of empire and its idolatrous values? Second, how do we discern such a critique in Paul's epistles where the ruler is nowhere explicitly named, in contrast to, for example, the savage anti-imperial diatribes of the Cynic-Stoic philosopher Epictetus (Arrian, *Epict.*

---

[20] Harrison, *Paul and the Imperial Authorities*, 101-2.
[21] Members of the *familia Caesaris* were not only located in Rome but were also stationed throughout the empire, including cities such as Corinth and Ephesus where Paul ministered.

diss. 3.13.9-13; 4.1.11-14, 41-50, 95)? Third, what voices within the academy regard recent studies of Paul in imperial context as methodologically unsound and, ultimately, theologically unbalanced? And, fourth, how have classical scholars recently interpreted the imperial cult? We turn to a brief examination of modern scholarship on the issue.

2. Modern Scholarship on Paul and Imperial Politics

Early last century Adolf Deissmann undertook a seminal investigation of the language of imperial cult and its intersection with the language of the LXX and the New Testament.[22] He argued that there existed a polemical parallelism between the language of the imperial cult and the cult of Christ. Honorific terminology formerly reserved for the deified ruler was now transferred to Christ in the early Christian preaching, with a view to demoting the cultic importance of the ruler and exalting instead Christ as Lord of all.[23] However, notwithstanding the fact that "an abhorrence of emperor worship" created "an upper line of demarcation" for the early believers, Paul remained, in Deissmann's view, a political conservative in his attitude towards the ruler.[24]

A trickle of publications canvassing the same issue appeared in the 1950s and 1970s,[25] but D. Georgi's 1987 monograph highlighted for the first time the way in which Paul's theocracy interacted with and subverted the imperial propaganda.[26] The momentum unleashed by Georgi's seminal monograph continues unabated to this day in a wide variety of publications. Several significant exegetical studies on Paul and imperial politics have appeared from 2008 onwards.[27] As far as commentaries, R. Jewett's magisterial work on Romans is characterized by its sensitivity to the Julio-Claudian context,[28] as is N. T. Wright's publication on the same epistle.[29] G. L. Green's discussion

---

[22] A. Deissmann, *Light from the Ancient East: The New Testament Illustrated by Recently Discovered Texts from the Graeco-Roman World* (London: Hodder & Stoughton, 1927 [repr. 1978]), 342.
[23] Deissmann, *Light from the Ancient East*, 343-78.
[24] Deissmann, *Light from the Ancient East*, 339-40.
[25] E. Stauffer, *Christ and the Caesars* (London: SCM, 1955); D. Cuss, *Imperial Cult and Honorary Terms in the New Testament* (Fribourg: Fribourg University Press, 1974).
[26] D. Georgi, *Theocracy in Paul's Praxis and Theology* (Minneapolis: Fortress, 1991 [Ger. orig. 1987]).
[27] N. Elliott, *The Arrogance of Nations: Reading Romans in the Shadow of Empire* (Minneapolis: Fortress, 2008); M. Gill, *Jesus as Mediator: Politics and Polemic in 1 Timothy 2:1-7* (New York: Peter Lang, 2008); J. Hardin, *Galatians and the Imperial Cult: A Critical Analysis of the First-Century Social Context of Paul's Letter* (Tübingen: Mohr [Siebeck], 2008); D. C. Lopez, *Apostle to the Conquered: Reimagining Paul's Mission* (Minneapolis: Fortress, 2008); B. Kahl, *Galatians Re-imagined: Reading with the Eyes of the Vanquished* (Minneapolis: Fortress, 2009); Harrison, *Paul and the Imperial Authorities*. See, too, the excellent unpublished doctoral thesis of I. E. Rock, *The Implications of Roman Imperial Ideology for an Exegesis of Paul's Letter to the Romans: An Ideological Literary Analysis of the Exordium, Rom 1:1-17* (Ph.D. diss., University of Wales, 2005).
[28] R. Jewett, *Romans: A Commentary* (Minneapolis: Fortress, 2007).
[29] N. T. Wright, "The Letter to the Romans," in N. T. Wright, J. P. Sampley, *The New Interpreter's Bible, Volume X* (Nashville: Abingdon, 2002), 395-770. For other publications of

of the imperial context of 2 Thess 2:1-10 contributes incisively to our exegetical understanding of a difficult passage.[30] Other publications have concentrated on how specific motifs from the Julio-Claudian propaganda would have engaged with Paul's theology, including, for example, lordship, fatherhood, and household language.[31] More general studies have also appeared,[32] as well as the three collections of (often pioneering) essays edited by R. A. Horsley.[33] This avalanche of scholarship—admittedly driven at times by modern reactions to the excesses of American foreign and economic policy in the Reagan and Bush eras[34]—has exposed the political context of Paul's proclamation of Christ as King (e.g. Acts 17:6-7). It has enabled us to see how first-century auditors might have responded to Paul's depiction of Christ's eschatological rule, as well unveiling for us his critique of the idolatrous mores of imperial society.[35] However, whether this was Paul's *deliberate* theological intention has recently come under scholarly challenge.

In a paper delivered at the SBL 2008 Annual Meeting (Boston, November 22-25), John Barclay debated N. T. Wright regarding the state of scholarship on "Paul and Empire."[36] He argued, over against the "coalition" of scholars endorsing the imperial perspective, that the Roman empire was insignificant

---

N. T. Wright on the issue, see "Paul's Gospel and Caesar's Empire," in R. A. Horsley, ed., *Paul and Politics:* Ekklesia, *Israel,* Imperium, *Interpretation. Essays in Honor of Krister Stendahl* (Harrisburg: Trinity Press International, 2000), 160-83; "A Fresh Perspective on Paul?," *BJRL* 83 (2001): 21-39; "Paul and Caesar: A New Reading of Romans," in C. Bartholemew, ed., *A Royal Priesthood: The Use of the Bible Ethically and Politically* (Carlisle: Paternoster, 2002), 173-93; *Paul: Fresh Perspectives* (London: SPCK, 2005), 59-79.

[30] G. L. Green, *The Letters to the Thessalonians* (Leicester: Apollos, 2002), 38-43, 307-13, 319-20.

[31] J. R. Hollingshead, *The Household of Caesar and the Body of Christ* (Lanham: University Press of America, 1998); J. L. White, *The Apostle of God: Paul and the Promise of Abraham* (Peabody: Hendrickson, 1999), 172-206; P. Oakes, *Philippians: From People to Letter* (Cambridge: Cambridge University Press, 2001), 147-74; J. D. Fantin, *The Lord of the Entire World: Lord Jesus, A Challenge to Lord Caesar?* (Sheffield: Sheffield Phoenix, 2011).

[32] J. D. Crossan and J. L. Reed, *In Search of Paul: How Jesus's Apostle Opposed Rome's Empire with God's Kingdom: A New Vision of Paul's Words and World* (New York: HarperSanFrancisco, 2004).

[33] R. A. Horsley, ed., *Paul and Empire: Religion and Power in Roman Imperial Society* (Harrisburg: Trinity Press International, 1997); Horsley, *Paul and Politics*; R. A. Horsley, ed., *Paul and the Roman Imperial Order* (Harrisburg: Trinity Press International, 2003). Most recently, see R. A. Horsley, ed., *In the Shadow of Empire: Reclaiming the Bible as a History of Faithful Resistance* (Louisville: Westminster John Knox, 2008). Additionally, see J. Meggitt, "Taking the Emperor's Clothes Seriously: The New Testament and the Roman Emperor," in C. Joynes, ed., *The Quest for Wisdom: Essays in Honour of Philip Budd* (Cambridge: Orchard Academic, 2002), 143-69; R. Saunders, "Paul and the Imperial Cult," in S. E. Porter, ed., *Paul and His Opponents* (Leiden: Brill, 2005), 226-38. An entire edition of *JSNT* (27.3 [2005]) was also devoted to imperial studies.

[34] Wright ("A Fresh Perspective on Paul?," 28) states in this regard: "There is a danger—and I think Horsley and his colleagues have not always avoided it—of ignoring the major theological themes in Paul and simply plundering parts of his writings to find help in addressing the political concerns of the contemporary Western world."

[35] B. W. Winter, "Roman Law and Society in Romans 12–15," in P. Oakes, ed., *Rome in the Bible and the Early Church* (Carlisle: Paternoster, 2002), 67-102.

[36] The paper is now available in J. M. G. Barclay, *Pauline Churches and Diaspora Jews* (Tübingen: Mohr [Siebeck]), 363-88.

to Paul. Barclay pointed out that the empire and its Julio-Claudian rulers were coopted under the tyranny of powers (sin, death, flesh) enslaving humanity. According to Barclay, Wright—the highest profile scholar of the coalition— works at times subjectively from nothing explicit in the text, resorting to expedients such as "hidden codes" to detect Paul's (alleged) allusions to empire in his letters. Barclay also proposes that the political situation in which Paul wrote in the early to late-fifties was more open than the coalition recognizes.

Seyoon Kim has also challenged the coalition, asserting that its scholars often fall into the trap of "parallelomania,"[37] depending upon hidden codes and proof-texting for their arguments,[38] with the result that self-contradictory portraits emerge. Although Paul realized the inadequacy of the *Pax Romana*, he did not propose the overthrow of the Roman ruler, a stance also endorsed by the church fathers. In sum, the debate has become sharply polarized in recent years, with Barclay and Kim vocalizing the unease that certain scholars were feeling about the overall theological direction of the "Paul and Empire" coalition and its methodology.[39] We will return briefly to assess some of the issues raised by Barclay and Kim in the section below.

Finally, we turn to several pivotal discussions of the imperial cult in the last three decades. First, S. R. F. Price's monumental work on the imperial cult in Asia Minor sparked a Copernican revolution in classical studies.[40] Price focused on the genuine religiosity animating the cult and its worshippers in the provinces, exploding the consensus that the imperial cult represented a debased form of Roman religion because of its (alleged) insincere flattery of the ruler. Rather the clients of the Julio-Claudian house in the provinces genuinely embraced the imperial cult because of the very considerable benefits it brought to their city-states and the upward mobility that it afforded clients through the ruler-sponsored *cursus honorum*. Of considerable importance, too, was the wide variety of genres of evidence (literary, documentary, numismatic, iconographic, archaeological) that Price employed in portraying the imperial cult of Asia. Second, D. Fishwick's multi-volumed corpus on the imperial cult in the Latin West represents the definitive counterpart to Price's seminal study of the Greek East.[41] Third, J. Sheid's publication on the priestly college of the Arval Brethren, as well as his invaluable translation of the inscriptions of its annual protocols, has provided

---

[37] On "parallelomania," see S. Sandmel, "Parallelomania," *JBL* 81 (1962): 1-13.
[38] See the searing review of Kim's monograph by Warren Carter in the SBL *Review of Biblical Literature* (July 2009), as well as that of J. D. Fantin, *Bryn Mawr Classical Review* (September 2009).
[39] For a critique of the arguments of Barclay and Kim, see Harrison, *Paul and the Imperial Authorities*, 5-8, 28-33.
[40] S. R. F. Price, *Rituals and Power: The Roman Imperial Cult in Asia Minor* (Cambridge: Cambridge University, 1985).
[41] D. Fishwick, *The Imperial Cult in the Latin West: Studies in the Ruler Cult of the Western Provinces of the Roman Empire* (3 vols.; Leiden: Brill, 1987–2005). See also D. Fishwick, "The Development of Provincial Ruler Worship in the Western Roman Empire," *ANRW* II 16.2:1201-53.

scholars invaluable insight into the priestly sacrifices offered each year to the ruler, his family, and the Roman gods.[42] Fourth, I. Gradel has explored the emergence of ruler worship in Rome, concluding with acts of deification in state religion.[43] He avoids the old simplistic Christian dichotomies of "man" or "god" in discussing the Roman ruler, skillfully investigating the "divine" status of various Julio-Claudian rulers within the protocols of benefaction parlance and the conventions of traditional Roman religion.

Given the controversy generated by recent New Testament scholarship on "Paul and Empire," how do we ensure that a methodologically responsible approach is undertaken in studying the ancient evidence and its intersection with Paul's epistles?

3. Important Methodological Questions: Locating Paul in His Imperial Context

In locating Paul's epistles in their imperial context, two important methodological issues are worth airing: whether Paul uses hidden transcripts in critiquing the imperial order and how we might responsibly detect imperial allusions in his epistles. We do not have to discuss in this instance the extent to which Paul's largely illiterate audiences and the apostle himself would have had access to the Julio-Claudian propaganda in the eastern and western Mediterranean basin. The ubiquity of the iconographic, numismatic, and architectural media of the Roman ruler, as well as his staged spectacles, ensured that the motifs associated with Julio-Claudian rule were visually familiar to those at the bottom of the social pyramid.[44] Paul would have had the opportunity to peruse the monument inscribed with the Latin text of the *Res Gestae* at Pisidian Antioch (Acts 13:13-52), presuming that Paul had rudimentary skills in the language,[45] and possibly even in Greek translation as well, although though no fragments of a Greek monument have survived at the site.[46] The wide range of honorific inscriptions erected in prominent locations by grateful clients of the ruler in the eastern Mediterranean basin would also have underscored for Paul the ubiquity of the Julio-Claudian χάριτες (favors), the chief first-century competitor to Paul's gospel of χάρις (grace).

---

[42] J. Scheid, *Romulus et ses frères: le collège des Frères Arvales, modèle du culte publique dans la Rome des empereurs* (Rome: École Française de Rome, 1990); J. Scheid, *Commentarii Fratrum Arvalium Qui Supersunt: Les copies épigraphiques des protocols annuels de la Confrérie Arvale (21 AV.–31 AP. J.-C)* (Rome: École Française de Rome, 1998).
[43] I. Gradel, *Emperor Worship and Roman Religion* (Oxford: Clarendon, 2002).
[44] Harrison, *Paul and the Imperial Authorities*, 19-27.
[45] S. E. Porter, "Did Paul Speak Latin?" in S. E. Porter, ed., *Paul: Jew, Greek, and Roman* (Leiden: Brill, 2008), 289-308.
[46] Harrison, *Paul and the Imperial Authorities*, 24-25.

3.1. Paul and "Hidden Transcripts": Evidence of Imperial Critique?

We saw in section 2 above that Barclay has challenged scholars who, drawing upon J. C. Scott's postcolonial studies, have proposed that Paul critiques the Roman empire in hidden transcript.[47] Scott argued that subordinate groups, when oppressed by their rulers or social superiors, create hidden transcripts that obliquely criticize their oppressors. These hidden transcripts are spoken offstage behind the backs of the politically and socially dominant. In response, Barclay suggests that Scott's case studies are inconclusive for Pauline studies because Paul's first-century context was politically more open than the situations Scott described. Barclay also disagrees with scholars such as N. Elliott who, supporting E. R. Goodenough, point to Philo's use of hidden "codes" when speaking of the Roman ruler.[48] According to Barclay, Goodenough's case for coding in Philo is vastly overstated. In sum, rather than looking for what is politically hidden behind Paul's texts, scholars should be discussing the face-value meaning of what the apostle actually says.

There is a cumulative force to Barclay's arguments. The idea of "coding" has perhaps assumed an axiomatic status in the minds of some Pauline interpreters, with the result that they do not argue their case with sufficient exegetical rigor. At times it has been employed artificially as a methodology for texts of Paul that resist its imposition. Moreover, what Paul *omits to say* about the status of the ruler in its first-century imperial context—informed by the LXX and by his gospel—is as significant as anything he *does say* in code about the ruler. Further, what Paul says *explicitly* about the transfer of the ruler's prerogatives to the reigning Christ and his church, the antitype to the Neronian "body of state," radically undermines the hierarchical social relations underlying the imperial conception of rule.

However, the use of anti-imperial codes in ancient literature and iconography is more widespread than Barclay allows and it opens up the possibility that Paul rhetorically employs the technique for his own pastoral purposes in restricted cases (e.g. Rom 13:1-13; 1 Thess 4:14–5:11; 2 Thess 2:1-12). For example, Philo's parable of the beasts of burden in the market place is very clear in proposing two strategies for dealing with the imperial authorities (*De somniis* 2.83-92). Philo advises that the authorities should be honored as the master of the beasts of burden in the market place.

---

[47] See J. C. Scott, *Domination and the Arts of Resistance: Hidden Transcripts* (New Haven: Yale University Press, 1990). Additionally, see J. C. Scott, *Weapons of the Weak: Everyday Forms of Peasant Resistance* (New Haven: Yale University Press, 1986). On Scott's importance to New Testament studies, see R. A. Horsley, ed., *Hidden Transcripts and the Arts of Resistance: Applying the Work of James C. Scott to Jesus and Paul* (Atlanta: Society of Biblical Literature, 2004).

[48] E. R. Goodenough, *The Politics of Philo Judaeus: Practice and Theory* (New Haven: Yale University, 1938), 21. See N. Elliott, "Romans 13:1-7 in the Context of Imperial Propaganda," in R. A. Horsley, ed., *Paul and Empire: Religion and Power in Roman Imperial Society* (Harrisburg: Trinity Press International, 1997), 184-204; R. A. Horsley, "Disciplining the Hope of the Poor in Ancient Rome," in R. A. Horsley, ed., *Christian Origins: A People's History of Christianity Volume 1* (Minneapolis: Fortress, 2005), 187-90; R. A. Horsley, *The Arrogance of Nations*, 57.

Alternatively, the beasts of burden themselves, like the authorities, should be regarded with "fear" because of their destructive potential. The relevance of Philo's text to Paul's rhetorical strategy in Rom 13:1-7 is pointed enough in its interplay of the motifs of honor and fear (cf. 13:3-4, 7b). It allows us to question whether Paul's endorsement of the imperial authorities in the pericope is as unqualified as some Romans interpreters suggest. Moreover, various Jewish and Greco-Roman texts speak of coded behavior being a necessity towards the authorities and their representatives on the part of subordinate groups (1QS 9.16-17, 21-23; Plutarch, *Mor.* 813D-F).

The anti-imperial propaganda could speak in hidden code, though it was also carried out in public with considerable venom by later generations (e.g. Pliny [the Elder], *Nat.* 7.45.147-150; Tacitus, *Ann.* 1.10). There are two important examples of this. First, the first-century A.D. *Culex* of pseudo-Virgil critiques the excessive and arbitrary rule of Augustus in hidden transcript by means of the engaging tale of the kindly gnat and the sleeping shepherd.[49] Second, whereas the Augustan propaganda depicted the ruler as the new Aeneas (e.g. in the *Ara Pacis*, the Augustan Forum, and Virgil, *Aen.* 8.720-28), the anti-Augustan propaganda parodied this claim through its subversion of Augustan iconography. A wall painting from a house in Pompeii depicts Aeneas fleeing from Troy, carrying his father Anchises and guiding his son Ascanius (the ancestor of the Julian family). But this famous image is caricatured in the anti-Augustan iconography of a wall painting from a villa near Stabiae: there each of the three figures, identical in pose to its Pompeii counterpart, is rendered as a dog-headed ape.[50] K. Scott also points to another humorous variation on the theme from Herculaneum, presently in the Museo Nazionale di Napoli, in which three dogs replace the apes just described.[51] In sum, we should not discount the possibility that Paul does work in hidden transcript where pastorally it was warranted. But why would Paul resort to such a tactic in Rom 13:1-13?

Paul's use of coded language in Rom 13:1-13 is probably driven not so much by the possible *external* threat of the ruler in the mid fifties—though Paul does not avoid the issue (Rom 8:35; 13:4: ἡ μάχαιρα ["the sword"])—but by the *internal* social reality that the early church contained slaves from the

---

[49] For discussion, see Harrison, *Paul and the Imperial Authorities*, 179-82.

[50] Zanker, *The Power of Images*, figures 156 (202) and 162 (209). The official description of the painting at Stabiae at the museum of Naples (K. Scott, "Humour at the Expense of the Ruler Cult," *CP* 27.4 [1932]: 327-28) states: "The monkey with the breastplate has an exaggerated *membrum virile*, as is also true of the monkey with the *pedum*" (328). For the portrait of Aeneas on the Ara Pacis, see Zanker, *The Power of Images*, figures 157 (204) and 204 (259). In a Neronian context, Suetonius (*Nero* 39) cites a puzzle based on the aggregate of the letters in Greek (1005), current in Nero's own lifetime, that unveils in hidden code the atrocities of Nero's rule:

    Count the numerical values
    Of the letters in Nero's name,
    And in "murdered his own mother"
    You will find that their sum is the same.

[51] Scott, "Humour," 328.

familia Caesaris (Phil 4:22) and from the households of powerful imperial freedmen (Rom 16:11b).[52] Moreover, within the body of Christ at Rome there would also have been believers who were either disenchanted with or antagonistic towards the ruler, or who were generally sympathetic to the anti-imperial propaganda.[53] We have to allow for the likelihood that, like believers in the twenty-first century, the first Christians came down on different sides of the political divide. Barclay is possibly correct in differentiating the politically sensitive situation necessitating the use of hidden transcripts in highly oppressive regimes from the more politically open situation confronting the house churches in the mid fifties. But, by A.D. 64, the political situation for Roman believers in the capital had dramatically changed. Tacitus underscores that the disclosures of some the Christians arrested by Nero had led inexorably to the arrest and execution of other believers (Tacitus, *Ann.* 15.44; cf. Mark 13:12a), with the inevitable recriminations that such betrayals would have brought. Since the Romans had perceived that the early believers, to some extent, stood at a distance from imperial society—an attitude styled by Tacitus as "hatred of the human race" (*Ann.* 15.44 [*odio humani generis*]; cf. Pliny, *Ep.* 10.96)[54]—it was easy enough for Nero to stereotype the early believers as the "culprits" responsible for the fire at Rome in A.D. 64.[55]

It is therefore likely that tensions between the early believers and the imperial authorities at Rome had begun to emerge earlier than has been traditionally believed.[56] Given that anti-Augustan sentiment was abroad in the

---

[52] For discussion, see Harrison, *Paul and the Imperial Authorities*, 21-22, 168-69 n. 15.

[53] See Jewett, *Romans*, 793 on the fears of Roman believers regarding the brutality of the Roman regime (Rom 13:3b).

[54] The term *odio humani generis* (Tacitus, *Ann.* 15.44) could refer to the early believers' self-distancing from various civic and religious ceremonies at Rome. Rhetorically, as P. Schafer points out (*Judeophobia: Attitudes toward the Jews in the Ancient World* [Cambridge, Mass.: Harvard University Press, 1997], 191), "Tacitus employs here the well-known accusation of *misanthropia*," a charge which he had used against the Jews in *Hist.* 5.5.1 (*adversus omnes alios hostile odium*: "toward every other people they only feel hate"). But, while the Christians are here being popularly stereotyped as "inferior Jews" (Schafer, *Judeophobia*), the fact that Nero distinguishes the Christians from the Jews demonstrates that the believers' distinctive outworking of community relations, intramural and extramural, in the capital had provoked anxiety among the Roman authorities. For alternate scholarly interpretations of *odio humani generis*, see S. Benko, *Pagan Rome and the Early Christians* (London: Batsford, 1984), 16-19 and R. M. Novak, *Christianity and the Roman Empire: Background Texts* (Harrisburg: Trinity Press International, 2001), 29-30.

[55] S. Spence (*The Parting of the Ways: The Roman Church as a Case Study* [Leuven: Peeters, 2004], 128, original emphasis) observes regarding the visibility of the early Christians as a group within Neronian Rome: "Both Suetonius and Tacitus refer to the Christians *by name* and indicate that the Roman population had developed a loathing for them. The reports of these two writers also indicate that the Roman authorities could identify Christians for specific persecution. Such a public profile requires that the Christians be distinct from the Jews, not as a separate faith but *as a separate social community*, for without social differentiation the Romans would have been at a complete loss to identify Jewish sects." I would also add that such "social differentiation" could have already occurred by the mid to late fifties, perhaps given initial impetus by Claudius' (limited) expulsion of the Jews from Rome in A.D. 49. See also G. Jossa, *Jews or Christians? The Followers of Jesus in Search of Their Own Identity* (Tübingen: Mohr [Siebeck], 2006 [Italian orig., 2004]), 133-34.

[56] See Jossa, *Jews or Christians?*, 127-31.

mid-fifties,[57] possibly infecting some members of the Roman house churches, Paul had to ensure that political divisions over the ruler, accompanied by attitudes of ethic superiority (Rom 11:17-24), did not split believers living in the capital. Undoubtedly, these attitudes are partially attributable to the arrogance associated with Roman conquest of the nations as much as the anti-Semitism infecting the Roman intelligentsia.[58] But because the slaves in the *familia Caesaris* and in the houses of imperial freedmen were totally dependent upon their patron,[59] it would be extremely unlikely that believing slaves would evince or subscribe to anti-imperial attitudes. Thus Paul proceeds delicately with coded diplomacy, so that believers, no matter their viewpoint concerning the Julio-Claudian house, would continue to submit to and honor the ruler, with wealthy Roman believers winning his praise for the benefactions and believers generally earning a reputation for civic cooperation by their payment of taxes (Rom 13:3-4, 7a). However, in so doing, Paul inculcates a clear understanding that the risen and reigning Lord of grace demanded the undivided allegiance of all believers over against the claims of the imperial rulers. Paul's prescient call to unreserved commitment to God in Romans (Rom 12:1-2) would be gloriously and tragically tested for believers in the capital a few years later.

3.2. Imperial Allusions in Paul's Epistles

Another important issue of methodology is how we detect imperial allusions in Paul's letters, given that the apostle does not accord the authority to the imperial texts that he does to the LXX. Kim and Barclay, as noted (section 2 above), have criticized the "Paul and Empire" coalition for its subjectivity in this regard. We face the problem that only rarely Paul does refer directly or indirectly to the Roman ruler (Rom 1:22-23; 13:1-7; 1 Cor 8:5-6). The following suggestions are not exhaustive, but they point to how we might detect collisions of ideology when Paul's gospel is heard against the backdrop of the imperial propaganda. It could be legitimately countered that these collisions merely represent inferences that Paul's audience drew from what he said rather than anything that Paul specifically intended. But the same might be equally said about the intertextual echoes from Second Temple Judaism—texts, stories, themes, and motifs—proposed by many scholars to be detected in Paul's letters. But there is little doubt that such an approach has been especially fruitful in further uncovering the Jewishness of Paul's exegesis.

It is therefore naïve for scholars to allow that Paul, the converted Pharisee,

---

[57] See Harrison, *Paul and the Imperial Authorities*, 177-83, 303-8.

[58] On anti-Semitism among the Roman intelligentsia, see W. Wiefel, "The Jewish Community in Ancient Rome and the Origins of Roman Christianity," in K. P. Donfried, ed., *The Romans Debate: Revised and Expanded Edition* [2nd ed.; Peabody: Hendrickson, 1991], 85-101).

[59] Note in this regard Seneca's advice to Polybius, the freedman of Claudius: "Long ago the love of Caesar lifted you to a higher rank, and your literary pursuits have elevated you . . . Think what loyalty, what industry, you owe him in return for his imperial favor to you . . . you owe the whole of yourself to Caesar" (Seneca, *Polyb.* 6.2; 7.1, 4).

spoke into the spiritual heart of Second Temple Judaism, while quibbling whether Paul, the apostle to the Gentiles and Roman citizen, was speaking *intentionally* into the most prominent and widespread example of idolatry of the Greco-Roman world, the imperial cult. We allow Paul's audience far too much prescience if we reduce the apostle's thought to an ideological cipher in this regard. Undoubtedly, Paul was casting his gospel in traditional Jewish terms for his Gentile auditors (Rom 1:13; 11:13; 15:15-16) so that they would know that they, as a wild olive shoot, had been graciously grafted into the olive root of Israel (11:17-21). But provincial believers in the West and East also needed to know that their incorporation into Christ was based on their elect status before God as the covenantal children of Abraham, the father of all nations (Rom 4:9-25; 9:6-10) rather than being one of the many humiliated nations conquered under the auspices of the elect ruler and the Roman gods. Alternatively, Gentiles believers living in the capital had to be instructed that the Julio-Claudian presumption about Rome's superiority as the conqueror of the nations, including Israel, was totally misplaced (Rom 11:17-21). All this speaks of deliberate intention on Paul's part in instructing his Gentile churches about their new covenantal identity and their responsibilities in acceptance of the "other,"[60] as well as obeying and honoring the ruler himself, within the idolatrous context of Julio-Claudian society.

What methodologies might be helpful in detecting collisions of ideology between Paul's gospel and the imperial world, with a view to uncovering Paul's personal critique of the empire? First, any unusual additions to traditional formulae (e.g. the addition of ἐν δυνάμει [in power] to υἱὸς θεοῦ [Son of God] in Rom 1:4; cf. section 4.1 below) may represent anti-imperial polemic on the part of Paul. Second, if Paul discusses motifs specific to the imperial context of the city to which his epistle is addressed, then he may be engaging in imperial critique (e.g. Nero and "the reign of death": section 4.5; Nero's mercy to his "body of state": section 4.7). Third, if Paul places a heavy or unusual emphasis on a theme that was prominent in the imperial propaganda (e.g. "glory": section 4.3; "grace": section 4:5; "election": section 4.6), it could well be anti-imperial, especially if the imperial version of the motif is critiqued in the Jewish literature. Fourth, the appearance of a phrase in a polemical context of Paul's epistles that is a commonplace of imperial propaganda (e.g. "whenever they say, 'Peace and security'": 1 Thess 5:3) could indicate a critique of the ruler's reign.[61] Fifth, the overlap of LXX and imperial terminology may be deliberate on Paul's part and could indicate a theological critique of the Julio-Claudian symbolic universe from the parameters of his Jewish worldview (section 4.3). Sixth, the intersection of the LXX and early Christian meta-narratives with the imperial "founder" narratives could also point to imperial critique (sections 4.4; 4.6).

The epistle to the Romans, it will be argued, is a potent example of how Paul taught Jewish and Gentile believers in the capital to renounce the idolatry

---

[60] On Roman attitudes to the "other," see E. S. Gruen, *Rethinking the Other in Antiquity* (Princeton: Princeton University Press, 2011), 115-96.
[61] See Harrison, "Paul and the Imperial Gospel," 86-87.

of the imperial cult and the self-serving mores of Julio-Claudian society, without unwisely provoking the Roman ruler, and, more positively, with the aim of winning his praise through the benefactions of wealthy believers (Rom 13:3b) and by submission to his God-given authority (13:2a, 3a, 4a, 5a, 6a, 7a). By calling believers to live transformed lives in loving service of their enemies as the "body of Christ" (Rom 12:1-21)—over against conformity to the Neronian "body of state" (12:2; Seneca, *Clem.* 1.4.1–1.5.1-2)—Paul highlighted the newness of the Spirit (Rom 2:29a; 7:6b; 8:4-17; 15:19) and the resurrection power of God animating those justified in Christ (4:25; 6:1-14). Thus, in view of the presence of the ruler and his family at Rome, as Paul's mission moved from the Greek East to the Latin West (Rom 1:5, 7,11-15; 15:17-29), the apostle considered a more holistic approach in engaging with the ideology of rule expressed in the imperial cult. In what follows (sections 4.1-7) we investigate seven profitable intersections of the Julio-Claudian propaganda with Paul's gospel, though other equally germane imperial motifs could have been discussed.[62] However, hopefully, the motifs chosen will illustrate the rich social and political hues of Paul's theology in Romans.

4. A Study in the Collision of Imperial Ideology with Paul's Gospel in the Epistle to the Romans

4.1. Paul and the Apotheosized Ruler

In Rom 1:2-4 Paul demonstrates how the resurrection of Jesus undermines the imperial propaganda about the apotheosis of Augustus and Claudius. There Paul compares the humble estate of the Son of God—the pre-existent One who was descended in his human nature from the house of David (Rom 1:3b: κατὰ σάρκα)[63]—with his divine exaltation as the victorious Son of God through the Holy Spirit (Rom 1:4a: κατὰ πνεῦμα ἁγιωσύνης). By virtue of his resurrection (Rom 1:4a: ἐξ ἀναστάσεως νεκρῶν), Paul asserts, Jesus was "appointed Son of God *in power*" (τοῦ ὁρισθέντος υἱοῦ θεοῦ ἐν δυνάμει).[64] In other words, Jesus was appointed to his messianic kingship heralded in the writings of the Old Testament and commented on in the literature of Second Temple Judaism (2 Sam 7:14; Ps 2:7; cf. 1QSa 2.11-12; 4Q521).[65] Paul's "enthronement" drama diverges from the humiliating submission of the

---

[62] See Harrison, *Paul and the Imperial Authorities*, 97-323.

[63] C. E. B. Cranfield (*Romans Volume 1: 1–8* [Edinburgh: T & T Clark, 1975], 58) and T. R. Schreiner (*Romans* [Grand Rapids: Baker, 1998], 38) observe that the placement of the words τοῦ υἱοῦ αὐτοῦ (Rom 1:3a) before the two participles (Rom 1:3a: τοῦ γενομένου; 1:4a: τοῦ ὁρισθέντος) suggests that Jesus existed as the pre-existent Son before his incarnation as the seed of David and prior to his appointment as the risen messianic king.

[64] J. D. G. Dunn (*Romans 1–8* [Waco: Word, 1988], 14): "Jesus did not become God's Son at the resurrection: but he entered upon a still higher rank of sonship at the resurrection."

[65] For this understanding of τοῦ ὁρισθέντος (Rom 1:4a), see Cranfield, *Romans*, 61-62 and Schreiner, *Romans*, 41-42.

nations to the ruler depicted in the Julio-Claudian propag/anda,[66] as well as from the belief that the ruler's sonship was the result of the apotheosis of his father.[67]

It is likely that Rom 1:3-4 is providing a different paradigm of rulership to its imperial counterpart. Paul's addition of the phrase ἐν δυνάμει ("in power") to the messianic title υἱὸς θεοῦ ("Son of God": Rom 1:4; cf. 2 Sam 7:14; Ps 2:7) elevates dramatically the status of Jesus, vindicating him as the risen and ruling Son of God in heaven over his imperial rivals on earth.[68] This strategy sidelines both Augustus and Nero, sons respectively of the apotheosized gods Caesar and Claudius.[69] As the vindicated and risen Son of God, Christ had returned to heaven—his original domain—in order to rule over all the nations through the obedience of faith (Rom 1:5: εἰς ὑπακοὴν πίστεως ἐν πᾶσιν τοῖς ἔθνεσιν). By contrast, in the imperial propaganda apotheosis was only ever extended to three rulers of the Julio-Claudian house (Caesar, Augustus, and Claudius), along with two other family members (Livia Augusta [wife of Augustus] and Poppaea [wife of Nero]).[70] Christ's resurrection, however, was more inclusive in its scope in that he was the "firstborn among many brothers" (Rom 8:29: πρωτότοκον ἐν πολλοῖς ἀδελφοῖς). In the present, as the divinely appointed benefactor of his siblings (Rom 8:31-35a), Christ provides access to his Father though the gift of the Spirit (8:14-16) and, in the future, seals their adoption as sons through the resurrection of the dead to eschatological glory

---

[66] J. Ziesler (*Paul's Letter to the Romans* [London: SCM, 1989], 63) argues that sonship, power and resurrection are interconnected. God sends his pre-existent Son (Rom 8:3). Thus "Jesus became, not Son of God, but Son of God *in power*" in his exaltation (original emphasis). Hence it is possible to view Rom 1:4 as "an enthronement formula". On the Old Testament "coronation" motif behind Rom 1:2-4, see Rock, *The Implications of Roman Imperial Ideology*, 157-61.

[67] From A.D. 64–68 Nero's portraiture undergoes a transformation to the eastern idea of divine royalty by being depicted in the tradition of Alexander and the Diadochi. See H. P. L'Orange, *Apotheosis in Ancient Portraiture* (New Rochelle: Caratzis Brothers, 1982), 57-63.

[68] Contra to Cranfield and Schreiner (n. 65 above), Jewett (*Romans*, 107) argues that ἐν δυνάμει ("in power") should be linked with τοῦ ὁρισθέντος ("appointed") as opposed to υἱὸς θεοῦ (Rom 1:4). Thus ἐν δυνάμει would be understood instrumentally, referring to Jesus' appointment through divine power.

[69] On Augustus as "Son of God," see L. R. Taylor, *The Divinity of the Roman Emperor* (Middletown: American Philological Association, 1931), 142-80. On Nero as "Son of God," see M. T. Griffin, *Nero: The End of a Dynasty* (New Haven: Yale University Press, 1984), 98. See now the major study by Michael Peppard, *The Son of God in the Roman World: Divine Sonship in Its Social and Political Context* (Oxford: Oxford University Press, 2011).

[70] For the Suetonian evidence for the apotheosis of Caesar, Augustus, and Claudius, see Suetonius, *Jul.* 88.1; *Aug.* 100 4 (cf. Tacitus, *Ann.* 1.10; Dio 41:9); *Claud.* 45 (cf. Dio 61.35.1-4; Seneca, *Apol.*). On the apotheosis of Livia Augusta and Poppaea, see Suetonius, *Claud.* 11; Dio 40.5; Tacitus, *Ann.* 16.21. For the numismatic and gem evidence of apotheosis, see L. J. Kreitzer, *Striking New Images: Roman Imperial Coinage and the New Testament* (Sheffield: Sheffield Academic, 1996), 69-98. Other members of the Julio-Claudian household were presented as apotheosized in the private gem evidence (e.g. Germanicus: see Kreitzer, *Striking New Images*, 79, 80, figure 6), though this does not constitute official recognition of apotheosis. Notwithstanding, the Greek East did not display the same reserve. See the inscription of Mytilene (D. C. Braund, *Augustus to Nero: A Sourcebook on Roman History 31 B.C.–A.D. 68* [London: Croom & Helm, 1985], §117; *DocsAug.* §95) referring to Nero Julius Caesar (A.D. 6–30) as the "son of new god (παῖς θέω νέω) Germanicus Caesar."

(8:11, 17, 23). Further, Augustus and Nero only *became* sons of god because of the apotheosis of their fathers. Jesus had *always possessed* the status of the eternal Son of God, but his power and glory had been immeasurably magnified through his death and resurrection.

In conclusion, the δύναμις (power) of the Davidic Son of God was demonstrated in God's gospel of justification (Rom 1:16: δύναμις θεοῦ) and in the Spirit's signs and wonders (15:13, 19: ἐν δυνάμει πνεύματος), with the purpose of bringing about the obedience of the Gentiles (1:5-6; 15:9-12, 18). This life-transforming δύναμις stands in contrast to the military *virtus* that the Roman ruler displays on the battlefield towards the enemy nations (ps.-Seneca, *Oct.* 440-44, 504-532).

4.2. Paul and the Idolatry of the Julio-Claudian Cult

A crucial text for Paul's attitude to the imperial cult is Rom 1:21-23. Here Paul focuses on the dishonorable response of the Gentile world to God's natural revelation, drawing from the semantic domains of honor (ἐδόξασαν) and benefaction (ηὐχαρίστησαν) to depict the sin of human ingratitude (Rom 1:21a).[71] Drawing upon the LXX traditions that speak of Israel exchanging the divine glory for idolatry (δόξα: Ps 4:2; 106 [LXX 105]:20; Jer 2:11; Hos 4:7; 9:11; 10:5; cf. Sir 49:5),[72] Paul states that Gentile idolaters make the same mistake in the present (Rom 1:23: ἤλλαξαν τὴν δόξαν τοῦ ἀφθάρτου θεοῦ ἐν ὁμοιώματι εἰκόνος).

Importantly, Paul nominates the types of image worshipped by the Gentiles: corruptible man, birds, quadrupeds, and reptiles. Jewish auditors familiar with the Genesis narrative would have spotted Paul's clear allusion to the subjugation of the created order (Gen 1:26b: birds, livestock, creeping things) that humankind, as the image of God (1:26a), was commanded to undertake. In an ironic reversal of the "dominion" mandate (Gen 1:26, 28), Paul implies, human beings are subjecting themselves to created beings, including their own species, instead of to the glorious Creator of all.

But, as I. E. Rock has demonstrated,[73] there is also imperial reference in Paul's critique which Roman auditors would have discerned. Caligula had recently attempted to install his image in the Jerusalem temple. Nero, too, was infamous for identifying himself with the Roman pantheon (Zeus, Apollo,

---

[71] See J. R. Harrison, *Paul's Language of Grace in Its Graeco-Roman Context* (Tübingen: Mohr [Siebeck], 2003), 214-19.

[72] G. K. Beale, *We Become What We Worship: A Biblical Theology of Idolatry* (Downers Grove: IVP, 2008), 203-16. For contemporary Jewish responses to imperial idolatry, see Philo, *Legat.*, passim; Philo, *Flacc.* 48-49; Josephus, *A.J.* 18.257-309; Josephus, *B.J.* 2.184-203; Josephus, *C. Ap.* 73-78. For discussion of Josephus, *C. Ap.* 73-78, see J. M. G. Barclay, "Snarling Sweetly: Josephus on Images and Idolatry," in S. C. Barton, ed., *Idolatry: False Worship in the Bible, Early Judaism and Christianity* (Edinburgh: T. & T. Clark, 2007), 73-87, esp. 77-81. For discussion of the imperial background to Paul's discussion of idolatry in 1 Corinthians 8:1–11:1, see D. Newton, *Deity and Diet: The Dilemma of Sacrificial Food in Corinth* (Sheffield: Sheffield Academic, 1998), passim.

[73] Rock, *The Implications of Roman Imperial Ideology*, 303-9.

Hercules) and for placing his statue in the temple of Mars Ultor. Rock notes how Seneca advised the young Nero that if he demonstrated *clementia* as ruler, then "all things will be molded into your likeness" (*Clem.* 2.2.1). For Paul, however, the Gentile world foolishly worshipped the "imperial likeness" instead of praising the glory and mercy of the immortal God (Rom 11:36; 16.27). In sum, the worship of the Roman ruler as godlike—along with the many other deities attached to the imperial cult—was but one example in a first-century context of the idolatry against which the Old Testament prophets had inveighed. Paul, as a first-century Jew, would not countenance his converts compromising on the issue.

Although a sidelight to our discussion of Romans, another important text of Paul relevant to the imperial cult, aired in a discussion of idolatry (1 Cor 8:1– 11:1), is 1 Corinthians 8:5-6. As B. W. Winter has convincingly shown,[74] Paul's christologically modified monotheism (v. 5) critiques the imperial cult with the telling phrase "many gods and many lords" who are present "in heaven" and "on earth" (v. 6). J. D. Fantin has correctly observed that the scope of Paul's polemic is "limitless": ἐν οὐρανῷ ("in heaven"). It captures not only the major and minor deities but also the apotheosized Roman rulers (Caesar, Augustus, and, depending on the time of 1 Corinthians' composition, Claudius) and their family members (Livia, Drusilla, and later in Nero's reign, Claudia and Poppaea), whereas ἐπὶ γῆς ("on earth") refers to the living ruler at Rome.[75] Indeed, Paul dismisses the gods wholesale as λεγόμενοι θεοί ("so-called gods"), a phrase that clearly carries a derogatory tone towards the Greco-Roman deities and their beneficent representatives, including the worship of Julio-Claudian family members as much as the ruler himself.[76] Thus Paul, while endorsing the appropriateness of imperial honorific culture in certain contexts (Rom 13:1-7: v. 7 [τῷ τὴν τιμὴν τὴν τιμήν: "honor to whom honor is due"]), dismisses its innate idolatry both from a Jewish and christological viewpoint. The heavy emphasis on the Lordship of Christ in particular (v. 5) also has imperial reference, given the increasing attribution of κύριος language to Nero in inscriptions and papyri from the sixties onwards.[77] It is likely that this language was already informally abroad in the early fifties.

---

[74] B. W. Winter, *After Paul Left Corinth: The Influence of Secular Ethics and Social Change* (Grand Rapids: Eerdmans, 2001), 269-86.
[75] Fantin, *The Lord of the Entire World*, 211. On the divinisation of female Julio-Claudian family members: Livia (Suetonius, *Claud.* 11; cf. Ovid, *Fasti* 1.536; Valerius Maximus 6.1*init.*), Drusilla (Dio 59.11.4), Claudia (Tacitus, *Ann.* 15.23) and Poppaea (Tacitus, *Ann.* 16.21).
[76] The sacrifices offered by the College of the Arval brethren to members of the Julio-Claudian family during the reign of Nero (Scheid, *Commentarii Fratrum Arvalium*, §24-39)—apart from those to the ruler himself — are initially only to those officially apotheosized by the Senate: namely, Augustus, Claudius, and Livia, as well as the Roman deities. Early in Nero's reign, care is taken in speaking of sacrifices to non-apotheosized family members: "and a cow to Concordia in honor of Agrippina Augusta" (Scheid, *Commentarii Fratrum Arvalium*, §27, 15 December A.D. 58, line 31). However, with the later divinisation of Claudia Augusta and Poppaea upon their deaths, both the daughter and wife of Nero are treated as divine: "a cow to the divine virgin Claudia, a cow to the divine Poppaea Augusta" (Scheid, *Commentarii Fratrum Arvalium*, §27, 11 January A.D. 66, line 27; April/May, line 7; etc.).
[77] Fantin, *The Lord of the Entire World*, 181-87.

In conclusion, it would be unwise to assume that Paul's view regarding the imperial cult commanded universal assent among the early Christians in the fifties of the first century. It is likely that some of the powerful and wealthy elite among the believers at Corinth thought that compromise with imperial idolatry was inconsequential (1 Cor 8:10; 10:14-22), being besotted by the opportunities that the imperial cult provided for social advancement.[78] The temptations posed for believers by the upwardly mobile perspective of imperial clients made Paul all the more determined to ensure that his converts should continue to flee idolatry (1 Cor 10:14).

4.3. Paul and the Quest for Ancestral Glory, Republican and Imperial

It is beyond the scope of this chapter to cover the heated quest for ancestral glory in the late republic that led to the social dislocation and heavy death toll of the civil wars.[79] With the triumph of the Julian family over the old noble houses, an intriguing social phenomenon emerges. Under the republic the language of glory was liberally applied to the forbears and descendants of the Roman nobility and, with the appearance of the *novi homines* (new men) on the political stage, also to those who had achieved the consulship for the first time for their house (e.g. Cicero). It was expected that each new generation of Roman nobles would compete for glory through the achievement of military victories and the acquisition of public magistracies in the *cursus honorum* (course of honor). Such careerists would not only replicate but also surpass the glory of their famous ancestors.

However, with the advent of the Julian principate from 31 B.C. onwards, the language of glory concentrated around Augustus and his family members. This meant that the traditional methods of self-advertisement could become precarious for the political competitors of Augustus if glory was pursued unwisely or outside of the ruler-sanctioned career paths in the imperial military and civil bureaucracy. However, Augustus did not intentionally set out to stifle his political competition by establishing a constitutional succession that would consolidate the Julian dynasty during his reign and after his death.[80] Rather, Augustus wanted to keep the traditional avenues of political competition open so that he and the future leaders of Rome would replicate the iconic leadership of the republican past (Suetonius, *Aug.* 31.5; cf. *Res Gestae* 8.5). But the political reality was that the overflowing χάριτες (favors) of Augustus ensured that the traditional clients of the old Roman nobles houses became attached to the Julian house, thereby diminishing the capacity of the nobility to compete as they had in the past. How, then, is glory spoken of in regards to the Julio-Claudian house?

---

[78] J. R. Harrison, "The Brothers as 'The Glory of Christ' (2 Cor 8:23): Paul's *Doxa* Terminology in Its Ancient Benefaction Context," *NovT* 52.2 (2010): 156-88, esp. 181-87.
[79] Harrison, *Paul and the Imperial Authorities*, 201-69.
[80] See J. R. Harrison, "Diplomacy over Tiberius' Accession," in S. R. Llewelyn and J. R. Harrison, eds., *New Documents Illustrating Early Christianity* (vol. 10; Grand Rapids: Eerdmans, 2012), 67-80.

Regarding the ascendancy of Julian house, Valerius Maximus (*Facta et Dicta Memorabilia* 3.2.19) refers to Augustus' apotheosized father, Caesar, in the language of glory: "let us set forth the bright glory of the stars (*siderum clarum decus*), as formerly of arms and the gown, the divine Julius, surest image of true valor." Ovid asserts that eternal glory resides permanently in the house of Caesar (*Tristia* 3.35-46; *Ex Ponto* 2.8.20-26).[81] Elsewhere, Ovid addresses Augustus as "you glory (*decus*), you image of a fatherland (*imago patriae*)" (*Tristia* 3.35-46). Similarly, Valerius Maximus (*Facta et Dicta Memorabilia* 2.8.7) speaks crisply of the civic crown awarded to Augustus in January 27 B.C. (*Res Gestae* 34.2) in these terms: "With it the doorposts of the August dwelling triumph in eternal glory" (*sempiterna gloria triumphant*).

More significantly, in a decree of Mytilene honoring the benefactions of Augustus, the city acknowledges that the honors returned to the ruler are vastly inferior when one remembers the enormity of the glorious honors that the ruler possesses as a godlike being. Consequently, Augustus:

> should ponder on his own self-esteem because it never is possible to match those honors which are insignificant both in accidence and in essence to those who have attained heavenly glory (τοῖς οὐρανίου τετε[υ]χόσι δόξης) and possess the eminence and power of gods. But if anything more glorious than those provisions is found hereafter the enthusiasm and piety of the city will not fail in anything that can further deify him.[82]

Augustus, in a personal letter to Tiberius (Suetonius, *Aug.* 71.3) about his gambling on the festival of Minerva (the Quinquatria, March 20–25), reveals how he lost a large amount of money. In language similar to the decree of Mytilene above, Augustus speaks humorously regarding his generosity at the gaming-board in the language of glory:

> For my part, I lost twenty thousand sesterces, but because I was extravagantly generous in my play (*sed cum effuse in lusu liberalis fuissem*), as usual. If I had demanded of everyone the stakes which I let go, or had kept all that I gave away, I should have won fully fifty thousand. But I like that better, for my generosity (*benignitas mea*) will exalt me to immortal glory (*me ad caelestum gloriam efferet*).

The language of glory is extended to the successors of Augustus and their immediate family circle. In an ode commemorating the deeds of Augustus' stepson Tiberius, Horace highlights how Fortuna had given Augustus unprecedented military glory since his victory at Actium:

---

[81] D. C. Earl (*The Moral and Political Tradition of Rome* [London: Thames and Hudson, 1967], 73) says: "It was not so much that Augustus . . . had all the pride of family typical of a Roman aristocrat. It was that when one *princeps* displaced the *principes*, he inevitably concentrated on himself all the privileges and prerogatives which they had shared and for which they had struggled. All real power and position, *auctoritas*, *dignitas* and *gloria*, had passed into the possession of one man."

[82] *OGIS* 456 lines 35-49.

... the troops, the plan, the favoring gods provided all by thee. For on the self-same day that suppliant Alexandria opened her harbors and her empty place to thee, propitious Fortune, three lustrums later, brought a happy issue to the war and bestowed fame and hoped-for glory upon deeds wrought in fulfilment of thy commands (*laudemque et optatum peractis imperiis decus adrogavit*).[83]

In an intriguing text, Valerius Maximus (*Facta et Dicta Memorabilia* 4.3.3; cf. Horace, *Carm.* 4.4.1-76) asserts that the glory of the Claudian branch of the imperial house—embodied in Drusus Germanicus, Livia's son by a previous marriage—equalled the prestige of the Julian rulers:

It is well known that Drusus Germanicus, the particular glory of the Claudian family (*eximiam Claudiae familiae gloriam*), his country's rare ornament, and, best of all, one who by the grandeur of his achievements, in the perspective of his years, marvelously matched the Augusti, his stepfather and his brother . . .

What is the significance of the explosion of δόξα (glory) language and its cognates in the epistle to Romans? In the epistle to the Romans the combined occurrences of δόξα (16), δοξάζω (5), and συνδοξάζω (1) exceed those in Paul's other letters, 2 Corinthians running a close second (δόξα [18]; δοξάζω [2]).[84] Perhaps one reason for the preponderance of glory terminology in Romans was Paul's awareness of the preoccupation of the Roman nobles with ancestral glory in the past and its decline in the first century A.D. because of the triumph of the all-glorious Caesars. What would Paul's gospel of the "Lord of glory" (1 Cor 2:8; 2 Cor 4:4, 6) have meant for Romans attached to the old republican perspectives of glory and for those who were grateful clients of the new imperial lords of glory at Rome?

At the outset, Paul underscores for his auditors the foolishness of humankind in exchanging the "glory" of God for "corruptible images" shaped in the form of humans, animals, birds, and reptiles (Rom 1:23). As noted (section 4.2 above), Paul's critique of the imperial cult in v. 23 (εἰκόνος φθαρτοῦ ἀνθρώπου ["an image of a mortal human being"])—along with his wholesale rejection of Gentile idolatry—would have been obvious enough to his auditors. The deep irony was that in the age of overflowing grace experienced under Augustus and Nero, humanity had forgotten to give glory and thanks to its true benefactor and Creator (Rom 1:21: οὐχ ὡς θεὸν

---

[83] Horace, *Carm.* 4.33-40. Ovid speaks of the deceased Drusus being the "glory" (*gloria*) of Livia, his aged mother (*Consolatio ad Liviam* 122) and affirms that the "hard-won glory of his exploits" (*operosaque gloria rerum*) would continue into posterity (*Consolatio ad Liviam* 365).
[84] δόξα: Rom 1:23; 2:7, 10; 3:7, 23; 4:20; 5:2; 6:4; 8:18, 21; 9:4, 23 (2x); 11:36; 15:7; 16:27; 2 Cor 1:20; 3:7 (2x), 8, 9 (2x), 10, 11 (2x), 18 (2x); 4:4, 6, 15, 17; 6:8; 8:19, 23; δοξάζω: Rom 1:20; 8:30; 11:13; 15:6, 9; 2 Cor 3:10; 9:13; συνδοξάζω: Rom 8:17. For discussion of the semantic range of δόξα and its cognates in Paul, see C. C. Newman, *Paul's Glory-Christology: Tradition and Rhetoric* (Leiden: Brill, 1992), 157-63.

ἐδόξασαν), the immortal God to whom all glory was due (11:36; 16:27). The so-called eternal glory of Augustus, the father of the fatherland, had fallen far short of the glory of God (Rom 3:23: τῆς δόξης τοῦ θεοῦ), as had the rest of humanity. By contrast, Abraham, the father of all believing Jews and Gentiles, had learned to give glory to God (Rom 4:20: δοὺς δόξαν) and is presented by Paul as the paradigm of persevering faith in God's promises for his Roman auditors.

Paul, however, does not dismiss the quest for glory as fundamentally mistaken, as had the Greek ethical tradition.[85] The quest for the lost glory of Adam was a legitimate object of pursuit for humankind (Rom 2:7). But the *shekinah* glory, associated in the Old Covenant with God dwelling in the temple (Rom 9:4: ἡ δόξα), was now located in the image of Jesus with the arrival of the New Covenant (8:29-30; cf. 2 Cor 3:7-18). The resurrection of Jesus "through the glory of the Father" (Rom 6:4: διὰ τῆς δόξης τοῦ πατρός) had testified to this dramatic shift in the ages. Believers, therefore, could be totally confident that they had been justified and glorified in advance of the eschaton (Rom 8:30: ἐδόξασεν).

Notwithstanding, the achievement of ultimate glory, in contrast to the triumphal boasting of the Julio-Claudians and the republican luminaries before them, would only be achieved at the resurrection (Rom 5:2b: καυχώμεθα ἐπ' ἐλπίδι τῆς δόξης τοῦ θεοῦ). The boasting culture of Roman society had been nullified by the gospel of divine grace in the crucified Christ (Rom 2:21-27). Therefore believers could boast in their present sufferings (Rom 5:3) because "we suffer with him so that we may also be glorified with him" (8:17: συνδοξασθῶμεν).

However, Paul presents his Roman auditors with a final surprise. Rather than the Julio-Claudian house and its family being the locus of all glory, the counter-imperial body of Christ has become the place where God demonstrates his glory in social relations. When Jewish and Roman Gentile believers unreservedly welcome each other, because Christ has welcomed them to the glory of God (Rom 15:7: εἰς δόξαν τοῦ θεοῦ), the Gentiles would glorify God for his mercy (15:9: δοξάσαι). Paul's dismantling of the ethnic divide points to a radically different understanding of glory than the triumph of Rome over the humiliated nations.

4.4. Paul and the Forum Augustum

The *forum Augustum* developed out of Augustus' desire at the Battle of Philippi in 42 B.C. to avenge his adoptive father's assassination. On the eve of the battle, Octavian vowed that he would construct a temple to Mars Ultor, should he be victorious (Suetonius, *Aug.* 29.2; Ovid, *Fasti* 5.569-78; cf. *Res Gestae* 21.1). Forty years later Augustus fulfilled his long-delayed vow when the temple was opened (2 B.C.), though in different form than he envisaged because the temple was now included as part of his forum project.

---

[85] See Harrison, *Paul and the Imperial Authorities*, 207-8.

More important is the design of the forum and the ideological purposes served by its portrait statue program. The temple of Mars Ultor faced the south-west, with the result that Mars Ultor faced the statue of Julius Caesar, Augustus' adoptive father, which was located prominently in the *forum Iulium*. The *forum Augustum* was set at right angles to the *forum Iulium*, with two semicircular bays jutting out on the south-east and north-west sides of the forum. Arrayed around the two bays and porticoes of the forum were statues of famous republican leaders and of the ancestors of the Julian nobility. Each line of republican and Julian luminaries radiated from a different founder of Rome (Aeneas or Romulus), the republican statues expanding outwards from the south-east bay, the Julian statues from the north-west bay.[86] As Ovid (*Fasti* 5.563-66) explains for the observer,

> On the one side (one) sees Aeneas laden with his precious burden, and so many members of Julian nobility. On the other (one) sees Ilia's son Romulus bearing on his shoulder the arms of the (conquered) general, and the splendid records of action (inscribed) beneath (the statues of the) men arranged in order.

Each statue was adorned with a distinctive emblem relevant to his career, and below each statue were boldly lettered laudatory inscriptions that catalogued each man's career achievements. While there is a heavy concentration upon magistracies and military triumphs in the catalogues—many of which prefigured Augustus' illustrious career in the *Res Gestae*—there are features in the careers of the republican luminaries that point forward to the civic and moral grounds for Augustus' unprecedented personal influence (*Res Gestae* 34.1–35.2). As E. A. Judge observes,[87] each inscription focused on an episode that involved the republican leader in political crisis management, that is, handling a desperate situation that imperiled Rome.

Augustus, therefore, had defined exemplary virtue for future generations. Roman history had found its culmination in him and he provided the yardstick of *virtus* (virtue, manliness) for the future rulers of Rome. A statue of Augustus riding in a triumphal chariot stood in the middle of the Forum. It celebrated the fact that he had been awarded the supreme honorific *pater patriae* (Father of the Fatherland: *Res Gestae* 35.1-2; cf. Ovid, *Fasti* 2:119-44).[88] Suetonius (*Aug.* 31.5) provides us insight into Augustus' motives in dedicating statues of famous Julian and republican leaders in triumphal form in the two porticoes of the forum. Augustus had declared in an edict:

---

[86] Judge, "The Eulogistic Inscriptions," 175-76 lists the republican leaders.

[87] Judge, "The Eulogistic Inscriptions," 169.

[88] A golden statue, dedicated by the province Hispania Baetica, also stood in the Forum, personifying either the province or Augustus himself. The gold base of the statue states: "To Imperator Caesar Augustus, Father of the Fatherland, Further Spain, Baetica, [set this up] because, through his good will and constant care, the province has been pacified. 100 pounds of gold" (*ILS* 103).

I have contrived this to lead the citizens to require me, while I live, and the rulers of later times as well, to attain the standard (*ad exemplar*) set by those worthies of old.[89]

How, then, does Paul undermine the supreme example of *virtus* for his Roman auditors? The iconic Augustus—the fulfillment of republican history and the yardstick of virtue for Roman leaders, past and future—had been outshone by the benefactor of the ages. Rom 5:12-21 explodes with the language of grace and overflow—formulaic in the imperial propaganda—as Paul describes the superiority of the reign of grace in Christ. Whereas Augustus had descended from the line of Romulus and the line of Aeneas, Paul reconfigures humanity in Rom 5:6-10 into two new lines of virtue that culminate in disappointment: one might conceivably die for the benefactor (ὑπὲρ γὰρ τοῦ ἀγαθοῦ) from the Greek world or the righteous man (ὑπὲρ δικαίου) from the Jewish world,[90] but no one would die for dishonorable humanity. Seemingly, in terms of crisis management of humanity, there was no hope of any solution to humankind's desperate plight. The reason was clear. In the Greco-Roman honor system, grace calculated the likelihood of its reciprocation in advance: Nero's mercy, for example, would only be extended to *worthy* citizens and allies in the imperial body (see section 4.8 below).

But, at the right time (Rom 5:6: ἔτι κατὰ καιρόν)—both in terms of God's timing and the desperate situation of his dependents—a dishonored benefactor chose to die in an act of grace for his impious enemies (5:6b [ὑπὲρ ἀσεβῶν], 8b [ἔτι ἁμαρτωλῶν], 10a [ἐχθροὶ ὄντες]). By means of this undiscriminating and foolish act of beneficence on behalf of ungrateful dependents (Rom 1:21; cf. 1 Cor 1:18-25), Christ managed the universal crisis that Augustus and the other heroes of the *forum Augustum* could not solve: the Adamic reign of sin and death and the universal suffering of all creation (Rom 5:12-21; 8:18-25).[91] Christ, the τέλος of salvation history (Rom 10:4: goal, end), fulfilled the law by absorbing its curse in his own person on the cross (Rom 3:23-24; 5:6-8, 18-19; 8:2-5; cf. Gal 3:10-14; Col 2:13-14), so that the blessing of Abraham might come by faith to all humanity through the promised Spirit (Rom 2:28-29; 7:6b; cf. Gal 3:14b). As a result, instead of the accolade *pater patriae* being the preserve of Augustus (*Res Gestae* 35:1), believers had the extraordinary privilege of addressing God as *abba*, Father, through the indwelling Spirit (Rom 4:16-18; 8:15-17; 9:6-10; cf. Gal 4:6; cf. Mark 14:36). Paul's counter-imperial family, which crossed the social and ethnic divide of antiquity, had supplanted the Julio-Claudian networks of privilege and obligation with a new set of social relations that would ultimately transform the ancient world.

---

[89] *Res Gestae* 8.5: "I myself left standards in many matters for the imitation of posterity."
[90] For discussion, see Harrison, *Paul and the Imperial Authorities*, 190-95.
[91] On Paul and the new creation in Julio-Claudian context, see Harrison, *Paul and the Imperial Authorities*, 123-28, 156-59.

4.5. Paul and "Age of Grace," Augustan and Neronian

In Romans 5:12-21 the familiar idea of *aeons* from Jewish apocalyptic underlies Paul's regnal imagery (βασιλεύειν: Rom 5:14a, 17a, 17b, 21a, 21b). However, the reign of Christ's grace (Rom 5:21) would have also recalled for Paul's auditors the Augustan "reign of grace" which had acquired iconic status as the age of unparalleled beneficence at Rome and which had established a yardstick of generosity against which all subsequent Roman rulers would be measured. In particular, the famous Priene inscription (9 B.C.) highlights the unsurpassable paradigm of generosity that Augustus had set for all time:

> ... since with his appearance Caesar exceeded the hopes of all those who had received glad tidings before us, not only surpassing those who had been benefactors before him, but not even leaving any hope of surpassing him for those who are to come in the future ...[92]

But the Golden Age inaugurated by Augustus' benefactions paled in comparison to Christ's grace displayed in his obedience unto death for his enemies (Rom 5:6-8, 18b, 19b), resulting in the liberation and transformation of his dependents (Rom 5:15-21). The language of overflow (περισσεύειν: Rom 5:15, 17, 20) and grace (χάρις: 5:15b, 17b, 20b, 21b; χάρισμα: 5:15a, 16b) throughout the pericope is found in the imperial propaganda—and in the Augustan inscriptions specifically—and would have resonated with first-century auditors familiar with the Augustan propaganda.[93] Undoubtedly, the motif of God's overflowing generosity towards sinners, articulated eloquently in the Psalms, is at the core of Paul's theological thought in this passage.[94] But that does not disqualify the resonances that would have been evoked by the Augustan age of grace for his auditors and its implied contrast with Christ's reign of grace.

In the Neronian context of Romans, there is a similar emphasis on the ruler's grace, although the most famous inscription in this regard postdates the epistle.[95] Notwithstanding, Paul's emphasis on the triumph of Christ's grace over death would also have resonated powerfully with later Neronian auditors. The military manliness of the ruler is powerfully displayed on a silver denarius of Nero (A.D. 63–64) from Rome. On the reverse side of the coin, Virtus is depicted, helmeted and in military dress, standing with the right foot on a pile of arms, holding a *parazonium* (a long triangular dagger) on the right knee and a vertical spear in the left hand.[96]

---

[92] *DocsAug.* §98b, lines 37-40.
[93] See Harrison, "Augustan Age of Grace," passim.
[94] In this regard, see C. Breytenbach's important correction to my arguments in Harrison, "CHARIS and ELEOS in Paul's Letter to the Romans," in U. Schnelle, ed., *The Letter to the Romans* (Leuven: Leuven University Press/Uitgenerij Peeters, 2009), 323-63.
[95] See the discussion of *SIG*³ 814 in Harrison, *Paul's Language of Grace*, 62.
[96] *RIC* I² "Nero," §41; cf. the Neronian aureus in *BMC* I "Nero" §27 (plate 38 no. 21).

But, in a chilling variation on the Virtus motif, an issue of a Neronian silver denarius depicts Virtus as standing on the severed head of a captive instead of the traditional pile of arms and helmet.[97] Here we see graphically depicted the reality of death for the humiliated enemies of the imperial ruler. It is important to realize, however, that it is a *personification* of the ruler's military might (Virtus) that is being depicted here and not the ruler himself. The coin could therefore be rendering, in continuity with republican and Augustan tradition, a traditional motif that expressed more the power of the Roman armies over the subdued nations than the military triumph of the ruler over his enemies. Either way, the victory of Rome and her armies, under the ruler, came at the expense of the lives of their captives. But for auditors of Romans, Paul's bold "death" and "life" contrasts (Rom 5:12, 14, 17, 21: θάνατος; 5:17, 18, 21: ζωή) would have spoken of a radically different hope (5:21; 8:18-25, 38) and the present availability of God's resurrection power over sin (6:1-13) for those under the patronage of Christ. The contrast between the reign of death under Nero and the reign of grace (Rom 5:21; 6:15) under Christ could not be sharper.

4.6. Paul and the Ruler a diis electus

What portrait of Augustus and Nero as divinely chosen rulers of the empire emerges from the imperial propaganda?[98] First, as regards the literary evidence, Vitruvius presents the gods congregating in heaven and deciding to apotheosize Julius Caesar as an immortal and to delegate his *imperium* to his adopted son, Augustus.[99] The evidence of Virgil, however, spells out in detail the relationship between the elect emperor and the gods.[100] In an extended speech, Jupiter explains that Augustus has been chosen by himself to establish a universal empire that would usher in the Golden Age:

> From this noble stock there will be born a Trojan Caesar to bound his empire by Oceanus at the limits of the world, and his fame by the stars. He will be called Julius, a name passed down to him from the great Julius. In a time to

---

[97] This issue of the Neronian silver denarius, with the severed head of a captive on its reverse, was for sale on www.oldmoney.com.au in February 2009. Walter Holt—the numismatist selling the coin at *M. R. Roberts Wynyard Coin Centre*, Sydney, Australia—proposed the identification of a captive's head on the coin. For further issues of such coins, see Harrison, *Paul and the Imperial Authorities*, 133 n. 61. For an image of Holt's coin, see Harrison, *Paul and the Imperial Authorities*, 338. For an imaginary discussion between Seneca and Nero on the ruler's ability to wield "death" or "mercy" and its relation to true *virtus*, see ps.-Seneca, *Oct.* 440-44.
[98] For a discussion of electing grace, covering the Jewish and Roman material, see J. R. Harrison, "Paul, Theologian of Electing Grace," in Porter, *Paul the Theologian*, 77-108.
[99] Vitruvius, *De arch.* praef. 2. For discussion of the evidence, see J. R. Fears, *PRINCEPS A DIIS ELECTUS: The Divine Election of the Emperor as Political Concept at Rome* (Rome: American Academy at Rome, 1977), 121-29.
[100] On the imperial ideology in Virgil's *Aeneid* and its relevance to Romans, see Rock, *The Implications of Roman Imperial Ideology*, 49-64.

come, have no fear, you will receive him in the sky, laden with the spoils of the East. He too will be called on in prayer.[101]

J. R. Fears sums up the significance of the text above succinctly: "Long before the foundation of Rome, before Aeneas had ever reached Italy, Augustus had been chosen by Jupiter."[102] Further, Virgil (*Aen.* 6.789-99) speaks later of the *imminent* fulfillment of Jupiter's prophecy with the coming of Augustus to establish his empire.

The decisive blow for Augustus in establishing his world rule is recounted by Virgil from a divine perspective. His famous naval victory at Actium over Antony and Cleopatra (31 B.C.) is achieved with the help of the Roman gods standing on the stern of his ship. A double flame emanates from Augustus' brow and his father's star dawns above his head.[103] Virgil's portrait of Augustus as the elect one is reinforced when the gods (Neptune, Venus, Minerva, Apollo) fight at Augustus' side and help him to defeat the Egyptian forces with their loathsome gods and commanders.[104] We are left in no doubt, therefore, that Augustus' election and the help given him by the gods prove the truth of Jupiter's prophecies a millennium ago. Propertius presents a similar scene regarding Augustus' victory at Actium, with Phoebus in that case delivering the divine help (*Elegies* 4.37-68).[105] Finally, the numismatic propaganda conveys a similar message. A denarius commemorates Augustus' victory at Actium by showing Apollo's protection of the princeps.[106]

By contrast, Ovid concludes his *Metamorphoses* by demonstrating that the fame of Augustus had now surpassed the fame of his father, Julius Caesar. In an impassioned prayer, Ovid invokes all the gods (including Vesta, Apollo, Jupiter) and depicts Augustus as Jupiter's vice-regent on earth:

> Jupiter controls the heights of heaven and the kingdom's of the triformed universe; but the earth is under Augustus' sway. Each is both father and ruler (*pater et rector*). O gods. I pray you, . . . far distant be that day and later than our own time when Augustus, abandoning the world he rules, shall mount to heaven and there, removed from our presence, listen to our prayers.[107]

Velleius Paterculus climaxes his *History of Rome* with a similar prayer for Augustus' successor, his adopted son Tiberius.[108]

---

[101] Virgil, *Aen.* 1.286-91. See also J. R. Fears, "The Cult of Jupiter and Roman Imperial Ideology," *ANRW* II 17.1:3-141, esp. 66-68 on the subordination of Augustus to Jupiter.

[102] Fears, *Divine Election*, 124.

[103] Virgil, *Aen.* 8.678-681. For a discussion of the literary and numismatic evidence relating to the *sidus Iulium*, see Harrison, *Paul's Language of Grace*, 230 n. 72, 232-33 n. 81.

[104] Virgil, *Aen.* 8.698-713.

[105] Horace (*Carm.* 4.2.41-56) gives thanks to the gods for Augustus' safe return to Rome.

[106] *RIC* I² "Augustus," §171a (14 B.C.), cited with a picture of the coin in D. Shotter, *Augustus Caesar* (2nd ed.; New York: Routledge, 2005), 34.

[107] Ovid, *Met.* 858-61, 868-70. Horace (*Carm.* 1.2.41-52) presents a scenario to Ovid, emphasizing that Augustus was "father and princeps" (*pater atque princeps*).

[108] Velleius Paterculus, *History of Rome* 2.136.1-2.

Horace, too, reiterates the theme of Augustus' vice-regency under Jupiter ("with Caesar next in power . . . second to thee alone").[109] As he pithily comments:

> We believe that Jove is king in heaven because we hear his thunders peal; Augustus shall be deemed a god on earth for adding to our empire the Britons and the dreaded Parthians.[110]

Second, as regards the documentary evidence, the fragments of twenty calendars on stone in Italian towns during the Julio-Claudian era provide us evidence regarding the divine protection of Augustus throughout his reign. The entry for 15 December 19 B.C. highlights the role that Fortuna Redux had in returning Augustus safely from the provinces: "On this day the altar of Fortuna Redux was dedicated, she having brought Caesar Augustus home from the overseas provinces: *supplicatio* to Fortuna Redux."[111]

Similarly, the famous Priene inscription refers to the role that Providence had in providing Augustus as the unsurpassed benefactor of the world:

> [S]ince Providence (ἡ πρόνοια), which has divinely (θείως) disposed our lives, having employed zeal and ardor, has arranged the most perfect (culmination) for life (τὸ τελητότατον τῶι βίωι) by producing Augustus, whom for the benefit of mankind she has filled with excellence (ἐπλήρωσεν ἀρετῆς), as [if she had granted him as a savior (σωτῆρα χαρισαμένη)] for us and our descendants, (a savior) who brought war to an end and set [all things] in peaceful order . . .[112]

Third, as regards the archaeological evidence, we briefly refer to the famous statue of Augustus at the Villa of Livia at Prima Porta.[113] On the cuirass of the statue, which celebrates Augustus' victory over the Parthians, we see in the center a Parthian looking up submissively at the Roman eagle. Below this central scene reclines Mother Earth, with Apollo and Diana riding nearby their cult animals (respectively, griffins and hinds). Above the central

---

[109] Horace, *Carm.* 1.12.49-60.
[110] Horace, *Carm.* 3.5.1-4.
[111] *DocsAug.* 55. Augustus (*Res Gestae* 11) refers to the establishment of the altar of Fortuna Redux at Porta Capena. The legends (FORT RED / FORTVN REDV) on Augustan coins commemorate the event as well (*RIC* I² "Augustus," §53a, 55, 56).
[112] *DocsAug.* §98b (lines 32-41; Priene: 9 B.C.). *BMI* 894 (Halicarnassus: 2 B.C.) speaks of Augustus' providential role thus: "in whom Providence has not only fulfilled but even surpassed the prayers of all men." A coin of Tiberius has *Providentia* as its legend (*RIC* I² "Tiberius," §80 [PROVIDENT]). Note how Velleius Paterculus depicts Augustus in providential terms (*History of Rome* 2.89.2). In similar vein, Valerius Maximus (*Facta et Dicta Memorabilia* 1. *Praef.*) says: "Caesar, surest foundation of the fatherland, in whose charge the unanimous will of the gods and men has placed the governance of land and sea, by whose celestial providence the virtues of which I shall tell are most kindly fostered and the vices most sternly punished."
[113] For discussion, see N. Hannestad, *Roman Art and Imperial Policy* (Aarhus: Aarhus University Press, 1988), 50-56. Sauron, QVIS DEVM?, 520-24. Price (*Rituals and Power*, 186) observes astutely regarding the *private* context of the Prima Porta statue: ". . . the statue was designed for a private context, which permitted much greater use of divine iconography."

scene the astral deities (*Sol* [Sun], *Luna* [Moon], *Caelus* [Sky], *Aurora* [Dawn]) are all busy with their cosmic tasks. P. Zanker sums up the significance of the scene in this way: "The princeps who wears this image of victory on his breastplate becomes the representative of divine providence and the will of the gods."[114]

Finally, although the motif of divine election does not feature as prominently in the propaganda of the Julio-Claudian rulers after Augustus, nevertheless we find echoes of "providential" motifs in Nero's famous A.D. 67 inscription in honor of the ruler's liberation of the province of Greece. Nero refers to his personal experience of the Greek gods' "forethought on land and sea,"[115] and, in response, the imperial high priest at Akraiphia eulogizes Nero in this manner:

> Since the lord of the whole world (παντὸς κόσμου κύριος), Nero, Imperator supreme, holding the tribunician power for the thirteenth time designate, father of his country (πατὴρ πατρίδος), New Sun shining upon the Greeks (νέος Ἥλιος ἐπιλάμψας τοῖς Ἕλλεσιν), has chosen to be a benefactor of Greece, requiting and reverencing our gods who stood by him at all times for care and deliverance ...[116]

By the time that Paul was writing Romans, the imperial gospel of divine election had held the East and the West enthralled for eight decades. The Roman gods had ensured the eternal perpetuity of the Roman empire through the Julio-Claudian dynasty. In constructing an alternate symbolic universe based around the divine election of Jews and Gentiles in Romans 9–11, Paul deconstructs the mythological universe of the ruler and thereby helps his auditors to discern the ruler's real status. The ruler is clay in the potter's hands (Rom 9:14-21), subject to the risen Lord of all (10:9-11) and to his glorious Father (11:36), and, at the very best, merely a servant appointed by God to administer justice (13:4), though without the eternal mandate asserted by the Julio-Claudian propaganda (13:11-12). However, given the potential for the ruler to wield the sword as much in persecution as in the maintenance of civil authority (Rom 8:35; 13:4), Roman believers needed a balanced appraisal of imperial rule.

What relevance, then, does the motif of the ruler being *a diis electus* ("chosen by the gods") have for Paul's depiction of electing grace in Romans 9–11? First, the Roman idea of Providence producing Augustus as "the most prefect (culmination) for life" (τὸ τελεότατον τῶι βίωι) is countered by the establishment of Jesus as the *telos* of salvation history (Rom 10:4: τέλος νόμου). Over against the providential strains of the imperial gospel, Paul heralds the eschatological return of the Messiah from Zion to redeem his elect

---

[114] Zanker, *The Power of Images*, 192.
[115] *SIG*³ 814 line 24. J. Malitz, *Nero* (Oxford: Blackwell, 2005 [Ger. orig. 1999]), 92 writes regarding Nero's self-perception in liberating Greece: "At the time (Nero) had become increasingly convinced of his own incomparable significance and the divine protection he thought was befitting of him."
[116] *SIG*³ 814 lines 30-37.

(Rom 11:26-27). Salvation comes through the Jews and the reigning Messiah of Israel (Rom 1:2-4, 16; 16:25-27)—crucified by the imperial authorities (1 Cor 2:8) but vindicated by God (Rom 4:25)—as opposed to the worldwide empire of Rome and the ruler's armies.

Second, whereas Augustus was designated the Father of the Country (5 February 2 B.C.: cf. *Res Gestae* 35.1; Suetonius, *Aug.* 58), God has established his own counter-imperial family who by faith have Abraham and Isaac as their "father" (Rom 4:12, 16-17; 9:10). As noted, those who have entered this new family have the privilege of calling God "Abba, Father"—Jesus' intimate address of God (Mark 14:36)—through the indwelling of the Holy Spirit (Rom 8:15) and by experiencing his new community into which they, as God's elect (8:29-30; 9:6-13), are incorporated by grace (10:12; 11:5 [κατ' ἐκλογὴν χάριτος]; 11:6 [χάριτι οὐκέτι ἐξ ἔργων]). Whereas only the divinely elected Augustus embodies excellence in the imperial gospel (ἀρετῇ), the process is democratized in Paul's thought with the "called" being justified and glorified in advance of the eschaton (Rom 8:30: . . . ἐδικαίωσεν καὶ ἐδόξασεν; 10:4b).

Moreover, the experience of grace is democratized in Paul's gospel, while in the Priene inscription Providence restricts its expression of grace to Augustus alone (σωτῆρα χαρισαμέμη). Grace, paradoxically, could only decline after the epiphany of Augustus because no benefactor afterwards, as the inscription notes (*DocsAug.* §98b [lines 32-41], *supra*), could ever compete again on such a large scale. For Paul, the overflowing grace of Christ continued to overflow into the international community of benefactors he established (Rom 5:17, 20; 2 Cor 4:15; 8:7; 9:8).[117]

Third, and last, Paul downgrades Augustus' Jupiter-like status and his priestly role in the Roman cult (*Res Gestae* 7; 10) by demonstrating Jesus' superior prophetic credentials (Rom 1:2-4; 16:25-27), his eternal deity and cosmic rule (8:18-21; 9:5; 15:13), his triumph over death and sin (Rom 5:12–6:10), and his continual intercession for his dependents before his Father in heaven (8:34). In particular, Jesus' heavenly intercession, supplemented by the earthly intercession of the Spirit though believers (Rom 8:26-27), stood over against the ruler's role as High Priest (Pontifex Maximus) mediating between the Roman gods and the inhabitants of the city.[118] Seen against the backdrop of Augustus' divine election, therefore, Paul's theology of electing grace dismantles the inflated claims of the imperial cult.

4.7. Paul and Believers Living under the Ruler at Rome

But how do we handle that *bête noire* of Pauline interpretation, Rom 13:1-7, which seems to endorse unequivocally the ruler's authority?[119] Paul clearly

---

[117] Harrison, *Paul's Language of Grace*, 226-27.
[118] On the priestly role of the ruler, see R. Gordon, "The Veil of Power: Emperors, Sacrificers and Benefactors," in Horsley, *Paul and Empire*, 126-37.
[119] For full discussion of the modern interpretation, see Harrison, *Paul and the Imperial Authorities*, 271-77.

demotes the imperial ruler in importance when we consider the Greek and Roman background evidence. The ruler is merely God's servant (Rom 13:4a, 4b [διάκονος], 6 [λειτουργοί]). The theocentric emphasis of the entire passage underscores that Paul had strongly imbibed the exilic traditions of the Hebrew Scripture regarding God's sovereign control of the Gentile nations and their rulers for his purposes.[120] The literature of Second Temple Judaism underscores the same point.[121] Further, in a pericope remarkably underplayed in secondary discussions of Rom 13:1-7, the Jesus tradition pivots the priority of obedience to God over against the claims of the ruling authorities, though affirming the legitimacy of their authority in civic administration (Mark 12:13-17). Undoubtedly, Paul's strong emphasis on the importance of the believer's submission (Rom 13:1, 5) to the authorities has to be understood against the teaching of the Old Testament, the literature of Second Temple Judaism, and the dominical traditions about the establishment of the authorities by God (13:1b, 1c, 2a). However, Paul's heavy emphasis on the "fear" of the ruler (Rom 13:3, 4, 7) and his "sword" (8:35; 13:4) also conveys in hidden transcript the importance of not provoking the ruler by unwise or contumacious behavior (section 3.1 above: Philo, *De somniis* 2.83-92). Significantly, the bloody results of disobedience to the ruler for his enemies was emphasized both in the pro and anti-imperial propaganda.[122] Paul, although not naming Augustus or Nero, showed the same awareness of the ruler's ruthlessness as his contemporaries had in this regard.

Moreover, Paul's approach contrasts markedly with the Greek and Roman sources that present the ruler in luminous hues. The Pythagorean political theorists (Diotogenes, Sthenidas, Ps.-Ecphantus) and other Greco-Roman writers (Dio Chrysostom, Plutarch, Musonius Rufus, Seneca) exalt the ruler as the image of God, the vice-regent of God who is foreknown and commissioned by him, the embodiment of animate law (νόμος ἔμψυχος), the priestly intermediary between his people and the gods, the summation of divine virtue and wisdom, the head of the body politic, the soul of the *res publica*, and, finally, the world benefactor and the dispenser of mercy.[123]

---

[120] See Harrison, *Paul and the Imperial Authorities*, 300-302; Wright, "The Letter to the Romans," 719. D. G. Horrell ("The Peaceable, Tolerant Community and the Legitimate Role of the State: Ethics and Ethical Dilemmas in Romans 12:1–15:13," *RevExp* 100.1 [2003]: 88) states: ". . . the (Jewish) strategy Paul adopts *both* legitimates *and* limits the state's authority at the one and the same time." P. H. Towner ("Romans 13:1-7 and Paul's Missiological Perspective: A Call to Political Quietism or Transformation?," in S. K. Soderlund and N. T. Wright, eds., *Romans and the People of God* [Grand Rapids: Eerdmans, 1999], 163), referring to the Old Testament prophetic writings and Jewish Wisdom literature, states that the "message of God's uninterrupted sovereignty in spite of pagan domination over Israel brought hope but also included the obligation to exhibit loyalty to the pagan state . . . (Jer 29:7; cf. Ezra 6:9-10; 1 Macc 7:33)."

[121] See Harrison, *Paul and the Imperial Authorities*, 302-3.

[122] For discussion of the pro-imperial propaganda regarding the military manliness (*virtus*) of the ruler, see our discussion of the Neronian silver denarius in section 4.5 above. For discussion of the Augustan literary and iconographic evidence, see Harrison, *Paul and the Imperial Authorities*, 313-16.

[123] See Harrison, *Paul and the Imperial Authorities*, 277-79.

Strikingly, Paul is deliberately silent about these accolades. In fact, the real emphasis of the passage is upon the obedience of believers to the ruler (Rom 13:1-5) rather than the transcendent status of the ruler.

Admittedly, Sthenidas calls the king the "servant of God" (Stob. 4.7.63) and Plutarch speaks of the ruler "serving" God (*Mor.* 780D). However, Sthenidas depicts the king as an imitator of God (Stob. 4.7.63) and Plutarch portrays him as the image of God (*Mor.* 780E, 780F–781A). Notably, both elements are missing from Paul's portrait of the authorities. Apart from servant function of the ruler (Rom 13:4, 6) and his being appointed by God (Rom 13:1b, 2b), little else remains in Paul consonant with the royal portrait found in the late Hellenistic and early imperial political theorists. Even the language of eternity, routinely associated with Julio-Claudian rule, is deflated by Paul's reference to the imminent arrival of the eschatological day (Rom 13:11b-12a), with the apostle further exhorting Roman believers to shun the immorality of Neronian Rome (13:13b-14).[124] Thus the apostle has effectively demythologized the status of the ruler in antiquity. Indeed, even believers as a group are corporately conformed to the image of Son (Rom 8:29: συμμόρφους τῆς εἰκόνος τοῦ υἱοῦ αὐτοῦ), whereas in the thought of the ancient political theorists the image of God is the preserve of the ruler alone. While this is a more subtle technique than the frontal attacks of the rabbis (e.g. *b. Shabbat* 33b) and Epictetus (section 1 above) against the imperial rulers, it is no less effective.[125]

Finally, Paul pioneered priestly benefactor communities—households of faith with new founding fathers, human (Rom 4:11-12, 16, 18; 9:10) and divine (8:15)—that would ultimately dethrone the ruler as Pontifex Maximus and world benefactor (section 4.6 above).[126] Wealthy believers would exercise beneficence towards the needy independently of the Julio-Claudian patronal networks (Rom 13:3-4), with a view to winning the ruler's praise (13:3b). More profoundly, the caring communities of the early believers expressed their indebtedness of love to all (Rom 13:8-10), including their enemies (12:14-21). The body of Christ, having experienced the mercies of God (Rom 11:30-32; 12:1), would exercise mercy impartially to everyone (12:8: ὁ ἐλεῶν ἱλαρότητι ["the one showing mercy in cheerfulness"]). This novel set of social relations stood in sharp contrast to those of Nero who demonstrated clemency only to those who were worthy of restoration in his "body of state" (*Clem.*

---

[124] See Harrison, *Paul and the Imperial Authorities*, 317-20. On the sexual immorality of Neronian Rome (Rom 13:13: μὴ κοίταις καὶ ἀσελγείαις), see Suetonius, *Nero* 28-29. More generally, see C. Edwards, *The Politics of Immorality in Ancient Rome* (Cambridge: Cambridge University Press, 1993).

[125] For discussion of the rabbinic evidence, see Harrison, *Paul and the Imperial Authorities*, 304-5.

[126] Note the comment of Wright regarding Romans 9–11 ("Paul and Caesar," 189): ". . . the story of Abraham's two sons, and of tracing the true lineage through the right ones in each case, could not but strike a Roman hearer as remarkably similar to the great founding stories of Rome itself, going back to Romulus and Remus. Paul is telling a much older story; like Josephus, he is suggesting that Rome's stories are upstaged by the far more antique Jewish story of origins." Wright makes a similar point about the meta-narratives of the Romans and the Jews in his *Paul*, 6-7, 9-10.

1.4.1–1.5.2).[127] What was remarkable about this social construct was that Paul had demoted the ruler and had reassigned his virtues throughout the body of Christ, without diminishing the importance of the rituals of imperial honorific culture (Rom 13:7b), and without bypassing the ruler's demand for taxes (13:7a).

5. Conclusion

How did Paul become "all things to all people" (1 Cor 9:19-23) in moving his mission from the Greek East to the Latin West (Rom 1:13-15; 15:18-29)? What was distinctive about Paul's critique of the imperial propaganda as it was articulated in Rome? How did his eschatological and apocalyptic gospel engage the Julio-Claudian conception of rule? It was easy enough for Paul to address the ubiquitous idolatry of the imperial cult, among other cults, as he moved through the provinces of the eastern Mediterranean (e.g. 1 Cor 8:5-6), but it was an entirely different matter to tackle the subtleties of its ideology in the capital, without ever having visited Rome. However, the widespread familiarity of the "founder" narratives of Rome, centered on Aeneas and Romulus and their culmination in Augustus and his house, allowed Paul to challenge the residents of the capital in Romans with a radically different narrative of human origins and destiny (Rom 4:1-25; 5:12-21; 15:7-13).[128]

The Julian propaganda—as expressed in the *forum Augustum* and in the *Res Gestae*—unfolds a grand narrative of power and grace that assigned to its loyal clients or defeated subjects either a position of privilege or humiliation in the empire. The Roman gods had providentially assigned eternal rule to the Julian house. It was the role of the ruler, as the embodiment of military manliness (*virtus*), to subjugate the enemy as quickly as possible and to dispense *clementia* (mercy) to those who deserved it, without thereby violating the demands of justice. In this regard, Augustus, the culmination of Roman history, managed the state crises in a way that outshone the exemplars of civic and military excellence of previous generations. He became thereby the paradigm of leadership for the Roman governing elite of the future.

The anti-imperial propaganda sought to counter this ideological construct by depicting Augustus as maintaining peace by fear of his sword. But Paul's counter-imperial benefaction communities, established through the soteriological obedience of a dishonored and vindicated benefactor, embraced a radically different narrative of power and grace that would empower and transform the weak and marginalized of all nations. Paul depicts Christ as simultaneously the fulfillment of universal world history and Jewish covenantal history in a rhetorical strategy designed to dismantle the ideology of rule articulated through the Roman "founder" narratives. Christ is the obedient anti-type of Adam—the disobedient founder of humanity—who had triumphed over the calamitous effects of the fall by his death and resurrection.

---

[127] See Harrison, *Paul and the Imperial Authorities*, 292-99.
[128] See Harrison, *Paul and the Imperial Authorities*, 330-32.

Equally, Christ is the atoning ἱλαστήριον (Rom 3:23), the grounds of justification for those with Abraham's faith (4:23-25), the τέλος of the law (10:4), and the risen messianic ruler of the nations (Rom 1:2-5; 15:12). In sharp contrast to the *clementia* of Nero, as expounded by Seneca in *De clementia*, the strictest demands of divine justice had been fully met by Christ (Rom 3:5-8, 25-26; 5:18-19; 8:3-4): but, paradoxically, mercy had been extended to ungrateful and unworthy recipients who had lost all hope of restoration (1:18–3:20; 5:6-8).

This intersection of two Jewish grand narratives—one the story of humanity in Adam, the other the story of Israel—must have challenged Roman auditors hearing the epistle for the first time. They would have had to consider whether the narrative of Roman origins and its fulfillment in the Julio-Claudian house really addressed the reign of death at Neronian Rome and the universal groaning of the fallen creation.[129] It is significant that Paul in his epistle to believers at Rome, where rulers were not divinized in the state cult until after their death, attributes to Christ his boldest accolade: θεὸς εὐλογητὸς εἰς τοὺς αἰῶνας (Rom 9:5: "God blessed forever"; cf. 1 Tim 2:5).[130] The risen and reigning Christ, the divine Son of the Father, had summoned the Romans and their provincial clients to abandon the idolatry of the imperial cult and the protection of the Roman gods, with a view to escaping God's wrath in the present and at the eschaton (Rom 1:18–3:20; 16:20). Instead they were to submit to God's King, whose offer of unconditional mercy had been extended to every nation and who would bless his dependents with eternal life (Rom 1:1-6; 15:7-13; 16:25-27). By becoming a "Roman to the Romans," Paul ensured the ultimate triumph of his gospel in the Greek East and in the Latin West.

Recommended Reading

Crossan, John Dominic, and John L. Reed. *In Search of Paul: How Jesus's Apostle Opposed Rome's Empire with God's Kingdom. A New Vision of Paul's Words and World.* New York: Harper San Francisco, 2004.

Elliott, Neil. *The Arrogance of Nations: Reading Romans in the Shadow of Empire.* Minneapolis: Fortress, 2008.

Fantin, Joseph D. *The Lord of the Entire World: Lord Jesus, A Challenge to Lord Caesar?* Sheffield: Sheffield Phoenix, 2011.

Georgi, Dieter. *Theocracy in Paul's Praxis and Theology.* Minneapolis: Fortress, 1991 (Ger. orig. 1987).

Gill, Malcolm. *Jesus as Mediator: Politics and Polemic in 1 Timothy 2:1-7.* New York: Peter Lang, 2008.

Gradel, Ittai. *Emperor Worship and Roman Religion.* Oxford: Clarendon, 2002.

---

[129] On the reign of death at Caligulan and Neronian Rome, see L. L. Welborn, "'Extraction from the Mortal Site': Badiou on the Resurrection in Paul," *NTS* 55.3 (2009): 295-314, esp. 301-3; J. R. Harrison, "Paul and the 'Social Relations' of Death at Rome (Rom 5:14, 17, 21)," in S. E. Porter, ed., *Paul and His Social Relations* (Pauline Studies 7; Leiden: Brill, 2012), 85-123.

[130] For a defence of θεός as referring to Christ in Rom 9:5, see M. J. Harris, *Jesus as God: The New Testament Use of Theos in Reference to Jesus* (Grand Rapids: Baker, 1992), 143-72.

Hardin, Justin. *Galatians and the Imperial Cult: A Critical Analysis of the First-Century Social Context of Paul's Letter.* Tübingen: Mohr (Siebeck), 2008.

Harrison, James R. *Paul and the Imperial Authorities at Thessalonica and Rome: A Study in the Conflict of Ideology.* Tübingen: Mohr (Siebeck), 2011.

Horsley, Richard A., ed. *Paul and Empire: Religion and Power in Roman Imperial Society.* Harrisburg: Trinity Press International, 1997.

Kahl, Brigitte. *Galatians Re-imagined: Reading with the Eyes of the Vanquished.* Minneapolis: Fortress, 2009.

Kim, Seyoon. *Christ and Caesar: The Gospel and the Roman Empire in the Writings of Paul and Luke.* Grand Rapids: Eerdmans, 2008.

Lopez, Davina C. *Apostle to the Conquered: Reimagining Paul's Mission.* Minneapolis: Fortress, 2008.

Price, Simon R. F. *Rituals and Power: The Roman Imperial Cult in Asia Minor.* Cambridge: Cambridge University Press, 1985.

Wright, N. T. "Paul's Gospel and Caesar's Empire." Pages 160-83 in *Paul and Politics: Ekklesia, Israel,* Imperium, *Interpretation. Essays in Honor of Krister Stendahl.* Edited by R. A. Horsley. Harrisburg: Trinity Press International, 2000.

Zanker, Paul. *The Power of Images in the Age of Augustus.* Ann Arbor: University of Michigan Press, 1999.

8. The Letter to the Romans

Michael F. Bird

> This letter is truly the most important piece in the New Testament. It is purest Gospel. It is well worth a Christian's while not only to memorize it word for word but also to occupy himself with it daily, as though it were the daily bread of the soul. It is impossible to read or to meditate on this letter too much or too well. The more one deals with it, the more precious it becomes and the better it tastes.
>
> Martin Luther, Preface to Romans

Paul's Letter to the Romans stands arguably as the pinnacle of Pauline thought. It is the longest letter in the Pauline corpus. Not only that, but it is arguably his most theologically erudite and pastorally applicable set of teachings about faith in Jesus Christ and all its implications. It is a letter that has had a monumental impact in the history of Christian thought. The rediscovery of Romans, time and again, has led to reformation and renewal in the Christian church.[1]

While spending time in Milan in A.D. 386, Augustine heard the words "Take up and read, take up read" from the chanting of a small boy or girl. He immediately looked for a Bible and opened it up at Romans, specifically to Rom 13:13-14, and there found rebuke for his behavior and hope for his soul. Soon after both he and his son were baptized by Ambrose of Milan. Martin Luther was Professor at Wittenberg and during 1515–1516 he began expounding Romans to his students, and so discovered that the "righteousness of God" was not the righteousness that condemned him, but the righteousness that acquitted him by faith alone. He wrote: "The whole of Scripture took on a new meaning, and whereas before 'the righteousness of God' had filled me with hate, now it became to me inexpressibly sweet in greater love. This passage of Paul became to me a gateway to heaven." John Wesley once

---

[1] Cf. J. D. Godsey, "The Interpretation of Romans in the History of the Christian Faith," *Int* 34 (1980): 3-16; Gerald Bray, ed., *Ancient Christian Commentary: Romans* (Downers Grove: IVP, 1998); Mark Reasoner, *Romans in Full Circle: A History of Interpretation* (Louisville: Westminster John Knox, 2005); Jeffery P. Greenman and Timothy Larsen, eds., *Reading Romans Through the Centuries: From the Early Church to Karl Barth* (Grand Rapids: Brazos, 2005); Kathy L. Gaca and L. L. Welborn, eds., *Early Patristic Readings of Romans* (London: T. & T. Clark, 2005); William S. Campbell, Peter S. Hawkins, and Brenda D. Schildgen, eds., *Medieval Readings of Romans* (London: T. & T. Clark, 2007); Kathy Ehrensperger and R. Ward Holder, eds., *Reformation Readings of Romans* (London: T. & T. Clark, 2008).

described how his heart was "strangely warmed" one evening at a Moravian meeting in Aldersgate on 24 May 1738 when he heard someone read the introduction to Luther's commentary on Romans. The effect it had upon Wesley was such that, "I felt I did trust in Christ, Christ alone, for salvation; and an assurance was given me that He had taken away my sins, even mine, and saved me from the law of sin and death." A suicidal young man named William Cowper was committed to St. Alban's Insane Asylum in 1763. Finding a Bible lying on a bench in the garden he read over Rom 3:21-26 and in his diary he wrote: "Immediately I received the strength to believe it, and the full beams of the Sun of Righteousness shone upon me. I saw the sufficiency of the atonement He had made, my pardon sealed in His blood, and all the fullness and completeness of His justification. In a moment I believed, and received the gospel." And so began the career of one of Britain's finest hymn writers. In 1921 Dumitri Cornilescu, a deacon in the Orthodox church, translated Romans into his native Romanian and through it he learned that God, in Christ, had secured salvation for him. His translation of the Bible is still used in Romania to this day. After the First World War a young Swiss pastor named Karl Barth rocked the theological faculties of twentieth-century Europe with his theological interpretation of Romans first published in 1919. Barth saw in Romans not the immanence of God in human society, but testimony to the transcendent God who was at work in Paul's gospel to reconcile sinful humanity to himself through Jesus Christ. According to Karl Adam, Barth's *Römerbrief* "fell like a bombshell on the playground of the theologians."

Studying Romans, then, is immensely profitable for theological reformation and spiritual renewal. However, engaging Romans is hard work as it requires concerted effort to analyze the text, purposes, argument, and themes of the letter. There are highly disputed matters in the letter such as the meaning of the "righteousness of God" (Rom 1:17; 3:21), the identity of the "wretched man" (Rom 7:24), the place of Romans 9–11 in the overall argument, and the very intention of the letter itself to name a few points of debate. In what follows, I will set out the context of how Christianity came to Rome, identify key critical issues that affect interpretation, and provide a summary of the argument of the letter.

1. How Christianity Came to Rome

Paul did not establish any churches in Rome. How then did Christianity come to Rome? Very probably it came through Jewish Christians travelling to Rome. Contact between the Jews of Palestine with Rome existed as early as 161 B.C. when Judas Maccabeus established an alliance between Rome and the Judean state (1 Macc 8:17-32; cf. 12:1-4; 14:24; 15:15-24). We also know that in 139 B.C. the Jews were expelled from Rome as part of a wider policy of expelling foreigners on account of spreading their rites and religion among the inhabitants.² There was a large influx of Jews into Rome as a result of Pompey's conquest of Palestine (68 B.C.) with many Jews brought to Rome as slaves, many of whom were later manumitted and gained Roman citizenship.³ Herod the Great and his dynasty secured Roman patronage that included Herod being declared "King of the Jews" by the Romans senate and the Herodian family were closely connected to the imperial household.⁴ Archaeological evidence has uncovered several Jewish synagogues and funeral inscriptions indicating a vibrant Jewish community in Rome in the first century.⁵ The fortunes of the Jews in Rome were positive under Julius Caesar and Augustus who granted them rights like freedom from participation in Roman religion, exemption from military service, and overall treated them fairly and with respect to their national customs.⁶ Things were considerably poorer under Tiberius (with his anti-Jewish advisor Sejanus) who in A.D. 19 deported four thousand Jews to Sardinia to fight bandits, and other Jews were banished from Rome as part of a suppression of foreign cults.⁷ The short reign of Gaius Caligula (A.D. 37–41) was traumatic for Jews in Egypt and Palestine. At this time there were anti-Jewish riots in Alexandria and Caligula attempted to have a statue of himself placed in the Jerusalem temple with only his death preventing its occurrence.⁸ The reign of Claudius (A.D. 41–54) was less tumultuous, but not less problematic for Jews in Rome, and it is probably during this time that Christianity first emerged in Rome. It may well have been travelling merchants like Priscilla and Aquila (Rom 16:1-16), or Roman Jews who visited Palestine for feasts like Pentecost and then returned to Rome, who brought Christianity to Rome (Acts 2:10-11).⁹

At an early point in Claudius' reign, Cassius Dio narrates how Roman Jews lost the right to assemble (ca. A.D. 41). Later (ca. A.D. 49) Suetonius reports how Claudius "expelled from Rome Jews who were constantly making disturbances at the instigation of Chrestus."¹⁰ The banishment of the Roman Jews is attested by Luke who reports that when Paul came to Corinth he met Aquila and Priscilla who had recently left Italy "because Claudius had ordered all the Jews to leave Rome."¹¹ We do not know why the Roman Jews lost the right to assemble. Nor do we know for sure if this "Chrestus" is a Latin

---

² Valerius Maximus, *Factorum et Dictorum Memorabilium* 1.3.3.
³ Philo, *Legat.* 155; cf. *Pss. Sol.* 2.6-7; 17.11-14.
⁴ Josephus, *B.J.* 1.284, 388; *A.J.* 18.179-94.
⁵ Harry J. Leon, *The Jews of Ancient Rome* (Peabody: Hendrickson, 1995); Peter Lampe, *Christians at Rome in the First Two Centuries* (London: Continuum, 2006).
⁶ Philo, *Legat.* 156-58.
⁷ Tacitus, *Ann.* 2.85.4; Suetonius, *Tib.* 36; Cassius Dio, *Hist. Rom.* 57.185.5; Josephus, *A.J.* 18.81-84; Philo, *Legat.* 159-60.
⁸ Philo, *Legat.* 188; Josephus, *A.J.* 18.257-309; *B.J.* 2.184-203.
⁹ Though Eusebius (*Hist. eccl.* 2.14.6) thinks that it was Peter who brought Christianity to Rome, more realistic is Ambrosiaster, *Commentaries on Romans and 1–2 Corinthians: Ambrosiaster* (Downers Grove: IVP, 2009) who wrote: "Those of them [i.e., Jews] who believed in Christ passed this belief on to the Romans, so that they too might keep the law by confessing Christ."
¹⁰ Suetonius, *Claud.* 25.4.
¹¹ Acts 18:1-2.

variation of "Christus" meaning "Christ."[12] What seems plausible is that many of the disputes within the Jewish communities in Rome were centered upon divisive issues occasioned by the influx of Jewish Christians to Rome, who began sharing their faith with fellows Jews, God-fearers, proselytes, and even pagans in Rome.

In addition, given that Paul writes largely to the Gentiles in Rome (see Rom 1:6, 13; 11:13; 15:16, 27), and that a number of the names in Rom 16:3-16 were probably of Gentile origin, we may assume that Jewish Christians won over a number of converts probably from the ranks of Gentile proselytes and God-fearers. The expulsion of Jews and Jewish Christians in A.D. 49, until their return in A.D. 54 at Claudius' death, may have impacted the shape of Christianity in Rome during that intervening period. We do not know for sure how connected Christian groups were with local synagogues and whether "all Jews" were really in fact expelled. Though the Gentile Christians could have become slightly more independent in the absence of their Jewish Christian colleagues, we have no firm reason to belief that Christianity became entirely Gentilized during the years following Claudius' expulsion.

2. Textual Issues

Before plunging into the argument of Romans we have to first recognize that the text of Romans constitutes a unique set of text-critical problems that require comment. These problems include possible interpolations, the absence of "in Rome" from Rom 1:7, 15 in some manuscripts, the place of the doxology in the letter, and the integrity of Romans 16.[13]

Since the nineteenth century some critical scholars have argued that Paul's letters comprise of an amalgamation of shorter letters artificially joined together, or include secondary glosses, and interpolations by subsequent editors of Paul's writings (esp. in 2 Corinthians and Philippians). Romans has not escaped conjecture in this area. Some have argued that Marcion's text of Romans was considerably shorter than canonical Romans and thus more original with additions made to Romans in response to Marcion's text.[14] Walter Schmithals advocated that Romans was a composite of two letters

---

[12] On identifying "Chrestus" with "Christ" see Robert E. Van Voorst, *Jesus Outside the New Testament: An Introduction to the Ancient Evidence* (Grand Rapids: Eerdmans, 2000), 29-39.

[13] Cf. Bruce M. Metzger, *A Textual Commentary on the Greek New Testament* (2nd ed.; Stuttgart: Deutsche Bibelgesellschaft, 1994), 446-77; Harry Gamble, *A Textual History of the Letter to the Romans: A Study in Textual and Literary Criticism* (Grand Rapids: Eerdmans, 1977); Robert K. Jewett, *Romans* (Minneapolis: Fortress, 2007), 4-18; Richard N. Longenecker, *Introducing Romans: Critical Issues in Paul's Most Famous Letter* (Grand Rapids: Eerdmans, 2011), 15-42.

[14] Cf. e.g., P-L. Couchoud, "Reconstitution et classement des Lettres de Saint Paul," *RHPR* 87 (1923): 8-31; P-L. Couchoud, "La première edition de Saint Paul," *RHPR* 94 (1926): 242-63; W. C. van Manen, *De Brief aan de Romeinen* (Leiden: Brill, 1891); W. C. van Manen, *Die Unechtheit des Römerbriefes* (Leipzig: G. Strübig [M. Altmann], 1906).

written to Gentile believers in Rome with two different purposes.[15] Though several interpolations have been proposed for Romans perhaps the most widely favored is that Rom 1:18–2:29 is secondary to the letter.[16]

There are a number of problems with these theories. First, concerning Marcion's text of Romans, it is quite possible that he was working with a shorter text than canonical Romans (there is a good chance that Rom 1:19–2:1 may not have been in his edition of Romans).[17] But the fragmentary and secondary nature of Marcion's text of Romans as we have access to it through the church fathers, and the fact that Marcion was suspected of excising parts of Romans that were not conducive to his interests, means that a Marcionite edition of Romans is not the surest grounds to build an edifice for the textual history of the letter. Second, on the compilation hypothesis, while in theory I think this possible, we are left with the question of why anyone would think to, want to, or need to compress separate letters together.[18] Third, with respect to Rom 1:18–2:29 being an interpolation, I find this quite improbable. For a start the themes and theology of Rom 1:18–2:29 are of a piece with what we find later in the letter. For instance, Rom 2:13-16 is expounded at length in Rom 8:1-16, while Rom 2:25-29 is arguably a compressed summary of Romans 9–11. In addition, the apparent non-Pauline style of Rom 1:18–2:29 needs to be countenanced with the fact that Paul is perhaps drawing on some traditional Jewish material (note especially the similarities with Wisdom of Solomon 11–15) and engaging in a diatribe rhetorical style with an imaginary Jewish interlocutor which accounts for the uniqueness of the language.[19] Fourth, our earliest papyrilogical evidence from ca. A.D. 200–250 (esp. P^{46} P^{40} P^{10} P^{26}) provide no textual grounds for supporting the interpolation theses concerning the earliest chapters of Romans.

The identification of the addresses in Rom 1:7, 15 is complicated by the fact that several textual witnesses (G 1739^{mg} 1908^{mg} it^g Origen) omit the phrase ἐν Ῥώμῃ ("in Rome"). Such an omission was probably deliberate and intended to render the letter universal rather than local in significance and

---

[15] Walter Schmithals, *Römerbrief als historisches Problem* (Gütersloh: Gütersloher Verlagshaus Mohn, 1975).

[16] Alfred Loisy, *The Origins of the New Testament* (trans. J. P. Jacks; New Hyde Park: University Book, 1962 [orig. 1936]), 250; J. C. O'Neil, *Paul's Letter to the Romans* (Baltimore: Penguin, 1975), 40-56; William O. Walker, *Interpolations in the Pauline Letters* (JSNTSup 213; Sheffield: Sheffield Academic Press, 2001), 166-89.

[17] Theodor Zahn, *Geschichte des neuentestamentlichen Kanon* (2 vols.; Erlangen: Deichert, 1888–1892), 2:516; Adolf von Harnack, *Marcion: The Gospel of the Alien God* (trans. J. E. Steeley and L. D. Bierman, Durham. Labyrinth, 1990 [orig. 1924]), 34.

[18] Cf. James D. G. Dunn, *Beginning from Jerusalem* (CITM 2; Grand Rapids: Eerdmans, 2009), 835.

[19] There are also other cogent explanations as to why Rom 1:18–2:29 might appear to be unique within the text of Romans. E. P. Sanders (*Paul, the Law, and the Jewish People* [Philadelphia: Fortress, 1983], 129) thinks Rom 1:18–2:29 was based on a synagogue sermon with no distinctively Pauline imprint; Douglas A. Campbell (*The Deliverance of God* [Grand Rapids: Eerdmans, 2009]) supposes that Paul is engaging in a speech-in-character that allows Paul to create a perspective on law and Sin attributed to false teachers in Rome only to invalidate it in the rest of the letter.

general rather than particular in relevance.[20] Textual support for the inclusion of ἐν 'Ρώμῃ is very strong (P[10, 26vid] ℵ A B C D[abs1] K L P ψ 6 33 81 88 104 181 256 330 424 436 451 459 614 629 1175 1241 1319 1506 1573 1739 1852 1877 1912[vid] 1962 2127 2200 2464 2492 vg sy[p,h,pal] sa bo arm eth geo slav Ambst Pel Aug). The Christians in Rome were undoubtedly then the addressees of the letter.

More problematic is the place of the doxology (Rom 16:25-27) in the original autograph. There are different text forms of Romans concerning the place of the doxology in the letter and none of them correspond to the current form of Romans as we have it in the NA[27], USB[4], and English versions. Traditionally the doxology has been printed after Rom 16:24 in vv. 25-27, but in some witnesses the doxology occurs after Rom 14:23, in other witness after Rom 15:33, and in other witnesses after Rom 16:23. What is more, several witnesses have it at the close of both Romans 14 and Romans 16, and in other witnesses it does not appear at all. Metzger tabulates the data like this:[21]

(a) 1.1–16.23 + doxology	P[61vid] a B C D 81 1739 it[d, 61] vg syr[p] cop[sa, bo] eth
(b) 1.1–14.23 + doxology + 15.1–16.23 + doxology	A P 5 33 104 arm
(c) 1.1–14.23 + doxology + 15.1–16.24	L Y 0209[vid] 181 326 330 614 1175 Byz syr[h] mss[acc. to Origenlat]
(d) 1.1–16.24	F[gr] G (perhaps the archetype of D) 629 mss[acc. to Jerome]
(e) 1.1–15.33 + doxology + 16.1-23	P[46]
(f) 1.1–14.23 + 16.24 + doxology	vg[mss] Old Latin[acc. to capitula]

One scenario is that: (1) the doxology was added in the second century to round off a version of Romans known to end at Romans 14; (2) the doxology was then placed at different locations in some manuscripts; and (3) the benediction in 16:24 was added to function as a bridge between 16:23 and the addition of the doxology at 16:25-27.[22] Another possibility is that the doxology is genuinely Pauline and echoes themes found in Romans 1–14. Afterwards the doxology was moved to 16:25-27 from an earlier point in the letter.[23]

---

[20] Metzger, *Textual Commentary*, 446-47; Gamble, *Textual History*, 29-33; Longenecker, *Romans*, 31-32.
[21] Metzger, *Textual Commentary*, 471.
[22] Cf. Kurt Aland, *Neutestamentliche Entwürfe* (Munich: Kaiser, 1979); Gamble, *Textual History*, 123-24; Peter Lampe, "Zur Textgeschichte des Römerbriefs," *NovT* 27 (1985), 273-77; Jewett, *Romans*, 8.
[23] In defense of the integrity of the doxology in Romans (though not necessarily its placement at 16:25-27) see Larry W. Hurtado, "The Doxology at the end of Romans," in G. D. Fee and E. J. Epp, eds., *New Testament Textual Criticism: Its Significance for Exegesis* (Oxford: Clarendon, 1981), 185-99; Douglas J. Moo, *The Epistle to the Romans* (Grand Rapids: Eerdmans, 1996),

The integrity of Romans 15–16 has been questioned given that its unity with Romans 1–14 is interrupted in some witnesses by the appearance of the doxology. F. C. Baur regarded Romans 15–16 as the interpolation of a Paulinist trying to smooth over Paul's tensions with Judaism.[24] Some scholars propose that Paul made two copies of Romans: Romans 1–15 sent to Rome and Romans 1–16 sent to Ephesus, rendering Romans 16 an appendix to a second copy.[25] It is possible that a shortened version of Romans 1–14 existed prior to Marcion as a "Romans-lite" meant for universal circulation as a general letter (and without the addresses "in Rome" in 1:7, 15).[26] More likely is the testimony of Origen that Marcion "took out the innermost part of this epistle"[27] and excised Romans 15–16 precisely because it was too Jewish. That is strengthened on the grounds that all complete textual witnesses include a sixteen chapter letter. What is more, Romans 14:1–15:13 constitute a literary unity that cannot be accidentally foisted as a secondary compilation. The recommendation and greetings in Romans 16 are far more appropriate if addressed to a group that Paul did not know from first hand acquaintance, rather than written to a church like the one in Ephesus that he knew intimately. Finally, the ending in Rom 16:22-23 constitutes a proper ending for the letter given ancient epistolary conventions.

3. Purpose of Romans

A deeply contested area of opinion is why Paul actually wrote Romans. It is roughly ten times longer than your average letter (like Philemon or 3 John). It is more like a letter-treatise than merely a piece of personal correspondence. Generally speaking, two primary questions have driven discussion: (1) Was the letter occasioned by circumstances specific to Paul's own situation and ministry? or (2) Was the letter occasioned by the perceived need to deal with some kind of internal problem in the Roman house churches? A such, several purposes for Romans have been proposed.

3.1. A Theological Treatise

The Muratorian Canon regards Romans as written "concerning the plan of the Scriptures showing that their foundation is Christ." Among the Reformers, Luther said in his preface to Romans, that Paul "wanted to compose a summary of the whole of Christian and evangelical teaching which would also

---

937; I. Howard Marshall, "Romans 16:25-27: An Apt Conclusion," in N. T. Wright and S. K. Soderlund, eds., *Romans and the People of God: Essays in Honor of Gordon D. Fee* (Grand Rapids: Eerdmans, 1999), 170-84.

[24] F. C. Baur, *Paul, the Apostle of Jesus Christ: His Life and Work, His Epistles and Doctrine* (2 vols.; trans. E. Zeller; Edinburgh: Edinburgh University Press, 1846), 1:352-65.

[25] See list of advocates in Joseph A. Fitzmyer, *Romans: A New Translation with Introduction and Commentary* (New York: Doubleday, 1993), 57.

[26] Gamble, *Textual History*, 113.

[27] Origen, *Commentary on Romans* 10.43.

be an introduction to the whole Old Testament."[28] Similarly, Luther's friend Melanchthon in his *Loci Communes Theologici* of 1521, labeled Romans a "compendium of Christian doctrine." John Calvin, in his introduction to Romans, regarded the letter as a methodological exposition of justification by faith.[29] Anders Nygren argued that Romans was a "doctrinal writing" or a "theological treatise" given in the form of a letter.[30] J. Christiaan Beker advocated that Romans is "in some sense a 'dogmatics in outline,' it is not a timeless theological product but a 'treatise.'"[31] Douglas Campbell even believes that in Romans 5–8, Paul "provisionally articulates a systematic theology."[32] While Romans is the most theologically intense and logically coherent writing on the Christian faith, it is unlikely to be a theological treatise for several reasons: (1) It fails to say much about key *loci* such as the Holy Spirit, Church, and Eschatology; (2) Paul's letters were always situational and Romans is no different as seen in the beginning (1:1-15) and ending (15:14–16:27) of the letter that focus on the details of Paul's ministry, his travel plans, digressions, warnings, and defensive remarks. Though Romans has great utility for Christian dogmatics, it is chiefly a situation letter.[33] That should be unsurprising because theological traction follows on from social reality.[34]

3.2. A Summary of Pauline Teaching

Another view is that although Romans is not a complete summary of the Christian faith, it is clearly a summary of Paul's articulation of the faith in the light of disputes that he had in Antioch, Galatia, and Corinth. That is why there are so many connections between Romans and Paul's other letters. For instance, there are similarities with Galatians, Philippians, and Romans 1–4 concerning justification, and similarities between 1 Corinthians 8 and Romans 14–15 concerning disputed matters of food and fellowship. William Sanday and Arthur Headlam regarded Romans as a conscious summing up of his past experiences.[35] Günther Bornkamm proposed that Romans was Paul's "Last Will and Testament," a summary and development of his doctrine as well as a dress rehearsal for the defense of his teaching as he prepared to go to

---

[28] Martin Luther, *Commentary on Romans* (trans. J. Theodore Miller; Grand Rapids: Zondervan, 1954), xxvi.
[29] John Calvin, *Commentary Upon the Epistle of Saint Paul to the Romans* (ed. Henry Beveridge; Edinburgh: Calvin Translation Society, 1844), xxiii-xxxi.
[30] Anders Nygren, *Commentary on Romans* (trans. C. C. Rasmussen; Philadelphia: Fortress, 1972), 6-8.
[31] J. Christiaan Beker, *Paul the Apostle: The Triumph of God in Life and Thought* (Philadelphia: Fortress, 1980), 77.
[32] Douglas A. Campbell, "Christ and the Church in Paul: A New 'Post-New Perspective' Account," in Michael F. Bird, ed., *Four Views of Paul* (Grand Rapids: Zondervan, 2012), 141.
[33] Cf. Baur, *Paul the Apostle of Jesus Christ*, 321-81.
[34] Cf. Philip F. Esler, *New Testament Theology: Communion and Community* (Minneapolis: Fortress, 2005).
[35] W. Sanday and A. C. Headlam, *A Critical and Exegetical Commentary on the Epistle to the Romans* (Edinburgh: T. & T. Clark, 1895), xlii.

Jerusalem to deliver the collection.[36] Eduard Lohse labels Romans a "summation of the gospel" as it takes up and utilizes motifs Paul had already used in his previous letters.[37] There is something right about this view since it reflects, in part, the theology of the Pauline mission in its mature form.[38] It does reflect key Pauline themes that have appeared in his earlier letters. In fact, James Dunn avers: "Paul's primary objective . . . was to think through his gospel in the light of the controversies which it had occasioned and to use the calm of Corinth to set out both his gospel itself and its ramifications in writing with a fullness of exposition which the previous trials and tribulations had made impossible and which would have been impossible to sustain in a single oral presentation."[39] However, there are also subtle differences. For instance, in Romans 6–8, Paul clearly has a more nuanced and positive view of the law, calling it "holy, righteous, and good" (Rom 7:12) compared to his rather point blank remarks that the law is not based on faith, it came indirectly through a mediator, it was like a penal colony, and obedience to its precepts is a form of slavery (Gal 3:15–4:12). Perhaps this change of tack in Romans was necessary because Paul was required to defend himself from suspicions that he was antinomian based on news of his views about the Mosaic law reaching the Roman house churches that were, in varying degrees, still entrenched in the Jewish way of life.[40] Likewise, while 1 Corinthians 8 deals with food sacrificed to idols and consuming meals at temples, Romans 14 is concerned with vegetarianism, wine, and holy days.[41] Furthermore, parts of the letter, like the analogy of the Olive Branch addressed to Gentiles (Rom 11:13-31), his remarks about taxes and government (Rom 13:1-7), and the warnings concerning false teachers (Rom 16:17-18), cannot emerge from Paul's context, or be part of his notes for an *apologia* in Jerusalem. So while Romans is a distillation of his missional theology, it still contains a specificity that cannot be explained purely by his reflections, or by his preparations to defend himself in Jerusalem.

3.3. A Letter of Introduction to the Roman Churches

Robert Jewett regards Romans as an "ambassadorial letter," akin to Agrippa's letter to Gaius that Philo records, mixed with paraenetic, rhetorical, and philosophical texturing. Paul advocates on behalf of the power of God to gain their support for a cooperative mission to evangelize Spain. Paul rehearses the

---

[36] Günther Bornkamm, "The Letter to the Romans as Paul's Last Will and Testament," in K. P. Donfried, ed., *The Romans Debate* (Peabody: Hendrickson, 1991), 16-28. Jacob Jervell ("The Letter to Jerusalem," in Donfried, *The Romans Debate*, 53-64) also emphasizes the role of Romans as a preparation for Paul's collections speech in Jerusalem.
[37] Eduard Lohse, *Der Brief an Die Römer* (Göttingen: Vandenhoeck & Ruprecht, 2003), 46.
[38] N. A. Dahl, "The Missionary Theology in the Epistle to the Romans," in *Studies in Paul: Theology for the Early Christian Mission* (Minneapolis: Augsburg, 1977), 70-94.
[39] Dunn, *Beginning from Jerusalem*, 867.
[40] Cf. Thomas H. Tobin, *Paul's Rhetoric in its Contexts: The Argument of Romans* (Peabody: Hendrickson, 2004), 76-78.
[41] Cf. Charles H. Talbert, *Romans* (Macon: Smyth & Helwys, 2002), 311-13.

gospel to be proclaimed and lived out there.[42] Though Paul does indeed introduce himself to the Romans and thought of himself as an "ambassador of Christ" (2 Cor 5:20; Eph 6:20), the style of letter is hardly diplomatic. There is a sense in which Paul wants, in all sincerity, to meet the Romans, to bless them by his ministry (Rom 15:29), so that they will reciprocate and help his mission. To that end, they can mutually help one another (Rom 1:10-12; 15:29-30). As such, Paul is also concerned with how the gospel is received and lived out in Rome, particularly given the challenges that Gentile believers face there.

3.4. A Letter Soliciting Support for the Pauline Mission

Paul probably lost Antioch as his base of missional operations in the east and had to rely on his own converts in Ephesus and Greece for support. As he intended to move westwards, he evidently required the support of the Roman churches for a mission to Spain (Rom 15:24-28). Several scholars have thought of Romans as principally designed to induce the Romans to support Paul's evangelistic endeavors in Spain.[43] Luke Timothy Johnson goes so far as to call Romans, in essence, a fund raising letter.[44] The problem of course is whether such an elaborate and lengthy letter would be required to solicit funds. In Philippians, Paul renews the bonds of fraternity with the audience and urges them to provide continued financial assistance to him, but with nowhere near as much theological density as Romans. Granted, that in order to get the support of the Roman churches, Paul would have to lay out his gospel at length to demonstrate its conformity to Scripture and to the Jewish Christian tradition, thus accounting for Romans 1–8. But such a purpose hardly warrants the inclusion of Romans 9–11 that deals with the problem of Israel's rejection of the message and the Gentiles' acceptance of it. Neither does it require the exhortations in Romans 12–15 that take on very specific character. The latter half of Romans must be explained by circumstances and exterior to Paul's own situation. Most likely, Paul writes such things because he has caught wind of events transpiring in Rome that he wishes to address before he arrives there. So I affirm a missionary purpose, but there is something else going on in Rome that occasions Paul's letter and its specific construction, apologia, and exhortations.

---

[42] Jewett, *Romans*, 44.
[43] Cf. e.g., G. Schrenk, "Der Römerbrief als Missionsdokument," in *Studien zu Paulus* (Zurich: Zwingli, 1954), 81-106; W. G. Kümmel, *Introduction to the New Testament* (trans. H. C. Kee; Nashville: Abingdon, 1975), 312-13.
[44] Luke Timothy Johnson, *Reading Romans: A Literary and Theological Commentary* (Macon: Smyth & Helwys, 2001), 6-9; Luke Timothy Johnson with Todd C. Penner, *The Writings of the New Testament: An Interpretation* (3rd ed.; London: SCM, 2003), 344-45.

3.5. A Letter to Bring Unity to the Roman Churches

There is a diverse array of suggestions that Paul wrote Romans in order to bring the potentially divisive ethnic groups in the Roman churches together. We have to remember that Romans is not Galatians. It was not written to attack Jewish Christian teachers for either their particularism or legalism.[45] There is a complete absence of specific names, peoples, or targets that Paul polemicizes against.[46] Consequently, in light of Romans 14–15, some see Paul as trying to bring reconciliation between the "strong" and the "weak." Also, in light of Romans 9–11, some perceive that Paul urges Gentile Christians not to imitate the anti-Judaism of Roman cultural elites.[47]

Wolfgang Wiefel, using a mixture of exegesis, archaeological data, and sociological analysis, argues that the ban of Jewish meetings and the expulsion of the Jews from Rome under Claudius significantly impacted the shape of Christianity in Rome between A.D. 49 and 54. Christianity came to Rome and to Gentiles via the synagogues, causing controversy within them over devotion to Christ, resulting in a ban on meetings, and then in an expulsion of Jewish Christians (or at least their leaders) in A.D. 49.[48] In the proceedings years, until the return of the Jewish Christians in A.D. 54, the Christian movement became largely separated from the synagogues and developed a largely Gentile leadership in house churches. The return of the Jewish Christians created internal tensions over the Jewish law and Jewish leadership of the Gentile house churches. The Roman house churches now included a Gentile majority, consisting of many of whom had never been involved with the synagogues. Paul wrote Romans to effect a reconciliation between them. The situation of the letter is that it was written to "assist the Gentile Christian majority, who are the primary addressees of the letter, to live together with the Jewish Christians in one congregation, thereby putting

---

[45] Contra Baur, *Paul the Apostle of Jesus Christ*, 1:309; Douglas A. Campbell, *Deliverance of God: An Apocalyptic Rereading of Justification in Paul* (Grand Rapids: Eerdmans, 2009), 499; see further Stanley E. Porter, "Did Paul Have Opponents in Rome and What were they Opposing?" in Stanley E. Porter, ed., *Paul and His Opponents* (Pauline Studies 1; Leiden: Brill, 2005), 149-68.

[46] Cf. E. P. Sanders, *Paul, the Law, and the Jewish People* (Philadelphia: Fortress, 1983), 148.

[47] Paul Minear, *The Obedience of Faith: The Purposes of Paul in the Epistle to the Romans* (London: SCM, 1979); Wolfgang Wiefel, "The Jewish Community in Ancient Rome and the Origins of Roman Christianity," in Donfried, *The Romans Debate*, 85-101; James D. G. Dunn, *Romans* (2 vols.; Dallas: Word, 1988), lvi-lviii; Dunn, *Beginning from Jerusalem*, 873-74; N. T. Wright, "The Letter to the Romans," *NIB* 10:406-8; J. P. Sampley, "The Weak and the Strong: Paul's Careful and Crafty Rhetorical Strategy in Romans 14:1–15:13," in L. M. White and L. Yarbrough, eds., *The Social World of the First Christians* (Minneapolis: Fortress, 1995), 40-52; W. L. Lane, "Social Perspectives on Roman Christianity During the Formative Years from Nero to Nerva," in K. P. Donfried and P. Richardson, eds., *Judaism and Christianity in First-Century Rome* (Grand Rapids: Eerdmans, 1998), 196-44 (esp. 199-202); Philip F. Esler, *Conflict and Identity in Romans: The Social Setting of Paul's Letter* (Minneapolis: Fortress, 2003), 133.

[48] For critical analysis of the sources and circumstances of the edict, see Rainer Riesner, *Paul's Early Period: Chronology, Mission Strategy, Theology* (Grand Rapids: Eerdmans, 1998), 157-201.

an end to their quarrels about status."[49]

Many scholars have argued similarly about divisions in Rome among Jewish and Gentile Christians. Paul Minear maintained that Paul wrote Romans as part of his preparation for his mission to Spain, but also to deal with disputes that arose in Rome that had been reported to him by some of those persons listed in Romans 16. Paul is trying to unite no less than five different groups in Rome according to Minear.[50] W. B. Russell saw Paul as opposing an ethnocentricism that exuded from both Jewish and Gentile elements. Russell contends that Paul exhorted the Romans to unity where God is glorified (Rom 12:1–15:7) and the revealing of the righteousness of God removes any smug racial superiority (Rom 1:18–8:39).[51] J. C. Walters acknowledges Paul's intent to solicit support for his mission. However, Christianity in Rome was not unified, and Paul's ministry was controversial. Therefore, Paul expounded upon the universality of the gospel and the priority of Israel. His argument served to deflate Gentile boasting and to quiet Jewish Christian concerns.[52] Francis Watson engaged in a mirror reading and sociological analysis of Romans where he proposed that Romans 14:1–15:13 presupposed two congregations in Rome separated by mutual hostility and shared suspicion over the question of Torah. Jewish Christianity came to Rome as a reforming movement and the character of relationships between both Jewish and Gentile groups was adversely effected by the banishment and return of the Jewish Christians under Claudius. According to Watson, Paul is commending to Jewish and Gentile believers a shared identity based on faith rather than law, and hopes that these two groups will worship together.[53]

The strengths of this thesis are that it identifies a plausible social context for the content in Romans 9–15, it demonstrates that the arguments in Romans 14–15 cannot be explained as general paraenesis based on 1 Corinthians 8 since the disputed issues are different,[54] and it makes sense of the emotive exhortations that appear at the end such as Paul's concern that his audience pursue the things of peace (Rom 14:19) and accept one another as Christ accepted them (Rom 15:7). There are, however, a few problems that plague this view. First, we cannot be certain that the "weak" were Jewish Christians and the "strong" were Gentile Christians. Paul (a Jewish Christian) considers himself to be one of the "strong" (Rom 15:1) and similar language concerning the "weak" was used in a Gentile majority church in Corinth (1 Cor 8:7, 10). There could be Gentile Christians with strong scruples about food, drink, and

---

[49] Wiefel, "Jewish Community in Ancient Rome," 96.
[50] Minear, *The Obedience of Faith*.
[51] W. B. Russell, "An Alternative Suggestion for the Purpose of Romans," *BSac* 45 (1988): 174-84.
[52] J. C. Walters, *Ethnic Issues in Paul's Letter to the Romans: Changing Self-Definition in Earliest Roman Christianity* (Valley Forge: Trinity Press International, 1993).
[53] Francis Watson, "The Two Roman Congregations: Romans 14:1–15:13," in Donfried, *The Romans Debate*, 203-15; *Paul, Judaism, and the Gentiles: Beyond the New Perspective* (2nd ed.; Grand Rapids: Eerdmans, 2007), 163-91.
[54] Contra Robert J. Karris, "Romans 14:1–15:13 and the Occasion of Romans," in Donfried, *The Romans Debate*, 65-84.

idolatry, just as there could be Jewish Christians who became lax in similar matters.[55] In fact, some scholars think that the entire letter is meant for digestion *within* Gentile churches in Rome.[56] Second, the equation of *Chrestus* with "Christ" in Suetonius (with *Chrestus* a mistranslation for the proper *Christus*) remains disputed, so there is no clear evidence for intra-Jewish rivalries in Rome about "Christ." Moreover, Acts depicts Paul arriving in Rome and meeting the Jewish leaders who turn out to be only vaguely aware of the messianic sect and are curious about Paul's gospel (Acts 28:21-22). That does not bode well for the presupposition that "Christ" was a hotbed of controversy amongst Roman Jews in the 40s. Third, the significance and extent of the expulsion of the Jews from Rome in A.D. 49 is over played. For a start, Paul nowhere mentions the expulsion explicitly or implicitly in the letter. It is also more likely that the ringleaders of those few synagogues known to be tumultuous were penalized with expulsion, not necessarily every Jew in Rome (some of whom were Roman citizens). It is unlikely that the expulsion of more than 50,000 Jews from Rome was complete and policed, since such expulsions were commonplace and primarily about political posturing and cultural pandering. The notion of a Jewish vacuum followed by a Gentile majority thereafter is more assumed than demonstrable.[57]

3.6. A Letter to Bring Unity to Christians and Jews in Rome

Mark Nanos innovatively proposed that Paul writes to urge the Gentile Christians in Rome to live in respectful harmony with non-Christian Jews.[58] As such, Paul was a Jewish teacher who functioned within the context of Judaism, he gave priority to Israel, and rallied against the ethnocentric exclusivism of his countrymen that prohibited Gentiles entering the community of the righteous. According to Nanos, the Gentile Christians in Rome were deeply embedded in the Jewish synagogues and Paul is not attempting to safeguard them from judaizing. Rather, Paul is concerned about the gentilizing of the Gentile Christians which would result in the fermentation of anti-Israel sentiment and render them as non-law observant. In

---

[55] Cf. F. F. Bruce, *Romans* (rev. ed.; Leicester: IVP, 1985), 236; Dunn, *Romans*, 2:802; Watson, *Paul, Judaism, and the Gentiles*, 175, 184; Longenecker, *Introducing Romans*, 144-45; Michele Murray, *Playing a Jewish Game: Gentile Christian Judaizers in the First and Second Centuries* (Waterloo: Wilfrid Laurier University Press, 2004), 29-100.

[56] A. Andrew Das, *Solving the Romans Debate* (Peabody: Hendrickson, 2007), 202, 263-64 (a Gentile audience for Romans is also advocated by Paul Achtemeier, Neil Elliott, Stanley Stowers, and Lloyd Gaston to name a few).

[57] Jerome Murphy O'Connor, *Paul: A Critical Life* (New York: Oxford University Press, 1996), 333; J. Ross Wagner, *Heralds of the Good News: Isaiah and Paul in Concern in the Letter to the Romans* (Leiden: Brill, 2003), 33-34; John M. G. Barclay, "Is it Good News that God is Impartial? A Response to Robert Jewett, Romans: A Commentary," *JSNT* 31 (2008): 91-94; Esler, *Conflict and Identity in Romans*, 102-6; Bruce N. Fisk, "Synagogue Influence and Scriptural Knowledge Among the Christians of Rome," in S. E. Porter and C. Stanley, eds., *As It is Written: Studying Paul's Use of Scripture* (Leiden: Brill, 2008), 160-71.

[58] Mark D. Nanos, *The Mystery of Romans: The Jewish Context of Paul's Letter* (Minneapolis: Fortress, 1996).

this sketch, the "weak" in Romans 14 are not Jewish Christians, but rather non-Christian Jews. What makes them weak is their failure to believe that through Christ, God has accepted the Gentiles. Thus, Nanos claims that Paul is seeking to restrain Gentile Christian freedom *halakhically* by ensuring that their practices remain within the orbit of accepted Jewish practices for Gentiles. Paul must do this because the Gentiles have an important role in enabling the restoration of Israel.

Intriguing as Nanos' position is, several pertinent criticisms have been leveled against it. Nanos' contention that the "weak" are non-Christian Jews is not convincing because Paul implies in Rom. 14:1–15:13 that the "strong" are in a position of ascendancy over the "weak."[59] In fact, Rom 14:23 suggests that the "strong" could get their way in forcing the "weak" to eat against their conscience. It is highly improbable to imagine Gentile Christians succeeding in getting Jews connected with a synagogue to abandon their law observances. The Pauline principle in Rom 14:14 also implies a complete relativization of the Jewish purity code, which Jews unfamiliar with the Jesus tradition (see Mark 7:15, 19), would be unlikely to accommodate. If the faith of the "weak" includes an attachment to Jewish boundary markers, then the absence of any mention of circumcision in Rom 14:1–15:13 is peculiar. Additionally, analogous language is used in 1 Corinthians 8, but without an intra-Jewish context.[60]

Purposes for Romans can be multiplied almost endlessly.[61] Sufficient criteria to determine a suitable purpose is hard to come by.[62] My own view, admittedly an eclectic one, is that Paul's reason for writing to the Romans includes both his own missionary situation and the pastoral circumstance of his audience.

3.7. An Eclectic Proposal

In my estimation, the reason for Romans are multiple and complex. Paul writes to the Roman churches, primarily to the Gentiles, but knowing full well that Jewish Christians in the city will hear about the letter, perhaps even from his delegate Phoebe (Rom 16:1-2). Paul wants the financial support of the Roman Gentiles for his planned journey to Spain and he also wants to return

---

[59] Robert A. J. Gagnon, "Why the 'Weak' at Rome Cannot be Non-Christian Jews," *CBQ* 62 (2000): 64-82; Ben Witherington, *Paul's Letter to the Romans: A Socio-Rhetorical Commentary* (Grand Rapids: Eerdmans 2004), 330-33.

[60] Michael F. Bird and Preston Sprinkle, "Jewish Interpretation of Paul in the Last Thirty Years," *CBR* 6 (2008): 365-67.

[61] Cf. Alexander J. M. Wedderburn, *The Reason for Romans* (Minneapolis: Fortress, 1991); L. Ann Jervis, *The Purpose of Romans: A Comparative Letter Structure Investigation* (JSNTSup 55; Sheffield: Sheffield Academic Press, 1991); George Smiga, "Romans 12:1-2 and 15:30-32 and the Occasion of the Letter to the Romans," *CBQ* 53 (1991): 257-73; James C. Miller, "The Romans Debate: 1991–2001," *CR:BS* 9 (2001): 306-49; James C. Miller, *The Obedience of Faith, the Eschatological People of God, and the Purpose of Romans* (SBLDS 177; Atlanta: Scholars, 2000); Das, *Solving the Romans Debate*, 26-52.

[62] Wedderburn, *Purpose*, 64; Longenecker, *Introducing Romans*, 128-33.

to Jerusalem to deliver the collection with all of the Gentile churches firmly behind him as the Apostle to the Gentiles (Rom 1:13; 15:24-25). In order to win their financial favor and their willingness to voluntarily come under his apostolate, Paul has two implied tasks. First, he must win them over to his version of the gospel that is announced to both Jews and Greeks (Rom 1:9, 15-16; 2:16; 15:15-21; 16:25). He does that by setting out his gospel at theological depth in order to better "establish" them (Rom 1:16; 16:25). He appeals to shared traditions (e.g., Rom 1:3-4, 3:22-25; 4:25; 6:17; 15:15) and makes apologetic remarks where necessary to assure them that he is not antinomian or anti-Israel, but is a kosher advocate of the Jewish Christian gospel about Israel's Messiah (Rom 3:8; 6:1-2; 9:1-5).[63] Paul's strength is that he is able to provide sophisticated scriptural and rhetorical arguments explaining how God, through the Messiah, welcomes Gentiles into the family of Abraham, and how believing Jews and Gentiles in the Messiah should equally welcome one another (Rom 4:16; 5:8-11; 15:6-7). Paul, in effect, "gospelizes" them, by which I mean that he endeavors to conform them to the evangelical character of his vision for Christian communities.[64] Paul wants to make the Romans a pristine example of a "faithful obedience" among the Gentiles (Rom 1:5; 16:26) which is precisely what his opponents believed that his converts lacked (Rom 3:7; Jas 2:14-26). Since Paul cannot be there in person to impart a spiritual gift to them, or reap a full harvest by preaching the gospel in Rome just yet, he does the next best thing. He imparts to them the blessing of his gospel, hoping that it will strengthen and encourage them, and also place them in his debt, a debt that will be repaid when he arrives in Rome (Rom 1:9-13).[65] This way we account for the themes of apostleship, Gentiles, gospel, mission, Rome, and Spain, which are so prominent at the beginning and end of the letter. A second implied task is some preventive pastoral care. Paul knows the dangers that the churches in Rome face. The possibility of anti-Paulinists arriving in Rome (Rom 16:17-18), the fragmentation of the house churches over Torah and halakhah perhaps exacerbated by the departure and return of Jewish Christians to Rome (Romans 14), the need for a strategy for negotiating the perils of living in a pagan society (Romans 12–13), preemptively countering the possibility of Gentile Christians imitating the rancorous anti-Judaism of Roman cultural elites (Romans 9, 11), affirming the interlocking nature of Jewish and Gentile missions (Rom 1:16; 10:14-21; 11:13-33; 15:8-9, 27), demonstrating a way of explaining to Jewish neighbors a messianic theodicy for the victory of God over suffering (Rom 8:18-39; 16:20),[66] and expositing God's faithfulness to Israel and his impartiality

---

[63] On the apologetic nature of Romans, see Wedderburn, *Purpose*, 104-12; Peter Stuhlmacher, "The Purpose of Romans," in Donfried, *The Romans Debate*, 238-42; Dunn, *Romans*, lvi; Longenecker, *Introducing Romans*, 126, 148-54.

[64] Cf. Eduard Lohse, "Das Evangelium für Juden und Grieschen," *ZNW* 92 (2001): 168-84.

[65] Bruce Lowe, "1½ Reasons for Romans (Debt Owed Turned to Debt Owing)" (Paper presented at the annual meeting of the SBL, Washington, 18 November 2006).

[66] Cf. Richard Hays, *Echoes of Scripture in the Letters of Paul* (New Haven: Yale University Press, 1989), 53; Beker, *Paul the Apostle*, 151.

towards Jews and Greeks in Jesus Christ (Romans 1–4, 9–10, 14:9-10). In sum, Romans is a word of exhortation,[67] a masterpiece of apologetics, missionary theology, christological exegesis, pastoral care, theological exposition, and artful rhetoric—all designed to win over the audience to Paul's gospel, to support his mission in Spain, to draw Jewish and Gentile Christians in Rome closer together, to strengthen them in the faith despite the perils of Roman culture, and for his audience to identify with the Apostle to the Gentiles as he goes to Jerusalem.

4. Structure

The structure of Romans is, for the most part, fairly agreed on with minor differences. Contentious points focus on whether Romans 5 belongs with Romans 1–4 concerning "justification," or whether Romans 5 belongs more properly with Romans 6–8 concerning "transformation." Most likely, Romans 5 is somewhat of a bridging section that summarizes what precedes it and prepares for what follow after.[68] Although Romans 9–11 is a recognizably distinct unit on its own, it also remains firmly connected with Romans 8 concerning eschatology and the people of God, and thus Romans 8 and 9–11 need to be closely aligned together.[69] Romans is not a rhetorical speech per se, but it contains a clear familiarity with several rhetorical forms. For instance, Rom 1:16-17 functions much like a *propositio* as a thesis statement and the entire letter has a feel of deliberative rhetoric in trying to persuade the audience to adopt Paul's view of the gospel and to support his mission.[70] An outline of Romans can be constructed as follows:

1. Salutation (1:1-7)
2. Thanksgiving (1:8-12)
3. *Narratio* (1:13-15)
4. *Propositio* (1:16-17)
5. Argument 1: The Shared Condemnation of Jews and Gentiles under God (1:18–3:20)
6. Argument 2: The Shared Justification of Jews and Gentiles by Faith in Jesus Christ (3:21–4:25)
7. Bridge Section 1: Peace and Reconciliation in Christ and the Beginnings of a New Humanity (5:1-21)
8. Argument 3: The Transforming Righteousness in Christ by Spirit not law (6:1–8:17)

---

[67] David E. Aune, "Romans as a *Logos Protreptikos*," in Donfried, *The Romans Debate*, 278-96.
[68] Cf. Dunn, *Romans*, 1:242-44.
[69] Tobin, *Paul's Rhetoric*, 254-72.
[70] Cf. Tobin, *Paul's Rhetoric*, 79-98; Michael F. Bird, "Reassessing a Rhetorical Approach to Paul's Letters," *ExpT* 119.8 (2008): 374-79; Ben Witherington III, *Paul's Letter to the Romans: A Socio-Rhetorical Commentary* (Grand Rapids: Eerdmans, 2004), 16-22; Ben Witherington III, *New Testament Rhetoric* (Eugene: Cascade, 2008), 94-157; Jewett, *Romans*, 23-46; Craig S. Keener, *Romans* (Eugene: Cascade, 2008), 2-9.

9. Bridge Section 2: The Victory of the Messiah over Suffering (8:18-39)
10. Argument 4: God's Faithfulness to Israel and the Interlocking Destiny of Israel and the Gentiles (9:1–11:36)
11. Argument 5: The Love-Ethics of the People of God in a Pagan City (12:1–13:14)
12. Argument 6: The Unity of the People of God within Halakhic Diversity (14:1–15:13)
13. Paul's Apostolate to the Gentiles (15:14-22)
14. Paul's Plan to Visit Rome (15:23-33)
15. Personal Greetings (16:1-16)
16. Concluding Exhortation (16:17-20)
17. Postscript (16:21-23)
18. Doxology (16:25-27)

5. Argument

Paul begins by announcing his apostolic call and expositing the gospel of God as containing the royal announcement about the identity of the risen Jesus as Son of David and Son of God in fulfillment of the scriptural promises (1:1-4). Paul's apostolic office was a grace given to him to bring the Gentiles to "the obedience of faith," and the Roman readers also belong to Jesus the Messiah. Thus, from the outset, the story of salvation is the story of Israel's Messiah, who is equally Lord of the nations (1:5-7).

Paul gives thanks for the news of the faith of the Roman churches and mentions his own prayers for them. Paul recounts that his prayers include the hope to visit them, to further establish them, and to impart a spiritual gift to them, so that he and they are mutually encouraged (1:8-12). As to why he has not visited already, Paul explains in a *narratio* how his previous plans to visit have been thwarted. Even so, he still intends to visit Rome in order to preach the gospel there and to have a harvest among the Barbarians and Greeks in the city (1:13-15).

Paul then sets forth the central thesis of the letter, namely, that the gospel is the power of God for the salvation of everyone who believes it, both Jew and Greek. What is more, Paul is not ashamed of this gospel, possibly a jibe against those who think that he should be. What makes the gospel so powerful is that in the gospel the "righteousness of God is revealed." Here the righteousness of God could be an objective genitive (righteousness from God, righteousness that avails before God) or a subjective genitive (righteous character of God, righteous activity of God). Most likely it is a subjective genitive that denotes the character of God embodied and enacted in his saving actions which means vindication for believers and condemnation for the wicked. This righteousness is apocalyptically revealed, an invasive power from God, which rectifies the status and state of believers, and conforms them to the reality of the new creation.[71] The purpose of the gospel is salvation and its scope includes both Jews and Gentiles. A near identical point is made in 15:8-9 where Christ became a servant of the circumcision in order to confirm the promises given to the Patriarchs and so that the Gentiles would glorify God for his mercy. I would argue that Romans has a double *inclusio*: salvation of the Gentiles through Israel's Messiah (1:2-4, 16-17; 15:8-9) and the obedience of faith as the goal of the gospel for Gentiles (1:5 and 16:26). Finally, this saving power of God is received by faith. A point emphasized with a citation of Hab 2:4, demonstrating the conformity of Paul's gospel to the pattern of Scripture.

Paul then identifies the punitive aspects of God's righteousness in the ongoing revelation of God's wrath against those who suppress the truth of God's revelation of himself in the created order. The idolatry and immorality of the pagan world fall under the judgment of God (1:18-31). Paul next shifts his focus from the Gentiles to the Jews in a *diatribe* where he makes four vital points about an imaginary Jewish opponent. For the Jew, even an acculturated Hellenistic Jew, has no claim to superiority due to God's impartiality. That implies that the Jewish interlocutor cannot appeal to a moral superiority based on performance of law due to his hypocrisy (2:1-11). He cannot appeal to his possession of law due to the existence of (Christian) Gentiles who fulfil the law in a manner superior to many Jews (2:12-16). Neither can inherited privileges of the Jewish people (2:17-24), nor even the badge of circumcision (2:25-29), establishes a claim before God for justification.[72] The priority of the Jew over the Greek is restated, but in negative terms, as the Jew is the one who stares first into the face of judgment (2:9).

So that Paul is not misunderstood, he immediately affirms the advantage of the Jew, the benefit of circumcision, and God's faithfulness to Israel (3:1-4). Paul also takes issue with a hypothetical objection that God is unjust to condemn those who by their iniquity and lying give occasion for God to prove his righteous character. God is not fickle, otherwise he could not judge the world (3:5-7). Unrighteous behavior may bring to the surface God's righteous judgments, but that in no way exonerates the guilty or gives anyone, even Paul, a license for sin (3:8). As Paul has now shown, Jews and Gentiles are equally under the power of sin and co-equally condemned in the economy of God's righteous wrath (3:9). This is proved with a cantata of citations from the Psalms (Ps 14:1-3; 5:9; 140:3; 10:7; 36:1) and Isaiah (Isa 59:7-8), which reinforces the wickedness of all human beings (3:10-18). The law speaks to those under its jurisdiction and it affirms the liability of the whole world to the judgment of God (3:19). This point is validated on the grounds that no "flesh" can make a claim before God to be justified on the basis of works of the law. Rather, the law brings knowledge of sin (not a means of release from sin).

---

[71] Michael F. Bird, *Saving Righteousness of God: Studies on Paul, Justification, and the New Perspective* (Milton Keynes: Paternoster, 2007), 12-18; *Bird's-Eye View of Paul: The Man, His Mission, and His Message* (Nottingham: Apollos, 2008), 93-98.

[72] Kent Y. Yinger, *Paul, Judaism, and Judgment* (SNTS 105; Cambridge: Cambridge University Press, 1999), 162-63.

Thus, Paul ends by affirming the faithfulness of God to Israel and the liability of Jews and Gentiles to the judgment of God (3:20).

Paul then begins to expound the central thesis initially set forth in 1:16-17, concerning the revelation of the "righteousness of God" (δικαιοσύνη θεοῦ) in the gospel (3:21-16). Wrath and condemnation are not the final words as God has done something dramatic to deliver believers from the power and penalty of sin. There is a logical and temporal contrast with the words "but now" (see Rom 16:23; Gal 4:9; Eph 2:13; 5:8; Col 1:22, 26) indicating a new epoch of redemptive history that brings salvation to those who have sinned and lack God's glory. The saving power of God (i.e. "the righteousness of God") is manifested apart from the covenantal strictures of the law, yet also intimated by the law and prophets. It is revealed through the πίστις Ἰησοῦ Χριστοῦ (faith of Jesus Christ), which could mean either the "faithfulness of Christ" or "faith in Christ."[73] More likely, it refers to human faith in the Christ event that includes the faithfulness of God operating through the faithfulness of Christ to bring salvation to believers. This deliverance is then described with three different types of metaphors: (1) a slave market metaphor: redemption; (2) a cultic sacrificial metaphor: propitiation; and (3) a legal metaphor: justification. Consequently all boasting, in election, ethnicity, or effort, are excluded because justification comes through faith not by works of the law. Righteousness by faith rules out any idea of a meritorious salvation, and it equally rules out a Jewish ethnocentrism that restricts salvation exclusively to ethnic Jews (Rom 3:27-31).

Paul's introduction of Abraham into his argument serves a dual role by establishing that faith is the mechanism for entrance into salvation and for determining membership in God's people. Thomas Schreiner comments that, "Paul is interested in the inclusion of Gentiles and the basis of their inclusion."[74] Paul insists that Abraham stood in the position of a Gentile when he was justified and was partner in a covenant wholly apart from circumcision. Paul cites Gen 15:6 and Ps 32:1-2 to reiterate what he has already said in 3:21-26, God justifies/credits righteousness by faith apart from works. By stressing that God justifies the "ungodly," Paul also refutes the attempt to cram Abraham's subsequent acts of obedience into his justification (see 1 Macc 2.52) or the notion that Abraham had a private revelation of the Mosaic law that he obeyed (see Sir 44:19-21; *Jub* 23.10; *2 Bar* 57.1-2). Abraham's faith was credited as righteousness without law obedience and given by sheer grace. This is a clear rejection of a work-for-reward view of salvation as one can imagine, but is also a penetrating riposte at those who contend that salvation is tied to Israel's covenantal election to the exclusion of Gentiles (Rom 4:1-8).

Paul repeats the theme of 3:29-30 that righteousness by faith applies equally to Jew and Gentile because Abraham was justified when he was still yet uncircumcised. Circumcision was the sign of the promise that was

---

[73] On this debate see Michael F. Bird and Preston M. Sprinkle, eds., *The Faith of Jesus Christ: Exegetical, Biblical and Theological Studies* (Peabody: Hendrickson, 2009).
[74] Thomas R. Schreiner, *Romans* (Grand Rapids: Baker, 1998), 228.

received by faith; circumcision did not establish the relationship or mark out who inherits the Abrahamic promises.[75] The Abrahamic narratives are enlisted in order to drive home the point that Gentiles are justified in the same way as Abraham and those who emulate the Abrahamic faith belong in the Abrahamic covenant. This justifying faith is directed at the life-giving power of God who raised Jesus from the dead. (4:9-17).[76] Following the Isaianic script, Jesus was handed over to deal with sins, and raised for the justification of believers (4:18-25).

Romans 5 is somewhat of a transition section which summarizes 3:21–4:25, while at the same time previewing Rom 6:1–8:17 where the sin-death-law nexus is broken. In 5:1-2, Paul recapitulates his *propositio* with reference to "having been justified by faith" and the "hope of glory" (5:1-2). Then he begins to admix themes of assurance in God's saving power and the virtues created by persevering under suffering. He introduces the imagery of reconciliation and reflects on the magnitude of divine grace and divine love. God justifies and reconciles the unrighteous by Christ's death and saves them on account of Christ's risen life (5:3-11). The Adam/Christ typology of 5:12-21 is really an extended commentary on 1 Cor 15:56: "The sting of death is sin, and the power of sin is the law." Paul moves to demonstrate how the law did not redeem Adam's fallen nature, but served only to antagonize the power of sin, activate sinful desire, and affirm the sentence of death due to Adam's progeny. Paul situates his argument about God's saving righteousness in the scope of humanity condemned and then justified, humanity enslaved in sin and set free in Christ; so that justification creates not only a world-wide Abrahamic family, but also a renewed humanity. Believers shift from the epoch of sin, death, and condemnation associated with Adam's transgression to the epoch of righteousness, life, and justification associated with the obedience of the new Adam.

The burden of Romans 6–7 is to anticipate several objections to Paul's message. If the law is not a means to attaining righteousness, and if law no longer marks out who are the children of Abraham, then it is legitimate to ask: what is the motivation for righteous behavior and what was the point of giving the law in the first place? The exhortation to righteousness in Romans 6 is predicated on one crucial premise: the transforming power of the gospel and the new obedience created by union with Christ. By union with Christ, believers are emancipated from the old age of sin and death and are uniquely empowered by baptism into Christ to live their lives in complete service to God. This thought is expressed most aptly as the indicative and imperative of Pauline ethics: because you have been united to Christ and died to sin, you need not offer your body into the service of sin; instead you are free to cultivate obedience that leads to righteousness (Rom 6:1-23).

---

[75] The discussion of Romans 4 by Peter T. O'Brien ("Was Paul Converted?" in D. A. Carson, Mark A. Seifrid, and Peter T. O'Brien, eds., *Justification and Variegated Nomism: Volume 2: The Paradoxes of Paul* [Grand Rapids: Baker, 2004], 376-88) is particularly helpful here.
[76] Cf. Esler, *Conflict and Identity in Romans*, 168-94.

Romans 7 addresses the issue of the role of the law in redemptive history and the believer's freedom from the law. The metaphor of a marriage covenant annulled by the death of the husband is used as an example of the believer's freedom from the law (Rom 7:1-5). The Christian has died from the age of sin and death that the law served. Paul is adamant though that this is no license for lawless behavior and believers are indebted to "bear fruit to God" (Rom 7:4) and to serve in the "new way of the Spirit" (Rom 7:6). The "wretched man" soliloquy in Rom 7:7-25 is among the most problematic sections of Romans and the most intellectually straining passage of the entire Pauline corpus. I am persuaded that this passage is not autobiographical of Paul either pre- or post-conversion,[77] but underscores the plight of the Jew under the law apart from Christ and the dark vestiges of the "Adamic self."[78] But such a plight is only evident when viewed retrospectively through the lens of faith. The purpose of the law was to mark out sin as sin; but law has no power to effect either redemption or transformation. In that sense the law points to salvation but does not provide it.

Romans 8 encapsulates a kaleidoscope of themes and arguments about the efficacy of God's saving righteousness, the outworking of righteousness in the life of the believer through the Spirit, and the vindication of God's people at the final assize. Paul begins by again recapitulating his *propositio* but in slightly different terms. Instead of "justification" we are presented with the obverse side, "no condemnation" for those in Christ Jesus (Rom 8:1). It is Spirit rather than law that sets believers free from sin and death. Whereas the law was impotent to effect anything on account of sin, God achieved it by sending his own Son to deal with the sin of humanity by condemning it in human flesh (Rom 8:1-3). Life in the Spirit effects the salvation and transformation of humanity that many thought the law would bring (Rom 8:4-11). Further to that, receipt of the Spirit is proof that believers have been adopted into God's family and possess the status of sons (Rom 8:12-17). In light of that, the sufferings that believers endure must be put into proper perspective (see earlier 5:3). Believers possess hope in the face of adversity because they are participants in the story of God's triumph over the world in Jesus Christ. Paul works out a messianic theodicy, so that the problems of death and affliction find their resolution in the atonement, resurrection, and new creation. The hope of believers is that they are part of God's eternal plan executed in Christ and nothing in the universe can thwart that plan (8:18-39).

This brings us to Romans 9–11 which are among the most disputed parts of Paul's letter. We can dismiss the view that these chapters are designed to give Paul's teaching on the election of individuals unto salvation (though I do think that Romans 8–9 certainly is of relevance for formulating a doctrine of predestination).[79] It was once common to think that these chapters constitute

---

[77] Bird, *Bird's-Eye View of Paul*, 140-43.
[78] Leander E. Keck, *Romans* (Nashville: Abingdon, 2005), 180.
[79] John Piper, *The Justification of God: An Exegetical and Theological Study of Romans 9:1-23* (2nd ed.; Grand Rapids: Baker, 1993), 56-73; Richard H. Bell, *Provoked to Jealousy: The Origin and Purpose of the Jealousy Motif in Romans 9–11* (WUNT 2.63; Tübingen: Mohr [Siebeck],

an excursus or a digression in Paul's train of thought.[80] Others argue that this section is in fact the climax of the epistle.[81] This section is neither "peripheral" nor "central," but is more accurately "integral" to Paul's argument.[82] Those who think that Romans 9–11 is the climax of the letter have mistaken the steepest incline for the peak, or make the assumption that after the most arduous terrain comes the summit. The bad news is that the peak of Romans is still four chapters away. Romans 9–11 is a false crest in the arduous yet scenic journey to the pinnacle of the letter in 15:8-9.[83] Whatever gravity we assign to Romans 9–11 we need not think of Romans 1–8 as a mere "preface."[84] There is an indelible connection between Romans 9–11 and what has gone before. Earlier Paul intimated the priority of the Jew in the gospel, Israel's disobedience of the law, and the faithfulness of God to Israel (1:16-17, 2:1-29; 3:1-4). Paul now brings those themes to a dramatic resolution. In addition, Romans 8 also ends on a triumphant note echoing the certainty of God's saving purposes and the inseparability of the believer from the love of God. That of course begs the question about the state and fate of Israel. In other words, can anyone really trust God and expect him to be faithful if the people of his promise are currently alienated from him? Running through the text then we find Paul's construction of a theodicy for God's faithfulness to Israel. In addition, an outstanding task for Paul is to reconcile the priority and privilege of the Jews with the impartiality of God and the universality of salvation. Paul's reflection on Israel comes in three distinct phases: (1) Israel in the past (9:6-29); (2) Israel in the present (9:30–10:21); and (3) Israel in the future (11:1-36).[85]

Despite the recalcitrance of national Israel, Paul takes solace from the fact that there is indeed a remnant of faithful Jews who have embraced God's

---

1994), 175-78; Charles H. Talbert, *Romans* (Macon: Smyth & Helwys, 2002), 230-31; Thomas R. Schreiner, "Does Romans 9 Teach Individual Election unto Salvation," in T. Schreiner and B. Ware, eds., *The Grace of God, The Bondage of the Will: Biblical and Practical Perspectives on Calvinism* (2 vols.; Grand Rapids: Baker Books, 1995), 1:89-106.

[80] W. Sanday and A. C. Headlam, *A Critical and Exegetical Commentary on the Epistle of the Romans* (Edinburgh: T. & T. Clark, 1896), 225; C. H. Dodd, *The Epistle of Paul to the Romans* (London: Hodder & Stoughton, 1932), 148-49; Rudolf Bultmann, *Theology of the New Testament* (2 vols.; trans. K. Grobel; London: SCM, 1952), 2:132; Otto Kuss, *Der Römerbrief* (3 vols.; Regensburg: Pustet, 1963–1978), 3:644-45.

[81] Baur, *Paul the Apostle of Jesus Christ*, 1:327-28; Krister Stendahl, *Paul Among Jews and Gentiles* (Philadelphia: Fortress, 1976), 4, 28, 85; J. Christiaan Beker, *Paul the Apostle: The Triumph of God in Life and Thought* (Philadelphia: Fortress, 1980), 87; Dunn, *Romans*, 1:lxii; 2.518-21; Fitzmyer, *Romans*, 539-43 (esp. 541); M. D. Hooker, "Introduction," in *From Adam to Christ: Essays on Paul* (Cambridge: Cambridge University Press, 1990), 3; N. T. Wright, *Climax of the Covenant* (Edinburgh: T. & T. Clark, 1991), 234; Wright, "Romans," 10:620-26; Brendan Byrne, *Romans* (Collegeville: Liturgical, 1996), 282; John G. Gager, *Reinventing Paul* (Oxford: Oxford University Press, 2000), 129; A. Katherine Grieb, *The Story of Romans: A Narrative Defence of God's Righteousness* (Louisville: Westminster John Knox, 2002), 87; Tobin, *Paul's Rhetoric in its Contexts*, 102.

[82] Talbert, *Romans*, 241.

[83] Cf. William J. Dumbrell, *Romans: A New Covenant Commentary* (Eugene: Wipf & Stock, 2005), 21.

[84] Stendahl, *Paul*, 29,

[85] Tobin, *Paul's Rhetoric*, 321.

grace, a grace that is now even extended to the Gentiles (9:6-29). In 9:30–10.4, we observe one of the crux passages as to whether or not Paul is denigrating "nationalism" or "legalism."[86] Contextually the passage is framed by an *inclusio* in 9:30-32 and 10:19-21 concerning the Gentiles' incorporation into the people of God set against the attitudes and activity of ethnic Israel. Paul's main point is not to compare Israel, who pursued salvation by works, with Gentiles, who pursued salvation by faith. Israel's biggest problem is not legalism but is their "stumbling" (9:32-33) and "ignorance" (10:3) of Christ. Paul has in mind Jews who have heard the kind of message outlined in 1:16–8:39 and yet still trust in the covenantal status quo and in their own law obedience.[87] Israel is "seeking to erect their own righteousness from the law."[88] A righteousness that is theirs by fact of obedience and a righteousness that is *exclusively* theirs by fact of election.[89] They are ignorant of God's impartiality as displayed towards Jew and Gentile and they have rejected the one who inaugurates salvation and brings the covenant to its appointed goal (10:4). Israel's privileged position and her performance of the law will ultimately amount to nothing, for she is unable to find in the law what the law does not have: life!

Paul focuses on the eschatological singularity of salvation in Christ for Jews and Gentiles without distinction (10:1-13) and the necessity of a continued mission to Israel because of the necessity of hearing the word of Christ (10:14-21). Yet Paul is quick to point out that Israel's rejection of the gospel does not entail God's rejection of Israel. God's call is irrevocable. Proof of that is a remnant of Jewish Christians who have believed in Jesus Christ (11:1-5, 29). Israel's failure is not final, but the salvation of Gentiles will drive Israel to jealousy so that "all Israel" may yet be saved. Since Israel's rejection of the message brought reconciliation to the Gentiles, their acceptance of the message will be a miracle on par with resurrection from the dead (11:15, 26). Paul counters a supersessionist ecclesiology with an analogy of an olive branch whereby some natural branches have been broken off and other wild olive branches have been grafted in. Paul makes several points from the analogy: If God can graft in the wild branches (Gentiles), how much more can he re-attach the natural branches (Israel); the root (Israel) supports the branches (Gentiles) and not the other way around; and if God can break off the natural branches due to unbelief (Israel), he can also do the same to the unnatural branches (Gentiles) which is a warning against unbelief (11:16-32). In the end it appears that: "The purposes of God are reducible to his will, a will that initially appears equally set to harden or to save, but turns out on closer inspection, and in the end, to harden only in order to save, to hate only in order to love, and to consign all to disobedience only in order to have

---

[86] Contrast Wright, *Climax*, 240-44 with Moo, *Romans*, 634-36.
[87] Cf. Frank Thielman, *Paul and the Law: A Contextual Approach* (Downers Grove: IVP, 1994), 239; Terence L. Donaldson, *Paul and the Gentiles: Remapping the Apostle's Convictional World* (Minneapolis: Fortress, 1997), 129-30.
[88] *T. Dan* 6.10-11 and Wis 2.11 refer to a "righteousness of the law."
[89] Cf. Colin Kruse, *Paul, the Law and Justification* (Peabody: Hendrickson, 1997), 225.

mercy on all."[90] That in turn is followed by a burst of doxological praise to the greatness and glory of God (11:33-36).

Romans 12–15 tease out the paramount implications of the preceding arguments as to how Paul's gospel is lived out among Jewish and Gentile Christians in the house churches and synagogues of Rome. This section constitutes Paul's blueprint for how an ethnically diverse, cosmopolitan community with competing convictions on law and liberty can live and worship together for the glory of God. His solution is that justification by faith implies fellowship by faith, therefore, accept those who have faith, be it strong or weak. Learn to differentiate between areas of conviction and areas of command, because the one Lord, Jesus Christ, is Lord of all.[91]

The gospel is fundamentally about transformation, the transformation of persons so that they become identifiable by their sacrificial service and worship to God over and against the pattern of the dominant culture around them (12:1-2). That transformation is worked out within the believing community by their humility and service rendered to each other in the body of Christ which makes them mutually interdependent upon one another (12:3-8). The central ingredient in the Christian life is the virtue of love and loving behavior. A praxis driven by love means redefining the way they understand honor, hospitality, grief, vengeance, and the triumph of good over evil (12:9-21). Paul then provides exhortations about how believers are to regard the governing authorities. It is difficult to discern the background to Paul's remarks here, whether he has in mind certain religious enthusiasts who no longer think of themselves as under the authority of the state, or perhaps Jewish Christians who have imbibed anti-Roman sentiments from Judea. In any case, Paul makes the point that government is divinely instituted, and rulers should be obeyed and respected (13:1-7). The reference to taxes leads Paul to remind his readers that they are indebted to love one another. Love is the fulfillment of the law (or at least the second half of the Decalogue). In particular, the Christian love ethic is lived out in the context of an eschatological expectation for the return of the Lord Jesus (13:8-14).

Paul next offers a plea for unity in a cluster of churches with contentions and suspicions of each other's commitment to the Jewish way of life and the gospel of Jesus Christ. The "weak" simply means those whose consciences are more easily offended by certain scruples, while the "strong" are those who have a more robust ability to exercise their freedom on the same matters. Paul pleads with them not to condemn each other over matters that he determines to be secondary, because they will all inevitably answer to the one Lord (14:1-12). He therefore urges believers to exercise their convictions about disputable matters (meat, holy days, or wine)[92] in a way that avoids causing others to

---

[90] John Barclay, "Two Versions of Grace: Romans 9–11 and the Wisdom of Solomon" (paper delivered at the British New Testament Conference, Durham, September 2008).
[91] Wright, "Romans," 10:733.
[92] Importantly these were a key means of avoiding idolatry in a pagan majority city. Meat was usually sacrificed to idols, wine was used in libations, and Sabbath and Roman holy days were days to be observed or ignored by faithful Jews in Rome.

stumble, but also prevents them from being bullied into adhering to regulations that impinge upon their freedom. Kingdom values and serving Christ ultimately transcends tertiary matters of food and drink (14:13-23). Paul makes a special exhortation to the "strong" to put the "weak" first, because this is the example given in Christ who did not please himself, but pleased God by bearing the shame of others. Crucial to the exhortation are his words: "[W]ith one mind and one voice you may glorify the God and Father of our Lord Jesus Christ. Accept one another, then, just as Christ accepted you, in order to bring praise to God" (15:6-7). Paul wants them to work for unity and a mutual acceptance of each other. Believers should receive one another because Christ received them. Paul affirms the priority of Israel in God's plan by noting that Christ himself became a servant to the circumcised, so that the promises made to the patriarchs would be confirmed, promises that pertained to the Gentiles receiving mercy and glorifying God. Scripture lays down a clear pattern for the Gentiles to come to the God of the patriarchs in faith and praise (15:7-13).

The foregoing arguments and exhortations are a reminder to his audience of the grace of Paul's apostleship to the Gentiles. Paul recounts the geographical arc of his ministry from Jerusalem to Illyricum and his continuing desire to preach Christ where Christ is not known (15:14-21). That explains Paul's future travel itinerary which involves visiting Jerusalem, Rome, and Spain. Paul also asks for their prayers for his safety in Jerusalem and his refreshment with the Roman believers (15:22-33). Paul begins a list of greetings including a commendation of Phoebe, a deacon from Cenchreae, the bearer of his letter (16:1-2). Greetings are passed on to several Roman Christians of whom Paul knows either directly or indirectly (16:3-16). That is followed with a final series of remarks that includes a warning against divisive teachers, an exhortation for continued obedience, and a promise of God's final victory over the Satan (16:17-20). There is a final greeting from Paul's companion and scribe, Tertius (16:21-23). The letter closes with a doxology about the plan of God revealed in the gospel for the glory of God (16:25-27).

6. Basic Themes

The main themes of Romans can be summarized around the two nodes of proclamation and praxis. First, in terms of proclamation, we could identify an overarching theme in Romans as "the apocalyptic power of the gospel for the salvation of Jews and Gentiles." The subject of Romans is not the "road" of salvation for individuals. It addresses the fundamental reality of God's faithfulness to Israel, God's impartiality in judging Jews and Gentiles, and the singularity of his salvation in Jesus Christ for Jews and Gentiles. The identity and deliverance of the people of God from sin, evil desire, and judgment remains a consistent theme throughout. God calls and creates a people in the Messiah from among both Jews and Greeks. Once we accept that Paul is narrating an apocalyptic story with corporate concerns it follows that the matter of fellowship between Jews and Gentiles cannot be regarded as ancillary to a more pervasive motif of the individual standing before God.[93] For Paul's Roman audience, they learn that "Evangelical persuasion rather than political and military power is thus the means whereby the salvation of the world is now occurring."[94] For Jews, God's faithfulness is demonstrated in the obedience, death, and resurrection of Jesus for the salvation of "all Israel." For Greeks, despite their idolatry and immorality, they have been engrafted into Israel in order to prompt Israel to jealously and conversion. The message of the gospel—bringing rectification, reconciliation, and redemption—must be lived out thereafter in Spirit-driven righteousness and in the unified fellowship of the messianic community that confesses the Lordship of Jesus Christ.

The history of interpretation is rather illuminating when it comes to highlighting how Romans is about how the gospel has come to both the Jew and the Greek. John Chrysostom (ca. A.D. 349–407) preached through Romans in his homilies. The Greek presbyter stated: "For these two things were what confused the Jews; one, if it were possible for men, who with works were not saved, to be saved without them, and another, if it were just for the uncircumcised to enjoy the same blessings with those, who had during so long a period been nurtured in the law."[95] Augustine of Hippo (A.D. 354–430) regarded Romans as a commentary on 2 Cor 3:6, "For the letter kills, but the Spirit gives life." The Letter to the Romans was Augustine's key weapon to undermine the works-salvation scheme of Pelagius. However, Augustine also knew the big picture of Romans, namely, the redemptive-historical context in which the gospel came to Gentiles:

> The Letter of Paul to the Romans, in so far as one can understand its literal content, poses a question like this: whether the Gospel of our Lord Jesus Christ came to Jews alone because of their merits through the works of the law, or whether the justification of faith that is in Christ Jesus came to all nations, without any preceding merits for works. In this last instance, people would believe not because they were just, but justified through belief; they would then begin to live justly. This then is what the apostle intended to teach: that the grace of the Gospel of Lord Jesus Christ came to all people. He thereby shows why one calls this "grace," for it was given freely, and not as a repayment of a debt of righteousness.[96]

In the modern era, the British philosopher John Locke (1632–1704), in his paraphrase and notes on Paul's letters, made this comment on Rom 3.26: "God rejected them [i.e. the Jews] for being his people, and took the Gentiles into his church, and made them his people jointly and equally with the few

---

[93] Contra Moo, *Romans*, 27-29.
[94] Jewett, *Romans*, 141.
[95] John Chrysostom, *Hom. Rom.* 7.
[96] Cited in Paula Fredriksen Landes, *Unfinished Commentary on the Epistle to the Romans* (Text and Translations 23; Early Christian Literature Series 6; Chico: Scholars, 1982), 53.

believing Jews. This is plainly the sense of the apostle here, where he is discoursing the nation of the Jews and their state in comparison with the Gentiles; not of the state of private persons. Let anyone without prepossession attentively read the context, and he will find it to be so."[97] Benjamin Jowett (1817–1893), a scholar of Plato, turned his hand to studying Paul's letters and found Romans not to be a doctrinal treatise, but fundamentally concerned with the unity of Jews and Gentiles: "it is union with Christ which breaks down all other ties of race and language, and knits men together into a new body which is His church."[98] Chrysostom, Augustine, Locke, and Jowett (as mere examples) show that it is possible to see a letter like Romans addressing an anthropological issue of human sin and divine redemption without divorcing it from the wider redemptive-historical theme of how the promises given to Israel result in the salvation of the Gentiles.

In the practical sense, Paul's two key exhortations are: "Let us therefore make every effort to do what leads to peace and to mutual edification" (14:19) and "Accept one another, then, just as Christ accepted you, in order to bring praise to God" (15:7). Paul labors to provide a theological rationale for a community to fully live out unity in diversity and to promote harmony with each other as a pathway to glorifying God. Paul's mandate for unity is not made in the abstract. The charge to "accept" one another (14:1) is rooted in God's acceptance of *both* those who eat and abstain from certain foods (14:3) and part of emulating Christ who "accepted you" (15:7).[99] The ultimate goal is the glorification of God by a community that is unified and in one mind.[100] Paul is showing that ethnicity and attitudes to legal observances, things that many Jews and their clientele of adherents treasured, do not establish any privilege over others. Similarly, many Gentiles may have accepted the message that most Jews rejected, but that does not entail a whole scale or permanent rejection of Israel. Christ was a servant to Israel, Jewish Christians brought the message to Rome, and the nation of Israel will yet return to the Lord at the final day. There are not two plans for two peoples. There is one covenantal promise running through Abraham to Moses to Christ. This singular purpose of God includes the interlocking destiny of Jews and Gentiles in Israel's Messiah. The community that confesses Christ must work out in its midst a way to embrace those whom God has embraced. An inherent bias against the Gentile world, or a cultural prejudice against the Jewish people, is not the means to God's glory. The gospel is about the lack of διαστολή ("difference") between Jews and Gentiles in salvation (Rom 3:22; 10:12), which should therefore result in an attitude of ἀδιάφορα ("indifference") to things that are not essential to their faith and fellowship (Rom 14:1; 1 Cor 8:8-9; Col 3:17). What matters is the common promises and

---

[97] John Locke, *A Paraphrase and Notes on the Epistles of St Paul to the Galatians, First and Second Corinthians, Romans, and Ephesians* (Cambridge: Brown, Shattuck, & Co., 1832), 277.
[98] William Baird, *History of New Testament Research* (2 vols.; Minneapolis: Fortress, 1992), 1:356.
[99] Keener, *Romans*, 170.
[100] Keck, *Romans*, 352.

mutual identity created by those who have been "baptized into Christ" (Rom 6:3) and have "put on Christ" (Rom 13:14).

7. Conclusion

Romans is the precipice of Pauline theology and the summit of early Christian thought. The challenge for contemporary readers of Romans is to get inside the story of the letter, to become conversant with its various background contexts, and to imagine the situation behind the text that called for its composition. Laboring hard in the vineyard of exegesis and theological interpretation of Romans will hopefully lead to a fruitful harvest of new wine for thirsty minds to drink. Then believing readers, having wrestled with Romans, may try to be like Paul and "glory in Christ Jesus in my service to God" (Rom 15:17).

Recommended Reading

Jewett, Robert. *Romans*. Minneapolis: Fortress, 2007.
Keener, Craig S. *Romans*. Eugene: Cascade, 2009.
Lampe, Peter. *From Paul to Valentinus: Christians at Rome in the First Two Centuries*. Translated by M. Steinhausen. Minneapolis: Fortress, 2003.
Longenecker, Richard N. *Introducing Romans: Critical Issues in Paul's Most Famous Letter*. Grand Rapids: Eerdmans, 2011.
Moo, Douglas. *The Epistle to the Romans*. Grand Rapids: Eerdmans, 1996.
Oakes, Peter. *Reading Romans in Pompeii*. London: SPCK, 2009.
Reasoner, Mark. *Romans in Full Circle*. Louisville: Westminster John Knox, 2005.
Rutledge, Flemming. *Not Ashamed of the Gospel: Sermons from Paul's Letter to the Romans*. Grand Rapids: Eerdmans, 2007.
Schreiner, Thomas R. *Romans*. Grand Rapids: Baker, 1998.

9. The Corinthian Correspondence

L. L. Welborn

1. Overview

Paul's letters to Corinth preserve the most extensive and eventful record of his relationship with any of the churches that he founded.[1] This fact attests Paul's recognition of the strategic importance of Corinth, "the promenade of Hellas,"[2] and "the passage for all mankind,"[3] to the realization of the ambitious goals of his apostolic mission (cf. Rom 15:19-29). The remarkable multiplicity of issues dealt with in the Corinthian correspondence—e.g., going to court before unbelievers, prostitution, eating meat sacrificed to idols, speaking in tongues, the resurrection of the dead—reflects the diverse social and ethnic makeup of the Christian groups at Corinth,[4] in contrast to Paul's more homogeneous assemblies in Macedonia,[5] and bespeaks the presence and influence of a group of strong-minded individuals whose opinions on a variety of subjects diverged sharply from Paul's own.[6] The arrival of other apostles and evangelists, such as Apollos, led to the formation of factions in the church at Corinth, with members declaring support for one teacher or another (1 Cor 1:10-12; 3:4).[7] Eventually, some in Corinth called into question the legitimacy of Paul's apostleship[8] and the probity of his administration of the collection for the poor in Jerusalem (2 Cor 12:16-18).[9] That Paul persevered in his

---

[1] See the classic account of the history of Paul's relationship with Corinth by Johannes Weiss, *The History of Primitive Christianity* (trans. F. C. Grant; 2 vols.; New York: Wilson-Erickson, 1937), 1.323-57.
[2] Dio Chrysostom, *Or.* 37.7.
[3] Aelius Aristides *Or.* 46.24.
[4] Gerd Theissen, *The Social Setting of Pauline Christianity: Essays on Corinth* (Philadelphia: Fortress, 1982).
[5] John M. G. Barclay, "Thessalonica and Corinth: Social Contrasts in Pauline Christianity," *JSNT* 15 (1992): 49-74.
[6] On the so-called "strong" in the church at Corinth, see Dale B. Martin, *The Corinthian Body* (New Haven: Yale University Press, 1999).
[7] L. L. Welborn, "Discord in Corinth," in *Politics and Rhetoric in the Corinthian Epistles* (Macon: Mercer University Press, 1997), 1-42.
[8] Ernst Käsemann, "Die Legitimität des Apostels. Eine Untersuchung zu II Korinther 10–13," *ZNW* 41 (1942): Georg Strecker, "Die Legitimität des paulinischen Apostolates nach 2 Korinther 10–13," *NTS* 38 (1992): 566-86.
[9] Hans Dieter Betz, *2 Corinthians 8 and 9: Two Administrative Letters of the Apostle Paul* (Philadelphia: Fortress, 1985), 76, 97.

relationship with the Corinthians, through all of its tumultuous stages, and despite a sense of being "wronged" by someone (2 Cor 7:12)[10] and "humiliated" before the congregation (2 Cor 10:1; 12:21),[11] was owing, in large measure, to the crucial role which Paul anticipated that the Corinthians would play in the success of the collection, on account of their material "abundance" (2 Cor 8:14).[12] Taken as a whole, the Corinthian correspondence is a chronicle of reconciliation.[13]

2. Paul's First Visit to Corinth

The date of Paul's arrival in Corinth is debated by scholars. The majority place the beginning of Paul's Corinthian mission in A.D. 50, correlating the account of Paul's trial before Gallio, the proconsul of Achaia, in Acts 18:12-17 with an inscribed letter of Claudius to Delphi, in which Gallio's name is mentioned.[14] But the narrative of Acts 18:1-18 is complex and multi-layered, evincing the author's usual tendency toward unified composition, with the resulting consolidation of facts.[15] It is possible that "Luke" has combined information about Paul's first and second visits to Corinth into a single, dramatic narrative; in that case, Paul might have stood trial before Gallio on the occasion of his second visit to Corinth, in A.D. 51.[16] Thus, a minority of scholars propose that Paul first visited Corinth in A.D. 41, correlating the edict of Claudius on the Jews, as reported in Suetonius (*Claud.* 25) and Cassius Dio (60.6.6), with the account in Acts 18:1-2 that Aquila and Priscilla had relocated from Italy to Corinth, "because Claudius had ordered all the Jews to leave Rome."[17] This early chronology, which brings Paul to Corinth in A.D. 41, will be presupposed in what follows.

The Corinth that Paul encountered was a Roman city,[18] having been re-founded by order of Julius Caesar in 44 B.C.,[19] after its brutal destruction by

---

[10] L. L. Welborn, *An End to Enmity: Paul and the "Wrongdoer" of Second Corinthians* (Berlin: de Gruyter, 2011).
[11] Weiss, *Primitive Christianity*, 1.343-44; Welborn, *An End to Enmity*, 67-80, 181, 425-26.
[12] Betz, *2 Corinthians 8 and 9*, 68; Welborn, *An End to Enmity*, 179.
[13] Margaret M. Mitchell, *Paul and the Rhetoric of Reconciliation: An Exegetical Investigation of the Language and Composition of 1 Corinthians* (Tübingen: Mohr [Siebeck], 1991); Welborn, *An End to Enmity*.
[14] Robert Jewett, *A Chronology of Paul's Life* (Philadelphia: Fortress, 1979), 38-40; Jerome Murphy-O'Connor, *Paul: A Critical Life* (Oxford: Oxford University Press, 1996), 18-22.
[15] Gerd Lüdemann, *Earliest Christianity according to the Traditions in Acts: A Commentary* (Philadelphia: Fortress, 1989), 10-12, 203-9; M.-E. Boismard and A. Lamouille, *Les Actes des deux apôtres* (Paris: Gabalda, 1990), 2.247-49, 300-303, 366.
[16] Gerd Lüdemann, *Paul, Apostle to the Gentiles: Studies in Chronology* (Philadelphia: Fortress, 1984), 171-73; J. J. Taylor, *Les Actes des deux apôtres, V. Commentaire historique (Act 9,1-18,22)* (Paris: Gabalda, 1994), 325-26.
[17] Lüdemann, *Paul, Apostle to the Gentiles*, 6-18, 157-77; David G. Horrell, *The Social Ethos of the Corinthian Correspondence: Interests and Ideology from 1 Corinthians to 1 Clement* (Edinburgh: T. & T. Clark, 1996), 73-74.
[18] Donald Engels, *Roman Corinth* (Chicago: University of Chicago Press, 1990); Jerome Murphy-O'Connor, "The Corinth That Saint Paul Saw," *BA* 47 (1984); 147-59.

Mummius in 146 B.C.[20] Caesar populated the colony with numerous freedmen,[21] but the ethnic mix was more diverse in Paul's day, including Syrians and Egyptians,[22] along with Greeks who immigrated from the surrounding cities.[23] Philo speaks of a sizeable Jewish community at Corinth.[24] The urban population of Roman Corinth may have approached 80,000, with a rural population of 20,000.[25] Corinth rapidly regained its ancient prosperity, owing to its favorable location, situated on the Isthmus: as Strabo succinctly puts it, "the master of two harbors."[26] By 27 B.C., Corinth was already the capital of the senatorial province of Achaia,[27] and became the judicial seat of the Roman proconsul.[28] Sharp contrasts between rich and poor were apparent in the city.[29] But opportunities for social advancement also existed, as demonstrated by the prominent role of freedmen in public life.[30] The Isthmian Games, hosted by Corinth every two years, drew large crowds.[31] The theater was rehabilitated at the end of the reign of Augustus and was fully operational in the time of Paul.[32] The structure held upwards of 15,000 spectators.[33] The Roman-style amphitheater at Corinth was one of the earliest built in the Greek world, probably dating to just after the foundation of the colony.[34] The gladiatorial games held there during the imperial cult festivals were criticized by moral philosophers, but were emulated by other Greek cities, such as Athens.[35] Corinth was sacred to the goddess Aphrodite,[36]

---

[19] Appian *Punica* 136; Strabo 8.6.23; Plutarch *Caes.* 57.5; Dio Cassius 43.50.3-5; Pausanias 2.1.2.

[20] Polybius 38.9.1-18.2; Diodorus Siculus 32.26.1-5; Strabo 8.6.23.

[21] Strabo 8.6.23. Cf. Benjamin W. Mills, "The Social and Ethnic Origins of the Colonists in Early Roman Corinth," in Steven J. Friesen, Daniel N. Schowalter, James C. Walters, eds., *Corinth in Context: Comparative Studies on Religion and Society* (Leiden: Brill, 2010).

[22] E.g., John H. Kent, *Corinth VIII.3: The Inscriptions 1926–1950* (Princeton: The American School of Classical Studies at Athens, 1966), no. 57; Dennis Edwin Smith, "The Egyptian Cults at Corinth," *HTR* 70 (1977): 201-31.

[23] Anthony J. S. Spawforth, "Roman Corinth: The Formation of a Colonial Elite," in A. D. Rizakis, ed., *Roman Onomastics in the Greek East: Social and Political Aspects* (Athens: Research Center for Greek and Roman Antiquity, 1996), 167-82.

[24] Philo *Legat.* 281.

[25] Engels, *Roman Corinth*, 84.

[26] Strabo 8.6.20.

[27] Tacitus, *Ann.* 1.76.4, returned to senatorial control by Claudius in A.D. 44, according to Suetonius *Claud.* 25.3.

[28] Acts 18:12.

[29] Alciphron, *Ep.* 3.60.

[30] E.g., Gnaeus Babbius Philinus in Kent, *Corinth VIII.3: The Inscriptions*, 73.

[31] Kent, *Corinth VIII.3: The Inscriptions*, 28-30; Engels, *Roman Corinth*, 51-52. Cf. Oscar Broneer, "The Apostle Paul and the Isthmian Games," *BA* 25 (1962): 1-31.

[32] Richard Stillwell, *Corinth II: The Theatre* (Princeton: The American School of Classical Studies at Athens, 1952), 135-41.

[33] Engels, *Roman Corinth*, 47.

[34] Katherine E. Welch, "Negotiating Roman Spectacle Architecture in the Greek World: Athens and Corinth," in Bettina Bergmann and Christine Kondoleon, eds., *The Art of Ancient Spectacle*, (New Haven: Yale University Press, 1999), 125-45, esp. 133-40.

[35] Apollonius of Tyana in Philostratus, *Vit. Apoll.* 4.22; Dio Chrysostom, *Or.* 31.121; Lucian, *Demonax* 57.

[36] Aelius Aristides, *Or.* 47.23. Cf. Engels, *Roman Corinth*, 56, 97-99.

protector of prostitutes,[37] whose famous sanctuary stood on the Acrocorinth.[38] The temple of Asclepius, the god of healing, enjoyed great popularity, as attested by numerous surviving donations replicating body parts.[39] The Asclepieion was equipped with dining facilities.[40] Numerous inscriptions and dedications attest to the importance of the worship of the Roman emperor.[41]

In Corinth, Paul found lodging with Aquila and Priscilla (Acts 18:1-3). As the reason for Paul's association with this couple, the author of Acts gives the circumstance that they were "of the same trade" (ὁμότεχνον). The term used by Acts to describe their occupation, σκηνοποιός, is traditionally translated "tent-maker"; but Frederick Danker, the editor of *A Greek-English Lexicon of the New Testament*, has recently argued, on the basis of contemporary usage, that readers of Acts in urban areas would have thought of σκηνοποιός in reference to matters theatrical, and so has proposed the translation "maker of stage properties."[42] Whether as a "tent-maker" or a "prop-maker," Paul lived and worked with Jewish artisans in one of the little shops scattered throughout the city, perhaps in the Peribolos of Apollo just off the Lechaeum Road,[43] or in the North Market,[44] or along East Theater Street.[45]

According to the author of Acts (18:4), Paul preached in the synagogue of Corinth every Sabbath for an unspecified number of weeks. The location of the synagogue in which Paul preached is uncertain. A broken lintel with the crude inscription [συνα]γωγη εβρ[αιων] ("Synagogue of the Hebrews") was found along the Lechaeum Road.[46] The lintel is a re-used stone, fashioned from the cornice of another building; the lettering suggests a date in the fourth century A.D.[47] If, as some archaeologists assume,[48] the synagogue of Paul's day stood at or near the place where the broken lintel was found, then the Jewish community had its meeting place along one of the principal arteries of the city, adjacent to some of Corinth's most important buildings.

---

[37] Alciphron, *Ep.* 3.60.
[38] Strabo 8.6.21; Pausanias 2.5.1.
[39] Bronwen Wickkiser, "Asklepius in Greek and Roman Corinth," in Friesen, Schowalter, and Walters, *Corinth in Context*, 37-64.
[40] Carl A. Roebuck, *Corinth XIV: The Asklepieion and Lerna* (Princeton: The American School of Classical Studies at Athens, 1951); John Fotopoulos, *Food Offered to Idols in Roman Corinth: A Socio-Rhetorical Reconsideration* (Tübingen: Mohr [Siebeck], 2003), 49-70.
[41] Engels, *Roman Corinth*, 101-2; Margaret L. Laird, "The Emperor in a Roman Town: The Base of the *Augustales* in the Forum at Corinth," in Friesen, Schowalter, and Walters, *Corinth in Context*, 67-116.
[42] Frederick Danker in Walter Bauer, *A Greek-English Lexicon of the New Testament and Other Early Christian Literature* (ed. F. W. Danker; 3rd and rev. ed.; Chicago: University of Chicago Press, 2000), 928-29 s.v. σκηνοποιός.
[43] Murphy-O'Connor, "The Corinth That Saint Paul Saw," 156.
[44] F. J. de Waele, "The Roman Market North of the Temple at Corinth," *AJA* 34 (1930): 432-54.
[45] Charles K. Williams, "Corinth, 1982: East of the Theater," *Hesperia* 52 (1983): 1-47, esp. 10-13; David G. Horrell, "Domestic Space and Christian Meetings at Corinth: Imagining New Contexts and the Buildings East of the Theatre," *NTS* 50 (2004): 349-59.
[46] A. B. West, *Corinth VIII: Latin Inscriptions 1896–1926* (Cambridge, Mass.: Harvard University Press, 1931), 78-79.
[47] West, *Corinth VIII: Latin Inscriptions*, 79.
[48] E.g., West, *Corinth VIII: Latin Inscriptions*, 79.

In response to opposition from some of the Jews, Paul withdrew from the synagogue at Corinth and began preaching in the house of a "God-fearer" named Titius Justus, whose house was next door to the synagogue (Acts 18:6-7).[49] It is safe to say that "Luke" would scarcely have invented the name or person of Titius Justus.[50] It is important to note the role that "God-fearers" played in the origin of the Christian community at Corinth.[51]

The author of Acts attributes sensational importance to the conversion of the "synagogue president" (ἀρχισυνάγωγος) Crispus in his account of the growth of the followers of Jesus in Corinth to a "large people" (Acts 18:10): "Crispus, the ruler of the synagogue, believed in the Lord, together with all of his household, and many of the Corinthians believed and had themselves baptized when they heard [of it]"—that is, of the conversion of Crispus (Acts 18:8).[52] Greater plausibility accrues to "Luke's" account of the influence of Crispus from Philo's reference to a Jewish "colony" at Corinth, which must have been of significant size and vitality, since it is one of only two Greek cities whose Jewish inhabitants Philo mentions by name.[53] That Paul made an exception to his customary practice of not baptizing new converts and personally administered baptism to Crispus (1 Cor 1:14) is further indication of the prominence of this individual.[54] To be sure, the majority of believers in Corinth were non-Jews, as demonstrated by Paul's reference in 1 Cor 12:1-2 to a past in which "you were Gentiles . . . and were led astray to dumb idols."[55] But the presence of an influential Jewish minority is one of the ways in which Christianity at Corinth differed from Pauline foundations in Galatia and Macedonia, and may account for the noticeable absence of "anti-Judaism" in 1 Corinthians.[56]

Among the early converts to Christianity at Corinth, Paul himself gives pride of place to Stephanas who, together with the members of his household, are described as "the first fruits of Achaia" (1 Cor 16:15-18). Paul commends

---

[49] Against the Western text (D), Paul did not change his residence, but only began to teach in a different location: thus, Ernst Haenchen, *The Acts of the Apostles: A Commentary* (Philadelphia: Westminster, 1971), 535; Murphy-O'Connor, *Paul*, 262-63; C. K. Barrett, *A Critical and Exegetical Commentary on the Acts of the Apostles, Vol. 2: Acts 15–28* (London: T. & T. Clark, 2004), 867.

[50] Lüdemann, *Early Christianity According to Acts*, 203.

[51] On the "God-fearers," see John Gager, "Jews, Gentiles and Synagogues in the Book of Acts," *HTR* 79 (1986): 91-99; Judith Lieu, "The Race of the God-fearers," *JTS* 46 (1995): 483-501; E. A. Judge, "Jews, Proselytes and God-fearers Club Together," in S. R. Llewelyn, ed., *New Documents Illustrating Early Christianity* (vol. 9; Grand Rapids: Eerdmans, 2002), 73-81.

[52] For this interpretation, which takes the report of the conversion of Crispus as the unexpressed object of the participle ἀκούοντες, see Haenchen, *The Acts of the Apostles*, 535; Barrett, *Acts 15–28*, 868-69.

[53] Philo, *Legat.* 281.

[54] Wayne A. Meeks, *The First Urban Christians: The Social World of the Apostle Paul* (New Haven: Yale University Press, 1983), 57.

[55] Cavan W. Concannon, "*Ecclesia laus Corinthiensis*: Negotiating Ethnicity under Empire" (Ph.D. diss., Harvard University, 2010).

[56] Cf. Peter Richardson, "On the Absence of 'Anti-Judaism' in 1 Corinthians," in P. Richardson and D. Granskou, eds., *Anti-Judaism in Early Christianity, Vol. I: Paul and the Gospels* (Waterloo: Wilfred Laurier University Press, 1986), 59-74, esp. 60-63.

the household of Stephanas because "they had assigned themselves to the ministry to the saints" (εἰς διακονίαν τοῖς ἁγίοις ἔταξαν ἑαυτούς); the vocabulary of the latter phrase suggests that they served as Paul's agents in the collection-work at Corinth.[57] Paul further reveals that Stephanas and his colleagues Fortunatus and Achaicus had visited him in Ephesus, and had alleviated his "lack" (ὑστέρημα), indicating that they brought him financial assistance.[58]

Also among the converts of Paul's first visit to Corinth was Gaius, who is mentioned in the same breath with Crispus in 1 Cor 1:14. In Rom 16:23, Paul sends greetings from a Gaius whom he describes as "my host and the host of the whole church." Although "Gaius" (Latin: *Caius*) was a common Roman *praenomen*,[59] especially common at Corinth owing to the history of the colony, there is no reason to doubt the identity of the two Gaii mentioned in 1 Cor 1:14 and Rom 16:23.[60] Paul's description of Gaius as "the host of the whole church" is crucial for determining Gaius' social status and role in the Christian community.[61] If Gaius served as "host" of the Corinthian Christians, whenever the house churches came together in common assembly,[62] then Gaius must have had a larger house than others.[63] Indeed, Gaius of Corinth is the only person in the early church of whom it is said that he hosted all of the Christians of a given city in his house as a central meeting place,[64] "which makes him perhaps the wealthiest person we know of from Paul's assemblies."[65]

The three Corinthians named thus far—Stephanas, Crispus, and Gaius—are all demonstrably persons of more than modest surplus resources. As the head of a "household" (1 Cor 1:16; 16:15), Stephanas would have had dependents, like Fortunatus and Achaicus, who were evidently his slaves or freedmen.[66] Stephanas was able to travel from Corinth to meet with Paul in

---

[57] Raymond F. Collins, *First Corinthians* (Collegeville: Michael Glazier, 1999), 587-88.
[58] Theissen, *Social Setting*, 88.
[59] Heikki Solin, "Names, personal, Roman," *OCD* 1024; Olli Salomies, *Die römischen Vornamen: Studien zur römischen Namengebung* (Helsinki: Societas Scientiarum Fennica, 1987).
[60] Theissen, *Social Setting*, 55; Meeks, *First Urban Christians*, 57. For a discussion of the nine people mentioned in 1 Corinthians and Romans in connection with Corinth, including Erastus, the financial manager of the city (οἰκονόμος τῆς πόλεως), see my *An End to Enmity*, 230-87.
[61] Theissen, *Social Setting*, 89; Meeks, *First Urban Christians*, 57-58.
[62] Robert Banks, *Paul's Idea of Community* (Peabody: Hendrickson, 1994), 34-36; Hans-Josef Klauck, *Hausgemeinde und Hauskirche im frühen Christentum* (Stuttgart: Katholisches Bibelwerk, 1981), 39.
[63] Theissen, *Social Setting*, 89; Murphy-O'Connor, *Paul*, 267.
[64] Meeks, *First Urban Christians*, 221 n. 7; Peter Lampe, "Paul, Patrons, and Clients," in J. Paul Sampley, ed., *Paul in the Greco-Roman World* (Harrisburg: Trinity Press International, 2003), 496.
[65] Steven J. Friesen, "Poverty in Pauline Studies: Beyond the So-called New Consensus," *JSNT* 26 (2004): 356.
[66] The names Fortunatus ("lucky") and Achaicus ("from Achaia") indicate servile origins: Heikki Solin, *Die stadtrömischen Sklavennamen: Ein Namenbuch* (Stuttgart: Franz Steiner, 1996); L. R. Taylor, "Freedmen and Freeborn in the Epitaphs of Imperial Rome," *AJP* 82 (1961): 125. Cf. Meeks, *First Urban Christians*, 56-57, 216 n. 30.

Ephesus, and he brought Paul a gift.[67] As the former "ruler of the synagogue," Crispus would have had considerable wealth, since the position entailed responsibility for the upkeep of the synagogue.[68] As noted above, Gaius was probably the wealthiest of the Corinthian Christians, since he served as "host of the whole assembly" (Rom 16:23). In sum, it seems that at Corinth the Pauline mission succeeded for the first time in winning a few adherents from the upper class. Yet, the majority of Christ-believers at Corinth were poor.[69] Paul reminds his Corinthian readers that "not many" of them were educated, powerful, or nobly-born (1 Cor 1:26-28). The social contrasts in the Christian assembly mirrored those in Corinthian society at large. Alciphron complains about "the sordidness of the rich" and "the misery of the poor" at Corinth.[70] He pictures the starvation of young men near the Craneum, in the very neighborhood where the rich "abounded in luxuries."[71]

According to the author of Acts, Paul resided in Corinth for eighteen months on the occasion of his first visit (Acts 18:11).[72] The church that Paul left behind is described by "Luke" as a "large people" (Acts 18:10). How many persons might have belonged to the Christian *ekklesia* in this early period? If one calculates on the basis of an average household size of named individuals, and makes allowances for individuals and household groups whom Paul does not mention by name, an estimate of 100 persons does not seem unreasonable.[73] It is not certain how much time passed between Paul's departure from Corinth and the inception of the correspondence, but it cannot have been long, because the issues addressed in the first phase of the correspondence attempt to define the boundary between the Christian church and the pagan world.

3. First Corinthians as a Letter Collection

The majority of interpreters regard 1 Corinthians as a single, unified composition. In support of this view is the early attestation of 1 Corinthians by the author of *1 Clement* (ca. A.D. 100),[74] and by Ignatius of Antioch (ca.

---

[67] Theissen, *Social Setting*, 91; Meeks, *First Urban Christians*, 58.
[68] Tessa Rajak and David Noy, "Archisynagogoi: Office, Title and Social Status in the Greco-Jewish Synagogue," *JRS* 83 (1993): 75-93; Tessa Rajak, "Archisynagogoi as benefactors" and "Archisynagogoi as patrons," in *The Jewish Dialogue with Greece and Rome: Studies in Cultural and Social Interaction* (Leiden: Brill, 2002), 416-19; Theissen, *Social Setting*, 74-75.
[69] Justin Meggitt, *Paul, Poverty and Survival* (Edinburgh: T. & T. Clark, 1998); Steven J. Friesen, "Prospects for a Demography of the Pauline Mission: Corinth Among the Churches," in Daniel N. Schowalter and Steven J. Friesen, eds., *Urban Religion in Roman Corinth* (Cambridge, Mass.: Harvard University Press, 2005), 351-70, esp. 367.
[70] Alciphron 3.60.
[71] Alciphron 3.60.
[72] On the "intrinsic plausibility" of the eighteen months, see Murphy-O'Connor, *Paul*, 264-65.
[73] Andreas Lindemann, *Der erste Korintherbrief* (Tübingen: Mohr [Siebeck], 2000), 13.
[74] L. L. Welborn, "'Take Up the Epistle of the Blessed Paul the Apostle': The Contrasting Fates of Paul's Letters to Corinth in the Patristic Period," in Gary A. Phillips and Nicole Wilkinson Duran, eds., *Reading Communities Reading Scripture* (Harrisburg: Trinity Press International, 2002), 345-57; L. L. Welborn, "On the Date of First Clement," *BR* 29 (1984): 29-54.

A.D. 130–140).[75] However, abrupt transitions, frequent changes of subject, and generally loose construction have invited questions about the literary integrity of 1 Corinthians by a minority of scholars.[76] The assignment of portions of 1 Corinthians to separate letters would be justified, only if the passages in question presupposed different situations.[77] This appears to be the case in three instances: Paul's attitude toward the factions (contrast 1:10-12 with 11:18-19), Paul's advice on food offered to idols (contrast 8:1-13 with 10:1-22), and Paul's announcement of his travel plans (contrast 4:17-21 with 16:5-9). Serious students of Paul's Corinthian correspondence, who are determined to comprehend the history of its composition, and who are not bound by the dogma of the *perfectio finalis scripturae*, will give attention to arguments on both sides of the debate over the literary unity of 1 Corinthians.

In 1 Cor 5:9-10, Paul mentions a letter that he had previously written on association with immoral and idolatrous persons: "I wrote to you in my letter not to associate with sexually immoral persons—not at all meaning the immoral of this world, or the greedy and robbers, or idolaters, since then you would need to go out of the world." Where is this letter? It is difficult to imagine that the Corinthians would have treated Paul's letters with such disregard that one of them would be entirely lost. Yet this is what most interpreters assume, rather than countenance the possibility that 1 Corinthians is a compilation of letters.[78]

The reliance of most scholars upon the canonical form of 1 Corinthians would represent admirable caution, if the composition of the epistle were unobjectionable. But, in fact, there are numerous difficulties. First, there are abrupt transitions which must be explained, if the text is to be made comprehensible as a single letter. To mention only the most noticeable, the abrupt beginning of 6:12, and differences of tone and content with 5:1–6:11, suggest that the paragraph 6:12-20 did not originally belong here, but between 10:22 and 10:23, with which 6:12-20 has much in common: in both passages, Paul quotes the Corinthian slogan, "All things are lawful for me" (6:12; 10:23); in both passages, the temptation to immorality is strong and the Corinthians are urged to "flee" (6:18; 10:23).[79]

Second, the situation presupposed in 11:17-22 is different from that reflected in 1:10-12, in respect to Paul's knowledge of the factions. In the

---

[75] William R. Schoedel, *Ignatius of Antioch: A Commentary on the Letters of Ignatius of Antioch* (Philadelphia: Fortress, 1985), 9; Timothy D. Barnes, "The Date of Ignatius," *ExpT* 120 (2009): 119-30.

[76] Johannes Weiss, *Der erste Korintherbrief* (Göttingen: Vandenhoeck & Ruprecht, 1910), xxxix-xliii; Wolfgang Schenk, "Der 1. Korintherbrief als Briefsammlung," *ZNW* 60 (1969): 219-43; Philip Vielhauer, *Geschichte der urchristlichen Literatur* (Berlin: de Gruyter, 1975), 140-41; Robert Jewett, "The Redaction of 1 Corinthians and the Trajectory of the Pauline School," *JAARSup* 46 (1978): 389-444; Christophe Senft, *La première épître de Saint Paul aux Corinthiens* (Neuchatel: Neuchatel-Delachaux, 1979), 17-25; Michael Bünker, *Briefformular und rhetorische Disposition im 1. Korintherbrief* (Göttingen: Vandenhoeck & Ruprecht, 1983), 51-59; Hans-Josef Klauck, *1. Korintherbrief* (Würzburg: Echter, 1984).

[77] Vielhauer, *Geschichte der urchristlichen Literatur*, 141.

[78] Weiss, *Der erste Korintherbrief*, xli.

[79] Weiss, *Der erste Korintherbrief*, xli.

former passage, Paul has only just "heard" that there are divisions among the Corinthians, and he allows that, "to some extent, I believe it" (11:18). But in 1:10-12, Paul shows himself very well informed about the factions, to the point of being able to parody their party slogans: "I am of Paul!" and "I am of Apollos!" It is difficult to explain how these passages could have belonged to the same writing.[80]

Third, there is a contrast between Paul's travel plans as announced in 4:19-21 and those communicated in 16:5-9. In the former passage, Paul threatens: "But I will come to you soon, if the Lord wills, and I will find out not the talk of these arrogant people but their power. . . . What do you wish? Shall I come to you with a rod, or with love in a spirit of gentleness?" But in 16:5-9, Paul outlines his plans very differently, much less definitively: "I will visit you after passing through Macedonia, and perhaps I will stay with you or even spend the winter, so that you may speed me on my journey, wherever I go. For I do not wish to see you now just in passing; I hope to spend some time with you, if the Lord permits. But I will stay in Ephesus until Pentecost, for a wide door for effective work has opened to me, and there are many adversaries." It is difficult to understand how the statements "I will come to you soon" (4:19) and "I will stay in Ephesus until Pentecost" (16:8) could have belonged to the same letter.[81]

Fourth, in 8:1-13 and in 10:1-22 Paul deals with the subject of food offered to idols. In the latter passage, Paul gives strict instructions aimed at separation: "I do not want you to be partners with demons. You cannot drink the cup of the Lord and the cup of demons. You cannot partake of the table of the Lord and the table of demons" (10:20-21). But in chapter 8, which also deals with idol meat, and eating in the temple of an idol (8:10), Paul's attitude is surprisingly liberal. Paul agrees in principle with those who possess the knowledge that "no idol in the world really exists" (8:4), so that "we are no worse off if we do not eat, and no better off if we do" (8:8). Paul only counsels that one should take care not to offend the conscience of a weaker brother or sister (8:11-13). Paul's outlook in the two passages is undeniably different. Paul's demand for a complete break with polytheistic sacrificial rituals in 10:1-22 is significantly more rigorous than his advice on food offered to idols in chapter 8, suggesting that 10:1-22 belonged, with 6:12-20, to the letter on association with the immoral and idolaters mentioned in 5:9-10. Defenders of the unity of 1 Corinthians must assume that Paul wavered in his judgment from one chapter to another within the same letter.[82]

Fifth, interpreters have noted that 1 Cor 4:14-21 has all of the formal features of the close of a letter body of a Pauline epistle: (a) 4:14—statement of Paul's purpose in writing; (b) 4:15-16—reminder of Paul's position in the community; (c) 4:17—announcement of Paul's plan to send a co-worker as envoy; (d) 4:18-19—communication of Paul's own plan to come to Corinth.[83]

---

[80] Vielhauer, *Geschichte der urchristlichen Literatur*, 141.
[81] Weiss, *History of Primitive Christianity*, 1.329.
[82] Weiss, *History of Primitive Christianity*, 1.332.
[83] Schenk, "Der 1. Korintherbrief als Briefsammlung," 236-40.

These elements are found at the close of the letter-body of 1Thessalonians, for example, in 1 Thess. 2:17-3:13, before the paraenesis offering instruction and exhortation on moral issues. Robert Funk established that this section is a recurring feature of Paul's epistles: at first, he called it the "travelogue"; then, more conscious of its "official" function, he described it as the "apostolic parousia."[84] But what is this section doing here toward the beginning of 1 Corinthians?

Finally, there are too many informants, sources, and occasions in 1 Corinthians for one letter: in 1:11, Paul echoes a report by Chloe's people; in 7:1, Paul refers to a letter from the Corinthians: "Now concerning the matters about which you wrote" (see also 8:1; 12:1; 16:1; 16:12); in 11:18, Paul makes reference to an anonymous report; in 16:17, Paul expresses joy over the arrival of Stephanas, Fortunatus, and Achaicus. John Hurd sought to explain the origin of this heterogeneous epistle by reference to these diverse sources and informants.[85] But if the composition of 1 Corinthians stretched out over a period of months, or even a year, to allow for the arrival of all these informants with fresh information about an evolving situation, in what sense is it meaningful to speak of 1 Corinthians as a single letter?

Hence, some scholars propose a division of canonical 1 Corinthians into three letters composed in the following order:

Letter A	On Association with the Immoral and Idolaters	1 Cor 10:1-22; 6:12-20; 10:23–11:34
Letter B	In Response to the Corinthians' Questions	1 Corinthians 7–9, 12–16
Letter C	Counsel of Concord	1 Cor 1:1–6:11

Although Letter A would appear to be the most fragmentarily preserved of the writings, in fact, only the epistolary prescript and postscript may be lacking. The removal of prescripts and postscripts was standard practice in the making of a letter compilation.[86] The redaction of 1 Corinthians is uncomplicated. The editor arranged the pieces according to a thematic principle, placing 6:12-20 (one papyrus page of text) after 5:1–6:11 because of the similarity of subject matter (sexual immorality), and affixed 10:1–11:34 to 12–16 because these chapters deal generally with participation in worship. The purpose of the redaction is indicated by an ecumenical gloss to the prescript in 1:2b—"together with all those who in every place call on the

---

[84] Robert W. Funk, "The Apostolic Parousia: Form and Significance," in W. R. Farmer, C. F. D. Moule, and R. R. Niebuhr, eds., *Christian History and Interpretation* (Cambridge: Cambridge University Press, 1967), 249-69.
[85] John C. Hurd, *The Origin of 1 Corinthians* (Macon: Mercer University Press, 1983).
[86] E.g., the letters of Isocrates and Apollonius of Tyana in *Epistolographi Graeci* (ed. R. Hercher; Paris: Didot, 1873), 319-36, 110-30. Cf. Vielhauer, *Geschichte der urchristlichen Literatur*, 154-55.

name of our Lord Jesus Christ, both theirs and ours"—which seeks to make the advice that follows applicable to Christians everywhere.[87]

The strongest argument for the unity of 1 Corinthians derives from rhetorical analysis, which identifies 1 Corinthians as a "deliberative appeal for concord" (1:1–4:21), with advice on divisive issues organized under subheadings (5:1–16:24). Margaret Mitchell has made a forceful presentation of this argument,[88] adducing numerous examples from deliberative rhetoric, and has persuaded the majority of interpreters. But critics have questioned whether all of 1 Corinthians can be subsumed under the species "deliberative" rhetoric: 1 Corinthians 9, for example, is explicitly characterized by Paul as an "apology."[89] Nor is it clear that the hypothesis of a single letter is consistent with the several occasions and sources of information evident in the text of 1 Corinthians: an anonymous report (11:18), the Corinthians' letter (7:1), a visit by Stephanas and his colleagues (16:17), and a report from Chloe's people (1:11).

In sum, the unity of 1 Corinthians, like the division of 1 Corinthians, must be regarded as a hypothesis in need of demonstration. The following exposition will operate on the basis of the three-letter hypothesis outlined above.

4. Letter A, On Association with the Immoral and Idolaters: 1 Cor 10:1-22; 6:12-20; 10:23–11:34

In light of the complex social and ethnic makeup of the early Christian groups at Corinth, it is not surprising that Paul's first communication with this congregation should be devoted to boundary-setting and integration, reflecting the moral and religious challenges faced by converts rooted in Greco-Roman polytheism, as well as the difficulty of forging a new identity among Jews and Greeks, slaves and free, men and women. Paul has heard of certain problems affecting the moral and cultic life of the community, and writes to offer instruction and correction. Note that the matters with which Paul deals in Letter A point to a yet unbroken connection with paganism—the lack of scruples about taking part in pagan offerings, eating idol meat, loose sexual morality, social relations with unbelieving neighbors, the persistence of conventional dining practices. Other matters, such as the ecstatic leadership of women in the church, signal intense experimentation with a new social identity in Christ. All of the issues reflect an early stage in the development of the Christian community at Corinth.

Paul undertakes the task of constituting a new people of God by means of a typological interpretation of the formative moment in Israel's history: the Exodus and the wilderness wandering (10:1-10). By speaking of the Israelites as "our ancestors" (10:1), Paul makes clear that he reckons Gentile Christians

---

[87] Vielhauer, *Geschichte der urchristlichen Literatur*, 140.
[88] Mitchell, *Paul and the Rhetoric of Reconciliation*.
[89] R. Dean Anderson, *Ancient Rhetorical Theory and Paul* (Kampen: Kok Pharos, 1996).

as belonging to Israel. In Paul's typology, Israel's passage through the cloud and the sea prefigures Christian baptism (10:2), just as Israel's "spiritual food and drink" prefigures the meal of the Christian community (10:3-4). Paul alludes to an apocryphal tradition found in *Targum Ps.-Jonathan* (on Num 20:19) that a rock followed Israel through the wilderness; but in a stunning typological substitution, Paul explains that "the rock was Christ" (10:4). The hortatory goal of Paul's typological interpretation is reached in 10:7, where Paul quotes Exod 32:6 ("The people sat down to eat and drink, and they rose up to play"), because it epitomizes Paul's concern with idolatry and immorality among the Corinthians.[90] Through typology, Paul discerns a deeper purpose in the things that happened to Israel: "These things happened to them to serve as an example, and they were written down to instruct us, upon whom the ends of the ages have come" (10:11). Paul's capacity to grasp such correspondences depends upon his eschatological perspective. Paul formulates the point of his typological interpretation as an urgent injunction: "Therefore, my beloved, flee from the worship of idols" (10:14).

In the following paragraphs of the letter (6:12-20; 10:23-30), Paul anticipates objections to his advice to shun immorality and idolatry by dealing with two disputed cases. In both cases, Paul begins by quoting a slogan of the Corinthians, "All things are lawful for me!" (6:12; 10:23)—a proud boast of freedom, asserting liberation from cultural taboos. The Corinthian slogan has a Cynic resonance, reminding us of the traditions which placed much of Diogenes' career in Corinth,[91] and of those which connected Demetrius, the famous Cynic of the first century A.D., with the city.[92] Both of the cases in which Paul anticipates objections—going to prostitutes and eating meat sacrificed to idols—had relevance at Corinth. Even if Strabo's tale of a thousand temple prostitutes associated with the cult of Aphrodite[93] is a product of Athenian propaganda and, in any event, refers to the city before 146 B.C.,[94] there can be little doubt that prostitution was as common at Corinth as in other Mediterranean cities. Corinth's reputation for unbridled sexuality persisted in the literature of the first and second century A.D.[95] Meat markets at Corinth, as in other cities, were often located in the vicinity of temples;[96] hence the relevance of the question whether all meat sold in the market should be regarded as "idol meat" (10:25). Paul counters the libertinism of the

---

[90] Wayne A. Meeks, "'And Rose Up to Play': Midrash and Paraenesis in 1 Corinthians 10:1-22," *JSNT* 5 (1982): 64-78.
[91] Diogenes Laertius 6.77.
[92] Philostratus, *Vit. Apoll.* 2.25; Lucian, *Adv. indoct.* 19. Cf. Margarethe Billerbeck, *Der Kyniker Demetrius: Ein Beitrag zur Geschichte der frühkaiserzeitlichen Popularphilosophie* (Leiden: Brill, 1979).
[93] Strabo 8.6.20.
[94] Hans Conzelmann, "Korinth und die Mädchen der Aphrodite. Zur Religionsgeschichte der Stadt Korinth," *Nachrichten von der Akademie der Wissenschaften in Göttingen* 8 (1967): 247-61; John Lanci, "The Stones Don't Speak and the Texts Tell Lies: Sacred Sex at Corinth," in Schowalter and Friesen, *Urban Religion in Roman Corinth*, 205-20.
[95] Cf. H. J. Mason, "Lucius at Corinth," *Phoenix* 25 (1971): 160-65.
[96] See Kent, *Corinth VIII.3: The Inscriptions*, 127, for a Latin inscription on the Lechaeum Road containing the term *macellum*.

Corinthians by insisting upon the "mutually beneficial" as the criterion of moral judgment (6:12; 10:23-24). Paul appeals to the idea of the church as the "body of Christ" in order to exclude the possibility of contact with dangerous polluting agents, such as prostitutes (6:15-17).[97] Meat that had been offered in sacrifice to idols should be avoided out of consideration for the conscience of others (10:28). For all such cases, Paul formulates a general rule: "Do everything for the glory of God. Give no offense to Jews or Greeks or to the church of God" (10:31-32).

The point at issue in the next paragraph of the letter (11:2-16) is difficult to determine. Paul seems to insist that women who lead in worship should wear the veil, in accordance with Jewish custom. But 11:15 allows that women have their hair as a covering. Hence, some interpreters construe "unveiled" (in 11:5, 13) more generally as "uncovered," in reference to the loose, disheveled hair of women in ecstatic cults such as those of Dionysus and Cybele.[98] But there is little support for this interpretation in the text. Paul's argument for the maintenance of tradition (11:2) with respect to gender differences is the weakest argument in the *corpus Paulinum*, in that it threatens to compromise his own insight into the new social identity given in Christ (cf. Gal. 3:28). Paul insists upon a hierarchy of beings (God, Christ, man, woman) and evokes the danger of disgrace for a woman without a veil, or with her hair cut short. Paul's argument reaches its nadir in 11:10, where he urges that a woman should keep her head covered "because of the angels," probably a reference to the "sons of God" in Gen 6:2, who had intercourse with mortal women and fathered a race of giants. Like other Jewish writers of the period (e.g., *Test. Reuben* 5:6), Paul evidently fears that the angels will be aroused to lust by the sight of exposed women.[99] At just this point (11:11), Paul catches himself: interjecting a strong sentence adverb (translated "nevertheless"), Paul breaks off the preceding argument, in order to emphasize what is essential—in the Lord, there is mutuality and reciprocity between women and men (11:11-12). Paul's argument having collapsed, he hands the decision on women's hair over to the Corinthians (11:13), invoking a Stoic argument from nature (11:14-15), and finally appealing to custom (11:16). More important than what Paul argues *for* in this passage is what he does *not argue against*: the Spirit-filled leadership of women in the church. It is assumed throughout Paul's argument that women will "pray" and "prophesy" in the worship assembly (11:5).

In the final section of the letter (11:17-34), Paul deals with the most pressing issue: divisions at the Lord's Supper. A gulf between the "haves" and the "have-nots" had emerged at the very place where the Corinthians should have been most capable of discerning the unity of the body of Christ—at the Lord's Supper. At Corinth, the house churches evidently came together for a weekly assembly (11:20; cf. 14:23; 16:2) in the home of a well-to-do member,

---

[97] Martin, *The Corinthian Body*, 163-97.
[98] Catherine Kroeger, "The Apostle Paul and the Greco-Roman Cults of Women," *JETS* 30 (1987): 25-38.
[99] Martin, *The Corinthian Body*, 243-45.

such as Gaius (Rom 16:23). According to the conventions of Greco-Roman dinner parties, the host apportioned the fare according to the status of his guests, reserving the best food and wine for his social equals and intimate friends.[100] The contrast that Paul draws between "the Lord's Supper" and "the private supper" in 11:20-21 makes clear how Paul sees the problem—the privatization of a meal intended for the community: "When you come together, it is not really to eat the Lord's Supper. For when the time comes to eat, each of you goes ahead with your own private supper, and one goes hungry and another becomes drunk." The Greek verb translated "goes ahead" is ambiguous: it may suggest that some (the leisure class) began to eat before others (slaves, laborers) had arrived, but also that some selfishly ate their food while others looked on.[101] In any case, the behavior of the rich made plain just how dependent the poor were upon their patronage. Paul protests: "You despise the church of God and humiliate those who have nothing!" (11:22). In correction of the Corinthians' practice, Paul reminds them of the act of self-giving which established the basis of their fellowship, recalling the tradition of Jesus' words on the night when he was betrayed: "This is my body that is for you. . . . This cup is the new covenant in my blood" (11:23-25). Paul's counsel that the Corinthians "wait for one another" when they come together to eat (11:34) implies sharing, so as to alleviate the hunger and humiliation of those who have nothing.

5. Letter B, In Response to the Corinthians: 1 Corinthians 7–9, 12–16

Paul's first letter to Corinth evidently raised more questions than it answered. As the opening words of Paul's next epistle reveal ("Now concerning the things about which you wrote"), the Corinthians had written Paul a letter seeking his advice on a number of matters: marriage, divorce and betrothal, food sacrificed to idols, spiritual gifts (especially tongue-speaking), the collection for the poor, etc. (7:1; 7:25; 8:1; 12:1; 16:1; 16:12).[102] The fact that the Corinthians should send to Paul in Asia (1 Cor 16:19) on matters of practical importance demonstrates that Paul was still regarded as an authority by the community. Yet, several of the statements quoted by Paul from the Corinthians' letter express views that diverge sharply from Paul's own: e.g., "It is well for a man not to touch a woman" (7:1); "All of us possess knowledge" (8:1); "There is no resurrection of the dead" (15:12). These strongly-worded opinions betray no lack of self-confidence! The group which speaks here seems to have regarded it as their duty to "build up" the conscience of "the weak" in the community, so that they would not cling to

---

[100] Theissen, *The Social Setting*, 145-74.
[101] Bruce W. Winter, "The Lord's Supper at Corinth: An Alternative Reconstruction," *RTR* 37 (1978): 73-82.
[102] Weiss, *History of Primitive Christianity*, 1.333-34. In her attempt to defend the unity of canonical 1 Corinthians, Margaret Mitchell explains the recurring formula "now concerning" (περὶ δέ) as a marker of topics, rather than responses to the Corinthians' questions in "Concerning ΠΕΡΙ ΔΕ in 1 Corinthians," *NovT* 31 (1989): 229-56.

superstitious scruples (8:10), so that they would strive to possess spiritual gifts (14:1), etc. Dale Martin has demonstrated that the attitudes of this minority group ("the Strong") correlate with high social status and high educational level.[103] In response to the Corinthians' questions, Paul rethinks the most basic human relationships and critiques the privileges and attainments of class, with the result that status is relativized in importance by the eschatological "calling" from the Lord.

Paul's warning against immorality in his previous epistle only served to generate more questions regarding sexual ethics among the Corinthians. The words "It is well for a man not to touch a woman" in 7:1 are a quotation from the Corinthians' letter. The quotation may be an expression of extreme asceticism, or may represent an ironic retort by those who claimed to have freedom from conventional morality (cf. 6:12). Against the temptation to immorality, Paul counsels monogamy and fidelity in marriage (7:2). Paul allows that the partnership of marriage includes the bodies of the husband and wife (7:4), a principle also affirmed by the Stoic philosopher Musonius Rufus.[104] Paul warns rather strongly against withholding conjugal relations, and allows for exceptions only within limits—"by agreement, for a season, to devote oneself to prayer" (7:5). To avoid the impression that he commands sexual relations within marriage, Paul clarifies the point of his previous statements: he has spoken "by way of concession," to prevent temptation on account of "lack of self-control" (7:6). Paul's wish is that all were as he is—unmarried yet self-controlled, a state which he regards as a "gift from God"; yet Paul acknowledges that others have different gifts (7:7). Paul counsels celibacy to the unmarried and widows (7:8) unless they prove incapable of "practicing self-control" and are "aflame with passion" (7:9). In advising the married against divorce (7:10-12), Paul was able to draw upon a "command of the Lord"—a reference to sayings about divorce like those attributed to Jesus in Mark 10:2-12. The advice which Paul gives to Christians in mixed marriages is naturally offered on his own authority (7:12), because such marriages were not envisioned by Jesus himself. If the non-Christian is sympathetically disposed to live with the believer, there should be no divorce (7:12-13). Paul's claim that an unbelieving husband can be made "holy" by a believing wife (7:14) rests upon the notion that "holiness," like "uncleanness," is a quality transferable within relationships.

Paul then seeks to enunciate a general rule of conditions and relations (7:17-24), of which the preceding advice on marriage has been a special application: the "call" of God does not remove a Christian from his or her situation in society, but intensifies obedience to God in the midst of life. Paul envisions the case of a Jewish believer who might seek to remove the marks of his circumcision, and of a Gentile believer who might seek circumcision, motivated in both cases by a desire for social acceptance (7:18). Paul insists that circumcision and un-circumcision amount to nothing; what matters is

---

[103] Martin, *The Corinthian Body*, xv-xviii and passim.
[104] Cora Lutz, *Musonius Rufus: The Roman Socrates* (New Haven: Yale University Press, 1942).

keeping the commandment of God (7:19). Paul plays in a profound way with the word "calling" (Greek: κλῆσις) to indicate that something has been added to every condition, by virtue of which a Christian can remain in his or her calling, yet with a higher vocation (7:20). A slave should not be concerned about his condition (7:21a). But what if he is able to become free? Paul's advice has puzzled interpreters: "Even if you are able to become free, rather make use of [it]" (7:21b). Since the Greek verb χρῆσαι ("make use of") lacks an object, one may supply either "slavery" or "freedom." Does Paul mean that, even if a slave has the resources to purchase his freedom, he should rather make use of his present condition? Or does Paul suggest that a slave who is able to become free should make use of the opportunity?[105] In any case, the "calling in the Lord" results in a status reversal: the Christian slave has become a "freed person of Christ," while the free man has become a "slave of Christ" (7:22). Paul's thought about slavery moves beyond the Stoic consolation of "inner freedom" and implies changes in social relationship and behavior.

Whether virgins should marry must have been a question raised in the Corinthians' letter to Paul, as indicated by the recurrence of the formula "now concerning" in 7:25. Paul acknowledges that the advice that follows is his own opinion, since he has no command of the Lord (7:25). What kind of "bond" is envisioned by Paul in the discussion of virgins in 7:25-38? Not, evidently, the bond of marriage, but a pledge to preserve the virginity of the young woman, to which the man addressed by Paul in 7:27 has committed himself. Paul reassures the man and his betrothed that the decision to marry is no sin, should they prove incapable of keeping their pledge to virginity (7:28). Paul explains that he wants the Corinthians to be "free from anxieties" (7:32). Epictetus counseled the ideal Cynic to avoid the distractions of marriage; but the goal of Paul's advice is not philosophical self-mastery, but "unhindered devotion to the Lord" (7:34-35). Paul gives particular consideration to a situation which posed a special danger, namely, when the desires of those who have pledged themselves to celibacy threaten to get out of control (7:36-38). In advising marriage in this case, Paul is not compromising his preference for the unmarried state. In Paul's hierarchy of virtue, marriage is good, but celibacy is better.[106]

In the course of his discussion of marriage and celibacy, Paul shares his belief about the foreshortening of time as justification for urging an adjustment in social relationships (7:29-31). Paul is convinced that "the appointed time has grown short" (7:29). The Greek participle that Paul chooses (συνεσταλμένος) to describe what has happened to time in the Christ-event is from a verb used elsewhere in Greek literature of the furling of a ship's sails, of the folding of a bird's wings, of curtains gathered together. In this "contracted" time, Paul urges that his readers should live according to the

---

[105] See the thorough discussion in S. Scott Bartchy, *Mallon Chrēsai: First Century Slavery and the Interpretation of 1 Corinthians 7:21* (Missoula: Scholars Press, 1972).
[106] Will Deming, *Paul on Marriage and Celibacy: The Hellenistic Background of 1 Corinthians 7* (Cambridge: Cambridge University Press, 1995).

principle of "as though not": "let those who have wives be as though they had none, and those who mourn as though they were not mourning, etc." An apocalyptic parallel to Paul's account of life in the "as though not" is found in 2 Esd 16:41b-44: "Let the one who buys be like the one who will lose, . . . those who marry like those who will have no children." But there are important differences: for Paul, the eschatological rupture occurs in the present, and is immanent to every action, whereas the author of 2 Esdras distinguishes present from future, and distributes the crisis across different actions.[107]

Paul next turns to the matter of eating meat offered to idols (8:1-13). The formula "now concerning" in 8:1 indicates that the matter had been raised in the Corinthians' letter to Paul. The background was apparently this: Paul's advice in the previous letter to shun the worship of idols (1 Corinthians 10) proved confusing and difficult for some to follow. What if one were invited to dine in the banquet hall of a sacred precinct? To decline such invitations would be socially disadvantageous (cf. 1 Cor 5:10). In reply, Paul quotes repeatedly from the Corinthians' letter (8:1, 4, 8), permitting a detailed reconstruction of the social status and religious beliefs of Paul's interlocutors. The words "All of us have knowledge" in 8:1 is a quotation from the Corinthians' letter. The content of their knowledge is specified by means of another quotation in 8:4: "no idol really exists." As a consequence, eating idol meat should be a matter of indifference (8:8). Perhaps the "strong" felt that it was their duty to build up the "conscience" of the "weak," so that they would not cling to superstitious scruples (8:10). In seeking to identify the "strong" and the "weak," one should bear in mind that the poor seldom had meat as part of their diet, except when it was distributed at public religious festivals, whereas the rich could afford to buy meat in the market, and would have received invitations to dine in temples like that of Asclepius, owing to their social status.[108] Paul counters the emphasis upon religious "knowledge" by exposing its tendency to self-inflation; "love" is the constructive force of Christian community (8:1-3). The "strong" have asserted that their consumption of idol meat did not convict them of any wrongdoing, and have alleged that the "conscience" of other Christians is "weak" for harboring such scruples (8:7-8). Paul confronts the "strong" with the reality that some do not share their enlightened attitude towards the gods (8:7). Paul appropriates the term "conscience" from the "strong" and uses it to express his own true concern that someone for whom the "so-called gods" have existence might be "defiled" by eating food sacrificed to an idol (8:7). Paul formulates a radical conclusion regarding the relationship between "knowledge" and "love": the proper object of religious concern is not an abstract truth about God, but "those weak believers for whom Christ died" (8:11-12). The general principle of Christian ethics is self-limiting regard for others (8:13).

---

[107] Cf. Wolfgang Schrage, "Die Stellung zur Welt bei Paulus, Epiktet und in der Apokalyptik: Ein Beitrag zu 1 Kor. 7,29-31," *ZTK* 61 (1964): 125-54.
[108] Theissen, *The Social Setting*, 121-43.

As if to illustrate the principle of renunciation articulated in 8:13, Paul launches into a spirited defense of his decision not to accept financial support from some at Corinth (9:1-27). The background of the controversy was as follows. While Paul was resident in Corinth on his first visit, he provided for his own needs by working with his hands (Acts 18:1-3). When other apostles and evangelists subsequently arrived, they accepted patronage from wealthy persons (Crispus? Gaius?). In retrospect, Paul's refusal of support appeared questionable. Did Paul know he was not entitled to support because he was not really an apostle? Moreover, labor of the sort by which Paul sustained himself was viewed as degrading by persons of high social status.[109] These doubts and questions must have found expression in the Corinthians' letter. Paul responds to the insinuation that he is not "free" to evangelize because he is a "slave" of his labor, and that he is not really an "apostle" (9:1) with an "apology," a speech of defense (9:3-27), such as one might give before a court. Paul argues that financial support is a "right" to which he, like other apostles, is legitimately entitled (9:4-6), but of which he has chosen to make no use, so as not to "put an obstacle in the way of the gospel of Christ" (9:12). Against those who find his occupation shameful, Paul asserts that it has provided him with "ground for boasting" (9:15), by enabling him to "make the gospel free of charge" (9:18). By means of a series of well-chosen economic terms, Paul reverses the values of his apostolic rivals and their Corinthian patrons (9:16-17): "Obligation is laid upon me, and woe to me if I do not proclaim the gospel! For if I do this of my own will, I have a reward (literally, "wages"); but if not of my own will, I am entrusted with a commission (Greek: οἰκονομία, "the work of a household-manager"). Paul's point is that evangelists who willingly accept financial support are mere "hirelings," whereas he is the trusted steward of the one true patron, God. Broadening his defense against the charge of "slavishness," Paul acknowledges, "I have made myself a slave to all, so that I might win more" (9:19). Paul portrays himself as a populist leader who identifies with the interests of the common people.[110] Paul justifies his self-lowering action "for the sake of the gospel" (9:23): by making himself a "slave to all," he hopes to "save some" (9:19, 22). Paul's upper-class critics may have regarded him as a demagogue, but the poor and weak would have found his self-presentation appealing. In an extended metaphor (9:24-27), Paul compares himself to an athlete in training for the games. His renunciation of financial support should be understood as a form of discipline, an exercise in "self-control."

Paul next turns to the subject of "spiritual gifts," which, judging from the formula "now concerning" in 12:1, must have been another question raised in the Corinthians' letter. Paul counters an over-emphasis on glossolalia (speaking in tongues). Judging from the amount of space devoted to the subject, the gift of tongues must have been highly prized by the Corinthians.

---

[109] Ronald F. Hock, *The Social Context of Paul's Ministry: Tentmaking and Apostleship* (Philadelphia: Fortress, 1980).

[110] Dale B. Martin, *Slavery as Salvation: The Metaphor of Slavery in Pauline Christianity* (New Haven: Yale University Press, 1990).

Not everyone in the church spoke in tongues (12:30); those who had the gift may have looked down upon those who did not. Paul does not deny the power of speaking in tongues, but interprets that power by ordering the gifts from the greatest (wisdom) to the least (tongues), while affirming that all are necessary for the body of Christ (12:8-11). Paul affirms the diversity of gifts within unity; the guiding principle should be the "common good" (12:7). Paul's metaphor of the church as a "body" in 12:12-26 is derived from Greco-Roman political discourse, where the figure functioned to urge concord.[111] In the well-known fable of Menenius Agrippa, the Roman senator compared a strike by common people to a revolt of the hands, mouth, and teeth against the belly, resulting in the death of the body.[112] In ancient politics, the body analogy was essentially conservative, portraying the established order as "natural."[113] Paul uses the metaphor subversively to question conventional assumptions about status and honor. Paul reverses the values of ancient political rhetoric, which figured the parts of the body representing the ruling class, such as the head and the belly, as most honorable and indispensable. Paul claims, scandalously, that the weaker parts are actually more indispensable and honorable—a fact we acknowledge when we clothe these private parts (12:22-23). Paul asserts that "God has arranged the body" in this paradoxical manner, "giving greater honor to the inferior member" (12:24). Because God has established the diversity of gifts in the body, one should not succumb to the ambition to have others' gifts, or to the tendency to privilege one gift over others (12:28-30).

In the context of the discussion of spiritual gifts, Paul's encomium of love in 1 Corinthians 13 serves to devalue the gift of tongues by showing the Corinthians "a more excellent way." Yet, chapter 13 is self-contained, and the transitions from 12:31 to 13:1 and from 13:13 to 14:1 are weak, so that some scholars conjecture that chapter 13 was conceived and written earlier and independently (perhaps as an essay for Paul's school in Ephesus; cf. Acts 19:9), and reused here because of its relevance.[114] It is illuminating to compare Paul's speech in praise of *agapē* with the encomia of *erōs* in Plato's *Symposium*. The qualities of love that Paul lists highlight love's power to nurture community (13:4-7). Paul emphasizes the imperishability of love, in contrast to the limitations of prophecies, tongues, and knowledge, which the Corinthians have overvalued (13:8-13).

Paul then seeks to establish that prophecy is more edifying to the church than tongues-speaking (14:1-40). Paul shares with Plato, Philo, and others the belief in a higher form of Spirit-inspired speech directed to the divine, but incomprehensible to normal human intelligence (14:2). Paul's concession, "I would like all of you to speak in tongues" (14:5a), reveals the high value that was set upon this gift, and how many Corinthians earnestly strove for it. By declaring that "one who prophesies is greater than one who speaks in tongues"

---

[111] Mitchell, *Paul and the Rhetoric of Reconciliation*, 157-64.
[112] Wilhelm Nestle, "Die Fabel des Menenius Agrippa," *Klio* 21 (1927): 350-60.
[113] Martin, *The Corinthian Body*, 38-68.
[114] See the literature cited by Hans Conzelmann, *1 Corinthians: A Commentary on the First Epistle to the Corinthians* (Philadelphia: Fortress, 1975), 217-18.

(14:5b), Paul reverses the hierarchy of speech-types assumed by the elite, elevating the comprehensible above the esoteric. The new criterion of value is whether the community is edified. Paul devalues the esoteric speech of tongues by comparing it with the sounds produced by lifeless instruments (14:6-12). In praying, singing, and other acts of worship, Paul counsels cooperation between spirit and mind (14:13-19). The Corinthians have been naïve in failing to consider the effects of speaking in tongues upon non-adept believers, as well as unbelievers (14:20-25). Tongues may lead outsiders to conclude that Christians are out of their minds (14:23). To avoid this danger, Paul gives instructions for an orderly procedure involving tongues and prophecy in the worship assembly (14:26-33a).

A number of scholars regard the paragraph instructing women to "keep silent" in the church in 14:33b-36 as a non-Pauline interpolation.[115] Scholars adduce the following reasons for this judgment: (1) the verses disrupt the flow of the argument from 14:33a to 14:37; (2) the instruction contradicts the assumption of 11:5 that women will pray and prophesy in the assembly; (3) the attitude resembles the viewpoint of the Deutero-Pauline letters (see esp. 1 Tim 2:9-15); (4) the paragraph exhibits non-Pauline sentiments, e.g., 14:34b, "as the law also says"; (5) verses 34-35 appear after 14:40 in some manuscripts.

The issue that evoked Paul's reasoned proof of the resurrection of the dead in 1 Corinthians 15 is identified in 15:12: some of the Corinthians have said, "There is no resurrection of the dead." Greeks and Romans were generally skeptical in the face of death.[116] Those who expressed hope tended to speak of a separation of the soul from the body, a belief sanctioned by the oracle at Delphi and popular philosophers.[117] Enlightened persons found the idea of the resurrection of the body laughable (cf. Acts 17:32). Paul constructs an argument for the resurrection of the body on the analogy of the philosophical proof of the immortality of the soul in Plato *Phaedrus* 245c-257d; Cicero *Tusculan Disputations*, bk. 1; Plutarch *On the Soul*, etc. The major divisions of Paul's discourse are easily recognized and correspond to the sections of his philosophical models: 15:1-34, proof of the *fact* of the resurrection, established by reasoned arguments; 15:35-38, discussion of the *manner* of the resurrection and the *nature* of the resurrection body, culminating in a "mythological hymn" (15:51-57).

Paul begins by reminding the Corinthians that the resurrection faith belongs to the foundation of Christian tradition (15:1-2). Paul quotes a primitive creedal formula in 15:3-4: "Christ died, ... was buried, ... and was raised" (cf. Rom 10:9-10). The phrase, "he was buried," is unique to this instance of the creed and may have been added by Paul with an eye to the context (cf. 15:12). Within the argument of chapter 15, the list of witnesses to Christ's resurrection in 15:5-7, which belonged to the tradition that Paul had

---

[115] Meeks, *First Urban Christians*, 220 n. 108.
[116] See the conclusions of Richard Lattimore, *Themes in Greek and Latin Epitaphs* (Carbondale: University of Illinois Press, 1962).
[117] See the texts cited in Martin, *The Corinthian Body*, 104-38.

received, provides the evidential basis for what follows. Paul employs a series of rhetorical syllogisms ("if . . . then") in 15:13-19 to refute the denial of the resurrection by some at Corinth. Paul then turns in 15:20-28 to argue positively for the resurrection based upon an "order" established by God. The resurrection of Christ as the "first fruits" guarantees the harvest to come (15:20). Having completed his reasoned proof, Paul adduces two examples of practices that would be futile, apart from the reality of the resurrection: the Corinthians' practice of baptizing on behalf of the dead (15:29), and his own daily exposure to mortal danger in fulfillment of his apostolic calling (15:30-32). In 15:35-50, Paul endeavors to explain the nature of the resurrection body. Through analogies (e.g., seed/grain), Paul seeks to make comprehensible that there can be types of bodies other than bodies of flesh (15:36-41). By means of four antitheses (perishable/imperishable, physical/spiritual, etc.), Paul contrasts the resurrected body with the present, mortal body (15:42-44). The point of these comparisons and contrasts is to establish that believers will be transformed in the resurrection: they will exchange the "image of the man of dust," which they currently bear as descendants of Adam, for the "image of the man of heaven," which they will receive through participation in Christ (15:49). In the final section of his argument (15:51-57), Paul discloses a "mystery" in the form of a lyrical account of the destiny of both the dead in Christ and those who will survive until the resurrection—a Pauline counterpart to the mythological hymn which concludes the philosophical proofs of the immortality of the soul.

The last portion of Letter B offers advice on administrative and personal matters (16:1-24). The formula "now concerning" in 16:1 indicates that a question about the collection had been raised in the Corinthians' letter to Paul. The instruction which Paul provides for the accumulation of monies includes a promissory incentive in the form of a proviso: "if [the collection] is sufficiently large," Paul himself will convey it to Jerusalem (16:4).[118]

The formula "now concerning" in 16:12 indicates that the Corinthians had asked about Apollos in their letter to Paul. The substance of their question is embedded in Paul's response: they wished to know when Apollos would be returning to Corinth. Paul's emphatic assurance that he had "often (or earnestly) exhorted" Apollos to return should probably be seen as a reflection of the urgency which Paul sensed in the Corinthians' request. The eagerness of some at Corinth for Apollos' speedy return is illuminated by Acts 18:27-28, which reports the powerful impression produced by Apollos' oratorical and dialectical skills.

Paul's appeal for recognition of Stephanas and his household in 16:15-18 is puzzling. Why should Paul need to appeal for recognition of the first converts in Achaia? Evidently, Paul assumed that the congregation, or some of its members, had no strong inclination to grant it. Because the words with which Paul commends Stephanas and his household—"they have devoted

---

[118] For this interpretation of the phrase ἐὰν δὲ ἄξιον ᾖ in 1 Cor 16:4, see Weiss, *Der erste Korintherbrief*, 382.

themselves to the service of the saints"—employ some of the same vocabulary used by Paul in describing the charitable collection in 16:1, one may conjecture that some of Stephanas' fellow Christians opposed his appointment as Paul's agent in this work.

6. Letter C, Counsel of Concord: 1 Cor 1:1–6:11

The next communication of the Corinthians with Paul signals the outbreak of a crisis. Chloe's "people" brought news of "quarrels" (ἔριδες) among the Corinthians (1:11). The term ἔρις that forms the substance of Chloe's report has its background in the political sphere where it is used by Greco-Roman historians to characterize conflicts between factions within city-states.[119] Paul presents the dispute as an incidence of partisanship: "What I mean is this: each of you says, 'I belong to Paul,' or 'I belong to Apollos,' or 'I belong to Cephas'" (1:12). Paul caricatures the Corinthians' quarrelsomeness using slogans like those shouted by the partisans of politicians in the assembly, or by the fans of star performers in the amphitheater.[120]

Apollos was evidently the focus of partisan spirit in the church at Corinth. This conclusion is an inference from several conspicuous features of Paul's discourse in 1 Corinthians 1–4. First, one notes the reduction in the number of the parties in the course of Paul's argument: only two slogans are repeated in 1 Cor 3:4—"I belong to Paul, . . . I belong to Apollos"—a clear indication that the preceding apology for the "foolishness" of Paul's gospel in 1:17-3:4 was written with a view to the Apollos faction. Second, Paul's summary of his purposes in the argument as a whole in 4:6 takes the avoidance of partisanship on behalf of Apollos as its object: "I have applied these things to myself and Apollos for your benefit, brothers and sisters, . . . so that none of you may be puffed up in favor of one against another." Finally, it is difficult to understand Paul's critique of eloquent wisdom in 1:17; 2:1, 4, in the context of his attempt to dissuade the Corinthians from faction, as directed at anyone other than the admirers of Apollos.[121] With respect to the identity of Apollos' partisans at Corinth, scholars have observed that Paul's thanksgiving in 1:14 that he "baptized none except Crispus and Gaius" has an unmistakable note of irony which suggests that Crispus and Gaius have been involved in the formation of factions.[122]

Analysis of Paul's argument in 1 Corinthians 1–4 makes it likely that partisanship on behalf of Apollos went beyond expressions of admiration for the gifted Alexandrian sophist, and took the form of opinions openly derogatory of Paul. First, the negative definition of the style and content of Paul's preaching in 1:17 ("not with eloquent wisdom") suggests that some in

---

[119] Welborn, *Politics and Rhetoric*, 3-4.
[120] Welborn, *Politics and Rhetoric*, 8-16.
[121] D. P. Ker, "Paul and Apollos: Colleagues or Rivals?" *JSNT* 77 (2000): 75-97; J. F. M. Smit, "What is Apollos? What is Paul? In Search of the Coherence of First Corinthians 1:10-4:21," *NovT* 44 (2002): 231-51.
[122] Welborn, *An End to Enmity*, 240-41, 248-49.

Corinth have found something wanting in Paul's proclamation, and indicates the respect in which they have found it deficient. Second, the concessive manner in which Paul introduces the subject of his rhetorical self-presentation in 2:1, 3 makes clear that someone in Corinth had put forward a negative evaluation of Paul's preaching: "*Indeed I did* come to you without eloquence or wisdom, ... *Indeed I did* come to you in weakness and fear and in much trembling." Finally, the label "fool" (μωρός) is so potently derogatory that it is unimaginable that the term originated with Paul himself, even if Paul proved capable of appropriating the term in a dialectical sense in the course of his argument (3:18; 4:10). One must conclude that the label "fool" was applied to Paul by certain members of the Christian community at Corinth to describe the impression that Paul made upon them.[123]

These conclusions are reinforced by the apologetic orientation of the entire discourse in 1 Cor 1:17–4:21, where Paul is clearly on the defensive when speaking of the "foolishness" of his preaching. The defensive tone is sharpest in those passages where Paul addresses himself in the first person singular to the Corinthians in the second person plural, that is, in 2:1-5, 3:1-4, and 4:1-5. In the latter passage, Paul explicitly rejects any judgment that the Corinthians may pass upon him (4:3). The reason for the apologetic stance of these passages may be inferred from the way in which Paul continues the discussion in 3:5-15 and 4:6-7: "What then is Apollos? What is Paul? ... I have applied all of this to Apollos and myself, etc." Clearly, some in Corinth have made invidious comparisons between Paul and Apollos. It is not difficult to reconstruct what the partisans of Apollos have said: "In comparison with our learned and eloquent teacher, Paul is a fool!"[124]

Paul's response to the report of Chloe's people takes the form of the powerful counsel of concord now preserved in 1:1–6:11, a letter that fully justifies the subsequent verdict of Paul's critic in terms of being "weighty and strong" (2 Cor 10:10).[125] In terms of rhetorical species, 1 Corinthians 1–4 belongs to the "deliberative genre" (συμβουλεθτικὸν γένος): it is Paul's purpose in writing to dissuade the Corinthians from their quarrelsome conduct.[126] Thus he urges them to consider that their actions are harmful and disgraceful (1:10-16; 3:1-4, 16-23; 4:8-14, 18-21), as writers on rhetoric recommend.[127] Narrative is kept to a minimum (1:11-16), since deliberative speech is concerned with the future and seeks to advise about things to come.[128] Like a good deliberative orator, Paul assigns blame where it is due (1:12-13; 3:1-4; 4:8-13, 18-19) and makes use of examples (e.g., 3:5-9; 3:10-15; 4:1-5).[129] Indeed, Paul's advice in 1 Corinthians 1–4 is related to a

---

[123] L. L. Welborn, *Paul, the Fool of Christ: A Study of 1 Corinthians 1–4 in the Comic-Philosophic Tradition* (London: T. & T. Clark, 2005), 50, 58, 60, 84, 90, 102-16, 110, 115, 128.
[124] Welborn, *Paul, the Fool of Christ*, 102-16.
[125] On the rhetorical artistry of many passages in 1 Corinthians 1–4, esp. 1:18–2:16, see Weiss, *Der erste Korintherbrief*, 27-36.
[126] Welborn, *Politics and Rhetoric*, 57-58.
[127] Aristotle *Rhet.* 1.3.5–4.7; Quintilian 3.8.22; 3.8.33; 3.4.16; *Rhet. ad Her.* 3.2.3–4.8.
[128] Aristotle *Rhet.* 1.3.4; Quintilian 3.8.6.
[129] Aristotle *Rhet.* 1.4.8-9; 1.9.28; Quintilian 3.7.28; 3.8.36.

particular type of deliberative discourse, namely, that which is customarily entitled "On Concord" (περὶ ὁμονοίας).¹³⁰ A number of examples of this genre have survived (e.g., Antiphon περὶ ὁμονοίας; Isocrates, *Or.* 4; Dio Chrysostom. *Or.* 38–41; Aelius Aristides, *Or.* 23–24), several in the form of epistles (e.g., Isocrates, *Ep.* 3, 8, 9; Demosthenes, *Ep.* 1; Socratic Ep. 30–32; *1 Clement*).¹³¹ Their authors, generally statesmen or philosophers, seek to conciliate rival factions by dissuading from strife (στάσις) and exhorting to concord (ὁμόνοια). Like Paul, they urge their hearers "that you all say the same thing and that there be no divisions among you, but that you be united in the same mind and the same judgment" (1:10).¹³²

Precisely when one recognizes the rhetorical genre which Paul is employing in 1 Corinthians 1–4, some significant departures from the paradigm of Greco-Roman political discourse become apparent. The *homonoia* discourses typically serve to reinforce the established relations of power, by portraying the body politic as a hierarchy, and by urging submission to the rulers (hegemonic concord).¹³³ Paul, by contrast, argues for a democratic path to concord. Paul reminds the Corinthians that the majority of members of their community who have been "called" by the gospel are persons lacking in education, power, and noble birth (1:26). Yet "God has chosen what is low and despised in the world, mere nothings" (1:27-28). Paul assures the Corinthians, "All things are yours, whether Paul or Apollos or Cephas, or the world or life or death, whether things present of things to come: all things are yours!" (3:21-22). Paul describes the leaders of the community—himself and Apollos—as merely "servants through whom you came to believe" (3:5). In a series of well-constructed metaphors, Paul portrays himself and Apollos as farm-workers (3:6-9), construction laborers (3:9-15), and household stewards (4:1-5), in order to emphasize collegiality against partisanship, and to diminish the importance attributed to leaders.

One should not fail to recognize how much of Paul's masterful appeal for concord would have been shocking and even offensive to members of the social elite. Paul not only asserts that God has chosen the nothings and the nobodies (1:27-28), Paul also accepts the "fool" label for himself, and then expounds the ways in which his social experience as an apostle of the crucified Christ corresponds to that of a low buffoon, with an explicitness that would have been shameful to an upper-class reader: "We are fools on account of Christ, . . . we are weak, . . . we are dishonored; we are hungry and thirsty, we are naked, we are beaten, we are homeless, and we toil, laboring with our own hands; [we are] reviled, . . . harassed, slandered; we have become like the refuse of the world, the scum of all things, to this very day" (4:9-13).¹³⁴

---

[130] Welborn, *Politics and Rhetoric*, 58-59.
[131] See the definition of the symbouleutic letter in Ps.-Demetrius τύποι Ἐπιστολικοί 11 and Ps.-Libanius Ἐπιστολιμαῖοι χαρακτῆρες 5 in Abraham J. Malherbe, *Ancient Epistolary Theorists* (Atlanta: Scholars Press, 1988).
[132] E.g., Dio Chrysostom, *Or.* 39.3, 8; Aelius Aristides, *Or.* 24.37.
[133] On the ideology of the *homonoia* discourses, see Martin, *The Corinthian Body*, 39-47.
[134] Welborn, *Paul, the Fool of Christ*, 50-86.

Moreover, Paul not only accepts the characterization of his discourse as "vulgar" and "simple" (1:18), but focuses upon the most scandalous element of his preaching—the cross (2:2). As Cicero attests (*Rab. Post.* 5.16), it was this cruel and disgusting term which the cultured elite of the Roman world least wanted to hear. The cross was an ominous lacuna at the center of public discourse.[135] When the cross was mentioned at all, it was generally as a subject of jest.[136] But Paul seizes upon this unspeakable word and pronounces it with a vengeance. Indeed, Paul summarizes the content of his gospel in a single phrase, "the word of the cross," a reduction of astonishing harshness. Paul's choice of the perfect participle "crucified" (ἐσταυρωμένος) to describe more precisely the Christ whom he proclaims (1:23; 2:2) can only be viewed as a deliberate provocation of those who hoped for a Messiah of resplendent glory: Paul insists that the continuing and present significance of Christ, even after his resurrection, consists in nothing other than the fact that he *is* "the crucified."

Paul sent the powerful epistle now preserved in 1 Cor 1:1–6:11 to Corinth by the hand of Timothy, who was charged with "reminding" the Corinthians of Paul's "ways in Christ Jesus" (4:17). Despite the polarization of the community and the open denigration of Paul as "foolish," Paul seems to have remained confident of his ability to restore order. Indeed, Paul concludes the body of the letter with a threat to come and impose discipline (4:18-21). Paul writes in full assurance of his authority as apostle, as the "father" of the community (4:15). Paul gives instructions for the expulsion of an incestuous man from the assembly (5:1-5), on the assumption that a judgment pronounced in his absence will be executed as if he were present (5:3-5). Paul counsels against lawsuits between believers (6:1-11) in the confidence that the Corinthians will be able to settle their own disputes without going to court (6:4-6). Even in the apologetic portion of the letter (1:17-2:16), Paul's tone is one of controlled excitement, a high irony that repeatedly breaks over into censure, rather than a mood of distress or grief. Nevertheless, Paul must have sensed an urgency to bring his work among the Corinthians to fruition, lest the partisanship on behalf of Apollos endanger the collection for Jerusalem, to which Paul hoped that the Corinthians would make a considerable contribution. In this situation, it is not surprising that Paul's next communication with Corinth should be an appeal for partnership in the collection—the letter now preserved in 2 Corinthians 8.

---

[135] Martin Hengel, *Crucifixion in the Ancient World and the Folly of the Message of the Cross* (Philadelphia: Fortress, 1977), 41-43.

[136] In comedy, farce and mime: e.g., Plautus, *Most.* 359-64; the *Laureolus* mime of Catullus, on which see Josephus, *A.J.* 19.94; Martial, *De spect.* 7. Cf. Welborn, *Paul, the Fool of Christ*, 99-101, 132-38.

7. Second Corinthians as a Letter Collection

The majority of scholars regard 2 Corinthians as a composite text, differing only with respect to the number and sequence of the letters.[137] Portions of canonical 2 Corinthians clearly reflect different situations in the relationship between Paul and the Corinthians. Indeed, the composition of 2 Corinthians is so problematic that the unity of 2 Corinthians must be regarded as a hypothesis in need of demonstration. A chapter such as this is not the place to examine the evidence for the various partition theories in detail. We must content ourselves with a summary of the textual features which lead scholars to conclude that 2 Corinthians is a collection of letters.

First, the discrepancy between chapters 10–13 and other portions of the canonical epistle is conspicuous. It is not only the reversal in tone between 9:15 and 10:1, but also the contrast in content that leads scholars to doubt that chapters 10–13 originally formed the continuation of chapters 1–9. One need only compare Paul's reference to "the obedience of you all" in 7:15 with his readiness to "punish every disobedience" in 10:6 to see that these statements presuppose different situations. One might also contrast Paul's account of the "godly grief" that has produced "repentance" in 7:10-11 with his fear that he will have to "mourn over many who previously sinned and have not repented" in 12:20-21. The various attempts at harmonization of these discrepancies have not proven convincing—from Lietzmann's famous "sleepless night,"[138] to recent appeals to the rhetorical structure of 2 Corinthians,[139] or to Paul's psychagogical purposes.[140] That statements so contrary originally stood in the same epistle seems impossible, and necessitates the partition of 2 Corinthians.

Second, chapters 8 and 9 are discrete appeals for partnership in the collection.[141] After a lengthy discussion of the collection in chapter 8, Paul introduces the subject anew in chapter 9, and treats it thoroughly, as if it had not been previously mentioned. Although both chapters treat the collection, they do not relate to one another, differing in tone, purpose, strategy, and style. Chapter 8 holds up the churches of Macedonia as models of generosity for the Corinthians, while chapter 9 boasts of the readiness of the Achaians in an appeal to the people of Macedonia. Thus, chapters 8 and 9 must have been originally independent pieces of correspondence.

Third, the passage 2:14–7:4 interrupts the account of Paul's search for Titus in 2:12-13, continued seamlessly in 7:5-6. As Johannes Weiss observed,

---

[137] See the extensive histories of research in Hans Dieter Betz, *2 Corinthians 8 and 9: Two Administrative Letters of the Apostle Paul* (Philadelphia: Fortress, 1985), 3-36; Reimund Bieringer and Jan Lambrecht, *Studies on 2 Corinthians* (Leuven: Leuven University Press, 1994), 67-130; Margaret E. Thrall, *A Critical and Exegetical Commentary on the Second Epistle to the Corinthians* (2 vols.; Edinburgh: T. & T. Clark, 1994), 1.3-49.

[138] Hans Lietzmann, *An die Korinther I/II* (Tübingen: Mohr [Siebeck], 1949), 139.

[139] E.g., Frederick J. Long, *Ancient Rhetoric and Paul's Apology: The Compositional Unity of 2 Corinthians* (Cambridge: Cambridge University Press, 2004).

[140] Ivar Vegge, *2 Corinthians: A Letter about Reconciliation: A Psychagogical, Epistolographical and Rhetorical Analysis* (Tübingen: Mohr [Siebeck], 2008).

[141] As demonstrated by Betz, *2 Corinthians 8 and 9*.

"This separation of what belongs together is unheard-of and intolerable from a literary point of view, since 2:13 and 7:5-7 fit onto each other as neatly as the broken pieces of a ring."[142] The attempt to construe Paul's apology for his apostolic office in 2:14–7:4 as a "digression"[143] within the narrative of 2:12-13; 7:5-6 fails to convince, since the apology has no point of departure in what precedes, and make no connection with what follows.[144] An excursus of such length (six pages in Nestle-Aland!) has no parallel in the letters of Paul. The judgment of Dieter Georgi remains valid: "The seams in 2:13/14 and 7:4/5 are the best example in the entire New Testament of one large fragment secondarily inserted into another text."[145]

Finally, the paragraph 2 Cor 6:14–7:1 tears apart the context of what may be the strongest peroration in the Pauline corpus in 6:11-13; 7:2-4.[146] The passage contains *hapax legomena* and stylistic peculiarities. The thought has more in common with the Qumran literature than the authentic letters of Paul.[147] Hence, 6:14–7:1 has long been recognized as an interpolation, probably non-Pauline in authorship.[148]

Thus, five authentic letters of Paul and one non-Pauline interpolation emerge from literary analysis of 2 Corinthians. The compelling rationale for the partition of canonical 2 Corinthians was clearly articulated by Philipp Vielhauer a generation ago: "The characteristic of 2 Corinthians which more than any other makes a literary-critical analysis necessary is that the incoherence lies in the composition of the whole, whereas the individual large sections, e.g., 2:17–7:4 and 10–13, are within themselves exceptionally well disposed."[149]

The single criterion for determining the original sequence of the letters collected in 2 Corinthians is the phenomenon of the "cross-references": that is, passages in later letters which refer back to earlier ones. On the basis of the most conspicuous of these cross-references, Adolf Hausrath identified 2 Cor 10–13 as the "letter of tears" mentioned in 2 Cor 2:3-4.[150] With subtle insight, James Kennedy disclosed the numerous cross-references that connect 2 Cor 1:1–2:13; 7:5-16 with chapters 10–13.[151] Consider, for example, 13:2 ("if I come again, I will not spare") and 1:23 ("it was to spare you that I did not

---

[142] Weiss, *History of Primitive Christianity*, 1.349.

[143] An explanation which goes back to J. A. Bengel, *Gnomon of the New Testament* (3 vols.; Edinburgh: T. & T. Clark, 1877), 2.361; trans. of *Gnomon Novi Testamenti* (1742).

[144] Welborn, *Politics and Rhetoric*, 95-131, esp. 114-18.

[145] Dieter Georgi, *The Opponents of Paul in Second Corinthians* (Philadelphia: Fortress, 1986), 335.

[146] See the discussion, with extensive bibliography, in Thrall, *Second Epistle*, 1.22-36.

[147] Joseph A. Fitzmyer, "Qumran and the Interpolated Paragraph in 2 Corinthians 6:14–7:1," *CBQ* 22 (1961): 271-80.

[148] Hans Dieter Betz, "2 Cor 6:14–7:1: An Anti-Pauline Fragment?" *JBL* 92 (1972): 88-108.

[149] Vielhauer, *Geschichte der urchristlichen Literatur*, 151.

[150] Adolf Hausrath, *Der Vier-Capitel-Brief des Paulus an die Korinther* (Heidelberg: Bassermann, 1870).

[151] James H. Kennedy, *The Second and Third Epistles of St. Paul to the Corinthians* (London: Methuen, 1900); James H. Kennedy, "The Problem of Second Corinthians," *Hermathena* 12 (1903): 340-76.

come again to Corinth"). Or, compare 13:10 ("So I write these things while I am away from you, so that when I come, I may not have to be severe") with 2:3 ("I wrote as I did, so that when I came, I might not suffer pain"). Or, compare 10:6 ("We are ready to punish every disobedience, when your obedience is complete") with 2:9 ("I wrote for this reason: to test you and know whether you are obedient in everything"). As Kennedy observed, "in each of these pairs—the act, or purpose, or feeling, which in 2 Corinthians 10–13 is present or future, in 2 Corinthians 1–9 is spoken of as belonging to the past."[152] In a number of instances, Paul can be seen to soften the harsh language of 2 Corinthians 10–13 by a conciliatory use of the same terms in 2 Corinthians 1–9: for example, in 10:1-2 Paul boasts, "I have confidence against you," but in 7:16 Paul reassures, "I have complete confidence in you." Kennedy observed that these cross-references "are like the valves of the heart which revealed to Harvey the secret of the circulation of the blood by opening in one direction only."[153]

Utilizing the criterion of the cross-references, Margaret Mitchell has recently argued that Paul's defense of the conduct of Titus and an unnamed brother in 2 Cor 12:18 refers back to the mission of Titus and the brother in 2 Cor 8:6, 22,[154] reviving an insight of Johannes Weiss. Thus, Mitchell has concluded that 2 Corinthians 8 is the earliest of the letters which make up canonical 2 Corinthians.[155]

A consequent application of the criterion of the cross-references would lead one to place 2 Cor 2:14–7:4 (minus the interpolated passage 6:14–7:1) after 2 Corinthians 10–13. An older generation of scholars, including Paul Schmiedel, Kirsopp Lake, and Alfred Plummer, among others, recognized several instances in 2:14–6:13; 7:2-4 where Paul refers back to statements in 10–13.[156] Thus, in 3:1 and 5:12, where Paul asks, "Are we beginning again to recommend ourselves?" and asserts, "We are not commending ourselves to you again," Paul is clearly referring back to passages in chapters 11 and 12 where he felt obliged to engage in "self-commendation" (cf. 12:11). As Kennedy observed, "The word 'again' (πάλιν) implies that Paul has done on a recent occasion that very thing which he now assures them that he will do no more."[157] In 5:13, where Paul alludes apologetically to a previous moment when he appeared to be "beside himself," he is probably referring to the experience described in 12:1-6. In 4:2, where Paul underlines his refusal to "practice cunning" or to "falsify the word of God," he is likely recalling his

---

[152] James H. Kennedy, "Are There Two Epistles in 2 Corinthians?" *The Expositor* 6 (1897): 231-38, 285-304, here 234.
[153] Kennedy, "Are There Two Epistles in 2 Corinthians?" 299.
[154] Margaret M. Mitchell, "Paul's Letters to Corinth: The Interpretive Intertwining of Literary and Historical Reconstruction," in *Urban Religion in Roman Corinth*, 307-38, here 326-33.
[155] Mitchell, "Paul's Letters to Corinth," 324, 328.
[156] Paul Wilhelm Schmiedel, *Die Briefe an die Korinther* (Freiburg: Mohr, 1891), 61; Kirsopp Lake, *The Earlier Epistles of St. Paul: Their Motive and Origin* (London: Rivingtons, 1914), 154; Alfred Plummer, *A Critical and Exegetical Commentary on the Second Epistle of St. Paul to the Corinthians* (Edinburgh: T. & T. Clark, 1915), xxxi-xxxiii.
[157] Kennedy, "The Problem of Second Corinthians," 350-51.

earlier rebuttal of the charge of being "crafty" and taking the Corinthians in "by deceit" in 12:16. Paul's retrospective assertion, "we defrauded no one," in 7:2 recalls his earlier denial that he had "defrauded" the Corinthians through Titus and the brother in 12:17-18. All of these cross-references were apparent to interpreters of previous generations, along with numerous, less conspicuous instances of "softening" of words and phrases, such as "boasting" and "confidence," used in a harsh and uncomplimentary fashion in chapters 10–13, but upon which Paul confers a new, conciliatory sense in 2:14–7:4.

Consistent application of the criterion of the cross-references establishes the following sequence of letters and letter fragments within 2 Corinthians:

Letter D	Appeal for Partnership in the Collection	2 Corinthians 8
Letter E	Polemical Apology	2 Corinthians 10–13
Letter F	Conciliatory Apology	2 Cor 2:14–6:13; 7:2-4
Letter G	Therapeutic Epistle	2 Cor 1:1–2:13; 7:5-16
Letter H	Appeal for Partnership in the Collection	2 Corinthians 9

The foregoing literary analysis will be presupposed in what follows.

8. Letter D, Appeal for Partnership in the Collection: 2 Corinthians 8

It is impossible to tell how much time passed between the dispatch of 1 Cor 1:1–6:11 and the composition of 2 Corinthians 8, but the interval cannot have been too great, because the vocabulary of 2 Corinthians 8 is remarkably close to 1 Corinthians in general. The purpose of 2 Corinthians 8 is to encourage the Corinthians to fulfill their commitment to partnership in the collection, and to mandate Paul's envoys to carry out the collection on Paul's behalf.[158] More particularly, the language of 8:6 and 8:11 makes clear that, in writing this letter and in commissioning Titus and the brothers, Paul aimed not merely at the continuation of the collection work in some further stage, but at the *completion* of the effort. This is the unambiguous meaning of the verb ἐπιτελεῖν in 8:6, which is "to finish something begun," "to bring to an end," a verb which has an established usage in legal and financial contexts for the execution of agreements such as deeds and contracts.[159]

Paul begins the letter now preserved in 2 Corinthians 8 by calling attention to the success of the collection among the churches of Macedonia, as the occasion for requesting that the Corinthians fulfill their commitment to his charitable project. Paul emphasizes the "abysmal poverty" of the Macedonians, which had "overflowed into the wealth of their generosity," and

---

[158] Betz, *2 Corinthians 8 and 9*, 41, 70 and passim.
[159] Betz, *2 Corinthians 8 and 9*, 54.

praises the Macedonians for acting "on their own initiative, petitioning ... for the favor of partnership in the charitable gift" (8:1-5). Noteworthy in this exordium is Paul's paradoxical assertion that the *poverty* of the Macedonians had become the source of *wealth* for the Jerusalem Christians. Paul develops this seemingly absurd proposition in the first of three proofs, appealing to the example of Jesus Christ, who "became poor, although he was rich, in order that by means of his poverty you might become rich" (8:9). Doubtless, Paul alludes here to the idea of the *kenosis* of the divine son, best known from the "Christ hymn" of Phil 2:6-11. But unique in 2 Cor 8:9 is the economic vocabulary, which evokes the image of Jesus living in circumstances of beggary, and attributes a soteriological function to Jesus' poverty.[160]

Yet, a full appreciation of the potential offensiveness of Paul's argument can be gained only from consideration of the third and final proof (8:13-15)—an appeal to the principle of "equality." Paul urges, "At the present time, your abundance should alleviate their lack, in order that their abundance may be for your lack, so that there may be equality" (8:14). The "equality" which Paul advocates is not a communism of the sort lampooned by Aristophanes in the *Ecclesiazusae*, but something more radical, amounting to the total upending of the traditional notion of the basis of friendship in "proportional equality." Greco-Roman thinkers such as Aristotle and Cicero held that, in a friendship between unequals, such as that between benefactor and beneficiary, equality could only be established and maintained if the inferior party rendered a proportionally larger share of honor, affection, or service to his benefactor.[161] Paul profoundly contradicts this assumption, arguing that the poor Jerusalem saints are in the position of the superior party, by virtue of their spiritual wealth, which has alleviated the Corinthians' deficiency; so now, as the beneficiaries, the Corinthians are obliged, by the logic of inverse proportion, to make a considerable gift to the Jerusalem Christians, in order to restore "equality" (cf. Rom 15:26-27). It is not difficult to imagine how perverse this argument must have seemed to anyone shaped by the conventional notion of obligations between benefactors and beneficiaries, when Paul first advanced it in 2 Cor 8:1-15.

In authorizing Titus and the brother to complete the collection on his behalf (8:16-24), Paul took extraordinary precautions to assure the Corinthians of the honesty of his administration of the collection, accepting the appointment of a "brother, elected by the churches" as an auditor, "to stave off the possibility that someone might complain against us in view of the large sum of money being administered by us" (8:19-20). Nevertheless, it seems evident that the collection collapsed at Corinth, and that Titus and the brothers returned to Paul empty-handed. The bitter invective against Paul that reverberates throughout 2 Corinthians 10–13 makes it unlikely that the collection failed on account of lethargy or indifference. Rather, the conclusion that seems best warranted by the evidence is that the collection collapsed

---

[160] Betz, *2 Corinthians 8 and 9*, 62.
[161] Aristotle, *Eth. nic.* 8.6.7; 8.7.2; 8.14.2; *Eth. eud.* 7.9.5; 7.10.10; 7.10.13.

because the Corinthians, or a few Corinthians with surplus resources, refused to contribute. It is not possible to determine whether Titus' report upon his return to Paul included mention of the Corinthians' suspicions of Paul's motives (cf. 2 Cor 12:16-18). But it stands to reason that the Corinthians would have given some cause for their refusal. What is clear, in any case, is that Paul decided, at this juncture, to go to Corinth in person.

9. Paul's Second Visit to Corinth

Although Acts is silent about Paul's second visit to Corinth, it is nevertheless certain that it took place—an inference required by Paul's references to an impending "third" visit in 2 Cor 12:14 and 13:1.[162] That this visit was intensely "painful" to both Paul and the Corinthians is evident from Paul's retrospective remarks in 2 Cor 2:1-3. What happened to cause so much pain? Detailed exegesis of 2 Cor 12:16-18 reveals that someone in the church at Corinth publically accused Paul of embezzlement in connection with the collection.[163] In all probability, this person was the one whom Paul later describes as "the wrongdoer" (2 Cor 7:12), the "one who caused pain" (2 Cor 2:5). It is not difficult to appreciate how serious the moment must have been for Paul, when someone leveled the accusation of embezzlement against him. Paul's rectitude and honor suffered a crushing blow. The fate of the collection hung in the balance. Most likely, Paul was stunned into silence. When Paul recovered his wits, he employed a skillful and entirely appropriate tactic: he invoked the protection of the Deuteronomic rule of judicial evidence: "By the mouth of two or three witnesses must every charge be substantiated! (2 Cor 13:1).[164] Evidently, no one rose to second the accusation. In any case, the assembly broke up in confusion. Paul recollects "strife, jealousy, angry outbursts, intrigues, slanders, whisperings, arrogant opinions, disorders" (2 Cor 12:20), in expressing his fear that the scenario might be repeated if he returned to Corinth. Paul departed Corinth in utter humiliation (2 Cor 12:21). It would not be surprising if the "pain" that bit into Paul's soul upon the return voyage to Ephesus and in the days that followed bordered upon what we would today call depression.[165] From Paul's retrospective explanation of his actions and motives in 2 Cor 1:23–2:4, one can form a clear image of what happened next: Paul resolved not to visit Corinth again under circumstances that might prove mutually painful. Instead, Paul decided to pursue reconciliation through letters.

---

[162] The occurrence of a second visit by Paul to Corinth was first hypothesized by Friedrich Bleek, "Erörterungen in Beziehung auf die Briefe Pauli an die Korinther," *ThStKr* 3 (1830): 614-32, esp. 614-24. The second visit was located between 1 and 2 Corinthians by Heinrich Ewald, *Die Sendschreiben des Apostels Paulus* (Göttingen: Dieterich, 1857), 220-27.
[163] Welborn, *An End to Enmity*, 164-81.
[164] Welborn, *An End to Enmity*, 182-94.
[165] David E. Fredrickson, "Paul, Hardships, and Suffering," in *Paul in the Greco-Roman World*, 172-97, esp. 181-82.

10. Letter E, Polemical Apology: 2 Corinthians 10–13

Paul describes the letter that he next wrote to Corinth in highly emotional terms: "I wrote you out of much affliction and anguish of heart, through many tears" (2 Cor 2:4). In accordance with the hypothesis embraced in this chapter, the "letter of tears" is to be identified with the writing preserved in 2 Corinthians 10–13. In this apologetic letter,[166] Paul not only defends the probity of his conduct in the matter of the collection against the specific charge of embezzlement (12:14-18), but also refutes the general insinuation that he lacked the apostolic "legitimacy" to make such a request.[167] Paul's references to "comparison" (10:12) and "self-commendation" (10:12, 18) reveal that Paul's critics had demanded of him that he demonstrate his apostolic legitimacy by comparing himself with other apostles who met with the Corinthians' approval (11:5, 12; 12:11). Paul makes clear that he regards the suggestion that he "commend" himself by comparing himself with others as unprincipled "boasting" (10:13, 15-17; 11:10, 16-18, 21, 30; 12:1, 5, 9). But what was Paul to do, given that no one in Corinth was willing to recommend him (12:11)?

From this seemingly hopeless situation, Paul found a way out. Paul hit upon an ingenious strategy: he would commend himself, as the Corinthians wanted, comparing his accomplishments and qualifications with those of other apostles, but he would speak in the role of a "fool" (11:1, 16-17, 21; 12:11)! Hans Windisch suggested that the "fool's speech" which Paul delivers in 11:21b–12:10, following a lengthy and apologetic prologue (11:1-21a), was modeled upon the performances of the fools in the mime,[168] a suggestion that may be confirmed by analyzing the surviving fragments of mime, as well as mime-inspired passages in satires and novels.[169] Paul's decision to play the "fool" was fraught with danger, because it risked confirming the impression of some of the Corinthians that Paul was "lowly" (10:1) and "weak" (10:10), a vulgar type. How painful and unnatural Paul found the role is indicated by numerous features of the text: the length and defensive tone of the prologue (11:1-21a), the self-contradictions (11:1, 16), the apologetic parentheses (11:17, 21b), and the startling interruptions (11:23a) that threaten to destroy the rhetorical schema. Paul makes it clear that the role has been forced upon him by others (12:11a), and places the blame for his actions upon the Corinthians (12:11b).

Nevertheless, the "fool's speech" held distinct advantages for Paul. Like other forms of satire, the "fool's speech" enabled Paul "to speak the truth laughingly."[170] Moreover, by means of irony, Paul was able to establish a

---

[166] Hans Dieter Betz, *Der Apostel Paulus und die sokratische Tradition: Eine exegetische Untersuchung zu seiner 'Apologie' in 2 Kor 10-13* (Tübingen: Mohr [Siebeck], 1972), 13-42 and passim.
[167] Betz, *Der Apostel Paulus*, 132-37.
[168] Hans Windisch, *Der zweite Korintherbrief* (Göttingen: Vandenhoeck & Ruprecht, 1924), 316.
[169] L. L. Welborn, "The Runaway Paul: A Character in the 'Fool's Speech,' 2 Cor 11:21b–12:10," *HTR* 92 (1999): 115-63.
[170] Horace, *Sat.* 1.1.23.

critical distance towards the role that he was forced to play. In a series of "asides" that punctuate the discourse (11:21b, 23b, 30; 12:1a, 5-6, 11a), Paul lifts the "mask" and shows his face, lest his hearers become so engrossed in the performance that they forget his true attitude. Throughout the "fool's speech," Paul undermines the values of his critics and the norms of his rivals by ironic treatment of the materials of the genre: his accomplishments are calamities (11:23-29); his revelations are unutterable (12:1-4); his healing is inefficacious (12:7-9); his power consists in weakness (12:5, 9-10). Paul's performance is virtuosic, by any standard. Paul combines elements of several types of "fools" in his speech, playing the "leading slave" in 11:21b-23, acting the "braggart warrior" in 11:24-27, evoking the "anxious old man" in 11:28-29, dramatizing the feckless "runaway" in 11:30-33, portraying the "learned impostor" in 12:1-4, and miming the "quack doctor" in 12:7-9.[171] The evocation of several types of "fools" in the performance of a single individual is not unique to Paul: in *Satire* 2.7, Horace permits his slave Davus to portray him as an adulterer, a leading slave, a braggart warrior, a learned impostor, a parasite, a runaway—all parts played by the "fool" in the mime.[172] Although Paul's "foolish discourse" is concise, it approximates the length of a recitation by a solo performer, judging from the *mimiambi* of Herodas. As an ironic defense of the legitimacy of his apostleship, Paul's "foolish discourse" must be judged a complete success.[173]

From what Paul says later (2 Cor 7:8-12), we learn that Paul was anxious about the Corinthians' response to the letter of 2 Corinthians 10–13. Paul knew that the letter was "severe" and that it would cause "pain." Moreover, Paul remained embarrassed about having engaged in "self-commendation," despite the cover provided by the paradoxical form of the "fool's speech," as the backward glancing disavowals of further exercises in "self-commendation" in 3:1 and 5:12 clearly reveal. Finally, Paul was concerned about the impression produced by his unrestrained display of powerful emotions such as anger and grief (2 Cor 2:4). Might not such displays of emotion be adduced by Paul's critics as evidence that Paul was "beside himself," as he later concedes that he appeared to be in 2 Cor 5:13? In anxiety over the outcome of his "painful epistle," Paul sent Titus as his envoy to Corinth (cf. 2 Cor 2:12-13; 7:5-6). Titus found the Corinthians is a state of "fear and trembling" (2 Cor 7:15) as a result of the "severe epistle."

11. Letter F, Conciliatory Apology: 2 Cor 2:14–6:13; 7:2-4

Paul did not send Titus on his delicate mission empty-handed, but with the letter now preserved in 2 Cor 2:14–6:13; 7:2-4. This letter is also an "apology": that is to say, Paul is still defending the legitimacy of his

---

[171] Welborn, "The Runaway Paul: A Character in the 'Fool's Speech'," 137-59.
[172] Karl Freudenberg, *The Walking Muse: Horace on the Theory of Satire* (Princeton: Princeton University Press, 1993), 225-26.
[173] Windisch, *Der zweite Korintherbrief*, 316.

apostleship and the probity of his ministry. But Paul's tone is far more conciliatory than in the apology of 2 Corinthians 10–13. In keeping with his conciliatory strategy, Paul focuses upon the theoretical basis of his ministry, deepening and intensifying his insight into the paradox of "power made perfect in weakness" (2 Cor 12:9) that formed the climax of his "letter of tears" (cf. 2 Cor 13:3-4). Breaking through the sea floor of his own being, so to speak, Paul now expounds an extreme form of the paradox of his apostolic ministry, indeed, as Paul understands it, the paradox of Christian existence as such—life made manifest in death: "But we have this treasure in earthen vessels, in order that it may be clear that the surpassing power belongs to God and does not come from us. We are afflicted in every way, but not crushed; perplexed, but not driven to despair; persecuted, but not forsaken; struck down, but not destroyed; always bearing about in the body the death of Jesus, in order that the life of Jesus may be made manifest in our bodies" (2 Cor 4:7-10).[174] The source of Paul's mysterious capacity to endure his paradoxical existence is not the concentrated inwardness of the Stoic, who has made himself invulnerable to life's adversities,[175] nor a psychic disposition gained through remaining aloof from bodily life, like a Platonic dualist,[176] but rather Paul's "death" to himself and to self-interest, accomplished through his participation in the death of Messiah Jesus. As Paul goes on to explain, those who have been grasped by the love of Christ have "died" with him, and no longer live for themselves: "For the love of Christ constrains us, because we are convinced of this—that one died for all, and therefore all died. And he died for all, so that those who live might live no longer for themselves, but for him who for their sake died and was raised" (5:14-15). The one who has been set free from the tyranny of self-interest is a "new creation," who has been "reconciled" to God, and who is the recipient of a "ministry of reconciliation" (5:17-19).[177] Paul's concluding defense of his apostolic ministry in 2 Cor 6:3-13 is a passionate and poetic self-portrait, in which endurance, love, and truth break through all suspicion and doubt, to provide a sincere and authentic self-commendation. The letter climaxes with the most direct and emotionally charged peroration in the Pauline corpus (7:2-4).

At some point during Titus' visit to Corinth, whether at the meeting when Titus presented Paul's conciliatory apology or on some later occasion, the *ekklesia* resolved to discipline the wrongdoer. It is this action to which Paul refers in a passage in his next letter: "Sufficient for such a one is this punishment by the majority" (2 Cor 2:6). In Troas, and then in Macedonia, Paul awaited Titus' report from Corinth. The account that Paul gives in 2 Cor 2:12-13 and 7:5 of the anxiety he endured while he awaited news of the

---

[174] See the insightful commentary on this passage by Rudolf Bultmann, *The Second Letter to the Corinthians* (Minneapolis: Augsburg, 1985), 110-20.
[175] Epictetus, *Diatr.* 2.19.24; Seneca, *Ep.* 41.4.
[176] Plato, *Phaedo* 66e-67a.
[177] Cilliers Breytenbach, *Versöhnung: Eine Studie zur paulinischen Soteriologie* (Neukirchen-Vluyn: Neukirchener Verlag, 1989), 125-32.

Corinthians' response is calculated to awaken the pity of his readers.[178] Yet there is no reason to doubt the genuineness of Paul's anxiety as he awaited Titus, or the exuberance of joy with which Paul greeted the news that the Corinthians were ready for reconciliation (2 Cor 7:6, 7, 9, 13, 16).

12. Letter G, Therapeutic Epistle: 2 Cor 1:1–2:13; 7:5-16

The letter that Paul wrote to Corinth in the afterglow of Titus' report is now preserved in 2 Cor 1:1–2:13; 7:5-16. Since the time of Günther Bornkamm, it has become customary to refer to 2 Cor 1:1–2:13; 7:5-16 as the "letter of reconciliation."[179] This usage may have encouraged the idea that all was now well between Paul and the Corinthians, and that Paul only needed to "set the seal" upon his conciliatory efforts, so to speak. But close reading of this epistle reveals that Paul still had work to do, in order to allay suspicions of insincerity and, above all, to heal his wounded friends at Corinth. As Johannes Weiss observed, "There is still some mistrust. The opinion still seemed to some extent to prevail that Paul had dealt with the Corinthians with worldly subtlety and not with complete sincerity, and that mental reservations were concealed beneath the words of his letters (2 Cor 1:12-13).[180]

Paul's assurance of the "simplicity and sincerity" of his conduct in 1:12-14 constitutes the proposition of this epistle—a sure indication that this letter, like the preceding two epistles, is "apologetic" in character. Accordingly, in the first argument (1:15-22), Paul appeals to his volition as proof of his sincerity against the charge of "foolish irresponsibility" (1:17) in his failure to keep his promise to return to Corinth. In the second argument (1:23-2:4), Paul explains that he exercised caution, "sparing" the Corinthians further grief by his decision not to come to Corinth. In the third argument (2:5-11), Paul proves his sincere goodwill by his magnanimous treatment of the one who had caused grief, recommending that the Corinthians "forgive" and "console" him, and that they "reaffirm love." Paul next (2:12-13; 7:5-7) adduces the anxious state in which he awaited news of the outcome of Titus' mission as proof of the genuineness of his affection. Paul's final argument (7:8-13a) appeals to the beneficial results of his painful epistle as proof of the integrity of his conduct: the grief of the Corinthians had produced repentance, salvation, and joy.

Yet, the overarching purpose of the epistle preserved in 1:1–2:13; 7:5-16 is the healing of Paul's wounded friends at Corinth, especially the wrongdoer. The Corinthians had been doubly grieved—first by the actions of the wrongdoer (2:5), then by Paul's severe response (7:8). So, from the first word of this epistle to the last, Paul offers consolation. Paul opens the exordium (1:3-7) with praise of God as the "God of all consolation." Paul represents

---

[178] L. L. Welborn, "Paul's Appeal to the Emotions in 2 Corinthians 1:1–2:13; 7:5-16," *JSNT* 82 (2001): 31-60, esp. 45-47.
[179] Günther Bornkamm, *Die Vorgeschichte des sogenannten Zweiten Korintherbriefs* (Heidelberg: Winter, 1961).
[180] Weiss, *History of Primitive Christianity*, 1.346.

himself as "afflicted" and "comforted" on behalf of the Corinthians, so that he may be able to extend consolation to his wounded friends. Equally, Paul portrays the Corinthians as the source of "consolation" and "joy" for himself and Titus (7:6-7). The jubilant peroration of this epistle (7:13b-16) reiterates Paul's consolation and joy in response to the good report of Titus.

The epistolary type which subsumes both the apologetic and the consolatory moments in 2 Cor 1:1–2:13; 7:5-16 is the "therapeutic" style of letter described in the handbook on epistolary types attributed to Libanius.[181] The agreement between the "therapeutic" letter in Ps.-Libanius' handbook and Paul's epistle in 2 Cor 1:1–2:13; 7:5-16 is striking.[182] A number of examples of this letter-type have survived, e.g., Apollonius of Tyana, *Ep.* 45, *BGU* II.531, Marcus Aurelius to Herodes Atticus (in Philostratus, *Vit. soph.* 2.1.562-63). When one compares 2 Cor 1:1–2:13; 7:5-16 with other letters of the therapeutic type, two features of Paul's epistle appear noteworthy: first, the intensity of Paul's appeal to the emotions, especially his willingness to acknowledge the mutual experience of "pain" or "grief" (λύπη);[183] second, Paul's insistence upon the forgiveness of the wrongdoer,[184] an attitude which has little precedent in Greco-Roman literature.[185]

13. Letter H, Appeal for Partnership in the Collection: 2 Corinthians 9

With renewed confidence in the Corinthians, Paul wrote one final letter to the churches of Achaia, before taking leave of the Macedonians—the letter now preserved in 2 Corinthians 9. Among the things that Titus reported to Paul upon his arrival in Macedonia must have been the Achaians' readiness to contribute to the collection for the poor in Jerusalem (9:2). Few echoes of the former conflict remain in Paul's well-calculated appeal for partnership in the collection: only the rhetorical contrast between the "gift of blessing" and "greediness" in the provision which Paul makes for the Achaians' contribution in 9:5 and the exclusion of "distress" and "compulsion" from the motives for giving in 9:7 recollect the former quarrels. Indeed, Paul portrays the Achaians as God-like in the abundance of their generosity, applying to his readers the words of Ps 111:9: "He scattered, he gave to the poor; his righteousness remains into eternity" (9:9). Noteworthy in Paul's argument is his assertion that the Achaians have entered into a contractual agreement by means of their donation, the substance of which is their submission to

---

[181] Ps.-Libanius, Ἐπιστολιμαῖοι χαρακτῆρες 19, 66 in Malherbe, *Ancient Epistolary Theorists*, 68-69, 76-77.
[182] Welborn, *An End to Enmity*, 464-65.
[183] Welborn, *An End to Enmity*, 466-75.
[184] Welborn, *An End to Enmity*, 476-78.
[185] David Konstan, "Remorse, Repentance and Forgiveness in the Classical World," *Phoenix* 62 (2008): 243-54.

Jerusalem (9:13).[186] Paul's final written word to the Corinthians is a prayer of thanksgiving for their anticipated contribution to the collection: "Thanks be to God for his indescribable gift!" (9:15).

14. Paul's Third Visit to Corinth

In the winter of A.D. 56, Paul arrived in Corinth for his third and final visit. The author of Acts (20:3) relates that Paul remained in Corinth for three months. During this period, Paul was a guest in the house of Gaius (Rom 16:23). The importance of Paul's reconciliation with the Corinthians is measured by the visionary quality of Paul's thought and the ethical consistency of his actions during the period of his final residence in Corinth; for it was there that Paul wrote his last and greatest epistle to the Romans (Rom 16:22-23); and it was then that Paul announced his audacious plan for a new mission in Rome and faraway Spain (Rom 15:23-24, 28); and it was then that Paul summoned the courage to accompany the collection to Jerusalem in person (Rom 15:25-27), even though he knew that his life was in danger (Rom 15:30-32). In sum, Paul's reconciliation with the Corinthians created the psychological conditions for the last and most productive period in Paul's life as an apostle of Christ.

Recommended Reading

Adams, E., and D. G. Horrell, eds. *Christianity at Corinth: The Quest for the Pauline Church*. Louisville: Westminster John Knox, 2004.

Cameron, Ron, and Merrill P. Miller. *Redescribing Paul and the Corinthians*. Leiden: Brill, 2011.

Concannon, Cavan. *"When You Were Gentiles": Ethnicity in Roman Corinth and Paul's Corinthian Correspondence*. New Haven: Yale University Press, 2013.

Friesen, Steven, Daniel N. Schowalter, and James Walters, eds. *Corinth in Context: Comparative Perspectives on Religion and Society*. Leiden: Brill, 2010.

Marquis, Timothy Luckritz. *Transient Apostle: Paul, Travel, and the Rhetoric of Empire*. New Haven: Yale University Press, 2013.

Martin, Dale B. *Slavery as Salvation: The Metaphor of Slavery in Pauline Christianity*. New Haven: Yale University Press, 1990.

Martin, Dale B. *The Corinthian Body*. New Haven: Yale University Press, 1999.

Mitchell, Margaret M. *Paul and the Rhetoric of Reconciliation: An Exegetical Investigation of the Language and Composition of 1 Corinthians*. Tübingen: Mohr (Siebeck), 1991.

Mitchell, Margaret M. *Paul, the Corinthians and the Birth of Christian Hermeneutics*. Cambridge: Cambridge University Press, 2010.

Schowalter, Daniel N., and Steven Friesen, eds. *Urban Religion in Roman Corinth: Interdisplinary Approaches*. Cambridge: Harvard University Press, 2005.

Welborn, L. L. *Politics and Rhetoric in the Corinthian Epistles*. Macon: Mercer University Press, 1997.

---

[186] See the detailed analysis of the technical vocabulary of 2 Cor 9:13 in Betz, *2 Corinthians 8 and 9*, 122-23.

L. L. Welborn

Welborn, L. L. *Paul, the Fool of Christ: A Study of 1 Corinthians 1–4 in the Comic-Philosophic Tradition*. London: T & T Clark, 2005.
Welborn, L. L. *An End to Enmity: Paul and the "Wrongdoer" of Second Corinthians*. Berlin: de Gruyter, 2011.

10. The Letter to the Galatians

Greg W. Forbes

Galatians finds the apostle Paul on the attack, vehemently opposing teaching that threatens not only the survival of the churches in this region, but undermines the gospel of Jesus Christ as proclaimed by him.

The severity of the situation is evident both in the way the letter is structured and in the way the apostle defends his apostolic credentials and his understanding of the gospel. This is no intimate letter of friendship. It is no letter of mild or even moderate correction. It is a full-on frontal assault written in an often ironic and sometimes sarcastic tone employing a wide range of the Pauline rhetorical arsenal.

The basic elements of the troublesome teaching are clear, although the origin and motives of the teachers themselves are somewhat disputed. The teachers have clearly infiltrated the churches in this region and have sought to undermine Paul's credibility and authority as an apostle. They have also denied the sufficiency of faith in Jesus for salvation by insisting on the continued validity and observance of the Mosaic law which includes the practice of circumcision.

Paul's response is unambiguous. He is a fully-fledged apostle, commissioned directly by Jesus himself and recognized as a co-worker by the Jerusalem apostles. The gospel he proclaims is of divine origin and is not to be undermined by any insidious human teaching that downplays the sufficiency of Christ's death and faith in him alone as the basis for forgiveness of sins.

The purpose of this chapter is to provide an introduction and overview of Paul's response to this crisis—the Letter to the Galatians. As authorship is rarely contested only a few brief comments will be offered, however the issues of date and recipients are complex and intertwined and will be discussed in some detail. We will then attempt to identify the opponents of Paul whose teaching necessitated the writing of the epistle. The purpose and theological content of Galatians will be summarized, followed by a discussion of the New Perspective on Paul. After some brief comments on the genre and structure of the book, we will conclude with an outline of contents. The outline is an attempt to provide an exegetical summary of sorts, tracing the apostle's flow of thought and highlighting the major interpretive issues that have arisen in the study of the epistle.

Greg W. Forbes

1. Authorship

Galatians is one of the undisputed Pauline epistles. The biographical details are consistent with what we find elsewhere, and the understanding of faith, justification, and the law, together with Paul's distinctive use of the OT, align with the other undisputed Pauline letters, namely, Romans, 1 and 2 Corinthians, and Philippians. Of course there are always dissenting voices, but Richard Longenecker is no doubt correct in stating: "If Galatians is not by Paul, no NT letter is by him, for none has any better claim."[1]

2. Date and Recipients

The question of the date of Galatians has shifted from a relatively settled issue to quite a complex and contested one over the past century or so. The solution is inseparably related to two other factors: (1) the identity and location of the recipients; and (2) the relationship between Gal 2:1-10 and Acts 15.

2.1. Traditional View: The North Galatian Hypothesis

The traditional view is that Paul wrote this epistle at some point during his third missionary journey (late 50s) to churches situated in north-central Asia Minor.[2] Consequently the letter was penned several years after the Jerusalem Council, with most adherents of this position equating Paul's visit to Jerusalem described in Gal 2:1-10 with the Council visit narrated by Luke in Acts 15. The main factors supporting this hypothesis are as follows.

1. The reference to "Galatia" most naturally refers to an ethnic group who were descendants of Celtic invaders from Gaul who lived in the central and northern part of Asia Minor.[3] This area was evangelized by Paul on the second missionary journey (Acts 16:6) and revisited on the third journey (Acts 18:23).
2. The similarities between Gal 2:1-10 and Acts 15 indicate that these are two depictions of the one event, with differences explained as either minor irrelevancies or the product of Luke's proclivity for placing theological concerns above historical accuracy.[4]

---

[1] R. N. Longenecker, *Galatians* (Dallas: Word, 1990), lviii. The dissenting voices are summarized on lviii-lix.
[2] Championed by J. B. Lightfoot, *Saint Paul's Epistle to the Galatians* (10th ed.; London: Macmillan, 1986); J. Moffatt, *An Introduction to the Literature of the New Testament* (3rd ed.; Edinburgh: T. & T. Clark, 1918), 83-107. See also H. D. Betz, *Galatians: A Commentary on Paul's Letter to the Churches in Galatia* (Philadelphia: Fortress, 1979), 81-83.
[3] On the history of the region, see T. George, *Galatians* (Nashville: Broadman & Holman, 1994), 38-46; F. F. Bruce, *Commentary on Galatians* (Grand Rapids: Eerdmans, 1982), 3-5; S. Mitchell, "Galatia," *ABD* 2.870-72. For map and discussion, see http://bibleatlas.org/regional/galatia.htm.
[4] See E. Haenchen, *The Acts of the Apostles* (trans. R. McL. Wilson; Oxford: Basil Blackwell, 1971), 455-72; R. Pervo, *The Mystery of Acts: Unravelling its Story* (Santa Rosa: Polebridge,

3. In his account of the meeting with the Jerusalem "pillars," Paul refers to previous work among the Gentiles (2:2), and indicates their confirmation of his ministry to the uncircumcised (2:7-8). This most naturally refers to the missionary activity of the First Journey and so correlates with the meeting of Acts 15 which appears to have taken place shortly after Paul returned to Antioch from that journey.
4. Style (defense of apostolic authority) and theological content (justification by faith, righteousness, role of the law) has more in common with Paul's later letters (2 Corinthians, Romans, Philippians) than with his earlier letters (1 and 2 Thessalonians).

2.2. South Galatian Hypothesis

The South Galatian theory was championed by W. M. Ramsay and has gained increasing support in recent times. Under this proposal Paul wrote to the churches in the south of the Roman province of Galatia. In other words, "Galatia" designates a Roman province rather than an area inhabited by a particular ethnic group, a province that by the time of Paul comprised a considerable portion of Asia Minor.[5]

The recipients of the letter would then be the churches evangelized by Paul on the First Missionary journey (Acts 13:13–14:28). This would allow the letter to be written prior to the Jerusalem Council and would make it the earliest extant letter of Paul (ca. A.D. 48). Consequently, Gal 2:1-10 does not equate with Acts 15 but with a previous visit to Jerusalem, most likely the "famine relief visit" described in Acts 11:27-30.

2.3. Assessing the Arguments

There are significant problems with the traditional view. First of all, working from the quite sustainable position of the general historical reliability of Acts,[6] the differences between Paul's visit to Jerusalem described in Gal 2:1-10 and Acts 15 can only, with undue optimism, be described as "minor." Galatians depicts a private meeting in response to a "revelation": Acts portrays a public assembly in response to a delegation. Furthermore, the qualification to remember the poor (Gal 2:10) bears no resemblance whatsoever with the conditions of the Apostolic Decree (Acts 15:19-21).

2008); J. D. G. Dunn, *Beginning from Jerusalem: Christianity in the Making Vol. 2* (Grand Rapids: Eerdmans, 2009), 446-69.
[5] See further C. J. Hemer, *The Book of Acts in the Setting of Hellenistic History* (WUNT 49; Tübingen: Mohr [Siebeck], 1989), 277-307; Longenecker, *Galatians,* lxii-lxiii.
[6] See Hemer, *Acts*; A. N. Sherwin-White, *Roman Society and Roman Law in the New Testament* (Grand Rapids: Baker, 1963); D. Marguerat, *The First Christian Historian: Writing the "Acts of the Apostles"* (SNTSMS 121; trans. K. McKinney, G. J. Laughery, and R. Bauckham; Cambridge: Cambridge University, 2002); D. L. Bock, Acts (Grand Rapids: Baker, 2007), 8-12; D. G. Peterson, *The Acts of the Apostles* (Grand Rapids: Eerdmans, 2009), 23-25.

Second, there are some historical and theological points that are more difficult to explain under the North Galatian than under the South Galatian hypothesis. These may be listed as follows:

1. The mention of Barnabas (2:1, 9) is difficult, given that the apostles had parted company prior to the Second Journey (Acts 15:36-41).
2. Paul under oath (1:20) describes the meeting with the Jerusalem pillars (2:1-10) as his second visit post-conversion. According to the North Galatian hypothesis it would be his third visit.[7]
3. Failure to mention the apostolic decree in Galatians is a significant issue. Although Paul does want to stress his independence from the Jerusalem apostles, it defies reason to imagine that this desire for independence should go so far as to omit the weightiest argument he could have utilized. Considering the fact that the Galatian Christians appear to have been so easily persuaded by an ultra-conservative Jewish Christianity, knowledge that the Jerusalem leaders themselves supported a law-free gospel could hardly have done Paul's argument much harm!
4. A "revelation" does fit with Acts 11:27-30. The "revelation" by which Paul went to Jerusalem could well have been intended to denote Agabus' prophecy of the famine (Acts 11:28).

In conclusion, although problems remain with either view, the South Galatian hypothesis better fits the available data. The Epistle to the Galatians would then be Paul's first letter, written ca. A.D. 48 shortly before the Jerusalem Council and sent to the churches recently evangelized on the First Missionary Journey.

3. The Opponents

Given that Paul does not address his opponents directly, their identity and teaching must necessarily be reconstructed from the allusions he makes to them and the response he makes to the Galatian churches (e.g. 1:6-9; 3:1-5; 4:17; 5:7-12; 6:12-15). Such a mirror-reading methodology does, however, have limitations.[8] It assumes that all issues addressed in the letter are linked to the false teachers and their teaching. Whereas some issues clearly stem from the false teachers others are less traceable. So, while the necessity of circumcision was obviously a key tenet of their teaching, it is hardly possible, on the basis of Paul's allegory of Hagar and Sarah (4:21-31), to state with

---

[7] Again, given the general historical credibility of Acts. The second visit was the so-called "famine relief visit" described in Acts 11:27-30.
[8] For a clear assessment of the problems and results of mirror reading with respect to Galatians, see J. M. G. Barclay, "Mirror-Reading a Polemical Letter," in M. D. Nanos, ed., *The Galatians Debate: Contemporary Issues in Rhetorical and Historical Interpretation* (Peabody: Hendrickson, 2002), 367-82; also I. J. Elmer, *Paul, Jerusalem, and the Judaisers: The Galatian Crisis in Its Broadest Historical Context* (WUNT 2.258; Tübingen: Mohr [Siebeck], 2009), 213.

much confidence that the opponents claimed "that his message represents an Ishmaelian form of truth."[9]

Another problem with mirror reading is that historical reconstructions have an uncanny tendency to reflect the historical milieu of the interpreter. Is it a coincidence, for example, that Walter Schmithals, writing in the 1950s and 60s when the influence of Gnosticism on the NT was in vogue, contended that the opponents were Jewish-Christian gnostics?[10]

These concerns aside, the following points seem reasonably assured:

1. The opponents were Jewish Christians,[11] conservative in bent, probably from Jerusalem.[12]
2. They were opposed to a law-free gospel, insisted on male circumcision for membership of God's people, and wanted to tie salvation to the law for both Jews and Gentiles.
3. They were not members of the Galatian churches, but itinerant Jewish Christian evangelists.[13]
4. They had an unflattering opinion of Paul and sought to discredit both him and his teaching.[14]

As we probe further, things become more uncertain. What relationship did the opponents have with the apostles in Jerusalem? Were they authorized by them (e.g. James), and/or had they overstepped the extent of their authorization? The dating of the epistle impinges on these questions; it is far more understandable that they acted with apostolic support prior to the Jerusalem Council.

---

[9] As does Longenecker, *Galatians*, xcvii, who considers it likely that this accusation stemmed from Paul's insistence that believers were sons of Abraham (3:6). This left open the question of which particular son, Isaac or Ishmael.

[10] W. Schmithals, *Paul and the Gnostics* (trans. J. E. Steely; Nashville: Abingdon, 1972), 13-64.

[11] There have been some suggestions by earlier commentators that the opponents were non-Christian Jews intent on proselytism to Judaism. See F. J. Foakes-Jackson and K. Lake, *The Acts of the Apostles* (Grand Rapids: Baker, 1979), 215; and more recently M. D. Nanos, *The Irony of Galatians: Paul's Letter in First-Century Context* (Minneapolis: Fortress, 2002). But this is highly unlikely given the fact that Paul refers to the teaching as "a different gospel" (1:6-9). Also unpersuasive is the view of J. H. Ropes, *The Singular Problem of the Epistle to the Galatians* (HTS 14; Cambridge, Mass.: Harvard University, 1929), 27-45, that Paul was battling both a Judaizing element as well as libertine Gentile Christians.

[12] J. C. Hurd, "Reflections concerning Paul's 'Opponents' in Galatia," in S. E. Porter, ed., *Paul and his Opponents* (Pauline Studies vol. 2; Leiden: Brill, 2005), 129-148, believes that the opponents were the two "brothers" mentioned in 2 Corinthians 8–9 entrusted with the collection for the Jerusalem church. They visited the Galatian churches on the way to Macedonia, presenting themselves as Paul's colleagues.

[13] The terms used for them are in the third person (1:7; 5:10, 12; 6:13) as opposed to the second person for congregation members.

[14] R. B. Cook, "Paul and the Victims of His Persecution: The Opponents in Galatia," *BTB* 32.4 (2002): 182-91, asserts that the opponents were his previous victims intent on discrediting him. Contrast this with M. Wigner, "Act One: Paul Arrives in Galatia," *NTS* 48.4 (2002): 548-67, who insists that these teachers did not know Paul's understanding of the law as he did not discuss it at any length in his initial evangelization of the region.

What were their motives? It could be that they were simply resistant to change and threatened by a large influx of Gentiles[15] into the people of God. Possibly the issue was theological/historical. Was not the Mosaic covenant permanent? Had it been abrogated? Jesus, in fact, was remembered as saying that he had not come to overthrow the law (Matt 5:17). Maybe they were apprehensive about decaying ethical standards, concerned to uphold the law as a regulatory system for moral and social behavior for both Jews and Gentiles. Possibly the issue was more structural, with Jerusalem (James?) wanting to gain control of the mission beyond Antioch and bring it under the auspices of the mother church.[16]

With respect to Paul and his teaching it is unlikely that this was a personal vendetta, but an attack on anyone who would erode what they saw as the fundamental requirements for belonging to God's people. It is possible they misunderstood his teaching and missed the ethical implications of living by the Spirit rather than by the law, but it is equally likely that they perceived the movement from law to Spirit as providing an unwelcome occasion for moral laxity.

It also appears as though the opponents perceived Paul to be somewhat fickle, willing to compromise his Jewish heritage and to package the gospel in ways conducive to audience acceptance (1:10). For the Gentiles, what better way than avoiding the painful and much maligned practice of circumcision.[17] Seen in this light, their actions may be understood more in terms of completing Paul's gospel than in correcting it.

Along different lines, J. K. Hardin has recently proposed that the Galatian crisis was purely a local affair. The agitators were local Jewish Christians who were concerned that association with Gentiles who no longer observed the imperial cult may result in severe reprisals (see 6:12-13). Consequently, the agitators sought to make Paul's converts appear more Jewish and so part of one of the two "normalized" groups of society. The vacillation of the Pauline converts in this respect is apparent in their return to observing the imperial cultic calendar (4:1-11).[18]

In weighing the evidence, the opponents would appear to be Jewish Christian evangelists active in the Greek speaking world. They are of the same mentality as those described in Acts 15:1-5[19], with the law being central to their doctrine of salvation. Hence the commonly ascribed term Judaizers is

---

[15] Bas Van Os, The Jewish Recipients of Galatians," in S. E. Porter, ed., *Paul: Jew, Greek, and Roman* (Leiden: Brill, 2008), 51-64, is one of the few to consider that the recipients were both Jewish and Gentile Christians.

[16] Elmer, *Judaisers*, 215.

[17] On the disdain of circumcision, see J. M. G. Barclay, *Jews in the Mediterranean Diaspora: From Alexander to Trajan (323 BCE–117 CE)* (Edinburgh: T. & T. Clark, 1996), 438-39.

[18] J. K. Hardin, *Galatians and the Imperial Cult: A Critical Analysis of the First-Century Social Context of Paul's Letter* (WUNT 2.237; Tübingen: Mohr [Siebeck], 2008), 85-115. Along similar lines B. Kahl, *Galatians Re-Imagined: Reading through the Eyes of the Vanquished* (Minneapolis: Fortress, 2010). See also A. E. Harvey, "The Opposition to Paul," in Nanos, *Galatians Debate*, 321-33.

[19] T. R. Schreiner, *Galatians* (Grand Rapids: Zondervan, 2010), 39-52. Schreiner also presents a rebuttal of Hardin's emphasis on the imperial cult (35-37).

apt.[20] Christ was probably understood as making a perfect sacrifice for sins according to the law,[21] rather than transcending the law. The fact that they are "troubling" the Galatian Christians (1:7; 5:10), indicates that the teaching was calling the confidence of their salvation into question (see 4:17). For Paul, this is a matter of the utmost seriousness that demands an urgent response.

4. Purpose and Theological Content

Paul's letter to the Galatian churches is a response to the destabilizing teaching described above. We can identify a threefold purpose: (1) to rescue the church from the teaching of the Judaizers; (2) to reassert his apostolic authority; (3) to instruct the Galatians regarding appropriate Christian living given a law-free gospel.

In achieving this purpose, Paul's argument is both biographical and theological. We will deal with the former first.

4.1. Paul's Biographical Argument

It is crucial that Paul re-establishes his apostolic authority at the outset, so in the opening verse (1:1) he vigorously defends his divine commission. In greater detail in 1:11-23 he insists that the gospel he proclaims is of divine origin, coming by direct revelation of Jesus.[22] It was not based on his background in Judaism and he was not taught it from a human source. Consequently he was not reliant on the apostles in Jerusalem. Furthermore, no matter what other Jewish-Christian factions may deem appropriate, the Jerusalem apostles acknowledged Paul's authority and certified his ministry to the Gentiles (2:1-10).[23]

Paul's lack of inferiority to the Jerusalem apostles is highlighted by the relating of an incident at Antioch where he rebuked Peter, one of the pillars (2:11-14).[24] Peter may well have taken what he believed to be the better of two options—segregation at meals rather than compel full proselytism of Gentiles. Nonetheless, Paul realized that this would not only damage Jewish Christian-Gentile Christian relationships, but virtually force Gentile Christians

---

[20] R. Jewett, "The Agitators and the Galatian Congregation," *NTS* 17 (1970-71): 198-212, maintains that the Judaizers were motivated by Zealot enthusiasts. They considered that Zealot fury at Jews who associated with Gentiles might be mitigated by demonstrating success with Gentile circumcision.

[21] J. Louis Martyn, *Galatians* (New York: Doubleday, 1997), 124-25.

[22] The Greek genitive is ambiguous here. It could be subjective, signifying that Jesus gave the revelation to Paul. Alternatively, it may be objective, indicating that the revelation was about Jesus. It is difficult to decide between these options and probably unnecessary to do so. Clearly Paul had an encounter with the risen Jesus on the Damascus road, an encounter that forced a dramatic reappraisal of his understanding of Jesus.

[23] M. D. Nanos, "'Intruding Spies' and 'Pseudo-Brethren'," in Porter, *Paul and his Opponents*, 54-97.

[24] Elmer, *Judaisers*, 163, believes that Paul's opponents may have been circulating a different version of this event.

to adopt circumcision in order to prevent a sense of inferiority and marginalization.[25] This section also demonstrates Paul's resolve in the face of a Judaizing threat which successfully engulfed Peter and even Barnabas. In this regard he functions as a model for the church to emulate in resisting such teaching.

Utilizing what Susan Eastman refers to as his "mother tongue",[26] the apostle also appeals to the relationship he shared in person with the Galatian Christians (4:12-20). This relationship began on good terms, all the more remarkable given the liability he was to them because of a physical infirmity of some sort.[27] Given that ill-health was considered a sign of weakness or divine displeasure in the ancient world,[28] this serves to underscore the genial reception he received.

4.2. Paul's Theological Argument

The topic of salvation by faith begins in earnest in 2:15-21. Salvation is by faith in Jesus Christ,[29] not by works of law, for if salvation was available by law observance then Christ died in vain.[30] Paul will explain in the following chapter why the law is ineffective with respect to justification; no one was able to observe it in its entirety (3:10).[31]

The apostle also invites the Galatians to recall their experience of the gospel. The reception of the Spirit was a sign of the new covenant, an eschatological experience[32] that involved the working of miracles among

---

[25] M. D. Nanos, "What Was at Stake in Peter's Eating with Gentiles," in Nanos, *Galatians Debate*, 282-318.

[26] S. Eastman, *Recovering Paul's Mother Tongue: Language and Theology in Galatians* (Grand Rapids: Eerdmans, 2007). By "mother tongue" she means Paul's use of maternal metaphors to convince his audience of the relational elements of their faith.

[27] We cannot specify the nature of this infirmity with any certainty. Seemingly, it would equate to his "thorn in the flesh" (2 Cor 12:7), with some considering that an eyesight problem was the issue given the following statement regarding the Galatians tearing out their eyes and giving them to him (see J. D. G. Dunn, *The Epistle to the Galatians* [Peabody: Hendrickson, 1993], 236). Of course, this might just be a metaphor indicating the extent of their affection. See Fung, *Galatians*, 199; Longenecker, *Galatians*, 193.

[28] Fung, *Galatians*, 198.

[29] Or alternatively, the faithfulness of Jesus Christ. See discussion in the summary of contents, below.

[30] Most interpreters understand this as an appeal to common ground. However, I. W. Scott, "Common Ground? The Role of Galatians 2:16 in Paul's Argument," *NTS* 53.3 (2007): 425-35, insists that Paul's thesis statement in 2:16 would not have been readily accepted by the Galatians.

[31] There has been extensive debate at this point as to whether the Jews would have understood the law as impossible to fulfill, and to what extent Paul echoes or departs from Jewish understanding. For a summary of the differing positions, see R. B. Matlock, "Helping Paul's Argument Work? The Curse of Galatians 3:10-14," in M. Tait and P. Oakes, eds., *Torah in the New Testament* (London: T. & T. Clark, 2009), 154-79.

[32] R. J. Morales, *The Spirit and the Restoration of Israel* (WUNT 2.282; Tübingen: Mohr [Siebeck], 2010) contends that the role of the Spirit in Galatians must be understood with reference to restoration themes from Isaiah. Similarly, M. S. Harmon, *She Shall and Must Go*

them. This occurred because of their positive response to the gospel, not by observing the law (3:1-5).

Because the Jews traced their lineage back to Abraham and understood themselves to be the rightful heirs of the Abrahamic promise, it is important that Paul draws Abraham into the discussion. As he also argues in Romans 4:1-25, Abraham's true descendants are to be numbered among those who believe, not those of physical lineage (3:6-9). As a consequence of this one family of faith there are no longer any racial, social or gender hierarchies in Christ (3:28).

Furthermore, the promise to Abraham predated the giving of the law thereby giving precedence to the promise. Consequently, inheritance of the blessing comes via the promise rather than via the law. Here the apostle also engages in a legal argument based on the comparison with human wills. The exegesis is literalistic and typically rabbinic. Paul construes the collective noun "seed" as singular,[33] arguing that the Abrahamic promise finds its fulfillment in Christ (in v. 29 he will then switch to the collective sense of "seed" to include all those who belong to Christ).

The Abrahamic traditions are further utilized in a rather complex allegory in 4:21-31. At this point Paul may be attempting to trump the Judaizers' own recourse to Abraham as the father of the nation of Israel by showing that the narrative can be seen in an entirely different light to that which mandates circumcision and law observance.[34] Drawing on the Genesis narrative Paul contends that Hagar, the slave woman, is mother of all those constrained by the law; i.e. Judaism. Sarah, on the other hand, is the mother of all those who are free and destined to share the inheritance. Consequently, just as Abraham and Sarah expelled Hagar, so the teaching of the Judaizers must be expelled from the churches,[35] for this teaching is nothing but a yoke of slavery.

As far as the law is concerned, it consigns its adherents to a curse, for it demands ruthless perfection (3:10-14). The allusion is to the final of the twelve curses found in Deut 27:11-26. The agitators may have used the passage as a threat or warning stressing the need to undergo circumcision to avoid a curse for failure to adhere to the Torah.[36] Although several difficulties have been identified in Paul's argument here,[37] the discussion serves to reinforce the previous point regarding the inability of the law to justify one before God. So the law is incompatible with faith because it is intrinsically linked with performance.

Free: Paul's Isaianic Gospel in Galatians (Berlin: de Gruyter, 2010), sees an "Isaianic substructure" in Galatians.

[33] See C. J. Collins, "Galatians 3:16: What Kind of Exegete Was Paul?" *TynB* 54.1 (2003): 75-86.

[34] J. D. G. Dunn, *The Theology of Paul's Letter to the Galatians* (Cambridge: Cambridge University Press, 1993), 96-97; Elmer, *Judaisers,* 136-37.

[35] Dunn, *Theology,* 97, believes the implication is that the Judaizers themselves should be expelled from the Christian assembly.

[36] T. A. Wilson, *The Curse of the Law and the Crisis in Galatia* (WUNT 2.225; Tübingen: Mohr [Siebeck], 2007), 47-68.

[37] These are discussed in the summary of contents section, below.

Having argued that the law is impotent with respect to justification and righteousness, the apostle needs to explain its purpose, especially given the central role it played in the life and thought of Judaism. His discussion in 3:19–4:7 is quite complex and interpretive problems arise once more.[38]

Nevertheless, the basic thrust of the passage is clear. The law was an integral part of God's purpose even though it could not lead to righteousness. The apostle presents three metaphors in order to stress the temporary nature of the law:[39] (1) jailor—the law had a protective function; (2) παιδαγωγός (paidagōgos), disciplinarian[40]—one who was entrusted with the supervision and custody of children until they come of age;[41] and (3) guardians and trustees who control the estate of a minor.[42] But now that redemption has been procured from the law by the Son of God, believers have received adoption as God's children, a status which carries the full privileges of a father-child relationship including inheritance.

In terms of the eschatological perspective of Galatians, the argument proceeds along realized eschatological lines in the main, but this is not the complete picture. The prospect of a negative evaluation at the final judgment of those who resort to circumcision bubbles beneath the surface of the text. Note, for example, the idea of Paul laboring in vain (4:11), the concept of a race (5:7), the shame of ending with the flesh (3:3), and the prospect of being cut off from Christ and grace (5:1-5). Future eschatology is therefore not an explicit motivating factor but is strongly alluded to in the above texts.[43]

4.3. The Role of Chapters 5:13–6:18

These verses are an integral part of the argument and not an ethical appendix. If the Judaizers are concerned about the possibility of moral decay in the church on the basis of a law-free gospel, then so too is Paul. Unlike them, however, the apostle's solution is not to hang onto the law but to explain the responsibilities of those who live by the Spirit. All this talk of freedom could easily be misconstrued, and the sense of freedom can easily be misused. So Paul needs to balance the freedom he has been discussing in 5:1-12.

Verse 13 summarizes the apostle's argument succinctly. Freedom must be used as an opportunity to serve those in the Christian community, not as an

---

[38] These are discussed in the summary of contents section, below.
[39] C. L. Blomberg, *From Pentecost to Patmos* (Nottingham: Apollos, 2006), 129. On Paul's argument concerning the lack of continuing significance of the law, see P. Oakes, "Law and Theology in Galatians," in Tait and Oakes, *Torah in the New Testament*, 143-53.
[40] The παιδαγωγός was not a teacher as such, but a guardian responsible for protection of minors until the age of maturity. This included behavioral restraint as well as protection.
[41] See Longenecker, *Galatians,* 146-49.
[42] There have been recent attempts to interpret the guardianship language typologically, but see J. K. Goodrich, "Guardians, not Taskmasters: The Cultural Resonances of Paul's Metaphor in Galatians 4.1-2," *JSNT* 32.3 (2010): 251-84, who argues that Paul's language and argument echoes contemporary Roman law and practice regarding the guardianship of minors.
[43] Y-G. Kwon, *Eschatology in Galatians: Rethinking Paul's Response to the Crisis in Galatia* (WUNT 2.183; Tübingen: Mohr [Siebeck], 2004).

occasion for self-indulgence. Paul's use of Lev 19:18 in the following verse regarding the summation of the law has parallels with the Synoptic tradition and in fact may be dependent upon it. The section concludes with a typical Pauline Spirit/flesh dichotomy, but unique to Galatians we find a list of the fruit of the Spirit; virtues which are to characterize those who belong to Christ.

5. The New Perspective on Paul

Until the mid-1970s it was generally agreed that in Galatians Paul was opposing a Judaism where law observance determined one's status before God. Thus the apostle was challenging a religious system where the law was understood and employed in legalistic terms. There were a few lone voices of dissent,[44] but in the main this approach was standard Protestant fare. "Ancient Judaism was simply sixteenth-century Roman Catholicism in different dress."[45]

It was E. P. Sanders who was responsible for a sea change in Pauline studies.[46] Based on a study of Jewish sources from 200 B.C. to A.D. 200, Sanders concluded that Judaism had been wrongly caricatured as a works-based religion. More appropriately, it should be understood as "covenantal nomism," whereby relationship with God is based on his gracious election. The law was an expression of this covenant relationship as well as a means of atonement for sin. In other words, the law does not put one in relationship with God, it keeps one in relationship with God. Paul however, is arguing at a completely different level. In his "participationist eschatology" righteousness is an entry term based on faith, whereas in Judaism righteousness is about maintenance of status among the elect.[47]

James D. G. Dunn is also one of the key figures in the new perspective.[48] While supporting Sanders' corrective approach to first-century Judaism, he is

---

[44] For example, Claude Montefiore insisted that rabbinic Judaism, as opposed to Hellenistic Judaism, was a more noble religion in the mid-first century than that portrayed by Paul. See C. G. Montefiore, *The Genesis of the Religion of St. Paul, Judaism and St. Paul: Two Essays* (London: Max Goschen, 1914). G. F. Moore, *Judaism in the First Centuries of the Christian Era* (Cambridge, Mass.: Harvard University, 1927–30) was critical of the long history of the Christian tradition for caricaturing Judaism to suit its apologetic and polemical purposes. H. J. Schoeps, *Paul: The Theology of the Apostle in the Light of Jewish Religious History* (Philadelphia: Westminster, 1961) contended that Paul misunderstood Jewish theology and misrepresented the role of the law. Anticipating the new perspective to some extent was Krister Stendahl, "Paul and the Introspective Conscience of the West," in *Paul among Jews and Gentiles and Other Essays* (London: SCM, 1977). Rather than dealing with the standing of the individual before God, Stendahl argued that Paul was primarily concerned with people groups. The focus on individual salvation is a product of the introspective conscience of the West.
[45] F. Thielman, *Paul and the Law* (Downers Grove: IVP, 1994), 29.
[46] E. P. Sanders, *Paul and Palestinian Judaism: A Comparison of Patterns of Religion* (London: SCM, 1977).
[47] Sanders, *Paul and Palestinian Judaism,* 544.
[48] See firstly, J. G. D. Dunn, "The New Perspective on Paul," *BJRL* 65 (1983): 95-122, now in *Jesus, Paul, and the Law: Studies in Mark and Galatians* (Louisville: Westminster John Knox, 1990), 183-206.

critical of his failure to integrate Paul's theology with Judaism's covenantal nomism. Rather than Paul's arguments being composed on a different plane to covenantal nomism, they should rather be understood in its context. When Paul speaks of "works of the law" he is primarily focused upon those elements of the law that fostered Jewish particularism. Consequently, Paul is not opposing the law as such, but Jewish exclusivism; he is opposing the social function of the law rather than its religious function. "What he (Paul) denies is that . . . God's grace extends only to those who wear the badge of the covenant."[49]

At the more extreme end of the spectrum, H. Räisänen contends that Paul constructed a set of *ad hoc* arguments to combat the Judaizing threat to the churches of Galatia. In doing so, he presents a distorted picture of Judaism. The apostle had no coherent theology of law and grace, hence his arguments are often contradictory and inconsistent.[50]

Thus the new perspective insists that Paul and first-century Judaism have been wrongly read through the lens of the Protestant Reformation. The extant Jewish literature does not support such a position, and such a reading has created a distorted picture of Jewish religion as legalistic and devoid of grace.

Response to Sanders, Dunn, and others has ranged from full-fledged support to outright rejection, and a number of positions in between.[51] F. Thielman, for example, while supporting Sanders' assessment of first-century Judaism to a large extent does acknowledge that Paul is combating genuine legalistic tendencies. However such legalism was hardly the prevailing *modus operandi*.[52]

Others have not at all been convinced by the proposals of the new perspective. T. Schreiner[53] and C. Kruse,[54] for instance, contend that although Judaism certainly possessed a theology of grace, Paul did identify genuine elements of legalism therein. This was a logical consequence of what Schreiner identifies as a "synergistic soteriology," where human merit works together with God's grace to achieve salvation.[55] Furthermore, Paul's arguments do not necessitate that all Jews were legalistic, only that some of them were.[56]

---

[49] Dunn, *Law*, 194. P. L. Owen, "The 'Works of the Law' in Romans and Galatians: A New Defense of the Subjective Genitive," *JBL* 126 (2007): 553-77, argues against both the traditional view and that of Dunn. He proposes that "works of law" should be understood as a subjective genitive indicating what the law itself accomplished in Israel.

[50] H. Räisänen, *Paul and the Law* (WUNT 29; Tübingen: Mohr [Siebeck], 1983).

[51] There have been several probing responses to the new perspective. See for example, S. Westerholm, *Israel's Law and the Church's Faith: Paul and His Recent Interpreters* (Grand Rapids: Eerdmans, 1988); C. G. Kruse, *Paul, the Law and Justification* (Leicester: Apollos, 1996); D. A. Carson, P. T. O'Brien, and M. A. Seifrid, eds., *Justification and Variegated Nomism* (2 vols.; Grand Rapids: Baker, 2001–2004).

[52] Thielman, *Paul*, 238-40.

[53] T. R. Schreiner, *The Law and its Fulfillment: A Pauline Theology of Law* (Grand Rapids: Baker, 1993), esp. 93-121.

[54] C. G. Kruse, *Paul, the Law, and Justification*.

[55] Schreiner, *Law*, 94.

[56] Schreiner, *Law*, 115; also Kruse, *Paul, the Law, and Justification*, 294-96.

Schreiner further maintains that Sanders is overly sympathetic in his evaluation of the Jewish source material. Even if grace is presupposed in the Jewish literature, "when people begin to stress complex and detailed prescriptions for obedience, then the primacy of grace is threatened, even if the specific laws are viewed as a divine gift."[57] Regrettably, human nature has the tendency to distort grace because of arrogance, pride or the need for control.[58]

One lesson of religious history is that official theological positions do not automatically translate into daily praxis. Religious leaders may espouse doctrinal particulars, but there is no guarantee that even they themselves will adhere to such. Undoubtedly the religion of the few does not necessarily equate with the religion of the masses.

The other main tenet of the new perspective is that justification by faith is not the center of Paul's theology, as it was only really pertinent for the Gentiles. Here Sanders picks up Albert Schweitzer's insistence that the doctrine is only a "subsidiary crater" in the apostle's overall thought. But it is difficult to understand how Paul's argument in Romans, Galatians, and Philippians addresses anything other than a universal human predicament. In terms of the ultimate question, it is not "what is wrong with the law?" so much as "what is wrong with human beings?" As far as the apostle is concerned justification by faith in Jesus is the only way to effectively deal with the sinful plight of humanity.

Although the center of Paul's theology is open to question, to downplay the importance of justification by faith ultimately and necessarily leads to a two covenant theory of salvation. Dunn, especially in his more recent work, has been careful to clarify his position and insists on the necessity of the doctrine.[59] But doubts remain. If Paul is only attacking Jewish exclusivism and is not opposed to covenantal nomism correctly understood and practiced, then salvation outside the Mosaic covenant works on a different basis to salvation inside the covenant. While Dunn may be correct in insisting that Paul argues against the law as a boundary marker, it is highly questionable that this is all he is doing.[60]

This raises another disputed issue: the definition of justification by faith in Paul. Adherents of the new perspective insist that Paul was addressing the particular problem of Jewish exclusivism based on covenant membership,[61] not the strivings of the individual to be accepted by God on the basis of meritorious works. Consequently, justification by faith is not about how an

---

[57] Schreiner, *Law,* 116.
[58] Schreiner, *Law,* 115; also Kruse, *Paul, the Law, and Justification,* 296; D. Hagner, "Paul and Judaism: Testing the New Perspective," in P. Stuhlmacher, ed., *The Challenge to the New Perspective: Revisiting Paul's Doctrine of Justification* (Downers Grove: IVP, 2001), 87-88.
[59] J. D. G. Dunn, "The New Perspective: whence, what, and wither?" in *The New Perspective on Paul, Revised Edition* (Grand Rapids: Eerdmans, 2005), 96.
[60] Hagner, "Paul and Judaism," 104; D. Hunn, "Christ versus the Law: Issues in Galatians 2:17-18," *CBQ* 72.3 (2010): 537-55.
[61] See D. B. Garlington, "Paul's 'partisan ἐκ' and the question of justification in Galatians," *JBL* 127.3 (2008): 567-89.

individual finds favor with God, but on what basis Gentiles can be admitted to the covenant people.[62] In this sense it is covenantal language;[63] it is the doctrine that emphasizes the equality of Jew and Gentile before God and excludes any merit on the basis of race or gender.[64]

As we have seen, the particular problem behind Galatians involved a disagreement between Paul and his opponents over the basis upon which Gentiles may be the recipient of covenant blessings. The Judaizers were not concerned with good works that the Gentiles may or may not do, but were concerned particularly with the boundary markers central to the Mosaic covenant.[65] Nonetheless, Westerholm is correct in insisting that:

> ... Galatians is misunderstood unless we realize that Paul attacked more than the notion that Jewish boundary markers needed to be observed by Gentiles. The Jewish law itself—of which the prescriptions of boundary markers were a small though contentious part—did not provide a basis by which *sinners* could be declared righteous; and Jews, for all their observance of boundary markers, were no less sinners than Gentiles. Paul does not fault the law for inviting self-reliance, self-righteousness, or boasting. He does, however, observe that its operative principle demands works: people must do what it commands if they are to enjoy life in God's favor. . . . Paul was not addressing Pelagianism or sixteenth-century disputes over works. But he responded to the insistence that Gentiles be circumcised by taking up the fundamental issue of how human beings, in spite of their sin, can experience life in God's favor. The "Lutherans" were not mistaken in finding an answer to that question in the epistle. Nor, in ascribing salvation to an initiative of divine grace that excludes any contribution from sinful human beings, did they misconstrue its terms (italics retained).[66]

Furthermore, Paul's discussion of justification by faith extends beyond Galatians, and any definition or understanding of justification must include the entire corpus.[67] Of course, there is disagreement about the extent of this corpus, but even the undisputed letters (particularly Romans and Philippians)

---

[62] Stendahl, *Paul*, 3, 131; E. P. Sanders, *Paul* (Oxford: Oxford University Press, 1991), 50, 66; Dunn, *Theology*, 340.

[63] N. T. Wright, *What St. Paul Really Said: Was Paul of Tarsus the Real Founder of Christianity?* (Grand Rapids: Eerdmans, 1991), 117.

[64] Wright, *Founder*, 160. In his more recent work, *Justification: God's Plan and Paul's Vision* (London: SPCK, 2009), Wright attempts to clarify his position in response to a number of evangelical critics, especially John Piper. He insists that the Lutheran view, while not incorrect, is shallow. It depicts justification in individual terms whereas it should more correctly be seen on a broader canvas as participation in the redemption of all creation.

[65] S. Westerholm, *Perspectives Old and New on Paul: The "Lutheran" Paul and His Critics* (Grand Rapids: Eerdmans, 2004), 383.

[66] Westerholm, *Perspectives*, 383-84.

[67] Westerholm, *Perspectives*, 407, also notes the relevance of Jas 2:14-26 to this issue. Given that James appears to be responding ultimately to a Pauline view, his response is centered on the necessity of works in general rather than distinctive Mosaic regulations.

provide enough material to challenge aspects of the new perspective.[68]

Although the new perspective claim that first-century Judaism has been unjustly caricatured has been both provocative and helpful to an extent, I remain unconvinced that justification by faith should be understood only in terms of Jew and Gentile equality. For Paul, justification is also a declaration by God of the righteousness of an individual in his sight. The basis for this declaration is not adherence to the law or anything to do with personal achievement or righteousness, but is totally dependent upon the atoning death and subsequent resurrection of Jesus Christ on behalf of humanity, and is appropriated by personal faith in Jesus. This declaration is a present reality but has an eschatological dimension bound up with the final judgment.

Undoubtedly the new perspective has forced a re-evaluation of first-century Judaism by exposing certain caricatures and prejudices. It has led to a helpful dialogue both in the NT academy as well as interfaith relations. It is not overstating the case to say that the topography of Pauline studies has forever changed. But it is doubtful whether Paul has been misread to the extent claimed by the new perspective. There is also a touch of arrogance in the claim that Paul had less of an idea about first-century Judaism than modern biblical scholarship. It is also clear that Judaism was not as monochrome as implied by Sanders and others.[69]

6. Genre and Structure of Galatians

Letters substitute for physical presence; they are a surrogate for oral communication. So in one sense Galatians is a letter, but it also is a rhetorical piece, as Paul employs various rhetorical tools to rebuke and convince his recipients.[70]

With respect to a rhetorical analysis of Galatians there are two basic camps; those who understand the epistle to be an example of forensic rhetoric,[71] and those who see it more as deliberative rhetoric.[72] Put simply, the former attempts to prove a case regarding past actions, whereas the latter attempts to persuade (or dissuade) regarding a future course of action.

Elements of both forms of rhetoric are present in Galatians. In terms of forensic rhetoric, Paul insists on his apostolic status and recalls the past experience of his Galatian converts. With respect to deliberative rhetoric he attempts to dissuade them from embracing the Jewish law and persuade them

---

[68] When it is all said and done, the validity of the new perspective rises or falls on its exegetical explanatory power. Whereas its proponents may be able to more readily explain passages such as Rom 2:6-10, 13-16; 3:31, ease turns to impediment with texts such as Gal 2:16; 3:10-14; Rom 3:20, 28; 4:4-6; 5:20; 11:6.
[69] See the extensive treatment in Carson, O'Brien and Seifrid, *Justification and Variegated Nomism*.
[70] See the collection of essays in Nanos, *Galatians Debate*. See also M. Hietanen, *Paul's Argumentation in Galatians: A Pragma-Dialectical Analysis* (London: T. & T. Clark, 2007).
[71] Betz, *Galatians*, c-cxix.
[72] B. Witherington III, *Grace in Galatia: A Commentary on St. Paul's Letter to the Galatians* (Edinburgh: T. & T. Clark, 1998), 25-36.

regarding freedom in the Spirit. Yet it is doubtful that Galatians can be squeezed into a rhetorical category.[73] J. L. Martyn's position is convincing: "... [the letter is] an argumentative sermon preached in the context of a service of worship—and thus in the acknowledged presence of God—not a speech made by a rhetorician in a courtroom."[74]

With these thoughts in mind, a basic outline of Galatians can be presented as follows.[75]

> Salutation (1:1-5)
> The Gospel Perverted (1:6-10)
> Paul's Vindication of his Apostleship (1:11–2:14)
>   Origin of the gospel (1:11-12)
>   Former life in Judaism (1:13-14)
>   Change in focus and early years as a follower of Jesus (1:15-24)
>   Meeting with the Jerusalem Apostles (2:1-10)
>   Rebuke of Peter at Antioch (2:11-14)
> Paul's Defence of the Gospel (2:15–4:7)
>   Faith in Jesus as Basis for Justification (2:15-21)
>   Spirit or Law (3:1-5)
>   Abraham's True Descendants (3:6-9)
>   The Curse of the Law (3:10-14)
>   The Promise to Abraham (3:15-19)
>   Purpose of the Law (3:19–4:7)
> Paul's Rebuke of and Appeal to the Galatians (4:8-20)
> Allegory of Hagar and Sarah (4:21–5:1)
> The Nature of Christian Freedom (5:2–6:10)
>   Circumcision Is Incompatible with Freedom in Christ (5:2-12)
>   Freedom means loving one another (5:13-15)
>   The Works of the Flesh (5:16-21)
>   The Fruit of the Spirit (5:22-26)
>   Living for the Good of Others (6:1-10)
> Closing Admonition (6:11-17)
> Benediction (6:18)

---

[73] So P. H. Kern, *Rhetoric and Galatians: Assessing an Approach to Paul's Epistle* (SNTSMS 101; Cambridge: Cambridge University Press, 1998).
[74] Martyn, *Galatians*, 21. See 20-27 for a discussion of rhetorical analysis and its limitations. Betz, *Galatians,* 14-25, has a thorough literary analysis of Galatians according to rhetorical conventions.
[75] For a further discussion of the structural features of the letter, see Betz; Witherington and Martyn cited above; R. A. Bryant, *The Risen Crucified Christ in Galatians* (SBL Dissertation Series 185; Atlanta: SBL, 2001). Longenecker, *Galatians,* c-cxix, has a helpful discussion that includes both diachronic and synchronic rhetorical analysis.

7. Outline of Contents

7.1. Salutation (1:1-5)

The uniqueness of the opening section of this epistle is underlined both by what it contains and what is omitted. Paul identifies himself in terms of his apostolic status, but right at the outset there is a stress on his divine commission. As the letter unfolds the reason for this will become apparent: the Judaizers are attempting to subvert his authority by drawing a distinction between him and the Jerusalem apostles.

Still within the prescript, the focus shifts quickly to the work of Christ and gives the impression of a corrective, or at least an emphasizing, theological statement. The thanksgiving section that traditionally follows on from the opening salutation of Paul's letters is entirely absent,[76] with the apostle moving straight from a brief doxology into a stinging rebuke of the Galatians churches. Obviously all is not well.

7.2. The Gospel Perverted (1:6-10)

Paul expresses his astonishment that the Galatian Christians would so quickly abandon the true gospel in favor of some perversion. The apostle is so confident of the truth of his gospel proclamation that he refuses to accommodate any conflicting message whether that be from a human or angelic source.

It would appear that criticism is being leveled against Paul by the Judaizers. They are attempting to undermine his authority by insinuating that his law-free gospel is nothing other than an attempt to win human approval. Paul vehemently denies this, pointing out that the strong rebuke he is delivering is hardly an attempt to please others. On the contrary, he is committed to serving Christ and seeking God's approval.

7.3. Paul's Vindication of his Apostleship (1:11–2:14)

(a) Origin of the Gospel (1:11-12)

Picking up his initial statement at the opening of the letter, Paul insists that the gospel he proclaims is of divine origin. This context implies that the ambiguous "a revelation of Jesus Christ" is to be understood as a revelation that Jesus gave rather than a revelation about him (although the latter is true as well).

---

[76] See R. E. Van Voorst, "Why is there no Thanksgiving Period in Galatians? An Assessment of an Exegetical Commonplace," *JBL* 129 (2010): 153-57, who contends that the absence of the thanksgiving can be explained not so much by the tone of what follows in verses 6-10, but by the unusual prescript itself.

(b) Former Life in Judaism (1:13-14)

Paul's statements here have a number of parallels with Philippians 3:4-6 where he also explains his Jewish pedigree. His zeal for his ancestral traditions led him to violent persecution of the followers of Jesus.

(c) Change in Focus and Early Years as a Follower of Jesus (1:15-24)

God had other plans for Paul that would involve not the destruction of the Jesus movement but its extension into the Gentile world. Again Paul stresses his independence from the Jerusalem apostles. He did not need or seek their approval, in fact he went nowhere near them. Rather, he journeyed to Arabia and subsequently returned to Damascus. The reference to Arabia lacks specificity with respect to both location and purpose. Arabia was east of the Jordan Valley rift and was part of the Natabean kingdom, at this time ruled by Aretas IV (9 B.C.–A.D. 40). Although Damascus was included in the Natabean kingdom for a portion of this period, the way Paul depicts his journey as from Damascus to Arabia tends to indicate their separateness at this point in time.[77] We can only conjecture regarding his purpose for the journey, but it probably had to do more with time for personal reflection than any evangelistic endeavor at this early stage.[78] In any event, the point is that given that he was in Damascus and Arabia he was nowhere near Jerusalem.

It was only after three years that Paul did visit Jerusalem and stayed with Peter for fifteen days. His only other contact was with James the brother of Jesus, whom he also terms an apostle.[79] This accords with other statements by both Paul (1 Cor 15:5-7; Rom 16:7) and Luke (Acts 14:4) which indicate that the term apostle was used not only of the 12, but of those who had seen the risen Jesus and been commissioned by him. That aside, Paul is stressing that his contact with the Jerusalem apostles was minimal. This brief visit did not allow him to become personally acquainted with churches in Judea, but they certainly were aware of his radical change of stance regarding Jesus.

(d) Meeting with the Jerusalem Apostles (2:1-10)

The temporal reference after 14 years is somewhat ambiguous. Commentators are divided as to whether it is to be reckoned from his encounter with Jesus on the Damascus Road or from his previously mentioned visit to Jerusalem. Coupled with the uncertain dating regarding Jesus' crucifixion and Paul's own encounter with the risen Jesus, the dating of the meeting depicted here becomes quite problematic. All these factors have bearing on the difficult

---

[77] Longenecker, *Galatians*, 34; R. H. Smith, "Arabia," *ABD* 1.324-27.
[78] Contra M. Hengel, "Paul in Arabia," *BBR* 12.1 (2002): 47-66.
[79] The Greek is somewhat ambiguous, but force of the statement would appear to number James among the apostolic group. See P. W. Barnett, "Apostle," in G. F. Hawthorne, R. P. Martin, and D. G. Reid, eds., *Dictionary of Paul and His Letters* (Downers Grove: IVP, 1993), 45-51; Longenecker, *Galatians*, 38-39.

interpretive issue surrounding the relationship between the meeting described here and the Jerusalem Council of Acts 15.

In Jerusalem Paul meets with those who had a reputation (vv. 2, 6), a common rhetorical term in the Greco-Roman world. It could be used neutrally, ironically or even derogatorily.[80] Here reputation of leadership is implied, and given the same term is used in v. 9 with reference to James, Cephas, and John as pillars, it is most likely that a private meeting with these three apostles is pictured throughout this section. It is hard to escape the presence of irony in Paul's voice. He is not being derogatory of the Jerusalem Apostles themselves, but seeks to downplay the lofty status they have obviously been bestowed by the Judaizers.[81]

Paul is fearful that he may have run in vain, not in the sense that his ministry was ineffective or illegitimate, but that his law-free gospel among the Gentiles may not be endorsed. But the respective ministries to both Jews and Gentiles were endorsed along with a plea for Paul to remember the poor. Given Romans 15:26, this expression primarily carries an economic sense rather than being self-designation of the Jerusalem Church, although it is hard to avoid the conclusion that it provided "an acknowledgement on the part of the Gentile churches of their indebtedness to Jerusalem as the origin of spiritual blessing . . . and a sign of unity between Jews and Gentiles in Christ."[82]

(e) Rebuke of Peter at Antioch (2:11-14)

Paul's lack of inferiority to the Jerusalem apostles is again underlined by the recounting of an incident at Antioch in which he rebuked Peter, one of the pillars. This section also has the additional function of illustrating Paul's resolution in the face of a Judaizing threat. He thus becomes a model for the church to emulate.[83]

7.4. Paul's Defense of the Gospel (2:15–4:7)

(a) Faith in Jesus as Basis for Justification (2:15-21)

This is, in effect, Paul's thesis statement (or *propositio* according to rhetorical conventions[84]) for this epistle. Justification is by faith in Christ, not by the works of the law. The reference to Gentile sinners in the opening verse, although a term characteristic of Judaism, may well be a derogatory slogan that the Judaizers used in the presence of the churches. Jews keep the law, so how could unrighteous Gentiles expect to be free from it? Paul counters this

---

[80] Witherington, *Grace in Galatia*, 134; Longenecker, *Galatians*, 48; Betz, *Galatians*, 86-87.
[81] M. C. de Boer, *Galatians* (Louisville: Westminster John Knox, 2011), 106-7.
[82] Fung, *Galatians*, 102-3.
[83] Dunn, *Theology*, 72, believes that Paul "lost out" to Peter here. This isolated Paul and marked the beginning of his distinctive theology. See also Elmer, *Judaisers*, 162-63.
[84] Witherington, *Grace in Galatia*, 169-94; Betz, *Galatians*, 18-19.

by contending that not all Jews, himself included, think this way.[85] The gospel shows all, even Jews, to be sinners in need of justification. This is the very reason Christ died, because the law could not bring about justification. Consequently the Christian life is characterized by faith in, and commitment to, the Son of God.

Over recent years the traditional understanding of Paul's expression "faith in Christ" (objective genitive) has been interpreted by many as faithfulness of Christ (subjective genitive). Most English versions retain the traditional translation and footnote the latter option. There are complex grammatical arguments involved, and important theological issues at stake. The issue is too complex for extensive discussion here and interested readers are referred to the notes for further resources.[86]

(b) Spirit or Law (3:1-5)

Employing rhetorical questions and outright sarcasm the apostle contrasts the Spirit and the law. The Spirit and accompanying divine supernatural activity is not a reward given for faithful law observance, but a gift in response to belief in the message of the gospel.

(b) Abraham's True Descendants (3:6-9)

Faith, rather than the law, as the basis for a declaration of righteousness is clearly seen in Abraham, and those who emulate his example of faith are his true descendants. Furthermore, the Abrahamic promise regarding the blessing of God upon the nations (Gen 12:3) is fulfilled in the gospel being offered to the Gentiles.

(d) The Curse of the Law (3:10-14)

By appeal to three OT texts, Paul continues to stress the superiority of faith over the law. First, with reference to Deut 27:26 he shows how human inability to keep the law results in being placed under a curse. Second, Hab 2:4 indicates that righteousness is linked to faith. Thus faith and law are in an

---

[85] There is some conjecture as to the precise identity of the "we" in 2:15-17. See W. O. Walker, "Does the 'we' in Gal 2:15-17 include Paul's opponents?" *NTS* 49.4 (2003): 560-65, who understands it primarily as a reference to Paul and Cephas.

[86] For an excellent summary of the issues—historical, grammatical, and theological—see the collection of essays in M. F. Bird and P. M. Sprinkle, eds., *The Faith of Jesus Christ* (Peabody: Hendrickson, 2009). See also R. Hays, *The Faith of Jesus Christ: The Narrative Substructure of Galatians 3:1–4:11* (2nd ed., Grand Rapids: Eerdmans, 2002), 141-62; B. R. Matlock, "The of Pistis in Paul: Galatians 2:16, 3:22, Romans 3:22, and Philippians 3:9," *JSNT* 30.2 (2007): 173-203; D. L. Stubbs, "The Shape of Soteriology and the 'pistis Christou' Debate," *SJT* 61.2 (2008): 137-57; D. M. Hay, "Paul's Understanding of Faith as Participation," in S. E. Porter, ed., *Paul and His Theology* (Pauline Studies vol. 3; Leiden: Brill, 2006), 65-75; B. W. Longenecker, *The Triumph of Abraham's God: The Transformation of Identity in Galatians* (Edinburgh: T. & T. Clark, 1998), 95-103; T. R. Schreiner, *Galatians* (Grand Rapids: Zonvervan, 2010), 163-66.

antithetical relationship. Third, the divine curse also applies to those who hang on a tree. By the first century, the original context regarding a corpse hanging on a tree overnight (Deut 21:23) had been extended to include crucifixion in general.[87] Thus Christ receives the divine curse in a substitutionary sense in order to secure the redemption of those cursed by their inability to keep the law.

(e) The Promise to Abraham (3:15-19)

Utilizing an exegetical technique that appears strange to modern readers, but not without precedent in rabbinic Judaism,[88] Paul interprets the collective noun "seed" as singular, arguing that the Abrahamic promise is fulfilled in Christ (in v. 29 he will then switch to the collective sense of "seed" to include all those who belong to Christ). As the promise to Abraham predates the Mosaic law the promise has precedence.[89] Consequently, inheritance of the blessing comes via the promise rather than via the law.

(f) Purpose of the Law (3:19–4:7)

Given the above argument, the obvious question remains as to the purpose of the law. Paul's answer to this question is reasonably complex, and there are several difficult interpretive problems. First, what is meant by the expression "because of transgressions"? Most commentators argue for a negative sense, either the law bringing consciousness of sin (cf. Rom 3:20), or the law causing sin to increase (cf. Rom 5:20).[90] However the immediate context does not favor such a negative focus. Dunn suggests that the idea is of the law providing remedy for sin,[91] but it is perhaps more likely that the idea is of the law restraining sin in some way.[92] This fits with the *paidagōgos* metaphor that follows.

Second, verse 20 is notoriously obscure. Without canvassing all the possibilities,[93] the most likely intention is a comparison between the law where God acts through a mediator (i.e. Moses) and the promise to Abraham where God acted directly. Furthermore, the fact that God is one is to be reflected in the one family of faith that comprises all nations.[94]

Third, there is uncertainty concerning the term στοιχεῖα (*stoicheia*) (4:3, 9), which is variously translated in the English versions as elemental spirits

---

[87] Fung, *Galatians*, 148.
[88] For discussion and examples, see Dunn, *Galatians*, 183-85.
[89] On the difficult chronological issue arising from "430 years later," see Longenecker, *Galatians*, 133; Betz, *Galatians*, 158.
[90] See Longenecker, *Galatians*, 138-39.
[91] Dunn, *Galatians*, 188-90.
[92] As Kruse, *Paul, the Law, and Justification*, 92-93.
[93] See Longenecker, *Galatians*, 141-43; Betz, *Galatians*, 171-72, for a discussion.
[94] Kruse, *Paul, the Law, and Justification*, 93.

(NRSV), powers (CEV), elements (KJV) basic principles (NIV).[95] A mere glance at the selection of English versions illustrates the problem. Basically it is a choice between four options: (1) basic elements of the universe (earth, air, fire, water);[96] (2) basic regulations or teaching; (3) heavenly bodies comprising basic elements of the universe; (4) a more sinister reference to malevolent spiritual forces.[97]

Many commentators argue for some sense of option 4,[98] although others are reticent on the basis that there is little or no lexical attestation for this sense before the third century.[99] The appeal of option 2 is that there is ample prior attestation for this sense of the word[100] and it admirably suits the point made about the temporary nature of the law. It also meshes with other NT uses of the term.[101]

Nevertheless, the basic thrust of the passage is clear. The law was an integral part of God's purpose even though it could not lead to righteousness. The apostle presents three metaphors in order to stress the temporary nature of the law:[102] (1) Jailor, the law had a protective function; (2) *paidagōgos* or disciplinarian, one who is entrusted with the supervision and custody of children until they come of age;[103] and (3) Guardians and trustees who control the estate of a minor. But this time is now past. Redemption has been secured from the law by the Son of God and believers have received adoption as God's children.

7.5. Paul's Rebuke of and Appeal to the Galatians (4:8-20)

The apostle is perplexed that religious slavery could be an attractive option to the Galatians. Relationship with God is incommensurate with legalistic religious observance, and his converts, on coming to faith, had already been freed from such a misguided piety. Had his work on their behalf been in vain (vv. 8-11)?

Perplexity becomes a plea, as Paul appeals to the initial positive relationship between himself and the churches.[104] This relationship began on

---

[95] The updated NIV (2011) now renders this word as "elemental spiritual forces."
[96] See more recently M. C. de Boer, "The Meaning of the Phrase τὰ στοιχεῖα τοῦ κόσμου," *NTS* 53 (2007): 204-24, who believes the expression is linked with religious beliefs and practices associated with these elements, in particular calendrical observances. See also de Boer, *Galatians*, 252-56; Schreiner, *Galatians*, 267-69.
[97] More recently, Hardin, *Imperial Cult*, 116-47, argues that the term represents adherence to the imperial cult and its calendar.
[98] For example Bruce, *Galatians*, 193-94, 202-4, "counterfeit deities"; George, *Galatians*, 295-99, 311-12, "demonic spiritual powers," as does Longenecker, *Triumph*, 46-51.
[99] Witherington, *Grace in Galatia*, 284-85.
[100] See Witherington, *Grace in Galatia*, 285.
[101] Col 2:8, 20 (arguably); Heb 5:12. In 2 Pet 3:10, 12 option 1 is in view.
[102] C. L. Blomberg, *From Pentecost to Patmos* (Nottingham: Apollos, 2006), 129.
[103] See Longenecker, *Galatians*, 146-49; Bruce, *Galatians*, 182-83.
[104] See T. W. Martin, "The Voice of Emotion: Paul's Pathetic Persuasion (Gal 4:12-20)," in Paul T. H. Olbricht and J. L. Sumney, eds., *Paul and Pathos* (Atlanta: Society of Biblical Literature, 2001), 181-202, who shows that far from being overcome by irrational emotion, his method of

good terms even given the liability he was to them (see 2 Cor 12:7). There has been much conjecture regarding the nature of the physical infirmity to which Paul refers here.[105] In any event, given that physical infirmity was considered a sign of weakness or divine displeasure in the ancient world,[106] Paul recalls that their initial friendship was not compromised on this basis.

There is also the issue of motive. The Judaizers ultimately seek to promote their own importance whereas Paul, like a woman in labor pains, struggles to produce Christian maturity in his readers.

7.6. Allegory of Hagar and Sarah (4:21–5:1)

To those who wish to be under the law Paul refers back to the law (in this case the Genesis narrative as part of the Pentateuch).[107] In a rather complex allegory[108] he insists that Hagar, the slave woman, is mother of all those bound by the law; i.e. Judaism. Sarah, on the other hand, is the mother of all those who are free and destined to share the inheritance. Consequently, just as Abraham and Sarah expelled Hagar, so the teaching of the Judaizers must be expelled from the churches, for it is nothing but a yoke of slavery.

7.7. The Nature of Christian Freedom (5:2–6:10)

(a) Circumcision is Incompatible with Freedom in Christ (5:2-12)

As circumcision was a mark of obedience to the old covenant, those who submit to it are obligated to keep the entire law. This is incompatible with living under grace and is, in effect, to separate oneself from Christ. Consequently, circumcision has nothing to do with Paul's gospel; if it did he would not be arousing the ire of unbelieving Jews. As far as the apostle is concerned, those who insist on circumcising others should castrate themselves!

(b) Freedom Means Loving One Another (5:13-15)

The section on Christian living is not just ethics as an afterthought. It is possible to misconstrue Paul's insistence on freedom from the law as freedom from moral obligation. On the contrary, Christian freedom is not a license for

---

argumentation follows a rhetorical strategy found in Aristotle's *Rhetoric* designed to appeal to the emotions of the audience.

[105] See n. 27 above.
[106] Fung, *Galatians*, 198; George, *Galatians*, 323-24.
[107] S. di Mattei, "Paul's Allegory of the Two Covenants (Gal 4:21-31) in light of first-century Hellenistic rhetoric and Jewish hermeneutics," *NTS* 52.1 (2006): 102-22, argues that here Paul is following Jewish exegetical practices that sought to interpret Torah in eschatological terms.
[108] A. Davis, "Allegorically speaking in Galatians 4:21–5:1," *BBR* 14.2 (2004): 161-174, concedes that the passage contains allegorical markers but should not strictly be labeled as narrative allegory.

self-indulgence or "back-biting power struggles"[109] but an opportunity for service.

(c) The Works of the Flesh (5:16-21)

Just as grace is incompatible with the law, so life in the Spirit is incompatible with both the law and the desires of the flesh. Thus, there is an implicit equation of fleshly living and living under the law, a juxtaposition that would have outraged the Jew, particularly given the content of the vice list in vv. 19-21 (sorcery, idolatry). Vice lists such as this were widely used in the Greco-Roman world in general, and Judaism and Christianity in particular.[110]

(d) The Fruit of the Spirit (5:22-26)

In contrast, a Spirit controlled life results in qualities that are neither mandated nor forbidden by the law.[111] Implicitly, therefore, it is useless to place oneself under the law in order to produce what only the Spirit can.

(e) Living for the Good of Others (6:1-10)

Paul now gives two practical examples of what it means to be a "servant to one another" (5:13). First, those caught in sin should be gently restored. Second, those who are experiencing difficulties in some way should be supported. Those who think they are above such service of others have a deluded opinion of their own self-importance (v. 3). The reference to "the law of Christ" (v. 2) is no doubt a reference to loving one's neighbor as oneself (5:14; cf. Jesus' words in Luke 10:27) and further reinforces the point that freedom from the law is not to be equated with antinomianism. All are responsible for their own actions (vv. 4-5). Self-serving motives will be exposed for what they are, whereas Spirit-directed and controlled actions will reap a due reward.

Paul's final statement in the section (v. 10) indicates that Spirit-controlled living results not only in an in-house ethic but also reaches into the unbelieving world.

7.8. Closing Admonition (6:11-17)

Paul concludes the letter with an identification of his own handwriting which obviously implies the use of an amanuensis up to this point. The "large

---

[109] Dunn, *Galatians*, 293. It is not necessary to conclude from this that the Galatian churches were characterized by such internal dissent. Nevertheless it is not difficult to imagine a scenario whereby the teachings of the Judaizers, garnering greater support in some areas of the Christian community, would result in factionalism and elitism.
[110] See Dunn, *Galatians*, 302.
[111] This appears to be the sense of the expression "against such as these there is no law."

letters" is generally considered as a means by which the importance of what follows is underlined.[112] And what follows is a restatement of the futility of circumcision, the improper motives of those who promote it, and the cross of Christ as the pivotal basis for both Paul's personal transformation, and implicitly, the new creation in its entirety.

The expression "the Israel of God" has been keenly debated, but it appears that Paul understands Christians in general as the new Israel. This does justice to the overall argument of the epistle and the specific statement of equality found in 3:28.[113]

7.9. Benediction (6:18)

The epistle concludes with a traditional blessing of peace (cf. Eph 6:23; 1 Cor 16:23; 2 Cor 13:13; Phil 4:23; 1 Thess 5:28; 2 Thess 3:18).

8. Conclusion

The Epistle to the Galatians is an important document. It is certainly of interest historically as it affords a particular window on the early church and its struggles with its parent faith Judaism. At a theological level, together with Romans, it provides the basis of the doctrine of justification by faith and sets out the apostle's understanding of the law in the divine plan. Although there has been, and continues to be, interpretive difficulties and differences of scholarly opinion here, it is clear that Paul was diametrically opposed to anything that compromised the total sufficiency of Jesus Christ for salvation.

On this basis I would maintain that the argument of Galatians has ramifications beyond its particular historical situation. Paul insists that the grace gift through Christ was unconditioned, that is, given not on the basis of any system of merit or privilege. Consequently any soteriological system constructed on law or "work," including Judaism but not confined to it, is ruled out.[114]

---

[112] So F. J. Matera, *Galatians, Revised ed.* (Sacra Pagina 9; Collegeville: Liturgical, 2007), 232; Betz, *Galatians,* 314; Dunn, *Galatians,* 335. Fung, *Galatians,* 301, states, "In conformity with the epistolary convention of the time, this orthographic postscript serves to authenticate the letter and sum up its main points..."

[113] Longenecker, *Galatians,* 298-99; Schreiner, *Galatians,* 381-83. Bruce, *Galatians,* 274-75 understands it as a prayer for the ultimate blessing of Israel as per Rom 11:26. Likewise M. Bachmann, *Anti-Judaism in Galatians? Exegetical Studies on a Polemical Letter and on Paul's Theology* (trans. R. L. Brawley; Grand Rapids: Eerdmans, 2008), 101-23, understands it as a reference to ethnic Israel. George, *Galatians,* 439-40, sees the reference to the entire eschatological people of God. Martyn, *Galatians,* 574-77, insists that the expression must be understood in context of this epistle only (i.e. Paul's battle with the Judaizers who may have been making much of the term Israel), and should not be construed as a theology of replacement. De Boer, *Galatians,* 405-10, understands the expression to refer to law observant Christian Jews.

[114] J. M. G. Barclay, "Paul, the Gift, and the Battle over Gentile Circumcision: Revisiting the Logic of Galatians," *ABR* 58 (2010): 36-56.

Paul was also fully cognizant of the fact that a law-free gospel was open to misinterpretation and abuse along antinomian lines. Followers of Christ may well be free from the law, but they are certainly not free from moral obligation. Consequently the letter provides clear guidelines for Christian living and rightly warrants the label "the charter of Christian liberty."

Recommended Reading

De Boer, M. C. *Galatians*. Louisville: Westminster John Knox, 2011.
Carson, D. A., P. T. O'Brien, and M. A. Seifrid, eds. *Justification and Variegated Nomism*. 2 vols. Grand Rapids: Baker, 2001–2004.
Dunn, J. D. G. *Beginning from Jerusalem: Christianity in the Making, Volume 2*. Grand Rapids: Eerdmans, 2009.
Dunn, J. D. G. *Jesus, Paul and the Law: Studies in Mark and Galatians*. Louisville: Westminster John Knox, 1990.
Dunn, J. G. D. *The Theology of Paul's Letter to the Galatians*. Cambridge: Cambridge University Press, 1993.
Elmer, I. J. *Paul, Jerusalem and the Judaisers: The Galatian Crisis in Its Broadest Historical Context*. Wissenschaftliche Untersuchungen zum Neuen Testament 2.258. Tübingen: Mohr (Siebeck), 2009.
Kwon, Y-G. *Eschatology in Galatians: Rethinking Paul's Response to the Crisis in Galatia*. Wissenschaftliche Untersuchungen zum Neuen Testament 2.183. Tübingen: Mohr (Siebeck), 2004.
Longenecker, R. N. *Galatians*. Dallas: Word, 1990.
Martyn, J. L. *Galatians*. New York: Doubleday, 1997.
Nanos, M. D., ed. *The Galatians Debate: Contemporary Issues in Rhetorical and Historical Interpretation*. Peabody: Hendrickson, 2002.
Porter, S. E., ed. *Paul and His Opponents*. Leiden: Brill, 2005.
Schreiner, T. R. *The Law and its Fulfillment: A Pauline Theology of Law*. Grand Rapids: Baker, 1993.
Schreiner, T. R. *Galatians*. Grand Rapids: Zondervan, 2010.

11. The Thessalonian Correspondence

Murray J. Smith

The two Thessalonian letters are among the earliest in the Pauline corpus, and provide a unique window on the apostolic proclamation in its earliest form. Together, they reveal a great deal about how earliest Christianity, with its roots in the Scriptures of Israel and the historic ministry of Jesus of Nazareth, first made its way in the Greco-Roman world. Despite being among the shortest of Paul's letters, 1 and 2 Thessalonians nevertheless provide us with a strikingly clear presentation of the gospel, a remarkably developed theological vision, and arguably the most extended reflection on the Christian hope to be found in any of the letters of Paul. For those who accept these letters as the "word of God" (cf. 1 Thess 2:13), their significance for Christian theology and service in a largely post-Christian culture is not hard to see. In what follows we offer, first, an account of the apostolic gospel mission in Thessaloniki and a description of the Christian community to which it gave rise, and second, an analysis of the letters themselves.[1]

1. The Apostolic Mission and the Christian Community in Thessaloniki

1.1. The Arrival of the Gospel in Thessaloniki

The gospel came to Thessaloniki in A.D. 49, when Paul, Silas, and Timothy arrived in the city.[2] The mission there formed part of a broader work in Macedonia and Achaia (modern Greece), to which Paul had been called in a vision (Acts 16:9-10). Having been mistreated and imprisoned in the Roman colony of Philippi (Acts 16:19-24; cf. 1 Thess 2:2), the three missionaries travelled 148 km west-south-west along the *Via Egnatia*, through Amphipolis and Apollonia, to Thessaloniki.[3] Consistent with Paul's mission strategy of

---

[1] For a review of recent research, see S. A. Adams, "Evaluating 1 Thessalonians: An Outline of Holistic Approaches to 1 Thessalonians in the Last 25 Years," *CBR* 8.1 (2009): 51-70.
[2] Silas had accompanied Paul from the beginning of his "second missionary journey" in Antioch (Acts 15:40). Timothy had joined the two missionaries in Lystra (Acts 16:1-4).
[3] For the road, and distances, see C. J. Hemer and C. H. Gempf, *The Book of Acts in the Setting of Hellenistic History* (Tübingen: Mohr [Siebeck], 1989), 115.

establishing a base for the gospel in the major centers, the apostolic trio did not stop until they reached the Macedonian capital.

1.2. The City of Thessaloniki before the Arrival of the Gospel

When the missionaries came to Thessaloniki, they encountered a cosmopolitan city with a proud Macedonian heritage, deep Roman connections, and a significant Jewish community.[4] The city's proud Macedonian heritage dates to 315 B.C. when Cassander, king of Macedonia, founded it on the site of ancient Therme, and named it after his wife, the daughter of Philip II, and half-sister of Alexander III ("the Great").[5] Situated at the head of the gulf of Therme, and boasting the best harbor in the Aegean, the city flourished throughout the Hellenistic period.[6]

As early as the first half of the second century B.C., however, Thessaloniki came under the influence of Rome. In 167 B.C., the Romans annexed Macedonia and made Thessaloniki the leading city in the second of four districts. In 148 B.C., they made Thessaloniki the capital of the newly united province of Macedonia.[7] In 42 B.C. Mark Antony granted Thessaloniki the status of "free city" (*civitas libera*), in thanks for the city's support for Antony and Octavian at the battle of Philippi.[8] Throughout this period, the location of the city on the *Via Egnatia*, which connected Rome with the cities of the East, further ensured its prosperity.

Indeed, the status of a Roman "free city" brought considerable benefits. It meant that Thessaloniki enjoyed imperial benefaction, while also retaining significant autonomy. In particular, the city (unlike Philippi and other Roman colonies) was free from military occupation, and did not have to integrate a large number of Roman veterans, or adjust to the imposition of Roman law (the *Ius Italicum*).[9] At the same time, it had the right to mint local and imperial coins, and received some tax concessions.[10] Significantly, local elites and local institutions, including the traditional body of five or six "city authorities" (the πολιτάρχαι of Acts 17:6, 8), remained in place.[11] This

---

[4] For details of the Thessalonian population, see D. W. J. Gill, "Macedonia," in D. W. J. Gill and C. Gempf, eds., *The Book of Acts in its First Century Setting, Volume 2: Graeco-Roman Setting* (Grand Rapids: Eerdmans, 1994), 406-8.
[5] Strabo, *Geogr*. VIII frgs. 21, 24.
[6] Cf. W. Elliger, *Paulus in Griechenland: Philippi, Thessaloniki, Athen, Korinth* (Stuttgarter Bibelstudien 92/93; Stuttgart: Verlag Katholisches Bibelwerk, 1978), 78.
[7] The administration of the province underwent several modifications during the Roman period. For the details, see D. Pandermalis and F. Papazoglou, "Macedonia under the Romans," in M. B. Sakellariou, ed., *Macedonia: 4000 Years of Greek History and Civilization* (Athens: Ekdotike Athenon S.A., 1983), 192-221; Gill, "Macedonia," 400-406.
[8] Pliny, *Nat*. 4.36.
[9] Gill, "Macedonia," 405-6.
[10] J. A. O. Larsen, "Roman Greece," in T. Frank, ed., *An Economic Survey of Ancient Rome IV* (Baltimore: Johns Hopkins, 1938), 449.
[11] The term πολιτάρχαι (sg. πολιτάρχης) appears at Acts 17:6, 8, but nowhere else in Acts or the surviving Greek literature. The term is, however, well known from Greek inscriptions and documentary papyri, where it refers to the ruling authorities of several Macedonia cities. Luke's

combination of Roman benefaction and local autonomy ensured that even after Macedonia was ravaged during the Roman civil wars (44–31 B.C.), Thessaloniki emerged relatively unscathed to enjoy a period of peace and prosperity during the Julio-Claudian era (27 B.C.–A.D. 68).[12]

Within this Roman free city with a proud Macedonian heritage, Paul found a significant Jewish population. The origins of the Jewish community in Thessaloniki are unknown, but the epigraphic evidence indicates that Jews were already in Greece-Macedonia in the third century B.C.[13] By the mid-first century A.D., Philo, citing a letter from Agrippa to the emperor Caligula, could list Thessaly, Boeotia, Macedonia, Aetolia, Attica, Argos, Corinth, and the Peloponnese as regions with a Jewish population.[14] Certainly, the account in Acts 17:1-9 indicates that by Paul's day Thessaloniki, like the other major cities of the eastern Mediterranean, was home to a strong Jewish community.

1.3. The Gospel in the Synagogue

The apostolic mission in Thessaloniki is narrated by the tantalisingly brief account in Acts 17:1-9, which indicates that Paul, consistent with his custom, took the gospel to the Jewish synagogue upon his arrival in the city. The apostle "reasoned" there "from the Scriptures" on three consecutive Sabbaths "explaining and proving that the Messiah had to suffer and rise from the dead," and so concluding that "this Jesus, who I am proclaiming to you, is the Messiah" (Acts 17:1-3). Some Jews, Acts continues, "were persuaded" to believe, and these "were joined" to the apostle and his companions (Acts 17:4). Most likely, these Jewish believers included Jason, who came to host the missionaries (Acts 17:5-7; cf. Rom. 16:21),[15] and Aristarchus (Acts 19:29; 20:4; 27:2; cf. Col 4:10-11; Phlm 24).[16] In addition, Acts 17:4 mentions that a "large number of God-fearing Greeks" and "quite a few prominent women" became believers. These God-fearing Greeks were Gentiles who worshipped the God of Israel, associated with the Jewish synagogue, and to some extent observed the Mosaic law, but who had not undergone the right of circumcision.[17] The prominent women were most probably either God-fearing

---

use of the term in this context and nowhere else is testimony to his meticulous concern for historical accuracy. For details see G. H. R. Horsley, "The Politarchs," in Gill and Gempf, *The Book of Acts*, 2:419-31.

[12] Larsen, "Roman Greece," 465.

[13] For sources and discussion see I. Levinskaya, *The Book of Acts in its First Century Setting, Volume 5: Diaspora Setting* (Grand Rapids: Eerdmans, 1996), 154.

[14] Philo, *Legatio* 281.

[15] Cf. F. M. Gillman, "Jason of Thessalonica," in Raymond F. Collins and Norbert Baumert, eds., *The Thessalonian Correspondence* (Louvain: Leuven University Press, 1990), 39-49.

[16] B. W. Winter, *Seek the Welfare of the City: Christians as Benefactors and Citizens* (Grand Rapids: Eerdmans, 1994), 46-47 suggests that this Aristarchus is also to be identified with the Aristarchus found in a list of Macedonian politarchs.

[17] Acts employs forms of φοβέω (10:2; 13:16, 26) and σέβω (13:43, 50; 16:14; 17:4, 17; 18:7) as semi-technical descriptions for such people. For discussion, see S. McKnight, "Proselytism and Godfearers," in C. A. Evans and S. E. Porter, eds., *Dictionary of New Testament Background* (Downers Grove: IVP, 2000), 835-47.

wives of some of the principal citizens of the city, or women who were leading citizens in their own right.[18] Either way, the Acts account records that Paul's gospel won at least some adherents in Thessaloniki from among those Jews and Gentiles who knew something of the Jewish Scriptures, and who worshipped the God of Israel.

1.4. The Gospel on the Streets

At some point, however, it seems that Paul and his companions took the gospel "to the streets."[19] The account in Acts provides no indication of a mission outside the synagogue, but the Thessalonian letters give the strong impression of a successful mission to the Gentiles of the city and are quite clearly addressed to people who had "turned to God from idols to serve the living and true God" (1 Thess 1:9).[20]

Indeed, four additional observations suggest not only that Paul and his companions conducted a successful mission outside the synagogue, but also that this mission lasted some time.[21] First, we must allow time for the fact that when the apostolic trio came to Berea, Athens, and Corinth, they found that the report of the conversion of the Thessalonians had preceded them (1 Thess 1:8). Second, the apostolic trio engaged in "tentmaking" work (1 Thess 2:9; 2 Thess 3:7-9; cf. Acts 18:2-3), which also seems to require a longer stay in the city. Third, at Phil 4:16 Paul speaks of how the Philippians sent him aid "more than once" while he was in Thessaloniki and, given the distances involved (about 148 km each way), it seems unlikely that this could have occurred within the space of "three sabbath days" (two weeks). Finally, at 1 Thess 2:7-8, 11-12, 17, 19-20 the apostolic trio speak of the great affection that exists between themselves and the Thessalonians, which also implies a stay longer than two weeks. Taken together, this evidence suggests that, even though the gospel "ran" among the Thessalonians (2 Thess 3:1), the apostolic proclamation to the Jews, which lasted "three Sabbath days," took place in the context of gospel work in the city lasting several weeks, or even months.[22]

---

[18] For discussion see C. K. Barrett, *A Critical and Exegetical Commentary on the Acts of the Apostles, Volume 2* (Edinburgh: T. & T. Clark, 1998), 812.

[19] R. F. Hock, *The Social Context of Paul's Ministry: Tentmaking and Apostleship* (Philadelphia: Fortress, 1980), 37-42 shows that Paul's workshop was almost certainly a primary site for his evangelistic activity among Gentiles. The homes of key individuals (such as Jason) most likely also provided a site from which Paul could preach and teach (see S. K. Stowers, "Social Status, Public Speaking, and Private Teaching: The Circumstances of Paul's Preaching Activity," *NovT* 26 [1984]: 65-68).

[20] It is probably significant, for example, that despite a range of intertextual echoes of the LXX, the letters nowhere explicitly cite the Scriptures of Israel.

[21] Cf. the case for a longer stay, first made by J. B. Lightfoot, *Biblical Essays* (London: Macmillan, 1893), 259.

[22] In order to reconcile the account in Acts with the evidence of the letters, we must posit a time lapse either between Acts 17:4 and 5 or, perhaps more likely, between Acts 17:1 and 2. Cf. B. Witherington III, *1 and 2 Thessalonians: A Socio-Rhetorical Commentary* (Grand Rapids: Eerdmans, 2006), 36-39 who argues that the ministry among the Gentiles of the city preceded, and was then contemporaneous with, the mission to the synagogue recorded in Acts 17.

1.5. The Gospel, the Church, and the Religio-political Culture of Thessaloniki

The earliest Christian community in Thessaloniki, then, seems to have comprised a majority of Gentiles (including some former God-fearers) and some Jews. Whatever the precise ethno-religious mix, the apostolic gospel provided an identity-shaping reference point for the whole church: it distinguished the nascent Christian community from both its Gentile environment and its Jewish roots.

On the one hand, for those of Gentile background, the gospel called for a significant re-orientation of life. The God revealed in Jesus Christ was utterly unlike the plethora of gods worshipped in the traditional Greco-Roman cults, the mystery religions, and the newly minted imperial cult, which filled the city. The archaeological evidence clearly demonstrates that Thessaloniki had devotees of the traditional cults of the region (especially that of the Cabiri), of the numerous gods and demi-gods imported from Greece (Zeus, Herakles, the Dioskouri, Apollo, Aphrodite, Dionysus, and Asclepius), and of the "mystery" cults of Serapis, Isis, and Mithras which came from Egypt and Persia.[23] Indeed, the numismatic evidence indicates that the cults of Cabirus and Dionysus were sponsored by the city authorities.[24] In this context, Paul reminds the Thessalonians that they had "turned to God from idols" when they embraced the gospel (1 Thess 1:9), and that this radical re-orientation of life had ethical implications: "each of you should learn to control your own body in a way that is holy and honorable, not in passionate lust like the Gentiles who do not know God" (1 Thess 4:4-5).[25] In contrast to the moral licence and cultic syncretism often associated with Greco-Roman religion, the God revealed in the gospel called for purity of life and exclusive devotion to one Lord, Jesus Christ.

This exclusive devotion to the Lord Jesus was particularly counter-cultural in the context of Roman rule. Roman benefaction had brought "peace and security" to Thessaloniki (cf. 1 Thess 5:2), and at least as early as the beginning of the first century B.C., the Thessalonian city authorities had added the cult of the "goddess Roma and the Benefactor Romans" to the range of other divinities worshipped in the city.[26] In the years following the establishment of Thessaloniki as a Roman free city (42 B.C.), the Thessalonians embraced the imperial cult, and gave it pre-eminence. The

---

[23] See especially C. Edson, "Cults of Thessalonica," *HTR* 41 (1948): 153-204 and Karl P. Donfried, "The Cults of Thessalonica and the Thessalonian Correspondence," *NTS* 31.3 (1985): 336-56.

[24] H. L. Hendrix, "Thessalonica," *ABD* 6:525.

[25] Donfried, "Cults," 337 suggests that Paul here deliberately critiques the cult of Dionysus, the god of wine and joy, which was often associated with phallic symbolism, when he calls to the Thessalonians to find joy and life in Christ while controlling their "member" (σκεῦος, 1 Thess 4:4).

[26] H. Hendrix, "Thessalonicans Honor Romans" (Th.D. Diss., Harvard University, 1984), 22 notes that the earliest extant inscription for this cult of "Roman benefactors" ('Ρωμαῖοι εὐεργέται) dates to 95 B.C.

epigraphic evidence demonstrates that they built a temple to "Imperator Caesar Augustus, son of god," provided a priest and "games superintendent" (ἀγωνοθέτης) for the cult of Augustus, and hosted annual games in his honor.[27] Significantly, they installed statues of the emperor,[28] and minted coins presenting Augustus as a "son of god."[29] As in other parts of the empire, the founding of imperial cults like this served to connect the social order of the city with the Roman imperial order and—through the Roman *princeps* (later emperor)—with the divinely established cosmic order.[30] Imperial cults thus gave divine sanction to the status quo, and it is no wonder that any challenge to the authority of the Roman emperor was treated with suspicion, and even violence. The apostolic gospel, which called for exclusive devotion to God's "Son," the "Lord Jesus Christ," thus sharply distinguished the newborn church from its Gentile environment.

On the other hand, for those who had come to faith in Christ from Judaism, the gospel revealed that the God of Israel's Scriptures had now acted in a new and decisive way through his Son, the Lord Jesus Christ (Acts 17:3). The gospel thus stood in deep continuity with Judaism, and Jews who accepted Christ did not encounter the same kind of radical re-orientation of life faced by their Gentile neighbors. Nevertheless, since the gospel relativized those aspects of the Jewish law which gave Jewish life its distinctive character (Sabbath, circumcision, food laws), it always had the potential to destabilize the Jewish community (cf. Acts 18:13). Indeed, this new development within deep continuity meant that the apostolic mission stood in direct competition with the mission of the synagogue, and was therefore opposed (cf. 1 Thess 2:16). The apostolic gospel thus sharply

---

[27] C. Edson, ed., *Inscriptiones graecae Epiri, Macedoniae, Thraciae, Scythiae, Pars II Inscriptiones Macedoniae, Fasciculus I Inscripitones Thessalonicae et viciniae* (Berlin: de Gruyter, 1972) = *IT* 31, 32, 132, 133. Hendrix, "Thessalonicans," 106-9, 312 notes that the significance of the new cult is evident in the fact that "every extant instance in which the 'priest and *agonothete* of the Imperator' is mentioned, he is listed first in what appears to be a strict observance of protocol".

[28] Archaeological Museum, Thessaloniki, Catalogue Number 1065. Images and discussion in Hendrix, "Thessalonicans," 45-54; cf. H. L. Hendrix, "Archaeology and Eschatology at Thessalonica," in B. A. Pearson et al., eds., *The Future of Early Christianity: Essays in Honor of Helmut Koester* (Minneapolis: Fortress, 1991), 116-18.

[29] Two series of coins are particularly significant: (1) the first series (*British Museum Catalogue* [= *BMC*] 115 nos. 16, 58-59, 61) quite possibly dates from as early as 29–28 B.C. and bears, on the obverse, the laureate head of Julius Caesar and the inscription ΘΕΟΣ ("god") and, on the reverse, the head of Augustus with the title ΣΕΒΑΤΟΥ ("of Augustus") or the name of the city ΘΕΣΣΑΛΟΝΙΚΩΝ ("of Thessaloniki"). Since Augustus was Julius Caesar's adoptive son, the coin clearly presents him as a "son of god," an epithet widely used of him during the principate. (2) The second series (H. Gaebler, *Die Antiken Münzen von Makedonia und Paionia* [Ger. orig. 1906], 2:125 no. 44) bears on the obverse the head of Augustus with the legend ΚΑΙΣΑΡ ΣΕΒΑΣΤΟΣ ("Caesar Augustus"), and on the reverse the prow of a ship with the city's name ΘΕΣΣΑΛΟΝΙΚΩΝ ("of Thessaloniki"). On this standard issue coin the place given to Augustus had previously belonged to Zeus. The coin may well, therefore, point to the divinization of Augustus. Images and discussion in Hendrix, "Thessalonicans," 170-73, 179.

[30] For this understanding of the imperial cults, see S. R. F. Price, *Rituals and Power: The Roman Imperial Cult in Asia Minor* (Cambridge: Cambridge University Press, 1984), 239-48.

distinguished the Thessalonian church not only from its Gentile environment, but also from its Jewish roots.

1.6. Opposition to the Gospel

It is no surprise, then, that opposition to the gospel in Thessaloniki first developed among the Jewish community, but quickly spread further afield to the Gentile inhabitants of the city (cf. 1 Thess 2:14). According to Acts 17.5, some unbelieving Jews, "jealous" of the missionaries' success, and no doubt "zealous" for the law (Acts 17:5: ζηλώσαντες; cf. Acts 5:17; 13:45: ζῆλος), gathered some men from the city marketplace and started a riot. This mob set out in search for Paul and Silas, and rushed to Jason's house where (presumably) the missionaries were staying and the first believers were known to meet (cf. Acts 17:7). Unable to find Paul and Silas, the mob forcibly dragged Jason and some of the other believers before the "city authorities" (the πολιτάρχης), and brought charges against them.[31]

The charges against Jason and the other believers were extremely serious: they had received Paul and Silas, who were "turning the world upside down" by acting "against the decrees of Caesar" in saying that "there is another king, Jesus" (Acts 17:6-7). Most likely, the Thessalonian Jews invoked here not merely the Roman law of treason (*maiestas*), but certain more specific "decrees of Caesar" (δογμάτων Καίσαρος). The Julio-Claudian emperors had, indeed, repeatedly forbidden astrologers and other magicians from all forms of prophecy, and especially prophecy related to the death of a ruler, or the coming of a new one.[32] Moreover, it is quite likely that the city authorities of Thessaloniki, together with the body of citizens (the δῆμος) had taken an oath of personal loyalty to the Roman emperor, by which they had bound themselves to "attack and pursue with arms and the sword by land and by sea" whomsoever was found to be an enemy of Caesar.[33] In this context, it is easy

---

[31] The vehemence of the Jewish opposition at this time may be further explained as a response to the actions of the emperor Claudius, which had placed Jews across the empire in a precarious position. In A.D. 41 Claudius banned meetings of Jews in Rome (Cassius Dio, *Hist*. 60.6.6). In the same year, he wrote to the Jews of Alexandria granting them freedom to worship, but warning them against welcoming those Jews who "stir up trouble throughout the whole world" (P.Lond. 1912). In A.D. 49 he expelled the Jews from Rome (Acts 18.2; Suetonius, *Claud*. 25.4; Orosius, *Hist. c. pag.* 7.6.15-16). Following these actions, the Jews of Thessaloniki no doubt feared the loss of their historic right to practice their ancestral religion (see Josephus, *A.J.* 14.211-16; 16.166; *C. Ap.* 2.37; Philo, *Legat*. 315-16; cf. Acts 16:21). In this context, it is easy to see why they distanced themselves from Paul and his companions.

[32] Cassius Dio, *Hist*., 56.25.5-6; 57.15.8. See E. A. Judge, "The Decrees of Caesar at Thessalonica," *RTR* 30 (1971): 1-7; repr. in E. A. Judge and J. R. Harrison, eds., *The First Christians in the Roman World: Augustan and New Testament Essays* (Tübingen: Mohr [Siebeck], 2008), 456-62.

[33] The language here is drawn from an oath of personal loyalty, binding of Roman citizens and non-Romans alike, from Paphlagonia (*Orientis Graeci Inscriptiones Selectae* [*OGIS*] 532: 6 March 3 B.C.). For discussion, see Judge, "Decrees," 5-7. J. R. Harrison, "Paul and the Imperial Gospel at Thessaloniki," *JSNT* 25.1 (2002): 79-80 demonstrates that there is widespread evidence for similar oaths being taken across the empire in the Julio-Claudian period. Although

to see how the apostolic proclamation in Thessaloniki, which included a pronounced eschatological element, and announced the enthronement and coming reign of the "Lord Jesus Christ" (1 Thess 1:10; 2:19; 3:13; 4:15; 5:23; 2 Thess 2:1, 8), could be understood as counter-imperial. Paul and his companions announced nothing less than "another King" (Acts 17:7) and so proclaimed the crucified Jesus as a rival to the Roman emperor Claudius! On this basis, then, the Jews of Thessaloniki sought to blacken Paul and Silas, and those who had received them, with the brush of political subversion.

1.7. After the Missionaries Left Thessaloniki: Persecution for the Gospel

This potentially explosive situation was only defused by the hasty departure of Paul and his companions from the city. The city authorities took monetary payment from "Jason and the rest" (Acts 17:9) to guarantee that they would keep the peace. Then, probably as a condition of the bail, "the brothers immediately sent Paul and Silas (and Timothy?) away by night to Berea" (Acts 17:9-10). Although the gospel was well received in Berea (Acts 17:11-12), the Jews of Thessaloniki vehemently pursued Paul and his companions there (Acts 17:13), forcing Paul to move on to Athens alone (Acts 17:14).

This premature departure was so traumatic that the missionary trio compare it to being "orphaned" (1 Thess 2:17). The trauma was exacerbated for the Thessalonians by the continuation of their persecution following the departure of the missionaries (2 Thess 1:4; cf. 1 Thess 2:14-16; 3:3-4). Indeed, it is possible that the persecution was so extreme that it led to the deaths of some in the church. This, at least, would help to explain why the death of some members had become such an issue so soon after the missionaries had left (1 Thess 4:13).[34]

Be that as it may, the missionary trio were clearly concerned for the suffering community in Thessaloniki. They had, to be sure, left behind some kind of rudimentary leadership structure (1 Thess 5:12), but they were all too aware that the apostolic mission in the Macedonian city had been cut short. In this context, the apostle and his companions sought continued personal contact with the young church. Paul himself made several attempts to return to Thessaloniki, but was unable to do so, being hindered by "Satan" (1 Thess 2:18).[35] Bereft of other options, therefore, and increasingly concerned about the state of the Thessalonian church, Paul sent Timothy back to the city from

---

we do not have direct evidence for Thessaloniki, such an oath was most likely part and parcel of the city's obligation as a "free city" of the empire.

[34] This was suggested by F. F. Bruce, *The Acts of the Apostles: The Greek Text with Introduction and Commentary* (2nd ed.; London: Tyndale Press, 1952), 327-28; cf. Donfried, "Cults," 349-50.

[35] The best explanation of this verse remains that of W. M. Ramsay, *St. Paul the Traveller and the Roman Citizen, Lewis Henry Morgan Lectures* (London: Hodder & Stoughton, 1895), 231 who suggested that the Thessalonian city authorities continued to oppose the presence in their city of one who had caused such a disturbance, and that Paul interpreted this ban as satanic opposition to the gospel.

Athens (Acts 17:15; 1 Thess 3:1-5),[36] while Silas was despatched to some other Macedonian destination (perhaps Berea or Philippi?).[37] This personal ministry through Timothy was, of course, supplemented by the ministry of the letters, and it is to them that we must now turn.

2. The Letters

2.1. The Authors

The Thessalonian letters were written by Paul, Silas, and Timothy.[38] Despite the tendency of modern scholarship to focus exclusively on Paul, the attribution of authorship to the three missionaries (1 Thess 1:1; 2 Thess 1:1), and the consistent use of the first person plural throughout both letters, should be given due weight. The ministry of letter writing, like that of the initial gospel proclamation in Thessaloniki, was collegial. It was together that these three missionaries had planted the church, and so together that they wrote to comfort and establish it in the faith.

At the same time, there should be no doubt that Paul was the leading author. Silas and Timothy were clearly subordinate to Paul in some ways (e.g. Acts 17:15; 1 Thess 3:1-6), and the emphatic greeting at 2 Thess 3:17, together with the occasional lapses into the first person singular throughout 1 Thessalonians (2:18; 3:5; 5:27) indicate that Paul was the one who actually dictated the letters. Just as he seems to have been the dominant evangelist and teacher during the mission in Thessaloniki (Acts 17:2), so he seems to have taken the lead role in writing to the church.

2.2. The Dates and Places of Writing

It is most commonly argued that both Thessalonian letters were written from Corinth some time between late A.D. 49/early 50, when Paul arrived in that city, and early A.D. 52, when he left.[39] On this view, the trio wrote 1

---

[36] Presumably, Timothy's presence was deemed less threatening than Paul's by the city authorities. Timothy's Greek patrilineage (Acts 16:1) and relatively junior status may have been factors here.

[37] It is difficult to be certain about Silas' movements. For this reconstruction, see J. B. Lightfoot, *Notes on Epistles of St Paul from unpublished commentaries* (2d ed.; London: Macmillan, 1904), 40; cf. T. W. Manson, "St. Paul in Greece: The Letters to the Thessalonians," *BJRL* 35 (1952-53): 435-36, 446-47.

[38] At least since J. E. C. Schmidt, *Vermutungen über die beiden Briefe an die Thessalonicher, Bibliothek für Kritik und Exegese des Neuen Testaments und ältesten Christengeschichte* (Hadamar: Gelehrtenbuchhandlung, 1801) and W. Wrede, *Die Echtheit des zweiten Thessalonicherbriefs* (Leipzig: Hinrichs, 1903) the authenticity of 2 Thessalonians has often been questioned. For a summary of the major arguments, and a convincing defense of the authenticity of 2 Thessalonians, see C. A. Wanamaker, *The Epistles to the Thessalonians: A Commentary on the Greek Text* (Grand Rapids: Eerdmans, 1990), 17-28.

[39] Paul's ministry in Corinth may be securely dated by a comparison of Acts 18:11-17 and the Delphic letter of Claudius which relates to Lucius Junius Gallio. See E. M. Smallwood, *Documents Illustrating the Principates of Gaius, Claudius, and Nero* (Cambridge: Cambridge

Thessalonians when Timothy returned from Thessaloniki with good news about the state of the church there (1 Thess 3:6; Acts 18:5), and wrote 2 Thessalonians shortly thereafter, when the missionaries became aware of renewed persecution, continued eschatological confusion, and a deterioration in the moral stance of some church members.[40]

It is perhaps more likely that 2 Thessalonians was written first.[41] The canonical order of the letters is, at any rate, no argument against this possibility, since it reflects only their relative length.[42] On this view, the missionary trio wrote 2 Thessalonians in anxiety and haste from Athens in late A.D. 49,[43] and sent it with Timothy on his first urgent return visit to Thessaloniki (1 Thess 3:1-5). 1 Thessalonians was then written from Corinth a short time later, probably in the early months of A.D. 50, after the missionary trio were reunited there (Acts 18:5), and in response to the good news Timothy brought back from the north (1 Thess 3:6).

In favor of this view, six considerations are noteworthy:

1. It seems quite probable that Paul and Silas would have sent a letter with Timothy from Athens expressing their own concern for the church.[44] In this connection, it is striking that the apostolic trio describe Timothy's mission (1 Thess 3:2) and the purpose of 2 Thessalonians (2 Thess 2:17) in identical terms, using a combination of the verbs "strengthen"

University Press, 1967), 105, no. 376; J. H. Oliver, "The Epistle of Claudius Which Mentions the Proconsul Junius Gallio," *Hesperia* 40 (1971): 239-40). For discussion, see Bruce, *Paul*, 253-55.

[40] Among the more recent commentaries, this view is adopted, with minor variations, by E. Best, *The First and Second Epistles to the Thessalonians* (London: Adams & Charles Black, 1972), 42-45; F. F. Bruce, *1 and 2 Thessalonians* (Grand Rapids: Word, 1982), xxxiv-v; I. H. Marshall, *1 and 2 Thessalonians* (London: Morgan and Scott, 1983), 20-23; A. J. Malherbe, *The Letters to the Thessalonians: A New Translation with Introduction and Commentary* (New York: Doubleday, 2000), 361-64; G. L. Green, *The Letters to the Thessalonians* (Grand Rapids: Eerdmans, 2002), 52-53; Witherington, *Thessalonians*, 10, 31, 183; G. D. Fee, *The First and Second Letters to the Thessalonians* (Grand Rapids: Eerdmans, 2009), 5.

[41] This view remains a minority position. It may be traced back at least as far as H. Grotius, *Annotations in Novum Testamentum I* (Amsterdam, 1641), 1032-42; H. Grotius, *Annotationes in Novum Testamentum II* (Amsterdam, 1646), 651. It has more recently been advocated by: J. C. West, "The Order of 1 and 2 Thessalonians," *JTS* 15 (1913): 66-74; J. Weiss, *Earliest Christianity: A History of the Period A.D. 30–150* (trans. Frederick C. Grant; 2 vols.; New York: Harper, 1959 [orig. 1937]), 286-91; Manson, "St Paul in Greece," 428-47; R. Gregson, "A Solution to the Problem of the Thessalonian Epistles," *EvQ* 38 (1966): 76-80; C. Buck and G. Taylor, *Saint Paul: A Study of the Development of His Thought* (New York: Scribner's, 1969), 150-62; R. W. Thurston, "The Relationship between the Thessalonian Epistles," *ExpT* 85 (1973–1974): 52-56; Wanamaker, *Thessalonians*, 37-45.

[42] Bruce, *1 and 2 Thessalonians*, xli.

[43] J. Calvin, *1, 2 Thessalonians* (Wheaton: Crossway, 1999 [orig. 1550]), in his discussion of "the argument" of 2 Thessalonians, notes "a very generally received opinion among the Latins, that it was written from Athens."

[44] Cf. Manson, "St Paul in Greece," 436; cf. J. L. White, *Light from Ancient Letters: Foundations and Facets* (Philadelphia: Fortress, 1986), 216 who notes that it was common practice in the first century to send a letter with a trusted representative authorized to interpret and elaborate on the letter's contents.

(στηρίξαι) and "encourage" (παρακαλέσαι), which occurs nowhere else in the Pauline corpus.[45]

2. The contrast between the urgent tone of 2 Thessalonians and the more irenic tone of 1 Thessalonians is well explained if 2 Thessalonians was written in haste and anxiety from Athens on the basis of limited information, while 1 Thessalonians was written some time later from Corinth, following the good report from Timothy (1 Thess 3:6), and when the apostolic trio had time and space to compose a more considered and polished letter.

3. The persecution of the Thessalonians is clearly a present and pressing reality in 2 Thess 1:4-7, but in 1 Thessalonians 1–3 it is, if not a thing of the past, at least a less pressing concern. If 1 Thessalonians was written first, we are forced to posit a renewal of persecution to account for 2 Thessalonians. While possible, this reconstruction lacks clear evidence. The only unambiguous evidence of persecution relates to the time of the apostolic mission and its immediate aftermath (Acts 17:5-9; 1 Thess 2:14-16).[46]

4. 2 Thess 3:6-15 provides an extended discussion on the problem of idleness, while 1 Thessalonians includes only brief references to the same issue (1 Thess 4:10-12; 5:14). The problem of idleness was addressed by the apostolic trio already during the initial mission (2 Thess 3:10), but there is no indication that they gave any instruction regarding how to discipline recalcitrant members. The command to "warn the idle" at 1 Thess 5:14 is somewhat cryptic on its own (warn them of what? admonish them how?) but makes good sense if the recipients have already read/heard the more detailed instructions about how to deal with recalcitrant members in 2 Thess 3:6-15.

5. The expression "now concerning" (περὶ δέ or περὶ τῶν) seems to have been something of a standard device for Paul when responding to oral or written questions (cf. 1 Cor 7:1, 25; 8:1; 12:1; 16:1, 12).[47] At 1 Thess 4:9, 13, and 5:1 this expression seems to refer to questions asked by the Thessalonians, and these questions can be related to issues discussed in 2 Thessalonians (1 Thess 4:9-12 with 2 Thess 3:6-15; 1 Thess 4:13-18 and 1 Thess 5:1-10 with 2 Thess 2:1-10).[48] It is certainly possible that the missionaries here simply refer to standing topics left over from their ministry in Thessaloniki, especially since both eschatology and idleness had been addressed during the original mission (2 Thess 2:5; 3:10).[49]

---

[45] So Wanamaker, *Thessalonians*, 44. Contra Green, *Thessalonians*, 66.

[46] A renewal of persecution is widely posited. See R. Jewett, *The Thessalonian Correspondence: Pauline Rhetoric and Millenarian Piety* (Philadelphia: Fortress, 1986), 24-25; C. R. Nicholl, *From Hope to Despair in Thessalonica: Situating 1 and 2 Thessalonians* (Cambridge: Cambridge University Press, 2004), 183-98; Witherington, *Thessalonians*, 15, 29-36. It is telling, however, that no evidence for such persecution can be adduced, beyond 2 Thess 1:4-7 itself, which merely begs the question.

[47] E. J. Richard, *First and Second Thessalonians* (Collegeville: Liturgical Press, 1995), 259.

[48] Cf. Manson, "St Paul in Greece," 445-46 and (following him) Wanamaker, *Thessalonians*, 39.

[49] So Witherington, *Thessalonians*, 15.

Alternatively, it is also possible that the missionary trio received such questions via a messenger or letter sent from Thessaloniki, although we have no firm evidence for this.[50] What we do know is that Timothy was sent to the church from Athens (1 Thess 3:1-5). It is eminently plausible, therefore, that having delivered the first letter to the Thessalonian congregation (2 Thessalonians), Timothy returned to Paul in Corinth with further questions relating to that letter, which the missionaries then addressed in 1 Thessalonians.

6. The abrupt change to the first person singular at 1 Thess 5:27 is unusual in the Pauline corpus in that the "I" is not clearly identified (cf. 1 Cor 16:21; Gal 6:11; Col 4:18; Phlm 19). In the light of the emphatic greeting at 2 Thess 3:17, however, it seems plausible to suggest that 1 Thess 5:27 was written in Paul's own hand,[51] and was intended as the "sign" of authenticity referred to in the earlier letter.[52]

These considerations carry varying weight, and yet provide a strong cumulative case.

The two main arguments against the view that 2 Thessalonians was written first appeal to indications of sequence in the letters themselves. First, proponents of the traditional view point to 2 Thess 2:15, which seems to refer to a previous letter, most likely (it is said) 1 Thessalonians.[53] The mention of "our letter" (singular) in this verse could, however, refer to 2 Thessalonians itself.[54] Second, proponents of the traditional view note that 1 Thessalonians does not refer to any previous correspondence, which seems strange given its extended review of the relationship between the missionaries and the church in 1 Thessalonians 1–3.[55] The references to Timothy's visit (1 Thess 3:1-5),

---

[50] A. J. Malherbe, "Did the Thessalonians Write to Paul?" in R. T. Fortuna and B. R. Gaventa, eds., *The Conversation Continues: Studies in Paul and John in Honor of J. Louis Martyn* (Nashville: Abingdon Press, 1990), 246-57 considers it likely the Thessalonians wrote to Paul.

[51] In the absence of the autograph of 1 Thessalonians, it is impossible to be certain that 1 Thess 5:27 was written in Paul's own hand. Given, however, that this was Paul's customary practice, it seems reasonable to assume that it was. cf. A. Deissmann, *Light from the Ancient East* (trans. L. R. M. Strachan; Grand Rapids: Baker, 1978 [orig. 1927]), 170-71 for an example of a first-century letter with a change in handwriting (but not a signature) as a mark of authenticity at the close.

[52] Manson, "St Paul in Greece," 442-43 argued that 2 Thess 3:17 itself indicates an initial letter. On its own, however, 2 Thess 3:17 may be simply explained as a response to the (real or imaginary) forged letter referred to at 2 Thess 2:2.

[53] Jewett, *Thessalonian Correspondence*, 27-28 also points to 2 Thess 2:2 and 3:17 as references back to 1 Thessalonians, but these are unlikely (cf. Wanamaker, *Thessalonians*, 40-41; Green, *Thessalonians*, 68, n. 8).

[54] Wanamaker, *Thessalonians*, 41 suggests that the governing verb ἐδιδάχθητε ("you were taught") may be taken either as an epistolary aorist, or as having the sense of a perfect passive, either of which allows for a reference to the present letter. Given, however, that the aorist tense-form by itself does not encode past time (eg. C. R. Campbell, *Verbal Aspect, the Indicative Mood, and Narrative: Soundings in the Greek of the New Testament* [New York: Peter Lang, 2008], 88-91), it is more likely that ἐδιδάχθητε simply refers to the apostolic teaching considered as a whole, whether given by word of mouth or through (the present?) letter.

[55] Cf. esp. Jewett, *Thessalonian Correspondence*, 29-30.

however, may well assume a letter sent with him, especially given the Greco-Roman and early Christian preference for a "living voice" over written communication.[56] At any rate, this argument can work both ways: when 2 Thessalonians discusses issues also addressed in 1 Thessalonians these refer not to a previous letter (as one would expect on this logic if 1 Thessalonians was already in existence), but to the initial oral instruction (cf. 2 Thess 2:5; 3:10).[57] In the end, therefore, it seems more likely that 2 Thessalonians was written first, even if the evidence does not allow certainty.

2.3. The Form and Purposes of the Letters

Whatever the order of their composition, the purposes of the Thessalonian letters come into sharp focus when their form and content are related to the concrete historical situations in which they were written. 1 Thess 5:27 makes it clear that these letters were intended to be read aloud to the congregation gathered in Thessaloniki and to meet the needs of the church there. It should be no surprise, then, that the form of the letters may be usefully compared with both Greco-Roman epistolary conventions and ancient rhetorical techniques.[58] The letters, indeed, integrate the conventions of ancient letter writing with those of ancient rhetoric to achieve their purposes, even as their distinctive Christian message breathes fresh life into both forms.[59] In what follows, then, we examine the form and purpose of each letter in turn.

(a) 2 Thessalonians

2 Thessalonians adopts the approach of deliberative rhetoric.[60] This form of rhetoric seeks to persuade an audience to embrace a particular course of action in the future. The letter thus opens with an epistolary prescript (1:1-2) and

---

[56] Galen, *De comp. med. sec. loc.* 6; Quintillian, *Inst.* 2.2.8; Pliny, *Ep.* 2.3; Seneca, *Ep.* 6.5; Papias in Eusebius *Hist. eccl.* 3.39.4. Cf. L. Alexander, "The Living Voice: Scepticism towards the Written Word in Early Christian and in Graeco-Roman Texts," in D. J. A. Clines, S. E. Fowl, and S. E. Porter, eds., *The Bible in Three Dimensions* (Sheffield: JSOT, 1990), 221-47.
[57] Cf. Wanamaker, *Thessalonians*, 43-44.
[58] For an introduction to ancient epistolary conventions as they relate to the NT, see D. E. Aune, *The New Testament in Its Literary Environment* (Philadelphia: Westminster, 1987), 158-225; H-J. Klauck, *Ancient Letters and the New Testament: A Guide to Content and Exegesis* (Waco: Baylor, 2006). For an introduction to rhetorical criticism of the New Testament letters, see G. A. Kennedy, *New Testament Interpretation through Rhetorical Criticism, Studies in Religion* (Chapel Hill: University of North Carolina Press, 1984); C. J. Classen, *Rhetorical Criticism of the New Testament* (Leiden: Brill, 2002).
[59] For this perspective, see especially C. Wanamaker, "Epistolary Analysis: Is a Synthesis Possible?," in Karl P. Donfried and Johannes Beutler, eds., *The Thessalonians Debate: Methodological Discord or Methodological Synthesis?* (Grand Rapids: Eerdmans, 2000), 255-86; R. F. Collins, "'I Command That This Letter Be Read': Writing as a Manner of Speaking," in Donfried and Beutler, *The Thessalonians Debate*, 319.
[60] The following analysis of the rhetorical form of the letters relies primarily on the discussions in Aristotle, *Rhetorica* 1.4-10; 3.14-19 and Cicero, *De inventione rhetorica* 1.19; *Partitiones oratoriae* 27.

exordium (1:3-12), which introduces the main theme of the letter as the future advent of the Lord in judgment, and indicates steadfast faith as the appropriate response to present persecution. The letter then introduces the primary problem in the *partitio* (2:1-2), namely, the false claim that the "Day of the Lord" has already come, which is then answered in the *probatio* or proof (2:3-12), which emphasizes the future advent of the Lord. A transitional prayer of thanksgiving (the *transitus:* 2:13-17) then leads to a twofold *exhortatio* (or exhortation) to prayer (3:1-5) and to faithful work (3:6-15). The *peroratio* contains the final wish prayer (3:16), before an epistolary greeting and blessing close the letter (3:17-18).[61]

This form was particularly well suited to the historical situation outlined above. The apostolic trio wrote from Athens (or perhaps Corinth), painfully aware of the persecution being faced by the church in Thessaloniki (2 Thess 1:4, 6-7), and having heard some disturbing reports about the situation there (2 Thess 2:1-2; 3:11), but lacking concrete information about the church they had left in such haste. In this context, Paul and his companions wrote 2 Thessalonians with a strong focus on the future: they wrote to "strengthen" and "encourage" (2 Thess 2:17) the Thessalonians to continue to "stand firm" (2 Thess 2:15) in their new faith and to continue to "walk worthy of their calling" (2 Thess 1:11-12), even despite intense persecution (2 Thess 1:4-5), in the knowledge that the coming of the Lord would bring comfort to them, and righteous condemnation to their enemies (2 Thess 1:3-12; 2:13–3:5). For this reason, it was a matter of great concern that some in the church had begun to claim that "the Day of the Lord has come," for in so doing they were undermining the hope provided by the gospel (2 Thess 2:2). No less serious was the continuation, and perhaps exacerbation, of a problem that had already surfaced while the missionaries were in Thessaloniki, namely, the refusal of some church members to work for their bread (2 Thess 3:10-11).

This analysis of the letter's form (future-focused deliberative rhetoric) and historical context leads to the conclusion that the apostolic trio wrote with a three-fold purpose. They wrote to persuade the Thessalonians: first, to continue standing firm amidst persecution (2 Thess 2:15-17); second, to reject mistaken beliefs regarding the "Day of the Lord" (2 Thess 2:1-12); and third, to discipline idle members of the community—to get them back to work so they could provide for themselves rather than being dependent on others (2 Thess 3:6-15). For each of these future-focussed goals, the form of deliberative rhetoric was an apt choice.

---

[61] Cf. similar outlines, each with its own distinctive emphases, in Jewett, *Thessalonian Correspondence*, 61-88; F. W. Hughes, *Early Christian Rhetoric and 2 Thessalonians* (Sheffield: Sheffield Academic Press, 1989), 68-73; Wanamaker, *Thessalonians*, 51; Witherington, *Thessalonians*, 31.

(b) 1 Thessalonians

1 Thessalonians, by contrast, is shaped by the conventions of epideictic or demonstrative rhetoric. This rhetorical form seeks, either through praise or blame, to encourage an appropriate response to the present situation.[62] Thus, in keeping with the conventions of epideictic rhetoric, after a brief epistolary prescript (1:1), 1 Thessalonians begins with an *exordium* or prologue that introduces the major themes of the letter in terms of active faith and love, and steadfast hope (1:2-3). The authors then tell the story of the apostolic gospel in Thessaloniki in the extended *narratio* (1:4–3:10). This element was a standard feature of epideictic rhetoric, but not required in deliberative rhetoric, which may go some way to explaining its inclusion here rather than in 2 Thessalonians.[63] Here it serves to emphasize the missionaries' commitment to the Thessalonians (1 Thess 2:17–3:5), and their exemplary behavior while among them (1 Thess 1:5; 2:1-12). This leads to a *transitus* (3:9-13), a transitional prayer of thanksgiving, which further highlights the themes of faith and love, but tellingly implies that somehow hope is lacking (see further below). The *probatio* or proof (4:1–5.22) then presents the main concerns of the letter in calling the Thessalonians to faithful holy living (4:1-8), brotherly love (4:9-12), and especially hope—even in the face of opposition and death—because of the coming "Day of the Lord" (4:13–5.11). The *exhortatio* then exhorts the Thessalonians to continue in the distinctive way of Christ (5:12-22), the *peroratio* expresses a final wish prayer, which again underscores the hope of the gospel (5:23-24), and the final epistolary greetings and charges close out the letter (5:25-28).[64]

This rhetorical form was well suited to the situation outlined above, in which the apostolic trio wrote to the church in Thessaloniki for a second time, now from Corinth, having finally received much-desired information about the health of the church, and celebrating the good report from Timothy (1 Thess 3:1-8). It seems that either the situation in Thessaloniki was not as serious as the missionaries had initially feared, or (perhaps more likely) that the initially intense persecution had died down, while Timothy's visit, and the letter he bore (2 Thessalonians), had gone at least some way towards addressing the internal problems being faced by the church. 1 Thessalonians is, accordingly, full of praise for the Thessalonians, and repeatedly affirms them in their current beliefs and behaviors (1:2-3, 6-10; 2:13-14, 19-20; 3:6-9; 4:1-2, 9-10; 5:11). The apostolic trio do not try to persuade the Thessalonians

---

[62] Aristotle, *Rhet.* 3.12.5-6 suggests this rhetorical form was particularly well suited to written compositions.
[63] Kennedy, *New Testament Interpretation*, 24.
[64] Cf. the similar outlines, each with its own distinctive emphases, offered by Jewett, *Thessalonian Correspondence*, 71-78; F. W. Hughes, "The Rhetoric of 1 Thessalonians," in Raymond F. Collins, ed., *The Thessalonian Correspondence* (Leuven: Leuven University Press, 1990) 97, 109-16; Wanamaker, *Thessalonians*, 49; Karl P. Donfried and I. H. Marshall, *The Theology of the Shorter Pauline Letters* (Cambridge: Cambridge University Press, 1993), 4; S. Walton, "What Has Aristotle to Do with Paul? Rhetorical Criticism and 1 Thessalonians," *TynB* 46 (1995): 234-38, 249-50; Witherington, *Thessalonians*, 21-29.

to change their beliefs or practices, but encourage them to continue in the way of faith, love, and hope as they wait for the Lord to come. At the same time, the letter starkly contrasts the Thessalonian believers with Satan, "the Jews," and their own "fellow countrymen" (1 Thess 2:14-18), on whom it heaps blame as those who oppose the gospel and who are destined for wrath (1 Thess 2:16; cf. 1:10; 5:3, 9).

These observations on the rhetorical form of the letter and the concrete historical situation in which it was written together suggest that its primary purpose was to encourage the Thessalonian believers to continue in faith and love and, especially, to bolster their hope in the God of the gospel as they look forward to the coming of the Lord. Indeed, this concern to bolster the hope of the church is evident not only in the prominence given to eschatological teaching throughout the letter (1 Thess 1:10; 2:19-20; 3:13; 4:13–5:10; 5:23), but also in three elements of the rhetorical strategy employed by Paul and his companions.

First, the missionaries strategically deploy the triadic formula of faith, love, and hope at the beginning and end of 1 Thessalonians (1 Thess 1:3; 5:8), but tellingly omit "hope" when they record Timothy's report about the church (1 Thess 3:6). The strong implication is that hope was lacking, and it was this that the missionaries longed to supply (1 Thess 3:10).[65] Second, the missionaries place emphasis throughout the first part of the letter on all that the Thessalonians "already know" (1 Thess 1:5; 2:1, 5, 9, 10, 11; 3:3-4 [2x]; 4:2, 9). This creates a clear contrast with their concern that the Thessalonians not remain ignorant about the fate of those who have died, or grieve as those who have "no hope" (1 Thess 4:13).[66] This contrast, then, strongly suggests that at least a key part of what was "lacking" in the Thessalonians' faith was the hope of the resurrection of the dead at the return of the Lord (1 Thess 4:13-18; cf. 5:9-10).[67] Third, as will be demonstrated shortly, the missionaries repeatedly present the return of the Lord in strongly polemical (i.e. counter-imperial) terms. This in turn suggests that the foundational social reality that stood behind the Thessalonian's lack of hope was the opposition to the gospel of the Roman-backed city authorities who had ejected the apostolic trio from the city, separated them from the church, and given tacit approval to the ongoing persecution. In all of this, the missionaries' choice of epideictic or demonstrative rhetoric was well suited to the purpose of the letter: by it they sought to confirm the Thessalonians in their newfound faith in Christ, to encourage them to continue as a distinctive community living in the way of

---

[65] So Donfried, "Cults," 347-48. Cf. the lack of "hope" at 2 Thess 1:3.

[66] Cf. Donfried, "Cults," 348 who notes further that the discursive prominence of the short paragraph at 1 Thess 4:13-18 is enhanced by the return, at 1 Thess 5:1, to matters about which the Thessalonians "have no need to have anything written" to them.

[67] It was not that the missionaries had neglected to teach the Thessalonians about the hope of the gospel in general. On the contrary, it is clear that the eschatological coming of Christ formed a central part of the initial gospel proclamation (2 Thess 2:5; 1 Thess 1:9-10). Rather, the missionaries had not had the chance to draw out all of the implications of this hope, especially as it relates to those who die before the Lord's return.

love, and especially to comfort them with the hope of the gospel even in the face of opposition and death.

2.4. The Christocentric Theological Worldview of the Letter

In order to achieve these purposes the apostolic trio provided the Thessalonians with a profoundly christocentric theological worldview. To be sure, the Thessalonian letters are no systematic theology textbook: the theological worldview they present is deeply embedded in the pastoral and polemical realities of the Thessalonian situation. Nevertheless, given that these are among our earliest extant letters from the apostle Paul, and therefore among the earliest Christian documents of any kind, it is striking that the theological worldview presented in them is so well-developed, including many of the major themes and emphases so characteristic of Paul's later letters. In what follows, we briefly outline the teaching of the Thessalonian letters on the gospel, the God of the gospel, the hope of the gospel, and gospel living.

(a) The Gospel

At the center of the theological worldview presented in these letters is "the gospel" (τὸ εὐαγγέλιον: 2 Thess 1:8; 2:14; 1 Thess 1:5; 2:2, 4, 8, 9; 3:2). Like so much of Paul's theological language, this terminology is rooted in the Scriptures of Israel, and speaks directly into the Greco-Roman world of his day.[68] In speaking of their message as "the gospel," the apostolic trio simultaneously evoke the biblical tradition about the "good news" of the coming kingdom of YHWH, the God of Israel,[69] and challenge the "good news" claims of the early Roman empire to have brought salvation and peace to the known world.[70]

The report in 1 Thess 1:9-10 indicates that the gospel Paul and his companions announced in Thessaloniki contained at least three key

---

[68] On the origins of the use of the term εὐαγγέλιον in antiquity, see G. Friedrich, "εὐαγγελίζομαι, εὐαγγέλιον, προευαγγελίζομαι, εὐαγγελιστής," in G. Kittell, ed., (Grand Rapids: Eerdmans, 1964), 2:707-37; cf. D. Dormeyer and H. Frankemölle, "Evangelium als literarischer Gattung und als theologischer Begriff," *ANRW* 2.25.2: 1543-1704; J. P. Dickson, "Gospel as News: εὐαγγελ- from Aristophanes to the Apostle Paul," *NTS* 51 (2005): 212-30.

[69] At several points in the LXX, the cognate verbs εὐαγγελίζομαι and εὐαγγελίζω refer to the announcement of God's victory over his enemies, or to the proclamation of the coming kingdom of YHWH. See Ps 39:10 (Eng. 40:9); 67:12 (= Eng. 68:11); 95:2 (= Eng. 96:2); Isa 40:9; 52:7 (cf. Nah 2:1 = Eng. 1:15); 61:1.

[70] For example, the Calendar Decree of the Asian League from Priene (9 B.C.), in the Roman province of Asia, announces that "the birthday of the god (Augustus) was the beginning for the world of the glad tidings (εὐαγγέλια) that have come to men through him." For the full text, see *OGIS* 2:458. A convenient translation is provided by V. Ehrenberg and A. H. M. Jones, eds., *Documents Illustrating the Reigns of Augustus and Tiberius* (2nd ed.; Oxford: Clarendon, 1976) §98b. For further examples, see Deissmann, *Light*, 366-67; Ehrenberg and Jones, *Documents*, nos. 14, 38, 41, 98, 99.

components:[71] the apostolic trio proclaimed the "living and true God" of Israel over against all idols (cf. Acts 14:15-17; 17:22-29); they declared that this God had acted decisively through the death and resurrection of his "Son," the Lord Jesus Christ (cf. 2 Thess 1:8; 1 Thess 3:2; 5:10); and, especially, they announced the good news that because Jesus died "for us" (cf. 1 Thess 5:10), he is also the one through whom God will bring eschatological salvation from the "wrath to come" (cf. 1 Thess 5:9; Acts 17:30-31).[72] This gospel, the apostolic trio affirm, had its origins in God (1 Thess 2:2, 8, 9; cf. 1 Thess 2:13) but was entrusted to Paul and his companions (1 Thess 2:4) so that they can speak of it as "our gospel" (2 Thess 2:14; 1 Thess 1:5). The significance of the gospel can be gauged from the fact that it was the means by which God, who had chosen the Thessalonians for himself, called them to salvation (2 Thess 2:14).

(b) The God of the Gospel: God our Father, the Lord Jesus Christ, and the Holy Spirit

The gospel that Paul and his companions proclaimed in Thessaloniki also opens up a vision of the one true God, who is at work in the lives of his people as Father, Son, and Spirit. The missionaries clearly embrace the fierce monotheism of the Hebrew Scriptures; they no less clearly include the Lord Jesus Christ and the Holy Spirit within the identity of God.[73] It is remarkable, then, that these very earliest of Christian documents contain all the essential building blocks for what would later become the characteristic Christian doctrine of the Trinity.

1. God our Father. To begin with, the "God" (θεός, 53x) of whom the missionaries regularly speak is, without question, the one "living and true God" of Israel, the great Creator and ruler of all (1 Thess 1:9 with Jer 10:10). Consistent with Paul's usage across the extant letters, however, θεός in the Thessalonian correspondence refers particularly to the "Father" (πατήρ: 2 Thess 1:1, 2; 2:16; 1 Thess 1:1, 3; 3:11, 13). This striking designation for God has its roots in the Hebrew Scriptures,[74] and more specifically in Jewish messianism,[75] but owes its major impetus to the teaching of Jesus, and to the early Christian recognition of him as the Son of God *par excellence*. The Thessalonians were no doubt familiar with the Greco-Roman habit of invoking Zeus, the gods of the mystery religions, and even the Roman

---

[71] Most likely, the report at 1 Thess 1:9-10 reflects the apostolic proclamation to the Gentiles (cf. Acts 14:14-18; 17:22-31). The preaching in the synagogue, briefly summarized at Acts 17:2-3, most probably followed the contours of the paradigmatic synagogue sermon from Pisidian Antioch reported in Acts 13:16-41.

[72] For similar conclusions see Wanamaker, *Thessalonians*, 9-10.

[73] For the language of "inclusion in the divine identity," see especially R. J. Bauckham, *God Crucified: Monotheism and Christology in the New Testament* (Carlisle: Paternoster, 1998).

[74] Exod 4:22; Deut 14:1; 32:6; Isa 1:2-4; 63:16; 64:8; Jer 3:19, 22; 4:22; 31:9, 20; Hos 11:1.

[75] See God's promise to David in 2 Sam 7:14; cf. Ps 2:7

emperor, as "father."[76] For Paul and his companions, however, there is only one true God and Father, who is first and foremost the Father of his Son, Jesus (1 Thess 1:10a; cf. Rom 15:6; 2 Cor 1:3; Eph 1:3; Col 1:3), and the one who raised Jesus from the dead (1 Thess 1:10b).[77]

Moreover, this God, the Father, loves his people (2 Thess 3:5; 1 Thess 1:4). He chose them for himself (2 Thess 2:13; 1 Thess 1:4) and destined them for salvation (1 Thess 5:9). He now calls them into his kingdom (1 Thess 2:12; cf. 2 Thess 1:5), and actively works in their lives (2 Thess 1:1, 4, 11; 1 Thess 1:1; 2:4, 12, 14; 4:1, 3, 7, 8; 5:18, 23). Ultimately, this God is also the righteous judge and defender of his people (2 Thess 1:5-6). He is displeased with those who do not know him and oppose his gospel (1 Thess 2:15; 2 Thess 1:8; cf. 1 Thess 4:5), and is already at work to harden his enemies for the judgment of the final day (2 Thess 1:6-8; 2:11-12), when he will vindicate his people by raising them from the dead (1 Thess 4:14).

2. God's Son: the Lord Jesus Christ. The Thessalonian letters also present a striking picture of God's Son, the Lord Jesus Christ. The missionaries presuppose the full humanity and historical career of Jesus (1 Thess 1:10; 2:15; 4:14) and, in characteristic Pauline fashion, invest these with soteriological significance (1 Thess 5:10). At the same time, however, without any hint that the monotheism just noted is being diminished or abrogated, the Lord Jesus Christ is consistently included in the identity of the one true God.

Jesus' identity as Son and Lord is particularly significant here. The first of these titles ("Son" = ὁ υἱός) is rooted in the biblical understanding of Israel (Exod 4:22-23; Hos 11:1; Ps 80:15), and then especially of Israel's King, the Davidic Messiah, as the "Son of God" (2 Sam 7:13-14; Ps 2:7). In appropriating this tradition, Paul elsewhere teaches that Jesus, by virtue of his resurrection from the dead, has now been enthroned as the "Son of God in power" (Rom 1:3-4; cf. 1 Cor 15:23-28; Col 1:12-15). Here, similarly, the designation of Jesus as Son enables Paul and his companions to combine Davidic messianism with the Danielic vision of the "son of man coming on the clouds" (Dan 7:13-14; cf. 1 Thess 4:17), to declare that Jesus, the resurrected Son, is now in heaven with the Father, from where he will come to bring eschatological deliverance to his people (1 Thess 1:10). In this way, the title "Son of God" takes on new significance, and begins to express something of Jesus' participation not only in the authoritative divine rule, but also in the very identity of God himself.[78]

---

[76] In his widely published *Res Gestae* (35.1) Augustus presents the award of the title *pater patriae* ("Father of the Fatherland") to him on 5 February 2 B.C. as the crowning moment of his career. For further evidence and discussion of Greco-Roman usage, see Schrenk, "πατήρ," *TDNT* 5:945-1014.

[77] For this most characteristic Pauline description of God, see 1 Cor 6:14; 2 Cor 4:4; Gal 1:1; Rom 4:24; 6:4; 8:11 (2x); 10:9; Col 2:12; Eph 1:20; cf. 1 Pet 1:21.

[78] Cf. Fee, *Thessalonians*, 48-49.

The second title applied to Jesus, "Lord" (ὁ κύριος), is particularly prominent in the Thessalonian correspondence (46x). It further develops the apostolic presentation of Jesus as one who is included within the identity of God. Indeed, the application of this title to Jesus is particularly striking given the usage of the LXX, where the Greek κύριος regularly translates the divine name (יהוה). In this context, it is significant that throughout the letters, God the Father and the Lord Jesus Christ share in a range of divine attributes and activities: the church exists "in God the Father and the Lord Jesus Christ" (2 Thess 1:1; 1 Thess 1:1); grace and peace come from God the Father and the Lord Jesus Christ (2 Thess 1:2, 12; 3:16; 1 Thess 5:23); divine glory and faithfulness belong both to God and the Lord Jesus Christ (2 Thess 1:9-10; 2:14; 1 Thess 2:12, and 2 Thess 3:3; 1 Thess 5:24); God's will finds expression "in Christ Jesus" (1 Thess 5:18); and, perhaps most striking of all, prayers are directed to both God the Father and the Lord Jesus (2 Thess 2:16-17; 3:3-5, 16; 1 Thess 3:11-13; 5:28). Similarly, the Thessalonian letters take a number of phrases which in the LXX regular apply to the LORD God, and effortlessly transpose them into references to the Lord Jesus. The missionary trio thus speak of the "name of the Lord" (2 Thess 1:12; 3:6), the "word of the Lord" (2 Thess 3:1; 1 Thess 1:8; 4:15), the "day of the Lord" (2 Thess 2:2; 1 Thess 5:2), and "the hope of our Lord" (1 Thess 1:3), in each case taking OT phrases pregnant with monotheistic significance and applying them to the Lord Jesus. Most significant of all, the Thessalonian letters also include a number of more extended, and seemingly deliberate, intertextual echoes, in which LXX texts that explicitly speak of the LORD God are now applied to the Lord Jesus. The most important of these relate to the "coming of the Lord" and are discussed below under "the hope of the gospel."

Paul's reasoning elsewhere reveals that this recognition of Jesus' inclusion in the identity of God was grounded in his resurrection from the dead, and facilitated by some remarkable christocentric exegesis of key LXX passages, especially Ps 110:1 (cf. 1 Cor 15:25; Rom 8:34; Eph 1:20; Col 3:1), Deut 6:4 (cf. 1 Cor 8:4-6), Isa 45:22-23 (cf. Phil 2:9-11), and Isa 28:16/Joel 2:32 (LXX Joel 3:5; cf. Rom 10:9-13). It is difficult to be certain how much of this understanding Paul had in place by the time the missionary trio first wrote to the church in Thessaloniki. Given, however, the presuppositional way in which Paul and his companions speak of Jesus as the Lord, and predicate of him a range of prerogatives that, from an OT perspective, belong to "the LORD" alone, it is highly likely that this exalted Christology predates not only the letters, but also the mission in Thessaloniki itself.

3. The Holy Spirit. The Holy Spirit is much less prominent in the Thessalonian letters—πνεῦμα occurs 5x in unambiguous reference to the Holy Spirit—than either God the Father (θεός, 54x; πατήρ, 8x) or the Lord Jesus Christ (κύριος, 46x; Ἰησοῦς, 29x; Χριστός, 20x in various combinations).[79]

---

[79] Cf. G. D. Fee, *God's Empowering Presence: The Holy Spirit in the Letters of Paul* (Peabody: Hendrickson, 1994), 40 who identifies six references to the Spirit: 1 Thess 1:5, 6; 4:8; 5:19; 2 Thess 2:2, 13.

Nevertheless, the Holy Spirit is closely associated with the work of the God the Father and the Lord Jesus, and he is clearly included with them in the identity of the one true God.

Indeed, already in these early letters, the contours of Paul's more fully developed doctrine of the Spirit may be clearly seen. The Thessalonians' conversion is attributed to God's work by his Spirit: the gospel came to them "not only in word, but also in power and in the Holy Spirit and with full conviction" (1 Thess 1:5) so that they "received the word," despite persecution, "with the joy of the Holy Spirit" (1 Thess 1:6). Likewise, the ongoing work of God in the Thessalonian community is attributed to the Spirit: God chose them to be saved "through sanctification by the Spirit and belief in the truth" (2 Thess 2:13); to disregard apostolic instruction regarding sexual immorality is to disregard "God, who gives his Holy Spirit to you" (1 Thess 4:8); and the church is commanded to "not quench the Spirit" (1 Thess 5:19).

The Thessalonian letters do not, of course, present a fully-developed Nicene doctrine of the Trinity. Nevertheless, the extent to which these two very brief and very early Christian letters present the one true and living God of Israel in proto-trinitarian terms should not be missed. The God who is at work through the gospel to save his people is a tri-une God. His actions as Father, Son, and Spirit provide the only hope for salvation in the face of sin, suffering, and death (see esp. 2 Thess 3:13-15; 1 Thess 1:2-10).

(c) The Hope of the Gospel: The Coming of the Lord Jesus Christ

The eschatology of the Thessalonian letters has excited as much interest—and created as much confusion—in the scholarly literature as it seems to have done among the Thessalonian believers.[80] Whatever else we might say about the striking eschatological vision presented in these letters, there is no doubt that its focal point is the personal coming and presence of the Lord Jesus Christ. The Lord Jesus, the apostolic trio announce, will "come" (ἔρχομαι: 2 Thess 1:10), "descend" from heaven (καταβαίνω: 1 Thess 4:16), and stage a "kingly arrival" (παρουσία: 2 Thess 2:1, 8; 1 Thess 2:19; 3:13; 4:15; 5:23).[81] This will be his "revelation" (ἀποκάλυψις: 2 Thess 1:7), or "manifestation" (ἐπιφάνεια: 2 Thess 2:8) on the "day of the Lord" (ἡ ἡμέρα τοῦ κυρίου: 2

---

[80] See especially now P. G. R. de Villiers, "In the Presence of God: The Eschatology of 1 Thessalonians," in Jan G. van der Watt, ed., *Eschatology of the New Testament and Some Related Documents* (Tübingen: Mohr [Siebeck], 2011), 302-32; de Villiers, "The Glorious Presence of the Lord: The Eschatology of 2 Thessalonians," in Watt, *Eschatology*, 333-61; D. Luckensmeyer, *The Eschatology of First Thessalonians* (Göttingen: Vandenhoeck & Ruprecht, 2009).

[81] The Thessalonian correspondence provides the first extant evidence of Christian use of the term παρουσία for Jesus' future advent, which may imply that the term (but not necessarily the concept) was coined by Paul (cf. R. H. Gundry, "The Hellenization of Dominical Tradition and Christianization of Jewish tradition in the Eschatology of 1–2 Thessalonians," *NTS* 33 [1987]: 162-69). Outside 1 and 2 Thessalonians, Paul employs the term παρουσία in this way only at 1 Cor 15:23.

Thess 1:10; 2:2; 1 Thess 5:2, 4, 5, 8). The Thessalonians, therefore, may be described as those who "turned to God . . . to wait for his Son from heaven" (ἐκ τῶν οὐρανῶν: 1 Thess 1:9-10). In these terms the two short letters furnish no less than seventeen unambiguous references to Jesus' final advent (cf. also 1 Thess 1:3; 2 Thess 2:14). The eschatological horizon of the Thessalonian letters is thus filled with the future or second coming of Jesus.[82]

This emphasis on Jesus' final advent has often been explained as a rush of "initial imminent eschatological fervor" later abandoned by the apostle Paul.[83] The evidence of the later letters, however, demonstrates that Paul never lost sight of Jesus' final advent.[84] The prominence of Jesus' future return in the Thessalonian letters, and the specific form it takes, is best explained, therefore, not by theories of radical development in Paul's theology, but by the dynamic interaction between the missionaries' Scripturally-rooted and Christ-centered theology, and the polemical and pastoral contexts of the letters. In what follows we explore this dynamic interaction via five observations regarding the apostolic teaching on Jesus' final advent in the Thessalonian letters.

First, the apostolic expectation that the Lord Jesus will "come" is rooted in the "coming of God" tradition of Israel's Scriptures.[85] This tradition simultaneously looks back to the great theophany at Sinai (Exod 19:7-20), and forward to the great and final "coming" of God to judge his enemies and vindicate his people (e.g. Ps 96:13; 98:9; Isa 40:1-11; 52:7-10; 66:12-16; Mic 1:3-4; Zech 14:1-9; Mal 3:1-5). It is closely associated with the prophetic expectation of the coming "day of the LORD" (יום יהוה),[86] and is further developed in the later Jewish literature.[87] The whole complex is, indeed,

---

[82] The explicit language of a "second coming" as distinct from a "first coming" does not appear in Christian sources until Justin Martyr in the second century (*1 Apol.* 52.3; *Dial.* 14.8; 32.3; 36.1; 40.4; 45.4; 49.2, 7; 52.1, 4; 53.1; 54.1; 69.7; 110.2, 5; 111.1; 121.3). The closest New Testament analogue is found at Heb 9:28: Christ "will appear a second time" (ἐκ δευτέρου). Nevertheless, the idea that Christ will come again is ubiquitous in the Pauline letters, as it is elsewhere in the NT.

[83] Most recently, P. Foster, "The Eschatology of the Thessalonian Correspondence: An Exercise in Pastoral Pedagogy and Constructive Theology," *JSPL* 1.1 (2011): 57; cf. C. L. Mearns, "Early Eschatological Development in Paul: The Evidence of I and II Thessalonians," *NTS* 27 (1981): 157.

[84] Clear references to the future advent of Jesus in the later Pauline letters include 1 Cor 1:7; 4:5; 11:26; 15:23; 16:22; Phil 3:20; Col 3:4; 1 Tim 6:14; 2 Tim 4:1, 8; Tit 2:13. References to "the day" of the Lord/Christ are probably also significant here. See Rom 2:16; 1 Cor 1:8; 5:5; 2 Cor 1:14; Phil 1:6, 10; 2:16; 2 Tim 4:8. cf. J. D. G. Dunn, *The Theology of Paul the Apostle* (Grand Rapids: Eerdmans, 1998), 313.

[85] On this theme, see esp. T. F. Glasson, "Theophany and Parousia," *NTS* 34 (1988): 259-70; E. Adams, "The Coming of God Tradition and its Influence on New Testament Parousia Texts," in C. Hempel and J. M. Lieu, eds., *Biblical Traditions in Transmission: Essays in Honour of Michael A.Knibb* (Leiden: Brill, 2006), 1-19.

[86] See esp. Isa 13:6, 9; 58:13; Jer 46:10; Ezek 13:5; 30:3; Joel 1:15; 2:1, 11, 31; 3:14; Amos 5:18, 20; Obad 15; Zeph 1:7, 8, 14; Mal 4:5. The two traditions are directly related at Zech 14:1-5 and Mal 3:1-2; cf. also *T. Mos.* 10.3-10.

[87] Cf. *2 Bar.* 48.39; *L.A.B.* 19.12-13; *1 En.* 1.2-9; 25.3; 90.15-17; 91.7; 100.4; 102.1-3; *2 En.* 32.1; *Jub.* 1.27-28; *Liv. Pro.* 13; *T. Abr.* 13.4; *T. Mos.* 10.3-10; *T. Levi* 8.11; *T. Jud.* 22.2; Sir 16:18-19.

nothing more than an outworking of the central covenant promise: "I will be your God and you will be my people, and I will dwell among you" (e.g. Exod 6:7; 29:45-46; Lev 26:12). In a world where the sovereign rule of the LORD God of Israel is contested and opposed, the prophets proclaim that God will again come down to establish his kingdom, judge his enemies, and vindicate his people.

The Thessalonian correspondence, however, takes this tradition in an unprecedented direction by declaring, without explanation or apology, that the "coming of the LORD" God is to be embodied in the future advent of the risen Lord Jesus. Thus, at 2 Thess 1:6-10, the apostolic trio employ OT texts that speak of the coming of the LORD God to announce the future advent of the Lord Jesus: he will be revealed from heaven "in blazing fire" (2 Thess 1:8; cf. Isa 66:15) with "his mighty angels" (2 Thess 1:7; cf. Zech 14:5); he will come "to be glorified in his saints" (2 Thess 1:10; cf. Ps 88:8 LXX [= Eng. 89:7]; Isa 49:3; so also 2 Thess 1:12 with Isa 66:5) and "marveled at among all who have believed" (2 Thess 1.10; cf. Ps 67.36 LXX [= Eng. 68:35]); he will "repay" those who "do not obey" the gospel (2 Thess 1:6, 8; cf. Isa 66:4, 6, 15), and these will suffer punishment "from the presence of the Lord (Jesus) and from the glory of his might" (2 Thess 1:9; cf. Isa 2:10, 19, 21). The great and final "day of the LORD" (2 Thess 1:10; 2:2; 1 Thess 5:2, 4, 5, 8) is therefore now centered on the "coming of our Lord Jesus Christ" (2 Thess 2:1).

The same phenomenon is evident in 1 Thessalonians. At 1 Thess 3:13 Zechariah's vision of the "coming of the LORD my God and all the holy ones with him" (Zech 14:5) is seen to reach its fulfilment in the "coming of the Lord *Jesus* with all *his* holy ones." Likewise, at 1 Thess 4:16-17, the promise that "the Lord himself will descend" (καταβήσεται) recalls the LORD's "descent" on Mount Sinai (Exod 19:11, 18, 20; 34:5 LXX: καταβαίνω),[88] when he came in "clouds" (1 Thess 4:17; Exod 19:9, 16), and with the sound of a "trumpet" (1 Thess 4:16; Exod 19:16, 19) to "meet" his people (1 Thess 4:17; Exod 19:17). Indeed, the apostolic proclamation here also evokes both the prophetic expectation that the LORD will "come down" again, just as he did at Sinai, to bring judgment and salvation (Mic 1:3; Isa 64:1-3) and the Danielic theophany in which the "Ancient of Days . . . comes" in judgment to vindicate the "son of man" who "comes" to him on the "clouds" (1 Thess 4:17; Dan 7:13-14, 18, 22, 27). In all of this, the apostolic trio never merely repeat the Scriptural data, but—as we will see—pass it through the filter of Jesus' own eschatological teaching, and rework it around Jesus himself, to show how all the hopes of Israel will reach their climax when *he* comes again.

---

[88] The verb καταβαίνω became the standard LXX translation of the Hebrew ירד in later allusions to the Sinai theophany (2 Sam 22:10; Ps 18:9; Neh 9:13; Ps 144:5; Mic 1:3). It is significant, therefore, that 1 Thess 4.16 is the only instance in the NT where the same verb is applied to the future "coming" of Christ. Since the word was not commonly used to speak of Christ's future advent, the choice of it here most likely reflects a deliberate allusion to the "descent" of the Lord at Sinai.

Second, this remarkable application of the "coming of God" tradition to Jesus is not arbitrary, but is grounded in Jesus' historic achievement as Israel's Messiah. For Paul and his companions, Jesus' future παρουσία as Lord is nothing more than the ultimate manifestation of his *messianic* victory, won at the resurrection.[89] There was in Second Temple Judaism no expectation that the Davidic Messiah, the son of God, should come *once* and then, after an interval, come *again* a second time. It was scarcely even imaginable that, having been crucified, the Messiah should come again "in glory" and "from heaven."[90] The apostolic trio, however, emphasize that the one who is to come is none other than the historical person Jesus, who was killed in Judea, and rose again (1 Thess 2:15-19; cf. 2 Thess 1:7; 2:1, 8; 1 Thess 1:10; 3:13; 5:23). It was Jesus' resurrection that made all the difference. Interpreted through the lens of Ps 110:1 and Dan 7:13-14, Jesus' resurrection allowed him who was crucified to be recognized as the enthroned Messiah, the Lord seated at the LORD's right hand, and thus the "Son" who will descend "from heaven" (1 Thess 1:10, ἐκ τῶν οὐρανῶν; cf. 2 Thess 1:7; 1 Thess 4:16, ἀπ' οὐρανοῦ) in "glory" (2 Thess 1:9, τῆς δόξης τῆς ἰσχύος αὐτοῦ). Once this was recognized, all the prophesies of a glorious messianic advent could be applied to Jesus' future coming. Accordingly, at 2 Thess 2:8 the apostolic trio proclaim that Jesus is the messianic "stump of Jesse" who at his future coming will destroy his enemies "with the breath of his mouth" (2 Thess 2:8; cf. Isa 11:4 with Ps 33:6 and Isa 30:27-28). Jesus' resurrection thus provides the crucial basis for the apostolic conviction that the crucified Messiah will come again as Lord.

This connection between Jesus' messianic identity and future παρουσία has, however, often been missed. Indeed, it is often asserted that the *only* Jewish background for early Christian "second coming" expectation is to be found in the "coming of God" and "day of the LORD" traditions.[91] What this reading misses, however, is that the application of the "coming of God" tradition to Jesus is grounded in the prior recognition that, through his resurrection, Jesus has been exalted to heaven to reign as Messiah at the Father's right hand (cf. 1 Cor 15:25; Rom 1:4; 8:34; Eph 1:20; Col 3:1 with Ps

---

[89] Cf. P. Ware, "The Coming of the Lord: Eschatology and 1 Thessalonians," *ResQ* 22 (1979): 111-12; Wanamaker, Thessalonians, 87.

[90] Cf. J. A. T. Robinson, *Jesus and His Coming: The Emergence of a Doctrine* (2nd ed.; London: SCM, 1979), 142; B. Witherington III, *Jesus, Paul and the End of the World: A Comparative Study of New Testament Eschatology* (Downers Grove: IVP, 1992), 178.

[91] T. F. Glasson, *The Second Advent: The Origin of the New Testament Doctrine* (3rd rev. ed.; London: Epworth, 1963), 176: "Jesus comes not because He is the Christ, but because He is Lord"; cf. Glasson, "Theophany and Parousia," 267: "He comes with angels to judge not because he is Messiah but because he is Lord"; R. J. Bauckham, *Jude, 2 Peter* (Waco: Word, 1983), 97: "much early Christian thinking about the parousia did not derive from applying OT messianic texts to Jesus but from the direct use of OT texts about the coming of God"; N. T. Wright, *Surprised by Hope: Rethinking Heaven, the Resurrection, and the Mission of the Church* (London: SPCK, 2007), 142: "Paul and the other writers regularly refer to 'the Day of the Lord,' and now of course they mean it in the Christian sense: 'the Lord' here is Jesus himself. In this sense, and in this sense only, there is a solid Jewish background for the Christian doctrine of the 'second coming' of Jesus."

110:1). Jesus' future coming as Lord is certain only because he has already been enthroned, by his resurrection, as Christ.

Third, the apostolic teaching regarding Jesus' final advent in the Thessalonian letters is not only rooted in the Scriptures and centered on Jesus' resurrection as Messiah, it is also clearly shaped by Jesus' own eschatological teaching. This is evident in both letters. In 2 Thessalonians, the coming of the "lawless one" to "deceive" through "signs and wonders" (2 Thess 2:9), while rooted in the Scriptural warning from Deut 13:1-3, has also been shaped by Jesus' teaching about the rise of "false messiahs and false prophets" who will come with "signs and wonders" before the end (Matt 24:24/Mark 13:22). In 1 Thessalonians, likewise, the declaration that the Lord will descend from heaven, call his people with the voice of an archangel and a trumpet, and gather them to himself on the clouds (1 Thess 4:16-17) most likely echoes not only Exodus 19 and Daniel 7, but also Jesus' application of the latter prophecy to himself in the saying about the "son of man" sending out his angels to gather the elect (Matt 24:30-31/Mark 13:26-27).[92] Similarly, the sudden arrival of the "day of the Lord . . . like a thief in the night . . . as labor pains on a pregnant woman" (1 Thess 5:2-4) draws not only on Jeremiah 6,[93] but probably also on Jesus' parable about the "thief" (Luke 12:39-40/Matt 24:43-44; cf. 2 Pet 3:10; Rev 3:3; 16:15), his eschatological sayings about "birth pains" (Matt 24:8/Mark 13:8), and his warnings about "sudden . . . destruction" from which there is no escape (Luke 17:26-27/Matt 24:37-39; Luke 21:34-36). Finally, the exhortation to be "awake and sober" as people who "belong to the day" (1 Thess 5:4-8) echoes Jesus' teaching in two parables closely related to the parable of the thief, namely those of the watchmen (Luke 12:36-38/Matt 24:42/Mark 13:34-7) and the steward (Luke 12:41-48/Matt 24:45-51).[94] In all of these instances the apostolic trio do not simply quote the Jesus tradition verbatim, but interpret both Israel's Scriptures and the "word of the Lord" (1 Thess 4:15) through the lens of the gospel (1 Thess 4:14), in order to apply them to the pastoral situation in Thessaloniki.[95]

---

[92] C. M. Tuckett, "Synoptic Tradition in 1 Thessalonians?" in R. F. Collins, ed., *The Thessalonian Correspondence* (Leuven: Peeters, 1990), 177-80 questions this connection on the basis that Matt 24:30-31/Mark 13:26-27 do not mention resurrection, which is "the key point of Paul's argument". In response, S. Kim, "The Jesus Tradition in 1 Thess 4:13–5.11," *NTS* 48 (2002): 234-35 plausibly suggests that Paul most likely considered the gathering of the elect to presuppose the resurrection of the dead, especially given the prominence of resurrection in the Danielic tradition on which Jesus' saying depends (Dan 12:1-3; cf. also John 5:27-29 which similarly connects the son of man's "voice" with "resurrection"). Cf. Witherington, *Thessalonians*, 133-37 who suggests that Paul here "combines a saying of Jesus with his own reflections on Dan 7:13-14 and 12:2-3" (135).

[93] G. K. Beale, *1–2 Thessalonians* (Leicester: IVP, 2003), 142 notes Jer 6.14: "saying 'peace, peace' when there is no peace" (cf. Jer 8:1; Ezek 13:10); Jer 6:24: "pain like that of a woman in labor;" 6:26: "suddenly the destroyer will come upon us;" and 6:4-5: "Let us attack at night."

[94] Cf. D. Wenham, *Paul: Follower of Jesus or Founder of Christianity?* (Grand Rapids: Eerdmans, 1995), 308-12.

[95] The "word of the Lord" at 1 Thess 4:15 has been variously interpreted as: (1) A pre-Easter *verbum Jesu*; (2) a post-Easter prophetic revelation; (3) the gospel of Jesus' death and resurrection. For a review of the literature, see M. W. Pahl, *Discerning the "Word of the Lord": The "Word of the Lord" in 1 Thessalonians 4:15* (London: T. & T. Clark, 2009), 6-34. All

Fourth, while the expectation of Christ's return in the Thessalonian letters is rooted in Israel's Scriptures, centered on the historic achievement of Messiah Jesus in his resurrection, and shaped by Jesus' own teaching, it is also cast in language designed to radically subvert Roman imperial claims.[96] At 1 Thess 1:9-10 Paul and his companions report how the Thessalonians had "turned to God . . . to wait for his Son from heaven." In doing so, they pit Jesus against Augustus, the deified "son" of the divine Julius Caesar,[97] who was in the first century widely believed, by virtue of his *apotheosis*, to be ruling the world from the heavens in the presence of his father.[98] The apostolic trio speak further of the "hope of salvation . . . through our Lord Jesus Christ" (1 Thess 5:8-9; cf. 1 Thess 1:3) and so directly challenge the claims of the Roman emperor to provide "hope" as the "savior" of the known world.[99] Similarly, at 1 Thess 2:12 the missionaries speak of God calling the Thessalonians into his kingdom, and thus implicitly contrast the kingdom of God with the Roman empire. At 1 Thess 5:2-3, moreover, they evoke the Augustan slogan "peace and security" (εἰρήνη καὶ ἀσφάλεια; Lat. *pax et securitas*) to show that the "day of the Lord" will bring sudden destruction on those who trust in the false peace and security provided by Rome.[100] Further,

---

things considered, it seems best to understand "the word of the Lord" here as a reference to Jesus' own teaching, interpreted in the light of both Scripture and the gospel message. For this understanding see Witherington, *Thessalonians*, 135.

[96] On this theme, see especially Harrison, "Imperial Gospel," 82-93; cf. N. T. Wright, "Paul's Gospel and Caesar's Empire," in Richard A. Horsley, ed., *Paul and Politics: Ekklesia, Israel, Imperium, Interpretation: Essays in Honor of Krister Stendahl* (Harrisburg: Trinity Press International, 2000), 160-83.

[97] For Augustus as, "son of god" see: *Inscriptiones latinae selectae* (*ILS*) 107, 113; *Corpus inscriptionum latinarum* (*CIL*) XI 0367; *Supplementum epigraphicum graecum* (*SEG*) XI 922-23; P.Ryl. 601; *Papiri Greci e Latini, Pubblicazioni della Societa italiana* (*PSI*) 1150; P.Tebt. 382; P.Oslo 26; *Sammelbuch griechischen Urkunden aus Ägypten* (*SB*) 8824; 8897. Discussion in T. H. Kim, "The Anarthrous υἱὸς θεοῦ in Mark 15:39 and the Roman Imperial Cult," *Biblica* 79.2 (1998): 225-36.

[98] For the heavenly rule of Augustus, see: Seneca, *Apol.* 8; *Oct.* 477-91, 504-33; *Clem.* 1.10.3-1.11.4; Manilius, *Astron.* 1.7-10, 384-86, 800-803, 915-16, 925-26; 4.551-52, 932-35, and *Insc. lat. sel.* 137. For discussion see Harrison, "Imperial Gospel," 93-95. It is significant, however, that there is no suggestion in the Roman imperial propoaganda that Augustus would ever "return" from the heavens to rule again on the earth.

[99] For the widespread application of "salvation" language to the Julio-Claudians from Augustus onwards, see W. Foerster and G. Fohrer, "σῴζω, σωτηρία, σωτήρ σωτήριος," *TDNT* 7:965-1024; J. Schneider and C. Brown, "Redemption," *NIDNTT* 3:205-21. For "hope", the sestertius minted by Claudius in A.D. 41 is particularly significant, in that it mentions "the hope of Augustus" (*Spes Augusti*). Discussion in M. E. Clark, "Images and Concepts of Hope in the Imperial Cult," in H. K. Richards, ed., *Society of Biblical Literature 1982 Seminar Papers* (Atlanta: Scholars Press, 1982), 39-43.

[100] The terms "peace" (Gk. εἰρήνη; Lat. *pax*) and "security" (Gk. ἀσφάλεια; Lat. *securitas*) were an important part of Roman imperial propaganda, and regularly appear (separately) on imperial coins (C. H. V. Sutherland and R. A. G. Carson, *The Roman Imperial Coinage* [rev. ed.; London: Spinks & Son, 1984] [= RIC], I.26, 38, 252, 253, 476) 38, 252, 253, 476) and monuments, esp. the "Altar of Peace" (*Ara Pacis*) 9 B.C., as well as in literary descriptions of the Julio-Claudian age (Ovid, *Ex Ponto* 2.5.18: "peace of Augustus;" Philo, *Legat.* 147: Augustus is "the guardian of the peace;" Martial, *Epigrams* 7.80.1; Tacitus, *Ann.* 12.29: "Roman peace;" Augustus, *Res Gestae* 12.2: "Augustan peace"). Significantly, the terms appear together as a

at 2 Thess 2:8 they speak of the "appearance" (ἐπιφάνεια) of Christ at his "coming" (παρουσία) using terms that were often applied to Roman rulers in the first century.[101]

Most striking of all, however, is the passage at 1 Thess 4:13-17 where Paul and his companions present the future advent of Jesus in what amounts to nothing less than a frontal assault on Roman imperial propaganda. To begin with, they speak of Jesus as "the Lord" (ὁ κύριος), and thus not only include him within the identity of the one true God of Israel, but also set him in direct competition with the Roman *princeps* (later emperor) who, from the time of Augustus onwards, could be honored (at least in the Mediterranean East) as the supreme Lord (κύριος) of the known world.[102] In addition, they speak of Jesus' "arrival" (παρουσία), using a term which not only described the "coming" of God in some Jewish texts,[103] but more prominently referred in the Greco-Roman world to the arrival of an emperor or other high-ranking dignitary in a city.[104] Moreover, they describe the "meeting" (ἀπάντησις) of the Lord and his people using a term which—especially in association with παρουσία[105]—could refer to the welcome extended by the citizens of a town to a visiting emperor or dignitary.[106]

---

description of the blessing of Roman rule in a number of important inscriptions and texts: *SEG* XLVI 1565; *CIL* 14, 2898-2899; *ILS* 3787-3788; *OGIS* 613; Josephus, *A.J.* 14.247-248; Velleius Paterculus, *Hist.* 2.98.2; 2.103.3-5; Tacitus, *Hist.* 2.12; 3.53; 4.74; Plutarch, *Ant.* 40.4. See J. A. D. Weima, "'Peace and Security' (1 Thess 5:3), Prophetic Warning or Political Propaganda?" *NTS* 58.3 (2012): 331-59.

[101] For παρουσία, see below. For ἐπιφάνεια: (1) *I.Eph.* II.251 has Julius Caesar as "god manifest" (θεὸν ἐπιφανῆ); (2) likewise Ernst Kalinka et al., eds., *Tituli Asiae Minoris* (Vienna: Hoelder, Pichler, Tempsky, 1901–) (= TAM), ii.760c and P.Oxy. 7 (1910), 1021.2 both have Claudius as "god manifest" (θεὸν ἐπιφανῆ). See S. R. F. Price, "Gods and Emperors: The Greek Language of the Roman Imperial Cult," *JHS* 104 (1984): 86; G. H. R. Horsley, *New Documents Illustrating Early Christianity* (vol. 4; Sydney: Macquarie University Ancient History Documentary Research Centre, 1987), §52.

[102] (1) Augustus: P.Oxy. 1143; (2) Tiberius and Livia: *OGIS* 606; Caligula: Aurelius Victor, *Caes.* 3; (3) Claudius: P.Oxy. 37; (4) Nero: P.Oxy. 246; SIG^2 376, 814; Deissmann ostraca 22, 23, 24, 25, 36a, 37, 39, 76 (in P. M. Meyer and A. Deissmann, *Griechische texte aus Ägypten, herausgegeben und erklärt* [Berlin: Weidmann, 1916]); Acts 25.26. Cf. discussion in Deissmann, *Light*, 351-57.

[103] *T. Jud.* 22.2; Josephus, *A.J.* 3.80; 9.55; *2 Bar.* 55:6; cf. 2 Pet 3:12 and *2 En.* 32:1 which speaks of God's "second coming" after his first visitation at creation (*2 En.* 58:1).

[104] For Hellenistic usage, see *BDAG* 2b, 780-81; cf. discussion in Deissmann, *Light*, 368-73. Examples of Roman imperial παρουσία language include: (1) Germanicus: *SB* I.3924, 34; (2) Nero: Latin adventus (= παρουσία) coins: *RIC* 95-97, 130-36, 371, 386-88, 429, 489-92, 564-65; cf. SIG^3 814; (3) Titus: Josephus, *B.J.* 7.100; (4) Hadrian: Latin adventus coins: *RIC* 224-27, 315-20, 374, 740-42, 793-94, 872-907; cf. *Bulletin de Correspondance Hellénique* 25 (1901): 275.

[105] The two terms (ἀπάντησις and παρουσία) appear together, for example, in Josephus' description of the entry of Alexander III ("the Great") to Jerusalem (*A.J.* 11.327-28).

[106] E.g. Cicero, *Att.* 8.16.2; 16.11.6; Josephus, *B.J.* 7.100. For this reading, see esp. E. Peterson, "Die Einholung des Kyrios," *ZST* 7 (1930): 682-702 (cf. already Chrysostom, *Homilies on 1 Thessalonians* 8 [*NPNF* 13:356]). Peterson's reading was challenged by J. Dupont, *SUN XRISTWI: L'union avec le Christ suivant saint Paul* (Bruges: Nauwelaerts, 1952), 66-73 who argued that Sinai theophany imagery provides a sufficient explanation for the language. For a comprehensive review of the ensuing debate, see Luckensmeyer, *The Eschatology of First*

In all of this, the apostolic trio directly challenge the realized eschatology of the Roman imperial gospel which served to legitimate the status quo.[107] Rome proclaimed Augustus (and his heirs) as "Lord," "Savior," and "son of god." The παρουσία of the Roman ruler and his representatives was celebrated in the provinces with great pomp and ceremony, for it was he who had brought "salvation," "peace," "security," and "hope" to the world.[108] Paul and his companions, by contrast, proclaim the present rule of the crucified and risen Lord Jesus, and announce the hope of his future παρουσία, when he will descend from heaven (1 Thess 4:16), execute wrath on the enemies of his people (2 Thess 1:5-10; 2 Thess 5:8; 1 Thess 1:10; 5:9), and bring lasting peace, salvation, and life in his presence to all who belong to him (1 Thess 2:19; 3:13; 4:17; 5:9-10, 23). In doing so, the apostolic trio not only redraw the monotheistic claims of Israel's Scriptures around Jesus they also bring them to bear, with striking polemical force, in the Greco-Roman world. Jesus, rather than Caesar, is the one true Lord of all.[109]

Fifth and finally, the significance of all of this for a fledgling Christian community subject to persecution should not be missed. It is, indeed, no accident that of Paul's seven uses of παρουσία ("arrival," "presence") for the future advent of Jesus, six occur in these letters to the Thessalonian churches (2 Thess 2:1, 8; 1 Thess 2:19; 3:13; 4:15; 5:23; cf. 1 Cor 15:23), where persecution by the Roman-sponsored city authorities had caused such trouble. The apostolic trio comfort the Thessalonians by declaring that Jesus' eschatological παρουσία will have opposite results for his people and their enemies. The wicked will receive "eternal destruction" from the presence of the Lord (2 Thess 1:8-9; cf. Isa 2:10, 19, 21),[110] but believers will enjoy that presence (2 Thess 1:10; 2:1; 1 Thess 4:17; cf. 1 Thess 2:19; 3:13; 4:17). The

---

Thessalonians, 260-68. In the end, there is no need to decide between Sinai/theophany imagery and Hellenistic ἀπάντησις patterns. Like so much of Paul's language in the Thessalonian correspondance, his description of the final advent in 1 Thess 4:13-18 is best understood as rooted in the Scriptures of Israel, and speaking (polemically) into the Greco-Roman world of the first century.

[107] J. R. Harrison, "Paul, Eschatology and the Augustan Age of Grace," *TynB* 50.1 (1999): 83-90; Harrison, "Imperial Gospel," 88-95.

[108] A prime example is provided by the Priene inscription (*OGIS* 2.458) which celebrates the "glad tidings" (εὐαγγέλια) of Augustus, who by his "appearance" (ἐπιφάνεια) as "savior" (σωτήρ) has brought "peace" (εἰρήνη) and "hope" (ἐλπίς). See also further examples in Harrison, "Imperial Gospel," 89-93.

[109] On the integration of Scripture, gospel, and counter-imperial polemics in Paul's letters, see esp. Wright, "Gospel and Empire," 182-83.

[110] Most English translations render the ἀπό in 2 Thess 1:9 with the sense of separation. The wicked will suffer eternal dustruction, "shut out from" (NIV), "separated from" (NRSV), "away from" (ESV) the presence of the Lord. Against this reading, however, it should be noted that in Isaiah 2, which manifestly provides the language here (Isa 2:10, 19, 21), the presence of the LORD is the source of the destruction coming on the wicked. For this reason, the preposition ἀπό at 2 Thess 1:9 should be rendered with a simple "from" to indicate that the "eternal destruction" of the wicked "comes from" the presence of the LORD. See C. L. Quarles, "The APO of 2 Thess 1:9 and the Nature of Eternal Punishment," *WTJ* 59 (1997): 201-11.

wicked will suffer "wrath" (1 Thess 2:16),[111] but believers will be rescued from it (1 Thess 1:10; 5:9).

In particular, not even death will ultimately be able to separate the Lord's people from his glorious presence. At 1 Thess 4:13-18 the apostolic trio explain that when the Lord Jesus descends, the dead will be raised so that all of Christ's people together will be "caught up in the clouds to meet the Lord in the air," and thus be "always . . . with the Lord" (1 Thess 4:6-17).[112] The connection made here between the "coming of the Lord" and the final resurrection has deep roots in Israel's Scriptures (cf. Isa 25:7-9; 26:19-21). Nevertheless, this passage is the first Christian text to connect the resurrection of God's people with the final advent of the Lord *Jesus* (cf. 1 Cor 15:23; Phil 3:20-21). Indeed, the real innovation here is the apostolic presentation of Jesus' resurrection as the prototype for the resurrection of his people: just as God raised Jesus from the dead so, through Jesus, God will also raise those who have died (1 Thess 4:14; cf. 1 Thess 5:10).[113] The purpose of all of this, it must be stressed, is to comfort the Thessalonians in their grief at the loss of some of the members of their community. Far from missing out on the life of the age to come, "those who have fallen asleep" will be raised first (1 Thess 4:16).[114] The Thessalonians, therefore, need not "grieve as others do who have no hope" (1 Thess 4:13). Instead they should "encourage one another" with the hope of the gospel (1 Thess 4:18; 5:11).

It should be clear, then, that there is no need to explain away the remarkable emphasis on Jesus final advent in these letters as a rush of "initial eschatological fervor" later abandoned by Paul. The prominence of Jesus'

---

[111] This fate will be shared by the "man of lawlessness" (2 Thess 2:8), whose identity is much debated. Given the evidence surveyed above, it is difficult to discount a reference to the Roman authority, through whom Paul sees Satan at work (2 Thess 2:9; cf. 1 Thess 2:18; 3:5), even if the Roman authority is only a prototype of the figure ultimately described here. For a helpful review of the options and insightful discussion, see esp. Green, *Thessalonians*, 300-325.

[112] The final destination of the Lord and his people is not made explicit in this text. Luckensmeyer, *The Eschatology of First Thessalonians*, 266 is correct to note that Paul's concern was to provide a "solution to the concrete problem of grief" rather than a fully developed eschatology. Nevertheless, contra J. Plevnik, "1 Thessalonians 4.17: The Bringing in of the Lord or the Bringing in of the Faithful?" *Biblica* 80.4 (1999): 537-46, three considerations strongly suggest that Lord's people are called to meet the Lord "in the air" in order to escort him back to the (re-)new(ed) earth: (1) Paul elsewhere emphasizes the terrestrial nature of the gospel hope when he speaks of the coming of Lord "from heaven" (1 Cor 15:20-28; Phil 3:20-21), the resurrection of "the body" (1 Cor 15:35-58), and the liberation of the entire created order (Rom 8:18-25); (2) the consistent biblical promise is that LORD will come to dwell with his people in a renewed heavens and earth (e.g. Exod 29:45-46; Lev 26:12; Isa 40:1-11; 52:1-10; 66:15; Ezek 43:1-5; 48:35; Zech 14:5; Rev 21:1-5); (3) the parallels with Hellenistic παρουσια and ἀπάντησις traditions suggest that an escort back to earth is evisaged (see above).

[113] Most English translations take διὰ τοῦ Ἰησοῦ ("through Jesus") as modifying the substantive participle τοὺς κοιμηθέντας ("the ones who have fallen asleep") and thus translate the phrase "God will bring with Jesus those who have fallen asleep in him" (NIV 2011). The translation cited above (ESV) is, however, to be preferred. The phrase διὰ τοῦ Ἰησοῦ ("through Jesus") modifies the verb ἄξει ("will bring") and thus makes Jesus the agent through whom God will bring the dead. Cf. Fee, *Thessalonians*, 172; contra Witherington, *Thessalonians*, 133.

[114] Contrast 2 Esd 13:24 which states that those who are alive at the end are more blessed than those who die before it arrives.

final advent in 1 and 2 Thessalonians is best explained by the dynamic interaction between, on the one hand, the apostle's Scripturally-rooted and Christ-centered theology, shaped by the teaching of Jesus himself and, on the other hand, the Thessalonian situation, to which this teaching was applied with pastoral sensitivity and polemical daring. These factors together provide ample explanation for both the prominence of the παρουσία in the Thessalonian letters, and the striking terms in which it is expounded.[115]

2.5. The Gospel Call to Live the Christian Life: The City within a City

Finally, and more briefly, the Thessalonian letters show how the gospel of hope calls the Thessalonians to live as an alternative society, a city within a city, demonstrating to the onlooking world the good news of the kingdom of God. The members of the fledgling messianic community at Thessaloniki were evidently still coming to grips with the significance of their new faith and its implications for their lives (1 Thess 1:9-10; 4:1-12). The apostolic trio, therefore, root their eschatological teaching in the Scriptures of Israel and the words of Jesus in order to deconstruct the Greco-Roman value system so prevalent in Thessaloniki, and to replace it with one grounded in the Creator God of Israel, and centered on the gospel of his Son, the Lord Jesus Christ.[116]

Within this new framework, Paul and his companions provide a brief, but remarkably full, account of the distinctive Christian life in community. They call the Thessalonians to faithfulness in marriage (1 Thess 4:1-8) and to brotherly love (1 Thess 4:9-10), as they work with their hands so as to "walk properly before outsiders and not be dependent on anyone" (1 Thess 4:11-12). They show, further how the gospel enables them to grieve with hope (1 Thess 4:13; 5:8) as they walk in faith and love confident in their salvation (1 Thess 5.6-10).[117] Finally, the apostolic trio provide an inspiring vision of Christian life and mission in community, as they exhort the Thessalonians to honor their leaders (1 Thess 5:12), to live at peace (1 Thess 5:13), to "admonish the idle" while also patiently "helping the weak" (1 Thess 5:14), to persist in "doing good . . . to one another and to everyone" (1 Thess 5:15) as they lead joy-filled, prayerful, thankful lives, overflowing with love by the power of the Spirit (1 Thess 5:16-22; cf. 3:11-13).[118] Indeed, one of the primary purposes of the pronounced eschatological emphasis we have explored above is to call the Thessalonians to a holy and blameless life in anticipation of the blessing they will receive at the coming of the Lord (1 Thess 3:11-13; 5:23-24).

---

[115] Cf. the similar assessment in R. F. Collins, "From παρουσία to ἐπιφάνεια: The Transformation of a Pauline Motif," in C. W. Skinner and K. R. Iverson, eds., *Unity and Diversity in the Gospels and Paul: Essays in Honor of Frank J. Matera* (Early Christianity and Its Literature 7; Atlanta: SBL, 2012), 299.

[116] Cf. Witherington, *Thessalonians*, 140.

[117] Indeed, the familiar Pauline triad of faith, hope, and love appears in these letters for the first time (1 Thess 1:3; 5:8; cf. 1 Cor 13:13; Col 1:4-5) as a characteristic description of the Christian life.

[118] On the Spirit here see Fee, *Empowering Presence*, 55-62.

The primary issue, however, on which the apostolic trio provide instruction is that of idleness. It appears that some in the Christian community in Thessaloniki were refusing to work for their bread (2 Thess 3:6-15; 1 Thess 4:11-12; 5:14). It has often been assumed that the source of this problem was a kind of over-realized eschatology: the belief that the "day of the Lord" was imminent, or had already arrived, had led some to abandon all work.[119] It is significant, however, that the apostolic trio never explicitly connect their instruction on the issue of idleness with their eschatological teaching. It seems just as likely, therefore, that the problem of idleness at Thessaloniki was unrelated to the eschatological confusion in the church.[120] Indeed, a strong case can be made that the primary target of the apostolic instruction is the patronage system which dominated ancient Mediterranean cultures.[121] In this system it was common for wealthy patrons to maintain a retinue of clients in return for political support.[122] Where this system continued within the church it could easily breed factionalism and division. Where Thessalonian believers remained the clients of unbelieving patrons, they could easily find their faith in Christ compromised by their prior obligations. The apostolic trio therefore call the Thessalonians to imitate their own practice: just as they worked to support themselves, so they expect the church to build a community upon principles of self-sufficiency and equity (2 Thess 3:7-10). Rather than spending their time as "busybodies" (2 Thess 3:11), engaged in political intrigue promoting the interests of their patrons by effusive praise in the public arena, the apostolic trio urge the Christians to "aspire to live quietly, and to mind your own affairs, and to work with your hands . . . so that you may walk properly before outsiders and be dependent on no one" (1 Thess 4:11-12). Indeed, Paul and his companions seek to imbue the Thessalonians with a vision of the church as a benefactor to the city, doing good in Jesus name, and overflowing in generosity towards those outside the community (2 Thess 3:13; 1 Thess 5:15).[123] The apostolic teaching on the idleness issue was, therefore, designed to call the Thessalonians out of the web of destructive reciprocal obligations involved in the Greco-Roman patron-client system, and to the kind of self-sufficiency that would allow to church to do good in the world.

---

[119] For an extended presentation of this widely assumed position, see especially Jewett, *Thessalonian Correspondence*, 159-78.
[120] Cf. Witherington, *Thessalonians*, 32-33
[121] See especially Winter, *Seek the Welfare of the City*, 41-60.
[122] See, for example, Juvenal, *Satires* I.V which provides a satirical window on patron-client relationships in the Roman world.
[123] Winter, *Seek the Welfare of the City*, 30-35, 58 demonstrates that the language of "doing good" at 2 Thess 3:13 (καλοποιοῦντες) and 1 Thess 5:15 (τὸ ἀγαθὸν διώκετε) would be readily recognized as "benefaction language" in the Greco-Roman world.

3. Conclusion

1 and 2 Thessalonians are among the earliest, and therefore most significant, documents for mapping the history and beliefs of the early church, especially Paul. They document the earliest Christian conviction that Jesus of Nazareth is the one in whom all the hopes and expectations of Israel reach their fulfilment. They record the way in which this very Jewish message first addressed the polytheistic cultures of the Greco-Roman world. They reveal much about the pastoral heart and collegial practice that shaped Paul's apostolic ministry. And they provide, for the first time, a brief but remarkably comprehensive vision of Christian life in community as a life of faith, hope, and love (1 Thess 1:3; 5:8).

More than all of this, however, as some of the oldest Christian texts in existence, these two letters preserve the heart of the Christian gospel in its earliest form. Together, 1 and 2 Thessalonians reveal that within twenty years of Jesus' crucifixion in Jerusalem, the apostolic trio could announce in distant Thessaloniki that Jesus, the Jewish Messiah, "died for us" (1 Thess 5:10), that he was "raised from the dead" so that "we might live together with him" (1 Thess 1:10; 5:10), that he is now ruling in heaven as the Son of the Father (1 Thess 1:10), and that he will come again in glory as Lord to judge the living and the dead (2 Thess 1:6-10; 1 Thess 4:13-17). These letters, moreover, present this gospel as the means by which the Creator, the one living and true God of Israel (1 Thess 1:9), is at work in his world, by his Holy Spirit (1 Thess 1:5-6; 4:8), to bring salvation (2 Thess 2:13; 1 Thess 5:8-9) to those from all the nations who trust in his Son (1 Thess 2:16). Stated in this way, it is abundantly clear that all of the major threads of Paul's theology, and of the orthodox Christian faith that later wove them together, are already laid out here in these very early letters to the church in Thessaloniki.

Recommended Reading

Best, E. *The First and Second Epistles to the Thessalonians*. London: Adams & Charles Black, 1972.
Bruce, F. F. *1 and 2 Thessalonians*. Waco: Word, 1982.
Donfried, Karl P. "The Cults of Thessalonica and the Thessalonian Correspondence." *New Testament Studies* 31.3 (1985): 336-56.
Donfried, Karl P., and J. Beutler, eds. *The Thessalonians Debate: Methodological Discord or Methodological Synthesis?* Grand Rapids: Eerdmans, 2000.
Fee, G. D. *The First and Second Letters to the Thessalonians*. Grand Rapids: Eerdmans, 2009.
Gundry, R. H. "The Hellenization of Dominical Tradition and Christianization of Jewish tradition in the Eschatology of 1–2 Thessalonians." *New Testament Studies* 33 (1987): 161-78.
Harrison, J. R. *Paul and the Imperial Authorities at Thessalonica and Rome: A Study in the Conflict of Ideology*. Wissenschaftliche Untersuchungen zum Neuen Testament 2.273. Tübingen: Mohr (Siebeck), 2011.
Jewett, R. *The Thessalonian Correspondence: Pauline Rhetoric and Millenarian Piety*. Philadelphia: Fortress, 1986.

Judge, E. A. "The Decrees of Caesar at Thessalonica." *Reformed Theological Review* 30 (1971): 1-7.
Kim, S., "The Jesus Tradition in 1 Thess 4:13–5:11." *New Testament Studies* 48 (2002): 225-42.
Luckensmeyer, D. *The Eschatology of First Thessalonians*. Göttingen: Vandenhoeck & Ruprecht, 2009.
Malherbe, A. J. *The Letters to the Thessalonians: A New Translation with Introduction and Commentary*. Anchor Bible 32B. New York: Doubleday, 2000.
Nicholl, C. R. *From Hope to Despair in Thessalonica: Situating 1 and 2 Thessalonians*. Cambridge: Cambridge University Press, 2004.
De Villiers, P. G. R. "In the Presence of God: The Eschatology of 1 Thessalonians." Pages 302-32 in *Eschatology of the New Testament and Some Related Documents*. Edited by Jan G. van der Watt. Wissenschaftliche Untersuchungen zum Neuen Testament 2.315. Tübingen: Mohr (Siebeck), 2011.
De Villiers, P. G. R. "The Glorious Presence of the Lord: The Eschatology of 2 Thessalonians." Pages 333-61 in *Eschatology of the New Testament and Some Related Documents*. Edited by Jan G. van der Watt. Wissenschaftliche Untersuchungen zum Neuen Testament 2.315. Tübingen: Mohr (Siebeck), 2011.
Wanamaker, C. A., *The Epistles to the Thessalonians: A Commentary on the Greek Text*. Grand Rapids: Eerdmans, 1990.
Witherington, B., III. *1 and 2 Thessalonians: A Socio-Rhetorical Commentary*. Grand Rapids: Eerdmans, 2006.

12. The Later Pauline Letters: Ephesians, Philippians, Colossians, and Philemon

Ian K. Smith

The four letters reviewed in this chapter are normally called "prison letters" or "captivity epistles" as the author regularly refers to his imprisonment (Eph 3:1, 13; 4:1; 6:20; Phil 1:7, 13, 14, 16; Col 4:3, 10, 18; Phlm 1, 9, 10, 23). The major theme of these letters is that the church as a community, as well as Christians as individuals, need to work out the practical and everyday implications of what it means to be united with Christ in his death and resurrection. Christians are to be those who reflect the reconciliation and new life achieved in these Easter events. Common among the recipients was the pressure of being a Christian in the world of the Roman Empire. Within this context, Paul is concerned that Christians, whose faith centers on the death and resurrection of Jesus, live out the faith which will be evidenced by their ethical standards within society. The application of the Christian gospel will impact every level of life, whether reconciliation between Jews and Gentiles within the church or an understanding of marriage, the family, and even of slavery. Through the centuries since these letters were written, they have been of great benefit to God's people, for although social circumstances have changed, the underlying premise of these letters remains: theology dictates practice.

Three of these letters (Ephesians, Colossians, and Philemon) were written to the context of churches in Asia Minor (modern day Turkey). The connections between these letters are apparent. Colossians and Philemon are written to Colossae; Ephesians and Colossians have strong similarities in structure, vocabulary, and content; Ephesians and Colossians wrestle with the question of how the Christian gospel impacts churches that are affected by a belief in mysticism with a focus on spiritual powers. Philippians, however, was addressed to a church in Macedonia and is more concerned with issues of Jewish legalism, similar to the issues discussed in Romans and Galatians. This may point to these churches facing different issues in different parts of the empire. Yet Ephesians, Philippians, and Colossians are all concerned with the same issue of Gentile incorporation into the church. The old division between Jews and Gentiles has been nullified through the ministry of Jesus; the dividing wall of hostility between Jews and Gentiles has been destroyed (Eph 2:14); there is no longer Greek or Jew, circumcised or uncircumcised (Col

3:11). Due to these similarities, and as shall be argued below, due to a belief that these letters were written from the same place at the same general time in the ministry of the apostle, we will not treat the letters in a piecemeal fashion as if they are unrelated. As far as possible we will consider them as a literary subset of the Pauline corpus of Scripture.

A true appreciation of these letters will only be achieved by placing them within their historical, socio-cultural, and literary contexts. The situation to which the letters were addressed was known to the writer and to the original readers, and so although at times there are explicit references to the situation, at other times there are only allusions. The task of the twenty-first-century reader is to piece together the clues that tell us something of the original situation. This process is known as "mirror reading," and its conclusions are not always accurate. It can be likened to listening to one side of a telephone conversation, a situation that can be either illuminating or deceiving, depending on the conclusions and inferences that are drawn. Significant background studies have taken place in Philippi and Ephesus, but Colossae has not been excavated since being destroyed by an earthquake in the first century. Care therefore needs to be taken in reconstructing the situation.[1]

We turn our attention to the critical issues concerning the historical context of these letters before addressing their content. The key historical issues to be resolved are who wrote these letters, to whom were they written and under what circumstances. There has been much debate on each of these issues. We commence with the issue of authorship.

1. Authorship

Each of the letters refers to Paul as the author (Eph 1:1; 3:1; Phil 1:1; Col 1:1, 23; 4:18; Phlm 1, 9, 19) and Timothy is also named in the opening of each of the letters except Ephesians. The mention of Timothy is normally taken as an indication that Timothy was with Paul when the letters were written, rather than Timothy being a co-author. The writer of these letters speaks in the first person singular "I" and Timothy is mentioned in the third person in Phil 2:19, 22. The mention of Timothy makes sense in the Letters to the Philippians and to the Ephesians as he is known to these people. Timothy accompanied Paul on the second missionary journey including the foundation of the church at Philippi. Furthermore, Acts 19:22 tells of how Paul sent Timothy from Ephesus to Macedonia (Acts 19:22), and there is mention of a visit by Timothy to Philippi in Acts 20:3-4. It is logical that Timothy be commissioned by Paul to go again to Philippi with the letter to the Philippians (Phil 2:19-23). We do not have an association of Timothy with Colossae, but neither do we know of a visit by Paul to that town.

---

[1] Jerry Sumney has extensively considered the issues of methodology in determining Paul's opponents in 2 Corinthians and in Colossians. See Jerry L. Sumney, *Identifying Paul's Opponents: The Question of Method in 2 Corinthians* (JSNTSup 40; Sheffield: JSOT Press, 1990); Jerry L. Sumney, "Those who 'Pass Judgment': The Identity of the Opponents in Colossians," *Bib* 74 (1993): 366-88.

Ian K. Smith

1.1. Philippians and Philemon

Of the four letters under discussion, scholars are generally in agreement that Paul is the author of Philippians and Philemon. Some have questioned Pauline authorship of Philippians, notably F. C. Baur,[2] but his doubts have not been sustained by later commentators.[3] Similarly Philemon is regarded as an undisputed Pauline epistle. C. H. Dodd writes of Philemon that the epistle "carries its authentication on its face. Nowadays, in fact, to reject it is a mere eccentricity of criticism."[4] Even P. N. Harrison, who denies Pauline authorship of Colossians, says of Philemon, "today not only Conservative but also Critical scholarship is practically solid in agreeing with Renan that 'only Paul could have written this little masterpiece.'"[5] Douglas Moo writes of Philemon, "the letter claims to be written by Paul (vv. 1, 19), and, in contrast to Colossians, there has been no serious challenge to this claim."[6]

1.2. Colossians and Ephesians

There is significant dispute, however, about the authorship of Colossians[7] and of Ephesians[8] and so we shall address these issues. It must be remembered that the authority of a Biblical text does not depend solely on identifying human authorship. No-one knows the identity of the author of Hebrews (despite numerous claims to knowledge) and the same anonymity is true of several sections of the Old Testament such as some of the psalms. Although, it must be remembered that unlike Hebrews and many of the Psalms, Colossians, and Ephesians are not anonymous; each claims Pauline authorship. Our issue, therefore, is not anonymity but pseudonymity.

The practice of composing a letter under the pseudonym of an influential person was not uncommon in the Greco-Roman world.[9] To what degree this

---

[2] F. C. Baur, *Paul: His Life and Works* (2 vols.; London: Williams and Norgate, 1875), 2.45-79.
[3] See Peter T. O'Brien, *The Epistle to the Philippians: A Commentary on the Greek Text* (Grand Rapids: Eerdmans, 1991), 9-10.
[4] C. H. Dodd, "Ephesians," in Frederick Carl Eiselen, E. Lewis, and David G. Downey, eds., *The Abingdon Bible Commentary* (Nashville: Abingdon-Cokesbury, 1929), 1221-37 (1223).
[5] P. N. Harrison, "Onesimus and Philemon," *ATR* 32 (1950): 268-94 (270).
[6] Douglas J. Moo, *The Letters to the Colossians and to Philemon* (Grand Rapids: Eerdmans, 2008), 361.
[7] For more information see Ian K. Smith, *Heavenly Perspective: A Study of the Apostle Paul's Response to a Jewish Mystical Movement at Colossae* (LNTS 326; London: T. & T. Clark, 2006), 6-16. See also Moo, *The Letters to the Colossians and to Philemon*, 29 n. 5.
[8] See H. W. Hoehner, *Ephesians: An Exegetical Commentary* (Grand Rapids: Baker Academic, 2002), 6.
[9] Frank S. Thielman, *Ephesians* (Grand Rapids: Baker Academic, 2010), 1. See B. M. Metzger, "Literary Forgeries and Canonical Pseudepigrapha," *JBL* 91, (1972): 3-24 (9-10), who comments, "Among the several kinds of literary forgeries in antiquity, arising from diverse motives, that of producing spurious epistles seems to have been most assiduously practiced. There is scarcely an illustrious personality in Greek literature or history from Themistocles down to Alexander, who was not credited with more or less extensive correspondence." See also P. A. Rosenmeyer, *Ancient Epistolary Fictions: The Letter in Greek Literature* (Cambridge: Cambridge University Press, 2001), 191-233.

pseudonymity was intentionally deceptive is a matter of debate. There is evidence of second-century forgeries such as the supposed Pauline letter to the Laodiceans.[10] However, there is no reason to believe that people in the first-century Roman world were any more tolerant of forgeries than we are today.[11]

Doubt about Pauline authorship of Ephesians and Colossians is multifaceted. Some have argued that the theology is too advanced to have been written in the apostle's lifetime. The theological emphases in these letters are said to represent "early Catholicism," especially the teachings on Christology with an emphasis on Christ's exaltation, on ecclesiology with emphasis on its unity with Christ as the head, and on eschatology which is more realized than earlier Pauline epistles. Such conclusions are built on the supposition that we can determine when doctrinal formulations arose. Furthermore, they do not take into account the particular nature of the situation Paul was addressing in Asia Minor, which differed from issues in other areas of the empire.[12]

The two principal quantifiable objections are: the language and style are different from the undisputed Pauline epistles, and the nature of the interdependence of Ephesians and Colossians. We will discuss these in greater detail.

On the first issue of language and style, both Ephesians and Colossians have very long sentences. Although the current punctuation of the Greek text of the New Testament is the work of later editors, the following sections of Ephesians could each be seen as one sentence: 1:3-14, 15-23; 2:1-7; 3:1-7; 4:11-16; 6:14-20.[13] Similarly in Colossians, in 2:8-15 one statement is loosely joined to the preceding one so that an unwieldy structure emerges; similarly 3:5-11 is a long sentence. In 1:3-23 "relative clauses, inserted causal phrases, participial phrases, and secondary notes inflate the sentence to a degree that its form almost collapses."[14]

The vocabulary of Colossians and of Ephesians differs from words Paul uses in other letters. In Colossians there are thirty-four words that appear

---

[10] See Thielman, *Ephesians*, 2, and B. M. Metzger, *The Canon of the New Testament: Its Origin, Development and Significance* (Oxford: Oxford University Press, 1987), 307. For a recent discussion of the authenticity of the Pauline corpus see Stanley E. Porter, "Paul and the Process of Canonization," in Craig A. Evans and Emanuel Tov, eds., *Exploring the Origins of the Bible: Canon Formation in Historical, Literary, and Theological Perspective* (Grand Rapids: Baker, 2008), 173-202.

[11] See Thielman, *Ephesians*, 2, 3. See also T. L. Wilder, *Pseudonymity, The New Testament, and Deception: An Inquiry into Intention and Reception* (Lanham: University Press of America, 2004), 35-73.

[12] See discussions of this in Moo, *The Letters to the Colossians and to Philemon*, 32-36; Peter T. O'Brien, *The Letter to the Ephesians* (Grand Rapids: Eerdmans, 1999), 21-33.

[13] The earliest manuscripts of the New Testament do not have punctuation, hence there are different interpretations about how to divide up sentences. For statistics and methodology of determining sentence length see A. Van Roon, *The Authenticity of Ephesians* (Leiden: Brill, 1974), 107 n. 3.

[14] See Smith, *Heavenly Perspective*, 10. Lohse notes that there are several instances of heavily laden sentences in Paul, to the point that he becomes almost incomprehensible (e.g. Gal 2:3-5, 6-9; Rom 1:1-7; 2:5-10, 14-16; 3:23-26). Eduard Lohse, *Colossians and Philemon: A Commentary on the Epistles to the Colossians and to Philemon* (Philadelphia: Fortress, 1971), 89.

nowhere else in the New Testament (*hapax legomena*) and twenty-eight words that do appear elsewhere in the New Testament but not in the other Pauline letters, ten words which are in common only with Ephesians, and fifteen words that appear in Colossians and Ephesians as well as the rest of the New Testament but not in the other Pauline letters.[15] In addition there are forty-one *hapax legomena* in Ephesians and a further eighty-four words that are found in Ephesians but nowhere else in Paul's writings.[16] Such statistics, however, do not produce water-tight conclusions. Galatians, a letter of a similar length to Ephesians, has thirty-five *hapax legomena* and yet its Pauline authorship is not disputed.[17]

The arbitrary nature of using style and vocabulary as a measure of authorship is usually discounted because of the circular nature of the arguments. For example, several scholars have denied the authenticity of Pauline authorship of Colossians because of the absence of particularly Pauline words such as ἁμαρτία (sin), δικαιοσύνη (righteousness), νόμος (law), πιστεύω (believe), σῴζω (save). These arguments seem convincing until one notices that all of these words appear in Ephesians, and yet many of the same scholars deny Pauline authorship of this epistle as well.[18]

The statistics of vocabulary need to take into account other variables, such as the education and linguistic facility of the author. In view of Paul's Pharisaic and Rabbinic education (Acts 22:3; Phil 3:5) it is not surprising that he could draw on a large pool of vocabulary. Vocabulary would be further expanded by the use of an amanuensis, a practice used by Paul in other letters (e.g. Rom 15:22) and implied in Col 4:18. An amanuensis may have had some input into the formation of sentences and the choice of vocabulary.[19] It is nowhere claimed that Paul used the same amanuensis for each of his letters.

We turn our attention to the second area commonly quoted when referring to doubt concerning Pauline authorship of Ephesians and of Colossians, namely: interdependence of Colossians and Ephesians.

The similarity between Colossians and Ephesians has often been noted. Both letters begin with a common introduction: Παῦλος ἀπόστολος Χριστοῦ Ἰησοῦ (Paul, an apostle of Christ Jesus) and conclude in a way similar to other Pauline letters: ἡ χάρις μεθ' ὑμῶν (grace be with you [Colossians]); ἡ χάρις μετὰ πάντων (grace be with all [Ephesians]). Other examples of Pauline style can be seen in the thanksgiving prayer (Col 1:3-8; Eph 1:15-23); the relationship between the indicative and the imperative in the paraenetic statements (e.g. Col 3:5-17; Eph 4:25–5:17); the use of statements about the contrast between the old and new person (Col 3:5-17; Eph 4:22-32). For this reason F. C. Baur asserts: "there can be no doubt of this, that the two (Colossians and Ephesians) are so much interwoven that they must stand or

---

[15] See a list of these words in Lohse, *Colossians and Philemon*, 85-86.
[16] O'Brien, *Ephesians*, 5.
[17] O'Brien, *Ephesians*, 6.
[18] For a more extended list see Lohse, *Colossians and Philemon*, 86-87.
[19] E. Randolph Richards, *The Secretary in the Letters of Paul* (WUNT 2.42; Tübingen: Mohr [Siebeck], 1991), 201.

The Later Pauline Letters

fall together in their claim to apostolic origin,"[20] although this opinion is not universally held.

Due to these similarities, several scholars have argued for a Pauline letter that pre-dates Colossians and Ephesians, which becomes the primitive source for the final form of the two letters, both of which are post-Pauline.[21] Such studies, however, are far from conclusive. When scholars seek to identify the original "Pauline" source of the letters, their conclusions are not uniform. Holtzmann sees the authentic Pauline sections of Colossians as 1:9b-12, 14-24, 26-28; 2:2b-3, 7a, 9-11, 15, 17-19, 22b; 3:1, 2, 4-11, 14-16, 18-25; 4:1, 9, 15-17;[22] whereas Masson sees them as 1:1-4, 7, 8; 2:6, 8, 9, 11a, 12a, 16, 20, 21; 3:3, 4, 12, 13a, 18-22a, 25; 4:1-3a, b, 5-8a, 9-12a, 14, (15), 17, 18.[23] This divergence shows the subjectivity of the task.

In favor of Pauline authorship of Ephesians and of Colossians, the relationship of Colossians to Philemon has been one of the strongest arguments. The two letters are concerned with the church in Colossae. The list of greeters in the two letters is very similar: Epaphras (Col 1:7; 4:12; Phlm 23), Aristarchus (Col 4:10; Phlm 24), Mark (Col 4:10; Phlm 24), Demas (Col 4:14; Phlm 24), and Luke (Col 4:14; Phlm 24). Both letters mention the sending of Onesimus (Col 4:9; Phlm 12) and have special words for Archippus (Col 4:17; Phlm 2).[24] This similarity points to the same author, namely Paul.

If we begin from the starting point of Pauline authorship, as clearly stated in the texts, there appears to be insufficient evidence to disprove this clear attestation to authorship within the four letters. On Ephesians, which is the "most disputed" of the four letters,[25] H. W. Hoehner has done an interesting statistical analysis of the significant scholarly exegetes of Ephesians throughout the history of the church. His findings are that those who agree with Pauline authorship outnumber those who disagree with it, hence his

---

[20] Baur, *Paul: The Apostle of Jesus Christ*, 2.44.
[21] Heinrich Julius Holtzmann, *Kritik der Epheser- und Kolosserbriefe: auf Grund einer Analyse ihres Verwandtschaftsverhältnisses* (Leipzig: Wilhelm Engelmann, 1872), 104-21. Charles Masson, *L'Epître de Saint Paul aux Colossiens* (CNT 10; Neuchâtel: Delachaux et Niestlé, 1950), 86, 159. Harrison argues that Colossians was completed by the author of Ephesians, namely Onesimus of Colossae. From word statistics he contends that the original Pauline letter consists of 1:1-6a, 6c-9a, 26–2:2a, 5, 6; 3:2-13, 17–4:18 (about half the current letter). He claims that 1:6b, 9b-25; 2:2b-4, 7–3:1; 3:14-16 are later interpolations. P. N. Harrison, *Paulines and Pastorals* (London: Villiers, 1964).
[22] Holtzmann, *Kritik der Epheser- und Kolosserbrief*, 104-21, as summarized in Lohse, *Colossians and Philemon*, 90.
[23] Masson, *L'Epître de Saint Paul aux Colossiens*, 159.
[24] Eduard Lohse has suggested that a disciple of Paul formed the list of greetings (Col 4:7-18) from names and information he found in Philemon is unconvincing, especially if, as Lohse suggests, Colossians is written as late as A.D. 80, fifteen years after Paul's death! Eduard Lohse, *The Formation of the New Testament* (Nashville: Abingdon, 1972), 92-93.
[25] Philippians and Philemon are normally regarded by critical scholars as "Pauline," Colossians as "disputed", and Ephesians as "deutero-Pauline." See David G. Meade, *Pseudonymity and Canon: An Investigation into the Relationship of Authorship in Jewish and Earliest Christian Tradition* (Grand Rapids: Eerdmans, 1986), 139-57, for a discussion of the pseudonymity of Ephesians.

conclusion that it is *not* the vast majority of critical scholars who disagree with Pauline authorship of the letter.[26]

We shall work on the assumption that all four letters, Ephesians, Philippians, Colossians, and Philemon, were written by the Apostle Paul. Most scholars see Colossians as prior to Ephesians,[27] and this conclusion will be argued below. Where and when Paul wrote these letters needs further discussion.

2. Provenance

As has been stated above, Paul was imprisoned at the time of writing these epistles (Eph 3:1, 13; 4:1; 6:20; Phil 1:7, 13, 14, 16; Col 4:3, 10, 18; Phlm 1, 9, 10, 23). Acts records three imprisonments of the apostle: in Philippi (16:23-40), in Caesarea (24:22–26:32), and in Rome (28:17-31). Of these three places, Philippi can be discounted as the origin of any epistle. Not only would it be an unlikely source for the Letter to the Philippians, but the night was so filled with activity (an earthquake, an attempted suicide, hymn singing followed by an evangelistic encounter, and a household baptism) that there would be little time left for letter writing! There is, however, no need to limit Paul's imprisonments to the three incarcerations mentioned in Acts. In 2 Cor 11:23 Paul states, "Are they ministers of Christ? I am talking like a madman—I am a better one: with far greater labors, far more imprisonments, with countless floggings, and often near death." This raises the prospect of more imprisonments than those mentioned in Acts, and several New Testament scholars have raised the possibility of an imprisonment at Ephesus (discussed below). This has led to three main theories for the provenance of these captivity epistles: Rome, Ephesus, and Caesarea.

There are good reasons to argue that Ephesians, Colossians, and Philemon were written from the same place, and that that place was Rome.[28] Both the Letter to the Colossians and the Letter to the Ephesians were entrusted to the same envoy: Tychicus (Col 4:7-8; Eph 6:21-22). The list of companions who send greetings in Col 4:10-14 and Phlm 23-24 is nearly identical (Aristarchus, Mark, Epaphras, Luke, and Demas are mentioned in both lists; Jesus Justus is only mentioned in Colossians). When we look at the fellow workers

---

[26] Hoehner, *Ephesians*, 6.
[27] A. T. Lincoln concludes his discussion on the interrelationship of the two letters by stating, "What has emerged from this overview is the dependence of Ephesians on a prior Colossians in terms of its overall structure and sequence, its themes, and its wording. Yet what is also absolutely clear is that this is a free and creative dependence, not a slavish imitation or copying." Andrew T. Lincoln, *Ephesians* (WBC 42; Dallas: Word, 1990), lv. Similarly James D. G. Dunn states, commenting on the similarities between Ephesians and Colossians, "this feature is best explained by Ephesians being written using Colossians as a kind of template (so most scholars)." James D. G. Dunn, *The Epistle to the Colossians and to Philemon: A Commentary on the Greek Text* (Grand Rapids: Eerdmans, 1996), 36. For the opposite view that Colossians presupposes Ephesians see J. Coutts, "The Relationship of Ephesians and Colossians," *NTS* 4 (1957–1958): 201-7.
[28] Moo, *The Letters to the Colossians and to Philemon*, 42.

mentioned in Colossians and in Philemon, Aristarchus accompanies Paul to Rome (Acts 27:2), as does John Mark (1 Peter 5:13 [interpreting Babylon as a reference to Rome]). Luke accompanies Paul to Rome (note the use of the first person plural in Acts 27:1–28:16), but not to Ephesus (see below for the discussion on an Ephesian provenance). In Colossians and Ephesians, Paul is writing on similar issues to churches in the same geographical area. As will be argued below, the Letter to the Ephesians may be general instructions sent to several churches, prompted by a more specific issue having arisen in Colossae.

Rome has been identified through the centuries as the most likely place for the writing of the captivity epistles and continues today to be the most widely attested theory.[29] Philippians gives us several clues to a Roman provenance. Paul was in a place where a trial could result in his death (1:19-20; 2:17) or acquittal (1:25; 2:24). As Paul was a Roman citizen, this seems to point to Rome. The Roman imprisonment described in Acts 28:30-31 indicates a form of arrest which allowed visitors to come and go which accords with what we read in the captivity Epistles. Paul is in contact with his co-workers while in prison (Col 4:7-14; Phlm 23-24) and has the freedom to proclaim the gospel (Eph 6:19-20; Col 4:3-4; Phil 1:12, 13). It could be argued that such a high level of freedom was inconsistent with someone being tried for a capital offence. However, when one considers the charges brought against Paul, namely a civil disturbance resulting from allowing Greeks into the Jerusalem temple (Acts 21:27-36), such a freedom is not inconsistent; this issue was of little concern to those in Rome as Paul did not bring a major threat to Roman society.

In Philippians Paul makes mention of the praetorium (1:12). The Greek word πραιτώριον can mean "palace guard" or "military headquarters". It is more likely that the term means "military headquarters," for it is "unlikely that Roman prisoners would be incarcerated in the emperor's own residence."[30] There is also a reference to "those of Caesar's household" (4:22), which need not be restricted to the Emperor's family or relatives, but may also refer to the large number of people, usually slaves or freedmen, who staffed the imperial civil service. They were scattered throughout the empire, but a large concentration of such people were found in Rome.[31]

A comparison between Philippians and Paul's Letter to the Romans produces some interesting results by contrasting the reference to Caesar's household in Phil 4:22 and the greetings in Rom 16:3-16. The household of Narcissus (Rom 16:11) may be among those from Caesar's household (Phil 4:22). Claudius Narcissus was a wealthy freedman under the Emperor Tiberius, but was executed after the accession of Nero in A.D. 54. This resulted in Narcissus' goods, including his slaves, being confiscated and made the property of the Emperor. These slaves would have been distinguished

---

[29] For a list of modern defenders of a Roman provenance see Moo, *The Letters to the Colossians and to Philemon*, 42 n. 37.
[30] M. Bird, *Colossians and Philemon* (Eugene: Cascade, 2009), 14.
[31] O'Brien, *Philippians*, 554.

from others in Caesar's household by the designation *Narcissiani*.[32] Furthermore, J. B. Lightfoot has suggested that the household of Aristobulus (Rom 16:10) may be a reference to the grandson of Herod the Great and the brother of Herod Agrippa I (referred to in Acts 12:1), and who is referred to by Josephus as a friend of the Emperor Claudius (*A.J.* 20.13).[33] It was not uncommon for a person to bequeath their slaves to the Emperor. We have no evidence of Aristobulus having done so, but if he had, his slaves would have been part of Caesar's household and designated *Aristobuliani*. This scenario is hypothetical and does not ultimately prove a link, but is an interesting possibility which gives a bit more weight to the theory of a Roman provenance for Philippians.

The arguments for a Roman provenance, however, are not universally held. Rome was not the only place in the empire to have a praetorium; one existed in Caesarea (Acts 23:35) and another in Jerusalem (Matt 27:27; Mark 15:16; John 18:28, 33; 19:9; Acts 23:35). We do not have evidence of a praetorian guard in the capital of a senatorial (rather than imperial) province of Asia, namely Ephesus.

When Paul was arrested in Jerusalem (Acts 21) and shut away in prison in Caesarea (Acts 23, 24), one could easily imagine that this was the end of his ministry, especially as this imprisonment dragged on for two years (Acts 24:27). Paul, however, could speak of his imprisonment being for the advancement of the gospel (Phil 1:12, 13). If Philippians was written from Caesarea, this imprisonment and the length of the imprisonment served to thrust the gospel into high levels of Roman society. Two Roman governors, Felix and Festus, along with King Herod Agrippa and their wives heard Paul speak about faith in Christ Jesus (Acts 24:24-27; 25:1–26:32). One of these governors, Felix, over a span of two years, often sent for Paul to converse with him (Acts 24:26). If Philippians was written from Rome, not only were there all these previous results from his earlier imprisonment at Caesarea, but Christ was also being declared at the center of the empire.

On the basis of a palace guard at Caesarea, J. A. T. Robinson suggests that Paul was in Caesarea at the time of writing the captivity epistles, thereby dating them in A.D. 58.[34] This view, however has not gained great acceptance, although some still hold to it as the origin of some of the captivity epistles.[35] At the time of the Caesarean imprisonment, the apostle was consumed by his desire to visit Rome, but this does not come out in the Philippian letter, in

---

[32] F. F. Bruce, *Philippians* (NIBC 11; Peabody: Hendrickson, 1983), 158.

[33] Aristobulus, with his brothers Agrippa (the later Agrippa I) and Herod (of Chalcis), was educated in Rome. For the argument plausibly identifying the two Aristobuli, see J. B. Lightfoot, *Saint Paul's Epistle to the Philippians* (London: Macmillan, 1913), 174-75. Cf. C. E. B. Cranfield, *Romans 9–16* (Edinburgh: T. & T. Clark, 1979), 791-92.

[34] J. A. T. Robinson, *Redating the New Testament* (London: SCM, 1976), 60-85.

[35] See for example B. Reicke, *Re-examining Paul's Letters: The History of the Pauline Correspondence* (Harrisburg: Trinity Press International, 2001), 73-102, who argues for a Caesarean provenance for Ephesians, Colossians, and Philemon but a Roman provenance for Philippians.

which he expresses a desire to return to Philippi (2:24).[36]

The major problem with Rome being the place of Paul's writing is its distance from the intended recipients of the letters. The Philippian letter refers to at least three items of correspondence between Paul and Philippi prior to Philippians: when the Philippians heard that Paul was imprisoned; when Paul received a gift through Epaphroditus (2:25, 4:18); and when the Philippians received news that Epaphroditus had fallen ill (2:26).[37] Some scholars argue that there is not enough time for this travel to have been completed prior to Paul penning Philippians if Paul was in Rome.[38] A trip between Rome and Philippi is a distance of 1200 kilometres (740 miles) over land and a two day trip across the Adriatic Sea, which would have taken between four and seven weeks.[39] Similar objections can be made against Caesarea, which is a similar distance from Philippi. These arguments are not convincing. With the traditional dating of the Roman imprisonment (A.D. 60–62), there is enough time for three return trips from Rome. Furthermore it is quite likely that the Philippians would have known of Paul's appeal to the Roman Emperor even before Paul arrived in Rome. They could have sent a gift with Epaphroditus at this stage, prior to Paul's arrival in Rome. Furthermore, Epaphroditus could have fallen ill during the journey to Rome which would have required much less time for the message to get back to Philippi. It is therefore possible to fit these journeys into a period of less than six months. Even with the maximum possible timeframe for the trips, they can certainly be accommodated within a timeframe of less than a year.[40] The most likely provenance for Philippians, therefore, is Rome, and, because of the trips between Philippi and Rome, the letter is probably to be dated towards the end of Paul's time of imprisonment there, possibly A.D. 61–62.

The distance from Rome to Ephesus and Colossae is even greater than the distance to Philippi. There was regular sea travel from Rome to Ephesus, Ephesus being a major "transport hub" in the first-century Roman world. D. H. French notes that the administrative center of the province was Ephesus and the paved roads started there and radiated outwards as "demonstrated by the high number of milestones . . . Mileages were measured from the *caput viae,* Ephesus."[41] From Ephesus it is less than 195 kilometers (120 miles) to

---

[36] Moisés Silva, *Philippians* (Grand Rapids: Baker Academic, 2005), 7.
[37] Some have argued for as many as five trips, although this is unlikely. For more detail see Gordon D. Fee, *Paul's Letter to the Philippians* (Grand Rapids: Eerdmans, 1995), 277 n. 28.
[38] See George S. Duncan, *St. Paul's Ephesian Ministry: A Reconstruction with Special Reference to the Ephesian Epistles* (London: Hodder and Stoughton, 1929). More recent proponents for an Ephesian provenance of Philippians include Frank S. Thielman, "Ephesus and the Literary Setting of Philippians," in Amy M. Donaldson and Timothy B. Sailors, eds., *New Testament Greek and Exegesis: Essays in Honor of Gerald F. Hawthorne* (Grand Rapids: Eerdmans, 2003), 205-23; Francis Watson, *Paul, Judaism, and the Gentiles: A Sociological Approach* (Cambridge: Cambridge University Press, 1986) 73-74.
[39] Silva, *Philippians*, 5 n. 5, for a discussion of travel times in the first century.
[40] Silva, *Philippians*, 6.
[41] D. H. French, "The Roman Road System of Asia Minor," *ANRW* II 7.2:698-729 (707). See also Clinton E. Arnold, *Power and Magic: The Concept of Power in Ephesians* (Grand Rapids: Baker, 1992), 13.

Colossae, the destination of both Colossians and of Philemon.[42]

Three journeys are assumed within Ephesians, Colossians, and Philemon: Epaphras' trip to Paul (Col 1:7-8); Onesimus' trip to Paul (Phlm 8-12); the trip of Tychicus to Ephesus and Colossae (Eph 6:22; Col 4:7-8).[43] There is also the trip of Onesimus to Colossae, which appears to have been at the same time as Tychicus' trip (Col 4:7-9; Phlm 12). In addition, there is Paul's expressed desire to visit Colossae in Phlm 22. The proximity of Colossae to Ephesus has resulted in a theory for an Ephesian provenance to these letters. Due to the circular nature of the Ephesian letter (argued below) it is not impossible that Ephesians was written in Ephesus. Although there is merit in many of these arguments, and it is hard to be overly dogmatic, the Ephesian hypothesis still lacks any evidence, whether textual, epigraphic or archaeological, of Paul being imprisoned in Ephesus.

The traditional view of a Roman provenance for these letters is more likely.[44] Onesimus, a runaway slave (the subject of Philemon), may have been attracted by the distance of Rome from Colossae,[45] as it minimized the possibility of him being found and returned to his master. The first two trips mentioned in the letters, that of Epaphras and that of Onesimus, are assumed to be prior to the sending of Colossians and Philemon respectively. Only one trip needs to be assumed from Rome to Asia Minor, that of Tychicus, the envoy of both the Letter to the Ephesians and the Letter to the Colossians (Eph 6:21-22; Col 4:7-8), accompanied by Onesimus (Col 4:7-9). A trip from Rome to Colossae would normally pass through Ephesus. It is probable that Tychicus carried both Ephesians and Colossians on the same voyage, delivering Ephesians *en route* to Colossae.[46]

We conclude that in the lack of any mention in the New Testament or in any other primary document of Paul being imprisoned in Ephesus, and due to the long tradition of Roman provenance and the internal evidence within the NT, it seems that Rome is the most likely provenance for all four letters under discussion in this chapter.

Once the place where the letters were written is determined, the dating of them is straightforward. If the letters came from Ephesus, they were written in the context of Paul's third missionary journey and are dated ca. A.D. 52–55. If the letter was written from the imprisonment in Caesarea recorded in Acts, the date is ca. A.D. 57–59, but if from Rome ca. A.D. 60–62. This is our preferred dating.[47]

---

[42] Note Col 4:9 which refers to Philemon's slave Onesimus as "one of you."

[43] Moo, *The Letters to the Colossians and to Philemon*, 44.

[44] For a list of modern scholars who assert a Roman provenance see Moo, *The Letters to the Colossians and to Philemon*, 42 n. 37.

[45] See S. Llewelyn, *New Documents Illustrating Early Christianity* (vol. 8; Grand Rapids: Eerdmans, 1998), 45.

[46] Moo, *The Letters to the Colossians and to Philemon*, 42.

[47] See O'Brien, *Philippians*, 19; Gerald F. Hawthorne, *Philippians* (WBC 43; Dallas: Word, 1983), xxxvi-xliv.

3. Destination

We now turn our attention to the destinations of the four captivity epistles. We shall look at Philippians first, followed by the letters addressed to the area of Asia Minor.

Philippi is in Macedonia and was named after Philip II, the father of Alexander the Great, who in 356 B.C. wrested the city from the Thracians. Macedonia became a part of the Roman Empire in 168–167 B.C. at the battle of Pydna.[48] Luke describes Philippi as a leading city in the district of Macedonia (Acts 16:11), however its distance of about sixteen kilometres (ten miles) from the port of Neapolis prevented it from achieving much importance and Roman administration settled in Amphipolis (Acts 17:1).

Philippi's significance in New Testament times lies in the fact that it was the site of a significant battle in 42 B.C. between the Republican forces of Brutus and Cassius and the imperial armies of Octavian (who later became the Emperor Augustus) and Mark Antony. Resulting from this victory, Octavian renamed Philippi *Colonia Augusta Julia Philippensis* and established it as a Roman colony for veterans from his victorious army. This resulted in not only the enlargement of the small settlement but ensured its allegiance to Rome. There was a further intake of soldiers into the new Roman colony after the defeat of Antony and Cleopatra at Actium by Octavian in 31 B.C. Due to these factors, by the time the Apostle Paul visited Philippi in A.D. 49 (Acts 16:11-15) it had become a site of significant Roman influence. Not only was it a Roman *colonia* but it also had the status of a *ius Italicum*, an area that was given the legal fiction of being on Italian soil. This meant there were certain tax exemptions, there was greater autonomy for citizens to be under direct Roman rule (rather than through a Hellenistic puppet king), Roman citizenship was bestowed on many people born in the city, and it would account for the presence of Roman officials in the city. Latin was the official language of Philippi, although it appears that Greek was more widely spoken. The apology that was given to Paul, a Roman citizen, after he was unjustly beaten in Philippi is due to this city's strong affiliation with Rome (Acts 16:35-39).

There is evidence of anti-Semitism in Philippi (cf. Acts 16:20). Paul's visit as recorded in Acts 16 is estimated at between A.D. 49 and A.D. 52.[49] In A.D. 49 the Emperor Claudius had taken steps to discourage the spread of Judaism which resulted in the expulsion of Jews from Rome. This may also have resulted in there being very few Jews in Philippi, a Roman *colonia*. When Paul arrived in Philippi in Acts 16, it appears there was no Jewish synagogue in that city and hence Lydia and some fellow Jews met by the river *outside the city* (Acts 16:13) each Sabbath. It was required that there be ten Jewish men to form a Jewish synagogue and the absence of even this number

---

[48] See J. E. Lendon, *Soldiers and Ghosts: A History of Battle in Classical Antiquity* (New Haven/London: Yale University Press, 2005), 193-211.
[49] For more detail on this see R. P. Martin, *New Testament Foundations: A Guide for Christian Students* (2 vols.; Grand Rapids: Eerdmans, 1978), 2.199-201.

of Jewish families in Philippi resulted in the riverside meeting each Sabbath morning. At this early stage of the development of Christianity, most Philippians would have seen Christianity as a sect of Judaism which would have resulted in hostility and persecution (Phil 1:28-30; 2:15). Furthermore, there appears to have been persecution from the small number of Jews in that city who saw Christians as a new heterodox sect. In this context, Paul calls upon the Philippians to stand firm (Phil 1:27; 2:16; 4:1) as they are a church undergoing trials (Phil 1:7).

In comparison to Philippi, there seems to have been a significant Jewish population in Colossae, a small town situated in Phrygia in the southern part of the Roman province of Asia in the Lycus Valley. The Jewish historian, Josephus, tells us that in the late third century B.C. Antiochus III brought two thousand Jewish families from Babylon and Mesopotamia and settled them in neighboring Lydia and in Phrygia in order to stabilize the region (*A.J.* 12.147-53). This re-population resulted in a significant Jewish population by the first century. These Jewish settlers had been granted land for homes, farming and viticulture, and exemptions from taxation to ensure their settlement became permanent.[50] It should be noted that on the day of Pentecost, Jews were gathered in Jerusalem from Asia and Phrygia (Acts 2:9-10). Colossae was thus a cosmopolitan town at the time of Paul, populated by both Jews and Gentiles.[51] It was probably the smallest town to which Paul wrote; it was overshadowed by nearby Hierapolis with its hot springs and Laodicea.

Colossae is not only the destination of Paul's Letter to the Colossians, but also of the Letter to Philemon. This letter concerns a runaway slave[52] named Onesimus who is identified in Phlm 10 and in Col 4:9 as a resident of Colossae. Four recipients are named in this letter: Philemon, Apphia, Archippus, and the church "in your house" (1-2). Whether the church met in the house of Philemon, or of Archippus, being the last named person in the list, is a matter of dispute.[53] The letter is primarily written to an individual, probably Philemon, as all the second person pronouns in vv. 1-22a and verbal forms in vv. 23-24 are singular.[54] However, it should also be noted that in v. 22b Paul uses to the second person plural for "your prayers" and similarly in v. 25 for "your spirit," indicating a broader audience at this point. Care should be taken with being too dogmatic in a distinction between private and public. As Douglas Moo asserts, "We may be injecting into the first-century Christian community a contrast of "private" versus "public" that was simply not present

---

[50] Paul Trebilco, *Jewish Communities in Asia Minor* (SNTSMS 69; Cambridge: Cambridge University Press, 1991), 6.
[51] For more detail see Smith, *Heavenly Perspective*, 3-6.
[52] For a discussion on first-century slavery in the Roman Empire, see Jennifer A. Glancy, *Slavery in Early Christianity* (Minneapolis: Fortress, 2006).
[53] J. Knox, *Philemon among the Letters of Paul* (London: Collins, 1960), 49-61 who asserts that it was Archippus, not Philemon, who was the owner of Onesimus and the prime person being addressed. For a discussion of this see Larry J. Kreitzer, *Philemon* (Sheffield: Sheffield Phoenix Press, 2008), 54-58.
[54] Moo, *The Letters to the Colossians and to Philemon*, 362.

there."[55]

The destination of the Ephesian letter has traditionally been seen as Ephesus. Ephesus was originally a Greek colony and by the time of the writing of this letter had become the capital of the Western province of Asia and was a busy commercial port.[56] It was also the headquarters of the cult of the goddess Artemis (also known by her Roman name of Diana), whose temple, after being destroyed in the middle of the fourth century B.C., had gradually been rebuilt to become one of the seven wonders of the ancient world. The temple was 130 metres (425 feet) long and 67 metres (220 feet) wide, having 127 marble columns each 19 metres (62 feet) high and less than 1.2 metres (4 feet) apart. In the inner sanctuary was the many-breasted image of Artemis, supposedly dropped from heaven. The impact of Paul's mission in Ephesus had been so great that it had even affected the earning capacity of the local silversmiths who made and sold models of the goddess (see Acts 19:23-27).

Paul knew the Ephesian Christians well. He visited them on at least two occasions, firstly in Ephesus where he ministered for two years (19:8–20:1), and then at Miletus where he met the Ephesian elders and bade farewell to them (Acts 20:17-38). The warmth of the farewell address at Miletus shows Paul's deep affection for the Ephesian church. It is surprising, therefore, that the Letter to the Ephesians is so impersonal, and unlike Paul's other letters addressed to congregations, lacks particular personal comments and greetings. Some parts of the letter seem to indicate Paul did not know his readers e.g. "I have heard of your faith in the Lord Jesus and your love toward all the saints" (1:15 see also 3:2; 4:21).

The reason for this impersonal tone may be explained by a textual variant in Eph 1:1. Most English translations point out (in a footnote) that several reliable Greek manuscripts do not have the words "in Ephesus" in 1:1. As there is no other designation within the letter of its destination, it raises doubts about the letter being addressed to Ephesus. Marcion claims the letter was written to the Laodiceans, and, if this is true, it may be the letter to the Laodiceans referred to in Col 4:16.[57] From the above evidence some have suggested that this letter was a general letter sent to several congregations in Asia Minor, including churches that met in Ephesus. The writing of letters in the first century was both expensive and time consuming, hence to write one letter, and then entrust it to an envoy such as Tychicus (Eph 6:20, 21), whose name is the only personal reference in the entire epistle, may prove expedient. Tychicus could have delivered this letter (either orally or in written form) to several congregations *en route* from Ephesus, where he disembarked from his ship from Rome, on his way to Colossae.

If we accept the theory that Ephesians is a more general letter written for the benefit of several congregations in Asia Minor, it may explain the

---

[55] Moo, *The Letters to the Colossians and to Philemon*, 362.
[56] See Anthony D. Macro, "The Cities of Asia Minor under the Roman Imperium," *ANRW* II 7.2:658-97.
[57] For a discussion of this see Moo, *The Letters to the Colossians and to Philemon*, 351.

similarities between it and the Letter to the Colossians. It may be that Paul has become aware of a specific situation in Colossae, which is being experienced more generally throughout the region. Thus having addressed the specific situation, Paul then writes a similar and more general "circular" letter. Both letters are then entrusted to Tychicus for delivery.

4. Literary Structure and Genre

We now turn our attention to the literary structure and genre of these letters. These epistles follow a traditional Hellenistic epistolary format, adapted for Paul's desire that theology inform practice. Each letter begins with the identification of the author (Paul and Timothy in Phlm 1; Col 1:1; Phil 1:1; and Paul in Eph 1:1). Paul asserts his apostolic authority in Colossians and Ephesians, but not in Philippians nor in Philemon. The salutation concludes with a prayer for those to whom the letter is addressed, which in each case is grace and peace (Eph 1:2, Phil 1:2; Col 1:2; Phlm 3). Grace (χάρις) is very similar to the usual Greek way of greeting (χαίρειν [rejoice]) but Paul can fill it here with a Christian content, as it alludes to the undeserved favor towards sinners. Paul adds the characteristic Hebrew salutation (*shalom*) of "peace" (εἰρήνη) which conveys the idea of reconciliation. Hence we have a summary statement of the gospel in these words "grace" and "peace."

In each of the letters, Paul proceeds from the initial greeting to a thanksgiving and prayer (Eph 1:15-23 [after a *berakah* in 1:3-14, outlining the spiritual blessings in Christ]; Phil 1:3-11; Col 1:3-14; Phlm 1:4-7). In each of the letters, the key content of Paul's intercession is that his recipients would grow in the knowledge of Christ (Eph 1:17, 18; Phil 1:9; Col 1:9; Phlm 6). The knowledge for which Paul prays is not just intellectual but relational, and leads to correct living. From these introductory remarks Paul continues to give theological interactions and teaching to the situation addressed (Eph 2:1–3:21; Phil 1:12-26; 3:1-21; Col 1:15–2:23; Phlm 8-16) which results in practical outworking of this teaching (Eph 4:1–6:20; Phil 1:27–2:18; 4:1-9; Col 3:1–4:6; Phlm 17-21), followed by personal comments (Eph 6:21-22; Phil 2:19-30; Col 4:7-17; Phlm 22), and a final greeting/benediction (Eph 6:23-24; Phil 4:21-23; Col 4:18; Phlm 23-24).[58] All four letters can therefore be categorized as having a Hellenistic epistolary genre, even the more general letter to the Ephesians. In a largely illiterate world, these letters would also have been intended to be read aloud and heard, but unlike the Letter to the Hebrews, they are not homilies.[59]

---

[58] Note the structure of Philippians is not totally consistent with the other three captivity epistles. For more detail on structure, see Ben Witherington III, *The Letters to Philemon, the Colossians and the Ephesians: A Socio-Rhetorical Commentary on the Captivity Epistles* (Grand Rapids: Eerdmans, 2007), 19-21; O'Brien, *Philippians*, 38-39.
[59] See discussion on genre, with specific reference to Ephesians, in O'Brien, *Ephesians*, 68-73.

5. Content

5.1. Colossians

1:1-14	Introductory greetings, thanksgiving and prayer
1:15-20	Christ the lord of creation and of redemption
1:21–2:5	Paul's mission
2:6-23	Response to the Colossian error concerning heavenly beings
3:1-4	A correct focus on things above
3:5–4:1	Christian behavior
4:2-18	Final instructions and greetings

We now turn our attention to the purposes for which these letters were written. Due to our theory that Ephesians may have been penned because of a specific situation in Colossae, we will depart from the canonical order of these epistles and start with Colossians.

It would appear that Paul wrote to the church in Colossae because he was concerned about a Jewish mystical group that was growing in influence and was affecting the Christians in that town. It is difficult to determine whether this group emanated from a Jewish synagogue[60] or from within the Christian church. This mystical group was concerned with celestial powers, focusing their attention on the elemental spirits of the universe (2:8), things above (3:2), and the principalities and powers (2:15), rather than upon Christ. It was concerned with Jewish practices such as circumcision (2:11), Sabbath and Jewish festivals (2:16), and food laws (2:16, 21); it encouraged asceticism and self-abasement (2:18); it spoke of the worship of angels (2:18), being understood as heavenly visions whereby adherents could witness the angels worshipping God. In short, the mystical group demonstrated a dualism whereby the celestial world is seen as determinative for earthly practices and access to this world was attained by asceticism and Jewish legalism. Those who adhered to the teachings of this group claimed superior spirituality and disqualified Christians who did not follow their mystical, dualistic, and legalistic practices.[61]

Paul centers his response to the Colossian philosophy on the crucifixion and the resurrection of Jesus. The cross is referred to as the true circumcision and baptism (2:11, 12); it is this work of Jesus and not rituals that gives significance and fullness. It is through the work of the cross that the powers of evil are conquered and sins are forgiven (2:14). It is through the resurrection that Christians participate in the life of heaven, in Christ, and there is hope for the renewal of all things (1:18; 2:12; 3:1). This understanding of the lordship of Christ has ramifications not only in the celestial realm but also in the earthly. Christians are to conduct their earthly lives in the light of liberation

---

[60] Dunn, *The Epistle to the Colossians and to Philemon*, 29-35.
[61] For more detail see Smith, *Heavenly Perspective*, esp. 143-46. See also Clinton E. Arnold, *The Colossian Syncretism: The Interface between Christianity and Folk Belief at Colossae* (WUNT 77; Tübingen: Mohr [Siebeck], 1995), esp. 103-243.

from the powers of evil and cosmic reconciliation.

This reconciliation is to be seen primarily within the church, between Jew and Gentile (3:11) evidenced through forgiveness (3:13) and love (3:14); the church is to be a society where the peace of Christ rules (3:15). In particular there is no place within the church for some to claim superior spirituality, whether because of legalism, asceticism, or mystical visions and heavenly ascents. Paul shows that those who boast in such beliefs and practices are, through their dependence on their own activities rather than the work of Christ, enslaved to the elemental spirits of the world. True heavenly mindedness is displayed by the faithful Christian life lived within society, in marriage (3:18-19), in family relationships (3:20-21), and in a manner by which Christians performed their duties within society (3:22–4:1).

It would appear that if such a problem occurred in a specific congregation like Colossae, it may also have been widespread throughout Asia Minor, an area renowned for its mystical practices.[62] As Tychicus sailed on the well-plied route of Rome to Ephesus and then continued along the Roman road to Colossae in order to deliver the Colossian letter, he would have passed through towns such as Ephesus, Hierapolis, and Laodicea. Each of these towns may have had Christian churches within them affected by similar beliefs and troubles to those that were affecting the Colossians. This would result in Paul writing the general letter now known as Ephesians.

5.2. *Ephesians*

1:1-23	Introductory greetings, thanksgiving and prayer
2:1-10	Salvation by grace
2:11-22	Inclusion of Gentiles
3:1-21	Divine mystery and Paul's ministry
4:1-16	Unity, diversity and maturity within the church
4:17–6:9	Christian lifestyle
6:10-20	Spiritual warfare
6:21-24	Final remarks

The emphasis in Ephesians upon the principalities and powers, and the rulers and authorities in the heavenly places, confirms what we know of the magic and mystical practices associated with the goddess Artemis in Ephesus, whose influence was felt throughout Asia Minor.[63] It would appear that the newly incorporated Gentile Christians in the churches of Asia Minor, sought to syncretize magical practices with their new-found Christian faith.[64]

It is not surprising, therefore, that words associated with power abound throughout Ephesians.[65] Paul responds by emphasizing the power of the

---

[62] See Arnold, *Power and Magic*, 5-40.
[63] For more detail see Arnold, *Power and Magic*, 20-28. See also Thielman, *Ephesians*, 20.
[64] O'Brien, *Ephesians*, 54.
[65] Arnold, *Power and Magic*, 1.

resurrection whereby all things, including principalities and powers, are put under Christ's feet (1:19-22). Indeed, Christians, through incorporation into Christ's resurrection, have been made to sit with Christ in the heavenly places (2:6). Through the victory of the risen Jesus, bondage to principalities and powers and the attendant mystical practices are nullified. The letter concludes with a call for Christians to put on the full armor of God in order to stand against these powers (6:10-20), thereby bringing the theme of Ephesians to its logical climax and conclusion.[66]

In a world that did not divide the secular from the sacred this focus on celestial power would also impact a Christian's attitude to the power of Rome and the imperial cult. Throughout Ephesians and Colossians Paul refers to how Christ's work has effected reconciliation both in heaven and on earth (Eph 1:10; Col 1:20). Whether it be the powers of Rome or the powers of heaven, Ephesians and Colossians remind the reader that Christ is preeminent over all powers, "whether thrones or dominions or rulers or powers" (Col 1:16).

By the middle of the first century, people within the Roman Empire were required to offer homage and devotion to the emperor. This was more than patriotism; it was religious, as the emperor was seen as divine. As a concession to their monotheistic beliefs, Jews were exempt from participation in certain aspects of this imperial cult.[67] In the early days of Christian expansion, when most Roman officials could not differentiate between Christians and Jews, Christians inadvertently fell under this protection. Jewish leaders, however, were quick to point out that Christianity should not fall under this Jewish exemption. This can be seen in Acts 18:12, 13 when the Jews of Corinth accused Paul before the Roman proconsul of Achaia of "persuading people to worship God in ways that are contrary to the law." Christians therefore found themselves threatened by the powers, both civil and celestial.[68]

The coming together of the issues of local mysticism associated with the Artemis cult and Jewish exemption from the imperial cult can be seen in the riot in Ephesus as described in Acts 19:23-27. This riot was initiated by the silversmiths who made silver shrines of Artemis (Acts 19:23). Although the Jewish population in Ephesus would not have condoned participation in the Artemis cult, they also wanted to distinguish themselves from the Christians and express their opposition to Paul and his followers. In the context of the riot the Jews put forward Alexander as their spokesperson in order to disassociate themselves from the Christians, and to protect their exemption

---

[66] Arnold, *Power and Magic*, 103-22.
[67] See Bruce W. Winter, *Seek the Welfare of the City: Christians as Benefactors and Citizens* (Grand Rapids: Eerdmans, 1994), 133-35, for an explanation of the status of Judaism as a *religio licita* within the Roman Empire, and the threat to Christianity being viewed as a *religio illicita*. See also Justin K. Hardin, *Galatians and the Imperial Cult: A Critical Analysis of the First-Century Social Context of Paul's Letter* (WUNT 2.237; Tübingen: Mohr [Siebeck], 2008), 102-10.
[68] See Winter, *Seek the Welfare of the City*, 136-37.

from certain practices associated with the imperial cult (Acts 19:33, 34).[69]

There are several examples of the association of the imperial cult with the celestial Greco-Roman pantheon. A temple in Ephesus was dedicated to Artemis and to the family of Augustus.[70] Visual depictions of Augustus' deity were seen throughout the Roman world.[71] Examples of the imperial cult have been found in coins from Hierapolis, where reverence for Dionysus (a Greek god) is worshipped alongside the family of the emperor.[72] The emperors were perceived as warrior gods who brought order to the world.[73] Of significance within the imperial cult is the decision by the provincial council of Asia in about 9 B.C. to reorder the calendar around the birthday of Augustus. It was perceived that Augustus had commenced a time of restoration, and in the decree of the council he is spoken of as σωτήρ (savior) and θεός (god), and the day of his birth was called ἦρξεν . . . τῷ κόσμῳ τῶν εὐαγγελίων (the beginning of good news [gospel] to the world).[74] Friesen argues that the imperial cult gave an explanation for how the current political situation was related to the ancient myths about the gods.[75] Whether through popular mysticism or Roman religion, or more probably a mixture of both, the issue facing Christians in Asia Minor was the need for cosmic reconciliation to ensure earthly peace.

This background helps to make sense of Paul leaving the Jewish synagogue in Ephesus and moving to the Hall of Tyrannus (Acts 19:9). Gentile inclusion within the church had real political ramifications for Jews in the first century as it threatened their exemption from the imperial cult. As the church continued to grow, especially among Gentiles, it was perceived more and more as a Gentile community. As the whole of Asia heard the gospel (Acts 19:10), this issue of the principalities and powers had become a pressing issue for newly planted churches.

Understanding this socio-political background helps to make sense of the teaching of reconciliation that is at the heart of both Colossians and Ephesians. Cosmic victory over the principalities and powers (Col 2:15)

---

[69] Paul Trebilco, *The Early Christians in Ephesus from Paul to Ignatius* (Grand Rapids: Eerdmans, 2004), 169-70. Thielman, *Ephesians*, 26. Lincoln, *Ephesians*, lxxiii-lxxxvii sees the backdrop as Christian struggles with Rome during the time of Domitian (A.D. 81–96), and therefore the letter, penned after Paul's death, is a pseudonymous encouragement to persevere against this time of persecution with the rise of the imperial cult. The issue of a Christian refusing to participate in certain expressions of the imperial cult, however, need not be dated after the death of Paul. This was a real issue in Ephesus and Asia Minor during the time of Paul.

[70] See S. J. Friesen, *Imperial Cults and the Apocalypse of John: Reading Revelation in the Ruins* (New York: Oxford University Press, 2001), 95-96. The temple is dedicated to Ephesian Artemis; to Emperor Caesar Augustus, son of god; to Tiberius Caesar, son of Augustus; and to the demos of the Ephesians. It was constructed between A.D. 11 and 13.

[71] M. Zanker, *The Power of Images in the age of Augustus* (Ann Arbor: University of Michigan Press, 1988), esp. 297-339.

[72] Friesen, *Imperial Cults and the Apocalypse of John*, 61.

[73] Thielman, *Ephesians*, 21.

[74] W. Dittenberger, ed., *Orientis graeci inscriptiones selectae: Supplementum sylloges inscriptionum graecarum* (2 vols.; Hildesheim: G. Olms, 1970 [orig. 1903–1905]), 458 lines 35, 40.

[75] Friesen, *Imperial Cults and the Apocalypse of John*, esp. 5-22.

results in the fact that one Christian should not disqualify another (Col 2:18).[76] Similarly Eph 2:2 sees that earthly rebellion is linked to the "ruler of the power of the air . . . at work among those who are disobedient". Jesus' victory is experienced in the resurrection (Eph 1:19-22) whereby he is seated "far above all rule and authority and power and dominion" (Eph 1:21). In Eph 4:8-10, drawing from Ps 68:18, a victory ode, Paul shows how the ascension of Jesus results in these powers being led as captives.[77] A similar picture of a victory procession is given in Col 2:15. The psalm envisions a military leader at the head of a procession, returning to Jerusalem after routing an enemy army and taking many prisoners. The victorious procession with the captives in its train makes its way up to the temple mount, preceded by the sacred ark which symbolizes the invisible presence of the God of Israel, to whom a sacrifice of thanksgiving will be offered when the procession reaches the temple precincts. The tribute received by the victor from the vanquished foe will be dedicated to God. This tribute is referred to as "gifts" which the victor has received "among men."[78] Paul adapts this Psalm by replacing "received" with its antonym "gave," which appears to follow the paraphrase of this psalm in an earlier Aramaic Targum.[79] He then applies it to officers in the church such as apostles, prophets, evangelists, and pastor/teachers. The whole existence of the church as God's new society is the result of the cosmic victory won in Christ's death and resurrection. The churches of Asia Minor are therefore not only encouraged to continue, they are also empowered through these gifts from the ascended Christ.

Despite this decisive victory in the death, resurrection, and ascension of Jesus, Christians continue to be attacked by the powers of evil and faithfulness is required. They are to put on the full armor of God with which they will be able to stand against the assault of these assailants (Eph 6:10-20). Within this context Christ is seen as preeminent over all (Col 1:15-20), and cosmic reconciliation finds its fruit in the church, a reconciled society where the alienation between Jews and Gentiles is overcome (Eph 2:11-18).[80]

The church therefore becomes "not only the pattern but also the means God is using to show that his purposes are moving triumphantly to their climax."[81] This then leads to a call for unity as an outworking of cosmic reconciliation. Unity is not to be created by the recipients of the letter, it is to

---

[76] Smith, *Heavenly Perspective*, 105-14.

[77] O'Brien, *Ephesians*, 61.

[78] There are many difficulties with the interpretation of Psalm 68, and this proposed setting is not beyond dispute. For more detail see Marvin E. Tate, *Psalms 51–100* (WBC 20; Dallas: Word, 1990), 159-86.

[79] The use of "gave" rather than "received" is supported neither by the Hebrew nor by the Greek wording (so far as extant copies go); it does occur, however, as a targumic rendering in the Peshitta which appears to represent an earlier text tradition. See R. A. Taylor, "The Use of Psalm 68:18 in Ephesians 4:8 in Light of Ancient Versions," *BSac* 148 (1991): 319-36. For a thorough examination of this see W. Hall Harris III, *The Descent of Christ: Ephesians 4:7-11 and Traditional Hebrew Imagery* (Grand Rapids: Baker, 1998), 64-142.

[80] See Chrys C. Caragounis, *The Ephesian* Mysterion*: Meaning and Content* (Lund: CWK Gleerup, 1977), 144-46.

[81] O'Brien, *Ephesians*, 63.

be maintained (4:1-6). Cosmic reconciliation has been achieved through the ministry of Christ (1:9-10, 20-23; 2:10-22; 3:6) for Christ has been victorious over all authorities (Eph 1:20-22 cf. 3:10; 4:8; 6:12), whether earthly or heavenly.

This resurrection ethic finds its outworking in the everyday life of Christians in Asia Minor. Rather than a focus on powers above or on heavenly ascents, as seen in the Colossian error (described above), the Ephesian and Colossian Christians were reminded of the victory of Christ in his death and resurrection. Through their union with Christ, emphasized by the expression ἐν Χριστοῦ (in Christ) (Col 1:2, 4, 26; Eph 1:1, 3; 2:6, 7, 10, 13; 3:6, 21; 4:32),[82] Christians are liberated to live the life of heaven on earth, not only when they meet together as the church but also in their everyday lives as seen in the household codes in both epistles (Col 3:18–4.1; Eph 5:22–6.9). An understanding of the crucified, resurrected, and exalted Christ works its way out in "personal, domestic, communal, and societal aspects of Christian living. It is because the Colossian believers participate in the triumph of the exalted Christ over the cosmic powers that they have been set free to claim the structures of the world for his kingdom and to live out the life of heaven within them."[83]

These similarities between Colossians and Ephesians, together with what we know of both the Roman Empire and of mysticism in Asia Minor, and the specific directions in Colossians as compared with the general instructions in Ephesians, support our theory that Ephesians is a general application of the specific response to the Colossian error.

5.3. Philemon

1-7   Introductory greetings, thanksgiving and prayer
8-20   Paul's plea to Onesimus
21-25   Final instructions and greetings

The Apostle Paul wrote a third letter to Asia Minor during his Roman imprisonment: Philemon. The traditional view is that the letter is about Onesimus, a runaway slave, who fled from the home of his master, Philemon of Colossae, and met Paul while the apostle was in prison. Onesimus was converted under Paul's ministry, and Paul is now sending him back to his master so that Philemon can make a final decision regarding him.[84]

---

[82] Note related expressions such as ἐν κυρίῳ (Eph 2:21; 4:1, 17; 5:8; 6:1, 10, 21; Col 3:18, 20; 4:7, 17); ἐν αὐτῷ (Eph 1:4, 9, 10; 2:10, 15, 16; 4:18, 21; 6:20; Col 1:16, 17, 19; 2:6, 7, 9, 10, 15); ἐν ᾧ (Eph 1:7, 11, 13; 2:2,3, 21, 22; 3:12; 4:30; 5:18; 6:16; Col 1:14; 2:3, 11, 12).

[83] Andrew T. Lincoln, *Paradise Now and Not Yet: Studies in the Role of the Heavenly Dimension in Paul's Thought with Special Reference to his Eschatology* (Grand Rapids: Baker, 1981), 130-31.

[84] See for example David E. Garland, *Colossians and Philemon* (Grand Rapids: Zondervan, 1998), 294-302; John G. Nordling, "Onesimus *Fugitivus*: A Defense of the Runaway Slave Hypothesis in Philemon," *JSNT* 41 (1991): 97-119.

Such a view involves an extraordinary chain of events including the possibility of Onesimus coming into contact with a friend of his master while in Rome, and the unlikely scenario of a slave being in the same prison as a Roman citizen. Although it is unlikely that Onesimus would have had the means to travel as far as Rome, he would have been highly motivated to get there by whatever means. We know that many runaway slaves in the first century attempted to flee to distant shores in order to disappear in the subcultures of large cities, as being caught would involve severe punishment.[85]

Some have doubted the traditional view of Onesimus' situation and so have suggested alternative views. One is that Onesimus fled from Philemon in pursuit of Paul in order that the apostle might assist as a mediator between Onesimus and Philemon.[86] This situation is more likely if Paul were in Ephesus than in Rome; Rome is a long way to go for mediation. Another view proposed by Sara Winter is that the Colossian church sent Onesimus to Paul while Paul was in prison in order to help him. Paul then requested that Onesimus be manumitted from his indenture to Philemon so he can stay with Paul as a brother.[87] The Torah teaches that runaway slaves deserve protection (Deut 23:15), but it is unlikely that this teaching had permeated early Christian teaching and practice to provide a reason for Onesimus fleeing to Paul.[88]

The most likely scenario is that Onesimus was a runaway slave, as Paul refers to his decision to return him to Philemon (v. 12) despite his desire to have Onesimus stay with him (v. 13). Now that Onesimus has become a Christian, Philemon is to treat him as a brother (vv. 15, 16). Whether this implies Onesimus' manumission is not stated, but it does suggest a change of relationship.

It is important for the reader of Philemon to understand the letter in its historical context, and not to impose later understandings of slavery upon it. Slavery was an accepted social norm in the Roman Empire. In the letters under discussion in this chapter, Paul commonly uses the word δοῦλος (slave) for a member of a household (Eph 6:5, 6, 8; Col 3:22; 4:1), a member of the church (Col 3:11; cf. Phlm 16), a follower of Jesus (Col 4:12), or even as a metaphor for Paul's own ministry (Phil 1:1), and even that of Jesus (Phil 2:7). Slavery in the Roman Empire was not racially determined. Many people became slaves involuntarily because of defeat in war, but many were sold voluntarily into slavery as a means of staying alive. Freedom did not have the same value in the first century as has been the case in recent Western societies; manumission often resulted in much difficulty for "freedmen," including poverty and starvation. Christians were a very small group within society, and Paul's call is for people to relate to each other and to the

---

[85] See Peter T. O'Brien, *Colossians and Philemon* (WBC 44; Waco: Word, 1982), 267, for the practices of runaway slaves in the first century.
[86] See Peter Lampe, "Keine 'Sklavenflucht' des Onesimus," *ZNW* 76 (1985): 135-37; Brian M. Rapske, "The Prisoner Paul in the Eyes of Onesimus," *NTS* 37 (1991): 187-203.
[87] Sara C. Winter, "Paul's Letter to Philemon," *NTS* 33 (1987): 1-15.
[88] Glancy, *Slavery in Early Christianity*, 92.

surrounding society on the basis of the gospel of Christ, whether they be slave or free.

We do not know Onesimus' fate. There is a tradition that he was freed and later became the Bishop of Ephesus, as Ignatius refers to an Onesimus in that role (Ign. *Eph.* 1.3). It is not possible, however, to determine whether this refers to the same Onesimus as in Paul's Letter to Philemon.

Through the centuries Christians have been responsible both for the practice of slavery and for its abolition. Whether the seeds of abolition are found within Paul's teaching that Onesimus be treated as a "beloved brother" (v. 16) is a matter of debate and is beyond our scope here.[89] Onesimus is seen by Paul as his child (v. 10), and therefore is to be treated by Philemon as a brother (v. 16). Believers are joined to each other in the intimacy of family bonds.

5.4. Philippians

1:1-11	Introductory greetings, thanksgiving and prayer
1:27-26	The importance of the gospel
1:27–2:18	Conduct that reflects the gospel
2:19-30	Timothy and Epaphroditus
3:1-11	Warning against Judaizers
3:12-21	Warning against libertinists
4:1-20	Final instructions and greetings

We now turn our attention to Philippians, where we note that two topics predominate: the gospel and joy. Paul mentions εὐαγγέλιον (gospel) nine times in the epistle. He speaks of "sharing in the gospel" (1:5); "the defense and confirmation of the gospel" (1:7); "the spread of the gospel" (1:12); "the defense of the gospel" (1:16); "worthy of the gospel" (1:27); "striving . . . for the faith of the gospel" (1:27); "work of the gospel" (2:22); "struggled beside me in the work of the gospel" (4:3); "the early days of the gospel" (4:15). Paul uses the term as a body of faith, a message, and a sphere of activity bounded by preaching. The use of the word εὐαγγέλιον (gospel/good news) needs to be understood within its context in the Roman Empire. The Roman Emperor was seen as a savior and had divine status. Significant events in the life of the Emperor, such as a birth or accession to the throne are accompanied by declarations of the gospel, or good news. The gospel is therefore that which is announced, not a means of responding to an announcement.

Similarly in the Greek Old Testament (LXX) the same word is used as an announcement that looks forward to the coming of the Messiah who will bring the time of salvation (e.g. Is 40:9; 52:7; 61:1). In the light of both the Roman and the Old Testament backgrounds, it can be seen that the gospel is the

---

[89] David Horrell, *Solidarity and Difference: A Contemporary Reading of Paul's Ethics* (New York: T. & T. Clark, 2005), esp. 111-15, looks at moves from community ethics to a broader understanding of social ethics.

declaration that Jesus has fulfilled God's promises to Israel, and that in his death and resurrection is the announcement of the forgiveness of sins and the renewal of life. It is not surprising therefore, that for Paul, the gospel centers on the death, burial, and resurrection of Jesus (1 Cor 15:1-5; Col 1:21-23; 2:11-12) that is the power of God for the salvation of all who believe (Rom 1:16), which includes the Gentiles who are heirs together with Israel (Eph 3:6).

Within the context of this gospel and the partnership implied by it, Philippians is a thank you letter and a letter of commendation. Paul is appreciative of the Philippians' remembrance of him (1:3, 4; 4:10, 14-20) as displayed through the sending of Epaphroditus and the gifts he carried (2:25). Paul also wants to commend his colleagues Timothy and Epaphroditus to the church in Philippi (2:19-30). Philippians is also an encouragement for the recipients to continue in the truth of the gospel. There appear to be two groups that seek to undermine the truth of the gospel with false practices and teaching.

The first group, described in 3:1-11, are called "evil workers . . . who mutilate the flesh" (3:2) by the practice of circumcision. As we have already noted, there were very few Jews in Philippi, and so it is interesting that there would be such Jewish opposition. This group appears to be Judaizing missionaries from elsewhere who insist on circumcision and thereby undermine the Gentile mission. They may be the same group as is mentioned in 2 Corinthians (2 Cor 11:13-22). Paul refers to these proponents of Jewish nomism as "dogs" (3:2). In light of the fact that Jews called Gentiles outside the law "dogs" (cf. Matt 15:21-28), Paul is now stating that the ones who are advocating such practices as circumcision are the ones who are outside God's covenant blessings.

The second group of those who would oppose the gospel are identified as those who "live as enemies of the cross" (3:18). There is significant debate about the identity of this group, of whom Paul says, "their god is their belly" (3:19). It would appear that they are a different group from those described in 3:1-11, in fact the very opposite. Rather than those who wish to adopt Jewish nomism, they appear to have taken Paul's teaching on grace to extremes and are living the libertine life of self-indulgence.[90] Paul calls on both groups to realize that they are citizens of heaven (3:20), and as we have seen in Ephesians and in Colossians, the heavenly life is that which motivates the Christian to stand firm (4:1).

The second major theme is that of joy. Despite his imprisonment, Paul rejoiced in the Philippians (1:3) because Christ was preached, whether sincerely or hypocritically (1:18). Paul rejoiced under diverse conditions: in the growth of humility in his followers (2:2), in his personal sacrifice for Christ (2:17), and in the gifts and goodwill of his friends (4:10). All through the epistle the brilliant joy of faith is contrasted with the somber background of untoward circumstances and impending disaster. Some have therefore

---

[90] For a summary of the views on these verses, see Fee, *Philippians*, 362-75.

concluded that the Philippian congregation was an ideal church and this epistle is the most positive letter penned by Paul. J. B. Lightfoot, for example states, "as we lay down the Epistle to the Galatians and take up the Epistle to the Philippians, we cannot fail to be struck by the contrast. We have passed at once from the most dogmatic to the least dogmatic of the apostle's letters, and the transition is instructive."[91] This, however, may be too positive a picture.

Not only is the gospel being undermined by Judaizing missionaries and by libertinists, but there also appears to be significant disunity within the congregation, as seen by the repeated appeal for unity (2:2-4, 14; 4:2). Epaphroditus' visit to Paul has clearly brought news of the outbreak of various troubles among church members, two of whom, Euodia and Syntyche, are named (4:2). Paul reproves them and calls them to agreement. Paul calls upon his co-workers to assist in this task as a disagreement between individuals affects the whole congregation and requires resolution. Whatever the disagreement, Paul still affirms Euodia and Syntyche as Christian sisters whose "names are in the book of life" (4:3).

Not only is there division within the Philippian church, there also appears to be persecution and attack from the outside world. There is a definite mention of the church's opponents in 1:28 and a scathing description of the society in which the church was called upon to live and bear witness to Christ (2:15). Amidst such opposition from without and division from within, the Philippians appear to be in danger of losing their confidence in the gospel and the joy it brings. They are therefore encouraged to run the race (3:13-15), to work out their salvation (2:12), to stand fast (1:27; 4:1), and to contend for the gospel. The paradox between the effort required on the part of the Philippians in their perseverance in the faith and the grace seen in the gospel is a hallmark of this epistle.

The suffering which the Philippian Christians underwent may be related to Philippi being a Roman colony and related to the emperor worship practised in the city. The primary titles for the emperor would have been κύριος (Lord) and σωτήρ (savior), the former term occurring fifteen times in the epistle (1:2, 14; 2:11, 19, 24, 29; 3:1, 8, 20; 4:1, 2, 4, 5, 10, 23), and the latter appearing in 3:20.[92] If our dating is correct at ca. A.D. 62, Nero would have been the Roman Emperor which would have meant that at public events he would have been acknowledged as lord and savior. In this context, it is significant that Paul writes: "Our citizenship is in heaven and it is from there that we are expecting a Savior, the Lord Jesus Christ" (3:20). The Christians would not have been able to participate in the imperial cult as citizens of Philippi, and therefore would have suffered at the hands of Roman authorities. In this context they are reminded of their true home. Paul reminds the Philippians that Christ has obtained the title of Lord, and every knee will bow to him (2:9-11), that Christ is also savior (3:20), and that the Philippian Christians have citizenship in heaven (3:20).

---

[91] Lightfoot, *Saint Paul's Epistle to the Philippians*, viii.
[92] For more detail see Hawthorne, *Philippians*, 169-72; Fee, *Paul's Letter to the Philippians*, 31.

6. Conclusion

We have found in our study of the captivity epistles that in order to understand them correctly the reader needs to have an appreciation of the world in which they were written. Each is written against the backdrop of the Roman Empire, with its societal and political structures. The reality of heaven is seen as determinative for the situation on earth, but this does not result in a deprecation of the physical. The reality of heaven is to be understood in the light of the reconciling work of the death and resurrection of Jesus. Christians are united to Christ in this work and are committed to reflecting reconciliation in the church, in their marriages, in the families, and in all relationships. Each of these letters causes the reader to reassess their theology and then allow those beliefs to be determinative for human behavior. The central tenet for the Christian focuses on the death and resurrection of Jesus Christ. It is these events, therefore, that become determinative for shaping the ethics of Christians, and of the Christian church.

Recommended Reading

Arnold, Clinton E. *The Colossian Syncretism: The Interface between Christianity and Folk Belief at Colossae.* Wissenschaftliche Untersuchungen zum Neuen Testament 77. Tübingen: Mohr (Siebeck), 1995.

Arnold, Clinton E. *Power and Magic: The Concept of Power in Ephesians.* Grand Rapids: Baker, 1992.

Bird, M. *Colossians and Philemon.* Eugene: Cascade, 2009.

Garland, David E. *Colossians and Philemon.* Grand Rapids: Zondervan, 1998.

Kreitzer, Larry J. *Philemon.* Sheffield: Sheffield Phoenix Press, 2008.

Lincoln, Andrew T. *Ephesians.* Word Biblical Commentary 42. Dallas: Word, 1990.

Moo, Douglas J. *The Letters to the Colossians and to Philemon.* Grand Rapids: Eerdmans, 2008.

Nordling, John G. "Onesimus *Fugitivus*: A Defense of the Runaway Slave Hypothesis in Philemon." Journal for the Study of the New Testament 41 (1991): 97-119.

O'Brien, Peter T. *The Epistle to the Philippians: A Commentary on the Greek Text.* Grand Rapids: Eerdmans, 1991.

O'Brien, Peter T. *The Letter to the Ephesians.* Grand Rapids: Eerdmans, 1999.

Silva, Moisés. *Philippians.* Grand Rapids: Baker Academic, 2005.

Smith, Ian K. *Heavenly Perspective: A Study of the Apostle Paul's Response to a Jewish Mystical Movement at Colossae.* Library of New Testament Studies 326. London: T. & T. Clark, 2006.

Thielman, Frank S. *Ephesians.* Grand Rapids: Baker Academic, 2010.

Trebilco, Paul. *The Early Christians in Ephesus from Paul to Ignatius.* Grand Rapids: Eerdmans, 2004.

Witherington, Ben, III. *The Letters to Philemon, the Colossians and the Ephesians: A Socio-Rhetorical Commentary on the Captivity Epistles.* Grand Rapids: Eerdmans, 2007.

13. The Pastoral Epistles

Mark Harding

1. Attestation

The two Letters to Timothy and the Letter to Titus have been collectively known as the Pastoral Epistles (PE) since the eighteenth century.[1] Unlike the other ten letters of the New Testament (NT) Pauline corpus, some or all of the PE were not accepted universally as genuine in the early church. Tertullian (fl. A.D. 200) writes that Marcion rejected the PE, refusing them a place in his Pauline canon on the spurious grounds that Paul did not write to individuals.[2] Jerome notes that Basilides (fl. A.D. 125–150) rejected the three PE and that Tatian (fl. A.D. 120–180) regarded some letters of Paul as spurious, but did accept Titus.[3]

The earliest unambiguous citation of any of the PE occurs in Athenagoras and Theophilus, both writing about or just before 180, and both citing 1 Tim 2:1-2.[4] The PE are known certainly as letters of Paul in the writings of Irenaeus (fl. A.D. 180) who cites the three PE frequently as such, and who is the first to do so unambiguously in the extant literature.

The earliest extant manuscript of any of the three letters is P[32] which is

---

[1] See Raymond F. Collins, *The Pastoral Epistles* (Louisville: Westminster John Knox, 2002), 1. Paul Anton applied the phrase to the letters in lectures delivered in 1726–1727 and published in two volumes between 1753 and 1755 under the titles *Exegetische Abhandlung der Pastoral-Briefe Pauli an Timotheum und Titum* and *Exegetische Abhandlung der Pastoral-Briefe, samt einem Anhange der Sieben Pastoral-Briefe Christi an die Sieben Gemeinden in Asia*.

[2] Tertullian, *Marc.* 5.21. It is not clear that Marcion knew the PE. F. C. Baur argues in his *Die sogennanten Pastoralbriefe des Apostels Paulus* (Stuttgart and Tübingen: J. G. Gotta'schen, 1835) that the PE were written to counter Marcion and Gnostic ideas about the value of asceticism. Note 1 Tim 6:20 which warns against the "contradictions" [ἀντιθέσεις; the title of a work by Marcion] of false knowledge (γνῶσις). See also John Knox, *Marcion and the New Testament* (Chicago: Chicago University Press, 1942), 74-75 noting that early opponents of Marcion identified him with the Gnostics; Martin Rist, "Pseudepigraphic Refutations of Marcionism," *JR* 22 (1942): 39-62 (esp. 50-62); H. Koester, *Introduction to the New Testament, Volume 2* (Philadelphia: Fortress, 1982), 297-305.

[3] See Jerome, "Prologue to Titus," in P. Scheck, *St Jerome's Commentaries on Galatians, Titus, and Philemon* (Notre Dame: University of Notre Dame Press, 2010). The fact that Tatian was an Encratite (i.e. he rejected marriage) suggests that 1 Timothy, with its acceptance of the normalcy of marriage, was one of those letters rejected. Note also Clement of Alexandria, *Strom.* 2.11.

[4] Athenagoras, *Supplicatio* 37; Theophilus, *ad Autolycum* 3.14.

dated to about A.D. 200 and consists of Tit 1:11-15 and 2:3-8.[5] The PE are not extant in the contemporaneous P^{46}. This is the earliest extant collection of the Pauline letters, though it should be noted that the text of the Letter to the Hebrews comes second in the manuscript after Romans. There is no way of knowing exactly which letters originally comprised the missing final seven leaves of that codex: the manuscript commences at Rom 5:17 and concludes at 1 Thess 5:28.[6] However, Jeremy Duff has argued that not long after reaching the halfway point in the codex it is apparent that the scribe began to condense his letters, so that it is possible that some of the PE might have been included.[7] With the addition of a short papyrus quire, Duff argues, all three PE might have been included in the codex. He concludes that the lack of the PE in P^{46} cannot be used conclusively to argue for the non appearance of the PE in the Alexandrian canon of about A.D. 200 and that P^{46} is evidence of a collection of Paul's letters to seven churches rather than to individuals.[8] Just as it is supposed that P^{46} is a collection of letters to churches, so it has been argued that the PE originally circulated as a corpus of Paul's letters to individuals, and that possibly P^{32} is a fragment of such a collection.[9] Neither the PE nor the Letter to Philemon are included in the fourth-century Codex Vaticanus, supporting the argument that the letters to churches and to individuals were in circulation as discrete collections, but the entire Pauline

---

[5] Kurt Aland and Barbara Aland, *The Text of the New Testament* (Grand Rapids: Eerdmans, 1997), 98.

[6] Consequently 2 Thessalonians, the PE, and Philemon do not appear. According to Frederic G. Kenyon, *The Chester Beatty Biblical Papyri: Descriptions and Texts of Twelve Manuscripts in Papyrus of the Greek Bible, Fasciculus III: Pauline Epistles and Revelation* (London: Emery Walker, 1934), vii, there would have been sufficient space for 2 Thessalonians but not enough space for the remaining Pauline letters, including the PE. Kenyon repeats this observation on x-xi in the *Supplement* to *Fasciculus III* of this work (London: Emery Walker, 1936).

[7] Jeremy Duff, "P46 and the Pastorals: A Misleading Consensus?" *NTS* 44 (1998): 578-90. Kenyon had already noted that the scribe had begun to lengthen and add lines in *Chester Beatty Biblical Papyri, Fasc. III, Supplement*, x and had made allowances for this in his conclusion that there was insufficient space in the codex for the PE.

[8] See Harry Y. Gamble, *The New Testament Canon: Its Making and Meaning* (Philadelphia: Fortress, 1985), 36-46; *Books and Readers in the Early Church: A History of Early Christian Texts* (New Haven: Yale University Press, 1995), 58-63. The PE, which were written to individuals, were not part of the corpus of letters to seven churches, a ten-letter corpus addressed to the churches in Rome, Corinth (two letters), Galatia, Ephesus, Colossae (with Philemon), Philippi, and Thessalonica (two letters). Gamble argues that there are two other seven-letter collections in the early second century: the corpus of Ignatian letters and the seven letters to the churches in the NT Apocalypse. These three collections of letters to seven churches claim catholic relevance and thus transcend the particularity of the letters read in isolation. Cf. Robert W. Wall, "The Function of the Pastoral Epistles within the Pauline Canon of the New Testament: A Canonical Approach," in Stanley E. Porter, ed., *The Pauline Canon* (Leiden: Brill, 2004), 135-36; John Knox, *Marcion*, 46. The Muratorian Canon also preserves the grouping of letters to churches and letters to individuals. For an insightful study of the particularity of the Pauline letters, see Nils A. Dahl, "The Particularity of the Pauline Epistles as a Problem in the Ancient Church," in David E. Aune, ed., *Neotestamentica et Patristica* (Leiden: Brill, 1962), 261-71.

[9] Jerome D. Quinn, "P^{46}: The Pauline Canon," *CBQ* 36 (1974): 379-85. Speculation about the scope of the codex of which P^{32} is a fragment is a fraught exercise given the fact that the papyrus consists of a small portion of Titus only.

corpus is included in the contemporaneous Codex Sinaiticus and the fifth-century Codex Alexandrinus.[10]

The Letters to Timothy were probably known to Polycarp (d. 156). His Letter to the Philippians (ca. A.D. 130) appears to cite 1 Tim 6:7, 10 at Pol. *Phil* 4:1 and 2 Tim 4:10 at 9:2 and may allude to other passages from those two the letters.[11] That Polycarp did know letters of Paul is certain since he cites 1 Cor 6:2 at 11.2, adding "as Paul teaches" (*sicut Paulus docet* [only the Latin text is extant at this point]). Kenneth Berding has argued that, although Polycarp does not cite 1 and 2 Timothy explicitly as letters of Paul, he probably does allude to these two letters. Moreover, Berding contends that the allusions to 1 and 2 Timothy appear in clusters of citations of and allusions to the Pauline corpus that follow the mention of the name of Paul in Pol. *Phil* 3:2; and 9:1. He therefore concludes that Polycarp considers 1 and 2 Timothy to be letters of Paul and that he is the "earliest external witness" of the Pauline authorship of the letters.[12]

The Oxford Committee responsible for compiling *The New Testament in the Apostolic Fathers* (Oxford: Clarendon Press, 1905) argues that any knowledge of the PE in writers earlier than Polycarp is doubtful. The Committee did conclude that letters of Paul are cited in *1 Clement*, the Ignatian letters, and other writings of the Apostolic Fathers. More specifically, there could be no reasonable doubt that the author of *1 Clement* knew Romans, the Corinthian letters, and Hebrews; that Ignatius knew 1 Corinthians; and that Polycarp knew 1 Corinthians and 1 Peter. As for the PE, *1 Clement* may allude to Titus (assessed at a "low degree of probability" by the Oxford Committee); Ignatius may have known all three PE ("low degree of probability") as might the author of the *Epistle of Barnabas* ("possible reference").[13]

In a collection of studies commemorating the centenary of *The New Testament in the Apostolic Fathers* and edited by Andrew F. Gregory and C. M. Tuckett, contributors evaluate the extent to which the New Testament is cited or alluded to in the Apostolic Fathers.[14] By and large, the contributors affirm the judgment of the Oxford Committee with respect to the use of the PE and other letters of the Pauline corpus by the Fathers. Thus Andrew Gregory on *1 Clement* concludes that Clement probably knew 1 Corinthians

---

[10] See Aland and Aland, *Text*, 107.
[11] Note the passages from 1 and 2 Timothy assembled in *The New Testament in the Apostolic Fathers* (Oxford: Clarendon, 1905), 95-98.
[12] Kenneth Berding, *Polycarp and Paul* (Leiden: Brill, 2002), 155. Cf. Paul Hartog, *Polycarp and the New Testament* (Tübingen: Mohr [Siebeck], 2002). Hartog concludes that Polycarp knew six Pauline letters: Romans, 1 Corinthians, Galatians, Ephesians, Philippians, and 1 Timothy, and possibly another three: 2 Corinthians, 2 Thessalonians, and 2 Timothy.
[13] In his essay on the use of the Pauline letters in *Diogn.* Michael Bird argues that *Diogn.* 12.5 cites 1 Cor 8:1, and that there are allusions to 1 Tim 2:7 (*Diogn.* 11.1), 1 Tim 3:16 (*Diogn.* 11.3), and 1 Tim 3:9 (*Diogn.* 7.2) and echoes of Tit 1:14 (*Diogn.* 1.1) and Tit 2:14; 3:4 (*Diogn.* 9.25). See Michael F. Bird and Joseph R. Dodson, eds., *Paul and the Second Century* (New York: T. & T. Clark, 2011), 70-90.
[14] *The Reception of the New Testament in the Apostolic Fathers* (New York: Oxford University Press, 2005).

and very likely knew Romans and Hebrews. Titus 3:1 is possibly alluded to in *1 Clem.* 2.7, but the evidence is thin.[15] Writing on the letters of Ignatius, Paul Foster concludes that the author knew 1 Corinthians, Ephesians, and 1 and 2 Timothy in descending order of likelihood.[16] Michael W. Holmes writing on Polycarp's letter to the Philippians concludes that the author probably knew 1 Corinthians, Ephesians, and 1 Peter. Less likely is his knowledge of 1 and 2 Timothy and 1 John.

The growth of the Pauline corpus and the status of the PE in that process is the subject of much scholarly debate.[17] We have referred above (see note 8) to the theory that the letters were grouped in two distinct collections—letters written to seven churches and letters written to individuals. But it seems doubtful that two *distinct* collections were circulating and accessible to Ignatius and Polycarp if it is the case that they cite or allude to letters in both. One would expect the collections to have been combined early if they ever existed concurrently and locally. Much more likely is the theory that a ten-letter corpus without the PE (because they had not yet been written) was circulating by the 80s and 90s of the first century. It is this collection that is represented in Marcion's Pauline corpus, P^{46} and Codex Vaticanus. This collection was followed by the dissemination of a thirteen-letter corpus once the PE had been written by the first decade of the second century. This corpus may have been familiar to Ignatius and, more certainly, Polycarp.[18] Both collections were the work of Paul's associates (of whom there were many) intent on extending the reach of the apostle and ensuring that his legacy was protected in the face of competing interpretations and teaching considered false.[19]

---

[15] Gregory and Tuckett, *Reception*, 151, 154-57.

[16] Gregory and Tuckett, *Reception*, 172, 185. Intriguingly, as Foster observes, these four letters all refer to Ephesus, thus satisfying the claim in Ign. *Eph.* 12.2 that Paul mentions the Ephesians "in every letter" (ἐν πάσῃ ἐπιστολῇ).

[17] For a summary of the debate, see Stanley E. Porter, "When and How was the Pauline Canon Compiled?: An Assessment of Theories," in Porter, *Pauline Canon*, 95-127 and his later "Paul and the Pauline Letter Collection," in Bird and Dodson, *Paul and the Second Century*, 19-36.

[18] Cf. F. F. Bruce, *The Canon of Scripture* (Downers Grove: IVP, 1988), 131: the ten-letter Pauline corpus, without the PE, was the "original edition" of Pauline letters.

[19] See Hans-Martin Schenke, "Das Weiterwirken des Paulus und die Pflege seines Erbes durch die Paulus-Schule," *NTS* 21 (1975): 505-18. Albert E. Barnett seeks to demonstrate that the PE are indebted to a ten-letter Pauline corpus, which it echoes and to which it alludes, in *Paul Becomes a Literary Influence* (Chicago: Chicago University Press, 1941), 251-77; but note the caveats of I. Howard Marshall, *A Critical and Exegetical Commentary on the Pastoral Epistles* (Edinburgh: T. & T. Clark, 1999), 66. E. Randolph Richards argues that the letters were collected early, Paul's own set of copies forming the first collection. See his "The Codex and the Early Collection of Paul's Letters," *BBR* 8 (1998); 151-66 which builds on his conclusions in *The Secretary in the Letters of Paul* (Tübingen: Mohr [Siebeck], 1991). In the latter work Richards argues that Paul, in keeping with the practice of contemporaneous letter-writers, would have kept copies of each letter he wrote. Whether such copies would have survived the vagaries of the apostle's tumultuous final years (shipwreck, imprisonment) to be passed on to his associates is by no means clear.

2. The Character of the Pastoral Epistles

The three letters are addressed to individuals, Timothy and Titus, who are delegated by the apostle to further the work Paul has left them to oversee in Ephesus and Crete respectively.[20] This has prompted scholars to note that, unlike the other letters of the NT Pauline corpus, the three PE are personal and private, and that this accounts for the emergence of themes and vocabulary not evidenced in the letters to churches. Paul, the argument proceeds, writes differently to churches than to individuals.[21] But Philemon, also classed as a letter addressed to an individual, is quite clearly Pauline in linguistic terms whereas the PE, as we shall see below, are marked by quite distinctive linguistic characteristics not encountered in the ten-letter corpus.

But the notion that there is a sharply delineated Pauline *persona* depending on whether or not the apostle is writing in personal and public contexts must be challenged on the grounds that there are no Pauline letters that are purely private. The evidence shows that all the letters of the NT that might be categorized as private are redolent of a public audience, 3 John being the only exception. The Letter to Philemon is addressed to "Philemon, Apphia, Archippus, and the church in his [Philemon's] house" (Phlm 1-2). The letter's exhortations (e.g., vv. 8, 12, 17, 21) and the final greeting are in the singular and addressed to Philemon (v. 23), but the final benediction is addressed to a plural audience (v. 25).[22] Similarly, though each of the greetings and exhortations in the PE are addressed to an individual the letters have a wider audience because each concludes with greetings in the plural (1 Tim 6:21; 2 Tim 4:22; Tit 3:15). We conclude that these are letters written not only for individuals but also for their communities; their author, from now on titled "the Pastor," wrote with an official and (to use William Doty's felicitous phrase) "public intent."[23]

It should also be noted that the three PE begin with very formal greetings that underscore Paul's apostolic credentials and his divinely appointed authority, a fact which further undermines the claim that these letters are private. Indeed the preface to Titus (1:1-3) is only second to that of Romans (1:1-6) in length among the 13 letters of the Pauline corpus. Consequently

---

[20] Timothy and Titus are members of the Pauline circle. For Timothy see Acts 16:1-4; 1 Cor 4:17; 16:10-11; 2 Cor 1:1; 1 Thess 3:2. For Titus see Gal 2:1, 3; 2 Cor 2:13; 7:6; 8:23.
[21] See, e.g., C. Spicq, *Les Épîtres Pastorales, Volume One* (Paris: Gabalda, 1969), 193-94; William D. Mounce, *The Pastoral Epistles* (Nashville: Thomas Nelson, 2000), ci-cii.
[22] See Joseph A. Fitzmyer, *The Letter to Philemon* (Anchor Bible 35C; New York: Doubleday, 2000), 23-24, 34.
[23] William Doty, *Letters in Primitive Christianity* (Philadelphia: Fortress, 1973), 26. See also the perceptive comments of James W. Aageson, "The Pastoral Epistles, Apostolic Authority, and the Development of the Pauline Scriptures," in Porter, *The Pauline Canon*, 8-9: "Eavesdropping on their epistolary monologue is the presumed audience that would also have entered into the exhortations, personal examples, ethical patterns, and theological claims of the epistle as it was read or heard." Cf. his *Paul, the Pastoral Epistles, and the Early Church* (Peabody: Hendrickson, 2008), 36, 41. Similarly Ignatius' letter to Polycarp is addressed to an individual (Polycarp), but has a clear public intent as can be seen by the frequency of plural forms of exhortation in the last three chapters.

Jerome Quinn argued that Titus should be placed first in the corpus of the three PE, as it is in the Muratorian Canon, its preface serving as the introduction to all three with its impressive articulation of the apostle's weighty authority.[24] In rhetorical terms the prefaces of the letters establish the "ethos," the moral character of Paul, and his right to address and to exhort his addressees. The current canonical order of the letters is based on their diminishing length.[25]

The PE purport to have been written by Paul during an imprisonment; indeed 2 Timothy registers the certainty that Paul will not survive the ordeal of the trial through which he is passing, and that its outcome will be the death sentence. "I am already being poured out as a libation," he writes in 2 Tim 4:6, "and the time of my departure (ἀνάλυσις) has come." Timothy and Titus are now more than Paul's delegates; they have become his successors. All three letters are imbued with a finality that renders the author's pronouncements fully authoritative.

3. Genre

The PE are letters in the formal sense that a letter identifies an addressee, a sender, an occasion for writing, and a farewell. But this is to say very little about the PE and about ancient letters in general. Letters mediated the presence (*parousia*) and hence the character of the writer, continued a conversation with the addressee(s) (*homilia*), and expressed a friendly relationship between the writer and the addressee(s) (*philophronesis*). Letters could give expression to strategies for persuasion and exhortation, especially when a greater addressed a lesser, or an older a younger.[26] In the case of the Pauline corpus, the letters continued Paul's ministry while he was absent. They embodied his apostolic presence and expressed his ongoing duty of care (psychagogy) for the congregations he had founded. Paul's practice is analogous with that of philosophers who sought to reform and counsel their protégés by means of letters of moral exhortation, or paraenesis.[27] Furthermore, the letters of Paul were soon gathered into collections, thus extending the authority of the apostle beyond his lifetime. In all likelihood,

---

[24] Jerome D. Quinn, *The Letter to Titus* (Anchor Bible 35; New York: Doubleday, 1990), 19-20. Cf. Hans-Josef Klauck, *Ancient Letters and the New Testament: A Guide to Content and Exegesis* (Waco: Baylor University Press, 2006), 327. In his commentary I. Howard Marshall treats the letters in the order Titus, 1 Timothy, and 2 Timothy, but does so because Titus addresses "a less developed and complex situation" than that encountered in 1 Timothy, and 2 Timothy may have been Paul's last letter. See his *Pastoral Epistles*, 2.

[25] Collins, *Pastoral Epistles*, 10; Klauck, *Ancient Letters*, 331 n. 24.

[26] See my *Tradition and Rhetoric in the Pastoral Epistles* (StudBL 3; New York: Peter Lang, 1998) following Heikki Koskenniemi, *Studien zur Idee und Phraseologie des griechischen Briefes bis 400 n. Chr.* (Helsinki/Wiesbaden: Suomalaien Tiedakatamie/Otto Harrassowitz, 1956), 35-47.

[27] Abraham J. Malherbe, *Paul and the Popular Philosophers* (Minneapolis: Fortress, 1989), 68; Mark Harding, *What Are They Saying About the Pastoral Epistles?* (Mahwah: Paulist Press, 2001), 73; Young Chul Whang, "Paul's Letter Paraenesis," in Stanley E. Porter and Sean A. Adams, eds., *Paul and the Ancient Letter Form* (Leiden: Brill, 2010), 255-58.

because of similarity of style and occasion, the three PE were written at much the same time and probably circulated only in a collection, thus ensuring that their exhortations assumed normative and public significance, transcending any perception that individually they were ephemeral.[28]

The style and content of the PE invite comparison with ancient letters that focus on moral exhortation. In his catalogue of 40 epistolary styles, Pseudo-Libanius (ca. A.D. 300–600), listing the paraenetic first, writes that the style is that "in which we give someone paraenesis, persuading him to pursue something or to avoid something."[29] Seneca's *Epistulae Morales*—letters of moral exhortation to his protégé Lucilius—provide near-contemporary stylistic analogies to the PE.[30] Stanley Stowers has argued that the PE are similar in style and character to letters written by way of advice to those about to embark on a major posting.[31] More boldly Luke Timothy Johnson has argued that 1 Timothy and Titus are best compared to an epistolary type he calls *mandata principis* (precepts of the ruler).[32] As an example he cites P.Tebt. 703, a memorandum sent from Alexandria by a third-century B.C. Ptolemaic official giving instructions to a manager (οἰκονόμος) in the Arsinoïte nome. Johnson allows that a pseudepigrapher might have used such a letter type, but hails the potential of the parallel to influence the debate over the authenticity of the PE.[33] However, Margaret M. Mitchell has exposed the dangers of using this papyrus for an understanding of the genre of 1 Timothy. She argues that P.Tebt. 703 is not a letter but a memorandum, that the original editor's translation of the text has exaggerated the element of personal exhortation that NT scholars have sometimes perceived to be analogous to the PE, and that there were no *mandata principis* letters that might constitute an epistolary type such as Johnson has argued.[34]

---

[28] See Jerome D. Quinn, "Parenesis and the Pastoral Epistles," in Maurice Carrez, Joseph Doré, and Pierre Grelot, eds., *De la Tôrah au Messie* (Paris: Desclée, 1981), 495-501.

[29] Abraham J. Malherbe, *Ancient Epistolary Theorists* (Atlanta: Scholars Press, 1988), 69; Harding, *What Are They Saying*, 75-78.

[30] See Spicq, *Les Épîtres Pastorales*, 1:38-39, 41-42; Benjamin Fiore, *The Function of Personal Example in the Socratic and Pastoral Epistles* (AnBib 105; Rome: Biblical Institute Press, 1986), 87-100. On 101-61 Fiore discusses the Socratic Epistles as helpful literary analogies to the PE.

[31] See Stanley K. Stowers, *Letter Writing in Greco-Roman Antiquity* (Philadelphia: Westminster, 1986), 103-4. Stowers cites Pliny's letter to Maximus (8.24, about A.D. 100) as an example.

[32] Luke Timothy Johnson, *The First and Second Letters to Timothy* (New York: Doubleday, 2001), 139-42. Johnson is not the first scholar to draw attention to the possibilities of P.Tebt. 703 for understanding 1 Timothy and Titus. Spicq, *Les Épîtres Pastorales*, 1:35, Michael Wolter, *Die Pastoralbriefe als Paulustradition* (Göttingen: Vandenhoeck & Ruprecht, 1988), 164-70 and Fiore, *Function*, 81-83 had all discussed the papyrus.

[33] Johnson, *1 and 2 Timothy*, 142. Johnson argues that it is no longer possible to characterize 1 Timothy and Titus as "strange combinations of elements" or as "clumsy" efforts of someone trying to imitate other letters, "but as belonging to the well-established convention of an epistolary form that Paul uses with the same flexibility and freedom that he did other conventional letter forms."

[34] Margaret M. Mitchell, "PTebt 703 and the Genre of 1 Timothy: The Curious Career of a Ptolemaic Papyrus in Pauline Scholarship," *NovT* 44 (2002): 344-70. Note Philip H. Towner's cautious comments on Johnson's use of P.Tebt. 703 in the wake of Mitchell's critique in his *The Letters to Timothy and Titus* (Grand Rapids: Eerdmans, 2006), 34-35.

The second Letter to Timothy is the most personal of the letters. James Aageson suggests that the letter is like Philippians, which Stanley Stowers argues is an hortatory letter of friendship.[35] However, the letter also has prominent testamentary features: the writer is about to die and passes on his final exhortation to his addressee(s). But again, few examples of testamentary letters are attested. Nevertheless, this characteristic of 2 Timothy intensifies the exhortations to the apostle's delegates, Timothy, and Titus. Such exhortations, Quinn aptly remarks, "admit of no refutation."[36] The closing of this letter, the longest of the PE, suggests that 2 Timothy was meant to conclude the corpus.[37]

In terms of their content the PE's closest analogies are with the ten-letter Pauline corpus. Like the letters of that collection, the PE contain weighty apostolic greetings, snatches of liturgical tradition and received wisdom, personal reminiscences consistent with the Pauline tradition, and the mention of individuals who are members of the Pauline circle. The three PE speak with all the authority of Paul for a new day and for times radically discontinuous with those of the apostle, but even more compellingly since the assumed author is about to be executed for his defense of the faith.

4. Authorship

The three PE are sufficiently similar in style to commend the view that they were written by the same person. Critical analysis of the PE in the late eighteenth century and early nineteenth centuries established the case for regarding these three letters not as works penned by Paul but by an admirer, perhaps a member of the apostles' circle, and written in about A.D. 100. For this reason scholars have long found it convenient to speak of "disputed" and "undisputed" letters of the Pauline corpus and class the PE (together with Ephesians, Colossians, and 2 Thessalonians) in the former category.[38]

---

[35] See James W. Aageson, *Paul, the Pastoral Epistles, and the Early Church* (Peabody: Hendrickson, 2008), 74-75. Cf. Stanley K. Stowers, "Friends and Enemies in the Politics of Heaven," in Jouette M. Bassler, David M. Hay, and E. Elizabeth Johnson, eds., *Pauline Theology, Volume 1* (Philadelphia: Fortress, 1991), 105-21.

[36] Note the major study by Seán Charles Martin, *Pauli Testamentum: 2 Timothy and the Last Words of Moses* (Rome: Pontifica Università Gregoriana, 1997). See also Quinn, "Parenesis," 499; Koester, *Introduction*, 2:300-301; Harding, *Tradition and Rhetoric*, 150-53. But note the caveats of Cynthia Long Westfall, "A Moral Dilemma? The Epistolary Body of 2 Timothy," in Porter and Adams, *Paul and the Ancient Letter Form*, 213-52 (esp. 223-25).

[37] Klauck, *Ancient Letters*, 327.

[38] See my "Disputed and Undisputed Letters of Paul," in Porter, *The Pauline Canon*, 129-68. Theories have been advanced that the PE were written by Luke (C. F. D. Moule, "The Problem of the Pastoral Epistles," *BJRL* 47 [1965]: 430-52, and Stephen G. Wilson, *Luke and the Pastoral Epistles* [London: SPCK, 1979]), though see George W. Knight III, *Commentary on the Pastoral Epistles* (Grand Rapids: Eerdmans, 1992), 48-52 for a negative evaluation; or that a secretary/amanuensis was given a particularly free hand under Paul's general direction to write the letters or that they were written by Polycarp, a view first advocated by Hans von Campenhausen, "Polykarp von Smyrna und die Pastoralbriefe," in *Aus der Frühzeit des Christentums: Studien zur Kirchengeschichte des ersten und zweiten Jahrhunderts* (Tübingen:

The arguments against the Pauline authorship of the PE are several. Cumulatively they make a strong case for the likelihood that Paul did not write these three letters. The arguments center on (1) Pauline chronology; (2) the language of letters; (3) the absence of distinctive themes encountered in the undisputed Pauline corpus; (4) the teaching of the opponents reported in the letters; and (5) the church order presupposed in the letters.

4.1. Pauline Chronology

The letters cannot be accommodated to the life of Paul as we know it. The book of Acts narrates three missionary journeys of Paul, the third culminating in his visit to Jerusalem, his arrest in the temple precincts on suspicion that he has compromised the sanctity of the Holy Place, and his imprisonment and subsequent appeal to the Emperor. The book ends with Paul in Rome in the early 60s awaiting trial, the author noting that Paul lived in Rome for two years at his own expense, preaching and teaching unhindered (Acts 28:30-31).

However, the PE speak of missionary excursions to Macedonia (1 Tim 1:3) and to Crete (Tit 1:5) which are not narrated in Acts and which presuppose a release from the Roman imprisonment recorded at the end of Acts. By contrast, in his Letter to the Romans Paul expresses his intention to proceed from Rome to Spain (Rom 15:23-24, 28), observing that he has completed his work in the east (v. 23).[39] Therefore, either the missions to Macedonia and Crete actually happened during an earlier missionary journey, but are not narrated,[40] or Paul was not only released from the Roman imprisonment of Acts 28 but, against all expectations of the book of Acts, resumed his missionary endeavors in the east prior to a second arrest and Roman imprisonment (2 Tim 1:17), this time ending with his death.[41] Clement

---

Mohr [Siebeck], 1963), 197-252 with more recent support from Helmut Koester (*Introduction*, 2:297-305, esp. 305) and R. Joseph Hoffmann (*Marcion: On the Restitution of Christianity* [AAR Academy Series 46; Chico: Scholars Press, 1984], 281-87 esp. 284). Generally, however, these theories have not commanded widespread support. Note, for example, the recent arguments against Polycarp's authorship by Hartog, *Polycarp*, 228-31.

[39] According to author of Acts, Paul knows that imprisonments and afflictions await him in every city (Acts 20:23) and that he will not see the Ephesians again (Acts 20:24-25, 38). It is therefore improbable that the author of Acts knew of Paul's resumption of his missionary endeavors in the east. Acts does not appear to know of Paul's intention to conduct a mission to Spain.

[40] In his *1 and 2 Timothy*, 67-68, Johnson argues that Acts is simply not exhaustive when it comes to giving an account of Paul's ventures, and that there is much in the letters that is not mentioned in Acts (such as the tribulations noted in 2 Cor 11:24-25). Towner, *Letters*, 12-15 argues that Paul may have undertaken a round trip from Ephesus to Corinth, including a mission in Macedonia (1 Tim 1:3), and dispatched Titus to Crete in the interval between Acts 19:20 and 21. Paul's presence in Crete (see Tit 1:5) is not necessary (see Towner, *Letters*, 678). But note the brief comments by Marshall, *Pastoral Epistles*, 71-72. Any theory that has the PE being written at the same time as the undisputed letters of Paul, he argues, only intensifies the problem of Paul writing contemporaneous letters in widely differing styles.

[41] The theory of a second career of Paul after release from the first imprisonment is favored by many scholars. E. Earle Ellis, for example, argues that the release explains the "peculiarities" of the PE: it accounts for the missions to Macedonia and Crete, and allows the use of a new

of Rome knows of Paul's martyrdom in Rome after he had reached "the furthermost limits of the west" (τὸ τέρμα τῆς δύσεως; *1 Clem.* 5.7), which Lightfoot and many scholars since understand as a reference to Spain; Clement is thus implying a release from the imprisonment narrated in Acts, and a mission to Spain followed by a subsequent arrest and execution.[42] The Muratorian Canon, perhaps of ca. A.D. 200, refers explicitly to Paul's departure from the city for Spain (line 26) as do the first three chapters of the late second-century *Acts of Peter (Actus Vercellenses)*.[43] The tradition of release from the first imprisonment, followed by a renewed ministry before a second imprisonment and execution in Rome, is known to Eusebius and Jerome *inter alia*.[44]

However, there is no evidence or trace in Spain of any mission of Paul there, though undoubtedly it was Paul's intention to visit there. It is best to assume, with the implication of the book of Acts, that after his arrival in Rome in 60 that Paul, unhindered from preaching and teaching for two years (Acts 28:30-31), was executed at the end of that time.[45]

4.2. Language

P. N. Harrison, whose work on the linguistics of the PE will be considered below, memorably contrasts the intense, dynamic, and even volcanic style of the undisputed letters of Paul with the style of the author of the PE. He characterizes the PE as "sober, didactic, static, conscientious, domesticated." The PE, Harrison continues, lack the "Pauline impetus, the drive and surge of

---

amanuensis with a distinctive style (Luke is a candidate) not used in the earlier letters of the corpus. See his "Traditions in the Pastoral Epistles," in Craig A. Evans and F. Stinespring, eds., *Early Jewish and Christian Exegesis: Studies in Memory of William Hugh Brownlee* (Atlanta: Scholars Press, 1987), 237-53 (esp. 252-53). For Paul's release and resumption of his missionary labor, see also J. B. Lightfoot, *Biblical Essays* (London: Macmillan, 1904), 423-24; J. N. D. Kelly, *A Commentary on the Pastoral Epistles* (New York: Harper & Row, 1963), 9-10; Jerome Murphy-O'Connor, *Paul: A Critical Life* (Oxford: Clarendon, 1996), 359-65. Murphy-O'Connor surmises that the Spanish mission was a failure, prompting a renewed mission by Paul first in Illyria and then the Aegean.

[42] J. B. Lightfoot, *The Apostolic Fathers* (vol. 2, part 1; Peabody: Hendrickson, 1989 [orig. 1889]), 30-31. However, it must be noted that Clement of Rome, after referring to Paul's reaching the "limits of the west" and the martyrdom of Paul and Peter, proceeds to mention the gathering to these men of a great multitude—presumably those put to death under Nero in A.D. 64 (see *1 Clem.* 6.1). The chronology implied here allows scant opportunity for Paul to resume his missionary labor in the east.

[43] For discussion, see David L. Eastman, *Paul the Martyr: The Cult of the Apostle in the Latin West* (Atlanta: Society of Biblical Literature, 2011), 144-48. It should be noted that, while Paul's *departure* for Spain is mentioned there is no account of his mission there.

[44] *Hist. eccl.* 2.22 and *Vir. ill.* 5 respectively.

[45] Robert Jewett, *Dating Paul's Life* (London: SCM, 1979), 45. On p. 102 Jewett places the arrival of Paul in Rome in March 60 and his execution in March 62. For the formidable political and linguistic challenges that Paul would have faced in his Spanish mission, see his, "Paul, Phoebe, and the Spanish Mission," in Jacob Neusner et al., eds., *The Social World of Formative Christianity and Judaism* (Philadelphia: Fortress, 1988), 144-64 and *Romans: A Commentary* (Minneapolis: Fortress, 2007), 74-91. The "uttermost parts of the west" in *1 Clem.* 5.7 is most likely hyperbolic.

mighty thoughts never spoken before." The letters preserve instead the author's concern for the transmission of the "deposit" (παραθήκη; a word occurring in the NT only at 1 Tim 6:20; 2 Tim 1:12, 14), which is the "correct pattern of sound words . . . the one duly authorized expression of saving truth."[46]

It has long been recognized that the existence of the large number of *hapax legomena*—words that occur only once in a text or body of literature (*hapaxes* for short)—in the PE militate against the view that the apostle Paul wrote them. Discounting proper names, of the 848 words used by the author, P. N. Harrison counted 306 which are not used in the ten-letter Pauline corpus. In addition there are 175 NT *hapaxes* in the PE of which 61 appear in the apostolic fathers and a further 32 in the apologists of the second century.[47] The remaining 82 appear in contemporary non-Christian writers of ca. A.D. 100 and after.[48] Per page of text these 82 NT *hapaxes* occur at the rate of 15.2 in 1 Timothy, 12.9 in 2 Timothy, and 16.1 in Titus. By contrast, Romans has on average 4 NT *hapaxes* to a page, 1 Corinthians 4.1 *hapaxes*, 2 Corinthians 5.6, Galatians 3.9, Ephesians 4.6, Philippians 6.2, Colossians 5.5, 1 Thessalonians 3.6, 2 Thessalonians 3.3, and Philemon 4.[49] Furthermore, in many cases words used in common by the author of the PE and the apostle are used with different meanings in the PE;[50] and there are occasions where the author of the PE and the ten-letter corpus say the same thing but in different words and phrases.[51] In addition there are stereotypical phrases and technical terms which do not appear at all in the ten-letter Pauline corpus. The author's failure to use 112 particles, enclitics, prepositions, and pronouns appearing in the ten-letter corpus also underscores the contrast between the PE and the style of the apostle in the undisputed letters.[52] Harrison also draws attention to

---

[46] P. N. Harrison, *The Problem of the Pastoral Epistles* (Oxford: University Press, 1921), 42.

[47] See Harrison, *Problem*, 67-82 for an analysis of the affinity of the language of the PE with second-century writings, especially the Apostolic Fathers.

[48] Harrison, *Problem*, 82-84. Importantly Donald Guthrie pointed out on 216-17 of *The Pastoral Epistles: An Introduction and Commentary* (Grand Rapids: Eerdmans, 1957) that 80 of Harrison's 175 NT hapaxes do occur in the Septuagint, thus undermining the argument that the language of the PE is oriented to the period of A.D. 100 and later.

[49] Harrison, *Problem*, 20.

[50] Harrison, *Problem*, 27-28.

[51] Harrison, *Problem*, 28-30. One example noted by Harrison is the use of παρουσία or ἀποκάλυψις for the coming of the Lord in the ten-letter corpus, but of ἐπιφάνεια for this concept in the PE, and for the incarnation as well as the "second" coming. The term does appear in 2 Thess 2:8, but pleonastically in the phrase ἡ ἐπιφάνεια τῆς παρουσίας αὐτοῦ ("the appearance of his coming").

[52] Harrison, *Problem*, 34-38. Of the 77 particles, enclitics, prepositions, and pronouns used by the author of the PE and found in the ten-letter corpus, all of them, Harrison notes, occur in the Apostolic Fathers, the Apologists, and in a majority of the books of the NT (Harrison, *Problem*, 38). See Walter Lock's unpersuasive argument in *A Critical and Exegetical Commentary on the Pastoral Epistles* (Edinburgh: T. & T. Clark, 1924), xxix: "Much change of vocabulary, including even particles, is due to the kind of letter, not argumentative or impassioned but full of practical warning and guidance, not written to churches or to private friends but to close intimate fellow-workers."

grammatical peculiarities between the PE and the ten-letter corpus.[53] Linguistically, Harrison concludes, the style of the PE is radically "peculiar" extending to their author's whole way of thinking and reasoning and to his temperament and personality.[54] There is a substantial affinity between the three PE, but a notable discontinuity between them and the ten-letter Pauline corpus.

Nevertheless, Harrison argued that the author of the PE had in his possession personal notes, *personalia*, written by the apostle to Timothy (2 Tim 4:6-22) and Titus (3:12-15) around which the second Letter to Timothy and the Letter to Titus were constructed.[55] The vocabulary and style of the *personalia* are consistent with Pauline usage in the ten-letter corpus.

Harrison's conclusions and methodology have not gone unchallenged. His statistical methodology was refined in an often-cited article by Grayston and Herdan, which resulted in the confirmation of Harrison's conclusions.[56] Defenders of the Pauline authorship of the PE have been particularly active in seeking to undermine the weight of Harrison's research. Among recent commentators, William Mounce devotes 20 close pages to a discussion of the vocabulary of the PE in the interests of demonstrating that the vast majority of the Pauline *hapaxes* occurring in the PE can be accounted for by the historical situation presupposed in the letters, the behavior and teaching of the false teachers (a unique Ephesian heresy not encountered in Paul's earlier ministry), "positive" teaching, the vocabulary relating to church leadership, the terms encountered in the vice lists, and the content of traditional material cited by the author—categories, which in my view, point to a post-Pauline situation and author.[57] With respect to the last of Mounce's categories, E. Earle Ellis had earlier propounded the view that a substantial proportion of the *hapaxes* appear in pre-formed traditions used by the author, and that such traditions account for 35% of the content of the PE.[58] More recently in a study of pre-formed traditions in 1 Timothy, inspired in part by Ellis's research, Mark M. Yarbrough has concluded that Paul used a significant number of these in the letter (though they do not account for as much as the content of 1 Timothy as

---

[53] Harrison, *Problem*, 38-40.
[54] Harrison, *Problem*, 40.
[55] Harrison, *Problem*, part 3 (87-135). In part, because of the personalia of 2 Timothy, Jerome Murphy-O'Connor argues that this is a genuine letter of Paul in *Paul: His Story* (Oxford: Oxford University Press, 2004), 231-33, and cf. "2 Timothy Contrasted with 1 Timothy and Titus," *RB* 98 (1991): 403-18.
[56] K. Grayston and G. Herdan, "The Authorship of the Pastorals in the Light of Statistical Linguistics," *NTS* 6 (1959): 1-15. See also the helpful survey in Anthony E. Bird, "The Authorship of the Pastoral Epistles: Quantifying Literary Styles," *RTR* 56 (1997): 118-37.
[57] Mounce, *Pastoral Epistles*, xcix-cxviii. Mounce concludes that 218 of the 306 Pauline hapaxes of the PE can be accounted for in this way, thus removing "the heart of Harrison's argument" (cix). He extends his accounting of the Pauline hapaxes in the PE by considering Latinisms, "topical groups" (by which he means words occurring in groups addressing a topic or using a metaphor), and Pauline hapaxes in the PE that are cognate with words used elsewhere by Paul.
[58] See Ellis, "Traditions," 247-48, 252-53. Ellis concludes that, counting repetitions of words, 157 of 437 hapaxes can be accounted for in the preformed traditions he identifies.

Ellis had calculated), that they are not Pauline in origin, and that they account for what he calls "the unique nuances atypical of the apostle's grammar and style."[59] Nevertheless, attempts to locate the distinctive language of the PE in the extensive use of traditions not originating with the apostle fail to persuade as an argument for Pauline authorship. We can give Grayston and Herdan the final word in this discussion. They conclude their article with this observation: "If ever a writer was in the grip of his own words, it was Paul, and that makes it highly improbable that he should change his style at will, and according to circumstances."[60]

4.3. Absence of Distinctive Pauline Themes

Several of the central themes of Pauline discourse in the undisputed letters, such as the cross, faith, righteousness, of being "in Christ," and imminent eschatological expectation, are absent in the PE.[61] The term "faith" (πίστις) does appear, but has generally become synonymous with what is believed or a set of creedal propositions ("the faith") rather than the confidence of the believer in the promises of God as in the undisputed Pauline letters.[62] Faith and righteousness are numbered among the virtues in 1 Tim 2:15 and 1 Tim 6:11 respectively. The author refers to the law (ὁ νόμος) in 1 Tim 1:8-9, but without any of the salvation-historical freight that renders Paul's discussion of the role of the law so fraught in Galatians and Romans (cf. Rom 7:8, 12). "We know that the law is good," the Pastor writes without nuance (1 Tim 1:8), "if any one uses it lawfully," that is, as a guide to godly living.

The language of Hellenistic ethical discourse appears prominently in the PE. The term εὐσέβεια, "religion," is especially common in the PE. Εὐσέβεια and its cognates εὐσεβεῖν (to act religiously) and εὐσεβῶς (religiously), all foreign to the ten-letter Pauline corpus, are encountered in the three PE and

---

[59] Mark M. Yarbrough, *Paul's Utilization of Preformed Traditions in 1 Timothy: An Evaluation of the Apostle's Literary, Rhetorical, and Theological Tactics* (New York: T. & T. Clark, 2009), 5. Yarbrough argues that Paul used preformed traditions that did not originate with him because he was appealing to common ground with the false teachers who had rejected his authority. See Yarbrough, *Preformed Traditions*, 170, 197. Both Ellis and especially Yarbrough carefully establish criteria for defining and identifying pre-formed traditions.

[60] Grayston and Herdan, "Authorship," 15. Note also the more nuanced conclusions of Marshall, *Pastoral Epistles*, 60-61.

[61] See my comments on the fact that the Paul of the PE has ceased to be impelled by the defining issues that are articulated in the undisputed corpus in Harding, *What are They Saying*, 22. Although there is an expectation in the PE that Christ will appear, the expectation of such an appearing (ἐπιφάνεια) is not as heightened as that in the undisputed letters of Paul (by contrast, see 1 Cor 7:29; 15:51; Rom 13:11-14; 1 Thess 4:17). Timothy is exhorted to plan for his own succession without any qualification that the "appearing" might intervene (2 Tim 2:2). Nevertheless, note the important corrective brought to bear by David J. Downs on the view that the PE are the prime examples of "early Catholicism" in the NT because of the receding of the imminent expectation of the parousia and the institution of a more ordered church order in his "'Early Catholicism' and Apocalypticism in the Pastoral Epistles," *CBQ* 67 (2005): 641-61.

[62] "I have kept the faith (ἡ πίστις)," the Pastor writes in 2 Tim 4:7. See also 1 Tim 3:9, 13; 4:1, 6; 5:8; Tit 1:13. This is not to deny that there are occasions in the PE where πίστις does not mean trust in the Pauline sense.

appear elsewhere in the NT only in Acts and 2 Peter.⁶³ They are common encountered in broadly contemporary Hellenistic literature (e.g. Philo and Josephus) and *1* and *2 Clement*. Likewise the frequently encountered term "appearance" (ἐπιφάνεια; 1 Tim 6:14; 2 Tim 1:10; 4:1, 8; Tit 2:13) and "rebirth" (παλιγγενεσία; Tit 3:5), which appear in key theological or ethical passages in the PE are unknown in the undisputed letters. Indeed the *hapaxes* of the PE appear prominently in ethical passages.⁶⁴

The PE also feature the use of σωτήρ (savior) used interchangeably of God and Christ.⁶⁵ The word occurs once in the undisputed corpus, at Phil 3:20 where Paul writes that our commonwealth is in heaven from which we await a σωτήρ, the Lord Jesus Christ, and at Eph 5:23 where Christ is the head of the church, its σωτήρ. The frequency of the use of word in the PE is distinctive, and was possibly influenced by claims made for the Roman emperor as savior of his people in the cult that honored him.⁶⁶

But this vocabulary, while it points away from the historical Paul as the author of the PE, discloses new themes that are important for an understanding of the theology of the letters.

4.4. The Teaching of the Opponents

The Paul of the undisputed letters argues dialogically with false teaching. This is particularly apparent in, say, 1 Corinthians where a number of false moral choices are addressed by theological argument, namely, going to law against believers (6:1-8), resorting to prostitutes (6:9-20). Paul also deals by reasoned argument with issues that relate to conjugal relations (7:1-7) and food offered to idols (chs. 8; 10). His concerns about action done in the body can be sheeted home to his core belief in the resurrection and the knowledge that there is a direct continuity between the physical body and the spiritual body (1

---

[63] Εὐσέβεια appears in Acts 3:12 and four times in 2 Peter; εὐσεβέω appears at Acts 17:23 and 1 Tim 5:4, and εὐσεβῶς at 2 Tim 3:12 and Tit 2:12. The adjective εὐσεβής (religious) appears at Acts 10:2, 7 and 2 Pet 2:9.

[64] Note the NT hapaxes πραϋπαθία (gentleness) in 1 Tim 6:11; ὑψηλοφρονεῖν (to be haughty), εὐμετάδοτος (generous), κοινωνικός (liberal) in 1 Tim 6:17-19; αὐθάδης (arrogant), ὀργίλος (quick-tempered), πάροινος (addicted to wine), πλήκτης (a bully), and several other terms in Titus 1:7-8; and σωφρόνως (showing self-control) and εὐσεβῶς (in a godly manner) in Tit 2:12.

[65] God is σωτήρ at 1 Tim 1:1; 2:3; 4:10; Christ is σωτήρ at 2 Tim 1:10; Both God and Christ are described as σωτήρ in Titus: God at Tit 1:3; 2:10; 3:4; Christ at 1:4; 2:13; 3:6. See discussion of the significance of the savior/epiphany language in the PE in Towner, *Letters*, 59-62.

[66] See the study by Malcolm Gill, *Jesus as Mediator: Politics and Polemics in 1 Timothy 2:1-7* (Oxford and New York: Peter Lang, 2008). Gill acknowledges that Ephesus became the center of the emperor cult in Asia Minor, especially after A.D. 89–90 when a new temple was dedicated to the emperor cult. This may be a possible further clue (my inference, not Gill's) to the post-Pauline situation of the letters. But see George Wieland, *The Significance of Salvation: A Study of Salvation Language in the Pastoral Epistles* (Milton Keynes: Paternoster, 2006) who is aware of the use of savior terminology in the imperial cult (22, 26), but does not connect its use in the PE with the emergent cult of the emperor. Wieland has also provided the chapter on the theology of salvation in the PE ("The Function of Salvation in the Letters to Timothy and Titus") in Andreas J. Köstenberger and Terry L. Wilder, eds., *Entrusted with the Gospel: Paul's Theology in the Pastoral Epistles* (Nashville: Baker Academic, 2010), 153-72.

Cor 15:42-44); 1 Cor 6:20—our bodies are not our own). But the Paul of the PE only rarely engages false teaching: his argument against asceticism in 1 Tim 4:3-5 is a rare, if not the only, example. The PE are notable for their vice lists which castigate the false teachers. There is a rhetorical technique at work here in which the Pastor seeks to create antipathy towards his opponents in the interests of protecting the teaching, the deposit, mandated in the letters.[67]

This aspect of the rhetoric of the PE led J. Christiaan Beker to observe that the argumentative style of the letters does not match what we encounter in the undisputed Paulines and commends the case for their pseudonymity.[68] Beker championed the idea that the Paul of the undisputed corpus engages dialogically with the contingent situations of his addressees, seeking to exhort, correct, and reform in a way that is grounded in his grasp of the gospel, his interpretation of the Christ event. In shorthand terms Beker used the terms "coherence and contingency" for this argumentative strategy. The coherence of Paul's gospel refers to the significance of the Christ-event in terms of the confirmation of his apocalyptic worldview, chiefly understood as the end-time triumph of God now confirmed in the death and resurrection of Christ, but awaiting actualization for believers. The author of the PE, on the other hand, defaults to issuing mandates and to vilifying his opponents.[69] However, Howard Marshall proposes to show that it is possible that the argumentative strategies of the author of the PE might be yet understood within the coherence and contingency model proposed by Beker for the undisputed Paulines. Marshall argues that the author engages with the new contingent situation encountered in the PE out of a coherent center that stresses the saving activity of God in history in the present rather than the end-time triumph of God.[70] As will become clear below, Marshall has correctly stressed the PE's focus on God's saving will which was made manifest in the first coming and is in the process of being actualized in the life of the believers until the resurrection.

It is impossible to know just what the opponents actually believed and whether those opposed are the same in each of the letters. The Jewishness of the false teachers is clear enough, at least as described in Tit 1:10, as is their desire to be "teachers of the law" (1 Tim 1:7). They are fixated on "myths and endless genealogies" (μύθοις καὶ γενεαλογίαις ἀπεράντοις, 1 Tim 1:4) and

---

[67] Robert J. Karris, "The Polemic of the Pastoral Epistles," *JBL* 92 (1973): 549-64; Luke Timothy Johnson, "II Timothy and the Polemic Against False Teachers: A Re-examination," *JRelS* 6.2/7.1 (1978-79): 1-26; Lloyd K. Pietersen, *The Polemic of the Pastoral Epistles: A Sociological Examination of the Development of Pauline Christianity* (New York: T. & T. Clark, 2004), 109-11.

[68] For extended discussion of the PE see J. Christiaan Beker, *Heirs of Paul: The Legacy of Paul in the New Testament and in the Church Today* (Minneapolis: Fortress, 1991), 36-47. Beker presented his coherence and contingency theory of the apostle's argumentative style in *Paul the Apostle: The Triumph of God in Life and Thought* (Philadelphia: Fortress, 1980).

[69] Beker, *Heirs of Paul*, 39-41 and his *The New Testament: A Thematic Introduction* (Minneapolis: Augsburg Fortress, 1994), 46-47.

[70] Marshall, *Pastoral Epistles*, 98-104. Marshall's formulation of the coherent center of the gospel in the PE is indebted to the summary of Paul's theology in Herman Ridderbos, *Paul: An Outline of His Theology* (London: SPCK, 1977), 39.

Jewish "myths" (Tit 1:14). Some false teachers advocate asceticism with respect to marriage, food, and drink (1 Tim 4:3). Some hold that the resurrection of believers is a past event (2 Tim 2:18). There is a fixation on "knowledge" (γνῶσις; *gnōsis*) in 1 Tim 6:20. The best guess of many scholars is that the opponents are Jewish Christians, with emancipist ideals with respect to women and slaves, who stand at the formative stage of the second-century obsession with *gnosis* and its power to enlighten and thus to save.[71] Those advocating Pauline authorship of the PE point to the presence in Corinth of teaching that is similar to that encountered in the PE, especially with respect to the contention that the resurrection is already part of current experience (see 2 Tim 2:18) and the Jewish-Christian identity of the opponents in the PE and the Corinthian correspondence.[72]

Lloyd Pietersen has recently advocated the position that the opponents attacked in the PE are pre-Montanists. In common with the Montanist movement that arose in the middle of the second century, the opponents of the PE accord women a prominent role in the Christian community, dissolve marriages, preach asceticism, and make laws concerning fasting.[73] Pietersen perceives traces of this teaching echoed in Ignatius' *Letter to the Philadelphians*, written more or less contemporaneously with the PE, and notes that Ammia, a prophetess possibly contemporaneous with Ignatius, who was esteemed as a predecessor of the later Montanist prophetesses,[74] was a Philadelphian. The PE function, Pietersen argues, as "literary versions of a status degradation ceremony" in which previously influential leaders are "transformed into outsiders."[75] Less bold is the contention of Michael Goulder that the opponents of the PE are Jewish-Christian visionaries who are also encountered in Col 2:16-18 and possibly in the church in Corinth.[76] Goulder explains the statement in 1 Tim 1:4 concerning the danger of myths and endless genealogies as a reference to Jewish speculation, encountered as early as Philo, about the process by which an impassible God might create the universe. Such speculation gave rise to the elaborate Gnostic systems encountered in the second century within a generation or so of the PE being written. Goulder argues that the Christology of the false teachers in the PE was Ebionite in character,[77] a Christology also espoused by the Ephesian

---

[71] See Karris, *Polemic*, 552-55; cf. Collins, *Pastoral Epistles*, 11-14.

[72] See Spicq, *Les Épîtres Pastorales*, 1:114 citing 1 Cor 4:18-20; 2 Cor 10:4-5. Cf. Philip H. Towner, "Gnosis and Realized Eschatology in Ephesus," *JSNT* 31 (1987): 95-124; Towner, *Letters*, 41-50.

[73] Pietersen, *Polemic*, 102-6. Pietersen draws attention to 1 Tim 4:3 as a reference to pre-Montanist teaching attacked in the PE. The silencing of women in 1 Tim 2:8-15 may be directed against the pre-Montanist value placed on the ministry of women. Pietersen also notes that Montanus paid preachers to disseminate his message. 1 Tim 6:5b and Tit 1:11 may target that characteristic, but among the pre-Montanists.

[74] See Eusebius, *Hist. eccl.* 5.17.4.

[75] Pietersen, *Polemic*, 1, 135.

[76] Michael Goulder, "The Pastor's Wolves: Jewish Christian Visionaries Behind the Pastoral Epistles," *NovT* 38 (1996): 242-56.

[77] The "Ebionites" (derived from the Hebrew word for the "poor"), Jewish-Christian sectarians of the second century, rejected the divinity of Christ and believed that Jesus was a human

teacher Cerinthus, possibly a contemporary of the Pastor. In general, therefore, the false teachers seems more closely aligned with a late first or early second-century date and are less likely to be situated within the life-span of the historical Paul.

4.5. The Church Order of the PE

In the undisputed Paulines the exercise of all ministries is charismatically endowed (Rom 12:6; 1 Cor 12:4-11), and apparently without gender restrictions, at least with respect to women prophesying (see 1 Cor 11:5). But the author of the PE knows of pastoral leadership which is restricted to males who are already governing their households well, with formal recognition of entry (almost ordination) to that office by a formal laying on of hands (1 Tim 5:22; 2 Tim 1:6). The church order presupposed in 1 Timothy emanates therefore from a later period than that of the historical Paul and has more in common with the church order glimpsed in the letters of Ignatius of Antioch where in each town a single bishop presides over a council of elders (presbyters) and from among whom he has been elevated.[78]

There is certainly no agreement about the nature of the church order of the PE, especially with respect to the relationship between elders (πρεσβύτεροι) and overseers (ἐπίσκοποι). Hans von Campenhausen championed the view that Paul only knew charismatic endowment of ministries in the church, and that where there is rudimentary organization the leaders are known as overseers (ἐπισκόποι), as in Phil 1:1, a term that is rooted to the oversight exercised in the Greco-Roman household. However, in churches that were Jewish-Christian in origin, leaders were termed elders (πρεσβύτεροι), as in 1 Pet 5:1 and James 5:14, and in the churches of Antioch (Acts 11:30) and Jerusalem (Acts 15:2) with corresponding indebtedness to the role of elders in the Jewish synagogue. While Paul is presented appointing elders in Acts in the churches he establishes (Acts 14:23), Gentile churches only knew of overseers (ἐπίσκοποι). In time both terms are to be found, even

---

inspired by the Holy Spirit. They also rejected the Pauline letters. See Irenaeus, *Haer*. 1.26.2. Note Irenaeus' linking of the teaching of Cerinthus and the Ebionites in *Haer*. 1.26.1-2.

[78] See A. T. Hanson, *The Pastoral Epistles* (Grand Rapids: Eerdmans, 1982), 32-34; William R. Schoedel, *A Commentary on the Letters of Ignatius of Antioch* (Philadelphia: Fortress, 1985), 22-23. There is support for this view in the PE insofar as the term ἐπίσκοπος always appears in the singular and πρεσβύτεροι appears in the plural (note 1 Tim 3:1; 5:17; Tit 1:5, 7). Note also the extensive comparison of the ecclesiology of the PE with that of the second century in Aageson, *Paul, the Pastoral Epistles, and the Early Church*, ch. 5 (122-56). Nevertheless, it must be pointed out that the church order in Ignatius, or better, the order for which Ignatius contends, is more developed than that of the PE especially with respect to the role of the bishop/overseer (ἐπίσκοπος). See the contrasts noted by Mounce, *Pastoral Epistles*, 186-92. For a helpful survey of church order in the NT, the later NT especially, see Kevin N. Giles, "Church Order, Government," in Ralph P. Martin and Peter H. Davids, eds., *Dictionary of the Later New Testament and Its Developments* (Downers Grove: IVP, 1997), 219-26; Joseph A. Fitzmyer, "The Structured Ministry of the Church in the PE," *CBQ* 66 (2004): 582-96.

in the churches that had been founded by Paul.[79]

Frances Young argues that the appearance of elders indicates that the embryonic church was adopting the social structures of the Jewish communities in which elders functioned as honored guardians of tradition and Jewish identity. In doing so the early Christians were signaling that they were beginning to think of themselves socially as God's *people* and not just God's *household*. The PE disclose the period of transition in which churches which operated with overseers and deacons (as in Phil 1:1), terms which betray their household origins, are integrating that structure with a "council" of elders, a presbyterate (πρεσβυτήριον, 1 Tim 4:14).[80] R. Alistair Campbell contends for an opposite point of view, namely, that the PE were written to legitimate an ecclesiology in which a single overseer (ἐπίσκοπος) is to exercise leadership in the church in each town and over other ἐπίσκοποι, heads of households, who were already known by the honorific title of elders (πρεσβύτεροι).[81] By and large, however, scholars continue to argue that the terminology of elder and overseer is interchangeable and synonymous. While the plural πρεσβύτεροι is used to indicate the honored *status* of the collective leadership of the churches, the singular ἐπίσκοπος is used when the *function* of elders is in view.[82] This may be true with respect to qualities of office since elders and overseer alike must evince sound moral qualities and be apt teachers. But the fact that the term ἐπίσκοπος only occurs in the singular strongly suggests the emergence of monepiscopal leadership to be exercised over elders in each locality.

Margaret Y. MacDonald argues that the PE embody third generation community-protecting strategies designed for churches founded by Paul and after the work of the consolidation of those churches in the second generation.[83] We concur with this assessment. In 2 Tim 2:2 Timothy is

---

[79] See Hans von Campenhausen, *Ecclesiastical Authority and Spiritual Power* (Peabody: Hendrickson, 1997 [Ger. orig. 1969]), 76-123.

[80] See Frances Young, *The Theology of the Pastoral Letters* (Cambridge: Cambridge University Press, 1994), 104-11. Young admits that her proposal is "tentative" (108); and note Marshall's caveats in his survey of theories of the relationship between elders and overseers in *Pastoral Epistles*, 177-81. A problem for Young's attractive theory is the author's abrupt change from speaking about the qualities of *elders* (pl.) in Tit 1:5 to those expected of the *overseer* (sing.) in 1:7. Young is not persuaded by the view that the overseer is simply a presbyter who presides (Young, *Theology*, 105). Rather, on the analogy of the Jewish elders appointing the synagogue ruler, the ἀρχισυναγωγός, the Pastor may be implying in Titus 1:5, 7 that from among the elders to be appointed by Titus one of their number will be elevated to the distinct and permanent office of overseer (Young, *Theology*, 109-11).

[81] R. Alistair Campbell, *The Elders: Seniority within Earliest Christianity* (Edinburgh: T. & T. Clark, 1994), esp. 196, 238-51.

[82] "The elder and an overseer are one and the same person. The man's status is that of elder; his function is that of overseer", Collins, *Pastoral Epistles*, 322. See also J. B. Lightfoot, *The Christian Ministry* (London: Macmillan, 1901), 20; Lock, *Pastoral Epistles*, xx; Marshall, *Pastoral Epistles*, 160; Towner, *Letters*, 685; Mounce, *Pastoral Epistles*, 390; Robert W. Wall (with Richard B. Steele), *1 & 2 Timothy and Titus* (Grand Rapids: Eerdmans, 2012), 340.

[83] Margaret Y. MacDonald, *The Pauline Churches: A Socio-Historical Study of Institutionalization in the Pauline and Deutero-Pauline Writings* (SNTSMS 60; Cambridge: Cambridge University Press, 1988), esp. 159-224.

charged to appoint his successors, entrusting to faithful men (πιστοὶ ἄνθρωποι) what he has heard from Paul before many witnesses. In a less developed communal environment that that of Ephesus, Titus is charged with appointing elders "in every town" (Tit 1:5). We understand the Pastor's rhetoric to be that of affirming and consolidating the Pauline character of the given (though contested) leadership of the communities that first received the PE.[84]

5. The PE as Pseudepigrapha

If Paul did not write the PE the letters must therefore be pseudonymous, i.e., written under an assumed name, since all three letters claim to be written by him (1 Tim 1:1; 2 Tim 1:1; Tit 1:1). Those in the second century who rejected the PE would, in my view, have concluded that that the letters were pseudonymous. If Tertullian is correct that Marcion knew the PE but did not accept them into his canon, then Marcion too must have rejected the letters as pseudonymous.

The writing of pseudepigrapha was common enough in the Greco-Roman world.[85] Some have been interpreted as epistolary exercises written in harmless imitation of famous philosophers,[86] thought is more likely that such letters were written by members of philosophical schools of to update the legacy of their particular founder.[87] Nevertheless, the writing of pseudepigrapha could be perceived as morally questionable because deception was involved. This extends to other works passed off as antique. Tertullian

---

[84] See Harding, *Tradition and Rhetoric*, 230-35. On the succession theme in the PE, see Perry L Stepp, *Leadership Succession in the World of the Pauline Circle* (Sheffield: Sheffield Phoenix Press, 2005).

[85] The literature on this subject is vast. For surveys Lewis R. Donelson, *Pseudepigraphy and Ethical Argument in the Pastoral Epistles* (HUT 22; Tübingen: Mohr [Siebeck], 1986), 23-54; Richard Bauckham, "Pseudo-Apostolic Letters," *JBL* 107 (1988): 469-94; James H. Charlesworth, "Pseudepigraphy," in Everett Ferguson, Michael P. McHugh, Frederick W. Norris, and David M. Scholer, eds., *Encyclopedia of Early Christianity* (2nd ed.; New York: Garland Publishing, 1997), 2:961-64; James D. G. Dunn, "Pseudepigraphy," in Martin and Davids, *Dictionary of the Later New Testament*, 977-84; David E. Aune, "Reconstructing the Phenomenon of Ancient Pseudepigraphy," in Jörg Frey et al., eds., *Pseudepigraphie und Verfasserfiktion in frühchristlichen Briefen* (WUNT 245; Tübingen: Mohr [Siebeck], 2009), 789-824. For more extensive surveys, see Norbert Brox, *Pseudepigraphie in der heidnischen und jüdisch-christlichen Antike* (Darmstadt: Wissenschaftliche Buchgesellschaft, 1977) and *Falsche Verfasserangaben: Zür Erklärung der frühchristlichen Pseudepigraphie* (Stuttgart: KBW Verlag, 1975).

[86] Klauck, *Letters*, 403.

[87] See the collection of mostly late first-century B.C. letters promoting Cynicism, written under the names of earlier representatives of the Cynic School and non-Cynics (such as Socrates) and brought together in Abraham J. Malherbe, ed., *The Cynic Epistles* (SBL Sources for Biblical Study 12; Atlanta: Scholars Press, 1977). See also Klauck, *Letters*, 403: "Readers were most inclined to accept pseudonymous publications within an established corpus of traditional literature when later members of a school wrote in the name of the founder of their school, such as the schools of the philosophers and the physicians. The pseudo-Pythagorean philosophical and scientific writings ... and the Hippocratic medical corpus may serve as examples."

tells of an Asian presbyter, a contemporary, who forged a treatise about Paul. He was subsequently removed from office even though he claimed to have written the work out of love for the apostle.[88] The presbyter Salvian (ca. A.D. 400–480) was discovered to have written in the name of Timothy a treatise entitled *Timothei ad ecclesiam* in which he exhorted his addressees to forgo love of money and material possessions, knowing that they would listen to Timothy but not to him, Salvian. Salvian was reprimanded and de-frocked for his deception even though he wrote the work from noble motives. There is no doubt that had the fathers suspected that the PE were pseudonymous they would have not accorded them value and worth as witnesses to the apostolic faith, but would have rejected them.[89]

The appearance of pseudepigrapha was clearly an issue with which the earliest church had to engage. The author of 2 Thessalonians warns his readers of a pseudepigraphon circulating in the name of Paul (2 Thess 2:2). Either 2 Thessalonians is a genuine letter and the now lost letter referred to here is the pseudepigraphon, or 2 Thessalonians is a pseudepigraphon.

The problem of the possible presence of pseudepigrapha in the Bible is not confined to the PE. In the OT, the book of Daniel is pseudonymous since the book emanates from the mid second century B.C., not from the time of the sixth-century B.C. exile as claimed in Dan 1:1-7. Isaiah 40–66, appended to a collection of oracles of the eighth-century B.C. prophet Isaiah ben Amoz which were included in chapters 1–39, is tantamount to being pseudonymous, as are other interpolations into biblical books.[90] In the Second Temple period works were written in the name of a venerable figure from the past as a way of actualizing the tradition associated with that person. This is perhaps the best way of understanding the pseudepigraphic apocalypses of the early Christian era (such as *1 Enoch*, *2 Baruch*, and *4 Ezra*). The *Wisdom of Solomon*, written in Solomon's name, is a conscious attempt by the author to locate the book in the wisdom tradition venerably associated with Solomon. *Wisdom* was accepted as part of the Christian OT and is included in the great codices Sinaiticus (א), Alexandrinus (A), and Vaticanus (B).[91] Many scholars

---

[88] *On Baptism* 17. The work referred to by Tertullian is the *Acts of Paul*. The identity of the work is clear enough given Tertullian's outrage that there were women appealing to the example of Paul's endorsement of the ministry of Thecla in the *Acts* as justification for their practice of teaching and baptizing. Note *Acts Paul* 3.34 (Thecla baptizes herself) and 3.41 (Paul commissions Thecla to teach). The apostle, Tertullian observes, did not permit a woman even to learn with "over-boldness." Dennis R. MacDonald, *The Legend and the Apostle: The Battle for Paul in Story and Canon* (Philadelphia: Westminster, 1983) argues that the PE were written to silence women who kept alive the memory of the apostle's encouragement of the ministry of women.

[89] See Donelson, *Pseudepigraphy*, 11-12.

[90] See Martin Rist, "Pseudepigraphy and the Early Christians," in David E. Aune, ed., *Studies in New Testament and Early Christian Literature: Essays in Honor of Allen P. Wikgren* (Leiden: Brill, 1972), 75-91. Rist argues that Isaiah 24–27 and John 7:53–8:11 can be classified as pseudepigraphical on the basis that they have been interpolated into established books.

[91] The compiler of the Muratorian Canon states that the book was written "by friends [*ab amicis*] of Solomon in his honor" [line 42].

argue that all the catholic epistles of the NT are pseudonymous; 2 Peter has especially been perceived as such.[92]

Why did our author not write in his own name? Why did he write pseudepigraphically? The reference to a Pauline pseudepigraphon in 2 Thess 2:2, the purpose of which was to correct the genuine teaching of the apostle, reveals how early pseudepigraphical strategies were adopted to protect the heritage of the apostle perhaps even during his lifetime, and certainly once he had died. Given his considerable authority in the churches, writing pseudepigraphically, a widespread strategy in the Greco-Roman world, presented a way of actualizing Paul's message for a new day and to counter teaching deemed false.[93] The PE testify to an overwhelming need to defy in Paul's own name the false teachers—teachers who no doubt appealed to Paul as their authority—and thus protect and preserve the Pauline identity of the churches for which the PE were written. In a time of competing interpretations of Paul's legacy, it was a culturally familiar strategy for the Pastor to write as Paul and articulate Paul's character in the letters such as to invest his writing with persuasive verisimilitude.[94] For the Pastor to write in his own name would have had no effect and put at risk the securing of the Pauline heritage, as the Pastor understood it. We have seen above that the writing of pseudepigrapha gave voice to a claim on the part of the actual authors to be actualizing or contemporizing what was implicit in the living tradition in which they stood. It is our view that the PE emanate from a member of a Pauline school operating in Ephesus who did precisely that.

But there are scholars who argue that there is a problem including pseudepigrapha in the NT. If pseudepigrapha are by definition fraudulent and written to deceive, they could not have been inspired by God. Consequently, if scholars insist that writings such as the PE are indeed pseudonymous, then they have no place in the canon and should now be rejected. Moreover, it is argued that had the early fathers suspected that the PE were pseudonymous they would have rejected them as unworthy of authoritative and canonical status. E. Earle Ellis is one who has championed this point of view.[95] It is well-represented in recent scholarship.[96]

---

[92] See, for example, Bart Ehrman, *The New Testament: An Historical Introduction to the Early Christian Writings* (New York: Oxford University Press, 2000), 394. Contra D. A. Carson, Douglas J. Moo, and Leon Morris, eds., *Introduction to the New Testament* (Grand Rapids: Zondervan, 1992), 433-37.

[93] See David G. Meade, *Pseudonymity and Canon* (Grand Rapids: Eerdmans, 1986). Meade's thesis is that attributing authorship, in our case, of Paul to the PE, "must be primarily regarded as a statement (or assertion) of authoritative tradition" (216). See also J. D. G. Dunn (Meade's doctoral supervisor), *The Living Word* (Philadelphia: Fortress, 1988), 65-85.

[94] See my *What Are They Saying*, 32-36.

[95] E. Earle Ellis, "Pseudonymity and Canonicity of New Testament Documents," in M. J. Wilkins and T. Paige, eds., *Worship, Theology, and Ministry in the Early Church: Essays in Honour of Ralph P. Martin* (JSNTS 87; Sheffield: JSOT Press, 1992), 212-24; Stanley E. Porter, "Pauline Authorship and the Pastoral Epistles: Implications for the Canon," *BBR* 5 (1995): 105-23.

[96] See Terry L. Wilder, "Pseudonymity, the New Testament, and the Pastoral Epistles," in Köstenberger and Wilder, *Entrusted with the Gospel*, 28-51. I. Howard Marshall advocates

However, the early fathers were neither infallible in their detection of pseudepigrapha nor did they respond consistently to the phenomenon. On the one hand Tertullian's presbyter and Salvian were punished for their deception; on the other the *Wisdom of Solomon* ("written by friends of Solomon in his honor," according to the Muratorian Canon) retained its canonical status, though admittedly this is the exception to the rule. The *Acts of Pilate* and the pseudonymous *Letters of Paul and Seneca* were received as genuine by Justin Martyr and Jerome respectively. The determination that works were genuinely apostolic did not commence with the weighing and scrutinizing of authorial claims. The fathers valued apostolic works, and some that we now know to be pseudepigraphical, because they were acknowledged to be venerable and widely used, and they articulated orthodox doctrine.[97] Works bearing the name of an apostle or of an associate that were perceived to be unorthodox in doctrine were quickly dismissed as pseudepigraphical.[98]

We have seen above that writing pseudepigraphically was a strategy designed to actualize living tradition and cause it to speak to new situations not originally envisaged. This explains the PE as Pauline pseudepigrapha. Paul, though dead, yet speaks through the Pastor out of the Pauline tradition that comes to speech in his letters to protect the Pauline heritage and the Pauline gospel. And thus it was that the PE were accepted as genuinely Pauline letters. If God caused Scripture to be written, then he did so by neither countervailing the constraints and exigencies under which the authors operated nor overruling the culturally determined methods by which ancient literary works come into being, including the use of pseudonymity.[99]

---

avoiding the pejorative term "pseudonymity" and adopting the neutral term "allonymity" or "allepigraphy" (emphasizing that a work has been written in the name of *another* person rather than written under a *false* name, without the intention to deceive the recipients) to explain the phenomenon in his *Pastoral Epistles*, 84. See also Harrison, *Problem*, 12-13. The PE are not deceptive, but in their origin they were a transparent representing of what the apostle might have said to the Timothys and Tituses of his day had he been alive. Over forty years later Harrison repeated this view in *Paulines and Pastorals* (London: Villiers Publications, 1964), 14 where he writes that the PE were neither "genuine," nor "spurious" (the work of a forger), but "pseudonymous." The author's purpose "was not to mislead, but to convey as true an account as possible of the Apostle's teaching in its relevance to the needs and conditions of the Sub-apostolic Age." Note the cautious assessment of the value of the term allepigraphy in Towner, *Letters*, 25-26.

[97] See the helpful discussion of the several criteria that determined what books would be regarded as authoritative and canonical in the emerging church in Lee M. McDonald, *The Formation of the Christian Biblical Canon* (Peabody: Hendrickson, 1995), 246-49. McDonald opts for usage as the most important of the five criteria he adduces (apostolicity, orthodoxy, antiquity, inspiration, and usage). He concludes: "It appears the writings that were best believed to have best conveyed the earliest Christian proclamation and that also best met the growing needs of the local churches in the third and fourth centuries were the writings they [the fathers] selected for their sacred scriptures" (248).

[98] To be noted in this regard is the story recounted by Eusebius, *Hist. eccl.* 6.12.6 in which Serapion, bishop of Antioch in about A.D. 200, finally condemns the *Gospel of Peter* used by the community at Rhossus because on closer examination he discovered docetic teaching in it. The work cannot have been written by Peter, Serapion concludes.

[99] See the helpful survey and conclusions by Harry Y. Gamble, "Pseudonymity and the New Testament Canon," in Frey, *Pseudepigraphie*, 333-62.

6. The Theology of the PE

As foreshadowed above we should now revisit I. Howard Marshall's contention that the theology of the PE proceeds on a coherence/contingency basis, albeit one that differs in focus from that of the apostle. The PE articulate a coherent theology of God's saving epiphany which informs the Pastor's engagement with the crisis that false teaching has precipitated in the Pauline communities addressed and provides the imperative for godly living (εὐσέβεια) to which all are called in their proper social station.[100] The author stresses the reality of the will of God for the salvation of all humankind (see 1 Tim 2:4; Tit 2:11) which has now been made manifest by the appearing (ἐπιφάνεια) of Christ. This saving appearing, the Pastor writes, has abolished death and brought immortality to light through the gospel (διὰ τοῦ εὐαγγελίου; 2 Tim 1:10). This gospel, Jouette Bassler argues, is itself an "epiphanic event" since the news of God's saving epiphany is brought to light in first Paul's and then his successors' proclamation; indeed all who proclaim this message and conduct their lives and teach in accordance with it are not only bearing witness to but are also embodying God's saving epiphany.[101] Moreover the PE themselves participate in this epiphany through their teaching and exhortation. They are "vehicles of intervention" in a critical situation in which the legacy of the apostle is being undermined.[102]

This theology is brought to bear on the urgent situation addressed in the letters. The first appearing has not exhausted the scope of God's will to save because there remains a second appearing to fully realize what God has intended such that no one could ever confess that the resurrection is past already (2 Tim 2:18). God's saving will is all-encompassing. Indeed it is the saving will of a Creator whose blessing extends to all that he has created—to food and marriage (1 Tim 4:3-5), to political realities (1 Tim 2:1-7), and to the time-honored moral conventions of society with its expectations of the submissive behavior of women (1 Tim 2:9-15) and slaves (Tit 2:9), the normativity of marriage (1 Tim 4:3; 5:14; cf. 1 Cor 7:25-27), and of the character that constitutes the morally commendable life. Only upright householders should expect to assume leadership in the "household of God" (οἶκος θεοῦ; 1 Tim 3:15, cf. 3:4, 5).[103] Salvation is not for the chosen few whose insight, whose *gnōsis* (γνῶσις), affords entitlement. Such teaching counters the exclusivity of the vision of the scope of salvation promulgated by the false teachers,[104] undermines the low esteem of the false teachers for the

---

[100] I am much indebted to Jouette M. Bassler's fine article "A Plethora of Epiphanies: Christology in the Pastoral Epistles," *PSB* 17 (1996): 310-25. For a study of the background of the epiphany language in the PE, see also Andrew Y. Lau, *Manifest in Flesh: The Epiphany Christology of the Pastoral Epistles* (WUNT 86; Tübingen: Mohr [Siebeck], 1996).
[101] Bassler, "Plethora," 320-23.
[102] Bassler, "Plethora," 323-24.
[103] For good character and moral attainment as key qualities of church leaders, not wealth and the accumulation of honors, see Reggie M. Kidd, *Wealth and Beneficence in the Pastoral Epistles* (SBLDS 122; Atlanta: Scholars Press, 1990).
[104] See e.g. Wieland, *The Significance of Salvation*, 57, 243.

created order, including its hierarchical social structures, and corrects the presumed license granted women (and possibly slaves) in the communities addressed.[105]

The can be no misunderstanding of the intention of the Pastor to mandate what Frances Young terms "correct relationships, duties, and obligations" for the emergent believing communities. They have their authoritative writings (she has in mind the Jewish Scriptures) and hierarchical social organization which is indebted both to the conventions of the Greco-Roman household and to the synagogue.[106] It is for this reason that the Pastor sets forth a church order in which upright male elders and overseers take responsibility for protecting and passing on the παραθήκη, the "deposit," taking care to preach and teach and to live in accordance with it. Set over the household of God (1 Tim 3:15), these leaders are to ensure that they and the communities they oversee mirror many of the ethical ideals affirmed in Greco-Roman culture and endorsed in the PE and continue to draw sharp distinctions between their teaching and that of false teachers. The PE thus set forth a vision of life for believers within the empire. That vision, as we have seen above, is grounded in the saving epiphany of God and his Christ, and amounts to a life-commitment that is consistent with Greco-Roman ideals and the notion of good citizenship—"quiet and peaceable," "godly and respectful in every way" (1 Tim 2:2b).[107]

Finally, relevant to the developing sense of what constitutes an orthodox community in 1 Timothy and Titus, it is important not to underestimate the requirements placed on those who aspire to be leaders. The personal characteristics that must be in evidence retain their force today. The ethos of the apostle, which is at the center of all three letters, but supremely so in 2 Timothy, legitimating all that is mandated therein, continues to exercise a profound hold on the formation of clergy and church leaders today, and indeed on all who would follow Paul's example.[108]

---

[105] See the important monograph of David Verner, *The Household of God: The Social World of the Pastoral Epistles* (SBLDS 71; Chico: Scholars Press, 1983). Studies of the interface between Greco-Roman society and the PE have been particularly common. Among the more recently published research note Marianne Bjelland Kartzow, *Gossip and Gender: Othering of Speech in the Pastoral Epistles* (Berlin: de Gruyter, 2009).

[106] See Young, *Theology*, 83.

[107] The phrase ἵνα ἤρεμον καὶ ἡσύχιον βίον διάγωμεν ἐν πάσῃ εὐσεβείᾳ καὶ σεμνότητι (1 Tim 2:2b) consists almost solely of NT hapaxes (in italics) and Pauline hapaxes (underlined). Note Martin Dibelius and Hans Conzelmann's comments on the moral vision of the PE in *The Pastoral Epistles* (Philadelphia: Fortress, 1972), 39-41, which they term "Christian citizenship" (bürgerliches Christentum), the direct result of the receding of the imminent παρουσία and the need for believers to accommodate themselves to the delay. This view has provoked several responses, notably Philip H. Towner, *The Goal of Our Instruction* (JSNTSup 34; Sheffield: JSOT Press, 1989). Towner contends that the moral instruction of the PE, far from being accommodationist, is proactively designed to enhance evangelistic enterprise.

[108] Note the comments on the formation of Christian character in the PE by Robert Wall in "Function," 34-44. See also the major study by Claire S. Smith, *Pauline Communities as "Scholastic Communities": A Study of the Vocabulary of Teaching in 1 Corinthians, 1 & 2 Timothy & Titus* (Tübingen: Mohr [Siebeck], 2012). She emphasizes the value of the PE for the formation of all believers, not just those in positions of leadership.

Recommended Reading

Aageson, James W. *Paul, the Pastoral Epistles, and the Early Church*. Peabody: Hendrickson, 2008.

Bassler, Jouette M. "A Plethora of Epiphanies: Christology in the Pastoral Epistles." *Princeton Seminary Bulletin* 17 (1996): 310-25.

Beker, J. Christiaan. *Heirs of Paul: The Legacy of Paul in the New Testament and in the Church*. Minneapolis: Fortress, 1991.

Collins, Raymond F. *The Pastoral Epistles*. Louisville: Westminster John Knox, 2002.

Frey, Jörg et al. *Pseudepigraphie und Verfasserfiktion in frühchristlichen Briefen*. Wissenschaftliche Untersuchungen zum Neuen Testament 245. Tübingen: Mohr (Siebeck), 2009.

Gill, Malcolm. *Jesus as Mediator: Politics and Polemic in 1 Timothy 2:1-7*. New York: Peter Lang, 2008.

Harding, Mark. *What Are They Saying About the Pastoral Epistles?* Mahwah: Paulist Press, 2001.

Köstenberger, Andreas J., and Terry L. Wilder, eds. *Entrusted with the Gospel: Paul's Theology in the Pastoral Epistles*. Nashville: Baker Academic, 2010.

Lau, Andrew Y. *Manifest in Flesh: The Epiphany Christology of the Pastoral Epistles* Wissenschaftliche Untersuchungen zum Neuen Testament 86. Tübingen: Mohr (Siebeck), 1996.

Marshall, I. Howard. *A Critical and Exegetical Commentary on the Pastoral Epistles*. Edinburgh: T. & T. Clark, 1999.

Pietersen, Lloyd K. *The Polemic of the Pastoral Epistles: A Sociological Examination of the Development of Pauline Christianity*. New York: T. & T. Clark, 2004.

Wall, Robert W., and Richard B. Steele. *1 and 2 Timothy and Titus*. Grand Rapids: Eerdmans, 2012.

Young, Frances. *The Theology of the Pastoral Letters*. Cambridge: Cambridge University Press, 1994.

14. Pauline Theology

Timothy J. Harris

It is an ambitious, and some would say perilous, exercise to attempt a synthesis of Pauline theology. Such a project is invariably reductionist in nature, and all too easily amounts to a summary overview. Our purpose here is more specific—to map and analyze something of the range, shape, and contours of Pauline theology, with a view to the interaction between Paul's theological thought and the range of cultural, social, and worldview issues that were frequently foremost in Paul's considerations.

Interpreters of Paul and his thought have been legion throughout history, and publications and studies engaging with his theology continue unabated. This chapter makes no attempt to provide a survey of the field regarding Pauline interpretation, nor does it seek to review publications on Pauline theology more specifically. Reference to secondary material will be kept to a minimum, and our focus will be on the correspondence associated with the name of Paul as contained in the New Testament canon.[1]

1. Methodology

Any notion of "Pauline theology" needs to consider a range of preliminary questions. Can we assume a direct correlation between the theology of Paul and the theology of letters that bear his name?[2] Can we determine a Pauline theology in terms greater than the particular expression in each letter—something that approximates to a more holistic "pattern of religion"?

---

[1] Unless otherwise indicated, all scriptural quotations in this chapter are taken from *The Holy Bible: New Revised Standard Version* (Nashville: Thomas Nelson Publishers, 1989).

[2] With the focus on "Pauline" theology, this chapter does not make specific delineation between the literature that is widely acknowledged as authentically from the authorial direction of Paul (Romans, 1 and 2 Corinthians, Galatians, Philippians, 1 Thessalonians, Philemon), and other letters that are subject to greater debate (Ephesians, Colossians, and 2 Thessalonians, and most extensively disputed, 1 and 2 Timothy, Titus). Whether they are directly composed by Paul at a later stage of his life, written with a greater degree of scribal discretion, or works attributed more loosely to the influence of Paul, they are all more broadly within a body of literature that we may more broadly consider "Pauline." The significant characteristics, themes, and terms that we will identify in this chapter are all reflected at some point in the undisputedly Pauline literature, even if given fuller expression in letters that are subject to greater dispute. For more detailed justification of the approach adopted here, see further Luke Timothy Johnson, *The Writings of the New Testament: An Interpretation* (3rd ed.; Minneapolis: Fortress, 2010), 239-42.

1.1. The Shaping of Pauline Theology

There is a range of approaches in the presentation of Pauline theology.[3] The most common is the identification of characteristically Pauline themes, motifs or terminology,[4] where the focus is directed to determining their interrelationship and whether there is a discernible "center" or overarching affirmation in Paul's theological canvas. On the other hand, there is the setting of Paul's theology into the context of his own life and experiences as they developed, whether personal or in relation to specific ministry contexts and circumstances.[5] This approach more readily accommodates the contingent nature of any and every expression of Paul's theological thought, together with the possibility of development in his thinking.

A number of factors need to be considered in approaching a "Pauline theology." Can coherence be detected?[6] And if so, is it capable of precise articulation in the language and terminology available to us?[7] Are there inconsistencies or contradictions?[8] Given the possibility of development in Paul's theological thinking,[9] can some dimensions of development be plotted? Are there "watershed" experiences, or further and deeper inspiration that modify previous statements or perspectives? In other words, we need to recognize that "Pauline theology" is neither static nor necessarily univocal.[10]

There are also inherent tensions between identifying Pauline theology as expressed contingently in particular contexts and addressing specific issues, over against some notion of a more generally identifiable pattern of thought. Is there such a thing as "Pauline theology" per se, other than its particular and specific contextual expression?

Moreover, there are questions of how Paul's theological thought-world might be organized.[11] Are we justified in seeking a "center" in Pauline theology, an underlying or definitive core affirmation around which all other

---

[3] See especially the opening section "Methodology" in Jouette M. Bassler, David M. Hay, and E. Elizabeth Johnson, eds., *Pauline Theology* (vol. 1; Minneapolis: Fortress, 1991).

[4] As an example see James D. G. Dunn, *The Theology of Paul the Apostle* (Grand Rapids: Eerdmans, 1998). It should also be noted, however, that Dunn adopts a narrative and developmental approach in his extensive "Christianity in the Making" series. With reference to Paul see especially James D. G. Dunn, *Beginning from Jerusalem, Christianity in the Making* (vol. 2, part 2; Grand Rapids: Eerdmans, 2008).

[5] A classic example is that by F. F. Bruce, *Paul, Apostle of the Heart Set Free* (Grand Rapids: Eerdmans, 1977).

[6] J. Christiaan Beker, "Recasting Pauline Theology: The Coherence-Contingency Scheme as Interpretive Model," in Bassler, Hay, and Johnson, *Pauline Theology*, 15-24.

[7] Paul J. Achtemeier, "Finding the Way to Paul's Theology: A Response to J. Christiaan Beker and J. Paul Sampley," in Bassler et al., *Pauline Theology*, 25-36.

[8] Note especially Heikki Räisänen, *Paul and the Law* (Tübingen: Mohr [Siebeck], 1987).

[9] Udo Schnelle, *Wandlungen im Paulinischen Denken* (Stuttgart: Verlag Katholisches Bibelwerk, 1989).

[10] By this we mean that the expression of Paul's theological thought may also reflect the terminology of differing scribes or amanuenses, or input from differing personalities amongst Paul's co-workers. The articulation of Paul's theology was not a solo exercise, and frequently picked up terms, categories, and paradigms specific to differing contexts.

[11] Udo Schnelle, *Apostle Paul: His Life and Theology* (Grand Rapids: Baker Academic, 2005).

dimensions are subsumed? Rather than seeking one central notion, J. Paul Sampley suggestively proposes a model on the analogy of electromagnetic fields in which for "something as complex as Paul's thought world one may imagine a series of electromagnetic fields, each in tension within itself and each field of force arrayed in tension with all the others."[12]

Given the largely antipodean provenance of this volume, the metaphor of Paul drawing on a great underground water reservoir through a range of boreholes is also suggestive. Such undercurrents have ancient origins, and are formed and hewn out of many theological streams and rivers sanctioned by the revelatory providence of the God of Israel, forming one multi-dimensional reality that is greater than any individual expression. Paul, in effect, accessed such a cavernous theological reservoir in many and varied contexts for purposes specific to each context or occasion. Paul's theological mode is dynamic and takes on a life of its own. As we shall suggest below, Paul as a theological thinker does more than draw on pre-existing wisdom or traditions: he contributes creatively and productively in applying such theological wellsprings to generate innovative and influential formulations that may be identified as characteristically and perhaps uniquely "Pauline." Paul takes theology into new territory, develops new conceptual paradigms, and in innovating a range of theological terms he shapes the way in which the gospel associated with Jesus of Nazareth is both perceived and proclaimed.[13]

There is no single or "correct" method of approach to delineating Pauline theology; differing modes of presentation often function in complementary fashion to highlight different aspects in the discernment of Paul's theological considerations.

1.2. Paul the "Theologian"

While drawing deeply on his memory and knowledge of Scripture and gospel traditions,[14] Paul also consciously develops new avenues of theological reflection and proclamation. Paul the educated Jew,[15] apparently well-versed

---

[12] J. Paul Sampley, "From Text to Thought World: The Route to Paul's Ways," in Bassler, *Pauline Theology*, 7.

[13] See for example Michael J. Gorman, *Apostle of the Crucified Lord: A Theological Introduction to Paul and His Letters* (Grand Rapids: Eerdmans, 2004). Gorman highlights the significance for Paul of the "cruciform" (crucified) character of God revealed in the person and mission of Christ. A further contribution in Gorman's work is the identification of a dozen "fundamental convictions" that are integral to Paul's theology, and subsequently explored with reference to the Pauline correspondence. Other scholars who follow a paradigmic mode of interpretation are Tom Holland, *Contours of Pauline Theology: A Radical New Survey of the Influences on Paul's Biblical Writings* (Fearn: Mentor, 2004) and Ben Witherington, *The Indelible Image: The Theological and Ethical Thought World of the New Testament* (Downers Grove: IVP Academic, 2009).

[14] This touches on significant questions about the relationship between Pauline Christianity and gospel traditions. See further Todd D. Still, ed., *Jesus and Paul Reconnected: Fresh Pathways into an Old Debate* (Grand Rapids: Eerdmans, 2007).

[15] Surprisingly little can be determined of the specifics of Paul's education (whether Greco-Roman or Jewish). It is saying too much to claim that Paul was formally trained as a "Rabbi"

in schools of interpretation, becomes Paul the apostle articulating a message of a new order emerging out of the former age and now inaugurated in the work of Christ;[16] a new cosmic reality no less.[17]

It is axiomatic that Paul's "theology," in the strictest sense of the word (his understanding of God), was grounded in his beliefs as affirmed within the people of Israel, especially as defined in association with the God of Abraham, Moses, David, and the prophets. His understanding of God, now identified with Christ, is no less than the God revealed to Israel. In Christ, however, this God is revealed in all-new and profoundly fuller ways. As Paul reflected on his former beliefs in the God of Israel, it is not so much that such beliefs were wrong, but that the apprehension of the God revealed to Moses is far eclipsed by God revealed in Christ (2 Cor 3:12-18).

The foundation of Paul's theology does not change: he remains fully committed to the one true and living God identified as YHWH, the covenantal God of Israel. While the terminology of "monotheism" has been challenged, we may rightly speak of the uniqueness of the God of Israel as reflected in the *Shema* (Deut 6:4). In one sense this can convey a strongly relational dimension ("the only one for me"), but the context of such affirmations is frequently covenantal, and very often associated with the sovereignty of God in the face of military threats and claims to supremacy by other nations in the name of their gods. Even when recognizing a variety of "agents" from the heavenly realm very closely associated with God as reflected in many Jewish writings, evidence for the "one and only" standing of the God of Israel in first-century Judaism is compelling.[18] YHWH is affirmed as both the sole Creator of all things and uniquely sovereign over all things.[19]

(and such usage is probably anachronistic for this period), although more regarding his education can be gleaned from the content of his correspondence: see Bruce Chilton, *Rabbi Paul: An Intellectual Biography* (New York: Doubleday, 2004); and Ronald Hock, "Paul and Greco-Roman Education," in J. Paul Sampley, ed., *Paul in the Greco-Roman World: A Handbook* (Harrisburg: Trinity Press International, 2003), 198-227.

[16] Behind this observation lie two areas of debate to be discussed further below: the place of narrative, and especially a narrative substructure, in Paul's thinking; and secondly the significance of Christology at the center of Paul's theological reappraisal.

[17] There is a connection between "cosmology" as a perception of ultimate reality, and the narratives that are told that underscore such realities. Thus the gospel narrative of Jesus Christ challenged the Roman imperial narrative that affirmed the centrality and authority of Caesar (see also chapter 7 of this volume). In profound ways, it is the influence of this alternative Judeo-Christian narrative that has shaped East and West more than propositions at the history of ideas level alone.

[18] See the summary of debates and evidence in Larry W. Hurtado, *Lord Jesus Christ: Devotion to Jesus in Earliest Christianity* (Grand Rapids: Eerdmans, 2003); Larry W. Hurtado, *How on Earth Did Jesus Become a God?: Historical Questions About Earliest Devotion to Jesus* (Grand Rapids: Eerdmans, 2005).

[19] Note especially the qualifications in defining monotheism (creational, providential, and covenantal monotheism) offered by N. T. Wright, *The New Testament and the People of God: Christian Origins and the Question of God* (vol. 1; London: SPCK, 1992), 248-52; compare Richard Bauckham, *God Crucified: Monotheism and Christology in the New Testament* (Grand Rapids: Eerdmans, 1999).

Given this strongly held foundational belief, the question then becomes where does devotion to Christ, and even more strikingly the attribution of worship of Christ in terms otherwise stringently reserved for YHWH, fit within such a faith framework? We shall address this further in considering Christology, but for now we may note that Paul's "conversion experience" was primarily a conversion to the person of Christ and especially his "Lordship" within this resolutely monotheistic affirmation.

1.3. Sources for Paul's Theological Outlook and Formulations

There are four main streams that inform Paul's thought-world, although each of these contains a variety of more specific influences.

1. The Jewish Scriptures[20] (generally the LXX in varying editions, although with occasional agreement with the Hebrew Bible against the LXX) and associated Jewish writings and traditions from a range of contexts (Dead Sea Scrolls, literature of Second Temple Judaism, Pharisaic Judaism, and some diaspora expressions of Jewish beliefs and religious observances[21]).
2. An awareness of Greco-Roman philosophical discourse, including contemporary expressions of Epicureanism, Stoicism, and the Cynics,[22] together with the socio-cultural environment of honor and shame, grace and benefaction, enmity and friendship.
3. Developing and foundational gospel traditions concerning Jesus, his manner of life, teachings, signs and miracles, death, resurrection, and eschatological pronouncements (such traditions including knowledge of sectarian claims concerning Jesus prior to his conversion, possible instruction in Damascus [Acts 9:19-22], association with Barnabas and other leaders in Syrian Antioch, and interaction with other apostles).
4. The Pauline ministry retinue and communities of discourse: in addition to the significant periods of time Paul spent in specific locations (e.g. Corinth and Ephesus). Paul's apparent mode of discourse was dialogue (Acts 20:7), and it is quite likely that his letters were "workshopped" in the context of his mission team and associated churches.[23]

---

[20] The classic text in this area is Richard B. Hays, *Echoes of Scripture in the Letters of Paul* (New Haven: Yale University Press, 1989).

[21] Note the extensive treatment of this area in the (provocatively titled) monograph by Pamela Eisenbaum, *Paul Was Not a Christian: The Real Message of a Misunderstood Apostle* (New York: HarperOne, 2009).

[22] A pioneering essay in this area is that of Abraham Malherbe, "Hellenistic Moralists and the New Testament," *ANRW* II 26.1: 267-333. See also essays in Troels Engberg-Pedersen, ed., *Paul in His Hellenistic Context* (Minneapolis: Fortress, 1995).

[23] See especially E. Randolph Richards, *Paul and First-Century Letter Writing: Secretaries, Composition, and Collection* (Downers Grove: IVP, 2004).

1.4. Early Creedal Confession

In many ways, a very early and profound stage of Pauline theology, notably grounded in an established and authoritative apostolic gospel tradition, can be detected in 1 Cor 15:1-5. This is the essential gospel as far as Paul is concerned, the only basis for salvation and belief (vv. 1-2). The language of "receiving" points unmistakably to a pre-existing affirmation, and the pithy outline of the death, burial, and resurrection appearances of Christ is interwoven with theological interpretation ("for our sins") articulated with reference to the Scriptures. The unit has both apologetic and kerygmatic character, and is incorporated into the epistle with personal reference to Paul's own experience, calling, and preaching (vv. 8-11).

Other possible creedal formulations have been detected and much debated (especially Phil 2:6-11 and Col 1:15-20), but enough has been noted to identify the interplay between early affirmations and Paul's presentation of the gospel.

2. Modes of Pauline Theology

2.1. The Writer of Letters and Discourses

The evidence for Paul's theology comes through to us in the general form of letters, but goes beyond personal or more formal expressions of letter writing. For the purposes of this chapter, our focus is less on the form of the Pauline letters[24] than the mode of theology conveyed therein. Epistles were composed to be communicated orally by the messenger, and therefore had significant rhetorical qualities that shape the mode of expression, even to the extent of being a type of substitute "conversation."[25] The reading of such a letter was to represent the author in their physical absence. Silent reading was a relatively rare and noteworthy skill in the ancient world to the extent that we need to approach the interpretation of Paul's letters with the assumption that they were not designed for private reflection and study. Reading was oral, and usually a communal activity. This is an important consideration in discerning the modes and forms of theological expression we encounter in Paul's letters.

Rhetoric—the skills of public address—was a prominent feature of communication in the ancient world, exercising a profound influence in terms of preparation, delivery, and reception. The form of rhetoric is a key indicator of the communicator's intent in any form of public address, and says much about the nature of the relationship between the communicator and the audience. While there are many more specific variations, there were three

---

[24] See Robert W. Wall, "Introduction to the Epistolary Literature," in *NIB* 10. More extensively, see the essays in Stanley E. Porter and Sean A. Adams, eds., *Paul and the Ancient Letter Form* (Pauline Studies 6; Leiden: Brill, 2010).

[25] Wall, "Introduction," 378-79; Richards, *Paul and First-Century Letter Writing*, 124-25.

main modes of ancient rhetoric:[26] forensic, deliberative, and epideictic. The discernment of Pauline theology needs to recognize the rhetorical mode employed at any given point.[27]

Given that Paul's letters were written with a view to being read aloud, recognizing the rhetorical mode is a helpful guide in the interpretive task. It is true that the language of formal rhetoric is not prevalent in the Pauline correspondence, yet in more general terms Paul does reflect rhetorical traits associated with the arts of persuasion. Paul's theology has a range of forms, tones, and purposes, and often cannot be reduced to a series of propositional statements alone without losing the point of relevance in any given context. The clearest indication of Paul's theological intent is found in the verbs of address, whether they be his most common terms of exhortation, urging or appeal, or the less frequent and therefore more striking use of the language of command and rebuke, usually reserved for occasions where Paul believed the gospel itself was under threat or compromised.

2.2. Pastoral Theology

Paul writes as a pastor, and much of the theology reflected in his correspondence derives from his responding and thinking theologically on everyday realities and questions of faith, identity, and lifestyle. Little if any of his theology is "abstract" or expressed in the form of a theological primer. Where Paul presents big picture dimensions to his theology, it is to inform very concrete and contentious issues of life. This in itself is an insight into the exercise of theology. The purpose of instruction is necessarily related to receiving, hearing, and responding to the word of God. The word of God is to be lived as a necessary part of its proclamation, something Paul sought to model as much as speak of (note, for example, how these various dimensions are reflected in 1 Thess 1:5-10).

In giving pastoral guidance and direction to a range of issues (whether asked of Paul or reported to him), the responses bear little resemblance to an identifiable "instruction manual"—although the household codes come close at points—and more to the "pastor-teacher" (Eph 4: 11). Paul wanted the hearers to recognize the theological thinking behind his responses, and to locate such questions or issues against the backdrop of a broader theological canvas, and one in which the person of Christ is central. It is also in this

---

[26] These three branches are derived from the classic treatment in Aristotle's *On Rhetoric*. For a well-respected treatment, see G. A. Kennedy, *Classical Rhetoric & Its Christian & Secular Tradition from Ancient to Modern Times* (2nd ed.; Chapel Hill: University of North Carolina Press, 1999). For a helpful treatment of the relevance of classical rhetoric with reference to the Pauline correspondence, see Stanley E. Porter and Dennis L. Stamps, eds., *Rhetorical Criticism and the Bible* (JSNTSup 195; New York: Sheffield Academic Press, 2002).

[27] The pioneering text in this field is that by Hans Dieter Betz, *Galatians: A Commentary on Paul's Letter to the Churches in Galatia* (Philadelphia: Fortress, 1979). Note also Lauri Thurén, *Derhetorizing Paul: A Dynamic Perspective on Pauline Theology and the Law* (Tübingen: Mohr [Siebeck], 2000).

context that much of Paul's pneumatology is expressed. The Spirit reveals, enlightens, guides, empowers, and consoles.

3. Theological Foundations

3.1. The Starting Point in Discerning Pauline Theology: Conversion of Worldview

Our understanding of "conversion" needs to be shaped less by modern psychological paradigms, and informed more by Greco-Roman perceptions of identity and social location within the realities of the social world of any given community.[28] Put more starkly, questions of authority, patronage, and obligation were reinforced (or subverted) by underlying worldviews.

Paul describes his encounter with Jesus on the road to Damascus as a revelatory experience. He moved from darkness to light, and such blindness is attributed to "the god of this world" blinding the minds of unbelievers, preventing them from seeing "the light of the gospel of the glory of Christ, who is the image of God" (2 Cor 4:4). This revelatory experience transformed Paul's mind—his worldview—so that he now proclaimed, "Jesus Christ as Lord and ourselves as your slaves for Jesus' sake" (2 Cor 4:5). It is in this sense that Pauline theology is essentially *apocalyptic*,[29] that is, grounded in God's revelation in Christ (see also Gal 1:15-16; Phil 3:3-11). Of Paul's encounter on the Damascus Road, J. Louis Martyn writes: "That event was the genesis of Paul's eschatological apocalyptic, for it was there that God opened his eyes to the presence of the risen Lord Jesus Christ in the Church . . . for Paul the cosmos in which he had been previously living met its end in God's apocalypse of Jesus Christ."[30]

A fruitful line of research is the exploration of engagement and potential confrontation between the proclamation of the gospel with its declaration that "Jesus is Lord" and Roman imperial claims.[31] While Paul gives no sign of

---

[28] Alan F. Segal, *Paul the Convert: The Apostolate and Apostasy of Saul the Pharisee* (New Haven: Yale University Press, 1990). See also Zeba A. Crook, *Reconceptualising Conversion: Patronage, Loyalty, and Conversion in the Religions of the Ancient Mediterranean* (Berlin: de Gruyter, 2004).

[29] Questions of definition are debated, but in general terms apocalyptic revelation may refer to truths known now, but not in former ages, or things not yet revealed, but will be in the age to come. The nature of the revelatory mode is complex, and can be through events (such as the cross) that reshape the cosmos and break into history. See Johan Christiaan Beker, *Paul the Apostle: The Triumph of God in Life and Thought* (Philadelphia: Fortress,1980). Consult also the essays in Joel Marcus, J. Louis Martyn, and Marion L. Soards, eds., *Apocalyptic and the New Testament: Essays in Honour of J. Louis Martyn* (JSNTSup 24; Sheffield: Continuum, 1989).

[30] J. Louis Martyn, *Galatians: A New Translation with Introduction and Commentary* (New York: Doubleday, 1997), 99.

[31] Indicative of such studies are the essays contained in Richard A. Horsley, ed., *Paul and Politics: Ekklesia, Israel, Imperium, Interpretation: Essays in Honor of Krister Stendahl* (Harrisburg: Trinity Press International, 2000). For a contrary perspective see Seyoon Kim, *Christ and Caesar: The Gospel and the Roman Empire in the Writings of Paul and Luke* (Grand Rapids: Eerdmans, 2008).

engaging with the political sphere in the Roman forum, and gospel mission as pursued by Paul has far greater horizons than seeking to challenge the Roman empire, it is nonetheless true that a fundamental conversion of worldview was an indispensible part of gospel allegiance.[32] It was not so much that Roman imperial claims are rejected, but rather subsumed within a much greater perception of authority and order understood in heavenly orientation (Rom 13:1-2).

The center of the universe is re-located around the Lordship of Christ, with such Lordship understood wholly and only with reference to the greater narrative of God's purposes reaching from creation to new creation. Absolutely pivotal to this narrative is the death and resurrection of Jesus, events Paul understood to be the working of God in Christ (2 Cor 5:19) attaining reconciliation and atonement, and thereby demonstrating the righteousness of God. The essence of Paul's theological outlook is stark: "I decided to know nothing among you except Jesus Christ, and him crucified" (1 Cor 2:2).

3.2. A (Retrospective) Diagnosis of the Human Condition

While a number of passages explore the origins and character of sin (in relation to Adam in Romans 5, and throughout Romans 5–8; Gal 3:22; 5:19-21; compare Eph 2:2-3; 4:17-18; 5:3-5; 1 Tim 4:2), Paul's most profound diagnosis of the human condition is found in Romans 1:18-32, operating at more levels than is often recognized. This is a passage that is to be seen retrospectively—Paul looking back on truths of which he was oblivious before his gospel enlightenment, and now revealed through his encounter with Christ and the illumination of the Spirit. In terms adopted in scholarly debates about schemas of salvation, Paul's own experience was less "from plight to solution," than a definitive insight into his theological and personal failures through encountering the living, glorious, and authoritative Christ in his own experience (2 Cor 4:4-6).[33]

Paul develops his treatment of the human condition in Romans 1 by noting the gospel as "the power of God for salvation for everyone who has faith, to the Jew first and also to the Greek" (1:16). The two hallmarks of this gospel are noted in terms of revelation: "the righteousness of God is revealed" (1:17), and "the wrath of God is revealed" (1:17). The latter is also "good news" (integral to the gospel), for it reveals a God who is passionate about upholding all that is right and who cannot tolerate "all ungodliness and wickedness." The expression of such ungodliness and wickedness is in exchanging "the truth of God for a lie," and worshipping and serving "the creature rather than the Creator" (1:25).

---

[32] For an analysis of Paul's conversion along similar lines to the view offered here, see Terence L. Donaldson, *Paul and the Gentiles: Remapping the Apostle's Convictional World* (Minneapolis: Fortress, 1997).
[33] Note especially the treatment in Seyoon Kim, *The Origin of Paul's Gospel* (Grand Rapids: Eerdmans, 1982).

In proceeding to name errant behavior characterizing sinful lifestyles in sexual spheres, Paul assumes ready agreement from his audience. Living in Rome, his audience could picture proponents of such behavior. They lived in the neighborhood and occupied the same tenement buildings, or perhaps observed such sexual practice in parties in which they served as slaves.

As Paul's list of sinful conduct continues, some unease would have set in. By the beginning of chapter 2, Paul's rhetorical trap is sprung. There is no "us" and "them" when it comes to complicity in sin. The indictment sheet is compelling, and all are guilty. However, more is going on in this section of Romans than the identification of sinful behavior. Paul is communicating with the "saints in Rome," not to bring them to faith or to spell out their need for salvation, but to locate this salvation within the one greater narrative of God's saving purposes since before time, to the Jew first and then to the Gentile. Furthermore, the spheres of sinfulness go beyond the individual. As reflected in the range of behaviors identified, sin has social expression; it involves families, households, and communities. Indeed, it impacts the whole of creation. Just as salvation has the most personal of reference, it also redresses the spread of sin in communal and global spheres.

Closer attention to Romans 1 reveals a deeper theological analysis. Paul explores the source of such behavior. How can it be that individuals and communities can manifest such evil? More than an indictment sheet, Paul offers both a diagnosis and prognosis. Such sinfulness, of which all are guilty, comes from a distortion of the mind (Rom 1:21; cf. v. 28), and living on the basis of a lie (Rom 1:25). The "mind" here is more than just a rational capacity as viewed in post-enlightenment perspective, but the entire outlook on life that draws together perception of truth, attitudes towards God, ambitions, passions, and life choices. Just as all have sinned, so also all have been afflicted with a distortion of mind. Salvation needs not only to bring about assurance of forgiveness and attainment of righteousness, it needs to transform the whole mindset that leads to this approach to life and idolatrous attitude towards God. The prognosis is stark: this manner of life is a dead-end (Rom 1:32).

Confirmation of this direction in Paul's thinking is found in the shape of his argument in Romans more broadly. The frustration of "sin that dwells within" (Rom 7:8, 11, 13) and the associated captivity that comes through the "law of my mind" gives way in chapter 8 to the work of the Spirit. The Spirit effects what the law could not do, namely, the replacing of the mind that is fixed on things of the "flesh" that lead to hostility to God (Rom 8:7) by a mind that is set on the things of the Spirit (Rom 8:5).[34]

All of this culminates in the reversals identified in Rom 12:1-2. While these verses are well known, their very specific correlation with the diagnosis of Romans 1 is frequently overlooked. In this summative statement, the gospel

---

[34] See further James M. Scott, *Adoption as Sons of God: An Exegetical Investigation into the Background of [Huiothesia] in the Pauline Corpus* (WUNT 2.48; Tübingen: Mohr [Siebeck], 1992).

as the power of God for salvation revealed in the mercies of God is depicted not only in the attainment of an acquittal, but addresses the source of such sinful life by underscoring nothing less than the complete transformation of the mind. In two profound verses, the state of affairs elaborated in Romans 1 is transformed in a whole new mindset, oriented to the discernment of the will of God and to what is "good and acceptable and perfect" (12:2).

Romans 1	Romans 12
wrath of God (v. 18)	mercies of God (v. 1)
refusal to thank or honor God (v. 21)	(thankful) pleasing sacrifice (v. 1)
dishonoring the body (v. 24)	presenting the body to God (v. 1)
impurity (v. 24)	holiness (v. 1)
foolish, idolatrous worship (vv. 21-23, 25)	reasonable worship (v. 1)
debased mind (v. 28)	renewed mind (v. 2)
refusal to acknowledge (v. 28)	discernment & obedience (v. 2)
the decree of God (v. 32)	the will of God (v. 2)

Just what this looks like in social and communal perspective in and through the body of Christ is addressed in the remainder of chapters 12 and 13. The contrast in values, attitudes, and manner of life compared to the behavior noted at the end of chapter 1 is stark. This is no less than "the gospel as the power of God for salvation, first to the Jews, and then to the Gentiles."

3.3. The Theological Significance of Jesus of Nazareth

It is well-recognized that discerning Pauline Christology needs to extend beyond a consideration of many of the titles Paul employed to designate Jesus of Nazareth. The location of Jesus within the greater biblical narrative, his association with doxology and worship, relational dimensions both within the God-head, and "in Christ" through the exercise of faith, all contribute to a much fuller perception of the theological significance of Jesus. The whole shape, mode, and nature of Jesus' life and ministry transformed Paul's worldview and established a paradigm around which his whole life and ministry was to be conformed.[35] The titles applied to Jesus are significant when perceived with reference to the greater theological narrative in which his person and works are given a unique and pre-eminent place.

(a) Christos

Writing in Greek, Paul used *Christos* as a curious lexical equivalent to the Hebrew *Māšīaḥ* with reference to Jesus. The pattern of use reflects the designation of "Christ" more as a name ("Jesus Christ") than a title ("the

---

[35] Michael J. Gorman, *Cruciformity: Paul's Narrative Spirituality of the Cross* (Grand Rapids: Eerdmans, 2001); Witherington, *Indelible Image,* ch. 2, "Paul the Paradigm Setter."

Christ"), although the titular dimension continues and the distinction is somewhat artificial.

In considering Paul's commonplace attribution [36] "Jesus Christ" (or "Christ Jesus"—there is no great difference), a number of issues need to be kept in mind. Firstly, there is no clear expectation that the figure of a "Messiah" was consistently or widely assumed. Different groupings within Judaism had differing expectations, with the terminology of an "anointed one" designating a broader genus of person raised and spiritually endowed by Yahweh to fulfill some aspect or role within the greater drama of salvation.[37]

The recognition of Jesus as "Christ" is an early one, and the association with the death and resurrection of Jesus a key affirmation in the gospel traditions that Paul repeats in 1 Cor 15:3-4. The fact that Paul sees no need to explain the term suggests that the association of Jesus as "Christ" was well established by the time of Paul's earliest correspondence.

We may note a pattern of usage emerging as early as 1 Thessalonians where the title and name are expressed in the phrase the "Lord Jesus Christ" (1 Thess 1:1), notably in conjunction with "God the Father," and together establishing the "church of the Thessalonians." A similar association is found in the closing prayer (5:23), with the characteristic reference to "the God of peace" set alongside an eschatological prayer-wish that "your spirit and soul and body be kept sound and blameless at the coming of our Lord Jesus Christ." This wish is coupled with the benediction "The grace of our Lord Jesus Christ be with you" (5:28). Also evident in 1 Thessalonians is the participatory "in Christ" (4:16) in which identification and union with Christ take on cosmic dimensions in which the same Jesus who "died and rose again" (4:14) will complete the raising of the dead "in Christ."

The association of "Christ" with the interlinking of the death and resurrection of Jesus, the identification and incorporation of believers "in Christ" in the present (whether physically alive or dead), and the cosmic and eschatological presence of Christ are profoundly Pauline. While the more cosmic dimensions are elaborated in notably exalted terms in the later epistles, the core affirmations are prominent in undisputed texts (Phil 2:5,11; Rom 10:6-7, and especially 1 Cor 15:12-25). So close is this identification that "Jesus Christ and him crucified" is synonymous with the gospel itself (1 Cor 2:2), especially when elaborated as the "Lord of glory" (1 Cor 2:8). Notably, the will and intent of God as revealed in the manner and ministry of Jesus is succinctly summed up in the phrase "the mind of Christ" (1 Cor 3:16; compare Phil 2:5-7) to the extent that the two are congruent.

---

[36] 270 times, out of 531 occurrences in the New Testament.
[37] For a helpful survey of background expectations regarding messianic figures, see chapter 2 in Michael F. Bird, *Are You the One Who Is to Come?: The Historical Jesus and the Messianic Question* (Grand Rapids: Baker Academic, 2009).

(b) Kyrios

Alongside Paul's frequent reference to Jesus as *Christos* is a more familiar and potentially subversive identification of Jesus as Lord (κύριος). The term itself had two distinctive spheres of usage. At one level, it was a common designation for a social superior to whom respect and some measure of obedience was due. It could be used of a great number of men in any given community. However, as the focus on the role of the *imperator* had developed since the time of Augustus, a political usage that assumed cosmic proportions was reserved for the emperor alone. The all-pervasive social world that was constructed and maintained in and through the elite of Rome had its epicenter in the person of the emperor.

This ultimate identification of "Lord" with the emperor defined all other lesser claimants. The propaganda of imperial lordship was pioneered by Augustus. By the time of Paul it was well established and prominent in every forum and urban center. Proclamation of the "good news" regarding the emperor was invariably as "Lord," terminology that also featured on many coins, inscriptions, and monuments.

As striking as the designation of Jesus as "Lord" would have been to Greek and Roman ears, the theological significance for Paul undoubtedly lay more with reference to Jewish traditions and Greek lexical equivalents to the Hebrew *'ăḏônay* and Aramaic *māryā'*, and also in some measure as an alternative for YHWH. Both the linguistic and oral background behind such usages is complex, and careful attention to context and the wider shape of the argument is essential. Along with *Christos*, the affirmation of "Jesus is Lord" is a major element in Paul's theology.

Of a number of passages in Paul's letters that reflect on the lordship of Jesus, one of the most striking and illuminating is found in the preface to Romans (1:1-7). The passage itself very likely incorporates elements of an early Jewish Christian confessional statement,[38] underscoring, on the one hand, Jesus' physical descent and continuity with David and, on the other, the royal title "son of God" status designated by decree in association with his resurrection. It is in this context that "the gospel of God" (1:1) takes focus, with the power of God manifested in and through "Jesus Christ our Lord" (1:4), and elaborated a few verses later as "the power of God for salvation" (1:16).

Just how much theological weight is to be given to the titular use of κύριος is much debated. At one end of the spectrum, the application to Jesus of Hebrew Bible texts that originally speak of YHWH suggests a very high Christology in which Jesus is attributed divine status (e.g. Phil 2:9-11, read with reference to Is 45:22-24). However, this line of interpretation is much debated, and depending on context the semantic sense of κύριος may also reflect a more socially defined sense of the term (a person of high social position or owner of property).

---

[38] See the discussion in Robert Jewett, *Romans: A Commentary* (Minneapolis: Fortress, 2007), 103-16.

Timothy J. Harris

Paul locates and advocates a place for Christ alongside the foundational affirmations concerning YHWH: "yet for us there is one God, the Father, from whom are all things and for whom we exist, and one Lord, Jesus Christ, through whom are all things and through whom we exist" (1 Cor 8:6), which some suggest is a profound re-working of the *Shema* (Deut 6:4) to incorporate Christ.[39]

(c) Other Expressions of Identity

Space does not allow a more extensive review of the presentation of Jesus within Pauline literature. Much more could be said of Jesus as "Savior,"[40] an attribution associated with God in both the Hebrew Bible and Second Temple writings, while also being very prominent in Greek and Roman mythology, and notably a much politicized and official designation of the Emperor.[41] A similar mix of association can be seen in the designation "Son of God," being both an honorific title associated with the king of Israel (for example, note Rom 1:4, with reference to Ps 2:7 and 2 Sam 7:12-14), as well as a specific claim of the Julio-Claudian emperors.[42]

Reference to Jesus as "seed" carried strong associations with covenantal ancestry (Gal 3:16) such that descent as the "seed of David according to the flesh" (Rom 1:4) identifies Jesus within the ongoing covenantal storyline connecting Christ with the programmatic Abrahamic promises. Yet the line of descent runs deeper, with the depiction of Jesus in terms of the "last" or "second" Adam (1 Cor 15: 45, 47; compare Rom 5:14), and with it much of the wider "old man/new man" typology (Rom 6:6; Eph 2:15; 4:22-24; Col 3:9-10) that points to a transformed mode of human existence established in Christ.

---

[39] N. T. Wright is the renowned exponent of the view that this verse amounts to "christological monotheism," and constitutes "one of the greatest pioneering moments in the entire history of Christology," N. T. Wright, *The Climax of the Covenant: Christ and the Law in Pauline Theology* (Minneapolis: Fortress, 1992), 136. This view is much debated.

[40] The term occurs twelve times in the wider Pauline corpus, ten of which are found in the Pastoral Epistles. About half of such references are to God as Savior; the others applied to Jesus. The two other notable instances outside the PE are Phil 3:20 in the context of eschatological expectation, and Eph 5:23 in a more realized sense of Christ as "Savior of the body."

[41] The profiling of Caesar as "Savior" is especially associated with the development of Julius Caesar's *persona* in *Bellum Gallicum* and the *Bellum Civile*, and subsequently became a prominent motif in the advertisement of imperial accomplishments. In similar terms, the Senate bestowed the title "Savior of the state" upon Augustus (*Senatus Consultum* of 13 January 27 B.C.), as symbolized in the laurel wreath and civic crown (Augustus, *Res Gestae* 34); see especially the treatment of Augustus in E. A. Judge and James R. Harrison, eds., *The First Christians in the Roman World: Augustan and New Testament Essays* (WUNT 229; Tübingen: Mohr [Siebeck], 2008), especially chapters 14–18.

[42] "*Divi filius*" was a title notably associated with Augustus with reference to his relationship with Julius Caesar, and subsequently officially conferred upon the male offspring of the emperors who were deified after their death (in Paul's time, Tiberius and Nero). The appellation "Son of God" would thus have carried strong political and imperial connotations to Greek and Roman ears.

The identification of Christ with the persona of "Wisdom" stands in contrast with the human dimensions of Pauline Christology and is more controversial, especially when associated with notions of pre-existence. Christ is designated the "wisdom of God" (1 Cor 1:24), whom God made "wisdom for us" (1 Cor 1:30). Activity often attributed to Wisdom is applied to Jesus in 1 Cor 8:6. The same line of thought is more fully developed in Col 1:15-20, again with qualities frequently associated with wisdom.

Persuasive cases have been made that Paul also speaks of Jesus as θεός.[43] While the syntax in Rom 9:5 can potentially be read in other ways, the introductory phrase and the syntactical balance of the sentence does incline towards reading the phrase as ". . . the Messiah, who is God over all . . ." (TNIV). However, all such considerations should be weighed in terms of wider context, the shape of the overall argument and the theological assumptions that underlie Paul's utterances. The same is true of much debated texts such as Phil 2:6-7 where Jesus is described as being "in the form of God," most likely designating that "form which truly and fully expresses the being which underlies it."[44] The profound association of Jesus, affirmed as Christ and Lord, with Paul's understanding of God is succinctly expressed in Second Corinthians: the God of creation and redemption (the God who brings light out of darkness) who has further shone through the greater glory of "the light of the knowledge of the glory of God in the face of Jesus Christ" (2 Cor 4:6). Christ, the "image of God" (4:2) is also the truest manifestation of God's glory.

(d) The Teaching of Jesus

The relative absence of direct quotations from the teachings of Jesus has given rise to much comment and discussion. There are differing levels in which teachings associated with Jesus can be discerned, ranging from direct quotation, allusion, to more loosely in the form of echoes.[45] It needs to be remembered that Paul wrote before any of the Gospels took shape, at a time when the teachings of Jesus were still largely retained in oral forms, and when written documentation was still largely localized.[46]

It is not only in quotations, allusions, and echoes that the teaching of Jesus can be discerned in Paul. An affinity with bigger picture dimensions of gospel traditions identified with Jesus, including wider themes and significant theological perspectives, can be noted.[47] Significant correlation between

---

[43] Murray J. Harris, *Jesus as God: The New Testament Use of Theos in Reference to Jesus* (Grand Rapids: Baker Book House, 1992).
[44] Moulton and Milligan, *s.v.* μορφή.
[45] A concise summary and helpful treatment is provided by S. Kim, "Sayings of Jesus," in Gerald F. Hawthorne, Ralph P. Martin, and Daniel G. Reid, eds., *Dictionary of Paul and His Letters* (Downers Grove: IVP, 1993), 472-92.
[46] Explored by James D. G. Dunn, *Jesus Remembered* (Christianity in the Making 1; Grand Rapids: Eerdmans, 2003), esp. 238-54.
[47] Note especially the helpful overview provided in James D. G. Dunn, *Jesus, Paul, and the Gospels* (Grand Rapids: Eerdmans, 2011).

Paul's thought and teachings subsequently identified with Jesus can be discerned with reference to the proclamation of the kingdom of God and Paul's presentation of the death and resurrection of Jesus, and more broadly by the whole manner and pattern of life associated with Christ and mirrored by Paul (e.g. 2 Cor 10:1-2; 11:10; compare also the parallels between Philippians 2 and 3).

(e) The Cross of Jesus

It is hard to overstate just how critical the work of Jesus upon the cross is for Paul's understanding of the gospel, and for his theology more generally. James D. G. Dunn observes that Paul, "having completed his indictment in Romans (1:18–3:20) turned at once, not to Jesus' life or teaching, but to his function as the God-provided "expiation" for sins past and present (Rom 3.25)."[48]

The enormity of this event in Paul's theological outlook defies brief description, but a few key features may be noted. The crucifixion of Jesus was no accidental development, but critical to the response of God to the human and creational predicament. God was at work in Christ, reconciling the world to himself by removing the offence and consequences of sin (2 Cor 5:19; compare Eph 2:3-5; Col 2:13-14). A range of images and qualities associated with the cross may be identified, but the significance of the sacrificial dimension is profound.[49] While the precise sense of ἱλαστήριον is much debated, the general allusion to the place and means of atonement is clear. In and through the cross, the righteousness of God was demonstrated and redemption attained.

It is also in this context that a notion of sacrificial "interchange" may be identified[50] where cultic language of atonement (e.g. Leviticus 4–5 passim; cf. 16:21) is used by Paul with reference to Christ's death achieving the removal of sin (Rom 3:25-26; 8:3; 2 Cor 5:21; compare Gal 3:13). The significance of Christ's death for those who are "in Christ" is conveyed through some notion of "substitution" and/or representation ("in the place of," 2 Cor 5:14-15[51]), but importantly also in terms of participation in his death and resurrection (Rom 6:6, 8; Gal 2:19; compare Col 2:12; 3:1).

If a center to Pauline theology is to be located, it must be identified with the person and work of Jesus. It was through engaging with the risen Jesus that Paul's theology was transformed, and his understanding of gospel traditions reshaped a profound insight into a "cruciform" God revealed in

---

[48] Dunn, *The Theology of Paul the Apostle*, 208.
[49] See further the summary in Dunn, *Theology of Paul*, 212-23.
[50] Morna D. Hooker, *Interchange and Atonement* (Manchester: John Rylands University Library of Manchester, 1978).
[51] Note also Rom 5:6, 8; compare 1 Tim 2:5-6; 5:10. On the significance of ὑπέρ in such contexts, see the treatment in Murray J. Harris, *Prepositions and Theology in the Greek New Testament* (Grand Rapids: Zondervan, 2012), 213-16.

Christ.[52]

3.4. The Pauline Meta-narrative: Creation, Redemption, and the Fullness of Time

In theological perspective, happenings in the present began before the foundation of the world (Eph 1:4) with the foreknowledge of God (Rom 8:28), and have proceeded according to God's counsel and will (Eph 1:11).

In seeking to delineate Paul's theology more comprehensively, a number of scholars have called for a greater appreciation of Paul's "narrative thought-world,"[53] shaped by the Jewish Scriptures and the story of Israel as rooted in creation, the promises to Abraham, Moses, and the events of the exodus, the Sinai and Davidic covenants, and the theological reflections associated with various prophetic traditions. As a schema, it is said that the story of Israel is taken up in the story of Christ, and all those who are "in Christ."[54]

Running alongside this ongoing story of Israel now identified with Christ, a more expansive biblical meta-narrative provides the framework for Paul's theological outlook. The outer parameters move from creation through to a new creation (Gal 6:15); a future reality that has broken into the present through the "first fruits" of Christ's resurrection (1 Cor 15:20; compare Rom 8:23). Creation has a goal and a purpose, closely identified with the mysteries of God now revealed as part of the divine economy (1 Cor 4:1; Eph 1:10; Col 1:25). The phrase "fullness of time" points to the climax of God's creational purposes, incorporating redemption but going beyond in realizing the full measure of all that creation was intended to become. The focus of all this is seeing "all things . . . things in heaven and things on earth" gathered or "summed up" in Christ (Eph 1:10).

Located within this overarching "creation to fullness" paradigm, Paul also traced an "Adam to last Adam" trajectory, not only giving expression to a significant dimension of his Christology but also identifying Christ within a profound and unique place in the story of redemption. The first Adam is primarily significant for characterizing the story of all humanity: the careful phrasing "as in Adam, all have died . . ." (1 Cor 15:22, cf. 15:45-48; Rom 5:12-14) depicts the identification of all humanity with the consequences of death following the same sinful disobedience, and this is set in contrast to the life attained "in Christ." The language of "first-fruits" used in 1 Cor 15:20, 23 is the language of harvest, not in a seasonal or cyclical sense, but more profoundly as the eschatological fullness that perceives the fruitfulness of creation realized in both the bestowing of the Holy Spirit (Rom 8:23) and in

---

[52] See especially Gorman, *Cruciformity: Paul's Narrative Spirituality of the Cross*.
[53] Ben Witherington, *Paul's Narrative Thought World: The Tapestry of Tragedy and Triumph* (Louisville: Westminster John Knox, 1994). For discussion on discerning different levels of narrative in Paul, see Bruce W. Longenecker, *Narrative Dynamics in Paul: A Critical Assessment* (Louisville: Westminster John Knox, 2002).
[54] Note the interpretive schema advocated by N. T. Wright, *Paul: Fresh Perspectives* (London: SPCK, 2005).

Christ the resurrection hope for those who have fallen asleep (1 Cor 15:20, 23).

In this context we may also note the significance of Paul's "apocalyptic" theology as a form of meta-narrative. The apocalyptic mode of expression underscores revelation in and through Christ, understood against the backdrop of the biggest of all perspectives, both in terms of time and space. Paul's apocalyptic theology locates the revelation of Christ (Gal 1:12) and the Spirit sent (Gal 3:23-25; 4:4, 6) as catalysts that divide the ages, distinguishing between the "present evil age" (Gal 1:3) and the age of the new creation. Such apocalyptic insight locates the gospel within a cosmic narrative that draws both past and future into the present.[55]

While it is true that reading Pauline theology in the mode of narrative can be overstated, and it would be a mistake to try and subsume every aspect of Paul's thought in such a paradigm, it is nevertheless also true that trying to interpret Paul without reference to this wider meta-narrative is to overlook key concerns that both inform and shape his theological outlook. It is the convergence and reframing of the story of Israel in and through the story of Christ that Paul develops some of his most profound theology.[56]

3.5. Theology of the Spirit

No consideration of Pauline theology can overlook the extent of his recognition of the essential and unique agency of the Spirit. Mapping qualities and actions identified with the Holy Spirit is a massive exercise,[57] and one that can never be fully exhausted. As Paul articulates it, the Spirit reveals the mysteries and wisdom of God, working within and transforming the lives of all those who are in Christ, both personally and corporately through the body of Christ.

The Spirit manifests the power of God, without being relegated to an intermediary of God but as the "one Spirit" that enables, empowers, and seals believers as they participate in the mission of God and constitute the body of Christ. It is not possible to distinguish the work and being of God in its many dimensions from the Spirit, and any understanding and experience of Christ is only possible through the Spirit (Rom 8:8; cf. 1 Cor 12:12-13).

At the same time, a distinctiveness is maintained in the sending of the Spirit (Gal 4:6; 1 Cor 2:12), the Spirit's intercessory work (Rom 8:26), and the uniqueness of the relationship of Jesus as the Father's Son who died upon the cross (Rom 5:8; 2 Cor 5:15). In Trinitarian terms, the Spirit is neither the

---

[55] This line of interpretation has been extensively explored by Martyn, *Galatians,* especially comment 3, 97-105.

[56] Note especially the narrative schema adopted by James D. G. Dunn, "The Story of God and Creation; The Story of Israel; The Story of Christ; The Story of Paul, as Developed in 'Paul's Theology'," in Scot McKnight and Grant R. Osborne, eds., *The Face of New Testament Studies: A Survey of Recent Research* (Grand Rapids: Baker Academic, 2004), 326-48.

[57] The classic work is that by Gordon D. Fee, *God's Empowering Presence: The Holy Spirit in the Letters of Paul* (Peabody: Hendrickson, 1994).

Father nor the Son, yet shares the fullness of "God-ness" with both. Much of the activity associated with "in Christ" is often in close correlation with "in the Spirit,"[58] something that reflects as much about their divine union and participation in the *missio Dei* as anything. For those who put their faith in Christ are baptized into the Spirit, who then "becomes the means through whom union with Christ is lived out."[59]

References to the Spirit appear consistently throughout Paul's letters. It is not possible to do justice to Pauline theology without recognition of the transformative and sanctifying work of the Spirit, and in equal measure identifying the Spirit as both "down-payment" of future inheritance (Eph 1:14) and defining presence in the present (especially Rom 8:1-17). Similarly, the fruit (Gal 5:22-23) and gifts of the Spirit (1 Cor 12:7-11) both testify to the working of God through the Spirit both personally and corporately, equipping the church for ministries within and through the body of Christ.

3.6. Ethos *as Theology*

The division between "theology" and "ethics" has resulted in the relegation of the latter to a secondary category of consideration. To a certain extent this may be explained on the basis of the perceived structure of Paul's letters, with the theological substance placed "up front" and the more pragmatic questions of lifestyle and conduct following in some form of application.

However, this is a false dichotomy. Consideration of the "ethos" of God as reflected in the person of Christ is revelatory, and in Pauline perspective this dimension provided a profound re-casting of his understanding of God.

"Ethos" may be defined as a "characteristic spirit," and in theological terms leads to a consideration of the *modus operandi* of God revealed in Christ—the distinctive and radical "ethos" revealed in the Christ story which becomes integral to the gospel itself. The God revealed in Christ is a cruciform God, where "being in the form of God" is associated with an attitude of mind that does not exploit, but embarks on a course of action characterized as "emptying" and taking human form, of a slave no less (Phil 2:5-8). The culmination of this course of action was obedience "to the point of death—even death on a cross" (Phil 2:8).

Debate around the significance of this famous Philippian "hymn" has revolved around its categorization as (variously) salvation history, doxology or ethical exhortation. Such distinctions are artificial. Taken in context, this wider passage (Phil 2:1-11) is a profound instance of "ethos as theology." Paul's reflection on the ethos manifest in Christ is part of his exhortation to be of the "same mind," and in and through this to experience a participation in the Spirit (Phil 2:1) and a "striving side by side with one mind for the sake of the gospel" (Phil 1:27b). Yet this is more than ethical exhortation: it is

---

[58] Constantine R. Campbell, *Paul and Union with Christ: An Exegetical and Theological Study* (Grand Rapids: Zondervan, 2012), 360-63.
[59] Campbell, *Union with Christ,* 362.

definitive of the gospel itself. Paul's reflection of the purpose and mode of ministry evident in Christ leads to doxology (2:9-11) and stands as a paradigm for the ongoing work of the gospel. The specific work of Christ is unique, and he alone was exclusively qualified to fulfill the work upon the cross within God's purposes. The "attitude of mind" exemplified in Christ redefines all perceptions of self-identity, value, and purpose (Phil 3:7-11). For Paul, it is integral to becoming like Christ in his death and the attaining of resurrection from the dead, and all this through faith in Christ, "the righteousness of God based on faith" (Phil 3:9b).

Paul's understanding of God and the gospel was deeply informed by the ethos of Christ. It is in this sense that a notion of *theosis* may also to be found in Paul.[60] The revelation of God's glory in Christ and through the Spirit is a transforming revelation so that those beholding such glory "are being transformed into the same image from one degree of glory to another" (2 Cor 3:18; cf. Rom 8:29). Indeed, to be "in Christ" is to be "in God."[61]

4. A Topography of Pauline Theology

Much of the popular philosophical advice in the ancient world on how to live well and the application of underlying foundational beliefs was frequently expressed in the form of essays or published speeches addressing a range of *topoi*—topics of public interest. It is notable that Paul does not shape his material in this format,[62] but it is possible to discern within the Pauline correspondence some significant motifs and themes. The outlining of a number of these will form the basis of this section on Paul's theological "topography."

4.1. A Multi-dimensional Model for Mapping Pauline Theology

Overviews of Pauline theology have traditionally been closely identified through significant terminology, whether organized thematically or as they feature within the contexts associated with each letter. There can be no doubting that a whole range of terms is of great significance in discerning a greater matrix of Pauline theology, but such terms, no matter how contextually construed, will only reflect limited dimensions of the modes and character of Pauline theology.

---

[60] M. David Litwa, *We Are Being Transformed: Deification in Paul's Soteriology* (Berlin: de Gruyter, 2012); Veli-Matti Kärkkäinen, *One with God: Salvation as Deification and Justification* (Collegeville: Liturgical Press, 2004).

[61] "For Paul, to be one with Christ is to be one with God; to be like Christ is to be like God; to be in Christ is to be in God. At the very least, this means that for Paul cruciformity—conformity to the crucified Christ—is really theoformity, or theosis"—so Michael J. Gorman, *Inhabiting the Cruciform God: Kenosis, Justification, and Theosis in Paul's Narrative Soteriology* (Grand Rapids: Eerdmans, 2009), 4.

[62] Andrew W. Pitts, "Philosophical and Epistolary Contexts for Pauline Paraenesis," in Porter and Adams, *Paul and the Ancient Letter Form*, 269-306.

In this section, a multi-dimensional model will be explored with reference to one well-recognized programmatic statement in Romans. As noted above, Rom 1:16-17 is well recognized as a summary statement of the gospel as expounded throughout the rest of Romans:

> For I am not ashamed of the gospel; it is the power of God for salvation to everyone who has faith, to the Jew first and also to the Greek. For in it the righteousness of God is revealed through faith for faith; as it is written, "The one who is righteous will live by faith."

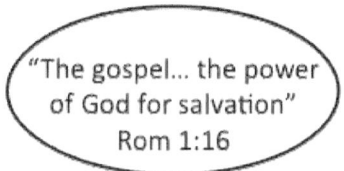

Within the context of Romans, it is as well to note that the explication of the "gospel as the power of God for salvation" does not trace Paul's own experiences other than retrospective perceptions, nor is it seeking to bring the "saints in Rome" (Rom 1:7) to faith. The articulation of the "gospel" does not end at the conclusion of chapter 3, nor even with the climactic affirmations that conclude chapter 8.[63] The entirety of chapters 1–11 is an expression of the gospel, with the following chapters grounding this gospel in very real communal and social realities.[64] In particular, it is important to note that Paul's perspective on the gospel is that of post-conversion enlightenment on theological issues that in many instances he had not recognized or personally struggled with prior to his conversion. Paul's "plight" was perceived essentially in hindsight.

The exploration of the "gospel as the power of God for salvation" is customarily presented through a range of significant terms, most of which we now hear as essentially "theological" terms, although they are drawn from a wider and more commonplace semantic stock.[65]

---

[63] Given that Romans was written with a view to being read aloud by a reader, it may be that it was read in sessions, with one session designed to conclude at the end of chapter 8.
[64] See further Peter Oakes, *Reading Romans in Pompeii: Paul's Letter at Ground Level* (Minneapolis: Fortress, 2009).
[65] Note for example more commonplace usage of many of the terms as identified in J. H. Moulton and G. Milligan, *The Vocabulary of the Greek Testament Illustrated from the Papyri and other Non-Literary Sources* (Peabody: Hendrickson, 1997) and the *New Documents Illustrating Early Christianity* series.

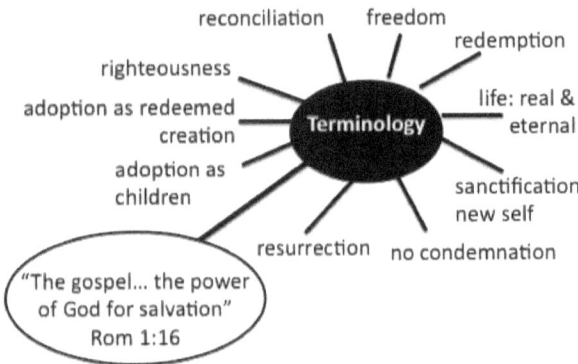

Some of these terms we explore below, and their inter-relationship, emphases, and coherence have been a major preoccupation in Pauline scholarship. Yet it is important to note that such terms are only one dimension of how such theological truths are conveyed in Romans. In a manner that goes beyond employing and developing a theological lexicon, Paul sets the gospel as the power of God for salvation against the backdrop of a range of word pictures and scenes,[66] and in a similar manner creatively employs a variety of images which are as much evocative as propositional.[67]

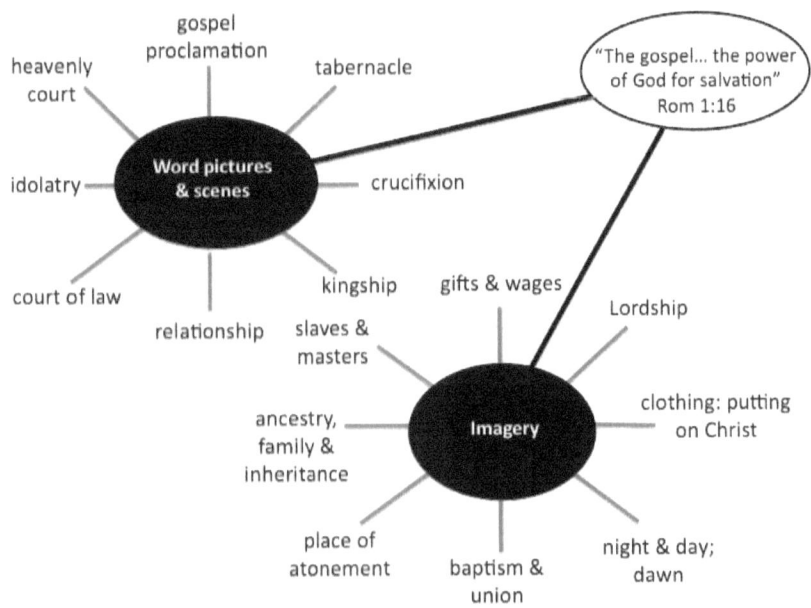

---

[66] An extensive survey of such imagery can be found in David J. Williams, *Paul's Metaphors: Their Context and Character* (Peabody: Hendrickson, 1999).
[67] Both categories overlap, but can be distinguished in that the former refers to identifiable scenarios and associated contexts that inform the allusion, while the latter employs imagery more generally.

As we analyze Paul's articulation of this gospel in Romans, we are also introduced to the centrality of God, as revealed more specifically in triune terms. The Creator God, Jesus as the Messianic king of the line of David, the transforming work of the Spirit that changes everything, including communicating between the adopted children and Abba Father: every aspect of the gospel as the power of God for salvation is identified with God as revealed in triune terms. The outcome of each work of God reflects the glory of God, from beginning to end.[68]

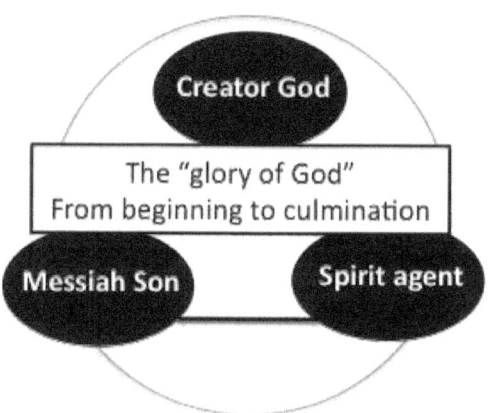

Running throughout this presentation are two other integral dimensions. On the one hand, it is very apparent that this work of salvation has a narrative, one that can be traced back to creation and the first Adam. The figure of Abraham stands tall in this narrative with a type of double ancestry: forefather of both those whose line of descent can be traced through his subsequent offspring, and equally (and no less legitimately) as forefather of the uncircumcised (Rom 4:11). Yet as the narrative progresses through Jesus, the defining center of the one people of God comes to be identified wholly with those who are "in Christ." In a closely related sense, it is therefore also important to note that just as the diagnosis of the human condition is both personal and social, the redemptive work of the gospel has both personal and communal dimensions. To experience salvation is necessarily to be drawn into the community of God's covenantal people.

---

[68] On the Trinitarian implications of understanding the "union with Christ" as much about Christ's indwelling with the Father as with believers, see Campbell, *Union with Christ,* 363-68.

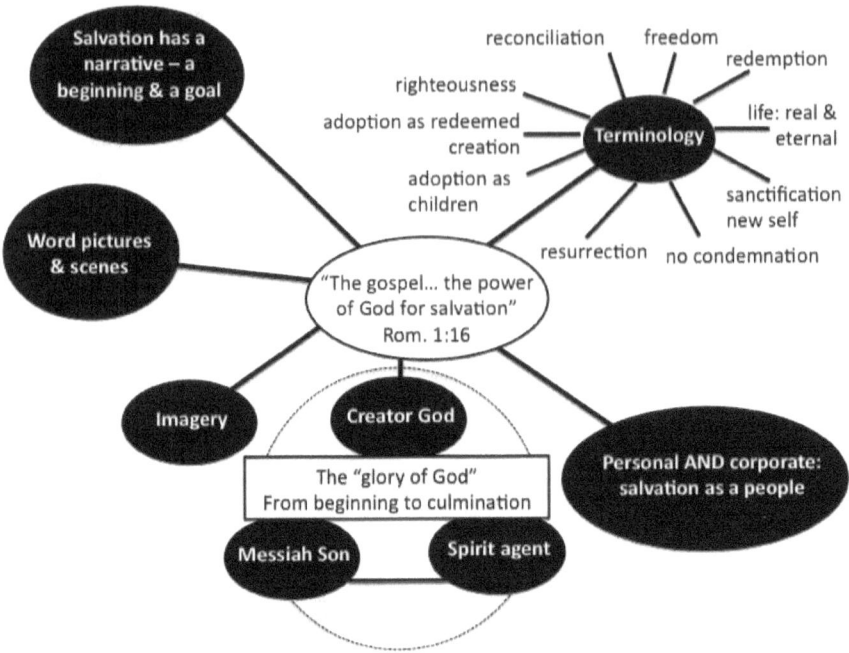

The purpose of this exercise is not to produce an exhaustive representation of the gospel as the power of God for salvation. It does open up, however, an alternative to the search for a "center" for Paul's theology, identifying instead something of the range and modes of expression of Paul's gospel, and brings into greater focus the multiple dimensions and features reflected in his theological artistry and exposition.

4.2. The Righteousness of God

Debate over the theological significance of this term is foundational to discerning Paul's theology more extensively. As is often the case, the danger emanates from being too specific, or in emphasizing one dimension to this polyvalent term to the neglect of others. It is another instance of "both-and," both a characteristic of God and a decisive act of intervention by God to bring about salvation.

The affirmation of the "righteousness of God" is grounded in an integral and defining attribute of God. It is related to a long history of covenantal fidelity that can be traced back to Abraham, and is orientated around the saving activity of God that culminates with the death and resurrection of Christ. The righteousness of God also involves the upholding of justice, the punishment of evil, and the vindication of the trust of the faithful over against the oppression afflicted upon them by the evildoers.

While it is rightly affirmed that the substantive background to the "righteousness of God" is primarily biblical and Hebrew,[69] it is also valid to point out that Paul would have also been very aware of Greek and Roman notions of righteousness. Coinage of this period highlights the associated qualities of justice, impartiality, and equity,[70] and Paul underscores the importance of God being recognized as "just" (Rom 3:26).

4.3. Righteousness and Justification

Regardless of whether the theme of "justification by faith" is to be regarded as the central affirmation and paradigm in Paul's theology, examination of its various senses and dimensions within the articulation of salvation surely continues as the epicenter of debate. Debate revolves around two spheres of questions: the nature of "righteousness"; and how it is attained.

In popular thinking, it is commonly misunderstood that the terminology of "righteousness" and "justification" are in fact one and the same in the Greek. To a certain degree, this may be addressed by seeking more consistent English renderings: to be "righteous," to act "righteously" or "rightly." This becomes more problematic however when it comes to verbal forms, especially in the passive ("to be justified"). In this latter sense, no recognized English term retains the overt association with "righteous," although some semantic innovations have been proposed. However, the issue is more profound.

Terms grounded in the δικ- root occupy a relatively broad semantic field, complicated by overlaps in meaning with notionally related terminology, and more specific senses depending on differing contexts, authors, and conceptual reference. Claims to a "core" meaning are hard to sustain, although an awareness of the complexity of reference (contextually considered) serves to illuminate the richness of the term rather than obscure its meaning.

In appreciating the theological richness of such terminology, care needs to be taken lest the positing of false dichotomies imposes unnecessary and potentially arbitrary specificity of meaning rather than appreciating the possibility of "both-and" dimensions. Thus to be "righteous" may indicate an ethical dimension—to act rightly or to conform to some standard or value of "rightness." It designates a manner of life. Ancillary to this, "righteous" may be attributed in association with a relationship of some description—to act rightly with reference to someone, a community, or even more broadly, to act rightly with regard to creation, the heavens and earth.[71] In another direction, to

---

[69] For a treatment that highlights a normative quality of righteousness with particular reference to creation (in priority over covenantal reference), see Mark A. Seifrid, "Righteousness Language in the Hebrew Scriptures and Early Judaism," in D. A. Carson, Peter Thomas O'Brien, and Mark A. Seifrid, eds., *Justification and Variegated Nomism, Volume 1* (WUNT 2.140, Tübingen: Mohr [Siebeck], 2001), 415-42.
[70] See the discussion in Frank Thielman, "God's Righteousness as God's Fairness in Romans 1:17: An Ancient Perspective on a Significant Phrase," *JSNT* 54.1 (2011): 41-43.
[71] Veli-Matti Kärkkäinen, "Deification View," in James K. Beilby and Paul R. Eddy, eds., *Justification: Five Views* (London: SPCK, 2012), 235-36.

be "righteous" can be regarded "forensically," and especially in the sense of a specific status as "publicly"[72] determined or affirmed.

With human reference, righteousness may be imputed (attributed or credited to) and/or imparted (a capacity that transforms and manifests righteous conduct). In Pauline theology, it cannot be earned or attained by merit, but is bestowed out of God's mercy and grace. It is to be received by faith, and lived out in obedience (the "indicative/imperative": that is, the status is a present reality that is to be lived out in ongoing conduct).

The "forensic" sense of attributed status has been charged by some as "legal fiction." Whatever its claims as a pronouncement, it does not reflect the reality of life or conduct, and calls into question the integrity of the upholding of right and just values. The evidence may be damning, and any verdict other than guilty may be tantamount to a miscarriage of justice. There is no doubt that popular presentations in terms of court scenarios in which a judge may set aside real wrong-doing as an act of personal grace are problematic, even with the caveat of paying the penalty themselves. Even as human analogy, this is not the same as a declaration of "righteousness," but functions more as "guilty yet expiated." Yet Pauline reference indicates righteousness as something that is real and effectively attributed, and only so through the very real events of the crucifixion and resurrection of Jesus Christ. To be declared righteous is to be acquitted, and the limitations of any analogy from the human realm need to be recognized. Paul's theology at this point draws on a range of biblical images to elucidate the significance of the cross: a ransom-payment has been paid (Rom 3:24), the "wrath of God" has been satisfied ("wrath" as carefully understood as righteous anger at all that is wrong and unjust), the offence of sin has been dealt with and sealed (atonement bringing expiation and propitiation[73]), as with the covenantal mercy-seat in the Tabernacle (Rom 3:25). Redemption is gained, freedom from tyranny attained, acquittal replaces condemnation, and reconciliation in the face of enmity is realized.

There are important eschatological dimensions to note as well. Righteousness is ultimately an "end-time" pronouncement affirmed in advance, to be lived out in the present age. This determination will be according to the totality of life, according to works—works that have resulted from the transforming activity of the Spirit and as the manifestation of spiritual fruit.[74] Amongst other things, it is in this way that the false dichotomy between faith and works is addressed, and the warning regarding "faith without works" in James 2:14-26 can be seen to be entirely consistent with Paul.

---

[72] Semantically, "forensic" is associated with the public "forum." Without overplaying such derivation, ongoing usage does retain a sense that is greater than a privatized dealing, especially if the court in view is ultimately a heavenly one. A "righteous" status is determined not as a private relationship but in the sphere of some identifiable community of reference.
[73] The meaning of ἱλαστήριον in the context of the wider argument of Romans is much debated.
[74] Paul's use of prepositions is significant at this point. Such judgment will be *according to* (κατά) works: Rom 2:6; 2 Cor 11:5.

Avoiding the narrowing of options as interpretive polarities (righteousness as imputed or imparted), Michael Bird has sought to bridge the alternative paradigms by proposing the notion of "incorporated righteousness."[75] Bird affirms both "vertical" and "horizontal" dimensions to righteousness, the former being the relationship with God whereby righteousness is attained (soteriology), while the latter reflects the reality of one people of God (ecclesiology), established in and through Israel as expanded with the inclusion of Gentiles and enhanced in its mission through the grace of being "in Christ" and empowered through the Spirit.

4.4. Paul, the Law, and Judaism: The "New Perspective"

The focus of this section is primarily on Paul's theology as discerned from the correspondence associated with his name, and not a review of secondary approaches to the interpretation of Paul. However, any discussion of Pauline theology needs to engage with the "New Perspective" debates. The term gathers and engages a number of key Pauline motifs, as understood and interpreted in Paul's own context and in the subsequent history of interpretation.

While commonly construed as "new perspectives on Paul," this was both historically and initially a new perspective on Jewish beliefs and practices in the experience and time of Paul. The classic 1977 critique by E. P. Sanders *Paul and Palestinian Judaism*[76] powerfully articulated claims by a number of scholars (frequently, although not exclusively, Jewish[77]) that much New Testament scholarship was predicated on a caricatured and fundamentally misunderstood notion of Judaism. Rather than its being grounded in justification by works and assumptions of merit-based righteousness, Sanders highlighted Judaism as a thorough-going theology of grace, and the place of Torah observance not as a means of "getting in," but of living within a covenantal relationship with the God of Israel (a paradigm summarized by Sanders as "covenantal-nomism").

While responses to Sanders' depiction of Judaism of this period have identified a greater diversity of belief and practice and a number of "exceptions,"[78] the main contours of his challenge (with regard to various forms of Palestinian Judaism) are widely respected. The question becomes: if this is so, what do we make of Paul's critique of Judaism?

Two related, but significantly distinct spheres of questions are to be identified: Paul's critique of Judaism in its various forms, over against faith in Jesus Christ (apologetic questions); and issues relating to Jewish and Gentile

---

[75] Michael Bird, *The Saving Righteousness of God: Studies on Paul, Justification, and the New Perspective* (Eugene: Wipf and Stock, 2007).
[76] E. P. Sanders, *Paul and Palestinian Judaism: A Comparison of Patterns of Religion* (London: SCM, 1977).
[77] Most notably George Foot Moore, "Christian Writers on Judaism," *HTR* 34 (1921): 197-254.
[78] Note especially the essays in Carson, O'Brien, and Seifrid, *Justification and Variegated Nomism*.

believers in Christ (conduct of life questions). In terms of issues "on the ground," foremost of these is the status of Gentile believers in Christ. Are they required to "Judaize," that is, to adopt Torah observance associated with Israel as the covenant people of God? There is also an associated question, although less recognized: were Jewish believers in Christ still required to maintain Torah observance?

Not far below the surface raised by this reconsideration of Paul's theology, an even more fundamental question is posed: is "justification by faith"—especially identified as the hallmark of Pauline theology in both the personal experience and theological controversies of the Reformation[79]—the crux of Pauline theology viewed as a whole, or a polemical response highlighted in particular contexts (i.e. Galatians and Romans), and less a feature in other contexts (e.g. 1 Thessalonians and Philippians)?

While the "New Perspective" is commonly referred to as one position, it is in fact a spectrum of views. Three trajectories can be identified in association with three renowned proponents, while there is also much common ground. In one direction, E. P. Sanders revisited the participationist reading of Paul, the view that being identified and incorporated "in Christ" was a more pervasive theme in Pauline theology, unduly neglected through the focus on justification. In another direction, James D. G. Dunn focused on the covenantal identity of Israel as God's chosen people. "Works of the law" were of less concern regarding gaining personal merit through law observance, but more in their role in identifying the cultural and covenantal boundary markers in affirming the particularity of God's saving purposes and the separateness of the Jews. Not unrelated to this, but with distinctive emphases and motifs, N. T. Wright highlighted Paul's location of Christ and the Spirit within the greater narrative of God's faithfulness to the covenantal promises given to Abraham, progressed through Moses, David, and the prophets, and now in an all-new era inaugurated by the life, cross, resurrection, and ascension of Christ. The story of Israel addressed the failures of Adam, which have only been truly redressed through Christ as the new man, through whom the re-creation of heaven and earth is being transformed into the fullness of a new creation. For Wright, the redemption of Israel was never the end of God's purposes, but always conceived as instrumental to the greater mission of drawing all nations into the greater eschatological purposes of God.

While consideration of the "New Perspective" can be identified by some particularly contentious questions, it may also be viewed as a catalyst for a range of considerations following through or responding to the perspectives highlighted by Sanders.

---

[79] It is important to note that the "doctrine of justification" is not one and the same as the Pauline notion of "justification," understood in its own context; see further Alister E. McGrath, *Iustitia Dei: A History of the Christian Doctrine of Justification* (2 vols.; New York: Cambridge University Press, 1986); N. T. Wright, *Justification: God's Plan & Paul's Vision* (Downers Grove: IVP Academic, 2009), 59-60.

4.5. Beyond the "New Perspective"

In recent times new avenues for understanding Pauline theology have been developed by Douglas A. Campbell and the publication his major monograph *The Deliverance of God*.[80] Campbell breaks new ground in a reframing of Paul's theology in what has been termed a "post-new perspective."[81] There are a number of elements to Campbell's proposal, and part of the debate is whether various elements can stand alone, or need to be viewed as a whole.

Space forbids an extensive overview or critique, but the main features of Campbell's treatment may be outlined.[82] A critical foundation in his argument is the construal of western views of "justification by faith" as "Justification Theory" (JT) as a particular model of salvation. This is a "forward looking" approach that moves from "problem" to "solution," in which the crisis that comes with the inability to fulfill the "works of the law" and in contrast finds a solution through "faith." A major clash is discerned between a retributive God before whom all are consigned to condemnation for the failure to achieve "100 percent righteousness," and the provision of undeserved and unmerited salvation. Against this foundation a "contract" is offered by the grace of God, attained by faith and not through merit.

Campbell regards JT as theologically inconsistent and ethically flawed. More to the point in terms of Pauline theology, he contends the expression of JT in Romans 1–4 is incompatible with the articulation of Paul's incorporative understanding of the gospel in Romans 5–8, salvation as an unconditional gift of deliverance grounded in divine initiative.

He resolves this apparent conflict of gospel presentations by identifying a substantial instance of *prosopopoeia,* commencing at Rom 1:18 and continuing until the end of chapter 3. Campbell contends that Paul's use of "speech-in-character" would have been readily perceived by the first auditors in Rome, as presenting the views of a recognizable Jewish Christian "Teacher" exercising significant influence amongst the house churches in Rome. Paul presents the alternative understanding of the gospel in Romans 1–4, before critiquing and presenting his understanding of the gospel as revealed in and through Christ in Romans 5–8.

While there have been some telling initial responses to Campbell's radical proposal,[83] it is too early to judge whether his views become a catalyst for a

---

[80] Beilby and Eddy, 235-36; Douglas A. Campbell, *The Deliverance of God: An Apocalyptic Rereading of Justification in Paul* (Grand Rapids: Eerdmans, 2009).

[81] Douglas A. Campbell, "Christ and the Church in Paul: A 'Post-New Perspective' Account," in Michael F. Bird, *Four Views on the Apostle Paul* (Grand Rapids: Zondervan, 2012), 113-43. A more extensive discussion is contained in chapter 6 of Campbell, *Deliverance,* "Beyond Old and New Perspectives" in which six areas of debate are identified and prepare the way for the new reading to follow.

[82] An accessible summary has been written by Campbell himself: "An Apocalyptic Rereading of 'Justification' in Paul: Or, an Overview of the Argument of Douglas Campbell's *The Deliverance of God,* by Douglas Campbell," *ExpT* 123 (May 2012): 382-93.

[83] Especially notable are articles in the *Journal for the Study of Paul and His Letters* 1.1 (Spring 2011): Chris Tilling, "The Deliverance of God, and of Paul?" 83-98; and Michael J. Gorman, "Douglas Campbell's *The Deliverance of God*: A Review by a Friendly Critic," 99-108;

genuine "post-new perspective" on Pauline theology. Campbell's construal of Romans 1–4 has yet to persuade many. However, there is greater support for the renewed emphasis on Romans 5–8 as integral to Paul's understanding of the gospel. Whether both are as incompatible as Campbell contends is yet to be resolved.

4.6. Participation and Union with Christ

The notions of being "in Christ" and "participating in Christ" carry much of the weight of Pauline theology. While the theological import of such terms goes well beyond grammatical forms and needs careful consideration in the context of wider material, something of the diversity of significance is sketched by reviewing the range of uses in a variety of contexts.[84]

Some form of the characteristic "in Christ" expression (or related variations) occurs 170 times in the Pauline literature. These refer to incorporative union, agency (accomplished by), mode (by being in), cause (because of), location, and sphere of reference. Similar senses apply to being "in the Lord," with an additional focus on personal identification (belonging to) and authority associated with the Lord Jesus.

Along with Luke-Acts, Paul also uses the prepositions "*syn*" and "*meta*" to indicate personal union, association or participation, especially with regard to dying, and being raised and living "with" Christ. *Syn* is also the most frequent compound prefix, with eleven verbal forms grouped around either the redemptive events of Christ's death and burial on the one hand, or the resurrection as a past and ongoing reality on the other. Many aspects of the Christian life and ministry are identified in similar terms.

Where such prepositions and related compounds flag the closeness and real participation that bind believer and Christ in a profound way, application of such terms showcases the theological treasury that constitutes Paul's understanding and articulation of the gospel.[85] As one recent writer puts it, the metatheme of *union, participation, identification, incorporation* does not constitute the center of Paul's theological framework, it is "the essential ingredient that binds all other elements together."[86]

Campbell responded in the same issue, "What Is at Stake in the Reading of Romans 1–3? An Elliptical Response to the Concerns of Gorman and Tilling," 109-32.

[84] Much that follows in this section is greatly indebted to Harris, *Prepositions and Theology in the Greek New Testament*, 122-30. Harris acknowledges that such categorizations can be somewhat arbitrary, but they do provide a convenient point of reference. Specific examples are provided in each category.

[85] See the extensive treatment in Campbell, *Paul and Union with Christ: An Exegetical and Theological Study*.

[86] Campbell, *Union with Christ*, 30. At a later point he suggestively describes the structure of Paul's thought as a web, and union with Christ as the webbing, 437-42.

4.7. Koinōnia, *Ecclesial Community, and Citizenship*

One of the biggest criticisms of the interpretation of Pauline theology is that it has been overly focused on the individual. While the personal dimension is certainly evident in Paul's correspondence, it is undoubtedly the case that Paul's concerns are much bigger than the eternal wellbeing of individuals. The gospel itself is inherently a process of the gathering of a people of God, and ultimately all creation will be drawn into the fulfillment of God's glorious purposes (Rom 8:21-25; Eph 1:10).

Communal imagery is extensive throughout Paul (especially body imagery), and even more deeply any incorporation or participation in Christ will invariably draw all involved into relationship with one another. The outworking of this in social contexts where masters and slaves, differing ethnic identities, and a strongly delineated culture of social orders and status are drawn together inevitably created tensions. At the same time, a profoundly counter-cultural social dynamic was established from the outset, and familiar expressions of partnership and association were applied to surprising and scandalous groupings in which there were neither Jew nor Greek, slave nor free, male nor female (Gal 3:28).

The *ecclesia* of Christ was also realized at different levels, from local gatherings to wider groupings, each also participating in the one heavenly and the ever-growing eschatological community. Yet one thing is ultimately clear: in the purposes of God there is only one body and one Spirit (Eph 4:4), and the calling of local expressions of church is to honor and reflect these heavenly realities. Relationships matter. Each church identified with the body of Christ (1 Cor 12:27) is to respect every member that makes up the body, while the outworking of reconciliation and hospitality is enhanced through the exercise of various *charisms* for the building up of the whole.

As new group identities are established "in Christ," a notion of dual citizenship (not unknown in the Greco-Roman world) is expressed by assurance of shared inheritance and an ultimate "seat of government" (rather than citizenship as such). This "seat of government" is a heavenly one, to which ultimate loyalty is exhorted and where true authority is located (Phil 3:20). It is from this cosmic center that the Savior will proceed and full benefits of the resurrection be realized (3:21).

Paul's theology has strong and integral communal dimensions. A range of relational categories is identified from the outset, where Paul's calling as an apostle and slave of Christ not only asserts a right to speak and instruct, but also locates his ministry as a herald of the gospel (1 Cor 1:17) and an instrument by whom unity is established in Christ—a unity that grows community.

In sociological terms, we can note how Paul's letters function to establish and maintain new social realities in the form of church communities. The validation of this role and function is found in Paul's appeal to a greater cosmology that transcends that proclaimed by the Roman empire, or any *polis* in association with that. It is at this point that Paul's theological horizon fuses heaven and earth, and identifies new communities established in Christ as belonging to a heavenly "citizenship."

A strong and pervasive cultural and political tension developed as a result. As Paul urged the recognition that believers gathered into church communities belong to God, so their lives should be holy just as they had been made holy "in Christ Jesus" (1 Cor 1:2). The "name of the Lord Jesus Christ" was not only a defining identity and common "lordship," it also called for a profound new loyalty and allegiance.

Much of the substance of letters such as 1 Corinthians, and also most other Pauline letters in their own contexts, reflects the very real conflict of social engagement and manner of life issues that threatened the integrity of the early churches.[87] A measure of cultural accommodation was modeled and commended by Paul (1 Cor 9:20-23), while disputes over leadership, the exercise of authority, and the pervasive challenges of sexual conduct and idolatry were presenting issues grounded in deeper questions of identity and cultural practice. Continuance in such behavior threatened their place within the kingdom of God (1 Cor 6:9), not only individually but also communally. Deep divisions in church communities saw the severing of relationships and the refusal to accept others who claimed an allegiance to Christ. The gospel ministry of reconciliation had very real urgency (2 Cor 5:11-21), with the need for repentance, transformation of the mind in no longer conforming to the world (Rom 12:2), and the setting aside of former patterns of life and behavior (1 Cor 6:11, Gal 4:8).

One other flashpoint that threatened community formation and unity revolved around deep differences in the observance (or non-observance) of various religious practices, such as diet (Rom 14:2) or special holy days (Rom 14:5). Paul's response is to distinguish between the "weak" and the "strong" in faith (Rom 14:1; 15:1; compare 1 Cor 8:7-13, with reference to conscience), but this begs the question as to the intended audience(s) and who would self-identify as "strong" and regard others as "weak." The terminology reflects commonplace usage and was employed in rhetorical forms when dealing with communal issues of some sensitivity.[88]

4.8. Grace, Mercy, and Peace

The frequency of these terms in the correspondence identified with Paul reflects how profound they are in his theology. Each term makes a strong statement about Paul's understanding of the gospel, understood in both Jewish and Greco-Roman perspectives. They identify the source of the gospel with attributes of God as revealed in the greater narrative of Scripture, and with particular reference to the person and ministry of Jesus Christ.

---

[87] On features of rhetoric in "political" mode (seeking to address community divisions), see especially L. L. Welborn, *Politics and Rhetoric in the Corinthian Epistles* (Macon: Mercer University Press, 1997).

[88] See further the treatment in Jewett, *Romans*, 841-44.

Grace (χάρις) features in the greetings of most of the Pauline letters (where ordinarily one would expect χαίρειν—"greetings"), and its connotations run in multiple directions. In Pauline usage it designates a disposition of favor towards someone where there is no obligation for the expression of such benevolence. To Jewish ears, grace speaks of the character of God despite unfaithfulness and transgression that deserves judgment.[89] This is true of Paul's own self-testimony, in which he recognized the horror of his own sinfulness in persecuting the church (1 Cor 15:10), only to be called as apostle in the grace of God ("But by the grace of God I am what I am, and his grace toward me has not been in vain.")

Grace reflects not only the disposition of God, but also the benefits that ensue, a status established in grace (e.g. Rom 5:2: "through whom we have obtained access to this grace in which we stand"), the ministry given to Paul (Gal 2:9), and a realm in which gospel life is to be lived (Rom 6:14: "For sin will have no dominion over you, since you are not under law but under grace").

To Roman ears, the language of grace spoke of protocols of friendship and benefaction. Social order was delineated and maintained around a clear understanding of status and the expectations in all directions. To receive some form of benefaction was to be brought under obligation, while the person who bestowed grace was honored for all they chose to give while being under no obligation. Benefaction is not the same as patronage, but both draw on the same cultural values of reciprocity and gratitude.[90]

To speak of "mercy" (ἔλεος) is more striking in Greco-Roman perspective. Such an attitude was regarded as contrary to strength of leadership, and likely to encourage insurrection and lack of respect for those in authority. Given that the "art of government" was predicated on dynamics of honor and shame, undue display of mercy was viewed negatively in social terms. Where one master demonstrated mercy, others would come under pressure to do likewise, and so "due order" within the whole social world was threatened. Those who fail to respect such order may be emboldened to rebel. The reality of honor and shame amounted to the exercise of fear and terror. However, such values were not universal. Julius Caesar for one modelled a policy of *clementia*, but only in as much as it suited his political purposes. However, the fact that Caesar was noteworthy for his exercise of *clementia* demonstrates the extent to which the reverse was common (especially cruelty and brutality). Where such qualities are displayed it is less an attribute of character and more a strategy for gaining loyalty or obligation.[91] Related qualities of pity (e.g. *misericordia*) do appear, but with great caution lest the

---

[89] Francis I. Andersen, "Yahweh, The Kind and Sensitive God," in P. T. O'Brien and D. G. Peterson, eds., *God Who is Rich in Mercy: Essays Presented to D. B. Knox* (Homebush West: Lancer Books, 1986), 41-88.

[90] See further Crook, *Reconceptualising Conversion*; James R. Harrison, *Paul's Language of Grace in its Graeco-Roman Context* (WUNT 2.172; Tübingen: Mohr [Siebeck], 2003).

[91] Caesar's affirmation of this virtue gave prominence to the deification of *Clementia*, Roman goddess of forgiveness and mercy, and counterpart to the Greek goddess *Eleos*.

"inner being" was disturbed and factors beyond the control of the individual impacted unduly on personal self-sufficiency and well-being. In the sphere of popular religious practice, notions of salvation and responses to pleadings for favor or rescue are also grounded in the character traits of the deities in view, but enter the realm of bargaining and seeking to gain favor.[92]

Against this background, the gospel attribute of mercy as articulated by Paul is significantly counter-cultural, although very much in line with the character of YHWH as understood within the faith of Israel. The "God who is rich in mercy" (Eph 2:4) is the theological explanation for the "why" of the gospel: it is undeserved in every way, cannot be achieved by contract, wage or effort, and is grounded only in a defining attribute of God (alongside righteousness, justice, and love). Again, it speaks deeply of Paul's own personal experience, yet embraces the breadth of the gospel by way of redemption and new life available to all, regardless of race or covenantal favor (Eph 2:4-9).

It is in this context that reference to "peace" was also highly significant. To Roman ears, it echoed (and perhaps subverted) the claim of the emperor to deliver empire-wide *Pax Romana*. The preceding century had been marked by relentless civil war and bloodshed, and the whole Mediterranean basin subjected to the threat of piracy and associated brigandry. The claims of Caesar Augustus, as denoted and paraded in his *Res Gestae Divi Augusti*, included his achievements in bringing peace and sustaining a state of order in which dissension and discord was suppressed. In this context of emerging victorious from various campaigns, Augustus was proclaimed *princeps pacis* ("prince of peace"), and the commissioning and dedication of the *Ara Pacis Augustae* ("altar of Augustan peace") provided a powerful visual statement associating the family and heirs of Caesar as the household responsible for enduring peace over the whole world.[93]

However, as significant as this imperial background was with regard to the attainment of peace, the richer Hebrew notion of *shalom* was more likely in Paul's mind when associating peace with the gospel. Again, the notion has a range of meanings. Finding peace through the cessation of hostilities and enmity is certainly a key element, especially when associated with the work of Christ on the cross.[94] The close association with reconciliation is evident in the way the two terms bracket Paul's treatment in Rom 5:1, 10, all of which underscores a strongly relational sense of the term. Broader dimensions of health, fullness, and all that creation was intended to be are also evident. In this sense, peace understood as *shalom* combines redemption with fulfillment, salvation with transformation.

---

[92] A helpful overview is provided by Bruce F. Harris, "Mercy in Its Graeco-Roman Context," in *God Who Is Rich in Mercy*, 89-105.

[93] Note Ovid's comment regarding this altar: "that the house which insures peace may last forever" *Fasti* 1.719, as rendered in Paul Zanker, *The Power of Images in the Age of Augustus* (Jerome Lectures; Ann Arbor: University of Michigan Press, 1988).

[94] See especially the treatment in Graham A. Cole, *God the Peacemaker: How Atonement Brings Shalom* (Downers Grove: IVP, 2009).

4.9. Reconciliation, Friendship, and Adoption

The language of reconciliation is inherently relational, and assumes a need for restoration. The breakdown of relationships was prominent and significant in ancient times, and especially so when understood against the backdrop of the social dynamics of friendship and enmity that created the social world in the Greco-Roman setting. Such dynamics extended well beyond the personal. Friendship and enmity were fundamental to the political realm,[95] and no less so in questions of patronage and civic loyalty. Oaths of allegiance to Caesar customarily included a declaration regarding friends and enemies. Whomever Caesar identified as a friend, so too did those declaring loyalty, and likewise enemies.[96]

Paul adopted such language when giving expression to the work of Christ as benefactor on behalf of all those who declared allegiance of faith in (and faithfulness to) Christ. So extensive and profound is the motif of reconciliation that some scholars have suggested it is the interpretive key to Paul's theology.[97] In the context of Romans, reconciliation is the resolution of the estrangement that follows God's righteous indignation or anger (ὀργή) over against "all ungodliness and wickedness," including idolatry (1:23), the "failure to acknowledge God" (1:28), and "having worshipped and served the creation rather than the Creator" (1:25). Just who is included in this indictment, and therefore not only estranged but facing God's wrath, is very much the focus of the rhetorical purposes of Romans 2–3.

It is alongside this profound statement of enmity before God, shared by all humanity, that the relational language of peace and reconciliation gives expression to the gospel as the power of God for salvation, achieved only through the death and resurrection life of his Son (Rom 5:10-11; see also 2 Cor 5 18-21).

A rich sequence of relational categories follows in Romans, with the newly reconciled relationship characterized (as spiritual realities, not just metaphors) as moving from a dominion of sin that brings condemnation, to receiving an abundance of grace and the free gift of righteousness (5:16-17), of slaves moving from the tyrannical mastery of sin to the righteous dominion

---

[95] On dynamics of friendship, see John T. Fitzgerald, *Greco-Roman Perspectives on Friendship* (Atlanta: Scholars Press, 1997).
[96] A typical example is found in an inscription at Phazimon-Neapolis (*OGIS* 532, available in Naphtali Lewis and Meyer Reinhold, *Roman Civilization: Selected Readings* [3rd ed.; 2 vols.; New York: Columbia University Press, 1990], 34-35). Dated 3 B.C., it notes an oath sworn by all the people of Phazimon, including all resident Roman businessmen "at the altars of Augustus in the temple of Augustus." The oath invokes the name of Jupiter and all other deities, a personal pledge of loyalty to Augustus and his house, a total commitment to protect his interests, reckoning the same friends and enemies; the undertaking to lay information against potential enemies, and to pursue and punish Augustus' foes "by land and sea, with weapons and sword."
[97] Ralph P. Martin, *Reconciliation: A Study of Paul's Theology* (rev. ed.; Grand Rapids: Academie Books, 1989). On the use of the terminology of reconciliation, see further Stanley E. Porter, *Katallasso in Ancient Greek Literature, With Reference to the Pauline Writings* (Estudios De Filologia Neotestamentaria 5; Cordoba: Almendro, 1994).

of grace in Christ (6:13-14); from redemption as slaves to adoption as children of God and joint heirs with Christ (8:14-17).

All of these are evocative terms drawn from the social realities experienced on an everyday basis in the lives of all in Rome, as well as profound theological truths on a cosmic scale. A place within a socially elite household figured high on the list of aspirations of most seeking a better life, and a subsequent formal adoption into the family was a rare but not unknown path to a whole new life. When such incorporation and adoption is into the household of Caesar, then the sons and daughters involved find themselves drawn into the realm of the gods.

Such is the strongly relational mode of Paul's articulation of the gospel. However, the relational dynamics go even deeper than socially identifiable categories: they are also construed in terms of identification with the profound realties of creation itself, from being "in Adam," through the gospel work of Christ, to becoming a new expression of humanity (1 Cor 15:21-23), even a "new creation" (2 Cor 5:17). This takes us to another level of theological analysis and application by Paul, drawing on socio-political terms of association and corporate membership, but applied as more fundamental categories of existence and allegiance.

5. The End of Pauline Theology

The heading of this section is intentionally ambiguous, picking up the notions of "*telos*" as both "conclusion" and "goal," and the wider sense of purpose underlying Paul's correspondence.

5.1. Telos *and Eschatology*

Paul's theological perspective on history is that life has a purpose which can only be discerned with reference to the "the will of God" (Rom 12:2; compare the elaboration in Eph 1:11 "the purpose of him who accomplishes all things according to his counsel and will"). Interest in this purpose was no theoretical exercise, and assumed a contentious nature with reference to the formation and inheritance of Yahweh's covenantal people. How does the story of the people of Israel intersect with the mission of Jesus Messiah, and how do the accomplishments of Christ relate to all those who are identified as being "in him"?

The hope and expectation of the presence or visitation (παρουσία) of Christ feature in early instances of Paul's correspondence (six times in 1 and 2 Thessalonians, once in 1 Corinthians). However, it is important to bear in mind that words are not the same as concepts, and Paul's end-time beliefs are conveyed through the shape and direction of his thought as much as specific terminology. Closely associated with the coming or return of Christ are notions of accountability and judgment on a cosmic scale. The origins of such a decisive moment in history can be traced back to earlier stages of the story of Yahweh and Israel, with the "day of the LORD" being at one and the same time an occasion of salvation and deliverance for Israel, and the exercise of judgment upon those who oppose the purposes of Yahweh. Expectation of a coming "Day" carries through into Paul's theological vista, characteristically formulated as "the day of Christ/the Lord" (1 Thess 5:2; Phil 1:6, 10; 2:16). This would be a time of unveiling, of revelation (2 Thess 1:7; 2:3, 6) of the mysteries of God (2:7), with language and imagery (in its own way common to other Jewish traditions as well) reflecting prophetic and apocalyptic modes of expression. As Paul's theological focus progresses beyond early concerns, the nature of Christ's return retains a strong association with final resurrection (1 Cor 15:23), while warnings of judgment and exposure of inner thoughts also feature (1 Cor 4:4-5).

Complicating Paul's expression of end time realities is the overlay of "ages." While the age of the chronically fallen world is still very much true of the present time, the new age has also been inaugurated in Christ and confirmed through the bestowing of the Holy Spirit. Both ages co-exist. The fruits of the crucified and resurrected Christ are at one and the same time "now, but not yet."

Without attempting a comprehensive review of Paul's eschatological thought that operates at multiple layers and in different directions (pastoral, kerygmatic, covenantal, and creational), it will suffice in this context to consider Greco-Roman socio-political resonances. The occasion of imperial visitations was a major feature in Roman propaganda. They developed the victory parade into an art-form in which the grandeur of the elite was publicly flaunted. In other words, such theater was not just an excuse for extravagance and display, but more profoundly made a statement about power, authority, salvation, peace, and hope. The fortunes of the civilized world were tied to the accomplishments and benevolence of the emperor.

The adoption of such terminology and imagery to express gospel visitation and triumph by Paul was not just a matter of literary convenience. All that the Roman imperial powers signified by such events is both subverted and overwhelmed in gospel theater on a cosmic scale. A number of motifs are adopted for this purpose. The athletic race or "contest" is introduced (e.g. 1 Cor 9:24-27; Phil 3:12-16; 1 Tim 6:12; 2 Tim 4:7; compare also Rom 9:30-33) to describe the ongoing life of faith, both personal and communal. The accolades and crowns that ensue reinforce perseverance and ultimate accomplishment, and with it a sharing in the glory bestowed by God in the company of the heavenly courts.

It is in this context that the direction of history, both as redemption and completion, is drawn together in the notion of τέλος, understood as both goal and conclusion (Rom 10:4; compare 1 Cor 1:8, 10:11). While more specific aspects are addressed ("end of the law"), the broader picture is clear. Life is neither static nor essentially cyclical, but moves inexorably towards the fulfillment of God's purposes. In Paul's theological perspective, salvation and redemption are located within this greater narrative of transformation and fulfillment.

5.2. Death, Resurrection, and Glorification of Christ

We have noted above the centrality of the death, burial, and resurrection of Christ in the earliest expressions of gospel traditions (1 Cor 15:3-5). The "cross" of Christ, as pivotal gospel event and integral to establishing redemption and victory over against all that oppose the reign of God, became synonymous with the gospel proclamation itself (1 Cor 1:17-18). In the same breath as such affirmations, Paul identified the power and glory of God at work in and through Christ. Without the cross, there is no gospel. In precisely the same terms the resurrection of Christ is foundational to any measure of hope, and with it, "all joy and peace in believing" (Rom 15:13). The multitudinous dimensions of the cross are complex and theologically rich. Any personal appropriation of the benefits of the cross is matched and transcended by the liberation of creation (Rom 8:21) and destruction of death. As all humanity identified with Adam were subject to death, so now in Christ "shall all be made alive" (1 Cor 15:24), with the transformation of "bodies of humiliation" into the "body of his glory" (Phil 3:21). In a manner fully consistent with prophetic vision, Paul's presentation of the gospel as manifest in the cross and resurrection of Christ assumes global and cosmic proportions, with "all things in subjection under his feet" (1 Cor 15:27; Phil 3:21; compare also Col 1:15-20).

5.3. Doxology

Almost invariably, Paul's reflection on the work of the cross, the resurrection and victory over "every ruler and every authority and power" (1 Cor 15:24) led to doxology. The fulfillment of God's purposes reveals the glory of God, a glory equally manifest in the work of Christ and the revelations of the Spirit. Doxology for Paul is not merely a way of "signing off," it is the goal that all true theology must attain.

As also with Paul's prayers, the doxological focus in and through Paul's letters is a profound dimension to his theological endeavors, and is too-often underestimated. For Paul, theology only had one end, and that is the praise and worship of God. This is especially so when we note the place of "glory" (δόξα) in Paul's theological canvas (e.g. 2 Cor 4:6: "the light of the knowledge of the glory of God in the face of Jesus Christ").

Paul's doxologies are expressions of his ultimate worldview and convictions. His perceptions of the greater realities embracing both heaven and earth are bonded in and through his doxology. It is at such points that Paul sums up the purpose and origin of all things, and all with reference to the great narrative of Scripture from creation to new creation. For Paul, any theological reflection that does not culminate in the praise of God is inherently flawed and fails to integrate faith, discipleship, and learning with the ultimate theological affirmations upheld in doxology.

Recommended Reading

Bassler, Jouette M., David M. Hay, and E. Elizabeth Johnson, eds. *Pauline Theology*. 4 vols. Minneapolis: Fortress, 1991–1997.

Beilby, James K., and Paul R. Eddy, eds. *Justification: Five Views*. Downers Grove: IVP, 2012.

Bird, Michael. *The Saving Righteousness of God: Studies on Paul, Justification, and the New Perspective*. Eugene: Wipf and Stock, 2007.

Donaldson, Terence L. *Paul and the Gentiles: Remapping the Apostle's Convictional World*. Minneapolis: Fortress, 1997.

Dunn, James D. G. *The Cambridge Companion to St. Paul*. New York: Cambridge University Press, 2003.

Engberg-Pedersen, Troels, ed. *Paul in His Hellenistic Context*. Minneapolis: Fortress, 1995.

Gorman, Michael J. *Apostle of the Crucified Lord: A Theological Introduction to Paul and His Letters*. Grand Rapids: Eerdmans, 2004.

Hawthorne, Gerald F., Ralph P. Martin, and Daniel G. Reid, eds. *Dictionary of Paul and His Letters*. Downers Grove: IVP, 1993.

Horsley, Richard A., ed. *Paul and Politics: Ekklesia, Israel, Imperium, Interpretation: Essays in Honor of Krister Stendahl*. Harrisburg: Trinity Press International, 2000.

Kim, Seyoon. *Christ and Caesar: The Gospel and the Roman Empire in the Writings of Paul and Luke*. Grand Rapids: Eerdmans, 2008.

Richards, E. Randolph. *Paul and First-Century Letter Writing: Secretaries, Composition, and Collection*. Downers Grove: IVP, 2004.

Witherington, Ben, III. *Paul's Narrative Thought World: The Tapestry of Tragedy and Triumph*. Louisville: Westminster John Knox, 1994.

APPENDIX 1: PAUL IN THE BOOK OF ACTS

Paul W. Barnett

There is sufficient information from Paul's own hand (Philippians, Galatians, Romans, First Corinthians) to point to his home background, subsequent career as Pharisee, scholar, "zealotic" persecutor, and "broad brush" career outline. But it is only Acts that gives any sense of sequence and chronology.

Scholars must engage with the centrality of the Damascus Event as the hinge around which Paul's career turned, and there is no way one can seriously engage with Paul apart from this. His letters are dotted with "a before and after" motif, e.g., εἴ τις ἐν Χριστῷ ("if anyone is in Christ, there is a new creation"; 2 Cor 5:17).[1]

1. The Acts of the Apostles

Only 2 Cor 11:32-33, which relates Paul's escape from Damascus under the eye of Aretas' ethnarch, provides any linkage to world history so as to allow us to "date" Paul.[2] If we were to depend only on Paul's letters we would have no absolutely no idea of the "when" and "how" of his journeys or his relationship with the churches of his mission. Based only on Paul's epistles, a Pauline chronology would not be possible without Acts.[3] So there is no option but to evaluate and use a number of texts from Acts. But if the historicity of the book is regarded as extremely problematic, how can Paul's escape from Damascus narrated in Acts 9:23-25 be linked with the event described by Paul in 2 Cor 11:32-33?

In this regard I believe there is an inconsistency for those who are skeptical about Acts, but who still (remarkably in my view) depend on Acts. It would be more historically acceptable for ultra-skeptical scholars to reject the book altogether, rather than to regard it as deeply flawed but to use it simply because there is nothing else. In my view, true scholarship, and the forensic trial process, would eschew the use of data if it were viewed as so flawed.

2. Paul in Acts: addressing the relationship between the Author of Acts and Paul

The author of Luke-Acts was Paul's companion in the "we"-passages (Acts 16:10-16; 20:5-21:18; 27:1–28:16), that is, for the period A.D. 57–62. This means (a) that the Author was contemporary with Paul in the events for those five years; but (b) through Paul he had inside access into Paul's entire former life, from the time of his birth through to the conclusion of the "third" missionary journey. In regards (b) Acts is a secondary primary source to be read alongside Paul.

---

[1] See Paul W. Barnett, *Paul, Missionary of Jesus* (Grand Rapids: Eerdmans 2008), 54-75.
[2] Cf. Douglas A. Campbell, "An Anchor for Pauline Chronology; Paul's Flight from 'the Ethnarch of King Aretas' (2 Corinthians 11:32-34)," *JBL* 121.2 (2002): 279-302.
[3] Contra the arguments of R. Pervo, *Acts* (Minneapolis: Fortress, 2009).

Appendix 1

Accordingly, the Author narrates (a) in considerable detail as of an eyewitness (Acts 21–28 is more intensely detailed than all that precedes), and narrates (b) with detail based on what Paul had told him between A.D. 57–62. As a consequence the whole of Acts is a good source for the life of Paul. The Author based his narrative of Acts 21–28 partly on his eyewitness observations, partly on Paul's information (about his early life). His narrative, Acts 9–20 (where it touches on Paul), was based on oral history from the mouth of Paul, but possibly also from written memoirs. How did the Author get the absolute plethora of information about Paul's missions in Pisidia/Lycaonia, Greece and Asia Minor—much of it unimaginable—if not from Paul? The major alternative is that the Author engaged in a *novelistic* enterprise in the writing of Acts 13–20.[4] I find that hypothesis quite incredible.

For example, in a recent article Clare K. Rothschild assumes a second century writing of Acts based on a reconstruction the course of Paul's travels from the corpus of Paul's letters that had been assembled by that time. Rothschild (following scholars such as Pervo and Betz[5]) asserts that "Acts is not historically accurate" (339) and that "the author knows little more about Paul in the region of Galatia than the duty to place him there" (340). She adds, "A writer in possession of a map or even just a list of the cities on this road might easily have selected them as an itinerant missionary's (or other traveler's) choices *in lieu of* sources" (341). In short, according to her Luke's narrative detail in Acts 13–14 is an invention and that it does not correspond to what happened, apart from the names of the places visited.

In response we note:

1. The creation of a Pauline corpus may or may not have occurred within the first part of the Second Century, but in any case it would not have been possible for "Luke" to recreate his narrative for Paul, based on a list of Paul's letters. Rothschild appears to be saying that Luke's detail in Acts 13–14 is fiction, pure and simple?
2. The actual routes that Paul took would not necessarily have been as predictable as Rothschild assumes. When Paul departed for Syria he re-embarked in Attalia where he would have been expected to arrive. Attalia was a major harbor city whereas Perge was a river port twenty kilometers inland. Further, the journey from Lystra on to Derbe (a minor settlement, not on the Via Sebaste) is inexplicable except to escape from the problems in Iconium and Lystra from which Paul had fled. Luke's reference to such an unimportant place as Derbe simply does not make sense unless Paul actually went there.
3. It is not appropriate to dismiss Luke's narrative about Paul's direct journey from Cyprus to Pisidia as due to "the connection, unifying Cyprus and Pisidian Antioch" (345). Through the discovery of the "Sergius Paulus" inscription in Pisidian Antioch we may now guess that Paul was keen to arrive in a region where there were relatives of the proconsul of Cyprus. But

---

[4] Clare K. Rothschild, "Pisidian Antioch in Acts 13: The Denouement of the South Galatian Hypothesis," *NovT* 54 (2012): 334-53.
[5] See Richard I. Pervo, *Acts*, 5–7 (on the historical accuracy of Acts), 392-96 (on the "we" passages); H. D. Betz, *Galatians* (Philadelphia: Fortress, 1979), 3-5.

if Luke knew this he does not say so. It is quite likely that this was, indeed, Paul's motive but it cannot be discerned from the text of Acts. Alternatively, a health issue may have been the reason (cf. Gal 4:13-14) Arguably Luke was faithfully narrating the expeditious journey from Cyprus to Antioch based on what he had been told without knowing the reason for the haste.

A number of leading authorities past and present have acknowledged this "we" relationship between the Author and Paul, for example:

> The Author of Acts was a companion of S. Paul... It is perhaps no exaggeration to say that nothing in biblical criticism is more important than this statement.[6]

> ...they [details in Acts] are drawn from a diary-like record that the author of Acts once kept and give evidence that he was for a time a companion of Paul.[7]

> ...the remarks in the first person plural refer to the author himself. They do not go back to an earlier independent source, nor are they merely a literary convention, giving the impression that the author was an eyewitness... "We" therefore appears in the travel narratives because Luke simply wanted to indicate that he was there.[8]

What else could "we" in the "we"-passages mean? The alternatives—that the author employed the second person for stylistic reasons or has reproduced "undigested" a diarist's source—seem far-fetched.[9]

3. "Luke" and Paul

Of course the Author of Acts will narrate his work according to his own salvation-history interest; he will not slavishly replicate Paul's versions, even though he greatly admires him. Accordingly the Author will emphasize, interpret his material accordingly to his worldview, and omit what does not fit in with his objectives in writing Luke-Acts. For example, Paul was preoccupied by "law" whereas Luke was not. But then Paul was a Pharisee and Luke a Gentile (God-fearer?).

Thus it is not difficult to find "loose ends" between Paul and the Author, such as his omission of Paul's sojourn in Arabia. But that is the nature of good but disparate sources. Nonetheless, the chronological agreement between e.g., Galatians and parallel passages in Acts is impressive. Likewise the pieces of

---

[6] A. Plummer, *St Luke* (Edinburgh: T. & T. Clark, 1901), xii.
[7] J. A. Fitzmyer, *Luke the Theologian: Aspects of His Teaching* (London: Geoffrey Chapman, 1989), 22.
[8] M. Hengel, *Acts and the History of Earliest Christianity* (London: SCM, 1979), 66.
[9] For an opposing point of view see E. Haenchen, "'We' in Acts and the Itinerary," *Journal for Theology and the Church* 1 (1965): 65-99; N. Hyldahl, *The History of Early Christianity* (Frankfurt: Peter Lang, 1997), 137-38.

historical information in 1 Thessalonians and 1 Corinthians in parallel with Acts are impressive.

While it has been argued that there is disagreement between Acts and the epistles on several biographical and chronological details, many leading authorities like Bruce, Hemer and Bauckham[10] argue for the *absence* of disagreement in their versions of Paul's visits to Jerusalem. Indeed no scholar, including me, approaches these texts without our preconceptions, but I would argue we need to engage with these and other leading scholars, and make a case that they are wrong if we wish to invalidate their views.

There is no good reason why Gal 2:1-10 and Acts 11:29 do not represent Paul's and the Author's idiosyncratic versions of Paul's Second Visit to Jerusalem, which was mainly a private meeting between Barnabas, Paul, Titus, and the Jerusalem Pillars, and which concludes by an agreement about remembering the poor, which the Antioch delegates had been eager to do (in their collection for Jerusalem).

---

[10] For extensive discussion in favor of Gal 2:1-10 and Acts 11:27-30 as Visit 2 see Richard Bauckham, T*he Book of Acts in its First Century Setting: Vol. 4, Palestinian Setting* (Grand Rapids: Eerdmans, 1995), 467-72. See also the important article by D. R. Catchpole, "Paul, James and the Apostolic Decree," *NTS* 23 (1977): 428-44.

APPENDIX 2: A TABULAR ANALYSIS OF PAUL'S ASIAN EPISTLES

Paul W. Barnett

The following tables set out an analysis of Paul's Asian Epistles—Philemon, Colossians, and Ephesians.

1. Pauline Authorship of the Asian Epistles[1]

Philemon: Pauline authorship not generally doubted.

Colossians: Pauline authorship doubted by a majority of scholars.

Ephesians: Pauline authorship is overwhelmingly doubted.
(1) Different vocabulary and literary style.
(2) Special cosmology ("principalities and powers").

2. Common to Philemon, Colossians, and Ephesians

1. Written from prison.

   Philemon: 9, 10, 13
   Colossians: 4:3, 18
   Ephesians: 3:1; 4:1; 6:20

2. Names common in Philemon and Colossians.

   (a) Greeting-senders:
       Epaphras, Mark, Aristarchus, Demas, Luke: Phlm 23.
       Aristarchus, Mark, Epaphras, Luke, Demas: Col 4:10-14.

   (b) Greeted one:
       Archippus: Phlm 2; Col 4:15-17.

   (c) Commonly mentioned one:
       Onesimus: Phlm 10; Col 4:8.

   Comment: Items (a)–(c) indicate that Philemon and Colossians were written at the same time, from the same place to the same destination, Colossae.

3. Common envoy (also amanuensis?) in Colossians and Ephesians.
   Tychicus: Col 4:7-8; Eph 6:21

---

[1] For discussion on authorship see e.g., L. M. McDonald and S. E. Porter, *Early Christianity and its Sacred Literature* (Peabody: Hendrickson, 2000), 482-85.

Appendix 2

Comment: The common envoy Tychicus indicates that Colossians and Ephesians were dispatched at the same or similar times.

3. Conclusion on Authorship

These three letters were written at the same time and from the same place. Since Philemon is authentically Pauline it follows that Colossians is likewise authentically Pauline. Because Colossians and Ephesians were delivered by the same envoy (Tychicus), as well as other verbal and theological elements in common, it follows that these letters have a common author. It is reasonable to conclude that each letter was written by Paul.

4. Place of Paul's Imprisonment

There are problems with places of known imprisonment:

Caesarea: No reason a fugitive slave, Onesimus, would go there.
Rome: Too great a coincidence that Onesimus met up with Paul in prison in so large a city as Rome.

Case for Ephesus as the place of imprisonment (even though not mentioned in Acts):

1. People in the letters who were in Ephesus/Asia:
   Aristarchus (Phlm 23; Col 4:10) was in Ephesus (Acts 19:29);
   Tychicus (Col 4:7; Eph 4:21) was an Asian (Acts 20:4).

2. Paul's ministry in Ephesus long enough (three years) and turbulent enough[2] to accommodate a brief imprisonment, perhaps under house arrest.

3. More readily imaginable for Paul to envisage release from Ephesus for hospitality-visit to Philemon in Colossae than from either Caesarea or Rome because of distance.

5. Problems of Non-Pauline Style

1. Since Paul was known to be opposed to letters "as if" written by him (2 Thess 2:2) the suggestion that Ephesians was pseudonymous (written by a friend) must be received with caution.

2. The presence of Paul's signature on Colossians (Col 4:18; cf. 2 Thess 3:17) and its absence from Ephesians as well as that letter's more general character is consistent if the latter was a circular letter.

---

[2] See Acts 19:23-41; 1 Cor 15:32; 16:9.

3. Imprisonment (in Ephesus) would imply an external amanuensis (Tychicus?) who came and went to see Paul in prison seeking his general ideas for Colossians and Ephesians which the scribe expressed in his own idiom (different from Paul's).

4. The unusual "principalities and powers" language of Ephesians and Colossians might be explained by the influence of (Jewish) Gnosticism (evident in Col 2:8-23) whose language Paul has adopted in that letter and which may have colored the language in Ephesians.

INDEX OF ANCIENT PEOPLE

Achaicus, 210, 214
Agabus, 45
Agrippa I, 121, 310
Agrippa II, 107, 122, 310
Alciphron, 211
Alexander the Great, 126-127, 270, 313
Ambrosiaster, 179n
Ammia, 343
Ananus (son of Ananus), 121
Antiochus III, 314
Antiochus IV, 128
Antony, 143, 168
Apollos, 205, 226
Apphia, 314, 332
Aquila, 48, 49, 60, 179, 206, 208
Archippus, 307, 314, 332
Aretas, 43, 52, 112, 260
Aristarchus, 271, 307, 308, 309, 396, 397
Aristobulus (brother of Agrippa I), 310
Aristophanes, 234
Aristotle, 234, 281n, 283n, 359n
Athenagoras, 328
Augustine, 11, 24, 25, 43, 177, 202
Augustus, 71, 73, 143, 144, 156, 157, 160, 161, 162, 163, 164, 165, 166, 167, 168, 169n, 171, 172, 174, 207, 294n, 313, 320, 366n, 386

Barnabas, 38, 45, 52, 103, 106, 113, 246, 250, 395
Basilides, 328

Cassander, 68, 270
Cassius Dio, 48, 179, 206, 275n
Cerinthus, 344
Chloe, 226
Cicero, 98-99, 160, 224, 229, 234, 281n
Claudius (emperor), 45, 46, 47, 48, 49, 52n, 122, 156, 179, 180, 187, 206, 275n, 276, 294n, 295n, 310, 313
Clement of Alexandria, 88, 328n
Clement of Rome, 41, 211, 330, 337
Cleopatra, 143, 168
Crispus, 209, 210, 211

Demas, 307, 308, 396
Demetrius the Cynic, 216
Dio Chrysostom, 130n
Diodorus Siculus, 125n
Diogenes, 216
Dionysius of Halicarnassus, 125n, 126
Drusilla, 159
Drusus Germanicus, 162

Epaphras, 307, 308, 312, 396
Epaphroditus, 311, 325, 326
Ephraem the Syrian, 91
Epictetus, 146, 173, 220
Epiphanius, 101n
Erastus, 62, 80-81
Euodia, 73, 74, 326
Eusebius of Caesarea, 41n, 43, 45n, 179, 337, 349n

Facundus Navius, 145
Felix (procurator), 49, 121, 122, 310
Festus (procurator), 49, 121, 122, 310
Fortunatus, 210, 214

Gaius (Caligula), 179, 271
Gaius, 210, 211, 218, 241
Galerius, 68
Gallio, 46, 47, 49, 50, 51, 62, 119, 121, 206, 277n
Gamaliel I, 104, 109

Helena of Adiabene, 45
Herod of Chalcis, 310
Herod the Great, 179
Herodas, 237
Herodotus, 125n
Hillel, 104, 108, 109
Horace, 168n, 169, 237

Ignatius, 43n, 100, 211, 330, 331, 332n
Irenaeus, 43, 101, 328, 344n

James (brother of Jesus), 38, 118, 112, 121
Jason, 271, 275, 276
Jerome, 88, 328n, 337, 349
Jesus Justus, 308
Johanan ben Zakkai, 104
John (the Apostle), 38
John Chrysostom, 43, 202
John Mark, 307, 308, 309, 396
John of Gischala, 111
Josephus, 43, 45n, 49, 76, 107, 110, 111, 121, 122, 125n, 135, 158n, 295n, 310, 314
Judas Maccabeus, 178
Judas the Galilean, 107, 110
Julius Caesar, 145, 157, 161, 163, 164, 167, 179, 206, 295n, 366n, 385n
Justin Martyr, 290n, 349

Livia Augusta, 157, 159
Luke, 45, 47, 104, 137, 209, 307, 308, 309, 313, 393, 394, 396
Lydia, 313

399

Manilius, 294n
Marcion, 100, 101, 180, 181, 183, 315, 328, 346
Marcus Aurelius, 72
Mark Antony, 270, 313
Martial, 294n
Menenius Agrippa, 223
Montanus, 343n
Mummius Archaicus, 207

Narcissus, 309
Nero, 55, 121, 122, 143, 146, 153, 155, 157, 159, 162, 165, 166, 167, 170, 172, 173, 175, 309, 326, 337n, 366n

Onesimus, 307, 312, 314, 322, 323, 324, 396, 397
Origen, 88-89, 90, 95, 96, 100, 183
Orosius, 48, 49
Ovid, 161, 162, 164, 168, 294n, 386n

Paullus Fabius Persicus, 77n
Pausanias, 78n
Pelagius, 202
Peter (Cephas), 38, 55, 112, 117, 250, 260
Philemon, 309, 314, 322, 323, 324, 332
Philip II, 71, 126, 270
Philo, 76, 124n, 127n, 151, 207, 209, 223, 271, 294n
Phoebe, 190, 201
Photius, 111
Plato, 223, 224
Pliny (the Elder), 45
Pliny (the Younger), 77, 99n, 153
Plutarch, 173, 224, 295n
Polycarp, 99n, 100, 330, 331, 332n
Pompey, 179
Poppaea, 157
Priscilla (Prisca), 48, 49, 60, 179, 206, 208
Propertius, 168

Salvian, 347, 349
Sejanus, 179
Seneca, 154n, 156, 175, 294n, 334
Serapion, 349n
Sergius Paulus, 45, 46, 393
Shammai, 104, 108, 109
Silas, 38, 119, 269, 275, 276, 277
Sosthenes, 61, 119, 121
Stephanas, 210, 214, 226
Stephen, 104, 105
Sthenidas, 173
Strabo, 125n, 132, 207, 215
Suetonius, 45, 48, 153n, 152n, 157n, 173n, 179, 189, 206
Syntyche, 73, 74, 326

Tacitus, 49, 153, 294n, 295n
Tatian, 328
Tertius, 201
Tertullian, 43, 101n, 328, 346-347, 349
Tertullus, 122
Thecla, 347n
Theophilus, 328
Tiberius (emperor), 49, 161, 168, 179, 309, 320n, 366n
Timothy, 39, 118, 119, 269, 276, 277, 283, 303, 316, 325, 332
Tiro, 99
Titius Justus, 119, 209
Titus (companion of Paul), 232, 234, 235, 238, 239, 332, 395
Titus (emperor), 110
Tychicus, 308, 312, 315, 316, 318, 396, 397, 398

Valerius Maximus, 161, 162, 169n
Valleius Paterculus, 168, 295n
Virgil, 167, 168
Vitruvius, 167

INDEX OF PLACES

Actium, 168
Alexandria, 127, 132, 179
Antioch (Syrian), 38, 39, 52, 106, 113, 120
Antioch of Pisidia, 114, 115, 116, 117, 119, 120, 150, 393
Arabia (Nabatea), 37, 43, 111, 112, 260, 394
Athens, 119, 132
Attalia, 393

Berea, 119, 276

Caesarea, 38, 39, 117, 121, 122, 310, 311, 312, 397
Capernaum, 40n
Cenchreae, 201
Colossae, 303, 311, 312, 314, 396, 397
Corinth, 41, 46, 47, 48, 49, 51, 54, 59n, 60, 61-63, 77-82, 119, 120, 179, 205, 207, 208, 209, 216, 241, 319
Crete, 336
Cyprus, 38, 45
Cyprus, 393

Damascus, 37, 43, 52, 105, 111, 112, 260, 357
Delphi, 47
Derbe, 393

Ephesus, 54, 74-77, 120, 303, 311, 312, 315, 319, 320, 323, 397, 398

Galatia, 53, 244-245
Galilee, 110
Gischala, 110, 111

Hierapolis, 314, 320

Illyricum, 201

Jamnia, 104
Jerusalem, 37, 38, 39, 40, 41, 45, 49, 51, 52, 53, 54, 104, 105, 112, 113, 120, 121, 131, 133, 191, 201, 241, 245, 260, 310, 314, 336, 395
Judea, 40, 45

Kenchreai, 60, 78

Laodicea, 314
Lechaion, 60, 78
Lystra, 393

Macedonia, 126, 205, 238, 240, 313, 336
Miletus, 74, 114, 315

Nazareth, 40n
Neapolis, 313

Perge, 393
Petra, 112
Philippi, 71-74, 99, 100, 119, 303, 311, 313-314, 326
Puteoli, 43

Rhossus, 349n
Rome, 40, 41, 42, 48, 49, 55, 60, 100, 103, 113, 121, 122, 123, 143, 144, 153, 168, 174, 178, 179, 180, 187, 189, 191, 201, 241, 308, 309, 310, 311, 312, 323, 336, 337, 397

Sardis, 74, 115, 116
Smyrna, 99, 100
Spain, 38, 42, 186, 191, 201, 241, 336, 337

Tarsus, 51, 104n, 110, 111, 113, 131, 132, 134
Thessalonica, 68-71, 75, 119, 270-271
Troas, 238

INDEX OF SCHOLARS

Aageson, J. W., 332n, 335, 344n
Achtemeier, P., 189n, 354n
Adamczewski, B., 55n
Adams, E., 290n
Adams, S. A., 269n, 358n
Agamben, G., 64n-65n
Alcoff, L. M., 138n
Alexander, L., 281n
Allison, Dale, 36n
Andersen, F. I., 385n
Anton, P., 328n
Arnold, C. E., 53n, 317n, 318n
Ascough, R. S., 71n
Aune, D. E., 1, 31, 281n, 346n
Aus, R. D., 140n

Bachmann, M., 267n
Bagnall, R., 86n
Barclay, J. M. G., 103, 105n, 106, 126n, 148-149, 151, 153, 154, 158n, 246n
Barnett, A. E., 331n
Barnett, P. W., 260n, 392n
Barrett, C. K., 272n
Barth, K., 178
Barthélemy, J-J., 58
Bassler, J. M., 350
Bauckham, R. J., 29, 286n, 292n, 346n, 356n, 395
Baur, F. C., 2, 4, 183, 304, 328n
Beale, G. K., 293n
Becker, J., 134n-135n
Beker, J. C., 30, 184, 342, 354n, 360n
Benko, S., 153n
Berding, K., 330
Best, E., 278n
Betz, H. D., 133n, 230n, 241n, 359n
Betz, O., 258n
Bird, A. E., 339n
Bird, M. F., 1, 22, 26n, 195n, 262n, 330n, 364n, 379, 381n
Blanton, W., 59n
Bleek, F., 235n
Bornkamm, G., 184, G., 239
Bousset, W., 4
Bowersock, G. W., 58n
Breytenbach, C., 166n
Broneer, O., 81n
Brown, C., 294n
Brox, N., 346n
Bruce, F. F., 244n, 267n, 276n, 278n, 331n, 354n, 395
Buck, C., 278n
Buell, D. K., 139n
Bultmann, R., 5, 6, 12

Buzard, J., 58n
Byrne, B., 22

Cadbury, H. J., 62n, 63, 81n
Callahan, A. D., 42n
Calvin, J., 8, 9, 24, 25, 184, 278n
Campbell, C. R., 280n, 371n, 375n, 382n
Campbell, D. A., 22, 30, 46n, 114-115, 181n, 184, 381-382, 392n
Campbell, R. A., 345
Campbell, W. S., 139
Campenhausen, H. von, 335n-336n, 344-345
Capps, E., 60n, 61
Caputo, D. J., 138n
Carson, D. A., 23, 27, 254n, 348n, 379n
Carter, W., 149n
Castelli, E. A., 67n
Catchpole, D. R., 395n
Charlesworth, J. H., 346n
Chilton, B. D., 135n, 356n
Clark, M. E., 294n
Clasen, C. J., 281n
Clish, M., 133n
Cohen, S. D., 118n
Cole, G. A., 386n
Collins, R. F., 31, 298n, 345n
Concannon, C. W., 57n
Conzelmann, H., 62n, 351n
Cook, R. B., 247n
Coutts, J., 308n
Cranfield, C. E. B., 156n
Crook, Z. A., 360n

Dahl, N. A., 138n, 329n
Danker, F. W., 208
Das, A. A., 189n
Davies, P. E. J., 145
Davies, W. D., 9-11
Davis, A., 265n
de Boer, M. C., 53n, 264n, 267n
de Villiers, P. G. R., 289n
De Vos, C. S., 72
Deissmann, A., 31, 59, 60n, 63, 64, 129, 147, 280n, 285n, 295n
DeMaris, R., 80n
di Mattei, S., 265n
Díaz-Andreu, M., 58n
Dibelius, M., 351n
Dickson, J. P., 285n
Dinkler, E., 63
Dmitriev, S., 74n
Dodd, C. H., 29, 304
Donaldson, T. L., 138n, 361n

Donelson, L, R., 346n
Donfried, K. P., 41, 53n, 56, 69, 273n, 283n, 284n
Dormeyer, D., 285n
Doty, W., 332
Downs, D. J., 340n
du Toit, A. B., 130n, 131n
Duff, J., 329
Dunn, J. D. G., 17-19, 20, 24, 27, 28, 131n, 156n, 185, 253-254, 255, 261n, 266n, 308n, 346n, 348n, 354n, 367n, 370n, 380
Dupont, J., 295n
Dyson, S. L., 58n

Earl, D. C., 161n
Eastman, D. L., 52, 54n, 55n, 337n
Eastman, S., 250
Edrei, A., 135n
Edwards, C., 173n
Ehrenberg, V., 285n
Ehrman, B., 85n, 348n
Eisenbaum, P., 103, 106, 357n
Elliott, N., 151
Ellis, E. E., 336n-337n, 339, 340, 348
Engberg-Pedersen, T., 132, 133n, 357n
Epp, E. J., 84n
Esler, P. F., 136n
Ewald, H., 235n

Fairchild, M. R., 110
Fantin, J. D., 149n, 159
Fears, J. R., 167n, 168
Fee, G. D., 278n, 288n, 298n, 311n, 325n, 326n, 370n
Fiore, B., 334n
Fishwick, D., 149
Fitzgerald, J. T., 132, 387n
Fitzmyer, J. A., 394
Foakes-Jackson, F. J., 247n
Foerster, W., 294n
Fohrer, G., 294n
Forbes, C., 129n, 133n, 134n
Foster, P., 290n, 331
Frankemölle, H., 285n
French, D. H., 311
Friedrich, G., 285n
Friesen, S., 76n, 80, 320
Fung, R., 267n
Funk, R. W., 214

Gamble, H. Y., 329n, 349n
Garlington, D., 22
Gathercole, S., 23, 27
Gempf, C. H., 269n
George, T., 244n, 267n
Georgi, D., 147, 231

Gerber, A., 75n
Giles, K. N., 344n
Gill, D. W. J., 270n
Gill, M., 341n
Given, M. D., 103
Glad, C. E., 132
Glasson, T. F., 290n, 292n
Goodenough, E. R., 151
Goodman, M., 108n, 135
Goodrich, J. K., 252n
Gordon, R., 171n
Gorman, M. J., 355n, 369n, 372n, 381n
Goulder, M., 343-344
Gradel, I., 150
Grayston, K., 339n, 340
Green, G. L., 147-148, 278n
Gregory, A. F., 330
Gregson, R., 278n
Grieb, K., 29
Grotius, H., 278n
Gundry, R. H., 26, 289n
Guthrie, D., 338n

Haenchen, E., 394n
Haines-Eitzen, K., 86n
Hannestad, N., 169n
Hanson, A. T., 344n
Hanson, J. S., 110
Hardin, J. K., 248, 264n, 319n
Harding, M., 333n, 340n
Harmon, M. S., 250n-251n
Harnack, A. von, 49n, 105
Harris, B. F., 386n
Harris, M. J., 367n, 368n, 382n
Harris, W. H., 321n
Harrison, J. R., 143n, 144n, 167n, 168n, 171n, 172n, 173n, 275n-276n, 294n, 296n, 366n, 385n
Harrison, P. N., 304, 307n, 337-339, 349n
Hartog, P., 330n, 336n
Hausrath, A., 231, 232
Hawthorne, G. F., 326n
Hays, R. B., 28, 262n, 357n
Headlam, A., 184
Hedrick, C. W., 106n
Heidegger, M., 6
Hemer, C. J., 245n, 269n, 395
Hendrix, H., 273n, 274n
Hengel, M., 395
Herdan, G., 339n, 340
Hingley, R., 79n
Hock, R. F., 130n, 272n, 356n
Hodge, C. J., 139n
Hoehner, H. W., 307-308
Hoffmann, R. J., 336n
Holland, T., 355n
Holmes, M. W., 331

Holtzmann, H. J., 307
Hooker, M. D., 28, 132n
Horrell, D. G., 172n, 324n
Horsley, G. H. R., 133n, 271n, 295n
Horsley, R. A., 110, 148, 360n
Horton, M., 22, 27
Hughes, F. W., 282n, 283n
Humphries, M., 58n
Hurd, J. C., 214, 247n
Hurtado, L., 29, 182n, 356n
Hyldahl, N., 394n

Jaster, R. A., 130n
Jeremias, J., 30, 109n
Jervell, J., 185n
Jewett, R., 52, 53, 54, 69n, 147, 157n, 249n, 279n, 282n, 283n, 299n, 337n, 365n, 384n
Johnson, L. T., 186, 334, 336n, 342n, 353n
Johnson-DeBaufre, M., 63-65, 68n
Jones, A. H. M., 285n
Jowett, B., 203
Judge, E. A., 31, 80, 116, 144n, 164, 275n, 366n

Kahl, B., 248n
Kärkkäinen, V-M., 372n, 377n
Karris, R. J., 342n
Kartzow, M. B., 351n
Käsemann, E., 11-13, 24, 25
Kasher, A., 127n
Keck, L. E., 137n
Kelly, J. N. D., 337n
Kennedy, G. A., 31, 130n, 281n, 359n
Kennedy, J. H., 231
Kidd, R. M., 350n
Kim, S., 30, 149, 154, 293n, 360n, 361n, 367n
Kirk, J. R. D., 27
Klauck, H-J., 281n, 346n
Knight, G. W., 335n
Knox, J., 113n, 314n, 328n
Koester, H., 66n, 67n, 104, 328n, 336n
Koskenniemi, H., 333n
Koukouli-Chrysantaki, C., 72n
Kraabel, A. T., 115
Kreitzer, L. J., 157n
Kreitzer, L., 314n
Kruse, C. G., 254
Kümmel, W. G., 30

Lake, K., 247n
Lau, A. Y., 350n
Lefebvre, H., 70
Levinskaya, I., 118n, 271n
Lewis, N., 387n

Lightfoot, J. B., 244n, 272n, 277n, 326, 337
Lincoln, A. T., 308n, 320n
Litwa, M. D., 372n
Lock, W., 338n
Locke, J., 202
Lohse, E., 185, 207n, 305n
Longenecker, B. W., 369n
Longenecker, R. N., 247n, 258n, 263n
Luckensmeyer, D., 289n, 295n, 297n
Lüdemann, G., 47n, 51n, 52, 53, 54
Luther, M., 24, 177

MacDonald, D. R., 347n
MacDonald, M. Y., 345-346
Mack, B., 129n
Magness, J., 115n
Malherbe, A. J., 132, 278n, 280n, 346n, 357n
Malina, B. J., 31
Malitz, J., 170n
Manson, T. W., 278n, 280n
Marchal, J. A., 72, 73-74
Marcus, J., 360n
Marshall, I. H., 278n, 283n, 331n, 333n, 336n, 342, 345n, 348n-349n, 350
Martin, D. B., 139n, 219
Martin, R. P., 313n, 387n
Martin, S. C., 335n
Martin, T. W., 264n
Martyn, J. L., 30, 258, 267n, 360, 370n
Mason, S., 124n
Masson, C., 307
Matlock, R. B., 250n
McDonald, L. M., 349n, 396n
McGrath, A. E., 380n
McKnight, S., 271n
Meade, D. G., 307n, 348n
Mearns, C. L., 290n
Meeks, W. A., 31, 80
Meggitt, J. J., 122
Melanchthon, P., 184
Mendels, D., 135n
Merritt, B. D., 62n
Metzger, B. M., 90, 95, 304n
Milligan, G., 373n
Millis, B., 78n
Minear, P., 188
Mitchell, M. M., 215, 218n, 232, 334
Mitchell, S., 244n
Montefiore, C. G., 9, 253n
Moo, D., 22, 304, 305n, 309n, 312n, 314-315, 348n
Moore, G. F., 9, 253n, 379n
Morales, R. J., 250n
Morris, L., 348n
Moule, C. F. D., 335n

Moulton, J. H., 373n
Mounce, W. D., 339, 344n
Murphy-O'Connor, J., 36n, 52, 53, 54, 55, 337n, 339n

Nanos, M. D., 116, 189-190, 247n
Nasrallah, L. S., 68n
Neusner, J., 107, 108, 117n, 135n
Newlands, C. E., 145
Newman, C. C., 162n
Newton, D., 158n
Nicholl, C. R., 279n
Nigdelis, P., 71
Nobbs, A., 46
Nock, A. D., 106
Novak, R. M., 153n
Nygren, A., 184

O'Brien, P. T., 196n, 254n, 305n, 316n, 323n, 379n
Oakes, P., 67n, 72, 81, 252n, 373n
Øklund, J., 82
Owen, P. L., 254n

Pahl, M. W., 293n
Pandermalis, D., 270n
Papazoglou, F., 270n
Parker, D. C., 92
Peppard, M., 157n
Pervo, R. I., 103, 105n, 118-119, 120, 392n, 393n
Peterson, E., 295n
Pfleiderer, O., 4
Pickering, S. R., 93n
Pietersen, L. K., 342n, 343
Pilhofer, P., 72
Piper, J., 22, 25, 27
Pitts, A. W., 130n, 131n
Pitts, A. W., 372n
Plevnik, J., 297n
Plummer, A., 394
Porter, S. E., 31, 130n, 131n, 135n, 305n, 331n, 348n, 358n, 359n, 387n, 396n
Price, S. R. F., 149, 274n

Quarles, C. L., 296n
Quinn, J. D., 329, 333, 335

Räisänen, H., 254, 354n
Ramsay, W. M., 245, 276n
Reicke, B., 310n
Reinhold, M., 387n
Reitzenstein, R., 4
Renan, E., 59
Richards, E. R., 331n, 357n
Richardson, R., 61
Ridderbos, H., 342n

Riesner, R., 34, 35, 51, 52, 187n
Rist, M., 328n, 347n
Robinson, J. A. T., 310
Rock, I. E., 147n, 158-159
Rosenmeyer, P. A., 304n
Rothschild, C. K., 393
Rudolph, D. J., 103
Russell, W. B., 188
Sanday, W., 184

Sanders, E. P., 13-16, 17, 20, 23, 103, 181n, 253, 255, 379, 380
Sandmel, S., 134n
Schafer, P., 153n
Schaner, K., 77
Scheck, P., 328
Schenke, H-M., 331n
Scherrer, P., 75n
Schmidt, J. E. C., 277n
Schmithals, W., 114n, 180-181, 247n
Schneider, J., 294n
Schnelle, U., 130n
Schoedel, W. R., 344n
Schoeps, H. J., 134n, 253n
Schreiner, T. R., 22, 53n, 156n, 248n, 254, 255
Schrenk, G., 287n
Schweitzer, Albert, 1, 2, 7-9, 10, 255
Schwindt, R., 76n
Scott, I. W., 250n
Scott, J. C., 151
Scott, J. M., 362n
Scott, K., 152
Segal, A. F., 106, 360n
Seifrid, M. A., 22, 26, 27, 254n, 377n, 379n
Sheid, J., 149
Slingerland, D., 47-48n
Smith, C. S., 351n
Smith, I. K., 304n, 314n, 317n
Snyder, G. E., 42n
Soards, M. L., 360n
Spawforth, A., 79
Spence, S., 153n
Spivak, G., 73
Sprinkle, P. M., 195n, 262n
Stamps, D. L., 359n
Stanley, C. D., 29, 128
Staples, J. A., 140n
Starling, D. I., 140n
Stemberger, G., 134n
Stendahl, K., 11, 15, 103, 105, 106, 115, 253n
Stepp, P. L., 346n
Sterling, G. E., 132n
Still, T. D., 355n
Stowers, S. K., 117, 129n, 334, 335

405

Stuhlmacher, P., 25
Sumney, J. L., 303n

Tate, M. E., 321n
Taussig, H., 67n
Taylor, G., 278n
Taylor, L. R., 157n
Taylor, R. A., 321n
Theissen, G., 31, 80, 81
Thielman, F., 254, 311n, 377n
Thomas, C. M., 69n, 70
Thompson, M. B., 22
Thurén, L., 359n
Thurston, R. W., 278n
Tilling, C., 381n
Towner, P. H., 172n, 334n, 336n, 341n, 349n, 351n
Trebilco, P., 74n, 76n-77n
Trobisch, D., 98n
Tuckett, C. M., 293n, 330

Unnik, W. C. van, 131n

Van Os, B., 248n
Van Roon, A., 305n
Van Voorst, R. E., 180n, 259n
Vanderspoel, J., 72n
Venema, C. P., 22
Verner, D., 351n
Vielhauer, P., 231

Walker, W. O., 262n
Wall, R. W., 329n, 351n, 358n
Walters, J. C., 138n, 188
Walton, S., 283n
Wanamaker, C. A., 277n, 278n, 280n, 281n, 282n, 283n, 286n
Watson, F., 22, 188
Wedderburn, A. J. M., 191n
Weima, J. A. D., 295n
Weiss, J., 205n, 225n, 230-231, 232, 239, 278n
Welborn, L. L., 98n, 112n, 175n, 211n, 384n
Wenham, D., 30
Wesley, J., 177-178
West, J. C., 278n
Westerholm, S., 254n, 256
Westfall, C. L., 335n
White, J. L., 31
Wiefel, W., 154n, 187
Wieland, G., 341n
Wigner, M., 247n
Wilder, T. L., 348n
Williams, D. J., 374n
Willoughby, H., 62, 81n
Wills, L. M., 118, 120

Wilson, S. G., 335n
Winter, B. W., 127n, 159, 271n, 299n, 319n
Winter, S., 323
Wire, A. C., 67n
Witherington, B. W., 29, 52, 53n, 54, 55, 272n, 278n, 279n, 282n, 293n, 294n, 316n, 355n
Wolter, M., 334n
Woolf, G., 78n
Wrede, W., 8, 277n
Wright, N. T., 1, 19-22, 24, 25, 26, 27, 28, 29, 105n, 109, 147, 148-149, 173n, 256n, 292n, 294n, 296n, 356n, 366n, 369n, 380n

Yarbrough, M. M., 339-340
Yinger, K., 22, 27
Young, F., 345, 351

Zanker, P., 152, 170, 386n
Zetterholm, M., 103, 112, 114n
Ziesler, J., 157n
Zunz, G., 100n

www.ingramcontent.com/pod-product-compliance
Lightning Source LLC
Chambersburg PA
CBHW021351290426
44108CB00010B/194